The Bedford Handbook

The Bedford Handbook

Eighth Edition

Diana Hacker
Nancy Sommers
Harvard University

Contributing Authors
Tom Jehn
Harvard University

Jane Rosenzweig
Harvard University

Contributing ESL Specialist
Marcy Carbajal Van Horn
St. Edward's University

BEDFORD / ST. MARTIN'S   BOSTON ◆ NEW YORK

For Bedford / St. Martin's

Executive Editor: Michelle M. Clark
Senior Development Editor: Barbara G. Flanagan
Development Editor: Mara Weible
Senior Production Editor: Anne Noonan
Senior Production Supervisor: Dennis Conroy
Executive Marketing Manager: John R. Swanson
Editorial Assistant: Alicia Young
Copyeditor: Linda McLatchie
Text Design: Claire Seng-Niemoeller
Cover Design: Donna Lee Dennison
Composition: Nesbitt Graphics, Inc.
Printing and Binding: RR Donnelley and Sons

President: Joan E. Feinberg
Editorial Director: Denise B. Wydra
Editor in Chief: Karen S. Henry
Director of Marketing: Karen R. Soeltz
Director of Editing, Design, and Production: Marcia Cohen
Assistant Director of Editing, Design, and Production: Elise S. Kaiser
Managing Editor: Elizabeth M. Schaaf

Library of Congress Control Number: 2009924937

For information, write: Bedford / St. Martin's, 75 Arlington Street, Boston, MA 02116   (617-399-4000)

ISBN-10:   ISBN-13:
0-312-54430-8   978-0-312-54430-0   (Instructor's Annotated Edition)
0-312-47974-3   978-0-312-47974-9   (hardcover Student Edition)
0-312-48013-X   978-0-312-48013-4   (softcover Student Edition)

Acknowledgments

Preface for Instructors

Hacker handbooks have long been recognized as the most innovative and practical college references—the ones that respond most directly to student writers' questions and challenges. In revising *The Bedford Handbook*, our goal was to continue to respond to students by helping them make the most of their college writing experiences. Part of our revision plan—crafted with my fellow contributors and Diana Hacker's longtime editorial team—was to learn firsthand what's happening in composition classrooms and writing centers across the country.

With our plan in mind, I visited more than thirty-five colleges and universities to listen to students, teachers, and tutors talk about the challenges facing today's college writers. Throughout my travels, I heard students puzzle out the unfamiliar elements of academic writing, particularly those related to working with sources. I watched creative teachers show their students how to build arguments, synthesize sources, and strengthen their ideas through revision. I observed writing center tutors responding to students' questions about thesis statements and research assignments. And I listened, everywhere, for clues about how to develop a better, more useful reference. The eighth edition is inspired by the students, teachers, and tutors at these schools—and by the candid feedback offered by users of *The Bedford Handbook*'s earlier editions.

As you look through this new edition, you'll find many innovations—large and small—that help students make the most of their experience as college writers. For example, new boxes called *Making the most of your handbook* pull together advice from different parts of the book to help students complete any college writing assignment. To help students make the most of their teachers' feedback as they revise, we have created a new feature, *Revising with comments*, that provides concrete strategies for revision. The comments in this new feature come directly from our interviews with sixty-five students about the comments they receive most frequently.

Teachers, students, and tutors asked for more instruction on academic writing and research. In response to their requests for a more detailed treatment of thesis, we expanded the coverage: Section 1e now helps students identify problems in a draft thesis, ask relevant questions, and then revise. Students asked for more guidance in finding, evaluating, and integrating scholarly sources, so we created a case study to illustrate steps in one student's research process. Teachers asked for attention to synthesis, a key academic skill. The eighth edition features new coverage that models how students use their own language and ideas to position sources in an academic conversation. Finally, teachers and tutors asked us for grammar coverage that's more accessible and relevant, so we added new hand-edited examples that show typical grammar errors that students make when they use sources. We also completely revised our ESL material.

Diana Hacker wanted her handbooks to provide clear, straightforward guidance in response to a college student's basic question: *How do I write a good college paper?* The eighth edition of *The Bedford Handbook* continues to respond, offering even more practical advice and useful models for today's college writers. Diana taught us well, and I am not alone in saying that her method of teaching one lesson at a time helped me become a more effective composition teacher. Now as lead coauthor on her handbooks, I am honored to continue the Hacker tradition, helping students make the most of their college writing experiences as they compose their way through college and into the wider world.

Features of the Eighth Edition

What's new

Navigation help that makes sense to students

- **Making the most of your handbook.** These new boxes, running throughout the book, help students to pull together the advice they need to complete writing assignments in composition and other classes. The boxes teach students to use their handbook as a reference by prompting them to consult related advice and examples from different parts of the book as they write and revise.

REFERENCES IN THE MARGIN HELP STUDENTS FIND RELATED MATERIAL

> **5b** View your audience as a panel of jurors
>
> Do not assume that your audience already agre
> instead, envision skeptical readers who, like a pa
>
> | Making the most of your handbook |
> | --- |
>
> You may need to consider
> a specific audience for your
> argument.
>
> ▶ Analyzing your audience: 1a
>
> ▶ Writing in a particular
>   discipline, such as business
>   or psychology: 7
>
> will make up their minds a
> to all sides of the argumer
> arguing a public policy iss
> paper at readers who repre
> of opinions. In the case of th
> offshore drilling, for examp
> jury representative of those
> stake in the matter: envir
> policymakers, and consume
>
> At times, you can deliberately narrow your
> you are working within a word limit, for exampl
> not have the space in which to address all the
> rounding the offshore drilling debate. Or you mig

See pages 6 and 109 for additional examples.

- **Plain-language navigation.** We have replaced traditional handbook section titles with familiar terms for quick and easy reference. Terms like *main idea*, *flow*, and *presenting the other side*, placed in the upper right-hand corners of the pages, will help students see at a glance the exact page they need. See page 47 for examples.

Concrete strategies for revising

- **Revising with comments.** Based on research with sixty-five students at colleges and universities across the country, this new boxed feature gives students targeted help with revising in response to instructors' comments on their drafts. Each box contains a sample student passage with a common instructor's comment, such as "unclear thesis," "develop more," or "cite your source." We help students understand similar comments by their instructors and give them strategies they can use to revise their own work. An example appears on page ix.   ▶ ▶ ▶

- **Specific strategies for revising thesis statements.** We know that college writers often need help reworking thesis statements, no matter the discipline. A new stepped-out approach helps students identify a problem in a draft thesis, ask relevant questions, and revise based on their own responses. See page 28.

- **New coverage of portfolio keeping.** For students who are asked to maintain and submit a writing portfolio, a new section (2c) covers types of portfolios and offers tips for writing a reflective cover document. See pages 59–61.

"REVISING WITH COMMENTS" PAGES PROVIDE CONCRETE STRATEGIES

Revising with comments | Unclear thesis

Understanding the comment

When a teacher or tutor points out that your thesis is unclear, the comment often signals that readers may have a hard time identifying your essay's main point.

> Fathers are more involved in the lives of their children today than they used to be. In the past, the father's primary role was as the provider; child care was most often left to the mother or other relatives. However, today's father drives to dance lessons, coaches his child's baseball team, hosts birthday parties, and provides homework help. Do more involved fathers help or hinder the development of their children?

Unclear thesis

One student wrote this introductory paragraph in response to an assignment that asked her to analyze the changing roles of mothers or fathers.

A writer's thesis, or main point, should be phrased as a statement, not a question. To revise, the student could answer the question she has posed, or she could pose a new question and answer it. After considering her evidence, she needs to decide what position she wants to take, state this position clearly, and show readers *why* this position—her thesis—matters.

Similar comments: vague thesis • state your position • your main point?

Revising when *your* thesis is unclear

1. *Ask questions.* What is the thesis, position, or main point of the draft? Can you support it with the available evidence?

2. *Reread your entire draft.* Because ideas develop as you write, you may find that your conclusion contains a clearer statement of your main point than your current thesis does. Or you may find your thesis elsewhere in your draft.

3. *Try revising your thesis* by framing it as an answer to a question you pose, the resolution of a problem you identify, or a position you take in a debate. And put your thesis to the "So what?" test: Why would a reader be interested in this thesis?

More help with writing a clear thesis: **1c** and **1e**

30

See pages 33, 110, and 502 for additional examples.

Targeted content for today's students:
Academic writing and research

- **A new case study** follows one student's research and
  writing process, providing a detailed, illustrated model
  for strategizing about sources, using search tools and
  techniques, evaluating sources, taking notes, thinking
  critically about how best to use sources in a paper, and
  integrating a source responsibly. This self-contained section (54b) includes marginal navigation aids directing
  students to more detailed information throughout the
  book. The first page of the case study is shown on
  page xi.   ▶▶▶

- **Synthesis, a requirement in academic writing.** More of
  today's college writing assignments require that students
  synthesize—analyze sources and work them into a conversation that helps develop an argument. New coverage
  of synthesis, with annotated examples in MLA and APA
  styles (pages 512–15 and 635–38), helps students work
  with sources to meet the demands of academic writing.

- **Integrating evidence in analytical papers.** New coverage in
  section 4, "Writing about Texts," shows students—at the
  sentence level—how to introduce, include, and interpret
  a passage in an analytical paper. See pages 94–97.

- **More help with writing assignments in other disciplines and
  in various genres.** For students who work with evidence
  in disciplines other than English, we have included
  annotated assignments and excerpts from model papers
  in psychology, business, nursing, and biology. For an
  example, see page 136.

- **New and up-to-date documentation models** for the sources
  students are using today—eighty-five new models across
  the three styles (MLA, APA, and *Chicago*)—with special
  attention to new sources such as podcasts, online videos,
  blogs, and DVD features. Detailed annotations for many

NEW CASE STUDY FOLLOWS ONE STUDENT'S RESEARCH AND WRITING PROCESS

Making the most of your handbook
Highlights of one student's research process (MLA style)

Anna Orlov, a student in a composition class, was assigned a research essay related to technology and the American workplace. The assignment called for her to use a variety of print and electronic sources and to follow MLA style. Orlov immediately thought of her summer internship at an insurance company and her surprise at the strict employee Internet use policy in place there. As she thought about how to turn her experience into a research project, she developed some questions and strategies to guide her research and writing.

"How do I begin a research paper?"

Before getting started, Orlov worked with a writing tutor to break her research plan into several stages. (Section numbers in blue refer to relevant discussions throughout the book.)

- Ask worthwhile questions about my topic.   1b, 46a
- Talk with a reference librarian about useful types of
  sources and where to find them.   46b
- Consider how each source can contribute
  to my paper.   47a
- Decide which search results are worth a
  closer look.   47b
- Evaluate the sources.   47d, 47e
- Take notes and keep track of the sources.   48
- Write a working thesis.   1c, 50a
- Write a draft and integrate sources.   1e–1g, 52, 53a
- Document sources.   49, 53b

Orlov began by jotting down the research question she wanted to investigate: *Is Internet surveillance in the workplace fair or unfair to employees?* She thought that the practice might be unfair but knew that she needed to consider all sides of the issue. Her instructor had explained that sources uncovered in the research process would both support and challenge her ideas and ultimately help shape the paper. Orlov knew she would have to be

1b and 46a:
Posing questions for a research paper

See pages 573–82 for the entire case study.

models help students see at a glance how to format their citations. See examples on page 553. **NOTE:** The eighth edition includes up-to-date guidelines for MLA (2009) and APA (2010).

- **New MLA-style research essay** (pages 583–88)

- **New flowchart on intellectual property** (pages 486–87)

New examples, more accessible grammar coverage

- **More ESL help, presented more accessibly.** Part VI, "Challenges for ESL and Multilingual Writers," now completely revised, offers more accessible advice and more support for multilingual writers across the disciplines.

- **Grammar basics content is more straightforward than ever.** Part XI, the handbook's reference within a reference, now teaches with everyday example sentences and exercise items.

- **More academic examples** reflect the types of sentences students are expected to write in college. A new type of hand-edited example ("Writing with sources") shows typical errors students make—and how they can correct them—when they integrate sources in MLA, APA, and *Chicago* papers. See page 240 for an additional example.

▼

Writing with sources MLA-style citation	▶ Deborah Tannen's research reveals that men and women have different ideas about communication. For example, *Tannen explains* that a woman "expects her husband to be a new and ‸ improved version of her best friend" (441).

A quotation must be part of a complete sentence. *That a woman "expects her husband to be a new and improved version of her best friend"* is a fragment—a subordinate clause. In this case, adding a signal phrase that includes a subject and a verb (*Tannen explains*) corrects the fragment and clarifies that the quotation is from Tannen.

A new collection of resources that helps instructors
make the most of their handbook

- ***Teaching with Hacker Handbooks,*** by Marcy Carbajal Van
  Horn, offers practical advice on common topics such as
  designing a composition course, crafting writing assignments, and teaching multilingual writers. Ten lesson
  plans, each including strategies and materials that are
  ready to use or customize, support common course goals
  such as teaching argument, teaching paragraphs, and
  teaching peer review. The collection also includes a
  wealth of handouts, syllabi, and other materials for integrating a Hacker handbook into your course. Available in
  print and online (hackerhandbooks.com/teaching).

What's the same

**Comprehensive coverage of grammar, academic writing, and re-
search.** A classroom tool and a reference, the handbook is designed to help students write well in any college course. This
edition includes nearly one hundred exercise sets, many with
answers in the back of the book.

A brief menu and a user-friendly index. Students will find help
fast by consulting either the brief list of contents on the inside
front cover or the user-friendly index, which works even for
writers who are unsure of grammar terminology.

Citation at a glance. Annotated visuals show students where to
find the publication information they need to cite common
types of sources in MLA and APA styles.

Quick-access charts and an uncluttered design. The eighth edition has what instructors and students have come to expect
of a Hacker handbook: a clear and navigable presentation of
information, with charts that summarize key content.

What's in the Student Center

hackerhandbooks.com/bedhandbook

The handbook's companion Web site has a new name but includes many of the resources students have used before.

Grammar, writing, and research exercises with feedback for every item. More than 1,400 items offer students plenty of extra practice, and our new scorecard gives instructors flexibility in viewing students' results.

Annotated model papers in MLA, APA, *Chicago*, and CSE styles. Student writers can see formatting conventions and effective writing in traditional college essays and in other common genres: annotated bibliographies, literature reviews, lab reports, business proposals, and clinical documents.

Research and Documentation Online. This award-winning resource, written by a college librarian, gives students a jump start with research in thirty academic disciplines.

Resources for writers and tutors. Checklists, hints, tips, and helpsheets are available in downloadable format.

Resources for ESL and multilingual writers. Writers will find advice and strategies for understanding college expectations and completing writing assignments. Also included are charts, exercises, activities, and an annotated student essay in draft and final form.

Language Debates. Twenty-two brief essays provide opportunities for critical thinking about grammar and usage issues.

Access to premium content. New copies of the print handbook can be packaged with a free activation code for premium content: *The Bedford e-Handbook*, a series of online video tutorials, and a collection of resources that includes games, activities, readings, guides, and more.

Supplements for instructors

Practical

Teaching with Hacker Handbooks: Topics, Strategies, and Lesson Plans

The Bedford Handbook instructor resources (at hackerhandbooks .com/bedhandbook)

Professional

Teaching Composition: Background Readings

The Bedford Guide for Writing Tutors, Fifth Edition

The Bedford Bibliography for Teachers of Writing, Sixth Edition

Supplements for students

Print

Developmental Exercises for The Bedford Handbook

Working with Sources: Research Exercises for The Bedford Handbook

Research and Documentation in the Electronic Age, Fifth Edition

Extra Help for ESL Writers: Supplement for Hacker Handbooks

Designing Documents and Understanding Visuals: Supplement for Hacker Handbooks

Writing in the Disciplines: Advice and Models

Online

The Bedford e-Handbook

CompClass for The Bedford Handbook

Acknowledgments

I am grateful for the expertise, enthusiasm, and classroom experience that so many individuals brought to the new edition.

Contributors

My fellow coauthors wrote new content and rethought existing content to make sure that *The Bedford Handbook* reaches an ever broader range of students and meets their various needs. Jane Rosenzweig, a composition teacher and writing center director, revised the coverage of thesis statements, wrote new content for the "Writing about Texts" section, and created many new examples for our innovative "Writing with sources" grammar coverage. Tom Jehn, a composition teacher and writing in the disciplines expert, refined our research coverage and drafted the new case study in the MLA section. Marcy Carbajal Van Horn, online writing lab director, ESL specialist, and experienced composition instructor, improved the ESL coverage in the book, wrote new ESL content for the companion Web site, and is lead author of the new collection of instructor resources, *Teaching with Hacker Handbooks*.

Reviewers

For her careful review of our coverage of research and documentation, I am grateful to Barbara Fister, academic librarian at Gustavus Adolphus College. I am also thankful to a group of colleagues who helped shape our new coverage of revision by talking with us about the comments they write on their students' papers: Steve Brahlek, Palm Beach Community College; Liz Canfield, Virginia Commonwealth University; Jon Cullick, Northern Kentucky University; Tiane Donahue, Dartmouth College; Anne Fernald, Fordham University; Holly McSpadden, Missouri Southern State University; and Jennifer Whetham, Green River Community College.

For their active engagement with new manuscript and for their willingness to share teaching ideas in a Boston-based focus group, I am grateful to the following instructors: Steve Brahlek and John Ribar, Palm Beach Community College; April Childress and Joanne Messman, Greenville Technical College; Beverly Holmes and James Suderman, Northwest Florida State College; Bobbie Kilbane, Volunteer State Community College; and Chris Twiggs, Florida Community College.

Many additional reviewers either answered a detailed questionnaire about the seventh edition or reviewed new manuscript for the eighth edition: Guy Aengus, University of California, Davis; Preston Allen, Miami Dade College; Sandy Archimedes, University of California, Santa Cruz; Chris Arevalo, Austin Community College; John Avery, Green River Community College; Diane Baird, Palm Beach Community College; April Baker, Greenville Technical College; Chelle Bernstein, St. Johns River Community College; Kristin Bivens, Harold Washington College; Laura Black, Volunteer State Community College; Deborah Borchers, Pueblo Community College; Laurie Buchanan, Clark State Community College; Karen Burge, Wichita State University; Nicole Buzzetto-More, University of Maryland Eastern Shore; Andrew Cavanaugh, University of Maryland University College; Pam Clark, Frederick Community College; Victoria Cliett, Henry Ford Community College; Mark Coley, Tarrant County College Southeast; Trish Conard, Hutchinson Community College; Janet Cook, Hutchinson Community College; Brian Cooney, Gonzaga University; Michael Cripps, York College CUNY; Margot Cullen, Ohio Northern University; Bonita Dattner-Garza, St. Mary's University; Rose Day, Central New Mexico Community College; Darren DeFrain, Wichita State University; Linda Didesidero, University of Maryland University College; Africa Fine, Palm Beach Community College; Bill Fisher, Pensacola Junior College; Jane P. Gamber, Hutchinson Community College; Grace Giorgio, University of Illinois; Shon Grant, Northern Virginia Community College; Miriam Gustafson, University of New Mexico; Karen Hall, Lewiston-Auburn College; Mickey Hall, Volunteer State Community College; Elisabeth

Heard, Harold Washington College; John Jebb, University of Delaware; Laura Jeffries, Florida Community College at Jacksonville; Nikki Johnson, University of Northern Iowa; Stephanie Kamath, University of Massachusetts Boston; Kathleen Keating, Greensboro College; Jana Kinder, Florida Community College at Jacksonville; Steven Knapp, Indian River Community College; Carol Koris, Johnson & Wales University; Robert Lietz, Ohio Northern University; Michelle Lisi-D'Alauro, Lewiston-Auburn College; Keming Liu, Medgar Evers College CUNY; Barbara Lutz, University of Delaware; Paul Madachy, Prince George's Community College; John Magee, Ohio Northern University; Caroline Mains, Palo Alto College; David Marlow, University of South Carolina; Tammy Mata, Tarrant County College; Linda McCloud-Bondoc, Athabasca University; Shellie Michael, Volunteer State Community College; Gayla Mills, Randolph-Macon College; Heidi Moore, Northern Virginia Community College; Rhonda Morris, Santa Fe College; Joan Nakke, Montgomery College; Betty Nelson, Volunteer State Community College; Tom O'Neal, St. Johns River Community College; Michelle Paulsen, Victoria College; Tammy Peery, Montgomery College; Susan Perry, Greenville Technical College; Sharon Prince, Wharton City Junior College; Roberta Proctor, Palm Beach Community College; Ellen Raphaeli, Northern Virginia Community College; Kent Richmond, California State University, Long Beach; Pearl Saunders, Palm Beach Community College; Lisa Shaw, Miami Dade College; Donald Skinner, Indian River Community College; Gary Sligh, Lake-Sumter Community College; Kate Spike, Bowling Green State University; Jeniffer Strong, Central New Mexico Community College; Rebecca Sullivan, St. Johns River Community College; Tom Treffinger, Greenville Technical College; Katherine Turner, Mary Baldwin College; April Van Camp, Indian River Community College; Susan Vergnani, Santa Fe College; Lisa Wilde, Howard Community College; Dennis Williams, College of Charleston; Rita Wisdom, Tarrant County College Northeast.

Students

A number of bright and willing students helped us see which instructor comments provide the best guidance for revision. From Green River Community College: Kyle Baskin, Josué Cardona, Emily Dore, Anthony Hines, Stephanie Humphries, Joshua Kin, Jessica Llapitan, James Mitchell, Derek Pegram, Charlie Piehler, Lindsay Allison Rae Richards, Kristen Saladis, Jacob Simpson, Christina Starkey, Ariana Stone, and Joseph Vreeburg. From Northern Kentucky University: Sarah Freidhoff, Marisa Hempel, Sarah Laughlin, Sean Moran, Laren Reis, and Carissa Spencer. From Palm Beach Community College: Alexis Day, Shawn Gibbons, Zachary Jennison, Jean Lacz, Neshia Neal, Sarah Reich, Jude Rene, and Sam Smith. And from the University of Maine at Farmington: Nicole Carr, Hannah Courtright, Timothy Doyle, Janelle Gallant, Amy Hobson, Shawn Menard, Jada Molton, Jordan Nicholas, Nicole Phillips, Tessa Rockwood, Emily Rose, Nicholas Tranten, and Ashley Wyman. We also thank the students who have let us use and adapt their papers as models in the handbook: Ned Bishop, Jamal Hammond, Albert Lee, Luisa Mirano, Anna Orlov, Emilia Sanchez, and Matt Watson.

Bedford / St. Martin's

A comprehensive handbook is truly a collaborative writing project, and it is a pleasure to acknowledge and thank the enormously talented Bedford/St. Martin's editorial team, whose deep commitment to students informs each new feature of *The Bedford Handbook*. Joan Feinberg, Bedford's president and Diana Hacker's first editor, asks tough questions and offers her superb judgment on every aspect of the book. Joan's graceful and generous leadership, both within Bedford and in the national composition community, is a never-ending source of inspiration for those who are fortunate to work with her. Michelle Clark, executive editor, combines wisdom with patience, creativity with practicality, and hard work with good humor. An author could not wish for a smarter editor and collaborator than Michelle. Her voice, vision, and elegance shape each page of the eighth edition. Barbara Flanagan, senior editor, has worked on Diana Hacker's handbooks for more than twenty-five years and brings to the eighth edition her unrelenting insistence on both clarity and precision as well as her expertise in documentation. Mara Weible, editor, is a close reader extraordinaire, whose intellectual patience and persistence shaped the new case study and synthesis sections. Denise Wydra, editorial director; Karen Henry, editor in chief; John Swanson, executive marketing manager; and Jimmy Fleming, senior English marketing specialist, are treasured sources of thoughtful and innovative ideas. Their passionate commitment to *The Bedford Handbook* ensures that it will meet the needs of today's students. Anne Noonan, senior production editor, kept us on schedule and turned a complex manuscript into a superior handbook. Alicia Young, editorial assistant, expertly managed the review process, prepared documents, and edited several ancillaries. And many thanks to Linda McLatchie, copyeditor, for her thoroughness and attention to detail; to Claire Seng-Niemoeller, text designer, who always has ease of use in mind as she designs a Hacker handbook; to Donna Dennison, art director, who has given the cover a fresh new look; and to Sarah Ferguson, new media editor, who developed the book's Student Center and e-book.

And last, but never least, I offer thanks to Maxine Rodburg and Kerry Walk, friends and mentors, for sustaining conversations about teaching writing; Joshua Alper, a most demanding—and forgiving—reader; and to my daughters, Rachel and Alexandra, whose good-natured and humorous observations about the real lives of college writers are a constant source of instruction and inspiration.

—*Nancy Sommers*

How to Use This Book and Its Student Center

Though it is small enough to hold in your hand, *The Bedford Handbook* will answer most of the questions you are likely to ask as you plan, draft, and revise a piece of writing:

How do I choose and narrow a topic?

How do I know when to begin a new paragraph?

Should I write *each was* or *each were*?

When should I place a comma before *and*?

What is counterargument?

What is the difference between *accept* and *except*?

How do I cite an online newspaper article?

The book's companion Web site, the Student Center, extends the book beyond its covers. See page xxvi for details.

How to find information with an instructor's help

When you are revising an essay that your instructor has marked, tracking down information is simple. If your instructor indicates problems with a number such as *16* or a number and letter such as *12e*, you can turn directly to the appropriate section of the handbook. Just flip through the tabs at the top of the pages until you find the number in question.

If your instructor uses an abbreviation such as *w* or *dm* instead of a number, consult the list of abbreviations and revision symbols at the end of the book. There you will find the name of the problem (*wordy*; *dangling modifier*) and the number of the section to consult.

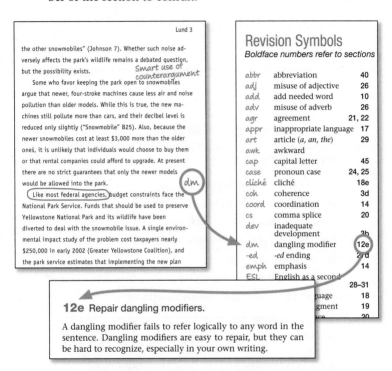

Lund 3

the other snowmobiles" (Johnson 7). Whether such noise adversely affects the park's wildlife remains a debated question, but the possibility exists.   *Smart use of counterargument*

Some who favor keeping the park open to snowmobiles argue that newer, four-stroke machines cause less air and noise pollution than older models. While this is true, the new machines still pollute more than cars, and their decibel level is reduced only slightly ("Snowmobile" B25). Also, because the newer snowmobiles cost at least $3,000 more than the older ones, it is unlikely that individuals would choose to buy them or that rental companies could afford to upgrade. At present there are no strict guarantees that only the newer models would be allowed into the park.   *dm*

Like most federal agencies, budget constraints face the National Park Service. Funds that should be used to preserve Yellowstone National Park and its wildlife have been diverted to deal with the snowmobile issue. A single environmental impact study of the problem cost taxpayers nearly $250,000 in early 2002 (Greater Yellowstone Coalition), and the park service estimates that implementing the new plan

Revision Symbols
Boldface numbers refer to sections

abbr	abbreviation	**40**
adj	misuse of adjective	**26**
add	add needed word	**10**
adv	misuse of adverb	**26**
agr	agreement	**21, 22**
appr	inappropriate language	**17**
art	article (*a, an, the*)	**29**
awk	awkward	
cap	capital letter	**45**
case	pronoun case	**24, 25**
cliché	cliché	**18e**
coh	coherence	**3d**
coord	coordination	**14**
cs	comma splice	**20**
dev	inadequate development	**3b**
dm	dangling modifier	**12e**
-ed	*-ed* ending	**27d**
emph	emphasis	**14**
ESL	English as a second	**28–31**
	...guage	**18**
	...gment	**19**
	...ce	**20**

12e Repair dangling modifiers.

A dangling modifier fails to refer logically to any word in the sentence. Dangling modifiers are easy to repair, but they can be hard to recognize, especially in your own writing.

How to find information on your own

This handbook is designed to allow you to find information without an instructor's help—usually by consulting the brief menu inside the front cover. At times, you may consult the detailed menu inside the back cover, the index, the Glossary of Usage, the list of revision symbols, or one of the directories to documentation models. The tutorials on pages xxviii–xxxi give you opportunities to practice finding information in different ways.

The brief menu. The brief menu inside the front cover displays the book's contents. Let's say that you want to find out how you can write with more active verbs. Your first step is to scan the menu for the appropriate numbered topic—in this case "8 Active verbs." Then you can use the blue and green tabs at the top of the pages to find section 8.

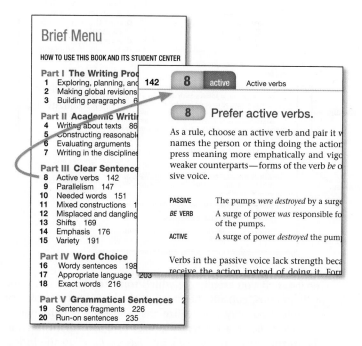

Brief Menu

142   **8**   active   Active verbs

8   Prefer active verbs.

As a rule, choose an active verb and pair it w
names the person or thing doing the action
press meaning more emphatically and vigo
weaker counterparts—forms of the verb *be* o
sive voice.

PASSIVE   The pumps *were destroyed* by a surge

BE VERB   A surge of power *was* responsible fo
of the pumps.

ACTIVE   A surge of power *destroyed* the pum

Verbs in the passive voice lack strength beca
receive the action instead of doing it. For

The detailed menu. The detailed menu appears inside the back cover. When the numbered section you're looking for is broken up into quite a few lettered subsections, try consulting this menu. For instance, if you have a question about the proper use of commas after introductory elements, this menu will quickly lead you to section 32b.

Once you find the right lettered subsection, you will see three kinds of advice to help you edit your writing—a rule, an explanation, and one or more hand-edited examples.

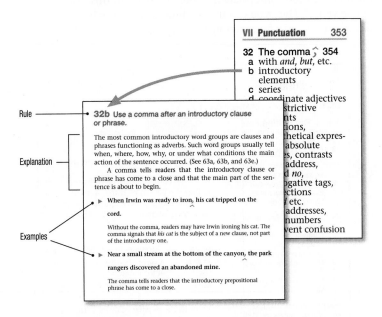

Rule

Explanation

Examples

> **VII Punctuation** 353
>
> **32 The comma ⌢ 354**
> a with *and, but,* etc.
> b introductory
>   elements
> c series
> d coordinate adjectives
>   restrictive
>   nts
>   ions,
>   thetical expres-
>   absolute
>   s, contrasts
>   address,
>   d *no,*
>   gative tags,
>   ctions
>   etc.
>   addresses,
>   numbers
>   vent confusion

> **32b** Use a comma after an introductory clause or phrase.
>
> The most common introductory word groups are clauses and phrases functioning as adverbs. Such word groups usually tell when, where, how, why, or under what conditions the main action of the sentence occurred. (See 63a, 63b, and 63e.)
>   A comma tells readers that the introductory clause or phrase has come to a close and that the main part of the sentence is about to begin.
>
> ▶ When Irwin was ready to iron, his cat tripped on the
>   cord.
>
>   Without the comma, readers may have Irwin ironing his cat. The comma signals that *his cat* is the subject of a new clause, not part of the introductory one.
>
> ▶ Near a small stream at the bottom of the canyon, the park
>   rangers discovered an abandoned mine.
>
>   The comma tells readers that the introductory prepositional phrase has come to a close.

The index. If you aren't sure which topic to choose from one of the menus, consult the index at the back of the book. For example, you may not realize that the issue of whether to use *have* or *has* is a matter of subject-verb agreement (section 21). In that case, simply look up "*has* vs. *have*" in the index. You will be directed to specific pages in two sections covering subject-verb agreement.

Making the most of your handbook. You will find your way to helpful advice by using the index, the menus, or the contents. Once you get to where you need to be, you may also find references to additional related advice and models. These boxes help you pull together what you need from the handbook for each assignment.

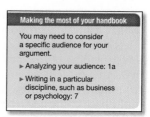

Making the most of your handbook

You may need to consider a specific audience for your argument.

▶ Analyzing your audience: 1a

▶ Writing in a particular discipline, such as business or psychology: 7

The Glossary of Usage. When in doubt about the correct use of a particular word (such as *affect* and *effect*), consult the Glossary of Usage at the back of the book. This glossary explains the difference between commonly confused words; it also includes words that are inappropriate in formal written English.

Directories to documentation models. When you are documenting a research paper with MLA, APA, or *Chicago* style, you can find documentation models by consulting the appropriate color-coded directories.

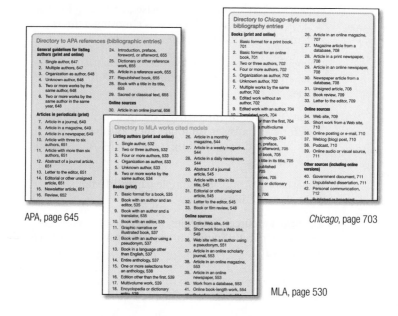

APA, page 645

Chicago, page 703

MLA, page 530

Answers to exercises. *The Bedford Handbook* has been designed so that you can learn from it on your own. By providing answers to some exercise sentences, it allows you to test your understanding of the material. Most exercise sets begin with five sentences lettered *a* through *e* and conclude with five or ten numbered sentences. Answers to lettered sentences appear in the back of the book, beginning on page 805.

Using the book's Student Center:
hackerhandbooks.com/bedhandbook

Throughout *The Bedford Handbook*, Eighth Edition, you will see references to exercises and model papers on the Student Center, the book's companion Web site. Here is a complete list of resources on the site. Your instructor may use some of this material in class; each area of the site, however, has been developed for you to use on your own whenever you need it.

- **Writing exercises** Interactive exercises, including feedback for every answer, on topics such as choosing a thesis statement and conducting a peer review

- **Grammar exercises** Interactive exercises on grammar, style, and punctuation, including feedback for every answer

- **Research exercises** Interactive exercises, including feedback for every answer, on topics such as integrating quotations and documenting sources in MLA, APA, and *Chicago* styles

- **Model papers** Annotated sample papers in MLA, APA, *Chicago*, and CSE styles

- **ESL help** Resources, strategies, model papers, and exercises to help multilingual students improve their college writing skills

- *Research and Documentation Online* Advice on finding sources in a variety of academic disciplines and up-to-date guidelines for documenting print and online sources in MLA, APA, *Chicago*, and CSE styles

- **Resources for writers and tutors** Revision checklists and helpsheets for common writing problems

- **Tutorials** Interactive resources that teach essential college skills such as integrating sources in a research paper and revising with peer comments (This area of the Web site requires an activation code.)

- **Language Debates** Mini-essays exploring controversial issues of grammar and usage, such as split infinitives

- **Additional resources** Print-format versions of the book's exercises and links to additional online resources for every part of the book

- *Re:Writing* A free collection of resources for composition and other college classes: help with preparing presentation slides, avoiding plagiarism, evaluating online sources, and more

Tutorials

The following tutorials will give you practice using the book's menus, index, Glossary of Usage, and MLA directory. Answers to the tutorials begin on page 804.

1 Using the menus

Each of the following "rules" violates the principle it expresses. Using the brief menu inside the front cover or the detailed menu inside the back cover, find the section in *The Bedford Handbook* that explains the principle. Then fix the problem. Example:

> *Tutors in*
> ~~In~~ the writing center/~~they~~ say that vague pronoun
> ^
> reference is unacceptable. 23

1. A verb have to agree with its subject.
2. About sentence fragments. You should avoid them.
3. Its important to use apostrophe's correctly.
4. If your sentence begins with a long introductory word group use a comma to separate the word group from the rest of the sentence.
5. When dangling, watch your modifiers.

2 Using the index

Assume that you have written the following sentences and want to know the answers to the questions in brackets. Use the index at the back of the book to locate the information you need, and edit the sentences if necessary.

1. Each of the candidates have decided to participate in tonight's debate. [Should the verb be *has* or *have* to agree with *Each*?]

2. We had intended to go surfing but spent most of our vacation lying on the beach. [Should I use *lying* or *laying*?]

3. We only looked at two houses before buying the house of our dreams. [Is *only* in the right place?]

4. In some cultures, it is considered ill mannered for you to accept a gift. [Is it okay to use *you* to mean "anyone in general"?]

5. In Canada, Joanne picked up several bottles of maple syrup for her sister and me. [Should I write *for her sister and I*?]

3   Using the menus or the index

Imagine that you are in the following situations. Using either the menus or the index, find the information you need.

1. You are a student studying health administration, and you're editing a report you've just written on the benefits of community-based urgent care clinics. You recall learning to put a comma between all items in a series except the last two. But you have noticed that most writers use a comma between all items. You're curious about the rule. Which section of *The Bedford Handbook* will you consult?

2. You are tutoring in your university's writing center. A composition student comes to you for help with her first college essay. She is revising a draft — and struggling with her use of articles (*a*, *an*, and *the*). You know how to use articles, but you aren't able to explain the complicated rules on their correct use. Which section in *The Bedford Handbook* will you and the student, a multilingual writer, consult?

3. You have been assigned to write in response to an essay you read for your composition class. Your instructor has asked that you use at least three quotations from the text in your response, which must be written in MLA style. You aren't quite sure how to integrate words from another source in your own writing. Which section in this handbook will help?

4. You supervise interns at a housing agency. Two of your interns have trouble with the *-s* endings on verbs. One tends to drop *-s* endings; the other tends to add them where they don't belong. You suspect that both problems stem from dialects spoken at home. The interns are in danger of losing their jobs because your boss thinks that anyone who writes "the tenant refuse . . ." or "the landlords insists . . ." is beyond hope. You disagree. Where can you direct your interns for help in *The Bedford Handbook*?

5. You are in a first-semester American literature course, which covers literature from the 1850s to World War II. On two different papers, your instructor has pointed out your tendency to shift between present tense and past tense as you write. When you consult your handbook, what do you discover about the rules for using verb tenses in papers about literature?

4 Using the Glossary of Usage

Consult the Glossary of Usage to see if the italicized words are used correctly. Then edit any sentences containing incorrect usage. If a sentence is correct, write "correct" after it. Example:

The pediatrician gave my daughter *a* injection for her
                                    an
allergy.

1. Changing attitudes *toward* alcohol have *effected* the beer industry.

2. It is *mankind's* nature to think wisely and act foolishly.

3. This afternoon I plan to *lie* out in the sun and work on my tan.

4. Our goal this year is to *grow* our profits by 9 percent.

5. Most sleds are pulled by no *less* than two dogs and no more than ten.

5 Using the directory to MLA works cited models

Let's say that you have written a short research essay on the origins of hip-hop music. You have cited the following five sources in your essay, using MLA documentation, and you are ready to type your list of works cited. Turn to page 530 and use the MLA directory to locate the appropriate models. Then write a correct entry for each source and arrange the entries in a properly formatted list of works cited.

A book by Jeff Chang titled *Can't Stop, Won't Stop: A History of the Hip-Hop Generation*. The book was published in New York by St. Martin's Press in 2005.

An online article by Kay Randall called "Studying a Hip Hop Nation." The article appeared on the University of Texas at Austin Web site. The title of the site is *University of Texas at Austin*. You accessed the site on August 13, 2009; the last update was October 9, 2008.

A journal article by H. Samy Alim titled "360 Degreez of Black Art Comin at You: Sista Sonia Sanchez and the Dimensions of a Black Arts Continuum." The article appears in the journal *BMa: The Sonia Sanchez Literary Review*. The article appears on pages 15–33. The volume number is 6, the issue number is 1, and the year is 2000.

A sound recording entitled "Rapper's Delight" performed by the Sugarhill Gang on the CD *The Sugarhill Gang*. The CD was released in 2008 by DBK Works.

A magazine article accessed online through the database *Expanded Academic ASAP*. The article, "The Roots Redefine Hip-Hop's Past," was written by Kimberly Davis and published in *Ebony* magazine in June 2003. The article appears on pages 162–64. You found this article on April 13, 2008.

Contents

Part IX Researched Writing   437

Part I
The Writing Process

Writing is not a matter of recording already developed thoughts but a process of figuring out what you think. Since it's not possible to think about everything all at once, most experienced writers handle a piece of writing in stages. You will generally move from planning to drafting to revising, but be prepared to return to earlier stages as your ideas develop.

1 Explore and plan; then rough out a first draft.

Before attempting a first draft, spend some time generating ideas. Mull over your subject while listening to music or driving to work, jot down inspirations, and explore your insights with a willing listener. Ask yourself questions: What do you find puzzling, striking, or interesting about your subject? What would you like to know more about? At this stage, you should be collecting information and experimenting with ways of focusing and organizing it to reach your readers.

1a Assess the writing situation.

Begin by taking a look at your writing situation. The key elements of a writing situation include the following:

- your subject
- the sources of information available to you
- your purpose
- your audience
- any constraints (length, document design, deadlines)

It is likely that you will make final decisions about all of these matters later in the writing process—after a first draft, for example. Nevertheless, you can save yourself time by thinking about as many of them as possible in advance. For a quick checklist, see the chart on page 3.

Academic English   What counts as good writing varies from culture to culture and even among groups within cultures. In some
situations, you will need to become familiar with the writing
styles — such as direct or indirect, personal or impersonal, plain
or embellished — that are valued by the culture or discipline for
which you are writing.

Checklist for assessing the writing situation

Subject

- Has the subject (or a range of possible subjects) been given to
  you, or are you free to choose your own?
- What interests you about your subject? What questions would
  you like to explore?
- Why is your subject worth writing about? How might readers
  benefit from reading about it?
- Do you need to narrow your subject to a more specific topic
  (because of length restrictions, for instance)?

Sources of information

- Where will your information come from: Reading? Personal
  experience? Observation? Interviews? Questionnaires?
- What documentation style is required: MLA? APA? *Chicago*?

Purpose and audience

- Why are you writing: To inform readers? To persuade them? To
  entertain them? To call them to action? Some combination of
  these?
- Who are your readers? How well informed are they about the
  subject? What do you want them to learn?
- How interested and attentive are they likely to be? Will they
  resist any of your ideas?
- What is your relationship to your readers: Student to instructor?
  Employee to supervisor? Citizen to citizen? Expert to novice?

Checklist for assessing the writing situation, *continued*

Length and document design

- Do you have any length specifications? If not, what length seems appropriate, given your subject, purpose, and audience?

- Is a particular document format required? If so, do you have guidelines to follow or examples to consult?

Reviewers and deadlines

- Who will be reviewing your draft in progress: Your instructor? A writing center tutor? Your classmates? A family member?

- What are your deadlines? How much time will you need to allow for the various stages of writing, including proofreading and printing the final draft?

Subject

Frequently your subject will be given to you. In a psychology class, for example, you might be asked to explain Bruno Bettelheim's Freudian analysis of fairy tales. In a composition course, assignments often ask you to respond to readings. In the business world, your assignment might be to draft a quarterly sales report.

When you are free to choose your own subject, it's a good idea to focus on something you are genuinely curious about. If you are studying television, radio, and the Internet in a communication course, for example, you might ask yourself which of these subjects interests you most. Perhaps you want to learn more about the role streaming video can play in activism and social change. Look through your readings and class notes to see if you can identify questions you'd like to explore further in an essay.

Making the most of your handbook

Effective research writers often start by asking a question.

▶ Posing questions for research: 46a

Make sure that you can reasonably investigate your subject in the space you have. If you are limited to a few pages, for

Ways to narrow a subject to a topic

Subdividing your subject

One way to subdivide a subject is to ask questions sparked by reading or talking to your classmates. If you are writing about teen pregnancy, for example, you might wonder why your city and a neighboring city have different rates of teen pregnancy. This question would give you a manageable topic for a short paper.

Restricting your purpose

Often you can restrict your purpose. For example, if your subject is preventing teen pregnancy, you might at first hope to call readers to action. Upon further reflection, you might realize that this goal is more than you could hope to accomplish, given your word limit. By adopting a more limited purpose—to show that an experimental health curriculum for sixth graders results in lower rates of teen pregnancy—you would have a manageable topic.

Restricting your audience

Consider writing for a particular audience. For example, instead of writing for a general audience on a broad subject such as teen pregnancy, you might address a group with a special interest in the subject: teens, parents, educators, or politicians.

Considering the information available to you

Look at the information you have collected. If you have gathered a great deal of information on one aspect of your subject (for example, counseling programs for pregnant teens) and less information on other aspects (such as birth control education), you may have found your topic.

example, you could not do justice to a subject as broad as "videos as agents of social change." You could, however, focus on one aspect of the subject—perhaps experts' contradictory claims about the effectiveness of "narrowcasting," or creating video content for small, specific audiences. The chart on this page suggests ways to narrow a subject to a manageable topic for a paper.

Whether or not you choose your own subject, it's important to be aware of the expectations of each writing situation. The chart on page 9 suggests ways to interpret assignments.

Sources of information

Where will your facts, details, and examples come from? Can you develop your topic from personal experience alone, or will you need to search for relevant information through reading, observation, interviews, or questionnaires?

Reading Reading is an important way to deepen your understanding of a topic and expand your perspective. Reading will be your primary source of information for many college assignments, which will generally be of two kinds: (1) analytical essays that call for a close reading of one book, essay, literary work, or visual and (2) research assignments that ask you to find and consult a variety of sources on a topic.

For an analytical essay, you will select details from the work, not to inform readers but to support an interpretation. You can often assume that your readers are familiar with the work and have a copy of it on hand, but be sure to provide enough context so that someone who doesn't know the work well can still follow your interpretation. When you quote from the work, page references are usually sufficient. When in doubt about the need for documentation, consult your instructor.

For a research paper, you cannot assume that your readers are familiar with your sources. Therefore, you must formally document all quoted, summarized, or paraphrased material.

Making the most of your handbook

Academic writing often requires that you read critically and cite your sources.

► Guidelines for active reading: page 87

► Analyzing an essay: 4d

► Interpreting literature: 55b

► Quoting, paraphrasing, and summarizing sources: 48c

Personal experience If your interest in a subject stems from your personal experience, you will want to ask what it is about your experience that would interest your audience and why. For example, if you volunteered at a homeless shelter, you might have spent some time talking to homeless children and learned about their needs. Perhaps you can use your experience to broaden your readers' understanding of the issues, to persuade an organization to fund an after-school program for homeless children, or to propose changes in legislation.

Observation   Observation is an excellent means of collecting information about a wide range of subjects, such as gender relationships on a popular television program, the clichéd language of sports announcers, or the appeal of a local art museum. For such subjects, do not rely on your memory alone; your information will be fresher and more detailed if you actively collect it, with a notebook, laptop, or tape recorder in hand.

Interviews and questionnaires   Interviews and questionnaires can supply detailed and interesting information on many subjects. A nursing student interested in the care of terminally ill patients might interview hospice nurses; a political science major might speak with a local judge about alternative sentencing for first offenders; a future teacher might conduct a survey on the use of computers in local elementary schools.

It is a good idea to record interviews to preserve any lively quotations that you might want to weave into your essay. Circulating questionnaires by e-mail or on a Web site will facilitate responses. Keep questions simple and specify a deadline to ensure that you get a reasonable number of replies. (See also 46g.)

Purpose

Your purpose will often be dictated by your writing situation. Perhaps you have been asked to draft a proposal requesting funding for a student organization, to report the results of a psychology experiment, or to write about the controversy surrounding genetically modified (GM) foods for the school newspaper. Even though your overall purpose is fairly obvious in such situations, a closer look at the assignment can help you make a variety of necessary decisions. How detailed should the proposal be? How technical does your psychology professor expect your report to be? Do you want to inform students about the GM food controversy or change their attitudes toward it?

In many writing situations, part of your challenge will be discovering a purpose. Asking yourself why readers should care about what you are saying can help you decide what your purpose might be. Perhaps your subject is magnet schools—schools that draw students from different neighborhoods because of features such as advanced science classes or a concentration on the arts. If you have discussed magnet schools in class, a description of how these schools work probably will not interest you or your readers. But maybe you have discovered that your county's magnet schools are not promoting diversity as had been planned and you want to call your readers to action. Or maybe you are interested in comparing student performance at magnet schools and traditional schools.

Although no precise guidelines will lead you to a purpose, you can begin by asking yourself which one or more of the following aims you hope to accomplish.

PURPOSES FOR WRITING

to inform	to evaluate
to persuade	to recommend
to entertain	to request
to call readers to action	to propose
to change attitudes	to provoke thought
to analyze	to express feelings
to argue	to summarize

Writers often misjudge their own purposes, summarizing when they should be analyzing, or expressing feelings about problems instead of proposing solutions. Before beginning any writing task, pause to ask, "Why am I communicating with my readers?" This question will lead you to another important question: "Just who are my readers?"

Understanding an assignment

Determining the purpose of an assignment

Usually the wording of an assignment will suggest its purpose. You might be expected to do one or more of the following in a college writing assignment:

- summarize information from textbooks, lectures, or research (See 4c.)
- analyze ideas and concepts (See 4d.)
- take a position on a topic and defend it with evidence (See 5.)
- synthesize (combine ideas from) several sources and create an original argument (See 52c and 56c.)

Understanding how to answer an assignment's question

Many assignments will ask you to answer a *how* or *why* question. Such questions cannot be answered using only facts; instead, you will need to take a position. For example, the question "*What* are the survival rates for leukemia patients?" can be answered by reporting facts. The question "*Why* are the survival rates for leukemia patients in one state lower than those in a neighboring state?" must be answered with both facts and interpretation. If a list of prompts appears in the assignment, be careful—instructors rarely expect you to answer all the questions in order. Look instead for topics, themes, or ideas that will help you ask your own questions.

Recognizing implied questions

When you are asked to *discuss*, *analyze*, *agree or disagree with*, or *consider* a topic, your instructor will often expect you to answer a *how* or *why* question.

Discuss the effects of the No Child Left Behind Act on special education programs.	=	*How* has the No Child Left Behind Act affected special education programs?
Consider the recent rise of attention deficit hyperactivity disorder diagnoses.	=	*Why* are diagnoses of attention deficit hyperactivity disorder rising?

Audience

Audience analysis can often lead you to an effective strategy for reaching your readers. A writer whose purpose was to persuade teenagers not to smoke began by making some observations about her audience (see the bottom of this page).

This analysis led the writer to focus on the social aspects of smoking rather than on the health risks. Her audience analysis also warned her against adopting a preachy tone that her readers might find offensive. Instead of lecturing, she decided to draw examples from her own experience as a smoker: burning holes in her best sweater, driving in zero-degree weather late at night to buy cigarettes, and so on. The result was an essay that reached its readers instead of alienating them.

Of course, in some writing situations the audience will not be neatly defined for you. Nevertheless, many of the choices you make as you write will tell readers who you think they are (novices or experts, for example), so it is best to be consistent.

For help with audience analysis, see the chart on page 3.

AUDIENCE ANALYSIS

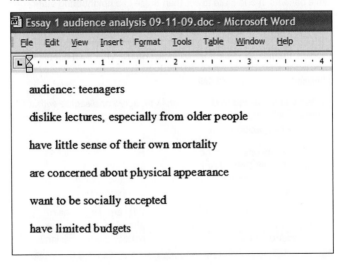

Academic audiences In the academic world, considerations of audience can be more complex than they seem at first. Your instructor will read your essay, of course, but most instructors play multiple roles while reading. Their first and most obvious roles are as coach and judge; less obvious is their role as an intelligent and objective reader, the kind of person who might reasonably be informed, convinced, entertained, or called to action by what you have to say.

Some instructors specify an audience, such as a hypothetical supervisor, readers of a local newspaper, or peers in a particular field. Other instructors expect you to imagine an audience appropriate to your purpose and your subject. Still others prefer that you write for a general audience of educated readers—nonspecialists who can be expected to read with an intelligent, critical eye.

Business audiences Writers in the business world often find themselves writing for multiple audiences. A letter to a client, for instance, might be distributed to sales representatives as well. Readers of a report might include persons with and without technical expertise or readers who want details and those who prefer a quick overview.

To satisfy the demands of multiple audiences, business writers have developed a variety of strategies: attaching cover letters to detailed reports, adding boldface headings, placing summaries in the margin, and so on.

Public audiences Writers in communities often write for a specific audience—the local school superintendent, a legislative representative, fellow members of a social group, readers of a local paper. With public writing, it is more likely that you are familiar with the views your readers hold and the assumptions they make, so you may be better able to judge how to engage those readers. If you are writing to a group of other parents to share ideas for lowering school bus transportation costs, for instance, you may have a good sense of whether to lead with a logical analysis of other school-related fees or with a fiery criticism of key decision makers.

Length and document design

Writers seldom have complete control over length. Journalists usually write within strict word limits set by their editors, businesspeople routinely aim for conciseness, and most college assignments specify an approximate length.

Your writing situation may also require certain document designs. Specific formats are used in business for letters, memos, and reports. In the academic world, you may need to learn precise conventions for lab reports, critiques, research papers, and so on. For most undergraduate essays, a standard format is acceptable (see 59).

In some writing situations, you will be free to create your own design, complete with headings, displayed lists, and perhaps visuals such as charts and graphs. For a discussion of the principles of document design, see 58.

Reviewers and deadlines

Professional and business writers rarely work alone. They work with reviewers, often called *editors*, who offer advice throughout the writing process. In college classes, too, the use of reviewers is common. Some instructors play the role of reviewer for you; others may ask you to visit your college's writing center. Still others schedule peer review sessions in class or online. Such sessions give you a chance to hear what other students think about your draft in progress—and to play the role of reviewer yourself.

Making the most of your handbook

Peer review can benefit student writers at any stage of the writing process.

▶ Guidelines for peer review: page 38

Deadlines are a key element of any writing situation. They help you plan your time and map out what you can accomplish in that time. For complex writing projects, such as research papers, you'll need to plan your time carefully. By working backward from the final deadline, you can create a schedule of target dates for completing parts of the process. (See p. 439 for an example.)

EXERCISE 1–1 Narrow five of the following subjects into topics that would be manageable for an essay of two to five pages.

1. Domestic violence and the courts
2. Performing as a musician
3. Treatments for mental illness
4. An experience with racism or sexism
5. Cell phones in the classroom
6. Images of women in video games
7. Mandatory drug testing in the workplace
8. Olympic swimmers
9. Presidential campaign funding
10. The films of the Coen brothers

EXERCISE 1–2 Suggest a purpose and an audience for five of the following subjects.

1. Graphic novels as literature
2. Genetic modification of cash crop foods
3. Government housing for military veterans
4. The future of online advertising
5. Working with special needs children
6. The challenges facing single parents
7. Obesity prevention and treatment
8. Growing up in a large family
9. The influence of African art on Picasso
10. Hybrid cars

hackerhandbooks.com/bedhandbook > Writing exercises > E-ex 1–4

1b Experiment with ways to explore your subject.

Instead of just plunging into a first draft, experiment with one or more techniques for exploring your subject, perhaps one of these:

- talking and listening
- annotating texts and taking notes
- listing
- clustering
- freewriting

- asking questions
- keeping a journal
- blogging (keeping a Weblog)

Whatever technique you turn to, the goal is the same: to generate ideas that will lead you to a question, a problem, or an issue that you want to explore further. At this early stage of the writing process, don't censor yourself. Sometimes an idea that initially seems trivial or far-fetched will actually turn out to be worthwhile.

Talking and listening

Because writing is a process of figuring out what you think about a subject, it can be useful to try out your ideas on other people. Conversation can deepen and refine your ideas before you even begin to set them down on paper. By talking and listening to others, you can also discover what they find interesting, what they are curious about, and where they disagree with you. If you are planning to advance an argument, you can try it out on listeners with other points of view.

Many writers begin a writing project by brainstorming ideas in a group, debating a point with friends, or chatting with an instructor. Others turn to themselves for company—by talking into a tape recorder. Some writers exchange ideas by sending e-mail or instant messages or by posting to discussion boards or blogs. You may be encouraged to share ideas with your classmates and instructor in an online workshop. One advantage of engaging in such discussions is that while you are "talking" you are actually writing.

Annotating texts and taking notes

When you write about a text, either a written work or a visual, one of the best ways to explore ideas is to mark up the work—on the pages of a print work (if you own a copy) or on a photocopy or printout. Annotating a text encourages you to look at it more carefully—to underline key concepts, to note contradictions in an argument, to raise questions for investigation. Here, for example, is a paragraph from an essay on medical ethics as one student annotated it.

What break-throughs?
Do all break-throughs have the same conse-quences?

Breakthroughs in genetics present us with a promise and a predicament. The promise is that we may soon be able to treat and prevent a host of debilitating diseases. The predicament is that our newfound genetic knowledge may also enable us to manipulate our own nature—to enhance our muscles, memories, and moods; to choose the sex, height, and other genetic traits of our children; to make ourselves "better than well." When science moves faster than moral understanding, as it does today, men and women struggle to articulate their unease. In liberal societies they reach first for the language of autonomy, fairness, and individual rights. But this part of our moral vocabulary is ill equipped to address the hardest questions posed by genetic engineering. The genomic revolution has induced a kind of moral vertigo.

Stem cell research?

What does he mean by "moral understanding"?

Which questions? He doesn't seem to be taking sides.

Is everyone really uneasy?
Is something a break-through if it creates a predicament?

—Michael Sandel, "The Case against Perfection"

After reading and annotating Michael Sandel's entire article, the student looked through his annotations for patterns. He noticed that several of his annotations pointed to the larger question of whether a scientific breakthrough should be viewed in terms of its moral consequences. He decided to reread the article, taking detailed notes with this question in mind.

> **Making the most of your handbook**
>
> Writing about a text or a visual is a common college assignment.
>
> ▶ Writing about texts: 4
> ▶ Advice on taking notes: 48c

Listing

Listing ideas—a technique sometimes known as *brainstorming*—is a good way to figure out what you know and what questions you have. Here is a list one student writer jotted down for an essay about funding for college athletics:

- Football receives the most funding of any sport.
- Funding comes from ticket sales, fundraisers, alumni contributions.
- Biggest women's sport is soccer.
- Women's soccer team is only ten years old; football team is fifty years old.
- Soccer games don't draw as many fans.
- Should funding be equal for all teams?
- Do alumni have the right to fund whatever they want?

The ideas and questions appear here in the order in which they first occurred to the writer. Later she rearranged them, grouped them under general categories, deleted some, and added others. These initial thoughts led the writer to questions that helped her narrow her topic. In other words, she treated her early list as a source of ideas and a springboard to new ideas, not as an outline.

Clustering

Unlike listing, clustering highlights relationships among ideas. To cluster ideas, write your topic in the center of a sheet of paper, draw a circle around it, and surround the circle with related ideas connected to it with lines. If some of the satellite ideas lead to more specific clusters, write them down as well. The writer of the diagram on page 17 was exploring ideas for an essay on obesity in children.

Freewriting

In its purest form, freewriting is simply nonstop writing. You set aside ten minutes or so and write whatever comes to mind, without pausing to think about word choice, spelling, or even meaning. If you get stuck, you can write about being stuck, but you should keep your fingers moving. If nothing much happens, you have lost only ten minutes. It's more likely, though, that something interesting will emerge—perhaps an eloquent sentence, an honest expression of feeling, or an idea worth further investigation. Freewriting also lets you

CLUSTER DIAGRAM

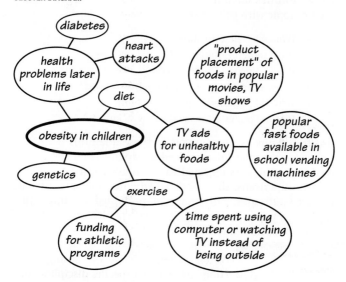

ask questions without feeling that you have to answer them. Sometimes a question that comes to mind at this stage will point you in an unexpected direction.

To explore ideas on a particular topic, consider using a technique known as *focused freewriting*. Again, you write quickly and freely, but this time you focus on a subject and pay attention to the connections among your ideas.

Asking questions

When gathering material for a story, journalists routinely ask themselves Who? What? When? Where? Why? and How? In addition to helping journalists get started, these questions ensure that they will not overlook an important fact.

Whenever you are writing about events, whether current or historical, asking questions is one way to get started. One student, whose topic was the negative reaction in 1915 to

D. W. Griffith's silent film *The Birth of a Nation*, began exploring her topic with this set of questions:

- *Who* objected to the film?
- *What* were the objections?
- *When* were protests first voiced?
- *Where* were protests most strongly expressed?
- *Why* did protesters object to the film?
- *How* did protesters make their views known?

As often happens, the answers to these questions led to another question the writer wanted to explore. After she discovered that protesters objected to the film's racist portrayal of
African Americans, she wondered whether their protests had
changed attitudes. This question prompted an interesting
topic for a paper: Did the film's stereotypes lead to positive, if
unintended, consequences?

> **Making the most of your handbook**
>
> Effective college writers begin by asking questions.
>
> ▶ Asking questions in academic disciplines: 7b

In the academic world, scholars
often generate ideas by posing questions related to a specific discipline: one
set of questions for analyzing literature,
another for evaluating experiments in
social psychology, still another for re-
porting field experiences in criminal justice. If you are writing
in a particular discipline, try to find out which questions its
scholars typically explore.

Keeping a journal

A journal is a collection of informal, exploratory, sometimes
experimental writing. In a journal, often meant for your eyes
only, you can take risks. In one entry, for example, you might
freewrite. In another, you might pose questions, whether or not
you have the answers. You might comment on an interesting
idea from one of your classes or keep a list of questions that
occur to you while reading. You might imagine a conversation
between yourself and your readers or stage a debate to understand positions counter to your own. A journal is also an excellent place to play around with language for the sheer fun of it.

Keeping a journal can be an enriching experience in its own right, since it allows you to explore issues without worrying about what someone else thinks. A journal can also serve as a sourcebook of ideas to draw on in future essays.

Blogging (keeping a Weblog)

Although a blog (Weblog) is a type of journal, it is a public writing space rather than a private one. In a blog, you can express opinions, release frustrations, make observations, recap an event, have fun with language, or do some combination of these. You can work through an idea for a paper by blogging about it in different ways or from different angles. One post might be your frustrated comments about the lack of parking for commuter students at your school. Maybe the next post shares a compelling statistic about competition for parking spaces at campuses nationwide. You can continue thinking about the topic as you respond to comments from other readers about alternatives to driving to campus.

1c Draft a working thesis.

As you explore your topic and identify questions to investigate, you will begin to see possible ways to focus your material. At this point, try to settle on a tentative central idea. The more complex your topic, the more your focus will change as your drafts evolve. For many types of writing, you will be able to assert your central idea in a sentence or two. Such a statement, which ordinarily appears in the opening paragraph of your finished essay, is called a *thesis statement*.

A thesis is often one or more of the following:

- the answer to a question you have posed
- the resolution of a problem you have identified
- a statement that takes a position on a debatable topic

A tentative, or working, thesis will help you organize your draft. Don't worry about the exact wording because your main point may change as you refine your efforts. Here, for example, are one student's efforts to pose a question and draft a thesis statement for an essay in his film course.

QUESTION

In *Rebel without a Cause*, how does the filmmaker show that Jim Stark becomes alienated from his family and friends?

WORKING THESIS

In *Rebel without a Cause*, Jim Stark, the main character, is often seen literally on the edge of physical danger—walking too close to a swimming pool, leaning over an observation deck, and driving his car toward a cliff.

The working thesis offers a useful place to start writing, but it doesn't give readers a reason to continue reading. The sentence includes an observation but no indication of why that observation matters. The student's final thesis is more engaging, reflects an evolution of his ideas, and is a better response to his question.

FINAL THESIS

The scenes in which Jim Stark is on the edge of physical danger—walking too close to a swimming pool, leaning over an observation deck, and driving his car toward a cliff— suggest that he is becoming more and more agitated by the constraints of family and society.

Here, another student identifies and responds to a problem in a thesis statement for an argument paper in her composition course.

PROBLEM

Americans who earn average incomes cannot run effective national political campaigns.

WORKING THESIS

Congress should pass legislation that would make it possible for Americans who are not wealthy to be viable candidates in national political campaigns.

The student has roughed out an idea for how to solve the problem—enacting federal legislation—but her working thesis

Testing a working thesis

Once you have come up with a working thesis, you can use the following questions to refine it.

- Does the thesis require an essay's worth of development? Or will you run out of points too quickly?

- Is the thesis too obvious? If you cannot come up with interpretations that oppose your own, consider revising your thesis.

- Can you support your thesis with the evidence available?

- Can you explain why readers will want to read an essay with this thesis? Can you respond when a reader asks "So what?" or "Why does it matter?"

isn't specific enough. The student's final thesis offers a specific solution to the problem she identifies and helps her focus her draft.

FINAL THESIS

By restricting campaign spending, Congress could enable candidates without personal wealth to compete more effectively in national elections.

Keep in mind as you draft your working thesis that a successful thesis is a promise to the reader; it points both the writer and the reader in a definite direction. For a more detailed discussion of the thesis, see 1e.

1d Sketch a plan.

Once you have generated some ideas and formulated a working thesis, you might want to sketch an informal outline to see how you will support your thesis and to figure out a tentative structure for your ideas. Informal outlines can take many forms. Perhaps the most common is simply the thesis followed by a list of major ideas.

Working thesis: Television advertising should be regulated to help prevent childhood obesity.

- Children watch more television than ever.
- Snacks marketed to children are often unhealthy and fattening.
- Childhood obesity can cause diabetes and other problems.
- Dealing with these problems costs taxpayers billions of dollars.
- Therefore, these ads are actually costing the public money.
- But if advertising is free speech, do we have the right to regulate it?
- We regulate alcohol and cigarette ads on television, so why not advertisements for soda and junk food?

If you began by jotting down a list of ideas (see p. 15), you can turn the list into a rough outline by crossing out some ideas, adding others, and putting the ideas in a logical order.

Planning with headings

When writing a long college paper or a business document, consider using headings to guide your planning and to help your readers follow the organization of your final draft. While planning, you can insert your working thesis, experiment with possible headings, and type chunks of text beneath each heading. You may need to try grouping your ideas in a few different ways to suit your purpose and audience.

Making the most of your handbook

Headings can help writers plan and readers understand a document.

▶ Using headings: 58b
▶ Papers organized with headings: 56f, 57f

When to use a formal outline

Early in the writing process, rough outlines have certain advantages: They can be produced quickly, they are obviously tentative, and they can be revised easily. However, a formal outline may be useful later in the writing process, after you have written a rough draft, especially if your topic is complex.

A formal outline helps you see whether the parts of your essay work together and whether your essay's structure is logical. A formal outline will often make clear which parts of your draft should be rearranged and which parts don't fit at all.

The following formal outline brought order to the research paper in 54c, on Internet surveillance in the workplace. The student's thesis is an important part of the outline. Everything else in the outline supports it, either directly or indirectly.

Thesis: Although companies often have legitimate concerns that lead them to monitor employees' Internet usage—from expensive security breaches to reduced productivity—the benefits of electronic surveillance are outweighed by its costs to employees' privacy and autonomy.

I. Although employers have always monitored employees, electronic surveillance is more efficient.
   A. Employers can gather data in large quantities.
   B. Electronic surveillance can be continuous.
   C. Electronic surveillance can be conducted secretly, with keystroke logging programs.
II. Some experts argue that employers have legitimate reasons to monitor employees' Internet usage.
   A. Unmonitored employees could accidentally breach security.
   B. Companies are legally accountable for the online actions of employees.
III. Despite valid concerns, employers should value employee morale and autonomy and avoid creating an atmosphere of distrust.
   A. Setting the boundaries for employee autonomy is difficult in the wired workplace.
      1. Using the Internet is the most popular way of wasting time at work.
      2. Employers can't easily determine if employees are working or surfing the Web.
   B. Surveillance can create resentment among employees.
      1. Web surfing can relieve stress, and restricting it can generate tension between managers and workers.
      2. Enforcing Internet usage can seem arbitrary.

IV. Surveillance may not increase employee productivity, and trust may benefit productivity.

    A. A company shouldn't care how many hours salaried employees work as long as they get the job done.

    B. Casual Internet use can actually benefit companies.

        1. The Internet may spark business ideas.

        2. The Internet may suggest ideas about how to operate more efficiently.

V. Employees' rights to privacy are not well defined by the law.

    A. Few federal guidelines on electronic surveillance exist.

    B. Employers and employees are negotiating the boundaries without legal guidance.

    C. As technological capabilities increase, there will be an increased need to define boundaries.

Guidelines for constructing an outline

1. Put the thesis at the top.
2. Make items at the same level parallel grammatically (see section 9).
3. Use sentences unless phrases are clear.
4. Use the conventional system of numbers, letters, and indents:

   I.

      A.

      B.

         1.

         2.

            a.

            b.

   II.

      A.

      B.

         1.

         2.

            a.

            b.

→

5. Always use at least two subdivisions for a category, since nothing can be divided into fewer than two parts.

6. Limit the number of major sections in the outline; if the list of roman numerals (at the first level) gets too long, try clustering the items into fewer major categories with more subcategories.

7. Be flexible; be prepared to change your outline as your drafts evolve.

1e For most types of writing, draft an introduction that includes a thesis.

Generally, the introduction to a piece of writing announces the main point; the body develops it, usually in several paragraphs; the conclusion drives it home. You can begin drafting, however, at any point. If you find it difficult to introduce a paper that you have not yet written, try drafting the body first and saving the introduction for later.

Your introduction will usually be a paragraph of 50 to 150 words (in a longer paper, it may be more than one paragraph). Perhaps the most common strategy is to open with a few sentences that engage the reader and establish your purpose for writing, your main point. The sentence stating the main point is called a *thesis*. (See also 1c.) In the following examples, the thesis has been italicized.

> The debate over athletes' use of performance-enhancing substances is getting more complicated as biotechnologies such as gene therapy become a reality. The availability of these new methods of boosting performance will force us to decide what we value most in sports—displays of physical excellence developed through hard work or victory at all costs. For centuries, spectators and athletes have cherished the tradition of fairness in sports. While sports competition is, of course, largely about winning, it is also about the means by which a player or team wins. *Athletes who use any type of biotechnology give themselves an unfair advantage and disrupt the sense of fair play, and they should be banned from competition.*   —Jamal Hammond, student

As the United States industrialized in the nineteenth century, using desperate immigrant labor, social concerns took a backseat to the task of building a prosperous nation. The government did not regulate industries and did not provide an effective safety net for the poor or for those who became sick or injured on the job. However, immigrants and the poor did have a few advocates. Settlement houses such as Hull-House in Chicago provided information, services, and a place for reform-minded individuals to gather and work to improve the conditions of the urban poor. Alice Hamilton was one of these reformers. Her work at Hull-House spanned twenty-two years and later expanded throughout the nation. *Hamilton's efforts helped to improve the lives of immigrants and drew attention to problems and people that until then had been virtually ignored.*

—Laurie McDonough, student

Ideally, the sentences leading to the thesis should hook the reader, perhaps with one of the following:

a startling statistic or an unusual fact

a vivid example

a description

a paradoxical statement

a quotation or a bit of dialogue

a question

an analogy

an anecdote

Whether you are writing for a scholarly audience, a professional audience, a public audience, or a general audience, you cannot assume your readers' interest in the topic. The hook should spark curiosity and offer readers a reason to continue.

Although the thesis frequently appears at the end of the introduction, it can just as easily appear at the beginning. Much work-related writing commonly begins with the thesis.

Flextime scheduling, which has proved its effectiveness at the Library of Congress, should be introduced on a trial basis at the main branch of the Montgomery County Public Library. By offering flexible work hours, the library can boost employee morale, cut down on absenteeism, and expand its hours of operation.

—David Warren, student

For some types of writing, it may be difficult or impossible to express the central idea in a thesis sentence; or it may be unwise or unnecessary to put a thesis sentence in the essay itself. A personal narrative, for example, may have a focus too subtle to be distilled in a single sentence. Strictly informative writing, like that found in many business memos, may be difficult to summarize in a thesis. In some academic fields, such as nursing, writers may produce reports that do not require a thesis. In such instances, do not try to force the central idea into a thesis sentence. Instead, think in terms of an overriding purpose, which may or may not be stated directly.

> **Making the most of your handbook**
>
> The thesis sentence is central to many types of writing.
> - ► Writing about texts: 4
> - ► Writing arguments: 5
> - ► Writing research papers: 50 (MLA), 56a (APA), 57a (*Chicago*)
> - ► Writing literature papers: 55c

> **Academic English**   If you come from a culture that prefers an indirect approach in writing, you may feel that asserting a thesis early in an essay sounds unrefined and even rude. In the United States, however, readers appreciate a direct approach; when you state your point as directly as possible, you show that you value your readers' time.

Characteristics of an effective thesis

An effective thesis sentence should be a central idea that requires supporting evidence; it should be of adequate scope for an essay of the assigned length; and it should be sharply focused. (See also 1c.)

When constructing a thesis sentence, you should ask yourself whether you can successfully develop it with the sources available to you and for the purpose you've identified. Also ask if you can explain why readers should be interested in reading an essay that explores this thesis. If your thesis addresses a question or problem that intrigues you, then it will probably interest your readers as well. If your thesis would be obvious to everyone, then your readers will be less compelled to read on.

A thesis must require proof or further development through facts and details; it cannot itself be a fact or a description.

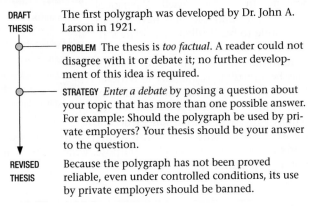

DRAFT THESIS The first polygraph was developed by Dr. John A. Larson in 1921.

PROBLEM The thesis is *too factual*. A reader could not disagree with it or debate it; no further development of this idea is required.

STRATEGY *Enter a debate* by posing a question about your topic that has more than one possible answer. For example: Should the polygraph be used by private employers? Your thesis should be your answer to the question.

REVISED THESIS Because the polygraph has not been proved reliable, even under controlled conditions, its use by private employers should be banned.

A thesis should be an answer to a question, not a question itself.

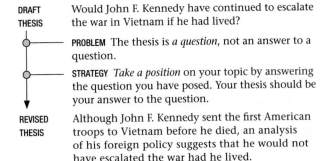

DRAFT THESIS Would John F. Kennedy have continued to escalate the war in Vietnam if he had lived?

PROBLEM The thesis is *a question*, not an answer to a question.

STRATEGY *Take a position* on your topic by answering the question you have posed. Your thesis should be your answer to the question.

REVISED THESIS Although John F. Kennedy sent the first American troops to Vietnam before he died, an analysis of his foreign policy suggests that he would not have escalated the war had he lived.

A thesis should be of sufficient scope for your assignment; it should not be too broad.

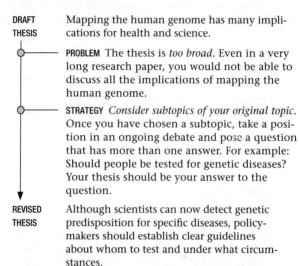

DRAFT THESIS Mapping the human genome has many implications for health and science.

PROBLEM The thesis is *too broad*. Even in a very long research paper, you would not be able to discuss all the implications of mapping the human genome.

STRATEGY *Consider subtopics of your original topic.* Once you have chosen a subtopic, take a position in an ongoing debate and pose a question that has more than one answer. For example: Should people be tested for genetic diseases? Your thesis should be your answer to the question.

REVISED THESIS Although scientists can now detect genetic predisposition for specific diseases, policy-makers should establish clear guidelines about whom to test and under what circumstances.

A thesis also should not be too narrow.

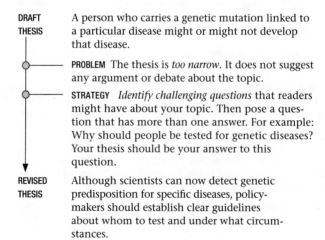

DRAFT THESIS A person who carries a genetic mutation linked to a particular disease might or might not develop that disease.

PROBLEM The thesis is *too narrow*. It does not suggest any argument or debate about the topic.

STRATEGY *Identify challenging questions* that readers might have about your topic. Then pose a question that has more than one answer. For example: Why should people be tested for genetic diseases? Your thesis should be your answer to this question.

REVISED THESIS Although scientists can now detect genetic predisposition for specific diseases, policy-makers should establish clear guidelines about whom to test and under what circumstances.

Revising with comments | Unclear thesis

Understanding the comment

When a teacher or tutor points out that your thesis is unclear, the comment often signals that readers may have a hard time identifying your essay's main point.

> Fathers are more involved in the lives of their children today than they used to be. In the past, the father's primary role was as the provider; child care was most often left to the mother or other relatives. However, today's father drives to dance lessons, coaches his child's baseball team, hosts birthday parties, and provides homework help. <u>Do more involved fathers help or hinder the development of their children?</u>

Unclear thesis

One student wrote this introductory paragraph in response to an assignment that asked her to analyze the changing roles of mothers or fathers.

A writer's thesis, or main point, should be phrased as a statement, not a question. To revise, the student could answer the question she has posed, or she could pose a new question and answer it. After considering her evidence, she needs to decide what position she wants to take, state this position clearly, and show readers *why* this position—her thesis—matters.

Similar comments: vague thesis • state your position • your main point?

Revising when *your* thesis is unclear

1. *Ask questions.* What is the thesis, position, or main point of the draft? Can you support it with the available evidence?

2. *Reread your entire draft.* Because ideas develop as you write, you may find that your conclusion contains a clearer statement of your main point than your current thesis does. Or you may find your thesis elsewhere in your draft.

3. *Try revising your thesis* by framing it as an answer to a question you pose, the resolution of a problem you identify, or a position you take in a debate. And put your thesis to the "So what?" test: Why would a reader be interested in this thesis?

More help with writing a clear thesis: **1c** and **1e**

A thesis should be sharply focused, not too vague. Avoid fuzzy, hard-to-define words such as *interesting*, *good*, or *disgusting*.

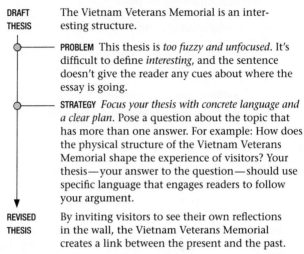

DRAFT THESIS   The Vietnam Veterans Memorial is an interesting structure.

PROBLEM This thesis is *too fuzzy and unfocused*. It's difficult to define *interesting*, and the sentence doesn't give the reader any cues about where the essay is going.

STRATEGY *Focus your thesis with concrete language and a clear plan.* Pose a question about the topic that has more than one answer. For example: How does the physical structure of the Vietnam Veterans Memorial shape the experience of visitors? Your thesis—your answer to the question—should use specific language that engages readers to follow your argument.

REVISED THESIS   By inviting visitors to see their own reflections in the wall, the Vietnam Veterans Memorial creates a link between the present and the past.

EXERCISE 1–3   In each of the following pairs, which sentence might work well as a thesis for a short paper? What is the problem with the other one? Is it too factual? Too broad? Too vague?

1. a. By networking with friends, a single parent can manage to strike a balance among work, school, a social life, and family.
    b. Single parents face many challenges as they try to juggle all of their responsibilities.
2. a. At the Special Olympics, athletes with disabilities show that, with hard work and support from others, they can accomplish anything—that they can indeed be winners.
    b. Working with the Special Olympics program is rewarding.
3. a. History 201, taught by Professor Brown, is offered at 10:00 a.m. on Tuesdays and Thursdays.
    b. Whoever said that history is nothing but polishing tombstones must have missed History 201, because in Professor Brown's class history is very much alive.
4. a. So far, research suggests that zero-emissions vehicles are not a sensible solution to the problem of steadily increasing air pollution.

    b. Because air pollution is of serious concern to many people today, several US government agencies have implemented plans to begin solving the problem.

5. a. Anorexia nervosa is a dangerous and sometimes deadly eating disorder occurring mainly in young, upper-middle-class teens.

    b. The eating disorder anorexia nervosa is rarely cured by one treatment alone; only by combining drug therapy with psychotherapy and family therapy can the patient begin the long, torturous journey to wellness.

hackerhandbooks.com/bedhandbook > Writing exercises > E-ex 1–5 to 1–7

1f Draft the body.

The body of the essay develops support for your thesis, so it's important to have at least a working thesis before you start writing. What does your thesis promise readers? Try to keep your response to that question in mind as you draft the body.

You may already have written an introduction that includes your thesis. If not, as long as you have a thesis you can begin developing the body and return later to the introduction. If your thesis suggests a plan (see 1e) or if you have sketched a preliminary outline, try to block out your paragraphs accordingly. Draft the body of your essay by writing a paragraph about each supporting point you listed in the planning stage. If you do not have a plan, pause for a few moments and sketch one (see 1d).

Keep in mind that often you might not know what you want to say until you have written a draft. It is possible to begin without a plan—assuming you are prepared to treat your first attempt as a "discovery draft" that will be radically rewritten once you discover what you really want to say. Whether or not you have a plan when you begin drafting, you can often figure out a workable order for your ideas by stopping each time you start a new paragraph to think about what your readers will need to know to follow your train of thought.

For more detailed advice about paragraphs in the body of an essay, see 3.

Understanding the comment

When a teacher or tutor indicates that you need to "be specific," the comment often signals that you could strengthen your writing with additional details.

> There are many cultural differences between the United States and Italy. Italian citizens do not share many of the same (attitudes) or (values) as American citizens. Such (differences) make it hard for some Italian students to feel comfortable coming to the United States for extended periods of time, even for an academic year.
>
> *Be specific!*

In this body paragraph, a student responds to an assignment that asked him to interview a group of international students and describe the challenges of studying in the United States.

The paragraph presents a student's claim but doesn't include specific examples or evidence to support the claim. To revise, the student might focus on *one* specific example of cultural differences between the United States and Italy. The student might then ask: What vivid details illustrate this cultural difference? The answer to that question will provide specific evidence to inform and persuade readers.

Similar comments: need examples • too general • evidence?

Strategies for revising when *your* writing needs to be more specific

1. *Reread your topic sentence* to understand the focus of the paragraph.

2. *Ask questions.* Does the paragraph contain claims that need support? Have you provided evidence—specific examples, vivid details and illustrations, statistics and facts—to help readers understand your ideas and find them persuasive?

3. *Choose exact, active, and engaging words* as you shape your evidence. And remember that details and examples don't speak for themselves. You'll need to interpret your evidence to show readers how it supports your claims.

More help with using specific evidence: **5e**

33

TIP: As you draft, keep careful notes and records of all the sources you read and consult. (See 48b.) If you quote, paraphrase, or summarize a source, include a citation, even in your draft. You will save time and avoid plagiarism if you follow the rules of citation and documentation while drafting.

1g Draft a conclusion.

A conclusion should remind readers of the essay's main idea without repeating it. Often the concluding paragraph can be relatively short. By the end of the essay, readers should already understand your main point; your conclusion drives it home and, perhaps, gives readers something more to consider.

In addition to echoing your main idea, a conclusion might briefly summarize the essay's key points, propose a course of action, offer advice, discuss the topic's wider significance, or pose a question for future study. To conclude an essay analyzing the shifting roles of women in the military, one student discusses her topic's implications for society as a whole.

> As the military continues to train women in jobs formerly reserved for men, our understanding of women's roles in society will no doubt continue to change. When news reports of women training for and taking part in combat operations become commonplace, reports of women becoming CEOs, police chiefs, and even president of the United States will cease to surprise us. Or perhaps we have already reached this point.   —Rosa Broderick, student

To make the conclusion memorable, you might include a detail, an example, or an image from the introduction to bring readers full circle; a quotation or a bit of dialogue; an anecdote; or a witty or ironic comment. To conclude an essay explaining how credit card companies hook college students, one student brings readers full circle by echoing his thesis and ending with a familiar phrase borrowed from popular culture.

> Credit cards are a convenient part of life, and there is nothing wrong with having one or two of them. Before signing up for a particular card, however, college students should

take time to read the fine print and do some comparison shopping. Students also need to learn to resist the many seductive offers that credit card companies extend to them after they have signed up. Students who can't "just say no" to temptations such as high credit limits and revolving balances could well become hooked on a cycle of debt from which there is no easy escape.   —Matt Watson, student

Whatever concluding strategy you choose, keep in mind that an effective conclusion is decisive and unapologetic. Avoid introducing wholly new ideas at the end of an essay. And because the conclusion is so closely tied to the rest of the essay in both content and tone, be prepared to rework it (or even replace it) when you revise.

2   Make global revisions; then revise sentences.

For most experienced writers, revising is rarely a one-step process. Global matters—focus, purpose, organization, content, and overall strategy—generally receive attention first. Improvements in sentence structure, word choice, grammar, punctuation, and mechanics come later.

Many of us resist making global revisions because we find it difficult to view our work from our audience's perspective. To distance yourself from a draft, put it aside for a while, preferably overnight or even longer. When you return to it, try to play the role of your audience as you read. Ask questions like the following:

> **Making the most of your handbook**
>
> Seeking and using feedback are critical steps in revising a college paper.
>
> ▶ Checklist for global revision: page 40
> ▶ Guidelines for peer reviewers: page 38
> ▶ Tips on using feedback: page 42

- Would readers disagree with my thesis? If so, how might I address their counterarguments?

- Would readers be confused by my organization?

- Have I provided enough evidence to inform or persuade readers?

EXAMPLE OF GLOBAL REVISIONS

Big Box Stores Aren't So Bad

In her essay *Big Box Stores Are Bad for Main Street*, Betsy Taylor shifts the focus away from the economic effects of these stores to the effects these stores have on the "soul" of America. She claims that stores like Home Depot and Target are bad for America, they draw people out of downtown shopping districts and cause them to focus on consumption. She believes that small businesses are good for America because they provide personal attention, encourage community interaction, and make each city different from the other ones. But Taylor's argument is not strong because it is based on nostalgic images rather than true assumptions about the roles that businesses play in consumers lives and communities. Taylor reveals that she has a nostalgic view of American society and does not understand economic realities. ~~She focuses~~ on idealized shoppers and shopkeepers interacting on Main Street ~~rather than the economic realities of the situation.~~ As a result, she incorrectly assumes that simply getting rid of big box stores would have a positive effect on us.

For example, in her first paragraph she refers to a big box store as a "25-acre slab of concrete with a 100,000 square foot box of stuff" that lands on a town, evoking images of something strong and powerful conquering something small and weak. But she oversimplifies a complex issue. *She ignores the complex economic relationship between large chain stores and the communities in which they exist.*

EXAMPLE OF SENTENCE-LEVEL REVISIONS

Rethinking Big-Box Stores
~~Big Box Stores Aren't So Bad~~ (no italics)

In her essay "Big Box Stores Are Bad for Main Street," Betsy Taylor ~~shifts~~ *focuses* ~~the focus away from~~ not on the economic effects of ~~these~~ *large chain* stores ~~to~~ but on the effects these stores have on the "soul" of America. She ~~claims~~ *argues* that stores like Home Depot, *and Wal-Mart* ~~and~~ Target, are bad for America *because* ~~they~~ draw people out of downtown shopping districts and cause them to focus on consumption. *In contrast, she* ~~She~~ believes that small businesses are good for America because they provide personal attention, encourage community interaction, and make each city *unique.* ~~different from the other ones.~~ But Taylor's argument is ~~not strong~~ *unconvincing* because it is based on *nostalgia* ~~nostalgic images~~—on idealized *images of* ~~shoppers and shopkeepers interacting on~~ Main Street—rather than ~~true assumptions about~~ *on* the roles that businesses play in consumers' lives and communities. *By ignoring* ~~She ignores~~ the complex economic relationship between large chain stores and ~~the~~ *their* communities, *Taylor* ~~in which they exist. As a result, she~~ incorrectly assumes that simply getting rid of big box stores would have a positive effect on ~~us.~~ *America's communities.*

Taylor's colorful use of language ~~Taylor~~ reveals that she has a nostalgic view of American society and does not understand economic realities. *In* ~~For example, in~~ her first paragraph, *Taylor* ~~she~~ refers to a big box store as a "25-acre slab of concrete with a 100,000 square foot box of stuff" that "lands on a town," evoking images of ~~something strong and powerful conquering something small and weak.~~ *a powerful monster crushing the American way of life* (1011). But she oversimplifies a complex issue.

Guidelines for peer reviewers

View yourself as a coach, not a judge.

Think of yourself as proposing possibilities, not dictating revisions. It is the writer, after all, who will have to grapple with the task of improving the essay. Work with the writer to identify the strengths and limitations of the draft.

Restate the writer's main ideas.

It's helpful for the writer to see if you understand the main point of the essay. Restate the thesis for the writer. And try to paraphrase each paragraph of the draft to help the writer see if the essay's points are clearly expressed.

Where possible, give specific compliments.

Vague compliments (such as "I liked your essay") sound insincere—and they aren't helpful. Point out specific successes. For example, you might mention that you particularly admire how the writer examines the opposing viewpoint in the second paragraph before challenging it in the third.

Link suggestions for improvement to the writer's goals.

Criticism is constructive when it is offered in the right spirit. For example, you might advise the writer to put the most dramatic example last, where it will have the maximum impact on readers. Or you might suggest that a passage would gain power if the writer replaced abstractions with concrete details.

Ask questions and tell the writer where you would like to hear more.

Note passages that you found either confusing or interesting. By asking for clarification, you will help the writer see what needs to be revised. Indicating an interest in hearing more about a topic will often inspire the writer to come up with useful and vivid details.

Express interest in reading the next draft.

When your interest is sincere, expressing it can be a powerful motivation for a writer.

If possible, enlist friends or family to play the role of audience for you, or perhaps visit your school's writing center to go over your draft with a writing tutor. Ask your reviewers to focus on the larger issues of writing, not on word- or sentence-level issues.

2a Approach global revision in cycles.

Making major revisions can be difficult, sometimes even painful. You might discover, for example, that an essay's first three paragraphs are merely padding, that its central argument tilts the wrong way, and that you sound pompous. But the fact that you can see such problems in your own writing is a sign of hope. Those opening paragraphs can be dropped, the argument's slant realigned, the voice made more approachable.

Because the process of global revision can be overwhelming, approach it in cycles. Five common cycles of global revision are discussed in this section:

- Engaging the audience
- Sharpening the focus
- Improving the organization
- Strengthening the content
- Clarifying the point of view

You can handle these cycles in nearly any order or even skip or combine some. See the chart on page 40.

Engaging the audience

Considerations of audience can contribute to global revision. Sometimes a rough draft needs an overhaul because it is directed at no audience at all for no apparent purpose. Readers are put off by such writing because they don't know *why* they are reading. A good question to ask yourself is the toughest question a reader might ask: "So what?" If your draft can't pass the "So what?" test, you may need to rethink your entire approach; in fact, you may even decide to scrap the draft and start over.

Checklist for global revision

Audience

- Does the draft address a question, a problem, or an issue that is of interest to readers?
- Is the tone diplomatic and respectful?

Focus

- Is the thesis clear? Is it prominently placed?
- If there is no thesis, is there a good reason for omitting one?
- Are any ideas obviously off the point?

Organization and paragraphing

- Are there enough organizational cues for readers (such as topic sentences and headings)?
- Are ideas presented in a logical order?
- Are any paragraphs too long or too short for easy reading?

Content

- Is the supporting material relevant and persuasive?
- Which ideas need further development?
- Are the parts proportioned sensibly? Do major ideas receive enough attention?
- Where might material be deleted?

Point of view

- Is the draft free of distracting shifts in point of view (from *I* to *you*, for example, or from *it* to *they*)?
- Is the dominant point of view—*I, we, you, he, she, it, one,* or *they*—appropriate?

Once you have made sure that your draft is directed at an audience—readers who stand to benefit in some way by reading it—you may still need to refine your tone. The tone of a piece of writing expresses the writer's feelings toward the audience, so it is important to get it right. If the tone seems too self-centered or too flippant, stuffy, bossy, patronizing, opinionated, or hostile, modify it.

For example, the following paragraph was drafted by a student who hoped to persuade his audience to buy organic produce.

A PARAGRAPH THAT ALIENATES READERS

If you choose to buy organic produce, you are supporting local farmers as well as demonstrating your opposition to chemical pesticides. As more and more supermarkets carry organic fruits and vegetables, consumers have fewer reasons not to buy organic. Some consumers do not buy organic produce because they are not willing to spend the extra money. But if you care at all about the environment or the small farmer, you should be willing to support organic farms in your area.

When he reviewed this draft, the writer saw the need to be more diplomatic. He didn't want to alienate his readers by accusing them of being unwilling to spend money or uninterested in helping the environment. He revised the paragraph to offer readers positive reasons to support his cause.

A PARAGRAPH THAT RESPECTS READERS

By choosing to buy organic produce, you have the opportunity to support local farmers, to oppose the use of chemical pesticides, and to taste some of the freshest produce available. Because more supermarkets carry organic produce than ever, you won't even have to miss out on any of your favorite fruits or vegetables. Although organic produce can be more expensive than conventional produce, the costs are not prohibitive. For example, a pound of organic bananas at my local grocery store is eighty-nine cents, while the conventional bananas are sixty-nine cents a pound. If you can afford this small price difference, you will have the opportunity to make a difference for the environment and for the small farmer.   —Leon Nage, student

Guidelines for using reviewers' comments

Don't take criticism personally.

Your reader is responding to your essay, not to you. It may be frustrating to hear that you still have more work to do, but taking feedback seriously will make your essay stronger.

Pay attention to ideas that contradict your own.

If comments show that a reviewer doesn't understand what you're trying to do, don't be defensive. Instead, consider why your reader is confused and figure out how to clarify your point. Responding to readers' objections—instead of dismissing them—will strengthen your ideas and make your essay more persuasive.

Look for global concerns.

Your reviewers will probably make more suggestions than you can use. To keep things manageable, focus on the comments that relate to your thesis, organization, and evidence. Do your readers understand your main idea? Can they follow your train of thought? Are they looking for more supporting ideas or facts?

Weigh feedback carefully.

As you begin revising, you may find yourself sorting through suggestions from many people, including instructors, writing tutors, and peer reviewers. Sometimes these readers will agree, but often their advice will differ. It's important to sort through all the comments you receive with your original goals in mind—otherwise you'll be facing the impossible task of trying to incorporate everyone's advice.

Keep a revision and editing log.

Make a clear and simple list of the global and sentence-level concerns that keep coming up in most of your reviewers' comments. That list can serve as a starting point each time you revise a paper. When you take charge of your own writing in this way, comments will become a valuable resource rather than something to dread.

Sharpening the focus

A clearly focused draft fixes readers' attention on one central idea and does not stray from that idea. You can sharpen the focus of a draft by clarifying the introduction (especially the thesis) and by deleting any text that is off the point.

Clarifying the introduction   Check to see whether the introduction clearly states the essay's main point. Does it let readers know what to expect as they read on? Does it make the significance of the subject clear so that readers will want to read on?

Can readers tell where the introduction stops and the body of the essay begins? Have you perhaps included material in the introduction that really belongs in the body? Is your introduction too broad or unfocused?

The most important sentence in the introduction is the thesis. (See 1e.) If your thesis is poorly focused or if it doesn't accurately state the real point of the essay, revise it. If your essay lacks a thesis, add one now or have a good reason for not including one.

Deleting text that is off the point   Compare the introduction, particularly the thesis sentence, with the body of the essay. Does the body fulfill the promise of the introduction? If not, you will need to adjust one or the other. Either rebuild the introduction to fit the body or keep the introduction and delete any body sentences or paragraphs that stray from its point.

Improving the organization

A draft is well organized when its major divisions are logical and easy to follow. To improve the organization of your draft, you may need to take one or more of the following actions: adding or sharpening topic sentences, moving blocks of text, and inserting headings.

Adding or sharpening topic sentences Topic sentences state the main ideas of the paragraphs in the body of an essay. (See 3a.) You can review the organization of a draft by reading only the topic sentences. Do they clearly support the essay's main idea? Do they make a reasonable sentence outline of the paper? If your draft lacks topic sentences, either add them or have a good reason for omitting them.

Moving blocks of text Improving the organization of a draft can be as simple as moving a few sentences from one paragraph to another or reordering paragraphs. You may also find that you can clarify the organization of a draft by combining choppy paragraphs or by dividing those that are too long for easy reading. (See 3e.) Often, however, the process is more complex. As you move blocks of text, you may need to supply transitions to make them fit smoothly in the new positions; you may also need to rework topic sentences to make your new organization clear.

Before moving text, consider sketching a revised outline. Divisions in the outline might become topic sentences in the restructured essay. (See 1d.)

Inserting headings In long documents, such as complex research papers or business reports, headings can help readers follow your organization. Typically, headings are presented as phrases, declarative or imperative sentences, or questions. To draw attention to headings, you can center them, put them in boldface, underline them, use all capital letters, or do some combination of these. (See also 58b.)

TIP: Construct an outline of your draft after you have written it (see 1d). By going through your draft paragraph by paragraph and listing the most important ideas in an outline, you can see how the parts work together and whether each paragraph has a clear focus.

Strengthening the content

In reviewing the content of a draft, first consider whether your argument is sound. You may need to rethink your argument

Understanding the comment

When a teacher or tutor points out that your introduction needs to be "narrowed," the comment often signals that the beginning sentences of your essay are not specific or focused.

> Sports fans are an interesting breed. They have many ways of showing support for the team they love. Many fans perform elaborate rituals before, during, or after a sporting event. These rituals are performed both privately in homes with family or friends and at the stadiums and arenas where the games take place. Experiencing a sports competition where the fans are participating in rituals to support the team makes the game exciting. Some fans even believe that rituals are necessary and that their actions influence the outcome of a game. However, some fans go beyond cheering, and their actions, verbal harassment, and chanted slurs reveal a darker side of sports.
>
> Narrow your introduction

One student wrote this introductory paragraph in response to an assignment that asked her to analyze a ritual.

This opening begins with such general statements that the purpose of the essay is unclear. To revise, the student might delete her first few sentences — generalizations about sports fans and rituals — and focus on one specific sports ritual. She might describe how fans who wear lucky clothes, eat certain foods, or chant a particular expression think they can influence the outcome of a game. Using a quotation, a vivid example, or a startling statistic, the student might show how a particular ritual not only unites fans but also reveals a dark side of sports. Whatever "hook" she chooses should lead readers to her thesis.

Similar comments: focus your intro • too general • engage your readers

Revising when you need to narrow *your* introduction

1. *Reread your introduction and ask questions.* Are the sentences leading to your thesis specific enough to engage readers and communicate your purpose? Do these sentences lead logically to your thesis? Do they spark your readers' curiosity and offer them a reason to continue reading?

2. *Try revising your introduction with a "hook"* that will engage readers — a question, quotation, paradoxical statement, or vivid example.

More advice on writing introductions: **1e**

as you revise. Second, consider whether any text (sentences, paragraphs, or longer passages) should be added or deleted, keeping in mind your readers' needs. Finally, if your purpose is to argue a point, consider how persuasively you have proved your point to an intelligent, discerning audience.

Rethinking your argument   A first draft presents you with an opportunity for rethinking your argument. You can often deepen your ideas about a subject by asking yourself some hard questions: Is your claim more sweeping than the evidence allows? Have you left out an important step in the argument? Have you dealt fairly with the arguments of the opposition? Is your draft free of faulty reasoning? The more challenging your subject, the more likely you will find yourself adjusting your early thoughts. (For more about writing arguments, see 5.)

Adding text   If any paragraphs or sections of the essay are too skimpy to be clear and convincing (a common flaw in rough drafts), add specific facts, details, and examples. You may need to go back to the beginning of the writing process: listing specifics, brainstorming ideas with friends or classmates, perhaps doing more research.

Deleting text   Look for sentences and paragraphs that can be cut without serious loss of meaning. Perhaps you have repeated yourself or strayed from your point. Maybe you have given too much emphasis to minor ideas. Cuts may also be necessitated by word limits, such as those imposed by a college assignment or by the realities of the business world, where readers are often pressed for time.

Clarifying the point of view

If the point of view of a draft shifts confusingly or if it seems not quite appropriate for your purpose, audience, and subject, consider adjusting it.

There are three basic points of view: the first person (*I* or *we*), the second person (*you*), and the third person (*he, she, it, one*, or *they*). Each point of view is appropriate in at least some contexts, and you may need to experiment before deciding which one best suits your needs.

The third-person point of view   Much academic and professional writing is best presented from the third-person point of view (*he*, *she*, *it*, *one*, or *they*), which puts the subject in the foreground. The *I* point of view is usually inappropriate in such contexts because, by focusing attention on the writer, it pushes the subject to the background. Consider one student's first-draft description of the behavior of a species of frog he had observed in the field.

> **INAPPROPRIATE FIRST PERSON**
> Each frog that *I* was able to locate in trees remained in its tree during *my* observation period. However, *I* noticed that there was considerable movement within the home tree.

Here the *I* point of view is distracting. The student's revision focuses more on the frogs and less on himself.

> **APPROPRIATE THIRD PERSON**
> Each frog located in a tree remained in that tree throughout the observation period. The frogs moved about considerably, however, within their home trees.

Just as the first-person *I* can draw too much attention to the writer, the second-person *you* can focus unnecessarily on the reader. In the following sentence from a memo, a supervisor writing to a sales manager needlessly draws attention to the reader.

> **INAPPROPRIATE SECOND PERSON**
> When *you* look at the numbers, *you* can clearly see that travel expenses must be cut back.

This sentence is clearer and more direct when it is revised without the distracting *you* point of view.

APPROPRIATE THIRD PERSON

The numbers clearly show that travel expenses must be cut back.

Although the third-person point of view is often a better choice than the *I* or *you* point of view, it is not trouble-free. Writers can run into problems when their writing requires many singular pronouns. Using the pronoun *he* to include both men and women is no longer acceptable, and using *one* as a gender-neutral alternative can sound stuffy. Writers should be aware of the awkwardness that third-person singular pronouns create and should try to find graceful alternatives (see 17f and 22a).

The second-person point of view The *you* point of view, which puts the reader in the foreground, is appropriate for advising readers directly, as in giving tips or instructions. All imperative sentences, such as the advice for writers in this book, are written from the *you* point of view, although the word itself is frequently omitted. "Sketch a plan" means "*You* should sketch a plan." (See 62a.)

In the course of giving advice or instructions, the actual word *you* may be appropriate and even desired. In a pamphlet designed to motivate students to vote, the second-person *you* is effective.

APPROPRIATE SECOND PERSON

If *you* have ideas about how the Student Senate should be run and *you* want *your* voice to be heard, vote on October 15 at the field house.

Written in the third-person point of view, the call to vote is far less motivating.

INAPPROPRIATE THIRD PERSON

Students who have ideas about how the Student Senate should be run and who want their voices to be heard should vote on October 15 at the field house.

Indefinite uses of *you* are inappropriate in formal writing. (See 23d.) The third person is usually more appropriate.

INAPPROPRIATE SECOND PERSON

Young Japanese women wired together electronic products on a piece-rate system: The more *you* wired, the more *you* were paid.

APPROPRIATE THIRD PERSON

The more *they* wired, the more *they* were paid.

The first-person point of view   If much of a writer's material comes from personal experience, the *I* point of view will be most natural.

Writers who are aware that the first-person point of view is sometimes seen as inappropriate in academic writing often go to extreme lengths to avoid it.

INAPPROPRIATE THIRD PERSON

Mama read with such color and detail that *one* could fancy *oneself* as the hero of the story.

Because the paper in which this sentence appeared was a personal reminiscence, the entire paper sounded more natural when the writer allowed himself to use the word *I*.

APPROPRIATE FIRST PERSON

Mama read with such color and detail that *I* could fancy *myself* as the hero of the story.

TIP: As you write in various disciplines and for a range of audiences, pay attention to the ways in which writers use the first-person or third-person point of view. For guidelines on point of view in various disciplines, see the chart on page 134.

hackerhandbooks.com/bedhandbook > Writing exercises > E-ex 2–1 and 2–2

2b Revise and edit sentences; proofread the final draft.

When you revise sentences, you focus on effectiveness; when you edit, you check for correctness. Proofreading is a slow and careful reading in search of spelling errors, typos, and other obvious mistakes.

Revising and editing sentences

Parts III–VIII in this book offer advice on revising sentences for clarity and on editing them for grammar, punctuation, and mechanics.

Some writers handle sentence-level revisions directly at the computer, experimenting on-screen with a variety of possible improvements. Other writers prefer to print out a hard copy of the draft, mark it up, and then return to the computer to enter their revisions. Here, for example, is a rough-draft paragraph as one student edited it on-screen for a variety of sentence-level problems.

> Although some cities have found creative ways to improve access to public transportation for passengers with physical disabilities, ~~and to fund other programs, there have been problems in~~ our city has struggled with ~~due to the need to address~~ budget constraints and competing ~~needs~~ priorities. ~~This~~ The budget crunch has led citizens to question how funds are distributed.~~?~~ For example, last year ~~when~~ city officials voted to use available funds to support ~~had to choose between allocating funds for accessible transportation or allocating funds to~~ after-school programs rather than transportation upgrades. ~~, they voted for the after-school programs.~~ It is not clear to some citizens why ~~these~~ after-school programs are more important.

The original paragraph was flawed by wordiness, a problem that can be addressed through any number of revisions. The following revision would also be acceptable.

> Some cities have funded improved access to public transportation for passengers with physical disabilities. Because of budget constraints, our city chose to fund after-school programs rather than transportation programs. As a result, citizens have begun to question how funds are distributed and why certain programs are more important than others.

Some of the paragraph's improvements do not involve choice and must be fixed in any revision. The hyphen in *after-school programs* is necessary; a noun must be substituted for the pronoun *these* in the last sentence; and the question mark in the second sentence must be changed to a period.

> **Grammar checkers** can help with some but by no means all of the sentence-level problems in a typical draft. Many problems—such as faulty parallelism and misplaced modifiers—require an understanding of grammatical structure that computer programs lack. Even if the grammar checker makes a suggestion for revision, it is your responsibility to decide whether the suggestion is more effective than your original.

Proofreading

After revising and editing, you are ready to prepare the final manuscript. (See 59 for guidelines.) Make sure to allow yourself enough time for proofreading—the final and most important step in manuscript preparation.

Proofreading is a special kind of reading: a slow and methodical search for misspellings, typographical mistakes, and omitted words or word endings. Such errors can be difficult to spot in your own work because you may read what you intended to write, not what is actually on the page. To fight this tendency, try proofreading out loud, articulating each word as it is actually written. You might also try proofreading your sentences in reverse order, a strategy that takes your attention away from the meanings you intended and forces you to think about surface features instead.

Although proofreading may be dull, it is crucial. Errors strewn throughout an essay are distracting and annoying. If the writer doesn't care about this piece of writing, thinks the reader, why should I? A carefully proofread essay, however, sends a positive message: It shows that you value your writing and respect your readers.

> **Spell checkers** are more reliable than grammar checkers, but they too must be used with caution. Many typographical errors (such as *quiet* for *quite*) and misused words (such as *effect* for *affect*) slip past the spell checker because it flags only words not found in its dictionary.

Student essay

Matt Watson wrote the essay "Hooked on Credit Cards" (pp. 56–59) in response to the following assignment.

> In an essay of 500–1,000 words, discuss a significant problem facing today's college students. Assume that your audience consists of general readers, not simply college students.
>
> If you use any sources, document them with in-text citations and a list of works cited in MLA style (see section 53 in *The Bedford Handbook*).

When he received the assignment, Watson considered several possibilities before settling on the topic of credit cards. He already knew something about the topic because

SAMPLE NOTES

Ideas for college problem essay 3.3.01.doc - Microsoft Word

File   Edit   View   Insert   Format   Tools   Table   Window   Help   Adobe PDF   Acrobat Comment

Ideas for college problem essay

Phone call with Rebecca Watson, 3.3.01

- Easy to get hooked on credit cards and run up huge debts
- Why do credit card companies try to sign up students? Aren't we a bad risk? But they must be profiting, or they'd stop.
- High interest rates
- Ads for credit cards appear all over campus and on the Web
- Using plastic doesn't seem like spending money
- Tactics used by the companies—offering low interest rates at first, setting high credit limits, allowing a revolving balance
- What happens to students who get in debt but don't have parents who can bail them out?

his older sister had run up large credit card bills while in college and was working hard to pay them off. Because the assignment required him to *discuss* a problem, he decided that a good strategy would be to identify a *how* or *why* question to answer.

To get started on his paper, Watson talked to his sister on the phone and typed some ideas on his laptop. (See p. 52.)

After he listed these ideas, Watson identified the question that would drive his essay:

> Why do credit card companies put so many resources into soliciting students, who often have poor credit profiles?

Watson decided that his purpose would be to answer this question for himself and his audience. He wrote his first draft quickly, focusing more on ideas than on grammar, style, and mechanics. Then he made some additions and deletions and fixed a few typos before submitting the draft for peer review. Here is the draft he submitted, together with the most helpful comments he received from classmates. The peer reviewers were asked to comment on global issues—audience appeal, focus, organization, content, and point of view—and to ignore any problems with grammar and punctuation.

ROUGH DRAFT

Hooked on Credit Cards

Credit card companies love to extend credit to college students. You see ads for these cards on campus bulletin boards and also on the Web. Why do companies market their product to a population that has no job and lacks a substantial credit history? They seem to be trying to hook us on their cards; unfortunately many of us do get hooked on a cycle of spending that leads to financial ruin.

Banks require applicants for a loan to demonstrate a good credit history and some evidence of a source of

Good question. Is there more to the answer than you've written here? That is, why are these companies trying to hook us? (Mark)

Some students do have jobs. (Sara)

The assignment asks for a general audience; your thesis shouldn't be about "us." (Sara)

Shouldn't your thesis also explain *how* the companies hook students? (Tim)

income, but credit card companies don't. On campus, students are bombarded with offers of preapproved credit cards. Then there are the Web sites. Sites with lots of student traffic are plastered with banner ads like this one: "To get a credit card, you need to establish credit. To establish credit, you need a credit card. Stop the vicious cycle! Apply for our student MasterCard."

Credit card companies often entice students with low interest rates, then they jack up the rates later. A student may not think about the cost of interest. That new stereo or back-to-school wardrobe can get pretty expensive at 17.9% interest if it's compounded over several months. Would you have bought that $600 item if you knew it would end up costing you $900?

Most cards allow the holder to keep a revolving balance, which means that they don't have to pay the whole bill, they just pay a minimum amount. The minimum is usually not too much, but a young person may be tempted to keep running up debt. The companies also give students an unrealistically high credit limit. I've heard of undergraduates who had a limit as high as $4,000.

Card companies make money not just from high interest rates. Often they charge fees for late payments. I've heard of penalties for going over the credit limit too.

Often students discover too late that they are thoroughly trapped. Some drop out of school, others graduate and then can't find a good job because they have a poor credit rating. There are psychological problems too. Your parents may bail you out of debt, but you'll probably feel guilty. On a Web site, I read that two students felt so bad they committed suicide.

Credit cards are a part of life these days, and everyone is probably wise to have a charge account for emergencies. But college students must take a hard look at their financial picture. The very things that make those cards so convenient and easy to use can lead to a mountain of debt that will take years to pay off.

Your paper focuses on the tactics that the companies use, but your conclusion doesn't mention them. (Tim)

After rereading his draft and considering the feedback from his classmates, Watson realized that he needed to develop his thesis further. He set out some goals for revising his essay.

MATT WATSON'S REVISION GOALS

Answer Mark's question about what credit card companies gain by hooking students.

Expand explanation of both why and how credit card companies market cards to students.

Include evidence to back up claims about how credit card companies hook students. Look at reputable Web sites: student loan provider Nellie Mae and the Consumer Federation of America.

Rework introduction to explain why credit card companies profit from students who have no steady source of income.

Adjust point of view so that essay is appropriate for a general audience, not just for other students.

When he was more or less satisfied with the paper as a whole, Watson worked to polish his sentences. His final draft begins on the next page.

Watson 1

Matt Watson

Professor Mills

English 101

12 March 2001

Hooked on Credit Cards

Introduction hooks readers with interesting details.

Credit card companies love to extend credit to college students, especially those just out of high school. Ads for credit cards line campus bulletin boards, flash across commercial Web sites for students, and get stuffed into shopping bags at college bookstores.

Introduction poses a question that leads readers to the thesis.

Why do the companies market their product so vigorously to a population that lacks a substantial credit history and often has no steady source of income? The answer is that significant profits can be earned through high interest rates and assorted penalties and fees.

Thesis announces Watson's main point.

By granting college students liberal lending arrangements, credit card companies often hook them on a cycle of spending that can ultimately lead to financial ruin.

Clear topic sentences guide readers through the body of the paper.

Whereas banks require applicants for a loan to demonstrate a good credit history and some evidence of income, credit card companies make no such demands on students. On campus, students find themselves bombarded with offers of preapproved cards—and not just on flyers pinned to bulletin boards. Many campuses allow credit card vendors to solicit applications during orientation week. In addition to offering preapproved cards, these vendors often give

Essay is double-spaced throughout.

away T-shirts or CDs to entice students to apply. Some companies even offer rewards program bonuses based on a student's GPA. Students are bombarded on the Web as well. Sites with heavy student traffic are emblazoned with banner ads like this one: "To get a credit card, you need to establish credit. To establish credit, you need a credit card. Stop the vicious cycle! Apply for our student MasterCard."

Marginal annotations indicate MLA-style formatting and effective writing.

Watson 2

Credit card companies often entice students with low "teaser" interest rates of 13% and later raise those rates to 18% or even higher. Others charge high rates up front, trusting that students won't read the fine print. Some young people don't think about the cost of interest, let alone the cost of interest compounding month after month. That back-to-school wardrobe can get pretty expensive at 17.9% interest compounded over several months. A $600 trip to Fort Lauderdale is not such a bargain when in the long run it costs $900 or more.

In addition to charging high interest rates, credit card companies try to maximize the amount of interest generated. One tactic is to extend an unreasonably high credit limit to students. According to Nellie Mae statistics, in 1998 undergraduates were granted an average credit limit of $3,683; for graduate students, the figure jumped to $15,721. Nearly 10% of the students in the Nellie Mae study carried balances near or exceeding these credit limits (Blair).

Another tactic is to allow students to maintain a revolving balance. A revolving balance permits the debtor to pay only part of a current bill, often an amount just a little larger than the accumulated interest. The indebted student is tempted to keep on charging, paying a minimum amount every month, because there aren't any immediate consequences to doing so.

Once a student is hooked on a cycle of debt, the companies profit even further by assessing a variety of fees and penalties. According to a press release issued by Consumer Action and the Consumer Federation of America, many credit card companies charge late fees and "over the limit" penalties as high as $29 per month. In addition, grace periods are often shortened to ensure that late fees kick in earlier. Many companies also raise interest rates for those who fail to pay on time or who exceed the credit limit. Those "penalty" rates can climb as high as 25% (1-2).

Body paragraphs are developed with details and examples.

Transition serves as a bridge between paragraphs.

Summary of the source is in Watson's own words.

Source is documented with an MLA in-text citation.

Watson cites a Web article from a reputable source.

Watson 3

Often students discover too late that they are thoroughly hooked. The results can be catastrophic. Some students are forced to drop out of school and take low-paying full-time jobs. Others, once they graduate, have difficulty landing good jobs because of their poor credit rating. Many students suffer psychologically as well. Even those who have parents willing to bail them out of debt often experience a great deal of anxiety and guilt. Two students grew so stressed by their accumulating debt that they committed suicide (Consumer Federation of Amer. 3).

Conclusion echoes Watson's main idea.

Credit cards are a convenient part of life, and there is nothing wrong with having one or two of them. Before signing up for a particular card, however, college students should take time to read the fine print and do some comparison shopping. Students also need to learn to resist the many seductive offers that credit card companies extend to them after they have signed up. Students who can't "just say no" to temptations such as high credit limits and revolving balances could well become hooked on a cycle of debt from which there is no easy escape.

Watson 4

Works Cited

Blair, Alan D. "A High Wire Act: Balancing Student Loan and Credit
Card Debt." *Credit World* 86.2 (1997): 15-17. *Business Source
Premier*. Web. 4 Mar. 2001.

Consumer Action and Consumer Federation of America. "Card Issuers Hike
Fees and Rates to Bolster Profits." *Consumer Federation of America*.
Consumer Federation of Amer., 5 Nov. 1998. Web. 4 Mar. 2001.

Consumer Federation of America. "Credit Card Debt Imposes Huge Costs
on Many College Students." *Consumer Federation of America*.
Consumer Federation of Amer., 8 June 1999. Web. 4 Mar. 2001.

Works cited page
follows MLA
format.

2c Prepare a portfolio; reflect on your writing.

At the end of the semester, your instructor may expect you
to submit a portfolio, or collection, of your writing. A writing portfolio often consists of drafts, revised pieces, and reflective entries that demonstrate a writer's thinking and
learning processes or that showcase the writer's best work.
Your instructor may give you the choice of submitting a paper
portfolio, often maintained and submitted in a folder or
binder, or an e-portfolio, maintained and submitted as a Web
site or as a collection of files on a flash drive or a CD.

Your instructor may distinguish between a *process portfolio*
and an *evaluation portfolio* (sometimes called an *assessment
portfolio*). A process portfolio allows you to demonstrate your
development as a writer; in it you will collect notes, outlines,
brainstorming, reflective journal or blog entries, multiple
drafts—in short, the messy stuff. In an evaluation portfolio,
you will include a few select final pieces that have perhaps
been revised multiple times, along with early drafts of those
pieces. At the end of the semester, you may be asked to re-
shape your process portfolio into an evaluation portfolio.

As early in the course as possible, be sure you know the answers to the following questions:

- Should the portfolio be a paper collection or an electronic one? Is it your choice?
- Will the portfolio be a process portfolio, an evaluation portfolio, or some combination of the two?
- Will the portfolio be checked or assessed before the end of the term? If so, when or how often?
- Are you free to choose any or all of the pieces to include?
- Are you free to include a variety of items (not just rough and final drafts of papers), such as outlines and notes, journal entries, photographs or other visuals, comments from readers, sound files, or video clips?
- Will your instructor be the primary or only audience for the portfolio? Or will the portfolio be shared with peers or with other instructors?
- Who will evaluate the portfolio?

Reflection—the process of stepping back periodically to examine your decisions, preferences, strengths, and challenges as a writer—is the backbone of portfolio keeping. Many instructors require writers to submit a number of reflective entries throughout the semester.

When you submit your portfolio for a final evaluation or reading, you may be asked to include a reflective opening statement—a cover letter, an introduction, a preface, or an essay. Whatever form your reflective piece takes, it could be your most important writing in the course. You will need to show that you can identify the strengths and weaknesses of your writing, comment on the progress you've made in the course, understand your own writing process, and make good writing decisions. Your instructor or other evaluator will expect you to reflect on how the specific pieces in the portfolio show your development as a writer.

Writing a reflective opening statement for your portfolio

Your instructor may require a reflective document in which you introduce the pieces in your portfolio and comment on your development as a writer throughout the course. Your document may take the form of an essay, a cover letter, or another introductory statement. Check with your instructor about the form this document should take.

For an effective portfolio cover document, you might try one or more of the following strategies:

- Discuss, in depth, your best entry. Explain why it is your best and how it reflects what you learned in the course.

- Discuss each piece of writing you've included, touching on its strengths.

- Describe in detail the revisions you've made to one key piece and the improvements and changes you want others to notice. Include specific passages from the piece.

- Demonstrate what this portfolio illustrates about you as a writer, student, researcher, or critical thinker.

- Acknowledge the readers or reviewers who have influenced your portfolio and describe their influence.

- Reflect on what you've learned about writing, reading, or other topics of the course.

- Acknowledge an important challenge you faced in your writing and show how you worked to overcome it. Where possible, include specific references to one or more pieces in your portfolio.

- Reflect on how you plan to take the skills and experiences from your writing course into other courses where writing will be assigned.

Keep in mind that it is critical to write multiple drafts of the reflective cover document, perhaps getting feedback from a peer, a tutor, or your instructor between drafts.

3 Build effective paragraphs.

Except for special-purpose paragraphs, such as introductions and conclusions (see 1e and 1g), paragraphs are clusters of information supporting an essay's main point (or advancing a story's action). Aim for paragraphs that are clearly focused, well developed, organized, coherent, and neither too long nor too short for easy reading.

3a Focus on a main point.

A paragraph should be unified around a main point. The point should be clear to readers, and all sentences in the paragraph should relate to it.

Stating the main point in a topic sentence

As readers move into a paragraph, they need to know where they are—in relation to the whole essay—and what to expect in the sentences to come. A good topic sentence, a one-sentence summary of the paragraph's main point, acts as a signpost pointing in two directions: backward toward the thesis of the essay and forward toward the body of the paragraph.

Like a thesis sentence (see 1c and 1e), a topic sentence is more general than the material supporting it. Usually the topic sentence (italicized in the following example) comes first in the paragraph.

> *All living creatures manage some form of communication.* The dance patterns of bees in their hive help to point the way to distant flower fields or announce successful foraging. Male stickleback fish regularly swim upside-down to indicate outrage in a courtship contest. Male deer and lemurs mark territorial ownership by rubbing their own body secretions on boundary stones or trees. Everyone has seen a frightened dog put his tail between his legs and run in panic. We, too, use gestures, expressions, postures, and movement to give our words point. [Italics added.] —Olivia Vlahos, *Human Beginnings*

Sometimes the topic sentence is introduced by a transitional sentence linking it to earlier material. In the following paragraph, the topic sentence has been delayed to allow for a transition.

> But flowers are not the only source of spectacle in the wilderness. *An opportunity for late color is provided by the berries of wildflowers, shrubs, and trees.* Baneberry presents its tiny white flowers in spring but in late summer bursts forth with clusters of red berries. Bunchberry, a ground-cover plant, puts out red berries in the fall, and the red berries of wintergreen last from autumn well into the winter. In California, the bright red, fist-sized clusters of Christmas berries can be seen growing beside highways for up to six months of the year. [Italics added.]   —James Crockett et al., *Wildflower Gardening*

Occasionally the topic sentence may be withheld until the end of the paragraph—but only if the earlier sentences hang together so well that readers perceive their direction, if not their exact point. The opening sentences of the following paragraph state facts, so they are supporting material rather than topic sentences, but they strongly suggest a central idea. The topic sentence at the end is hardly a surprise.

> Tobacco chewing starts as soon as people begin stirring. Those who have fresh supplies soak the new leaves in water and add ashes from the hearth to the wad. Men, women, and children chew tobacco and all are addicted to it. Once there was a shortage of tobacco in Kạobawä's village and I was plagued for a week by early morning visitors who requested permission to collect my cigarette butts in order to make a wad of chewing tobacco. Normally, if anyone is short of tobacco, he can request a share of someone else's already chewed wad, or simply borrow the entire wad when its owner puts it down somewhere. *Tobacco is so important to them that their word for "poverty" translates as "being without tobacco."* [Italics added.]
> —Napoleon A. Chagnon, *Yanomamö: The Fierce People*

You will find that some professional writers, especially journalists and informal essayists, do not always use clear topic sentences. In college writing, however, topic sentences are often necessary for clarifying the lines of an argument or reporting the research in a field. In business writing, topic sentences (along with headings) are essential because readers often scan for information.

Sticking to the point

Sentences that do not support the topic sentence destroy the unity of a paragraph. If the paragraph is otherwise focused, such sentences can simply be deleted or perhaps moved elsewhere. In the following paragraph describing the inadequate facilities in a high school, the information about the chemistry instructor (in italics) is clearly off the point.

> As the result of tax cuts, the educational facilities of Lincoln High School have reached an all-time low. Some of the books date back to 1990 and have long since shed their covers. The few computers in working order must share one printer. The lack of lab equipment makes it necessary for four or five students to work at one table, with most watching rather than performing experiments. *Also, the chemistry instructor left to have a baby at the beginning of the semester, and most of the students don't like the substitute.* As for the furniture, many of the upright chairs have become recliners, and the desk legs are so unbalanced that they play seesaw on the floor. [Italics added.]

Sometimes the solution for a disunified paragraph is not as simple as deleting or moving material. Writers often wander into uncharted territory because they cannot think of enough evidence to support a topic sentence. Feeling that it is too soon to break into a new paragraph, they move on to new ideas for which they have not prepared the reader. When this happens, the writer is faced with a choice: Either find more evidence to support the topic sentence or adjust the topic sentence to mesh with the evidence that is available.

Revising with comments

Understanding the comment

When a teacher or tutor tells you that you have "more than one point in this paragraph," the comment often signals that not all sentences in your paragraph support the topic sentence.

> Bringing casino gaming to Massachusetts would benefit the state in a number of ways. First, it would provide needed property tax relief for many of the state's towns and cities. Casino gaming would also bring in revenue needed to fix the state's roads and bridges. The speaker of the House of Representatives is blocking the governor's proposal because he believes the social costs are greater than the economic benefits. Many people agree with the speaker. Most important, casino gaming would provide jobs in areas of the state that have suffered economically in recent years. *More than one point in this paragraph*

One student wrote this body paragraph in response to an assignment that asked him to take a position on a current issue.

The topic sentence promises a discussion of benefits, but the detour into risks strays from the point. To revise, the student should focus on the key word in his topic sentence—*benefit*—because that signals to readers that the paragraph will examine the advantages of casino gaming. He might focus his paragraph by providing specific examples of benefits and deleting references to risks, perhaps using risks as counterpoints in a separate paragraph.

Similar comments: unfocused • lacks unity • hard to follow

Strategies for revising when *you* have more than one point in a paragraph

1. *Reread your paragraph and ask questions.* What is the main point of the paragraph? Is there a topic sentence that signals to readers what to expect in the rest of the paragraph? Does each sentence support the topic sentence and logically follow from the one before? Have you included sentences that perhaps belong elsewhere in your paper?

2. *Remember the purpose of topic sentences*; they serve as important signposts for readers. Make sure that the wording of your topic sentence is precise and that you have enough evidence to support it in the paragraph.

More advice on unifying paragraphs: **3d**

EXERCISE 3–1 Underline the topic sentence in the following paragraph and cross out any material that does not clarify or develop the central idea.

Quilt making has served as an important means of social, political, and artistic expression for women. In the nineteenth century, quilting circles provided one of the few opportunities for women to forge social bonds outside of their families. Once a week or more, they came together to sew as well as trade small talk, advice, and news. They used dyed cotton fabrics much like the fabrics quilters use today; surprisingly, quilters' basic materials haven't changed that much over the years. Sometimes the women joined their efforts in support of a political cause, making quilts that would be raffled to raise money for temperance societies, hospitals for sick and wounded soldiers, and the fight against slavery. Quilt making also afforded women a means of artistic expression at a time when they had few other creative outlets. Within their socially acceptable roles as homemakers, many quilters subtly pushed back at the restrictions placed on them by experimenting with color, design, and technique.

hackerhandbooks.com/bedhandbook > **Writing exercises** > E-ex 3–2

3b Develop the main point.

Though an occasional short paragraph is fine, particularly if it functions as a transition or emphasizes a point, a series of brief paragraphs suggests inadequate development. How much development is enough? That varies, depending on the writer's purpose and audience.

For example, when health columnist Jane Brody wrote a paragraph attempting to convince readers that it is impossible to lose fat quickly, she knew that she would have to present a great deal of evidence because many dieters want to believe the opposite. She did *not* write only the following:

When you think about it, it's impossible to lose—as many diets suggest—10 pounds of *fat* in ten days, even on a total fast. Even a moderately active person cannot lose so much weight so fast. A less active person hasn't a prayer.

This three-sentence paragraph is too skimpy to be convincing. But the paragraph that Brody did write contains enough evidence to convince even skeptical readers.

> When you think about it, it's impossible to lose—as many . . . diets suggest—10 pounds of *fat* in ten days, even on a total fast. A pound of body fat represents 3,500 calories. To lose 1 pound of fat, you must expend 3,500 more calories than you consume. Let's say you weigh 170 pounds and, as a moderately active person, you burn 2,500 calories a day. If your diet contains only 1,500 calories, you'd have an energy deficit of 1,000 calories a day. In a week's time that would add up to a 7,000-calorie deficit, or 2 pounds of real fat. In ten days, the accumulated deficit would represent nearly 3 pounds of lost body fat. Even if you ate nothing at all for ten days and maintained your usual level of activity, your caloric deficit would add up to 25,000 calories. . . . At 3,500 calories per pound of fat, that's still only 7 pounds of lost fat.
>
> —Jane Brody, *Jane Brody's Nutrition Book*

3c Choose a suitable pattern of organization.

Although paragraphs (and indeed whole essays) may be patterned in any number of ways, certain patterns of organization occur frequently, either alone or in combination: examples and illustrations, narration, description, process, comparison and contrast, analogy, cause and effect, classification and division, and definition. These patterns (sometimes called *methods of development*) have different uses, depending on the writer's subject and purpose.

Examples and illustrations

Examples, perhaps the most common pattern of development, are appropriate whenever the reader might be tempted to ask, "For example?" Though examples are just selected instances, not a complete catalog, they are enough to suggest the truth of many topic sentences, as in the following paragraph.

> Normally my parents abided scrupulously by "The Budget," but several times a year Dad would dip into his battered black strongbox and splurge on some irrational, totally satisfying luxury. Once he bought over a hundred comic books at a flea market, doled out to us thereafter at the tantalizing rate of two a week. He always got a whole flat of pansies, Mom's favorite flower, for us to give her on Mother's Day. One day a boy stopped at our house selling fifty-cent raffle tickets on a sailboat and Dad bought every ticket the boy had left—three books' worth. —Connie Hailey, student

Illustrations are extended examples, frequently presented in story form. Because they require several sentences apiece, they are used more sparingly than examples. When well selected, however, they can be a vivid and effective means of developing a point. The writer of the following paragraph uses illustrations to demonstrate that Harriet Tubman, the underground railroad's most famous conductor, was a genius at eluding her pursuers.

> Part of [Harriet Tubman's] strategy of conducting was, as in all battle-field operations, the knowledge of how and when to retreat. Numerous allusions have been made to her moves when she suspected that she was in danger. When she feared the party was closely pursued, she would take it for a time on a train southward bound. No one seeing Negroes going in this direction would for an instant suppose them to be fugitives. Once on her return she was at a railroad station. She saw some men reading a poster and she heard one of them reading it aloud. It was a description of her, offering a reward for her capture. She took a southbound train to avert suspicion. At another time when Harriet heard men talking about her, she pretended to read a book which she carried. One man remarked, "This can't be the woman. The one we want can't read or write." Harriet devoutly hoped the book was right side up. —Earl Conrad, *Harriet Tubman*

Narration

A paragraph of narration tells a story or part of a story. Narrative paragraphs are usually arranged in chronological order, but they may also contain flashbacks, interruptions that take the story back to an earlier time. The following paragraph, from Jane Goodall's *In the Shadow of Man*, recounts one of the author's experiences in the African wild.

> One evening when I was wading in the shallows of the lake to pass a rocky outcrop, I suddenly stopped dead as I saw the sinuous black body of a snake in the water. It was all of six feet long, and from the slight hood and the dark stripes at the back of the neck I knew it to be a Storm's water cobra— a deadly reptile for the bite of which there was, at that time, no serum. As I stared at it an incoming wave gently deposited part of its body on one of my feet. I remained motionless, not even breathing, until the wave rolled back into the lake, drawing the snake with it. Then I leaped out of the water as fast as I could, my heart hammering.
>
> —Jane Goodall, *In the Shadow of Man*

Description

A descriptive paragraph sketches a portrait of a person, place, or thing by using concrete and specific details that appeal to one or more of our senses—sight, sound, smell, taste, and touch. Consider, for example, the following description of the grasshopper invasions that devastated the midwestern landscape in the late 1860s.

> They came like dive bombers out of the west. They came by the millions with the rustle of their wings roaring overhead. They came in waves, like the rolls of the sea, descending with a terrifying speed, breaking now and again like a mighty surf. They came with the force of a williwaw and they formed a huge, ominous, dark brown cloud that eclipsed the sun. They dipped and touched earth, hitting objects and people like hailstones. But they were not hail. These were *live* demons. They popped, snapped, crackled, and roared. They were dark brown, an inch or longer in length, plump in the middle and tapered at the ends. They had transparent wings, slender legs, and two black eyes that flashed with a fierce intelligence.
>
> —Eugene Boe, "Pioneers to Eternity"

Process

A process paragraph is structured in chronological order. A writer may choose this pattern either to describe how something is made or done or to explain to readers, step by step, how to do something. The following paragraph describes what happens when water freezes.

> In school we learned that with few exceptions the solid phase of matter is more dense than the liquid phase. Water, alone among common substances, violates this rule. As water begins to cool, it contracts and becomes more dense, in a perfectly typical way. But about four degrees above the freezing point, something remarkable happens. It ceases to contract and begins expanding, becoming less dense. At the freezing point the expansion is abrupt and drastic. As water turns to ice, it adds about one-eleventh to its liquid volume.
> —Chet Raymo, "Curious Stuff, Water and Ice"

Here is a paragraph explaining how to perform a "roll cast," a popular fly-fishing technique.

> Begin by taking up a suitable stance, with one foot slightly in front of the other and the rod pointing down the line. Then begin a smooth, steady draw, raising your rod hand to just above shoulder height and lifting the rod to the 10:30 or 11:00 position. This steady draw allows a loop of line to form between the rod top and the water. While the line is still moving, raise the rod slightly, then punch it rapidly forward and down. The rod is now flexed and under maximum compression, and the line follows its path, bellying out slightly behind you and coming off the water close to your feet. As you power the rod down through the 3:00 position, the belly of line will roll forward. Follow through smoothly so that the line unfolds and straightens above the water.
> —*The Dorling Kindersley Encyclopedia of Fishing*

Comparison and contrast

To compare two subjects is to draw attention to their similarities, although the word *compare* also has a broader meaning that includes a consideration of differences. To contrast is to focus only on differences.

Whether a paragraph stresses similarities or differences, it may be patterned in one of two ways. The two subjects may be presented one at a time, as in the following paragraph of contrast.

> So Grant and Lee were in complete contrast, representing two diametrically opposed elements in American life. Grant was the modern man emerging; beyond him, ready to come on the stage, was the great age of steel and machinery, of crowded cities and a restless, burgeoning vitality. Lee might have ridden down from the old age of chivalry, lance in hand, silken banner fluttering over his head. Each man was the perfect champion of his cause, drawing both his strengths and his weaknesses from the people he led.
> —Bruce Catton, "Grant and Lee: A Study in Contrasts"

Or a paragraph may proceed point by point, treating the two subjects together, one aspect at a time. The following paragraph uses the point-by-point method to contrast speeches given by Abraham Lincoln in 1860 and Barack Obama in 2008.

> Two men, two speeches. The men, both lawyers, both from Illinois, were seeking the presidency, despite what seemed their crippling connection with extremists. Each was young by modern standards for a president. Abraham Lincoln had turned fifty-one just five days before delivering his speech. Barack Obama was forty-six when he gave his. Their political experience was mainly provincial, in the Illinois legislature for both of them, and they had received little exposure at the national level—two years in the House of Representatives for Lincoln, four years in the Senate for Obama. Yet each was seeking his party's nomination against a New York senator of longer standing and greater prior reputation—Lincoln against Senator William Seward, Obama against Senator Hillary Clinton. They were both known for having opposed an initially popular war—Lincoln against President Polk's Mexican War, raised on the basis of a fictitious provocation;

> Obama against President Bush's Iraq War, launched on false claims that Saddam Hussein possessed WMDs [weapons of mass destruction] and had made an alliance with Osama bin Laden.   —Garry Wills, "Two Speeches on Race"

Analogy

Analogies draw comparisons between items that appear to have little in common. Writers turn to analogies for a variety of reasons: to make the unfamiliar seem familiar, to provide a concrete understanding of an abstract topic, to argue a point, or to provoke fresh thoughts or changed feelings about a subject. In the following paragraph, physician Lewis Thomas draws an analogy between the behavior of ants and that of humans.

> Ants are so much like human beings as to be an embarrassment. They farm fungi, raise aphids as livestock, launch armies into wars, use chemical sprays to alarm and confuse enemies, capture slaves. The families of weaver ants engage in child labor, holding their larvae like shuttles to spin out the thread that sews the leaves together for their fungus gardens. They exchange information ceaselessly. They do everything but watch television.
>
> —Lewis Thomas, "On Societies as Organisms"

Although analogies can be a powerful tool for illuminating a subject, they should be used with caution in arguments. Just because two things may be alike in one respect, we cannot conclude that they are alike in all respects. (See "false analogy," p. 121.)

Cause and effect

When causes and effects are a matter of argument, they are too complex to be reduced to a simple pattern (see p. 121). However, if a writer wishes merely to describe a cause-and-effect relationship that is generally accepted, then the effect may be stated in the topic sentence, with the causes listed in the body of the paragraph.

The fantastic water clarity of the Mount Gambier
sinkholes results from several factors. The holes are fed
from aquifers holding rainwater that fell decades—even
centuries—ago, and that has been filtered through miles
of limestone. The high level of calcium that limestone
adds causes the silty detritus from dead plants and animals
to cling together and settle quickly to the bottom. Abun-
dant bottom vegetation in the shallow sinkholes also helps
bind the silt. And the rapid turnover of water prohibits
stagnation.
   —Hillary Hauser, "Exploring a Sunken Realm in Australia"

Or the paragraph may move from cause to effects, as in
this paragraph from a student paper on the effects of the in-
dustrial revolution on American farms.

The rise of rail transport in the nineteenth century forever changed American farming—for better and for worse.
Farmers who once raised crops and livestock to sustain just
their own families could now make a profit by selling their
goods in towns and cities miles away. These new markets
improved the living standard of struggling farm families and
encouraged them to seek out innovations that would increase
their profits. On the downside, the competition fostered by
the new markets sometimes created hostility among neighboring farm families where there had once been a spirit of
cooperation. Those farmers who couldn't compete with their
neighbors left farming forever, facing poverty worse than they
had ever known.   —Chris Mileski, student

Classification and division

Classification is the grouping of items into categories according to some consistent principle. For example, an elementary school teacher might classify children's books
according to their level of difficulty, but a librarian might
group them by subject matter. The principle of classification
that a writer chooses ultimately depends on the purpose of
the classification. The following paragraph classifies species
of electric fish.

Scientists sort electric fishes into three categories. The first comprises the strongly electric species like the marine electric rays or the freshwater African electric catfish and South American electric eel. Known since the dawn of history, these deliver a punch strong enough to stun a human. In recent years, biologists have focused on a second category: weakly electric fish in the South American and African rivers that use tiny voltages for communication and navigation. The third group contains sharks, nonelectric rays, and catfish, which do not emit a field but possess sensors that enable them to detect the minute amounts of electricity that leak out of other organisms.

—Anne and Jack Rudloe, "Electric Warfare:
The Fish That Kill with Thunderbolts"

Division takes one item and divides it into parts. As with classification, division should be made according to some consistent principle. The following passage describes the components that make up a baseball.

Like the game itself, a baseball is composed of many layers. One of the delicious joys of childhood is to take apart a baseball and examine the wonders within. You begin by removing the red cotton thread and peeling off the leather cover—which comes from the hide of a Holstein cow and has been tanned, cut, printed, and punched with holes. Beneath the cover is a thin layer of cotton string, followed by several hundred yards of woolen yarn, which makes up the bulk of the ball. Finally, in the middle is a rubber ball, or "pill," which is a little smaller than a golf ball. Slice into the rubber and you'll find the ball's heart—a cork core. The cork is from Portugal, the rubber from southeast Asia, the covers are American, and the balls are assembled in Costa Rica.

—Dan Gutman, *The Way Baseball Works*

Definition

A definition puts a word or concept into a general class and then provides enough details to distinguish it from others in the same class. In the following paragraph, the writer defines *envy* as a special kind of desire.

Envy is so integral and so painful a part of what animates
behavior in market societies that many people have forgotten
the full meaning of the word, simplifying it into one of the
synonyms of desire. It is that, which may be why it flourishes
in market societies: democracies of desire, they might be
called, with money for ballots, stuffing permitted. But envy is
more or less than desire. It begins with an almost frantic sense
of emptiness inside oneself, as if the pump of one's heart were
sucking on air. One has to be blind to perceive the emptiness,
of course, but that's just what envy is, a selective blindness. *In-
vidia*, Latin for envy, translates as "non-sight," and Dante has
the envious plodding along under cloaks of lead, their eyes
sewn shut with leaden wire. What they are blind to is what
they have, God-given and humanly nurtured, in themselves.

—Nelson W. Aldrich Jr., *Old Money*

3d Make paragraphs coherent.

When sentences and paragraphs flow from one to another
without discernible bumps, gaps, or shifts, they are said to be
coherent. Coherence can be improved by strengthening the
ties between old information and new. A number of techniques
for strengthening those ties are detailed in this section.

Linking ideas clearly

Readers expect to learn a paragraph's main point in a topic sentence early in the paragraph. Then, as they move into the body
of the paragraph, they expect to encounter specific details,
facts, or examples that support the topic sentence—either directly or indirectly. In the following paragraph, all of the sentences following the topic sentence directly support it.

A passenger list of the early years [of the Orient Express]
would read like a *Who's Who of the World*, from art to politics. Sarah Bernhardt and her Italian counterpart Eleonora
Duse used the train to thrill the stages of Europe. For musicians there were Toscanini and Mahler. Dancers Nijinsky
and Pavlova were there, while lesser performers like Harry
Houdini and the girls of the Ziegfeld Follies also rode the rails.

Violinists were allowed to practice on the train, and occasionally one might see trapeze artists hanging like bats from the baggage racks.   —Barnaby Conrad III, "Train of Kings"

If a sentence does not support the topic sentence directly, readers expect it to support another sentence in the paragraph and therefore to support the topic sentence indirectly. The following paragraph begins with a topic sentence. The italicized sentences are direct supports, and the rest of the sentences are indirect supports.

Though the open-space classroom works for many children, it is not practical for my son, David. *First, David is hyperactive.* When he was placed in an open-space classroom, he became distracted and confused. He was tempted to watch the movement going on around him instead of concentrating on his own work. *Second, David has a tendency to transpose letters and numbers, a tendency that can be overcome only by individual attention from the instructor.* In the open classroom he was moved from teacher to teacher, with each one responsible for a different subject. No single teacher worked with David long enough to diagnose the problem, let alone help him with it. *Finally, David is not a highly motivated learner.* In the open classroom, he was graded "at his own level," not by criteria for a certain grade. He could receive a B in reading and still be a grade level behind, because he was doing satisfactory work "at his own level." [Italics added.]
            —Margaret Smith, student

Repeating key words

Repetition of key words is an important technique for gaining coherence. To prevent repetitions from becoming dull, you can use variations of a key word (*hike, hiker, hiking*), pronouns referring to the word (*gamblers . . . they*), and synonyms (*run, spring, race, dash*). In the following paragraph describing plots among indentured servants in the seventeenth century, historian Richard Hofstadter binds sentences together by repeating the key word *plots* and echoing it with a variety of synonyms (which are italicized).

Plots hatched by several servants to run away together occurred mostly in the plantation colonies, and the few recorded servant *uprisings* were entirely limited to those colonies. Virginia had been forced from its very earliest years to take stringent steps against *mutinous plots*, and severe punishments for *such behavior* were recorded. Most servant *plots* occurred in the seventeenth century: a contemplated *uprising* was nipped in the bud in York County in 1661; apparently led by some left-wing offshoots of the *Great Rebellion*, servants *plotted* an *insurrection* in Gloucester County in 1663, and four leaders were condemned and executed; some discontented servants apparently joined *Bacon's Rebellion* in the 1670's. In the 1680's the planters became newly apprehensive of discontent among the servants "owing to their great necessities and want of clothes," and it was feared they would *rise up* and *plunder* the storehouses and ships; in 1682 there were plant-cutting *riots* in which servants and laborers, as well as some planters, took part. [Italics added.]

—Richard Hofstadter, *America at 1750*

Using parallel structures

Parallel structures are frequently used within sentences to underscore the similarity of ideas (see 9). They may also be used to bind together a series of sentences expressing similar information. In the following passage describing folk beliefs, anthropologist Margaret Mead presents similar information in parallel grammatical form.

Actually, almost every day, even in the most sophisticated home, something is likely to happen that evokes the memory of some old folk belief. The salt spills. A knife falls to the floor. Your nose tickles. Then perhaps, with a slightly embarrassed smile, the person who spilled the salt tosses a pinch over his left shoulder. Or someone recites the old rhyme, "Knife falls, gentleman calls." Or as you rub your nose you think, That means a letter. I wonder who's writing?

—Margaret Mead, "New Superstitions for Old"

Maintaining consistency

Coherence suffers whenever a draft shifts confusingly from one point of view to another or from one verb tense to another. (See 13.) In addition, coherence can suffer when new information is introduced with the subject of each sentence. As a rule, a sentence's subject should echo a subject or an object in the previous sentence.

The following rough-draft paragraph is needlessly hard to read because so few of the sentences' subjects are tied to earlier subjects or objects. The subjects appear in italics.

> *One* goes about trapping in this manner. At the very outset *one* acquires a "trapping" state of mind. A *library* of books must be read, and preferably *someone* with experience should educate the novice. *Preparing* for the first expedition takes several steps. The *purchase* of traps is first. A *pair* of rubber gloves, waterproof *boots*, and the grubbiest *clothes* capable of withstanding human use come next to outfit the trapper for his adventure. Finally, the *decision* has to be made on just what kinds of animals to seek, what sort of bait to use, and where to place the traps. [Italics added.]

Although the writer repeats a number of key words, such as *trapping*, the paragraph seems disconnected because new information is introduced with the subject of each sentence.

To improve the paragraph, the writer used the first-person pronoun as the subject of every sentence. The revision is much easier to read.

> *I* went about trapping in this manner. To acquire a "trapping" state of mind, *I* read a library of books and talked at length with an experienced trapper, my father. Then *I* purchased the traps and outfitted myself by collecting a pair of rubber gloves, waterproof boots, and the grubbiest clothes capable of withstanding human use. Finally, *I* decided just what kinds of animals to seek, what sort of bait to use, and where to place my traps. [Italics added.]
>
> —John Clyde Thatcher, student

Notice that Thatcher combined some of his original sentences. By doing so, he was able to avoid excessive repetitions of the pronoun *I*. Notice, too, that he varied his sentence openings (most sentences do not begin with *I*) so that readers are not likely to find the repetitions tiresome.

Providing transitions

Transitions are bridges between what has been read and what is about to be read. Transitions help readers move from sentence to sentence; they also alert readers to more global connections of ideas—those between paragraphs or even larger blocks of text.

Academic English   Choose transitions carefully and vary them appropriately. Each transition has a different meaning (see the chart on p. 81). If you do not use a transition with an appropriate meaning, you might confuse your readers.

▶ **Although taking eight o'clock classes may seem**

 unappealing, coming to school early has its advan-
      For example,
 tages. ~~Moreover~~, students who arrive early typically

 avoid the worst traffic and find the best parking spaces.

Sentence-level transitions   Certain words and phrases signal connections between (or within) sentences. Frequently used transitions are included in the chart on page 81.

Skilled writers use transitional expressions with care, making sure, for example, not to use *consequently* when *also* would be more precise. They are also careful to select transitions with an appropriate tone, perhaps preferring *so* to *thus* in an informal piece, *in summary* to *in short* for a scholarly essay.

In the following paragraph, taken from an argument that dinosaurs had the "'right-sized' brains for reptiles of their body

Revising with comments | Need a transition

When a teacher or tutor points out that you "need a transition," the comment often signals that readers need bridges—transitional words—to follow the progression from one idea to the next.

> The United States of America is one of many countries in the world that were created by immigration. This essential characteristic is perhaps America's greatest weakness and its greatest strength. Our country has the potential to be swallowed up by the diverse beliefs, values, and social practices of its immigrants so that nothing is common to anyone. America can benefit from embracing the amazing cultural diversity within itself. **?** **Need a transition**

In this body paragraph, a student responded to an assignment that asked him to analyze a central feature of American identity.

Transitional words or phrases help readers follow the connections between sentences and ideas. To revise, the student might begin by asking: What idea is expressed in each sentence? Does each sentence point clearly back to the previous one? If not, what words or phrases might be added to help readers see how one idea moves to the next? The answers to these questions will help the student recognize that his last two sentences contrast with each other (one about weaknesses, one about strengths) but that he needs to provide a transitional word or phrase, such as *however*, before the last sentence to make the contrast clear.

Similar comments: something missing? • missing connection • transition?

Revising when *you* need a transition between sentences

1. *Read your paragraph aloud* to a peer or a tutor. Ask your listeners what is missing between sentences that would help them follow the progression from one idea to the next.

2. *Ask questions.* What words or phrases might be added to help readers move from sentence to sentence? For instance, do you need transitions to show addition (*furthermore*), to give examples (*specifically*), to compare (*similarly*), to contrast (*however*), or to summarize (*in summary*)?

3. *Revise with an appropriate transition* to show connections between ideas.

More help with transitions: pages **79–83**

Common transitions

To show addition: and, also, besides, further, furthermore, in addition, moreover, next, too, first, second

To give examples: for example, for instance, to illustrate, in fact, specifically

To compare: also, in the same manner, similarly, likewise

To contrast: but, however, on the other hand, in contrast, nevertheless, still, even though, on the contrary, yet, although

To summarize or conclude: in short, in summary, in conclusion, to sum up, therefore

To show time: after, as, before, next, during, later, finally, meanwhile, then, when, while, immediately

To show place or direction: above, below, beyond, nearby, opposite, close, to the left

To indicate logical relationship: if, so, therefore, consequently, thus, as a result, for this reason, because, since

---

size," biologist Stephen Jay Gould uses transitions (italicized) with skill.

> I don't wish to deny that the flattened, minuscule head of large bodied Stegosaurus houses little brain from our subjective, top-heavy perspective, *but* I do wish to assert that we should not expect more of the beast. *First of all*, large animals have relatively smaller brains than related, small animals. The correlation of brain size with body size among kindred animals (all reptiles, all mammals, *for example*) is remarkably regular. *As* we move from small to large animals, from mice to elephants or small lizards to Komodo dragons, brain size increases, *but* not so fast as body size. *In other words*, bodies grow faster than brains, *and* large animals have low ratios of brain weight to body weight. *In fact*, brains grow only about two-thirds as fast as bodies. *Since* we have no reason to believe that large animals are consistently stupider than their smaller relatives, we must conclude that large animals require

relatively less brain to do as well as smaller animals. *If* we do not recognize this relationship, we are likely to underestimate the mental power of very large animals, dinosaurs *in particular.* [Italics added.]

> —Stephen Jay Gould, "Were Dinosaurs Dumb?"

hackerhandbooks.com/bedhandbook > Writing exercises > E-ex 3–3

Paragraph-level transitions   Paragraph-level transitions usually link the *first* sentence of a new paragraph with the *first* sentence of the previous paragraph. In other words, the topic sentences signal global connections.

Look for opportunities to allude to the subject of a previous paragraph (as summed up in its topic sentence) in the topic sentence of the next one. In his essay "Little Green Lies," Jonathan H. Alder uses this strategy in the following topic sentences, which appear in a passage describing the benefits of plastic packaging.

> Consider aseptic packaging, the synthetic packaging for the "juice boxes" so many children bring to school with their lunch. One criticism of aseptic packaging is that it is nearly impossible to recycle, yet on almost every other count, aseptic packaging is environmentally preferable to the packaging alternatives. Not only do aseptic containers not require refrigeration to keep their contents from spoiling, but their manufacture requires less than one-10th the energy of making glass bottles.
>
> What is true for juice boxes is also true for other forms of synthetic packaging. The use of polystyrene, which is commonly (and mistakenly) referred to as "Styrofoam," can reduce food waste dramatically due to its insulating properties. (Thanks to these properties, polystyrene cups are much preferred over paper for that morning cup of coffee.) Polystyrene also requires significantly fewer resources to produce than its paper counterpart.

Transitions between blocks of text   In long essays, you will need to alert readers to connections between blocks of text that are more than one paragraph long. You can do this by inserting transitional sentences or short paragraphs at key points in the essay. Here, for example, is a transitional paragraph from a student research paper. It announces that the first part of the paper has come to a close and the second part is about to begin.

> Although the great apes have demonstrated significant language skills, one central question remains: Can they be taught to use that uniquely human language tool we call grammar, to learn the difference, for instance, between "ape bite human" and "human bite ape"? In other words, can an ape create a sentence?

Another strategy to help readers move from one block of text to another is to insert headings in your essay. Headings, which usually sit above blocks of text, allow you to announce a new topic boldly, without the need for subtle transitions. (See 58b.)

3e If necessary, adjust paragraph length.

Most readers feel comfortable reading paragraphs that range between one hundred and two hundred words. Shorter paragraphs require too much starting and stopping, and longer ones strain readers' attention span. There are exceptions to this guideline, however. Paragraphs longer than two hundred words frequently appear in scholarly writing, where scholars explore complex ideas. Paragraphs shorter than one hundred words occur in newspapers because of narrow columns; in informal essays to quicken the pace; and in business writing and Web sites, where readers routinely skim for main ideas.

In an essay, the first and last paragraphs will ordinarily be the introduction and the conclusion. These special-purpose paragraphs are likely to be shorter than the paragraphs in the body of the essay. Typically, the body paragraphs will follow the essay's outline: one paragraph per point in short essays, several paragraphs per point in longer ones. Some ideas require more development than others, however, so it is best to be flexible. If an idea stretches to a length unreasonable for a paragraph, you should divide the paragraph, even if you have presented comparable points in the essay in single paragraphs.

Paragraph breaks are not always made for strictly logical reasons. Writers use them for the following reasons as well.

REASONS FOR BEGINNING A NEW PARAGRAPH

- to mark off the introduction and the conclusion
- to signal a shift to a new idea
- to indicate an important shift in time or place
- to emphasize a point (by placing it at the beginning or the end, not in the middle, of a paragraph)
- to highlight a contrast
- to signal a change of speakers (in dialogue)
- to provide readers with a needed pause
- to break up text that looks too dense

Beware of using too many short, choppy paragraphs, however. Readers want to see how your ideas connect, and they become irritated when you break their momentum by forcing them to pause every few sentences. Here are some reasons you might have for combining some of the paragraphs in a rough draft.

REASONS FOR COMBINING PARAGRAPHS

- to clarify the essay's organization
- to connect closely related ideas
- to bind together text that looks too choppy

Part II
Academic Writing

4 Writing about texts

The word *texts* can refer to a variety of works, including essays, periodical articles, government reports, books, Web sites, and even visuals such as advertisements and photographs. Most assignments that ask you to respond to a text call for a summary or an analysis or both.

A summary is neutral in tone and demonstrates that you have understood the author's key ideas. Assignments calling for an analysis of a text vary widely, but they usually ask you to look at how the text's parts contribute to its central argument or purpose, often with the aim of judging its evidence or overall effect.

Making the most of your handbook

Knowing the expectations for a writing assignment is a key first step in drafting.

▶ Understanding an assignment: page 9

When you write about a written text, you will need to read it several times to digest its full meaning. Two techniques will help you move beyond a superficial first reading: (1) annotating the text with your observations and questions and (2) outlining the text's key points. The same techniques will help you analyze visual texts.

4a Read actively: Annotate the text.

Read actively by jotting down your questions and thoughts in the margins of the text or visual or in a notebook. When you annotate a text as you read, you are engaging with the work, not just letting the words slip past you. Use a pencil instead of a highlighter; with a pencil you can underline key concepts, mark points, or circle elements that intrigue you. If you change your mind, you can erase your early annotations and replace them with new ones. (See the chart on the following page for advice about active reading.)

On pages 88 and 89 are an article from a consumer-oriented newsletter and a magazine advertisement, both annotated by students. The students, Emilia Sanchez and Albert Lee, were assigned to write both a summary and an analysis. Each began by annotating the text.

Guidelines for active reading

Familiarize yourself with the basic features and structure of a text.

- What kind of text are you reading? An essay? An editorial? A scholarly article? An advertisement? A photograph?
- What is the author's purpose? To inform? To persuade? To call to action?
- Who is the audience? How does the author appeal to the audience?
- What is the author's thesis? What question does the text attempt to answer?
- What evidence does the author provide to support the thesis?

Note details that surprise, puzzle, or intrigue you.

- Has the author revealed a fact or made a point that runs counter to your assumptions? What exactly is surprising?
- Has the author made a generalization you disagree with? Can you think of evidence that would challenge the generalization?
- Are there any contradictions or inconsistencies in the text?
- Does the text contain words, statements, or phrases that you don't understand? If so, what reference materials could you consult?

Read and reread to discover meaning.

- What do you notice on a second or third reading that you didn't notice earlier?
- Does the text raise questions that it does not resolve?
- If you could address the author directly, what questions would you pose? Where do you agree and disagree with the author? Why?

Apply critical thinking strategies to visual texts.

- What first strikes you about the visual text? What elements do you notice immediately?
- Who or what is the main subject of the visual text?
- What colors and textures dominate?
- What is in the background? In the foreground?
- What role, if any, do words play in the visual text?

ANNOTATED ARTICLE

Big Box Stores Are Bad for Main Street

BETSY TAYLOR

Opening strategy—the problem is not x, it's y.

There is plenty of reason to be concerned about the proliferation of Wal-Marts and other so-called "big box" stores. The question, however, is not whether or not these types of stores create jobs (although several studies claim they produce a net job loss in local communities) or whether they ultimately save consumers money. The real concern about having a 25-acre slab of concrete with a 100,000 square foot box of stuff land on a town is whether it's good for a community's soul.

Sentimental—what is a community's soul?

Lumps all big boxes together.

The worst thing about "big boxes" is that they have a tendency to produce Ross Perot's famous "big sucking sound"—sucking the life out of cities and small towns across the country. On the other hand, small businesses are great for a community. They offer more personal service; they won't threaten to pack up and leave town if they don't get tax breaks, free roads and other blandishments; and small-business owners are much more responsive to a customer's needs. (Ever try to complain about bad service or poor quality products to the president of Home Depot?)

Assumes all small businesses are attentive.

Logic problem? Why couldn't customer complain to store manager?

Yet, if big boxes are so bad, why are they so successful? One glaring reason is that we've become a nation of hyper-consumers, and the big-box boys know this. Downtown shopping districts comprised of small businesses take some of the efficiency out of overconsumption. There's all that hassle of having to travel from store to store, and having to pull out your credit card so many times. Occasionally, we even find ourselves chatting with the shopkeeper, wandering into a coffee shop to visit with a friend or otherwise wasting precious time that could be spent on acquiring more stuff.

True?

Nostalgia for a time that is long gone or never was.

Community vs. economy. What about prices?

But let's face it—bustling, thriving city centers are fun. They breathe life into a community. They allow cities and towns to stand out from each other. They provide an atmosphere for people to interact with each other that just cannot be found at Target, or Wal-Mart or Home Depot.

Ends with emotional appeal.

Is it anti-American to be against having a retail giant set up shop in one's community? Some people would say so. On the other hand, if you board up Main Street, what's left of America?

ANNOTATED ADVERTISEMENT

What signals is McDonald's giving customers about its menu?

Is McDonald's trying to remake its image with lettuce?

A real customer?

Repetition of "real."

Ask M:
A series of real answers to real questions asked by our customers.

WHAT MAKES YOUR LETTUCE SO CRISP?

Our lettuce is fresh, so the crunch you hear is pure, fresh lettuce from the same place you buy yours. Simply put, the only unusual thing about our lettuce is the speed at which it travels from the farm to the restaurant. For more real answers to real questions, give us a call at 1-877-623-3663 or write us at mcdonalds.com.

Local vs. corporation, McDonald's as family restaurant.

Open, nothing to hide.

Trying to show its commitment to customer service.

i'm lovin' it

4b Sketch a brief outline of the text.

After reading, rereading, and annotating a text, attempt to outline it. Seeing how the author has constructed a text can help you understand it. As you sketch an outline, pay special attention to the text's thesis (central idea) and its topic sentences. The thesis of a written text usually appears in the introduction, often in the first or second paragraph. Topic sentences often can be found at the beginning of body paragraphs, where they announce a shift to a new topic. (See 1e and 3a.)

In your outline, put the author's thesis and key points in your own words. Here, for example, is the outline that Emilia Sanchez developed as she prepared to write her summary and analysis of the text printed on page 88. Notice that the outline does not simply trace the author's ideas paragraph by paragraph; instead, it sums up the article's central points.

OUTLINE OF "BIG BOX STORES ARE BAD FOR MAIN STREET"

Thesis: Whether or not they take jobs away from a community or offer low prices to consumers, we should be worried about "big-box" stores like Wal-Mart, Target, and Home Depot because they harm communities by taking the life out of downtown shopping districts.

I. Small businesses are better for cities and towns than big-box stores are.
   A. Small businesses offer personal service, and big-box stores do not.
   B. Small businesses don't make demands on community resources as big-box stores do.
   C. Small businesses respond to customer concerns, and big-box stores do not.

II. Big-box stores are successful because they cater to consumption at the expense of benefits to the community.
   A. Buying everything in one place is convenient.
   B. Shopping at small businesses may be inefficient, but it provides opportunities for socializing.
   C. Downtown shopping districts give each city or town a special identity.

Conclusion: Although some people say that it's anti-American to oppose big-box stores, actually these stores threaten the communities that make up America by encouraging buying at the expense of the traditional interactions of Main Street.

A visual often doesn't state an explicit thesis or an explicit line of reasoning. Instead, you must sometimes infer the meaning beneath the image's surface and interpret its central point and supporting ideas from the elements of its design. One way to outline a visual text is to try to define its purpose and sketch a list of its key elements. Here, for example, are the key features that Albert Lee identified for the advertisement printed on page 89.

OUTLINE OF MCDONALD'S ADVERTISEMENT

Purpose: To persuade readers that McDonald's is concerned about its customers' health.

Key features:
- A close-up of a fresh, green lettuce leaf makes up the entire background.
- Near the center is a comment card with a handwritten question from a "real" McDonald's customer: "What makes your lettuce so crisp?"
- A photograph of a smiling woman is clipped to the card.
- Beneath the comment card is the company's response, which emphasizes the farm-fresh quality and purity of its vegetables and urges customers to ask other candid questions.
- At the bottom of the ad is the McDonald's slogan "I'm lovin' it."

4c Summarize to demonstrate your understanding.

Your goal in summarizing a text is to state the work's main ideas and key points simply, briefly, and accurately in your own words. If you have sketched a brief outline of the text (see 4b), refer to it as you draft your summary.

Summarizing a written text

To summarize a written text, first find the author's central idea—the thesis. Then divide the whole piece into a few

Making the most of your handbook

Knowing how to summarize a source is a key research skill.

▶ Using summaries in researched writing: 48c

major and perhaps minor ideas. Since a summary must be fairly short, you must make judgments about what is most important. Following is Emilia Sanchez's summary of the article that is printed on page 88.

In her essay "Big Box Stores Are Bad for Main Street," Betsy Taylor argues that chain stores harm communities by taking the life out of downtown shopping districts. Explaining that a community's "soul" is more important than low prices or consumer convenience, she argues that small businesses are better than stores like Wal-Mart, Target, and Home Depot because they emphasize personal interactions and don't place demands on a community's resources. Taylor asserts that big-box stores are successful because "we've become a nation of hyper-consumers" (1011), although the convenience of shopping in these stores comes at the expense of benefits to the community. She concludes by suggesting that it's not "anti-American" to oppose big-box stores because the damage they inflict on downtown shopping districts extends to America itself.

Summarizing a visual text

To summarize a visual text, begin with essential information such as who created the visual, who the intended audience is, where the visual appeared, and when it was created. Then, in a few sentences, explain the visual's main point or purpose and describe the image by pointing to its key features.

Following is Albert Lee's summary of the McDonald's advertisement printed on page 89.

An advertisement for McDonald's in the July-August 2004 issue of *Men's Health* magazine represents an attempt by the restaurant chain to remake its image. The implicit reason for the ad is that McDonald's world-famous fast food has come under increasingly harsh attack for

> ### Guidelines for writing a summary
>
> - In the first sentence, mention the title of the text, the name of the author, and the author's thesis or the visual's central point.
> - Maintain a neutral tone; be objective.
> - Use the third-person point of view and the present tense: *Taylor argues.* . . .
> - Keep your focus on the text. Don't state the author's ideas as if they were your own.
> - Put all or most of your summary in your own words; if you borrow a phrase or a sentence from the text, put it in quotation marks and give the page number in parentheses.
> - Limit yourself to presenting the text's key points.
> - Be concise; make every word count.

unhealthful processing and preparation. The fresh, spring-green lettuce that dominates this ad is a signal to customers that McDonald's has changed its menu and now offers food as fresh and healthful as any found in a supermarket. By publicizing this new direction, McDonald's clearly hopes to attract health-conscious customers. Moreover, by framing this advertisement as a response to an individual customer's question, McDonald's attempts to show that the vast size of the chain does not prevent it from tending personally to its customers' concerns.

4d Analyze to demonstrate your critical thinking.

When you analyze, you separate the whole to study the parts. Whereas a summary most often answers the question of *what* a text says, an analysis looks at *how* a text makes its point. When an assignment calls for an analysis, read the whole

Making the most of your handbook

Writing about a text often requires you to quote directly from the text.

▶ Guidelines for using quotation marks: 48c

Making the most of your handbook

When you analyze a text, you weave words and ideas from the source into your own writing.

► Quoting or paraphrasing: 51 (MLA), 56b (APA), 57b (*Chicago*)

► Using signal phrases: 52b (MLA), 56c (APA), 57c (*Chicago*)

► Using details for support: 50c (MLA), 56a (APA), 57a (*Chicago*)

► Analyzing literature: 55

assignment carefully, along with any models provided, to see what your instructor expects.

Typically, an analysis takes the form of an essay that makes its own argument about a text. Include an introduction that briefly summarizes the text, a thesis that states your own judgment about the text, and body paragraphs that support your thesis with evidence. If you are analyzing a visual, examine it as a whole and then reflect on how the individual elements contribute to its overall meaning. If you have written a summary of the text or visual, you may find it useful to refer to the main points of the summary as you write your analysis.

Within your body paragraphs, include and interpret individual passages from the text to help support your overall analysis of the text. The following steps can help you do this:

1. In a topic sentence, include a claim about the author's text.

2. Use a signal phrase to introduce exact language or ideas from the text. Place any exact language in quotation marks.

3. Follow the quotation or ideas with your interpretation. To interpret the text, you may explain its significance, define one of its important terms, or point out what the author is assuming or implying in the passage.

4. Provide a transition to the claim in your next paragraph. (See 3d.)

Using interpretation in an analysis

In her paper analyzing the article by Betsy Taylor that appears on page 88, student writer Emilia Sanchez begins by

Guidelines for analyzing a text

Written texts

Instructors who ask you to analyze an essay or an article often expect you to address some of the following questions.

- What is the author's thesis or central idea? Who is the audience?
- What questions does the author address (implicitly or explicitly)?
- How does the author structure the text? What are the key parts, and how do they relate to one another and to the thesis?
- What strategies has the author used to generate interest in the argument and to persuade readers of its merit?
- What evidence does the author use to support the thesis? How persuasive is the evidence (5e)?
- Does the author anticipate objections and counter opposing views (see 6c)?
- Does the author fall prey to any faulty reasoning (see 6a)?

Visual texts

If you are analyzing a visual text, the following additional questions will help you evaluate an image's purpose and meaning.

- What surprises, perplexes, or intrigues you about the image?
- What clues suggest the visual text's intended audience? How does the image appeal to its audience?
- If the text is an advertisement, what product is it selling? Does it attempt to sell an idea or a message as well?
- If the visual text includes words, how do the words contribute to its meaning?
- How do design elements—colors, shapes, perspective, background, foreground—shape the visual text's meaning or serve its purpose?

When a teacher or tutor points out that you need to "summarize less, analyze more," the comment often signals that your readers want to hear your interpretation of a text, not a summary of the text itself.

> Growing up as a borderlander, I have always considered myself bilingual. Reading "How to Tame a Wild Tongue" by Gloria Anzaldúa made me rethink that label. In the "*El lenguaje de la frontera*" section of the essay, Anzaldúa explains the origins of Chicano Spanish, a "border tongue" (326). Then she says that most Chicanos actually speak as many as eight languages. Anzaldúa lists these languages and then tells which languages she speaks with which people in her life. For example, she speaks Tex-Mex with friends, Chicano Texas Spanish with her mother, and working-class English at school (327). Finally, she talks about her experience with speaking made-up languages.

Summarize less, analyze more

One student wrote this body paragraph in response to an assignment that asked students to analyze Gloria Anzaldúa's essay "How to Tame a Wild Tongue."

The student writer needs to go beyond summary to offer his insights about Anzaldúa's text. To revise this paragraph, the student might begin by underlining the verbs in his own sentences: *explains, says, lists, tells,* and *talks*. These sentences simply restate what Anzaldúa has written. Although the student needs a brief summary to help his readers understand the basis of his analysis, he should move quickly to exploring the meaning of Anzaldúa's text. In his analysis, the student might ask questions about Anzaldúa's strategies. For instance, why does she combine Spanish with English? Or why does she list the eight separate languages that most Chicanos speak?

Similar comments: too much summary • show, don't tell • go deeper

Revising when *you* need to summarize less and analyze more

1. *Reread your paragraph* and highlight the sentences that summarize. Then, in a different color, highlight the sentences that contain your analysis. (Think about the differences between summary and analysis: Summary

answers the question of *what* a text says; analysis offers a judgment or interpretation of the text.)

2. *Reread the text* (or passages of the text) that you are analyzing, paying attention to the language and structure of the text.
3. *Ask questions.* What strategies does the author use? How do these strategies convey the meaning of the text? What insights can you convey to your readers about the text? How can you deepen your readers' understanding of the text?

More advice on analyzing a text: **4d** and **55b**

summarizing Taylor's argument. She then states her own thesis, or claim, which offers her judgment of Taylor's article, and begins her analysis. In her first body paragraph, Sanchez interprets Taylor's use of language.

Topic sentence includes Sanchez's claim.

Quoted material shows the author's language in quotation marks.

Transition to Sanchez's next point.

Taylor's use of colorful language reveals that she has a nostalgic view of American society and does not understand economic realities. In her first paragraph, Taylor refers to a big-box store as a "25-acre slab of concrete with a 100,000 square foot box of stuff" that "land[s] on a town," evoking images of a powerful monster crushing the American way of life (1011). But she oversimplifies a complex issue. Taylor does not consider. . . .

Signal phrase introduces a quotation from the text.

Quotation is followed by Sanchez's interpretation of the author's language.

4e Sample student essay: Analysis of an article

Following is Emilia Sanchez's complete essay. Sanchez used Modern Language Association (MLA) style to format her paper and cite the source.

Sanchez 1

Emilia Sanchez

Professor Goodwin

English 10

23 October 2009

Rethinking Big-Box Stores

Opening briefly summarizes the article's purpose and thesis.

In her essay "Big Box Stores Are Bad for Main Street," Betsy Taylor focuses not on the economic effects of large chain stores but on the effects these stores have on the "soul" of America. She argues that stores like Home Depot, Target, and Wal-Mart are bad for America because they draw people out of downtown shopping districts and cause them to focus on consumption. In contrast, she believes that small businesses are good for America because they provide personal attention, encourage community interaction, and make each city unique.

Sanchez begins to analyze Taylor's argument.

But Taylor's argument is unconvincing because it is based on nostalgia—on idealized images of a quaint Main Street—rather than on the roles that businesses play in consumers' lives and communities.

Thesis expresses Sanchez's judgment of Taylor's article.

By ignoring the complex economic relationship between large chain stores and their communities, Taylor incorrectly assumes that simply getting rid of big-box stores would have a positive effect on America's communities.

Taylor's use of colorful language reveals that she has a nostalgic view of American society and does not understand economic realities.

Signal phrase introduces quotations from the source; Sanchez uses an MLA in-text citation.

In her first paragraph, Taylor refers to a big-box store as a "25-acre slab of concrete with a 100,000 square foot box of stuff" that "land[s] on a town," evoking images of a powerful monster crushing the American way of life (1011). But she oversimplifies a complex issue.

Sanchez begins to identify and challenge Taylor's assumptions.

Taylor does not consider that many downtown business districts failed long before chain stores moved in, when factories and mills closed and workers lost their jobs. In cities with struggling economies, big-box

Marginal annotations indicate MLA-style formatting **and** effective writing.

Sanchez 2

stores can actually provide much-needed jobs. Similarly, while Taylor blames big-box stores for harming local economies by asking for tax breaks, free roads, and other perks, she doesn't acknowledge that these stores also enter into economic partnerships with the surrounding communities by offering financial benefits to schools and hospitals.

> Transition to another point in Sanchez's analysis.

Taylor's assumption that shopping in small businesses is always better for the customer also seems driven by nostalgia for an old-fashioned Main Street rather than by the facts. While she may be right that many small businesses offer personal service and are responsive to customer complaints, she does not consider that many customers appreciate the service at big-box stores. Just as customer service is better at some small businesses than at others, it is impossible to generalize about service at all big-box stores. For example, customers depend on the lenient return policies and the wide variety of products at stores like Target and Home Depot.

> Clear topic sentence announces a shift to a new topic.

> Sanchez refutes Taylor's claim.

Taylor blames big-box stores for encouraging American "hyper-consumerism," but she oversimplifies by equating big-box stores with bad values and small businesses with good values. Like her other points, this claim ignores the economic and social realities of American society today. Big-box stores do not force Americans to buy more. By offering lower prices in a convenient setting, however, they allow consumers to save time and purchase goods they might not be able to afford from small businesses. The existence of more small businesses would not change what most Americans can afford, nor would it reduce their desire to buy affordable merchandise.

Taylor may be right that some big-box stores have a negative impact on communities and that small businesses offer certain advantages. But she ignores the economic conditions that support big-box stores as well as the fact that Main Street was in decline before

> Sanchez treats the author fairly.

Sanchez 3

Conclusion returns to the thesis and shows the wider significance of Sanchez's analysis.

the big-box store arrived. Getting rid of big-box stores will not bring back a simpler America populated by thriving, unique Main Streets; in reality, Main Street will not survive if consumers cannot afford to shop there.

Sanchez 4

Work Cited

Work cited page is in MLA style.

Taylor, Betsy. "Big Box Stores Are Bad for Main Street." *CQ Researcher* 9.44 (1999): 1011. Print.

4f Sample student essay: Analysis of an advertisement

On the following pages is Albert Lee's analysis of the McDonald's ad that appears on page 89.

Albert Lee

Professor McIntosh

English 101

4 November 2009

The Golden Arches Go Green: McDonald's and Real Lettuce

Dominating a McDonald's advertisement in the July-August 2004 issue of *Men's Health* magazine is a highly magnified head of lettuce, the centerpiece of a healthful menu that McDonald's was promoting. The lettuce looms over the ad's two other elements, a comment card from a smiling female customer with a question about lettuce and a friendly note in reply from McDonald's. For a restaurant chain known for its supersized meals of Double Quarter Pounders with Cheese, the close-up of a lettuce leaf might come as a surprise. A superficial interpretation of the McDonald's ad would point out that the fast-food giant is attempting to remake its image into a health-conscious restaurant. After all, the greening of the Golden Arches follows a shift in public attitudes toward diet and a sometimes environmentally unfriendly food industry.

Less obvious are the associations that the ad creates to persuade people that McDonald's is committed to a product—an entire experience—not usually offered by fast-food restaurants. If fast food has become synonymous in many consumers' minds with the impersonal and artificial conditions of modern life—from assembly-line food to robotic exchanges at the counter or drive-through window—then the McDonald's ad seeks to replace those associations with images of authenticity and familiarity.

The ad's underlying message emphasizes for viewers the real over the artificial, a quality in both McDonald's food and its relationship with its customers. Through vivid graphics McDonald's shows, rather than tells, viewers that its ingredients are wholesome. The head of lettuce

Marginal annotations:

Lee briefly summarizes the content of the ad.

Lee suggests a simple interpretation to highlight his more compelling interpretation.

Lee's thesis offers his analysis of the ad's message.

Marginal annotations indicate MLA-style formatting and effective writing.

Lee 2

Lee describes the dominant image in the visual text.

that creates the ad's entire background is the picture of mouthwatering wholesomeness. Enlarged to many times its natural size, the lettuce reveals its sharp, spring-green edges and beads of water standing on its leaves, presumably from recent washing. The fast-food chain could have bombarded the public with nutritional statistics about its food items, as many other restaurants do, but it seems to recognize that numbers can begin to read like cold data from a science textbook. Instead, McDonald's invites us to take a closer look at its ingredients, a chance to verify

Lee quotes words from the text.

for ourselves that the lettuce is as "pure" and "fresh" as it claims. The lettuce does in fact look "so crisp" that we can easily believe it would produce a "crunch" if we bit into it, just as McDonald's reports.

Clear topic sentence announces a shift to a new topic.

The ad's copy suggests that McDonald's wishes to convince viewers that its commitment to serving customers' needs is as genuine as its lettuce. The prominent repetition of the word *real* in the tagline expresses McDonald's policy of plain dealing with individual customers. The picture of a supposedly real customer, a paper clip holding her photograph, and the ragged left edge of the comment card all contribute to a sense that this exchange between customer and McDonald's is as real, as "pure," as McDonald's claims its lettuce is.

Lee analyzes the ad's language.

Indeed, the heading to the comment card, "Ask M," gives McDonald's a personal identity, which intensifies the impression of the company's accessibility. "Ask M" conjures up the image of a straight-shooting, small-town newspaper advice columnist. McDonald's lettuce, "M" says, comes "from the same place you buy yours." This comparison with the neighborhood market emphasizes the local presence of the restaurant by association. The lettuce we eat at McDonald's, the ad suggests, is in fact the very same we would feel confident putting on our family's plate at home. The opening phrase of the second sentence, "Simply put," is a signal that McDonald's earnestly desires to explain its operations to its

Lee 3

customers. As with the close-up of the lettuce, the wording suggests
that the company has nothing to hide.

It might be difficult to imagine that people will be persuaded
to abandon their local markets for McDonald's. But then again, we
cannot easily forget the ad's image of lettuce, its curling, serrated
edges and finely branched veins, enlarged to a slightly unsettling
size. And if this green image conjures up in our minds a golden
"M"—a place where we can reconnect with real people and the bounty
of the land—then maybe one of the most successful companies in
history has done it again.

Lee concludes with his
interpretation of the
ad's overall effect.

Lee 4

Work Cited

McDonald's Corporation. Advertisement. *Men's Health* July-
    Aug. 2004: 95. Print.

Work cited page is in
MLA style.

5 Constructing reasonable arguments

In writing an argument, you take a stand on a debatable issue. The question being debated might be a matter of public policy:

Should religious groups be allowed to meet on public school property?

What is the least dangerous way to dispose of hazardous waste?

Should a state require its citizens to have health insurance?

On such questions, reasonable people may disagree.

Reasonable men and women also disagree about many scholarly issues. Psychologists debate the role of genes and environment in determining behavior; historians interpret the causes of the Civil War quite differently; biologists challenge one another's predictions about the effects of global warming.

When you construct a *reasonable* argument, your goal is not simply to win or to have the last word. Your aim is to explain your understanding of the truth about a subject or to propose the best solution available for solving a problem — without being needlessly combative. In constructing your argument, you join a conversation with other writers and readers. Your aim is to convince readers to reconsider their opinions by offering new reasons to question an old viewpoint.

5a Examine your issue's social and intellectual contexts.

Arguments appear in social and intellectual contexts. Public policy debates obviously arise in social contexts, conducted among groups with competing values and interests. For example, the debate over offshore oil drilling has been renewed in the United States in light of skyrocketing energy costs

---

Academic English   Some cultures value writers who argue with force; other cultures value writers who argue subtly or indirectly. Academic audiences in the United States will expect your writing to be assertive and confident—neither aggressive nor passive. You can create an assertive tone by acknowledging different opinions and supporting your view with specific evidence.

TOO AGGRESSIVE	Of course prayer should be discouraged in public schools. Only foolish people think that organized prayer is good for everyone.
TOO PASSIVE	I might be wrong, but I think that organized prayer should be discouraged in public schools.
ASSERTIVE TONE	Organized prayer should be discouraged in public schools because it violates the religious freedom guaranteed by the First Amendment.

If you are uncertain about the tone of your work, ask for help at your school's writing center.

---

and terrorism concerns—with environmentalists, policymakers, and consumers all weighing in on the argument. Most public policy debates also have intellectual dimensions that address scientific or theoretical questions. In the case of the drilling issue, geologists, oceanographers, and economists all contribute their expertise.

Making the most of your handbook

Supporting your claims with evidence from sources can make your argument more effective.

▶ Conducting research: 46

Scholarly debates clearly play themselves out in intellectual contexts, but they have a social dimension too. Scholars respond to the contributions of other specialists in the field, often building on others' views and refining them, but at times challenging them.

Because many of your readers will be aware of the social and intellectual contexts in which your issue is grounded, you will be at a serious disadvantage if you are not informed. That's why it is a good idea to conduct some research before preparing your argument; consulting even a few sources can help. For example, the student whose paper appears on pages 115–18 became more knowledgeable about his issue—the ethics of performance-enhancing procedures in sports—after consulting several brief sources.

5b View your audience as a panel of jurors.

Do not assume that your audience already agrees with you; instead, envision skeptical readers who, like a panel of jurors,

Making the most of your handbook

You may need to consider a specific audience for your argument.

▶ Analyzing your audience: 1a

▶ Writing in a particular discipline, such as business or psychology: 7

will make up their minds after listening to all sides of the argument. If you are arguing a public policy issue, aim your paper at readers who represent a variety of opinions. In the case of the debate over offshore drilling, for example, imagine a jury representative of those who have a stake in the matter: environmentalists, policymakers, and consumers.

At times, you can deliberately narrow your audience. If you are working within a word limit, for example, you might not have the space in which to address all the concerns surrounding the offshore drilling debate. Or you might be primarily interested in reaching one segment of a general audience, such as consumers. In such instances, you can still view your audience as a panel of jurors; the jury will simply be a less diverse group.

In the case of scholarly debates, you will be addressing readers who share your interest in a discipline such as literature or psychology. Such readers belong to a group with an agreed-upon way of investigating and talking about issues. Though they generally agree about procedures, scholars in an academic discipline often disagree about particular issues. Once you see how they disagree about your issue, you should be able to imagine a jury that reflects the variety of opinions they hold.

5c In your introduction, establish credibility and state your position.

When you are constructing an argument, make sure your introduction contains a thesis sentence that states your position on the issue you have chosen to debate. In the sentences leading up to the thesis, establish your credibility with readers by showing that you are knowledgeable and fair-minded. If possible, build common ground with readers who may not at first agree with your views, and show them why they should consider your thesis.

> **Making the most of your handbook**
>
> When you write an argument, you state your position in a thesis.
>
> ▶ Writing effective thesis statements: 1c, 1e

In the following introduction, student Kevin Smith presents himself as someone worth listening to. Because Smith introduces both sides of the debate, readers are likely to approach his essay with an open mind.

> Although the Supreme Court has ruled against prayer in public schools on First Amendment grounds, many people still feel that prayer should be allowed. Such people value prayer as a practice central to their faith and believe that prayer is a way for schools to reinforce moral principles. They also compellingly point out a paradox in the First Amendment itself: at what point does the separation of church and state restrict the freedom of those who wish to practice their religion? What proponents of school prayer fail to realize, however, is that the Supreme Court's decision, although it was made on legal grounds, makes sense on religious grounds as well. Prayer is too important to be trusted to our public schools. —Kevin Smith, student

Writer is fair-minded, presenting the views of both sides.

Smith shows that he is familiar with the legal issues surrounding school prayer.

Smith's thesis builds common ground.

TIP: A good way to test a thesis while drafting and revising is to imagine a counterargument to your argument (see 5f). If you can't think of an opposing point of view, rethink your thesis or ask a classmate to respond to your argument.

5d Back up your thesis with persuasive lines of argument.

Arguments of any complexity contain lines of argument that, when taken together, might reasonably persuade readers that the thesis has merit. The following, for example, are the main lines of argument that Jamal Hammond used in his paper on performance-enhancing practices in sports (see pp. 115–18).

CENTRAL CLAIM	Thesis: Athletes who use any type of biotechnology give themselves an unfair advantage and disrupt the sense of fair play, and they should be banned from competition.
SUPPORTING CLAIMS	• Athletic achievement nowadays increasingly results from biological and high-tech intervention rather than strictly from hard work.
	• There is a difference between the use of state-of-the-art equipment and the modification of the body itself.
	• If the rules that guarantee an even playing field are violated, competitors and spectators alike are deprived of a sound basis of comparison on which to judge athletic effort and accomplishment.
	• If we let athletes alter their bodies through biotechnology, we might as well dispense with the human element altogether.

If you sum up your main lines of argument, as Hammond did, you will have a rough outline of your essay. In your paper, you will provide evidence for each of these claims.

5e Support your claims with specific evidence.

You will need to support your central claim and any subordinate claims with evidence: facts, statistics, examples and illustrations, expert opinion, and so on. Most debatable topics require that you consult some written sources. As you read through the sources, you will learn more about the arguments and counter-arguments at the center of your debate.

Remember that you must document your sources. Documentation gives credit to the authors and shows readers how to locate a source in case they want to assess its credibility or explore the issue further.

Using facts and statistics

A fact is something that is known with certainty because it has been objectively verified: The capital of Wyoming is Cheyenne. Carbon has an atomic weight of 12. John F. Kennedy was assassinated on November 22, 1963. Statistics are collections of numerical facts: Alcohol abuse is a factor in nearly 40 percent of traffic fatalities. More than four in ten businesses in the United States are owned by women. As of 2007, more than 50 percent of US households owned a digital television.

> **Making the most of your handbook**
>
> Sources, when used responsibly, can provide evidence to support an argument.
>
> ▶ Paraphrasing, summarizing, and quoting sources: 48c
>
> ▶ Punctuating direct quotations: 37a
>
> ▶ Citing sources: 51 (MLA), 56b (APA), 57b (*Chicago*)

Most arguments are supported at least to some extent by facts and statistics. For example, in the following passage the writer uses statistics to show that college students carry unreasonably high credit card debt.

> A 2001 study by Nellie Mae revealed that while the average credit card debt per college undergraduate is $2,327, more than 20% of undergraduates who have at least one credit card maintain a much higher debt level, from $3,000 to $7,000 (Barrett).

Writers often use statistics in selective ways to bolster their own views. If you suspect that a writer's handling of statistics is not quite fair, read authors with opposing views, who may give you a fuller understanding of the numbers, or track down the original sources for those statistics.

Using examples and illustrations

Examples and illustrations (extended examples, often in story form) rarely prove a point by themselves, but when used in combination with other forms of evidence they flesh out an argument and bring it to life. Because they often have an emotional dimension, they can reach readers in ways that statistics cannot.

When a teacher or tutor suggests that you "develop more," the comment often signals that you stopped short of providing a full and detailed discussion of your idea.

> Distancing ourselves from our family is a natural part of growing up. There are many ways in which we try doing so. For essayist Richard Rodriguez, it was his drive for academic success that separated him from his parents and his past (195). In his desire to become educated, he (removed himself) from his family and (distanced himself) from his culture. In his essay "The Achievement of Desire," he admits regretting the separation from his family and acknowledges the particular challenges of growing up between two cultures.

Develop more

In this body paragraph, a student responded to an assignment that asked her to explore one theme in Richard Rodriguez's essay "The Achievement of Desire."

The student has not included enough evidence or developed a thorough analysis of that evidence. To revise, she might look for specific examples and details from Rodriguez's essay to support her claim that Rodriguez "removed . . . and distanced himself" from his family. Then she might develop the claim by analyzing *how* and *why* Rodriguez's "desire to become educated" removed him from his family.

Similar comments: undeveloped • give examples • explain • expand

Revising when *you* need to develop more

1. *Read your paragraph to a peer or a tutor* and ask specific questions: What more is needed? More evidence? If so, what kind of evidence— specific examples, vivid details, statistics, or facts? Or more analysis? If so, how might you explain the meaning of the evidence you provide?

2. *Keep your purpose in mind.* You aren't being asked to restate what you've already written or what the author has written.

3. *Consider including more evidence* from the text and a more thorough exploration of why or how your evidence supports your claims.

More advice on using specific evidence: **5e**

In a paper arguing that any athletes who use gene therapy should be banned from competition, Jamal Hammond gives a thought-provoking example of how running with genetically modified limbs is no different from riding a motorcycle in a footrace.

Citing expert opinion

Although they are no substitute for careful reasoning of your own, the views of an expert can contribute to the force of your argument. For example, to help him make the case that biotechnology could degrade the meaning of sports, Jamal Hammond quotes the remarks of an expert.

> Thomas Murray, chair of the ethics advisory panel for the World Anti-Doping Agency, says he hopes, not too optimistically, for an "alternative future . . . where we still find meaning in great performances as an alchemy of two factors, natural talents . . . and virtues" (qtd. in Jenkins D11).

When you rely on expert opinion, make sure that your source is an expert in the field you are writing about. In some cases, you may need to provide credentials showing why your source is worth listening to. When including expert testimony in your paper, you can summarize or paraphrase the expert's opinion or you can quote the expert's exact words. You will of course need to document the source, as Hammond did in the example just given.

5f Anticipate objections; counter opposing arguments.

Readers who already agree with you need no convincing, but indifferent or skeptical readers may resist your arguments. To be willing to give up a position that seems reasonable, a reader has to see that there is an even more reasonable one. In addition to presenting your own case, therefore, you should review the opposing arguments and attempt to counter them.

It might seem at first that drawing attention to an opposing point of view or contradictory evidence would weaken your argument. But by anticipating and countering objections to your argument, you show yourself as a reasonable and well-informed writer. You also establish your purpose, demonstrate the significance of the issue you are debating, and ultimately strengthen your argument.

There is no best place in an essay to deal with opposing views. Often it is useful to summarize the opposing position early in your essay. After stating your thesis but before developing your own arguments, you might have a paragraph that takes up the most important counterargument. Or you can anticipate objections paragraph by paragraph as you develop your case. Wherever you decide to deal with opposing arguments,

---

Anticipating and countering objections

To anticipate a possible objection, consider the following questions:

- Could a reasonable person draw a different conclusion from your facts or examples?
- Might a reader question any of your assumptions?
- Could a reader offer an alternative explanation of this issue?
- Is there any evidence that might weaken your position?

The following questions may help you respond to a potential objection:

- Can you concede the point to the opposition but challenge the point's importance or usefulness?
- Can you explain why readers should consider a new perspective or question a piece of evidence?
- Should you explain your position in light of contradictory evidence?
- Can you suggest a different interpretation of the evidence?

When you write, use phrasing to signal to readers that you're about to present an objection. Often the signal phrase can go in the lead sentence of a paragraph:

Critics of this view argue that. . . .

Some readers might point out that. . . .

But isn't it possible that . . . ?

When a teacher or tutor suggests that you "consider opposing viewpoints," the comment often signals that you need to recognize and respond to possible objections to your argument.

> For many American workers, drug testing is a routine part of their working life. In her book *Nickel and Dimed*, Barbara Ehrenreich observes how random drug testing leads to a hostile work environment (128). In addition, researchers Shepard and Clifton have found that companies using drug-testing programs are likelier to have lower productivity levels than those that have not adopted such practices (1). Drug testing in the workplace has shown no benefits for employers or employees.

consider opposing viewpoints

In response to an assignment about changes in the workplace, one student wrote this body paragraph.

The student jumps to a conclusion too quickly without recognizing any opposing points of view. To revise, the student might begin by reading two or more sources to gain a different perspective and to learn more about the debate surrounding her topic. As she reads more sources, she might ask: What evidence do those in favor of drug testing provide to support their point of view? How would they respond to my conclusion against drug testing? By anticipating and countering opposing views, she will show herself as a fair and reasonable writer.

Similar comments: what about the other side? • counterargument?

Revising when *you* need to consider other points of view

1. *Read more* to learn about the debates surrounding the topic. Ask questions: Are there other sides to the issue? Would a reasonable person offer an alternative explanation for the evidence or provide counterevidence?

2. *Be open-minded.* Although it might seem counterintuitive to introduce opposing arguments, you'll show your knowledge of the topic by recognizing that not everyone draws the same conclusion.

3. *Try these (or similar) phrases* to introduce and counter objections: "Some readers might point out that . . ." or "Critics of this view argue that. . . ."

4. *Revise your thesis,* if necessary, to account for multiple points of view.

More advice on considering opposing viewpoints: **5f** and **6c**

do your best to explain the arguments of others accurately and fairly (see 6c).

5g Build common ground.

As you counter opposing arguments, try to seek out one or two assumptions you might share with readers who do not initially agree with your views. If you can show that you share their concerns, your readers will be more likely to acknowledge the validity of your argument. For example, to persuade people opposed to shooting deer, a state wildlife commission would have to show that it too cares about preserving deer and does not want them to die needlessly. Having established these values in common, the commission might be able to persuade critics that a carefully controlled hunting season is good for the deer population because reducing the total number of deer prevents starvation caused by overpopulation.

People believe that intelligence and decency support their side of an argument. To be persuaded, they must see these qualities in your argument. Otherwise they will persist in their opposition.

5h Sample argument paper

In the paper that begins on the following page, student Jamal Hammond argues that athletes who enhance their performance through biotechnology should be banned from athletic competition. Notice that he is careful to present opposing views fairly before providing his counterarguments.

In writing the paper, Hammond consulted three newspaper articles, two in print and one online. When he quotes or uses information from a source, he cites the source with an MLA (Modern Language Association) in-text citation. Citations in the paper refer readers to the list of works cited at the end of the paper. (See 53.)

hackerhandbooks.com/bedhandbook > Model papers
> MLA argument papers: Hammond; Lund; Sanghvi
> MLA papers: Orlov; Daly; Levi

Jamal Hammond

Professor Paschal

English 102

19 March 2007

Performance Enhancement through Biotechnology

Has No Place in Sports

The debate over athletes' use of performance-enhancing substances is getting more complicated as biotechnologies such as gene therapy become a reality. The availability of these new methods of boosting performance will force us to decide what we value most in sports—displays of physical excellence developed through hard work or victory at all costs. For centuries, spectators and athletes have cherished the tradition of fairness in sports. While sports competition is, of course, largely about winning, it is also about the means by which a player or team wins. Athletes who use any type of biotechnology give themselves an unfair advantage and disrupt the sense of fair play, and they should be banned from competition.

Researchers are experimenting with techniques that could manipulate an athlete's genetic code to build stronger muscles or increase endurance. Searching for cures for diseases like Parkinson's and muscular dystrophy, scientists at the University of Pennsylvania have created "Schwarzenegger mice," rodents that grew larger-than-normal muscles after receiving injections with a gene that stimulates growth protein. The researchers also found that a combination of gene manipulation and exercise led to a 35% increase in the strength of rats' leg muscles (Lamb 13).

Such therapies are breakthroughs for humans suffering from muscular diseases; for healthy athletes, they could mean new world records in sports involving speed and endurance—but at what cost to

Opening sentences provide background for Hammond's thesis.

Thesis states the main point.

Hammond establishes his credibility by summarizing medical research.

Source is cited in MLA style.

Marginal annotations indicate MLA-style formatting and effective writing.

Hammond uses specific evidence to support his thesis.

the integrity of athletic competition? The International Olympic Committee's World Anti-Doping Agency has become so alarmed about the possible effects of new gene technology on athletic competition that it has banned the use of gene therapies and urged researchers to devise a test for detecting genetic modification (Lamb 13).

Opposing views are presented fairly.

"Qtd. in" is used for an indirect source: words quoted in another source.

Some bioethicists argue that this next wave of performance enhancement is an acceptable and unavoidable feature of competition. As Dr. Andy Miah, who supports the regulated use of gene therapies in sports, claims, "The idea of the naturally perfect athlete is romantic nonsense. . . . An athlete achieves what he or she achieves through all sorts of means—technology, sponsorship, support and so on" (qtd. in Rudebeck). Miah, in fact, sees athletes' imminent turn to genetic modification as "merely a continuation of the way sport works; it allows us to create more extraordinary performances" (qtd. in Rudebeck). Miah's approval of "extraordinary performances" as the goal of competition reflects our culture's tendency to demand and reward new heights

Hammond counters opposing arguments.

of athletic achievement. The problem is that achievement nowadays increasingly results from biological and high-tech intervention rather than strictly from hard work.

Hammond develops the thesis.

Better equipment, such as aerodynamic bicycles and fiberglass poles for pole vaulting, have made it possible for athletes to record achievements unthinkable a generation ago. But athletes themselves must put forth the physical effort of training and practice—they must still build their skills (Jenkins D11). There is a difference between the use of state-of-the-art equipment and the modification of the body itself. Athletes who use medical technology, including drugs, to alter their bodies can bypass the hard work of training by taking on the powers of a machine. If they set new records this way, we lose the opportunity to witness sports as a spectacle of human effort and are left marveling at scientific advances, which have little relation to the athletic tradition of fair play.

Hammond 3

Such a tradition has long defined athletic competition. Sports rely on equal conditions to ensure fair play, from regulations that demand similar equipment to referees who evenhandedly apply the rules to all participants. If the rules that guarantee an even playing field are violated, competitors and spectators alike are deprived of a sound basis of comparison on which to judge athletic effort and accomplishment. When major league baseball rules call for solid-wood bats, the player who uses a corked bat enhances his hitting statistics at the expense of players who use regulation equipment. When Ben Johnson tested positive for steroids after setting a world record in the 100-meter dash in the 1988 Olympics, his "achievement" devalued the intense training that his competitors had undergone to prepare for the event. The International Olympic Committee responded by stripping Johnson of his medal and his world record. Likewise, athletes who use gene therapy to alter their bodies and enhance their performance will create an uneven playing field.

> Transition moves from the writer's main argument to specific examples.

If we let athletes alter their bodies through biotechnology, we might as well dispense with the human element altogether. Instead of watching the 100-meter dash to see who the fastest runner in the world is, we might just as well watch the sprinters mount motorcycles and race across the finish line. The absurdity of such an example, however, points to the damage that we will do to sports if we allow these therapies. Thomas Murray, chair of the ethics advisory panel for the World Anti-Doping Agency, says he hopes, not too optimistically, for an "alternative future . . . where we still find meaning in great performances as an alchemy of two factors, natural talents . . . and virtues" (qtd. in Jenkins D11).

> A vivid example helps the writer make his point.

Unless we are willing to organize separate sporting events and leagues—an Olympics, say, for athletes who have opted for a boost from

> Conclusion echoes the thesis without dully repeating it.

Hammond 4

the test tube and another for athletes who have chosen to keep their
bodies natural—we should ask from our athletes that they dazzle us less
with extraordinary performance and more with the fruits of their hard work.

Hammond 5

Works Cited

Jenkins, Sally. "The First Item in a Pandora's Box of Moral
        Ambiguities." *Washington Post* 4 Dec. 2004: D11. Print.

Lamb, Gregory M. "Will Gene-Altered Athletes Kill Sports?" *Christian
        Science Monitor* 23 Aug. 2004: 12-13. Print.

Rudebeck, Clare. "The Eyes Have It." *Independent* [London]. Independent
        News and Media, 27 Apr. 2005. Web. 1 Mar. 2007.

Works cited page
uses MLA style.

6 Evaluating arguments

In your reading and in your own writing, evaluate all arguments
for logic and fairness. Many arguments can stand up to critical
scrutiny. Often, however, a line of argument that at first seems
reasonable turns out to be illogical, unfair, or both.

6a Distinguish between reasonable and fallacious argumentative tactics.

A number of unreasonable argumentative tactics are known as
logical fallacies. Most of the fallacies—such as hasty generalizations and false analogies—are misguided or dishonest uses
of legitimate argumentative strategies. The examples in this
section suggest when such strategies are reasonable and when
they are not.

Generalizing (inductive reasoning)

Writers and thinkers generalize all the time. We look at a sample of data and conclude that data we have not observed will most likely conform to what we have seen. From a spoonful of soup, we conclude just how salty the whole bowl will be. After numerous bad experiences with an airline, we decide to book future flights with a competitor.

When we draw a conclusion from an array of facts, we are engaged in inductive reasoning. Such reasoning deals in probability, not certainty. For a conclusion to be highly probable, it must be based on evidence that is sufficient, representative, and relevant. (See the chart on p. 120.)

The fallacy known as *hasty generalization* is a conclusion based on insufficient or unrepresentative evidence.

HASTY GENERALIZATION

In a single year, scores on standardized tests in California's public schools rose by ten points. Therefore, more children than ever are succeeding in America's public school systems.

Data from one state do not justify a conclusion about the whole United States.

A *stereotype* is a hasty generalization about a group. Here are a few examples.

STEREOTYPES

Women are bad bosses.

Politicians are corrupt.

Asian students are exceptionally intelligent.

Stereotyping is common because of our human tendency to perceive selectively. We tend to see what we want to see; we notice evidence confirming our already formed opinions and fail to notice evidence to the contrary. For example, if you have concluded that politicians are corrupt, your stereotype will be confirmed by news reports of legislators being indicted—even though every day the media describe conscientious officials serving the public honestly and well.

Testing inductive reasoning

Though inductive reasoning leads to probable and not absolute truth, you can assess a conclusion's likely probability by asking three questions. This chart shows how to apply those questions to a sample conclusion based on a survey.

CONCLUSION   The majority of students on our campus would volunteer at least five hours a week in a local organization if the school provided a placement service for volunteers.

EVIDENCE   In a recent survey, 723 of 1,215 students questioned said they would volunteer at least five hours a week in a local organization if the school provided a placement service for volunteers.

1. Is the evidence sufficient?

   That depends. On a small campus (say, 3,000 students), the pool of students surveyed would be sufficient for market research, but on a large campus (say, 30,000), 1,215 students are only 4 percent of the population. If that 4 percent were known to be truly representative of the other 96 percent, however, even such a small sample would be sufficient (see question 2).

2. Is the evidence representative?

   The evidence is representative if those responding to the survey reflect the characteristics of the entire student population: age, sex, race, field of study, overall number of extracurricular commitments, and so on. If most of those surveyed are majors in fields like social work or counseling, however, the researchers would be wise to question the survey's conclusion.

3. Is the evidence relevant?

   Yes. The results of the survey are directly linked to the conclusion. A question about the number of hours students work for pay, by contrast, would not be relevant because it would not be about *choosing to volunteer*.

> **Academic English**   Many hasty generalizations contain words such as *all*, *ever*, *always*, and *never*, when qualifiers such as *most*, *many*, *usually*, and *seldom* would be more accurate.

Drawing analogies

An analogy points out a similarity between two things that are otherwise different. Analogies can be an effective means of arguing a point. Our system of judicial decision making, or case law, which relies heavily on previous decisions, makes extensive use of reasoning by analogy. One lawyer may point out, for example, that specific facts or circumstances resemble those from a previous case and will thus argue for a similar result or decision. In response, the opposing lawyer may maintain that such facts or circumstances bear only a superficial resemblance to those in the previous case and that in legally relevant respects they are quite different and thus require a different result or decision.

It is not always easy to draw the line between a reasonable and an unreasonable analogy. At times, however, an analogy is clearly off base, in which case it is called a *false analogy*.

FALSE ANALOGY

If we can send a spacecraft to Pluto, we should be able to find a cure for the common cold.

The writer has falsely assumed that because two things are alike in one respect, they must be alike in others. Exploring the outer reaches of the solar system and finding a cure for the common cold are both scientific challenges, but the problems confronting medical researchers are quite different from those solved by space scientists.

Tracing causes and effects

Demonstrating a connection between causes and effects is rarely simple. For example, to explain why a chemistry course has a high failure rate, you would begin by listing possible causes: inadequate preparation of students, poor teaching, lack of qualified tutors, and so on. Next you would investigate each possible cause. Only after investigating the possible causes would you be able to weigh the relative impact of each cause and suggest appropriate remedies.

Because cause-and-effect reasoning is so complex, it is not surprising that writers frequently oversimplify it. In particular, writers sometimes assume that because one event follows another, the first is the cause of the second. This common fallacy is known as *post hoc*, from the Latin *post hoc, ergo propter hoc*, meaning "after this, therefore because of this."

> ### POST HOC FALLACY
>
> Since Governor Cho took office, unemployment among minorities in the state has decreased by 7 percent. Governor Cho should be applauded for reducing unemployment among minorities.

The writer must show that Governor Cho's policies are responsible for the decrease in unemployment; it is not enough to show that the decrease followed the governor's taking office.

Weighing options

Especially when reasoning about problems and solutions, writers must weigh options. To be fair, a writer should mention the full range of options, showing why one is superior to the others or might work well in combination with others.

It is unfair to suggest that there are only two alternatives when in fact there are more. Writers who set up a false choice between their preferred option and one that is clearly unsatisfactory are guilty of the *either . . . or* fallacy.

> ### EITHER . . . OR FALLACY
>
> Our current war against drugs has not worked. Either we should legalize drugs or we should turn the drug war over to our armed forces and let them fight it.

Clearly there are other options, such as increased funding for drug abuse prevention and treatment.

Making assumptions

An assumption is a claim that is taken to be true—without the need of proof. Most arguments are based to some extent on assumptions, since writers rarely have the time and space to prove all of the conceivable claims on which their argument is based. For example, someone arguing about the best means of limiting population growth in developing countries might well assume that the goal of limiting population growth is worthwhile. For most audiences, there would be no need to articulate this assumption or to defend it. Some religious audiences, however, argue that bringing children into the world is an act of faith. It is a good idea to think through your own assumptions and imagine where they might conflict with those of your audience.

There is a danger in failing to spell out and prove a claim that is clearly controversial. Consider the following short argument, in which a key claim is missing.

ARGUMENT WITH MISSING CLAIM
Violent crime is increasing. Therefore, we should vigorously enforce the death penalty.

The writer seems to be assuming that the death penalty deters violent criminals—and that most audiences will agree. The writer also assumes that the death penalty is a fair punishment for violent crimes. These are not safe assumptions.

When a missing claim is an assertion that few would agree with, we say that a writer is guilty of a *non sequitur* (Latin for "does not follow").

NON SEQUITUR
Leah loves good food; therefore, she will be an excellent chef.

Few people would agree with the missing claim—that lovers of good food always make excellent chefs.

Deducing conclusions (deductive reasoning)

When we deduce a conclusion, we—like Sherlock Holmes—put things together. We establish that a general principle is true, that a specific case is an example of that principle, and that therefore a particular conclusion about that case is a certainty. In real life, such absolute reasoning rarely happens. Approximations of it, however, sometimes occur.

Deductive reasoning can often be structured in a three-step argument called a *syllogism*. The three steps are the major premise, the minor premise, and the conclusion.

1. Anything that increases radiation in the environment is dangerous to public health. (Major premise)
2. Nuclear reactors increase radiation in the environment. (Minor premise)
3. Therefore, nuclear reactors are dangerous to public health. (Conclusion)

The major premise is a generalization. The minor premise is a specific case. The conclusion follows from applying the generalization to the specific case.

Deductive arguments break down if one of the premises is not true or if the conclusion does not logically follow from the premises. In the following short argument, the major premise is very likely untrue.

UNTRUE PREMISE

The police do not give speeding tickets to people driving less than five miles per hour over the limit. Sam is driving fifty-nine miles per hour in a fifty-five-mile-per-hour zone. Therefore, the police will not give Sam a speeding ticket.

The conclusion is true only if the premises are true. If the police sometimes give tickets for driving less than five miles per hour over the limit, Sam cannot safely conclude that he will avoid a ticket.

In the following argument, both premises might be true, but the conclusion does not follow logically from them.

CONCLUSION DOES NOT FOLLOW

All members of our club ran in this year's Boston Marathon.
Jay ran in this year's Boston Marathon. Therefore, Jay is a
member of our club.

The fact that Jay ran the race is no guarantee that he is a member of the club. Presumably, many runners are nonmembers.

Assuming that both premises are true, the following argument holds up.

CONCLUSION FOLLOWS

All members of our club ran in this year's Boston Marathon.
Jay is a member of our club. Therefore, Jay ran in this year's
Boston Marathon.

6b Distinguish between legitimate and unfair emotional appeals.

There is nothing wrong with appealing to readers' emotions.
After all, many issues worth arguing about have an emotional
as well as a logical dimension. Even the Greek logician Aristotle lists *pathos* (emotion) as a legitimate argumentative tactic. For example, in an essay criticizing big-box stores, writer
Betsy Taylor has a good reason for tugging at readers' emotions: Her subject is the decline of city and town life. In her
conclusion, Taylor appeals to readers' emotions by invoking
their national pride.

LEGITIMATE EMOTIONAL APPEAL

Is it anti-American to be against having a retail giant set up
shop in one's community? Some people would say so. On
the other hand, if you board up Main Street, what's left of
America?

As we all know, however, emotional appeals are frequently
misused. Many of the arguments we see in the media, for instance, strive to win our sympathy rather than our intelligent
agreement. A TV commercial suggesting that you will be thin
and sexy if you drink a certain diet beverage is making a pitch

to emotions. So is a political speech that recommends electing a candidate because he is a devoted husband and father who serves as a volunteer firefighter.

The following passage illustrates several types of unfair emotional appeals.

> **UNFAIR EMOTIONAL APPEALS**
>
> This progressive proposal to build a ski resort in the state park has been carefully researched by Western Trust, the largest bank in the state; furthermore, it is favored by a majority of the local merchants. The only opposition comes from narrow-minded, do-gooder environmentalists who care more about trees than they do about people; one of their leaders was actually arrested for disturbing the peace several years ago.

Words with strong positive or negative connotations, such as *progressive* and *do-gooder*, are examples of *biased language*. Attacking the persons who hold a belief (environmentalists) rather than refuting their argument is called *ad hominem*, a Latin term meaning "to the man." Associating a prestigious name (Western Trust) with the writer's side is called *transfer*. Claiming that an idea should be accepted because a large number of people (the majority of merchants) are in favor of it is called the *bandwagon appeal*. Bringing in irrelevant issues (the arrest) is a *red herring*, named after a trick used in fox hunts to mislead the dogs by dragging a smelly fish across the trail.

6c Judge how fairly a writer handles opposing views.

The way in which a writer deals with opposing views is telling. Some writers address the arguments of the opposition fairly, conceding points when necessary and countering others, all in a civil spirit. Other writers will do almost anything to win an argument: either ignoring opposing views altogether or misrepresenting such views and attacking their proponents.

In your own writing, you build credibility by addressing opposing arguments fairly. (See also 5f.) In your reading, you can assess the credibility of your sources by looking at how they deal with views not in agreement with their own.

Describing the views of others

Writers and politicians often deliberately misrepresent the views of others. One way they do this is by setting up a "straw man," a character so weak that he is easily knocked down. The *straw man* fallacy consists of an oversimplification or outright distortion of opposing views. For example, in a California debate over attempts to control the mountain lion population, pro-lion groups characterized their opponents as trophy hunters bent on shooting harmless lions and sticking them on the walls of their dens. In truth, such hunters were only one faction of those who saw a need to control the lion population.

During the District of Columbia's struggle for voting representation, some politicians set up a straw man, as shown in the following example.

STRAW MAN FALLACY
Washington, DC, residents are lobbying for statehood. Giving a city such as the District of Columbia the status of a state would be unfair.

The straw man wanted statehood. In fact, most District citizens lobbied for voting representation in any form, not necessarily through statehood.

Quoting opposing views

Writers often quote the words of writers who hold opposing views. In general, this is a good idea, for it assures some level of fairness and accuracy. At times, though, both the fairness and the accuracy are an illusion.

A source may be misrepresented when it is quoted out of context. All quotations are to some extent taken out of context, but a fair writer will explain the context to readers. To select a provocative sentence from a source and to ignore the more moderate sentences surrounding it is both unfair and misleading. Sometimes a writer deliberately distorts a source through the device of ellipsis dots. Ellipsis dots tell readers that words have been omitted from the original source. When those words are crucial to an author's meaning, omitting them is obviously unfair. (See also 39d.)

ORIGINAL SOURCE

Johnson's *History of the American West* is riddled with inaccuracies and astonishing in its blatantly racist description of the Indian wars.   —B. R., reviewer

MISLEADING QUOTATION

According to B. R., Johnson's *History of the American West* is "astonishing in its . . . description of the Indian wars."

EXERCISE 6–1   Explain what is illogical in the following brief arguments. It may be helpful to identify the logical fallacy or fallacies by name. Answers to lettered sentences appear in the back of the book.

a. My roommate, who is an engineering major, is taking a course called Structures of Tall Buildings. All engineers have to know how to design tall buildings.
b. If you're old enough to vote, you're old enough to drink. Therefore, the drinking age should be lowered to eighteen.
c. Cable stations that rely on nauseating reality shows, annoying infomercials for useless products, idiotic talk shows, and second-rate movies should have their licenses pulled.
d. Most young people can't afford to buy a house in Silicon Valley because they spend too much money on new clothes and computer games.
e. If you're not part of the solution, you're part of the problem.

1. Whenever I wash my car, it rains. I have discovered a way to end all droughts—get all the people to wash their cars.
2. Either you can learn how to build a Web site or you won't be able to get a decent job after college.
3. College professors tend to be sarcastic. Three of my five professors this semester make sarcastic remarks.

4. Although Bell's book on Joe DiMaggio was well researched, I doubt that an Australian historian can contribute much to our knowledge of an American baseball player.

5. Slacker co-workers and crazy, big-mouthed clients make our spineless managers impose ridiculous workloads on us hard-working, conscientious employees.

6. If professional sports teams didn't pay athletes such high salaries, we wouldn't have so many kids breaking their legs at hockey and basketball camps.

7. Ninety percent of the students oppose a tuition increase; therefore, the board of trustees should not pass the proposed increase.

8. If more people would take a long, close look at businesses like Microsoft and Amazon, they could reorganize their family lives to run successfully.

9. A mandatory ten-cent deposit on bottles and cans will eliminate litter because everyone I know will return the containers for the money rather than throw them away.

10. Researching what voters think during an election campaign is useless because most citizens don't vote anyway.

7   Writing in the disciplines

Writing is a fact of college life. No matter what you study, you will be expected to write for a variety of audiences in a variety of formats. College courses expose you to the thinking of scholars in many disciplines, such as the humanities (literature, music, art), the social sciences (psychology, anthropology, sociology), and the sciences (biology, physics, chemistry). Writing in any discipline provides the opportunity to practice the methods used by scholars in these fields and to enter into their debates. Each field has its own questions, evidence, language, and conventions, but all disciplines share certain expectations for good writing.

7a Find commonalities across disciplines.

If you understand the features that are common to writing in all disciplines, you will have an easier time sorting out the unique aspects of writing in a particular field.

Making the most of your handbook

When writing for any course, keep in mind the steps needed to write a strong academic paper.

▶ Communicating a purpose: 1a

▶ Determining your audience: 1a

▶ Asking an academic question: 7b

▶ Making and supporting a claim: 5c, 5e

▶ Citing sources: 51 (MLA), 56b (APA), 57b (*Chicago*)

In every discipline, scholars write about texts. For example, in the humanities scholars write about texts such as novels, poems, paintings, and music. In the social sciences, texts include journal articles, books and field accounts by researchers, census reports, case studies, and reports on experiments. In the sciences, researchers write about data taken from reports that other researchers have published and about data drawn from site results, site surveys, and laboratory experiments.

A good paper in any field needs to communicate a writer's purpose to an audience and to explore an engaging question about a subject. Effective writers make an argument and support their claims with evidence. Writers in most fields need to show readers the thesis they're developing (or, in the sciences, the hypothesis they're testing) and how they counter the opposing explanations or objections of other writers. In some fields, such as nursing and business, writers may not put forth an explicit claim or thesis but will still communicate a clear purpose and use evidence to support their ideas. All disciplines require writers to document where they found their evidence and from whom they borrowed ideas.

7b Recognize the questions that writers in a discipline ask.

Disciplines are characterized by the kinds of questions their scholars attempt to answer. Social scientists, who analyze human behavior, might ask about the factors that cause people to act in certain ways. Humanities scholars interpret texts within their cultural contexts; they ask questions about the society at the time a text was written or about the connections between an author's life and work. Historians, who seek an understanding of the past, ask questions about the causes and effects of events and about connections between current and past events. Scientists collect data and ask questions to help them interpret the data.

One way to understand how disciplines ask different questions is to look at assignments on the same topic in various fields. Many disciplines, for example, might be interested in the subject of disasters. The following are some questions that writers in different fields might ask about this subject.

EDUCATION	Should the elementary school curriculum teach students how to cope in disaster situations?
FILM	How has the disaster film genre changed since the advent of computer-generated imagery (CGI) in the early 1970s?
HISTORY	How did the formation of the American Red Cross change this country's approach to natural disasters?
ENGINEERING	What recent innovations in levee design are most promising?
PSYCHOLOGY	What are the most effective ways to identify and treat post-traumatic stress disorder (PTSD) in disaster survivors?

The questions you ask in any discipline will form the basis of the thesis for your paper. The questions themselves don't communicate a central idea, but they may lead you to one. For an education paper, for example, you might begin with the question "Should the elementary school curriculum teach students how to cope in disaster situations?" After considering the issues involved, you might draft the following thesis.

School systems should adopt age-appropriate curriculum units that introduce children to the risks of natural and human-made disasters and that allow children to practice coping strategies.

Whenever you write for a college course, try to determine the kinds of questions scholars in the field might ask about a topic. You can find clues in assigned readings, lecture or discussion topics, e-mail discussion groups, and the paper assignment itself. When in doubt, ask your instructor for guidance.

7c Understand the kinds of evidence that writers in a discipline use.

Regardless of the discipline in which you are writing, you must support any claims you make with evidence—facts, statistics, examples and illustrations, expert opinion, and so on. Familiarize yourself with the kinds of evidence most writers use to support claims in your field.

- For an English paper that examines three types of parent-child relationships in Shakespeare's *King Lear*, you would look closely at lines from the play.

- For a psychology paper on the connection between certain medications and suicidal impulses, you might study the results of clinical trials.

- For a nursing practice paper about the medical condition of a particular patient, you would review the patient's chart as well as any relevant medical literature.

- For a history paper on Renaissance attitudes toward marriage, you might examine historical documents such as letters, diaries, and church records.

The kinds of evidence used in different disciplines often overlap. Students of geography, media studies, and political science, for example, might use census data to explore different topics. The evidence that one discipline values, however, might not be sufficient to support an interpretation or a conclusion in another field. You might use anecdotes or interviews in an anthropology paper, for example, but such evidence would be irrelevant in a biology lab report. The chart

Evidence typically used in various disciplines

Humanities: Literature, art, film, music, philosophy

- Passages of text or lines of a poem
- Details from an image or a work of art
- Passages of a musical composition
- Critical essays that analyze original works

Humanities: History

- Primary sources such as photographs, letters, maps, and government documents
- Scholarly books and articles that interpret evidence

Social sciences: Psychology, sociology, political science, anthropology

- Data from original experiments
- Results of field research such as interviews, observations, or surveys
- Statistics from government agencies
- Scholarly books and articles that interpret data from original experiments and from other researchers' studies

Sciences: Biology, chemistry, physics

- Data from original experiments
- Scholarly articles that report findings from experiments

at the top of this page lists the kinds of evidence accepted in various disciplines.

7d Become familiar with a discipline's language conventions.

Every discipline has a specialized vocabulary. As you read the articles and books in a field, you'll notice certain words and phrases that come up repeatedly. Sociologists, for example,

Point of view and verb tense in academic writing

Point of view

- Writers of analytical or research essays in the humanities usually use the third-person point of view: *Austen presents* . . . or *Castel describes the battle as.* . . .

- Scientists and most social scientists, who depend on quantitative research to present findings, tend to use the third-person point of view: *The results indicated.* . . .

- Writers in the humanities and in some social sciences occasionally use the first person in discussing their personal experience or in writing a personal narrative: *After spending two years interviewing families affected by the war, I began to understand that* . . . or *Every July as we approached the Cape Cod Canal, we could sense.* . . .

Present or past tense

- Literature scholars use the present tense to discuss a text: *Hughes effectively dramatizes different views of minority assertiveness.* (See 52b.)

- Science and social science writers use the past tense to describe experiments and the present tense to discuss the findings: *In 2003, Berkowitz released the first double-blind placebo study.* . . . *These results paint a murky picture.* (See 56c.)

- Writers in history use the present tense or the present perfect tense to discuss a text: *Shelby Foote describes the scene like this* . . . or *Shelby Foote has described the scene like this.* . . . (See 57c.)

use terms such as *independent variables, political opportunity resources,* and *dyads* to describe social phenomena; computer scientists might refer to *algorithm design* and *loop invariants* to describe programming methods. Practitioners in health fields such as nursing use terms like *treatment plan* and *systemic assessment* to describe patient care. Use discipline-specific terms only when you are certain that you and your readers fully understand their meaning.

In addition to vocabulary, many fields of study have developed specialized conventions for point of view and verb tense. See the chart at the top of the previous page.

7e Use a discipline's preferred citation style.

In any discipline, you must give credit to those whose ideas or words you have borrowed. Whenever you write, it is your responsibility to avoid plagiarism by citing sources honestly and accurately.

While all disciplines emphasize careful documentation, each follows a particular system of citation that its members have agreed on. Writers in the humanities usually use the system established by the Modern Language Association (MLA). Scholars in some social sciences, such as psychology and anthropology, follow the style guidelines of the American Psychological Association (APA); scholars in history and some humanities typically follow *The Chicago Manual of Style*.

> **Making the most of your handbook**
>
> You will need to document your sources in the style preferred by your discipline.
>
> ▶ Documenting sources: MLA (humanities), 53; APA (social sciences), 56d; *Chicago* (history), 57d; CSE (sciences), online at hackerhandbooks .com/resdoc

7f Respond to writing assignments in the disciplines.

When you are asked to write in a specific discipline, become familiar with the distinctive features of the writing in that discipline. Then read the assignment carefully and try to identify the purpose of the assignment and the type of evidence you are expected to use.

On the following pages are examples of assignments in four disciplines—psychology, business, biology, and nursing—along with excerpts from student papers that were written in response to the assignments.

Psychology

ASSIGNMENT: LITERATURE REVIEW

———— 1 ————   —— 2 ——
Write a literature review in which you report on and

— 2 —   ——— 3 ———   ———— 1 ————
evaluate the published research on a behavioral disorder.

1 Key terms

2 Purpose: to report on and evaluate a body of evidence

3 Evidence: research of other psychologists

ADHD in Boys vs. Girls   1

Always Out of Their Seats (and Fighting):

Why Are Boys Diagnosed with ADHD More Often Than Girls?

Background and
explanation of writer's
purpose.

Attention deficit hyperactivity disorder (ADHD) is a commonly
diagnosed disorder in children that affects social, academic, or
occupational functioning. As the name suggests, its hallmark
characteristics are hyperactivity and lack of attention as well as

Evidence from
research the writer
has reviewed.

impulsive behavior. For decades, studies have focused on the causes,
expression, prevalence, and outcome of the disorder, but until recently
very little research investigated gender differences. In fact, until the
early 1990s most research focused exclusively on boys (Brown,

APA citations and
specialized language
(*ADHD, comorbid*).

Madan-Swain, & Baldwin, 1991), perhaps because many more boys
than girls are diagnosed with ADHD. Researchers have speculated on
the possible explanations for the disparity, citing reasons such as true
sex differences in the manifestation of the disorder's symptoms,
gender biases in those who refer children to clinicians, and possibly
even the diagnostic procedures themselves (Gaub & Carlson, 1997).

Thesis: writer's
argument.

But the most persuasive reason is that ADHD is often a comorbid
condition—that is, it coexists with other behavior disorders that are
not diagnosed properly and that do exhibit gender differences.

Marginal annotations indicate appropriate formatting and effective writing.

Business

ASSIGNMENT: PROPOSAL

Write a proposal, as a memo, for improving or adding a service at a company where you have worked. Address the pros and cons of your proposal; draw on relevant studies, research, and your knowledge of the company.

1 Key terms
2 Purpose: to analyze certain evidence and make a proposal based on that analysis
3 Appropriate evidence: relevant studies

Memorandum

To: Jay Crosson, Senior Vice President, Human Resources

From: Kelly Ratajczak, Intern, Purchasing Department

Subject: Proposal to Add a Wellness Program

Date: April 24, 2009

Health care costs are rising. In the long run, implementing a wellness program in our corporate culture will decrease the company's health care costs.

> Writer's main idea.

Research indicates that nearly 70% of health care costs are from common illnesses related to high blood pressure, overweight, lack of exercise, high cholesterol, stress, poor nutrition, and other preventable health issues (Hall, 2006). Health care costs are a major expense for most businesses, and they do not reflect costs due to the loss of productivity or absenteeism. A wellness program would address most, if not all, of these health care issues and related costs.

> Data from recent study as support for claim.
>
> APA citation style, typical in business.
>
> Business terms familiar to readers (*costs, productivity, absenteeism*).

Biology

ASSIGNMENT: LABORATORY REPORT

Write a report on an experiment you conduct on the distribution pattern of a plant species indigenous to the Northeast. Describe your methods for collecting data and interpret your experiment's results.

1 Key terms
2 Purpose: to interpret the results of an experiment
3 Evidence: data collected during the experiment

CSE style, typical in sciences.

Distribution Pattern of Dandelion (*Taraxacum officinale*)
on an Abandoned Golf Course

ABSTRACT

Abstract: an overview of hypothesis, experiment, and results.

This paper reports our study of the distribution pattern of the common dandelion (*Taraxacum officinale*) on an abandoned golf course in Hilton, New York, on 10 July 2005. An area of 6 ha was sampled with 111 randomly placed 1×1 m^2 quadrats. The dandelion count from each quadrat was used to test observed frequencies against expected frequencies based on a hypothesized random distribution. [Abstract continues.]

Specialized language (*aggregated*, *random*, *uniformly distributed*, and so on).

INTRODUCTION

Introduction: context and purpose of experiment. Instead of a thesis, or main claim, a lab report interprets the data in a later Discussion section.

Theoretically, plants of a particular species may be aggregated, random, or uniformly distributed in space [1]. The distribution type may be determined by many factors, such as availability of nutrients, competition, distance of seed dispersal, and mode of reproduction [2].

The purpose of this study was to determine if the distribution pattern of the common dandelion (*Taraxacum officinale*) on an abandoned golf course was aggregated, random, or uniform.

Nursing

ASSIGNMENT: NURSING PRACTICE PAPER

Write a client history, a nursing diagnosis, recommendations for care, your rationales, and expected and actual outcomes. Use interview notes, the client's health records, and relevant research findings.

1 Key terms

2 Purpose: to provide client history, diagnosis, recommendations, and outcomes

3 Evidence: interviews, health records, and research findings

---

ALL and HTN in One Client   1

Acute Lymphoblastic Leukemia and Hypertension in One Client:
A Nursing Practice Paper

Physical History

    E.B. is a 16-year-old white male 5'10" tall weighing 190 lb. He was admitted to the hospital on April 14, 2006, due to decreased platelets and a need for a PRBC transfusion. He was diagnosed in October 2005 with T-cell acute lymphoblastic leukemia (ALL), after a 2-week period of decreased energy, decreased oral intake, easy bruising, and petechia. The client had experienced a 20-lb weight loss in the previous 6 months. At the time of diagnosis, his CBC showed a WBC count of 32, an H & H of 13/38, and a platelet count of 34,000. His initial chest X-ray showed an anterior mediastinal mass. Echocardiogram showed a structurally normal heart. He began induction chemotherapy on October 12, 2005, receiving vincristine, 6-mercaptopurine, doxorubicin, intrathecal methotrexate, and then high-dose methotrexate per protocol. During his hospital stay, he

Evidence from client's medical chart for overall assessment.

Specialized nursing language (*echocardiogram, chemotherapy,* and so on).

required packed red cells and platelets on two different occasions. He was diagnosed with hypertension (HTN) due to systolic blood pressure readings consistently ranging between 130s and 150s and was started on nifedipine. E.B. has a history of mild ADHD, migraines, and deep vein thrombosis (DVT). He has tolerated the induction and consolidation phases of chemotherapy well and is now in the maintenance phase, in which he receives a daily dose of mercaptopurine, weekly doses of methotrexate, and intermittent doses of steroids.

Instead of a thesis, or main claim, the writer gives a diagnosis, recommendations for care, and expected outcomes, all supported by evidence from observations and client records.

hackerhandbooks.com/bedhandbook > Model papers
> APA literature review: Charat
> APA business proposal: Ratajczak
> CSE laboratory report: Johnson and Arnold
> APA nursing practice paper: Riss

Part III
Clear Sentences

8   Prefer active verbs.

As a rule, choose an active verb and pair it with a subject that names the person or thing doing the action. Active verbs express meaning more emphatically and vigorously than their weaker counterparts—forms of the verb *be* or verbs in the passive voice.

PASSIVE	The pumps *were destroyed* by a surge of power.
***BE* VERB**	A surge of power *was* responsible for the destruction of the pumps.
ACTIVE	A surge of power *destroyed* the pumps.

Verbs in the passive voice lack strength because their subjects receive the action instead of doing it. Forms of the verb *be* (*be, am, is, are, was, were, being, been*) lack vigor because they convey no action.

Although passive verbs and the forms of *be* have legitimate uses, choose an active verb if it can carry your meaning. Even among active verbs, some are more active—and therefore more vigorous and colorful—than others. Carefully selected verbs can energize a piece of writing.

▶ The goalie crouched low, ~~reached~~ out his stick, and ~~sent~~ the

rebound away from the mouth of the net.

swept

hooked

> **Academic English**   Although you may be tempted to avoid the passive voice completely, keep in mind that some writing situations call for it, especially scientific writing. For appropriate uses of the passive voice, see page 144; for advice about forming the passive voice, see 28c and 62c.

Grammar checkers are fairly good at flagging passive verbs, such as *is used* or *had been tried*. However, because passive verbs are sometimes appropriate, you—not the computer program—must decide whether to change a verb from passive to active.

8a Use the active voice unless you have a good reason for choosing the passive.

In the active voice, the subject does the action; in the passive voice, the subject receives the action (see also 62c). Although both voices are grammatically correct, the active voice is usually more effective because it is simpler and more direct.

ACTIVE   Hernando *caught* the fly ball.

PASSIVE   The fly ball *was caught* by Hernando.

Passive sentences often identify the actor in a *by* phrase, as in the preceding example. Sometimes, however, that phrase is omitted, and who or what is responsible for the action becomes unclear: *The fly ball was caught.*

Most of the time, you will want to emphasize the actor, so you should use the active voice. To replace a passive verb with an active one, make the actor the subject of the sentence.

▶ A bolt of lightning struck the transformer.
    ~~The transformer was struck by a bolt of lightning.~~
    ^

The active verb (*struck*) makes the point more forcefully than the passive verb (*was struck*).

▶ The settlers stripped the land of timber before realizing
    ~~The land was stripped of timber before the settlers realized~~
    ^

the consequences of their actions.

The revision emphasizes the actors (*settlers*) by naming them in the subject.

▶ ~~The debris was removed~~ from the construction site.
The contractor removed the
⌃

Sometimes the actor does not appear in a passive-voice sentence. To turn such a sentence into the active voice, the writer must determine an appropriate subject, in this case *contractor*.

Appropriate uses of the passive

The passive voice is appropriate if you wish to emphasize the receiver of the action or to minimize the importance of the actor.

APPROPRIATE PASSIVE	Many Hawaiians *were forced* to leave their homes after the earthquake.
APPROPRIATE PASSIVE	As the time for harvest approaches, the tobacco plants *are sprayed* with a chemical to retard the growth of suckers.

The writer of the first sentence wished to emphasize the receiver of the action, *Hawaiians*. The writer of the second sentence wished to focus on the tobacco plants, not on the people spraying them.

In much scientific writing, the passive voice properly emphasizes the experiment or process being described, not the researcher. Check with your instructor for the preference in your discipline.

APPROPRIATE PASSIVE	The solution *was heated* to the boiling point, and then it was reduced in volume by 50 percent.

8b Replace *be* verbs that result in dull or wordy sentences.

Not every *be* verb needs replacing. The forms of *be* (*be, am, is, are, was, were, being, been*) work well when you want to link a subject to a noun that clearly renames it or to an adjective that describes it: *Orchard House was the home of Louisa May Alcott. The harvest will be bountiful after the summer rains.* And *be* verbs are essential as helping verbs before present participles (*is flying, are disappearing*) to express ongoing action: *Derrick was fighting the fire when his wife went into labor.* (See 27f.)

If using a *be* verb makes a sentence needlessly dull and wordy, however, consider replacing it. Often a phrase following the verb will contain a noun or an adjective (such as *violation, resistant*) that suggests a more vigorous, active verb (*violate, resist*).

▶ Burying nuclear waste in Antarctica would ~~be in violation of~~ *violate*

an international treaty.

Violate is less wordy and more vigorous than *be in violation of.*

▶ When Rosa Parks ~~was resistant to~~ *resisted* giving up her seat on the

bus, she became a civil rights hero.

Resisted is stronger than *was resistant to.*

> **Grammar checkers** usually do not flag wordiness caused by *be* verbs. Only you can find ways to strengthen your sentences by using vigorous, active verbs in place of *be.*

8c As a rule, choose a subject that names the person or thing doing the action.

In weak, unemphatic prose, both the actor and the action may be buried in sentence elements other than the subject and the verb. In the following sentence, for example, both the actor and the action appear in prepositional phrases, word groups that do not receive much attention from readers.

WEAK   The institution of the New Deal had the effect of reversing some of the economic inequalities of the Great Depression.

EMPHATIC   The New Deal reversed some of the economic inequalities of the Great Depression.

Consider the subjects and verbs of the two versions—*institution had* versus *New Deal reversed.* The latter expresses the writer's point more emphatically.

> P
> ~~The use of~~ pure oxygen can ~~cause~~ healing ~~in~~ wounds that
> are otherwise untreatable.

In the original sentence, the subject and verb—*use can cause*—
express the point blandly. *Pure oxygen can heal* makes the point
more emphatically and directly.

Writing with sources

Chicago-style citation

> Francis Lowell built
> In 1813, a large mill ~~was built by Francis Lowell~~ along the
> Charles River in Waltham, Massachusetts.[1]

When you are writing about historical events, naming the actor
in the subject is the clearest and most direct way to get your point
across. Instead of burying the actor (*Francis Lowell*) in a prepositional phrase, the writer has made *Francis Lowell* the subject and
has changed the verb *was built* from passive to active voice. (See
also 8a on active voice and 57d on *Chicago* documentation style.)

EXERCISE 8–1   Revise any weak, unemphatic sentences by replacing be verbs or passive verbs with active alternatives and, if necessary, by naming in the subject the person or thing doing the action.
Some sentences are emphatic; do not change them. Revisions of lettered sentences appear in the back of the book. Example:

> The ranger doused the campfire before giving us
> ~~The campfire was doused by the ranger before we were given~~
> a ticket for unauthorized use of a campsite.

a.   The Prussians were victorious over the Saxons in 1745.

b.   The entire operation is managed by Ahmed, the producer.

c.   The sea kayaks were expertly paddled by the tour guides.

d.   At the crack of rocket and mortar blasts, I jumped from the top
     bunk and landed on my buddy below, who was crawling on
     the floor looking for his boots.

e.   There were shouting protesters on the courthouse steps.

1.   A strange sound was made in the willow tree by the monkey
     that had escaped from the zoo.

2.   Her letter was in acknowledgment of the student's participa-
     tion in the literacy program.

3.   The bomb bay doors rumbled open, and freezing air whipped
     through the plane.

4. The work of Paul Oakenfold and Sandra Collins was influential in my choice of music for my audition.
5. The only responsibility I was given by my parents was putting my little brother to bed when they had to work late.

hackerhandbooks.com/bedhandbook > Grammar exercises > Clear sentences
> E-ex 8–2 to 8–5

9 Balance parallel ideas.

If two or more ideas are parallel, they are easier to grasp when expressed in parallel grammatical form. Single words should be balanced with single words, phrases with phrases, clauses with clauses.

A kiss can be a comma, a question mark, or an exclamation

point.   —Mistinguett

This novel is not to be tossed lightly aside, but to be hurled

with great force.   —Dorothy Parker

In matters of principle, stand like a rock; in matters of taste,

swim with the current.   —Thomas Jefferson

Writers often use parallelism to create emphasis. (See p. 190.)

> **Grammar checkers** only occasionally flag faulty parallelism because they cannot assess whether ideas are parallel in grammatical form.

9a Balance parallel ideas in a series.

Readers expect items in a series to appear in parallel grammatical form. When one or more of the items violate readers' expectations, a sentence will be needlessly awkward.

▶ **Children who study music also learn confidence,**

creativity.

discipline, and ~~they are creative.~~
        ^

The revision presents all the items in the series as nouns: *confidence*, *discipline*, and *creativity*.

▶ **Impressionist painters believed in focusing on ordinary**

subjects, capturing the effects of light on those subjects,

using

and ~~to use~~ **short brushstrokes.**
      ^

The revision uses *-ing* forms for all the items in the series: *focusing*, *capturing*, and *using*.

▶ **Racing to get to work on time, Sam drove down the middle**

ignored

of the road, ran one red light, and two stop signs.
                                  ^

The revision adds a verb to make the three items parallel: *drove*, *ran*, and *ignored*.

In headings and lists, aim for as much parallelism as the content allows. (See 58b and 58c.)

9b Balance parallel ideas presented as pairs.

When pairing ideas, underscore their connection by expressing them in similar grammatical form. Paired ideas are usually connected in one of these ways:

- with a coordinating conjunction such as *and*, *but*, or *or*
- with a pair of correlative conjunctions such as *either . . . or* or *not only . . . but also*
- with a word introducing a comparison, usually *than* or *as*

Parallel ideas linked with coordinating conjunctions

Coordinating conjunctions (*and*, *but*, *or*, *nor*, *for*, *so*, and *yet*) link ideas of equal importance. When those ideas are closely parallel in content, they should be expressed in parallel grammatical form.

▶ **Emily Dickinson's poetry features the use of dashes and**
the capitalization of
~~capitalizing~~ **common words.**
^

The revision balances the nouns *use* and *capitalization*.

▶ **Many states are reducing property taxes for home owners**
extending
and ~~extend~~ financial aid in the form of tax credits to
^
renters.

The revision balances the verb *reducing* with the verb *extending*.

Parallel ideas linked with correlative conjunctions

Correlative conjunctions come in pairs: *either . . . or, neither . . . nor, not only . . . but also, both . . . and, whether . . . or.* Make sure that the grammatical structure following the second half of the pair is the same as that following the first half.

▶ **Thomas Edison was not only a prolific inventor but also ~~was~~**

a successful entrepreneur.

The words *a prolific inventor* follow *not only*, so *a successful entrepreneur* should follow *but also.* Repeating *was* creates an unbalanced effect.

to
▶ **The clerk told me either to change my flight or take the train.**
^

To change my flight, which follows *either,* should be balanced with *to take the train,* which follows *or.*

Comparisons linked with than or as

In comparisons linked with *than* or *as,* the elements being compared should be expressed in parallel grammatical structure.

to ground
▶ **It is easier to speak in abstractions than ~~grounding~~ one's**
^
thoughts in reality.

To speak is balanced with *to ground.*

Writing with sources

MLA-style citation

▶ In Pueblo culture, according to Silko, ~~to write~~ *writing* down the

stories of a tribe is not the same as "keeping track of all the

stories" (290).

When you are quoting from a source, parallel grammatical structure—such as *writing . . . keeping*—helps create continuity between your sentence and the words from the source.

Comparisons should also be logical and complete. (See 10c.)

9c Repeat function words to clarify parallels.

Function words such as prepositions (*by, to*) and subordinating conjunctions (*that, because*) signal the grammatical nature of the word groups to follow. Although you can sometimes omit them, be sure to include them whenever they signal parallel structures that readers might otherwise miss.

▶ Our study revealed that left-handed students were more likely

to have trouble with classroom desks and *that* rearranging

desks for exam periods was useful.

A second subordinating conjunction helps readers sort out the two parallel ideas: *that* left-handed students have trouble with classroom desks and *that* rearranging desks was useful.

EXERCISE 9–1 Edit the following sentences to correct faulty parallelism. Revisions of lettered sentences appear in the back of the book. Example:

Rowena began her workday by pouring a cup of coffee and ~~checked~~ *checking* her e-mail.

a. Police dogs are used for finding lost children, tracking criminals, and the detection of bombs and illegal drugs.

b. Hannah told her rock-climbing partner that she bought a new harness and of her desire to climb Otter Cliffs.

c. It is more difficult to sustain an exercise program than starting one.

d. During basic training, I was not only told what to do but also what to think.

e. Jan wanted to drive to the wine country or at least Sausalito.

1. Camp activities include fishing trips, dance lessons, and computers.

2. Arriving at Lake Powell in a thunderstorm, the campers found it safer to remain in their cars than setting up their tents.

3. The streets were not only too steep but also were too narrow for anything other than pedestrian traffic.

4. More digital artists in the show are from the South Shore than the North Shore.

5. To load her toolbox, Anika the Clown gathered hats of different sizes, put in two tubes of face paint, arranged a bundle of extra-long straws, added a bag of colored balloons, and a battery-powered hair dryer.

hackerhandbooks.com/bedhandbook > Grammar exercises > Clear sentences
> E-ex 9–2 to 9–5

10 Add needed words.

Do not omit words necessary for grammatical or logical completeness. Readers need to see at a glance how the parts of a sentence are connected.

> **ESL** Languages sometimes differ in the need for certain words. In particular, be alert for missing articles, verbs, subjects, or expletives. See 29, 30a, and 30b.

> Grammar checkers do not flag the vast majority of missing words. They can, however, catch some missing verbs (see 27e). Although they can flag some missing articles (*a, an,* and *the*), they often suggest that an article is missing when in fact it is not. (See also 29.)

10a Add words needed to complete compound structures.

In compound structures, words are often left out for economy: *Tom is a man who means what he says and* [*who*] *says what he means.* Such omissions are acceptable as long as the omitted words are common to both parts of the compound structure.

If a sentence defies grammar or idiom because an omitted word is not common to both parts of the compound structure, the simplest solution is to put the word back in.

▶ Successful advertisers target customers whom they identify

  who

  through demographic research or have purchased their

  product in the past.

  The word *who* must be included because *whom . . . have purchased* is not grammatically correct.

▶ Mayor Davis never has and never will accept a bribe.

  accepted

  Has . . . accept is not grammatically correct.

▶ Many South Pacific islanders still believe and live by ancient

  in

  laws.

  Believe . . . by is not idiomatic in English. (For a list of common idioms, see 18d.)

NOTE: Even when the omitted word is common to both parts of the compound structure, occasionally it must be inserted to avoid ambiguity.

  My favorite *professor* and *mentor* influenced my choice of a career. [Professor and mentor are the same person.]

  My favorite *professor* and *my mentor* influenced my choice of a career. [Professor and mentor are two different people; *my* must be repeated.]

10b Add the word *that* if there is any danger
of misreading without it.

If there is no danger of misreading, the word *that* may be
omitted when it introduces a subordinate clause. *The value
of a principle is the number of things* [*that*] *it will explain.*
Occasionally, however, a sentence might be misread without
that.

▶ In his famous obedience experiments, psychologist Stanley
    that
  Milgram discovered ˄ ordinary people were willing to inflict

  physical pain on strangers.

  Milgram didn't discover ordinary people; he discovered that
  ordinary people were willing to inflict pain on strangers. The word
  that tells readers to expect a clause, not just *ordinary people*, as the
  direct object of *discovered*.

10c Add words needed to make comparisons
logical and complete.

Comparisons should be made between items that are alike. To
compare unlike items is illogical and distracting.

▶ The forests of North America are much more extensive than
  those of
  ˄ Europe.

  Forests must be compared with forests, not with all of Europe.

▶ ~~The death rate of~~ |infantry soldiers in the Vietnam War ~~was~~ died
  at a   rate   ˄
  ˄ much higher than ˄ the other combat troops.

  The death rate cannot logically be compared to troops. The writer
  could revise the sentence by inserting *that of* after *than*, but the
  preceding revision is more concise.

▶ Some say that Ella Fitzgerald's renditions of Cole Porter's

                                   singer's.

  songs are better than any other ~~singer.~~

Ella Fitzgerald's renditions cannot logically be compared with a
singer. The revision uses the possessive form *singer's,* with the word
renditions being implied.

Sometimes the word *other* must be inserted to make a
comparison logical.

                      other

▶ Jupiter is larger than any planet in our solar system.

Jupiter is a planet, and it cannot be larger than itself.

Sometimes the word *as* must be inserted to make a comparison grammatically complete.

                            as

▶ The city of Lowell is as old, if not older than, the neighboring

  city of Lawrence.

The construction *as old* is not complete without a second *as: as old
as . . . the neighboring city of Lawrence.*

Comparisons should be complete enough to ensure clarity.
The reader should understand what is being compared.

INCOMPLETE   Brand X is less salty.

COMPLETE   Brand X is less salty than Brand Y.

Finally, comparisons should leave no ambiguity for readers. If more than one interpretation is possible, revise the
sentence to state clearly which interpretation you intend. In
the following ambiguous sentence, two interpretations are
possible.

AMBIGUOUS   Ken helped me more than my roommate.

CLEAR   Ken helped me more than *he helped* my roommate.

CLEAR   Ken helped me more than my roommate *did.*

10d Add the articles *a, an,* and *the* where necessary for grammatical completeness.

It is not always necessary to repeat articles with paired items: *We bought a computer and printer.* However, if one of the items requires *a* and the other requires *an,* both articles must be included.

> We bought a computer and ^an^ antivirus program.

Articles are sometimes omitted in recipes and other instructions that are meant to be followed while they are being read. Such omissions are inappropriate, however, in nearly all other forms of writing, whether formal or informal.

> **ESL**   Choosing and using articles can be challenging for multilingual writers. See 29.

EXERCISE 10–1 Add any words needed for grammatical or logical completeness in the following sentences. Revisions of lettered sentences appear in the back of the book. Example:

The officer feared ^that^ the prisoner would escape.

a. A grapefruit or orange is a good source of vitamin C.
b. The women entering VMI can expect haircuts as short as the male cadets.
c. Looking out the family room window, Sarah saw her favorite tree, which she had climbed as a child, was gone.
d. The graphic designers are interested and knowledgeable about producing posters for the balloon race.
e. Reefs are home to more species than any ecosystem in the sea.

1. Very few black doctors were allowed to serve in the Civil War, and their qualifications had to be higher than white doctors.
2. Rachel is interested and committed to working at a school in Ecuador next semester.
3. Vassily likes mathematics more than his teacher.

4. The inspection team saw many historic buildings had been damaged by the earthquake.

5. Lila knows seven languages, but she found English harder to learn than any language.

hackerhandbooks.com/bedhandbook > Grammar exercises > Clear sentences
> E-ex 10–2 to 10–4

11 Untangle mixed constructions.

A mixed construction contains sentence parts that do not sensibly fit together. The mismatch may be a matter of grammar or of logic.

> **Grammar checkers** can flag *is when, is where,* and *reason . . . is because* constructions (11c), but they fail to identify nearly all other mixed constructions, including sentences as tangled as this one: *Depending on our method of travel and our destination determines how many suitcases we are allowed to pack.*

11a Untangle the grammatical structure.

Once you head into a sentence, your choices are limited by the range of grammatical patterns in English. (See 62 and 63.) You cannot begin with one grammatical plan and switch without warning to another. Often you must rethink the purpose of the sentence and revise.

MIXED   For most drivers who have a blood alcohol content of .05 percent double their risk of causing an accident.

The writer begins the sentence with a long prepositional phrase and makes it the subject of the verb *double*. But a prepositional phrase can serve only as a modifier; it cannot be the subject of a sentence.

REVISED   For most drivers who have a blood alcohol content of .05 percent, the risk of causing an accident is doubled.

REVISED   Most drivers who have a blood alcohol content
                 of .05 percent double their risk of causing an
                 accident.

In the first revision, the writer begins with the prepositional
phrase and finishes the sentence with a proper subject and
verb (*risk . . . is doubled*). In the second revision, the writer
stays with the original verb (*double*) and heads into the sentence
another way, making *drivers* the subject of *double*.

▶ ~~When the country elects~~ *Electing* a president is the most important

   responsibility in a democracy.

The adverb clause *When the country elects a president* cannot serve
as the subject of the verb *is*. The revision replaces the adverb
clause with a gerund phrase, a word group that can function as a
subject. (See 63e and 63b.)

▶ Although the United States is one of the wealthiest nations

   in the world, ~~but~~ more than twelve million of our children

   live in poverty.

The coordinating conjunction *but* cannot link a subordinate clause
(*Although the United States . . .*) with an independent clause (*more
than twelve million of our children live in poverty*).

Occasionally a mixed construction is so tangled that it
defies grammatical analysis. When this happens, back away
from the sentence, rethink what you want to say, and then
rewrite the sentence.

MIXED   In the whole-word method, children learn to recog-
                 nize entire words rather than by the phonics method
                 in which they learn to sound out letters and groups of
                 letters.

REVISED   The whole-word method teaches children to recognize
                 entire words; the phonics method teaches them to
                 sound out letters and groups of letters.

ESL   English does not allow double subjects, nor does it allow an object or an adverb to be repeated in an adjective clause. Unlike some other languages, English does not allow a noun and a pronoun to be repeated in a sentence if they have the same grammatical function. See 30c and 30d.

▶ My father ~~he~~ moved to Peru before he met my mother.

▶ ~~The final exam~~ I should really study for ~~it~~ to pass the
  the final exam

  course.

11b Straighten out the logical connections.

The subject and the predicate (the verb and its modifiers) should make sense together; when they don't, the error is known as *faulty predication*.

▶ We decided that ~~Tiffany's welfare~~ would not be safe living
  Tiffany

  with her mother.

Tiffany, not her welfare, may not be safe.

▶ Under the revised plan, the elderly/~~who now receive a double~~
  double personal exemption for the

  ~~personal exemption,~~ will be abolished.

The exemption, not the elderly, will be abolished.

An appositive is a noun that renames a nearby noun. When an appositive and the noun it renames are not logically equivalent, the error is known as *faulty apposition*. (See 63c.)

▶ ~~The tax accountant,~~ a very lucrative profession, requires
  Tax accounting,

  intelligence, patience, and attention to mathematical detail.

The tax accountant is a person, not a profession.

11c Avoid *is when*, *is where*, and *reason . . . is
because* constructions.

In formal English, many readers object to *is when, is where,*
and *reason . . . is because* constructions on either grammatical
or logical grounds. Grammatically, the verb *is* (as well as *are,
was,* and *were*) should be followed by a noun that renames the
subject or by an adjective that describes the subject, not by an
adverb clause beginning with *when, where,* or *because.* (See 62b
and 63e.) Logically, the words *when, where,* and *because* suggest relations of time, place, and cause—relations that do not
always make sense with *is, are, was,* or *were.*

▶ Anorexia nervosa is ~~where people~~ think they are too

  a disorder suffered by people who

  fat and diet to the point of starvation.

  Where refers to places. Anorexia nervosa is a disorder, not a place.

▶ The ~~reason the~~ experiment failed ~~is~~ because conditions in

  the lab were not sterile.

  The writer might have changed *because* to *that* (*The reason the experiment failed is that conditions in the lab were not sterile*), but the
  preceding revision is more concise.

EXERCISE 11–1   Edit the following sentences to untangle mixed
constructions. Revisions of lettered sentences appear in the back of
the book. Example:

  Taking
  ~~By taking~~ the oath of allegiance made Ling a US citizen.

a.   Using surgical gloves is a precaution now worn by dentists to
     prevent contact with patients' blood and saliva.
b.   A physician, the career my brother is pursuing, requires at least
     ten years of challenging work.
c.   The reason the pharaohs had bad teeth was because tiny par-
     ticles of sand found their way into Egyptian bread.

d. Recurring bouts of flu among team members set a record for number of games forfeited.
e. In this box contains the key to your future.

1. Early diagnosis of prostate cancer is often curable.
2. Depending on our method of travel and our destination determines how many suitcases we are allowed to pack.
3. Dyslexia is where people have a learning disorder that impairs reading ability.
4. Even though Ellen had heard French spoken all her life, yet she could not speak it.
5. In understanding artificial intelligence code is a critical skill for computer game designers.

hackerhandbooks.com/bedhandbook > Grammar exercises > Clear sentences
> E-ex 11–2 to 11–4

12 Repair misplaced and dangling modifiers.

Modifiers, whether they are single words, phrases, or clauses, should point clearly to the words they modify. As a rule, related words should be kept together.

Grammar checkers can flag split infinitives, such as *to carefully and thoroughly sift* (12d). However, they don't alert you to other misplaced modifiers (*I only ate three radishes*) or dangling modifiers (*When a boy, my mother enrolled me in tap dance classes*).

12a Put limiting modifiers in front of the words they modify.

Limiting modifiers such as *only, even, almost, nearly,* and *just* should appear in front of a verb only if they modify the verb: *At first, I couldn't even touch my toes, much less grasp them.* If they limit the meaning of some other word in the sentence, they should be placed in front of that word.

▶ The literature reveals that students ~~only~~ learn new vocabulary

   only

   words when they are encouraged to read.

   ⌃

   Only limits the meaning of the *when* clause.

▶ St. Vitus Cathedral, commissioned by Charles IV in the

   almost

   mid-fourteenth century, ~~almost~~ took six centuries to

   ⌃

   complete.

   Almost limits the meaning of *six centuries*, not *took*.

   just

▶ If you ~~just~~ interview chemistry majors, your picture of the

   ⌃

   student body's response to the new grading policies will

   be incomplete.

   The adverb *just* limits the meaning of *chemistry majors*, not *interview*.

When the limiting modifier *not* is misplaced, the sentence usually suggests a meaning the writer did not intend.

   not

▶ In the United States in 1860, all black southerners were ~~not~~

   ⌃

   slaves.

   The original sentence says that no black southerners were slaves. The revision makes the writer's real meaning clear: Some (but not all) black southerners were slaves.

12b Place phrases and clauses so that readers can see at a glance what they modify.

Although phrases and clauses can appear at some distance from the words they modify, make sure your meaning is clear. When phrases or clauses are oddly placed, absurd misreadings can result.

MISPLACED	The soccer player returned to the clinic where he had undergone emergency surgery in 2004 in a limousine sent by Adidas.
REVISED	Traveling in a limousine sent by Adidas, the soccer player returned to the clinic where he had undergone emergency surgery in 2004.

The revision corrects the false impression that the soccer player underwent emergency surgery in a limousine.

▶ *On the walls*
~~There~~ are many pictures of comedians who have performed ∧

at Gavin's.~~on the walls.~~ ∧

The comedians weren't performing on the walls; the pictures were on the walls.

▶ *170-pound,*
The robber was described as a six-foot-tall man with a heavy ∧

mustache .~~weighing 170 pounds.~~ ∧

The robber, not the mustache, weighed 170 pounds.

Occasionally the placement of a modifier leads to an ambiguity—a squinting modifier. In such a case, two revisions will be possible, depending on the writer's intended meaning.

AMBIGUOUS	The exchange students we met for coffee occasionally questioned us about our latest slang.
CLEAR	The exchange students we occasionally met for coffee questioned us about our latest slang.
CLEAR	The exchange students we met for coffee questioned us occasionally about our latest slang.

In the original version, it was not clear whether the meeting or the questioning happened occasionally. Both revisions eliminate the ambiguity.

12c Move awkwardly placed modifiers.

As a rule, a sentence should flow from subject to verb to object, without lengthy detours along the way. When a long adverbial word group separates a subject from its verb, a verb from its object, or a helping verb from its main verb, the result is often awkward.

▶ ~~Hong Kong,~~ ^Aafter more than 150 years of British rule, was ^{Hong Kong}

transferred back to Chinese control in 1997.

> There is no reason to separate the subject, *Hong Kong*, from the verb, *was transferred*, with a long phrase.

▶ ~~Jeffrey Meyers discusses,~~ in his biography of F. Scott
Jeffrey Meyers discusses
Fitzgerald, the writer's "fascination with the superiority,

the selfishness, and the emptiness of the rich" (166).

> When you quote from a source, the phrase or clause that you use to introduce the source should be as straightforward as possible. There is no reason to separate the verb, *discusses*, from its object, *fascination*, with two prepositional phrases.

EXCEPTION: Occasionally a writer may choose to delay a verb or an object to create suspense. In the following passage, for example, Robert Mueller inserts the *after* phrase between the subject *women* and the verb *walk* to heighten the dramatic effect.

> I asked a Burmese why women, after centuries of following their men, now walk ahead. He said there were many unexploded land mines since the war.   —Robert Mueller

ESL English does not allow an adverb to appear between a verb and its object. See 30f.

▶ Yolanda lifted ^{easily}~~easily~~ the fifty-pound weight.

Writing with sources

MLA-style citation

12d Avoid split infinitives when they are awkward.

An infinitive consists of *to* plus the base form of a verb: *to think*, *to breathe*, *to dance*. When a modifier appears between *to* and the verb, an infinitive is said to be "split": *to carefully balance*, *to completely understand*.

When a long word or a phrase appears between the parts of the infinitive, the result is usually awkward.

> ▶ ~~The~~ **patient should try to** ~~if possible~~ **avoid going up and**
>
> *If possible, the*
>
> **down stairs.**

Attempts to avoid split infinitives can result in equally awkward sentences. When alternative phrasing sounds unnatural, most experts allow—and even encourage—splitting the infinitive.

AWKWARD   We decided actually to enforce the law.

BETTER   We decided to actually enforce the law.

At times, neither the split infinitive nor its alternative sounds particularly awkward. In such situations, it is usually better to unsplit the infinitive, especially in formal writing.

> ▶ **Nursing students learn to** ~~accurately~~ **record a patient's vital**
>
> **signs./**
>
> *accurately.*

EXERCISE 12–1   Edit the following sentences to correct misplaced or awkwardly placed modifiers. Revisions of lettered sentences appear in the back of the book. Example:

> *in a telephone survey*
>
> **Answering questions can be annoying.** ~~in a telephone~~
>
> ~~survey.~~

a.   More research is needed to effectively evaluate the risks posed by volcanoes in the Pacific Northwest.

b. Many students graduate with debt from college totaling more than fifty thousand dollars.

c. It is a myth that humans only use 10 percent of their brains.

d. A coolhunter is a person who can find in the unnoticed corners of modern society the next wave of fashion.

e. All geese do not fly beyond Narragansett for the winter.

1. The flood nearly displaced half of the city's residents, who packed into several overcrowded shelters.

2. Most lions at night hunt for medium-size prey, such as zebra.

3. Several recent studies have encouraged heart patients to more carefully watch their cholesterol levels.

4. The garden's centerpiece is a huge sculpture that was carved by three women called *Walking in Place*.

5. The old Marlboro ads depicted a man on a horse smoking a cigarette.

hackerhandbooks.com/bedhandbook > Grammar exercises > Clear sentences
> E-ex 12–3 to 12–5

12e Repair dangling modifiers.

A dangling modifier fails to refer logically to any word in the sentence. Dangling modifiers are easy to repair, but they can be hard to recognize, especially in your own writing.

Recognizing dangling modifiers

Dangling modifiers are usually word groups (such as verbal phrases) that suggest but do not name an actor. When a sentence opens with such a modifier, readers expect the subject of the next clause to name the actor. If it doesn't, the modifier dangles.

▶ Understanding the need to create checks and balances on
   the framers of
   power, the Constitution divided the government into three
   ⌃
   branches.

The framers of the Constitution (not the document itself) understood the need for checks and balances.

> *women have often been denied*
>
> **After completing seminary training,** ~~**women's**~~ **access to the**
>
> **priesthood.** ~~**has often been denied.**~~

Women (not their access to the priesthood) complete the training.

The following sentences illustrate four common kinds of dangling modifiers.

DANGLING   *Deciding to join the navy*, the recruiter enthusiastically pumped Joe's hand. [Participial phrase]

DANGLING   *Upon entering the doctor's office*, a skeleton caught my attention. [Preposition followed by a gerund phrase]

DANGLING   *To satisfy her mother*, the piano had to be practiced every day. [Infinitive phrase]

DANGLING   *Though not eligible for the clinical trial*, the doctor was willing to prescribe the drug for Ethan on compassionate grounds. [Elliptical clause with an understood subject and verb]

These dangling modifiers falsely suggest that the recruiter decided to join the navy, that the skeleton entered the doctor's office, that the piano intended to satisfy the mother, and that the pharmaceutical company was not eligible for the clinical trial.

Although most readers will understand the writer's intended meaning in such sentences, the inadvertent humor can be distracting.

Repairing dangling modifiers

To repair a dangling modifier, you can revise the sentence in one of two ways:

- Name the actor in the subject of the sentence.
- Name the actor in the modifier.

Checking for dangling modifiers

Depending on your sentence, one of these revision strategies may be more appropriate than the other.

ACTOR NAMED IN SUBJECT

▶ Upon entering the doctor's office, a skeleton ~~caught my attention.~~

I noticed

▶ To satisfy her mother, the piano ~~had to be practiced~~ every day.

Jing-mei had to practice

ACTOR NAMED IN MODIFIER

▶ ~~Deciding~~ to join the navy, the recruiter enthusiastically pumped ~~Joe's~~ hand.

When Joe decided

his

▶ Though not eligible for the clinical trial, the doctor *Ethan was*
was willing to prescribe the drug for ~~Ethan~~ *him* on

compassionate grounds.

NOTE: You cannot repair a dangling modifier just by moving it. Consider, for example, the sentence about the skeleton. If you put the modifier at the end of the sentence (*A skeleton caught my attention upon entering the doctor's office*), you are still suggesting—absurdly, of course—that the skeleton entered the office. The only way to avoid the problem is to put the word *I* in the sentence, either as the subject or in the modifier.

▶ Upon entering the doctor's office, a skeleton. *I noticed* ~~caught my attention.~~

▶ ~~Upon entering~~ *As I entered* the doctor's office, a skeleton caught my attention.

EXERCISE 12–2 Edit the following sentences to correct dangling modifiers. Most sentences can be revised in more than one way. Revisions of lettered sentences appear in the back of the book. Example:

To acquire a degree in almost any field, *a student must complete* two science courses. ~~must be completed.~~

a. Though only sixteen, UCLA accepted Martha's application.
b. To replace the gear mechanism, attached is a form to order the part by mail.
c. Settled in the cockpit, the pounding of the engine was muffled only slightly by my helmet.
d. After studying polymer chemistry, computer games seemed less complex to Phuong.
e. When a young man, my mother enrolled me in tap dance classes.

1. While working as a ranger in Everglades National Park, a Florida panther crossed the road in front of my truck one night.
2. By following the new recycling procedure, the city's landfill costs will be reduced significantly.
3. Serving as president of the missionary circle, one of Sophia's duties is to raise money for the church.
4. After buying an album by Ali Farka Toure, the rich and rolling rhythms of Malian music made more sense to Silas.
5. Opening the window to let out a huge bumblebee, the car swerved into an oncoming truck.

hackerhandbooks.com/bedhandbook > Grammar exercises > Clear sentences
> E-ex 12–6 to 12–8

13 Eliminate distracting shifts.

> **Grammar checkers** usually do not flag shifts in point of view or in verb tense, mood, or voice. Even obvious errors, like the following shift in tense, slip right past the grammar checker: *My three-year-old fell into the pool and to my surprise she swims to the shallow end.*
>
> Sometimes grammar checkers mark a shift from a direct to an indirect question or quotation but do not make any suggestions for revision. You must decide where the structure is faulty and how to fix it.

13a Make the point of view consistent in person and number.

The point of view of a piece of writing is the perspective from which it is written: first person (*I* or *we*), second person (*you*), or third person (*he, she, it, one, they,* or any noun).

The *I* (or *we*) point of view, which emphasizes the writer, is a good choice for informal letters and writing based primarily on personal experience. The *you* point of view, which emphasizes the reader, works well for giving advice or explaining how to do something. The third-person point of view, which emphasizes the subject, is appropriate in formal academic and professional writing.

Writers who are having difficulty settling on an appropriate point of view sometimes shift confusingly from one to another. The solution is to choose a suitable perspective and then stay with it.

▶ Our class practiced rescuing a victim trapped in a wrecked

car. We learned to dismantle the car with the essential

          We   our   our
tools. ~~You~~ were graded on ~~your~~ speed and ~~your~~ skill in

freeing the victim.

The writer should have stayed with the *we* point of view. *You* is inappropriate because the writer is not addressing readers directly. *You* should not be used in a vague sense meaning "anyone." (See 23d.)

    You need
▶ ~~One needs~~ a password and a credit card number to access

the database. You will be billed at an hourly rate.

You is an appropriate choice because the writer is giving advice directly to readers.

▶ According to the National Institute of Mental Health

            children
(2007), ~~a child~~ with attention deficit hyperactivity disorder

may have trouble sitting still and may gradually stop

paying attention to their teachers (Symptoms section,

para. 2).

In describing reports or results of studies, writers are often tempted to generalize with singular nouns, such as *child*, and then later in the passage find themselves shifting from singular to plural. Here the writer might have changed *their* to the singular *his or her* to agree with *child*, but the revision making both terms plural is more concise. (See also 17f and 22a.)

Writing with sources

APA-style citation

point of view • *I*, *you*, *he* •
singular vs. plural • consistent tense
shift **13b** **171**

EXERCISE 13–1 Edit the following paragraph to eliminate distracting shifts in point of view (person and number).

When online dating first became available, many people thought that it would simplify romance. We believed that you could type in a list of criteria—sense of humor, college education, green eyes, good job—and a database would select the perfect mate. Thousands of people signed up for services and filled out their profiles, confident that true love was only a few mouse clicks away. As it turns out, however, virtual dating is no easier than traditional dating. I still have to contact the people I find, exchange e-mails and phone calls, and meet him in the real world. Although a database might produce a list of possibilities and screen out obviously undesirable people, you can't predict chemistry. More often than not, people who seem perfect online just don't click in person. Electronic services do help a single person expand their pool of potential dates, but it's no substitute for the hard work of romance.

hackerhandbooks.com/bedhandbook > Grammar exercises > Clear sentences
> E-ex 13–5

13b Maintain consistent verb tenses.

Consistent verb tenses clearly establish the time of the actions being described. When a passage begins in one tense and then shifts without warning and for no reason to another, readers are distracted and confused.

▶ There was no way I could fight the current and win. Just as I

was losing hope, a stranger ~~jumps~~ *jumped* off a passing boat and

~~swims~~ *swam* toward me.

The writer thought that the present tense (*jumps, swims*) would convey immediacy and drama. But having begun in the past tense (*could fight, was losing*), the writer should follow through in the past tense.

Writers often encounter difficulty with verb tenses when writing about literature. Because fictional events occur outside the time frames of real life, the past tense and the present tense may seem equally appropriate. The literary convention, however, is to describe fictional events consistently in the present tense. (See 55.)

▶ The scarlet letter is a punishment sternly placed on Hester's
breast by the community, and yet it ~~was~~ a fanciful and
  _is_
imaginative product of Hester's own needlework.

EXERCISE 13–2 Edit the following paragraphs to eliminate distracting shifts in tense.

The English colonists who settled in Massachusetts received assistance at first from the local Indian tribes, but by 1675 there had been friction between the English and the Indians for many years. On June 20 of that year, Metacomet, whom the colonists called Philip, leads the Wampanoag tribe in the first of a series of attacks on the colonial settlements. The war, known today as King Philip's War, rages on for more than a year and leaves three thousand Indians and six hundred colonists dead. Metacomet's attempt to retain power in his native land failed. Finally he too is killed, and the victorious colonists sell his wife and children into slavery.

The Indians did not leave records of their encounters with the English settlers, but the settlers recorded some of their experiences at the hands of the Indians. One of the few accounts to survive was written by a captured colonist, Mrs. Mary Rowlandson. She is a minister's wife who is kidnapped by an Indian war party and held captive for eleven weeks in 1676. Her history, *A Narrative of the Captivity and Restoration of Mrs. Mary Rowlandson,* tells the story of her experiences with the Wampanoags. Although it did not paint a completely balanced picture of the Indians, Rowlandson's narrative, which is considered a classic early American text, showed its author to be a keen observer of life in an Indian camp.

13c Make verbs consistent in mood and voice.

Unnecessary shifts in the mood of a verb can be distracting and confusing to readers. There are three moods in English: the *indicative*, used for facts, opinions, and questions; the *imperative*, used for orders or advice; and the *subjunctive*, used in certain contexts to express wishes or conditions contrary to fact (see 27g).

The following passage shifts confusingly from the indicative to the imperative mood.

▶ The counselor advised us to spread out our core requirements over two or three semesters. ~~Also,~~ *She also suggested that we* pay attention to prerequisites for elective courses.

The writer began by reporting the counselor's advice in the indicative mood (*counselor advised*) and switched to the imperative mood (*pay attention*); the revision puts both sentences in the indicative.

A verb may be in either the active voice (with the subject doing the action) or the passive voice (with the subject receiving the action). (See 8a.) If a writer shifts without warning from one to the other, readers may be left wondering why.

▶ Each student completes a self-assessment, *gives it* ~~The self-assessment is then given~~ to the teacher, and a copy *exchanges* ~~is exchanged~~ with a classmate.

Because the passage began in the active voice (*student completes*) and then switched to the passive (*self-assessment is given, copy is exchanged*), readers are left wondering who gives the self-assessment to the teacher and the classmate. The active voice, which is clearer and more direct, leaves no ambiguity.

13d Avoid sudden shifts from indirect to direct questions or quotations.

An indirect question reports a question without asking it: *We asked whether we could visit Miriam.* A direct question asks directly: *Can we visit Miriam?* Sudden shifts from indirect to direct questions are awkward. In addition, sentences containing such shifts are impossible to punctuate because indirect questions must end with a period and direct questions must end with a question mark. (See 38b.)

▶ I wonder whether Karla knew of the theft and, if so, ~~did~~
　　　　　　　　　　　　　 whether she reported
　~~she report~~ it to the police~~?~~.

The revision poses both questions indirectly. The writer could also ask both questions directly: *Did Karla know of the theft and, if so, did she report it to the police?*

An indirect quotation reports someone's words without quoting word for word: *Annabelle said that she is a Virgo.* A direct quotation presents the exact words of a speaker or writer, set off with quotation marks: *Annabelle said, "I am a Virgo."* Unannounced shifts from indirect to direct quotations are distracting and confusing, especially when the writer fails to insert the necessary quotation marks, as in the following example.

▶ The patient said she had been experiencing heart palpitations
　　　asked me to　　　　　　　　　　　　　　　　 was
　and ~~please~~ run as many tests as possible to find out what~~'s~~

wrong.

The revision reports the patient's words indirectly. The writer also could quote the words directly: *The patient said, "I have been experiencing heart palpitations. Please run as many tests as possible to find out what's wrong."*

EXERCISE 13–3 Edit the following sentences to make the verbs consistent in mood and voice and to eliminate distracting shifts from indirect to direct questions or quotations. Revisions of lettered sentences appear in the back of the book. Example:

> As a public relations intern, I wrote press releases, managed
> the Web site, and ~~all phone calls were fielded by me.~~ *fielded all phone calls.*

a. An incredibly talented musician, Ray Charles mastered R&B, soul, and gospel styles. Even country music was performed well by him.

b. Environmentalists point out that shrimp farming in Southeast Asia is polluting water and making farmlands useless. They warn that action must be taken by governments before it is too late.

c. The samples were observed for five days before we detected any growth.

d. In his famous soliloquy, Hamlet contemplates whether death would be preferable to his difficult life and, if so, is he capable of committing suicide?

e. The lawyer told the judge that Miranda Hale was innocent and allow her to prove the allegations false.

1. When the photographs were taken on the beach at sunset, I intentionally left the foreground out of focus.

2. If the warning sirens sound, evacuate at once. It is not advised that you return to the building until the alarm has stopped.

3. Most baby products warn parents not to leave children unattended. Also, follow all directions carefully.

4. The advertisement promised that results would be seen in five days or consumers could return the product for a full refund.

5. Investigators first need to determine whether there was a forceful entry and then what was the motive?

EXERCISE 13–4 Edit the following sentences to eliminate distracting shifts. Revisions of lettered sentences appear in the back of the book. Example:

> For many first-year engineering students, adjusting to a
> rigorous course load can be so challenging that ~~you~~ *they*
> sometimes feel overwhelmed.

a.   A courtroom lawyer has more than a touch of theater in their blood.

b.   The interviewer asked if we had brought our proof of citizenship and did we bring our passports?

c.   The reconnaissance scout often has to make fast decisions and use sophisticated equipment to keep their team from being detected.

d.   After the animators finish their scenes, the production designer arranges the clips according to the storyboard. Synchronization notes must also be made for the sound editor and the composer.

e.   Madame Defarge is a sinister figure in Dickens's *A Tale of Two Cities*. On a symbolic level, she represents fate; like the Greek Fates, she knitted the fabric of individual destiny.

1.   Everyone should protect yourself from the sun, especially on the first day of extensive exposure.

2.   Our neighbors told us that the island was being evacuated because of the coming storm. Also, take the northern route to the mainland.

3.   Rescue workers put water on her face and lifted her head gently onto a pillow. Finally, she opens her eyes.

4.   In my first tai chi class, the instructor asked if I had ever done yoga stretches and did I have good balance?

5.   The artist has often been seen as a threat to society, especially when they refuse to conform to conventional standards of taste.

hackerhandbooks.com/bedhandbook > Grammar exercises > Clear sentences
> E-ex 13–7 to 13–9

14   Emphasize key ideas.

Within each sentence, emphasize your point by expressing it in the subject and verb of an independent clause, the words that receive the most attention from readers (see 14a–14e).

Within longer stretches of prose, you can draw attention to ideas deserving special emphasis by using a variety of techniques, often involving an unusual twist or some element of surprise (see 14f).

14a Coordinate equal ideas; subordinate minor ideas.

When combining two or more ideas in one sentence, you have two choices: coordination or subordination. Choose coordination to indicate that the ideas are equal or nearly equal in importance. Choose subordination to indicate that one idea is less important than another.

> Grammar checkers do not catch the problems with coordination and subordination discussed in this section. Not surprisingly, computer programs have no way of sensing the relative importance of ideas.

Coordination

Coordination draws attention equally to two or more ideas. To coordinate single words or phrases, join them with a coordinating conjunction or with a pair of correlative conjunctions: *bananas and strawberries; not only a lackluster plot but also inferior acting* (see 61g).

To coordinate independent clauses—word groups that express a complete thought and that can stand alone as a sentence—join them with a comma and a coordinating conjunction or with a semicolon:

, and	, but	, or	, nor
, for	, so	, yet	;

The semicolon is often accompanied by a conjunctive adverb such as *moreover, furthermore, therefore,* or *however* or by a transitional phrase such as *for example, in other words,* or *as a matter of fact.* (For a longer list, see p. 179.)

Assume, for example, that your intention is to draw equal attention to the following two ideas.

> Web sites like *Facebook* and *MySpace* offer ways for people to connect in the virtual world. They do not replace traditional forms of social interaction.

To coordinate these ideas, you can join them with a comma and the coordinating conjunction *but* or with a semicolon and the conjunctive adverb *however.*

> Web sites like *Facebook* and *MySpace* offer ways for people to connect in the virtual world, but they do not replace traditional forms of social interaction.

> Web sites like *Facebook* and *MySpace* offer ways for people to connect in the virtual world; however, they do not replace traditional forms of social interaction.

It is important to choose a coordinating conjunction or conjunctive adverb appropriate to your meaning. In the preceding example, the two ideas contrast with each other, calling for *but* or *however.* (For specific coordination strategies, see the chart on p. 179.)

Subordination

To give unequal emphasis to two or more ideas, express the major idea in an independent clause and place any minor ideas in subordinate clauses or phrases. (For specific subordination strategies, see the chart on p. 180.)

Let your intended meaning determine which idea you emphasize. Consider the two ideas about social networking Web sites.

> Web sites like *Facebook* and *MySpace* offer ways for people to connect in the virtual world. They do not replace traditional forms of social interaction.

If your purpose is to stress the ways that people can connect in the virtual world rather than the limitations of these connections, subordinate the idea about the limitations.

> Although they do not replace traditional forms of social interaction, Web sites like *Facebook* and *MySpace* offer ways for people to connect in the virtual world.

Using coordination to combine sentences of equal importance

1. Consider using a comma and a coordinating conjunction. (See 32a.)

, and	, but	, or	, nor
, for	, so	, yet	

▶ In Orthodox Jewish funeral ceremonies, the shroud is
a simple linen vestment. *and the* ~~The~~ coffin is plain wood.

2. Consider using a semicolon with a conjunctive adverb or transitional phrase. (See 34b.)

also	however	next
as a result	in addition	now
besides	in fact	of course
consequently	in other words	otherwise
finally	in the first place	still
for example	meanwhile	then
for instance	moreover	therefore
furthermore	nevertheless	thus

▶ Alicia scored well on the SAT. *moreover, she* ~~She also~~ had excellent
grades and a record of community service.

3. Consider using a semicolon alone. (See 34a.)

▶ In youth we learn. *in* ~~In~~ age we understand.

To focus on the limitations of the virtual world, subordinate the idea about the Web sites.

> Although Web sites like *Facebook* and *MySpace* offer ways for people to connect in the virtual world, they do not replace traditional forms of social interaction.

Using subordination to combine sentences of unequal importance

1. Consider putting the less important idea in a subordinate clause beginning with one of the following words. (See 63e.)

after	before	that	which
although	even though	unless	while
as	if	until	who
as if	since	when	whom
because	so that	where	whose

▶ *When*
Elizabeth Cady Stanton proposed a convention to discuss the

status of women in America/, Lucretia Mott agreed.

▶ My sister owes much of her recovery to a yoga program/. ~~She~~ *that she*

began ~~the program~~ three years ago.

2. Consider putting the less important idea in an appositive phrase. (See 63c.)

▶ Karate, ~~is~~ a discipline based on the philosophy of nonviolence/,

~~It~~ teaches the art of self-defense.

3. Consider putting the less important idea in a participial phrase. (See 63b.)

▶ *Noticing*
~~I noticed~~ the EpiPen in her tote bag/, I asked her if she has

food allergies.

▶ ~~American essayist Cheryl Peck was~~ ~~e~~ncouraged by friends to
American essayist Cheryl Peck
write about her life/, ~~She~~ began combining humor and irony

in her essays about being overweight.

EXERCISE 14–1   Use the coordination or subordination technique in brackets to combine each pair of independent clauses. Revisions of lettered sentences appear in the back of the book. Example:

> Ted Williams was one of the best hitters in the history of
> ~~baseball. He~~ *baseball, but he* never won a World Series ring. [*Use a comma and a coordinating conjunction.*]

a.   Williams played for the Boston Red Sox from 1936 to 1960. He managed the Washington Senators and Texas Rangers for several years after retiring as a player. [*Use a comma and a coordinating conjunction.*]

b.   In 1941, Williams finished the season with a batting average of .406. No player has hit over .400 for a season since then. [*Use a semicolon.*]

c.   Williams acknowledged that Joe DiMaggio was a better all-around player. Williams felt that he was a better hitter than DiMaggio. [*Use the subordinating conjunction* although.]

d.   Williams was a stubborn man. He always refused to tip his cap to the crowd after a home run because he claimed that fans were fickle. [*Use a semicolon and the transitional phrase* for example].

e.   Williams's relationship with the media was unfriendly at best. He sarcastically called baseball writers the "knights of the keyboard" in his memoir. [*Use a semicolon.*]

1.   Williams took time out from his baseball career to serve in the Marines during World War II. He went on active duty a second time during the Korean War. [*Use a semicolon and the transitional phrase* in addition.]

2.   Williams was named most valuable player twice in his career. He was listed as the eighth-best baseball player of all time by the *Sporting News* in 1999. [*Use the relative pronoun* who.]

3.   Williams hit a home run in his final at bat in September 1960. Then he retired as a player. [*Use a comma and a coordinating conjunction.*]

4.   Williams surprised many people with his 1966 Hall of Fame induction speech. It called for recognition of Negro League players and their inclusion in the Hall of Fame. [*Use the relative pronoun* which.]

5. At the 1999 All-Star game, Ted Williams returned to Fenway Park in Boston to throw out the ceremonial first pitch. For the first time he waved his hat to the cheering fans. [*Use a comma and a coordinating conjunction.*]

14b Combine choppy sentences.

Short sentences demand attention, so you should use them primarily for emphasis. Too many short sentences, one after the other, make for a choppy style.

If an idea is not important enough to deserve its own sentence, try combining it with a sentence close by. Put any minor ideas in subordinate structures such as phrases or subordinate clauses. (See 63.)

▶ The Parks Department keeps the use of insecticides to a
  because the
  minimum. ~~The~~ city is concerned about the environment.

The writer wanted to emphasize that the Parks Department minimizes its use of chemicals, so she put the reason in a subordinate clause beginning with *because*.

▶ The Chesapeake and Ohio Canal, ~~is~~ a 184-mile waterway

  constructed in the 1800s. ~~It~~ was a major source of

  transportation for goods during the Civil War.

A minor idea is now expressed in an appositive phrase (*a 184-mile waterway constructed in the 1800s*).

                                          E
▶ ~~Sister Consilio was~~ ~~E~~nveloped in a black robe with only her
                          Sister Consilio
  face and hands visible. ~~She~~ was an imposing figure.

Because Sister Consilio's overall impression was more important to the writer's purpose, the writer put the description of the clothing in a participial phrase beginning with *Enveloped*.

Although subordination is ordinarily the most effective technique for combining short, choppy sentences, coordination is appropriate when the ideas are equal in importance.

▶ At 3:30 p.m., Forrest displayed a flag of truce./ ~~Forrest~~ sent
                                                    and

in a demand for unconditional surrender.

Combining two short sentences by joining their predicates (*displayed . . . sent*) is an effective coordination technique.

ESL Unlike some other languages, English does not repeat objects or adverbs in adjective clauses. The relative pronoun (*that, which, whom*) or relative adverb (*where*) in the adjective clause represents the object or adverb. See 30d.

▶ The apartment that we rented ~~it~~ needed repairs.

The pronoun *it* cannot repeat the relative pronoun *that*.

▶ The small town where my grandfather was born ~~there~~ is

now a big city.

The adverb *there* cannot repeat the relative adverb *where*.

EXERCISE 14–2 Combine the following sentences by subordinating minor ideas or by coordinating ideas of equal importance. You must decide which ideas are minor because the sentences are given out of context. Revisions of lettered sentences appear in the back of the book. Example:

Agnes, ~~was~~ another girl I worked with,/ ~~She~~ was a hyper-

active child.

a. The X-Men comic books and Japanese woodcuts of kabuki dancers were part of Marlena's research project on popular culture. They covered the tabletop and the chairs.

b. Our waitress was costumed in a kimono. She had painted her face white. She had arranged her hair in a lacquered beehive.

c. Students can apply for a spot in the leadership program. The program teaches thinking and communication skills.

d. Shore houses were flooded up to the first floor. Beaches were washed away. Brant's Lighthouse was swallowed by the sea.

e. Laura Thackray is an engineer at Volvo Car Corporation. She addressed women's safety needs. She designed a pregnant crash-test dummy.

1. I noticed that the sky was glowing orange and red. I bent down to crawl into the bunker.

2. The Market Inn is located on North Wharf. It doesn't look very impressive from the outside. The food, however, is excellent.

3. He walked up to the pitcher's mound. He dug his toe into the ground. He swung his arm around backward and forward. Then he threw the ball and struck the batter out.

4. Eryn and Maeve have decided to start a business. They have known each other since kindergarten. They will renovate homes for people with disabilities.

5. The first football card set was released by the Goudey Gum Company in 1933. The set featured only three football players. They were Red Grange, Bronko Nagurski, and Knute Rockne.

hackerhandbooks.com/bedhandbook > Grammar exercises > Clear sentences
> E-ex 14–5 and 14–6

14c Avoid ineffective or excessive coordination.

Coordinate structures are appropriate only when you intend to draw readers' attention equally to two or more ideas: *Professor Sakellarios praises loudly, and she criticizes softly.* If one idea is more important than another—or if a coordinating conjunction does not clearly signal the relationship between the ideas—you should subordinate the less important idea.

INEFFECTIVE COORDINATION	Closets were taxed as rooms, and most colonists stored their clothes in chests or clothespresses.
IMPROVED WITH SUBORDINATION	Because closets were taxed as rooms, most colonists stored their clothes in chests or clothespresses.

The revision subordinates the less important idea (*closets were taxed as rooms*) by putting it in a subordinate clause. Notice that the subordinating conjunction *Because* signals the relation between the ideas more clearly than the coordinating conjunction *and.*

Because it is so easy to string ideas together with *and,* writers often rely too heavily on coordination in their rough drafts. The cure for excessive coordination is simple: Look for opportunities to tuck minor ideas into subordinate clauses or phrases.

▶ *When shareholders*
~~Shareholders~~ exchanged investment tips at the company's

annual meeting, ~~and~~ they learned that different approaches

can yield similar results.

The minor idea has become a subordinate clause beginning with *When.*

▶ *noticing*
My uncle, ~~noticed~~ my frightened look, ~~and~~ told me that

Aunt Edna had to feel my face because she was blind.

The less important idea has become a participial phrase modifying the noun *uncle.*

▶ *After four hours,*
~~Four hours went by, and~~ a rescue truck finally arrived, but

by that time we had been evacuated in a helicopter.

Three independent clauses were excessive. The least important idea has become a prepositional phrase.

EXERCISE 14–3 The following sentences show coordinated ideas (ideas joined with a coordinating conjunction or a semicolon). Restructure the sentences by subordinating minor ideas. You must decide which ideas are minor because the sentences are given out of context. Revisions of lettered sentences appear in the back of the book. Example:

> *where they*
> **The rowers returned to shore, ~~and~~ had a party on the beach**
> *to celebrate*
> **~~and celebrated~~ the start of the season.**

a. These particles are known as "stealth liposomes," and they can hide in the body for a long time without detection.

b. Irena is a competitive gymnast and majors in biochemistry; her goal is to apply her athletic experience and her science degree to a career in sports medicine.

c. Students, textile workers, and labor unions have loudly protested sweatshop abuses, so apparel makers have been forced to examine their labor practices.

d. IRC (Internet relay chat) was developed in a European university; it was created as a way for a group of graduate students to talk about projects from their dorm rooms.

e. The cafeteria's new menu has an international flavor, and it includes everything from enchiladas and pizza to pad thai and sauerbraten.

1. Victor switched on his remote-control lawn mower, and it began to shudder and emit clouds of smoke.

2. Iguanas are dependent on ultraviolet rays from the sun, so in the winter months they must be put under ultraviolet-coated lights that can be purchased at most pet stores.

3. The Civil War Trust was founded in 1991; it spearheads a nationwide campaign to protect America's Civil War battlefields.

4. We did not expect to receive so many large orders so quickly, and we are short on inventory.

5. Mother spread her love equally among us all, but she made each of us feel special in our own way.

14d Do not subordinate major ideas.

If a sentence buries its major idea in a subordinate construction, readers may not give the idea enough attention. Make sure to express your major idea in an independent clause and to subordinate any minor ideas.

defeated Thomas E. Dewey,

▶ **Harry S. Truman, who ^ was the unexpected winner of the 1948 presidential election,. ~~defeated Thomas E. Dewey.~~**

The writer wanted to focus on Truman's unexpected victory, but the original sentence buried this information in an adjective clause. The revision puts the more important idea in an independent clause and tucks the less important idea into an adjective clause (*who defeated Thomas E. Dewey*).

As

▶ **^ I was driving home from my new job, heading down Ranchitos Road, ~~when~~ my car suddenly overheated.**

The writer wanted to emphasize that the car overheated, not the fact of driving home. The revision expresses the major idea in an independent clause and places the less important idea in an adverb clause (*As I was driving home from my new job*).

14e Do not subordinate excessively.

In attempting to avoid short, choppy sentences, writers sometimes go to the opposite extreme, putting more subordinate ideas into a sentence than its structure can bear. If a sentence collapses of its own weight, occasionally it can be restructured. More often, however, such sentences must be divided.

▶ **In *Animal Liberation,* Peter Singer argues that animals possess nervous systems and can feel pain. ~~and that~~ H~~he~~ therefore believes that "the ethical principle on which human equality rests requires us to extend equal consideration to animals" (1).**

Writing with sources
MLA-style citation

Excessive subordination makes it difficult for the reader to focus on the quoted passage. By splitting the original sentence into two separate sentences, the writer draws attention to Peter Singer's main claim, that animals should be given "equal consideration" to humans.

EXERCISE 14–4 In each of the following sentences, the idea that the writer wished to emphasize is buried in a subordinate construction. Restructure each sentence so that the independent clause expresses the major idea, as indicated in brackets, and lesser ideas are subordinated. Revisions of lettered sentences appear in the back of the book. Example:

> *Although*
> **Catherine has weathered many hardships, ~~although~~ she has**
> **rarely become discouraged. [*Emphasize that Catherine has***
> ***rarely become discouraged.*]**

a. Gina worked as an aide for the relief agency, distributing food and medical supplies. [*Emphasize distributing food and medical supplies.*]

b. Janbir spent every Saturday learning tabla drumming, noticing with each hour of practice that his memory for complex patterns was growing stronger. [*Emphasize Janbir's memory.*]

c. The rotor hit, gouging a hole about an eighth of an inch deep in my helmet. [*Emphasize that the rotor gouged a hole in the helmet.*]

d. My grandfather, who raised his daughters the old-fashioned way, was born eighty years ago in Puerto Rico. [*Emphasize how the grandfather raised his daughters.*]

e. The Narcan reversed the depressive effect of the drug, saving the patient's life. [*Emphasize that the patient's life was saved.*]

1. Fatima, who studied Persian miniature painting after college, majored in early childhood education. [*Emphasize Fatima's studies after college.*]

2. I was losing consciousness when my will to live kicked in. [*Emphasize the will to live.*]

3. Using a sliding compound miter saw, the carpenter made intricate edges on the cabinets. [*Emphasize the carpenter's use of the saw.*]

4. Ernie was using origami to solve some tricky manufacturing problems when he decided to leave engineering and become an artist. [*Emphasize Ernie's decision.*]

5. As the undulating waves glinted in the sun, the paddlers synchronized their strokes. [*Emphasize the brightness of the waves.*]

14f Experiment with techniques for gaining special emphasis.

By experimenting with certain techniques, usually involving some element of surprise, you can draw attention to ideas that deserve special emphasis. Use such techniques sparingly, however, or they will lose their punch. The writer who tries to emphasize everything ends up emphasizing nothing.

Using sentence endings for emphasis

You can highlight an idea simply by withholding it until the end of a sentence. The technique works something like a punch line. In the following example, the sentence's meaning is not revealed until its very last word.

> The only completely consistent people are the dead.
> —Aldous Huxley

Two types of sentences that withhold information until the end are the inversion and the periodic sentence. The *inversion* reverses the normal subject-verb order, placing the subject at the end, where it receives unusual emphasis. (Also see 15c.)

> In golden pots are hidden the most deadly poisons.
> —Thomas Draxe

The *periodic* sentence opens with a pile-up of modifiers and withholds the subject and verb until the end. It draws attention to itself because it contrasts with the cumulative sentence, which is used more frequently. A *cumulative* sentence begins with the subject and verb and adds modifying elements at the end.

PERIODIC

Twenty-five years ago, at the age of thirteen, while hiking in the mountains near my hometown of Vancouver, Washington, I came face-to-face with a legend.   —Tom Weitzel, student

CUMULATIVE

A metaphysician is one who goes into a dark cellar at midnight without a light, looking for a black cat that is not there.
— Baron Bowan of Colwood

Using parallel structure for emphasis

Parallel grammatical structure draws special attention to paired ideas or to items in a series. (See 9.) When parallel ideas are paired, the emphasis falls on words that underscore comparisons or contrasts, especially when they occur at the end of a phrase or clause.

> We must *stop talking* about the *American dream* and *start listening* to the *dreams of Americans*.   — Reubin Askew

In a parallel series, the emphasis falls at the end, so it is generally best to end with the most dramatic or climactic item in the series.

> Sister Charity enjoyed passing out writing punishments: translate the Ten Commandments into Latin, type a thousand-word essay on good manners, copy the New Testament with a quill pen.   — Marie Visosky, student

Using punctuation for emphasis

Obviously the exclamation point can add emphasis, but you should not overuse it. As a rule, the exclamation point is more appropriate in dialogue than in ordinary prose.

> I oozed a glob of white paint onto my palette, whipped some medium into it, loaded my brush, and announced to the class, "Move over, Michelangelo. Here I come!"
> — Carolyn Goff, student

A dash or a colon may be used to draw attention to word groups worthy of special attention. (See 35a, 35b, and 39a.)

> The middle of the road is where the white line is — and that's the worst place to drive.   — Robert Frost

I turned to see what the anemometer read: The needle had pegged out at 106 knots. —Jonathan Shilk, student

Occasionally, a pair of dashes may be used to highlight a word or an idea.

They carried the land itself—Vietnam, the place, the soil—a powdery orange-red dust that covered their boots and fatigues and faces. —Tim O'Brien

Using an occasional short sentence for emphasis

Too many short sentences in a row will fast become monotonous (see 14b), but an occasional short sentence, when played off against longer sentences in the same passage, will draw attention to an idea.

The great secret, known to internists and learned early in marriage by internists' wives [or husbands], but still hidden from the general public, is that most things get better by themselves. Most things, in fact, are better by morning. —Lewis Thomas

15 Provide some variety.

When a rough draft is filled with too many sentences that begin the same way or have the same structure, try injecting some variety—as long as you can do so without sacrificing clarity or ease of reading.

15a Vary your sentence openings.

Most sentences in English begin with the subject, move to the verb, and continue to the object, with modifiers tucked in along the way or put at the end. For the most part, such sentences are fine. Put too many of them in a row, however, and they become monotonous.

Adverbial modifiers are easily movable when they modify verbs; they can often be inserted ahead of the subject. Such modifiers might be single words, phrases, or clauses.

► *Eventually a*
  A̶ few drops of sap ~~eventually~~ began to trickle into the
  bucket.

Like most adverbs, *eventually* does not need to appear close to the verb it modifies (*began*).

► *Just as the sun was coming up, a*
  A̶ pair of black ducks flew over the pond. ~~just as the sun was~~
  ~~coming up.~~

The adverb clause, which modifies the verb *flew*, is as clear at the beginning of the sentence as it is at the end.

Adjectives and participial phrases can frequently be moved to the beginning of a sentence without loss of clarity.

► *Dejected and withdrawn,*
  Edward/~~dejected and withdrawn,~~ nearly gave up his search
  for a job.

►   *A*   *John and I*
  ~~John and I,~~ anticipating a peaceful evening, sat down at the
  campfire to brew a cup of coffee.

TIP: When beginning a sentence with an adjective or a participial phrase, make sure that the subject of the sentence names the person or thing described in the introductory phrase. If it doesn't, the phrase will dangle. (See 12e.)

15b Use a variety of sentence structures.

A writer should not rely too heavily on simple sentences and compound sentences, for the effect tends to be both monotonous and choppy. (See 14b and 14c.) Too many complex or

compound-complex sentences, however, can be equally monotonous. If your style tends to one or the other extreme, try
to achieve a better mix of sentence types.

The major sentence types are illustrated in the following
sentences, all taken from Flannery O'Connor's "The King of
the Birds," an essay describing the author's pet peafowl.

SIMPLE	Frequently the cock combines the lifting of his tail with the raising of his voice.
COMPOUND	Any chicken's dusting hole is out of place in a flower bed, but the peafowl's hole, being the size of a small crater, is more so.
COMPLEX	The peacock does most of his serious strutting in the spring and summer when he has a full tail to do it with.
COMPOUND-COMPLEX	The cock's plumage requires two years to attain its pattern, and for the rest of his life, this chicken will act as though he designed it himself.

For a fuller discussion of sentence types, see 64a.

15c Try inverting sentences occasionally.

A sentence is inverted if it does not follow the normal subject-
verb-object pattern (see 62c). Many inversions sound artificial
and should be avoided except in the most formal contexts.
But if an inversion sounds natural, it can provide a welcome
touch of variety.

> Opposite the produce section is a
> ▶ A refrigerated case of mouthwatering cheeses; is opposite
> the produce section; a friendly attendant will cut off just
> the amount you want.

The revision inverts the normal subject-verb order by moving the
verb, *is*, ahead of its subject, *case*.

▶ *Set at the top two corners of the stage were huge*
~~Huge~~ lavender hearts outlined in bright white lights. ~~were~~
   ^   ^

~~set at the top two corners of the stage~~.

In the revision, the subject, *hearts*, appears after the verb, *were set*. Notice that the two parts of the verb are also inverted—and separated from each other (*Set . . . were*)—without any awkwardness or loss of meaning.

Inverted sentences are used for emphasis as well as for variety (see 14f).

15d Consider adding an occasional question or quotation.

An occasional question can provide a change of pace, especially at the beginning of a paragraph, where it engages the reader's interest.

> Virginia Woolf, in her book A *Room of One's Own*, wrote that in order for a woman to write fiction she must have two things, certainly: a room of her own (with key and lock) and enough money to support herself.
> *What then are we to make of Phillis Wheatley, a slave, who owned not even herself*? This sickly, frail black girl who required a servant of her own at times—her health was so precarious—and who, had she been white, would have been easily considered the intellectual superior of all the women and most of the men in the society of her day. [Italics added.]
> —Alice Walker

Quotations can also provide variety, for they add other people's voices to your own. These other voices might be bits of dialogue.

> When we got back upstairs, Dr. Haney and Captain Shiller, the head nurse, were waiting for us by the elevator. As the nurse hurried off, pushing Todd, the doctor explained to us what would happen next.

"Mrs. Barrus," he began, "this last test is one we do only when absolutely necessary. It is very painful and hard on the patient, but we have no other choice." Apologetically, he went on. "I cannot give him an anesthetic." He waited for the statement to sink in.   —Celeste L. Barrus, student

Or they might be quotations from written sources.

Even when she enters the hospital on the brink of death, the anorexic will refuse help from anyone and will continue to deny needing help, especially from a doctor. At this point, reports Dr. Steven Levenkron, the anorexic is most likely "a frightened, cold, lonely, starved, and physically tortured, exhausted person—not unlike an actual concentration camp inmate" (29). In this condition she is ultimately force-fed through a tube inserted in the chest.   —Jim Drew, student

Notice that the quotation from a written source is documented with a citation in parentheses. (See 53a.)

EXERCISE 15–1   Improve sentence variety in each of the following sentences by using the technique suggested in brackets. Revisions of lettered sentences appear in the back of the book. Example:

To protect endangered marine turtles, fishing
~~Fishing~~ crews place turtle excluder devices in fishing nets.
~~to protect endangered marine turtles.~~ [*Begin the sentence*

with the adverbial infinitive phrase.]

a.   The exhibits for insects and spiders are across the hall from the fossils exhibit. [*Invert the sentence.*]

b.   Sayuri becomes a successful geisha after growing up desperately poor in Japan. [*Move the adverb clause to the beginning of the sentence.*]

c.   It is interesting to consider what caused Mount St. Helens to erupt. Researchers believe that a series of earthquakes in the area was a contributing factor. [*Change the first sentence to a question.*]

d.   Ice cream typically contains 10 percent milk fat. Premium ice cream may contain up to 16 percent milk fat and has considerably less air in the product. [*Combine the two sentences as a compound sentence.*]

e. The economy may recover more quickly than expected if home values climb. [*Move the adverb clause to the beginning of the sentence.*]

1. The Dust Bowl farmers, looking wearily into the cameras of US government photographers, represented the harshest effects of the Great Depression. [*Move the participial phrase to the beginning of the sentence.*]

2. The Trans Alaska Pipeline was completed in 1977. It has moved more than fifteen billion barrels of oil since 1977. [*Combine the two sentences into a complex sentence.*]

3. Mr. Guo habitually dresses in loose clothing and canvas shoes for his wushu workout. [*Move the adverb to the beginning of the sentence.*]

4. A number of obstacles are strategically placed throughout a firefighter training maze. [*Invert the sentence.*]

5. Ian McKellen is a British actor who made his debut in 1961 and was knighted in 1991, and he played Gandalf in the movie trilogy *The Lord of the Rings*. [*Make a simple sentence. See also 64a.*]

EXERCISE 15–2   Edit the following paragraph to increase sentence variety.

Making architectural models is a skill that requires patience and precision. It is an art that illuminates a design. Architects come up with a grand and intricate vision. Draftspersons convert that vision into blueprints. The model maker follows the blueprints. The model maker builds a miniature version of the structure. Modelers can work in traditional materials like wood and clay and paint. Modelers can work in newer materials like Styrofoam and liquid polymers. Some modelers still use cardboard, paper, and glue. Other modelers prefer glue guns, deformable plastic, and thin aluminum and brass wire. The modeler may seem to be making a small mess in the early stages of model building. In the end the modeler has completed a small-scale structure. Architect Rem Koolhaas has insisted that plans reveal the logic of a design. He has argued that models expose the architect's vision. The model maker's art makes this vision real.

Part IV
Word Choice

16 Tighten wordy sentences.

Long sentences are not necessarily wordy, nor are short sentences always concise. A sentence is wordy if it can be tightened without loss of meaning.

> Grammar checkers flag wordy constructions only occasionally. They sometimes alert you to common redundancies, such as *true fact*, but they overlook more than they catch. They may miss empty or inflated phrases, such as *in my opinion* and *in order that*, and they rarely identify sentences with needlessly complex structures. Grammar checkers are very good, however, at flagging and suggesting revisions for wordy constructions beginning with *there is* and *there are*.

16a Eliminate redundancies.

Writers often repeat themselves unnecessarily, thinking that expressions such as *cooperate together*, *yellow in color*, or *basic essentials* add emphasis to their writing. In reality, such redundancies do just the opposite. There is no need to say the same thing twice.

▶ Twentysomethings are often ~~thought of or~~ stereotyped as apathetic even though many are active in political and service groups.

▶ Daniel ~~is now employed~~ works at a private rehabilitation center ~~working~~ as a registered physical therapist.

Though modifiers ordinarily add meaning to the words they modify, occasionally they are redundant.

▶ Sylvia ~~very hurriedly~~ scribbled her name, address, and phone number on a greasy napkin.

The word *scribbled* already suggests that Sylvia wrote *very hurriedly*.

▶ Gabriele Muccino's film *The Pursuit of Happyness* tells the

story of a single father determined ~~in his mind~~ to pull

himself and his son out of homelessness.

The word *determined* contains the idea that his resolution formed
in his mind.

16b Avoid unnecessary repetition of words.

Though words may be repeated deliberately, for effect, repetitions will seem awkward if they are clearly unnecessary. When a more concise version is possible, choose it.

▶ Our fifth patient, in room six, is a mentally ill. ~~patient.~~

▶ The best teachers help each student ~~become a better~~ grow

    ~~student~~ both academically and emotionally.

▶ A study by the Henry J. Kaiser Family Foundation (2004)

    ~~studied~~ measured the effects of diet and exercise on childhood

    obesity.

Writing with sources

APA-style citation

The repetition of *study . . . studied* is awkward and redundant. By using the descriptive verb *measured* instead, the writer conveys more precisely the purpose of the study and suggests its function in her paper.

16c Cut empty or inflated phrases.

An empty phrase can be cut with little or no loss of meaning. Common examples are introductory word groups that weaken the writer's authority by apologizing or hedging: *in my opinion, I think that, it seems that, one must admit that,* and so on.

▶ ~~In my opinion,~~ Our current immigration policy is misguided.

Readers understand without being told that they are hearing the writer's opinion.

Inflated phrases can be reduced to a word or two without loss of meaning.

INFLATED	CONCISE
along the lines of	like
as a matter of fact	in fact
at all times	always
at the present time	now, currently
at this point in time	now, currently
because of the fact that	because
by means of	by
by virtue of the fact that	because
due to the fact that	because
for the purpose of	for
for the reason that	because
have the ability to	be able to, can
in light of the fact that	because
in order to	to
in spite of the fact that	although, though
in the event that	if
in the final analysis	finally
in the nature of	like
in the neighborhood of	about
until such time as	until

▶ ~~At this point in time~~ M̂y skills and experience are a perfect

match for the position of assistant manager.

16d Simplify the structure.

If the structure of a sentence is needlessly indirect, try simplifying it. Look for opportunities to strengthen the verb.

▶ The financial analyst claimed that because of volatile market

conditions she could not ~~make an~~ estimate ~~of~~ the company's

future profits.

The verb *estimate* is more vigorous and concise than *make an estimate of*.

The colorless verbs *is*, *are*, *was*, and *were* frequently generate excess words.

▶ Investigators ~~were involved in~~ studying the effect of classical

music on unborn babies.

> The revision is more direct and concise. The action (*studying*), originally appearing in a subordinate structure, has become a strong verb, *studied*.

The expletive constructions *there is* and *there are* (or *there was* and *there were*) can also generate excess words. The same is true of expletive constructions beginning with *it*. (See 62c.)

▶ ~~There is~~ Another module ~~that~~ tells the story of Charles

Darwin and introduces the theory of evolution.

▶ ~~It is imperative that~~ All night managers must follow strict

procedures when locking the safe.

Finally, verbs in the passive voice may be needlessly indirect. When the active voice expresses your meaning as effectively, use it. (See 8a.)

▶ All too often, athletes with marginal academic skills our coaches have recruited ~~. have~~

~~been recruited by our coaches.~~

16e Reduce clauses to phrases, phrases to single words.

Word groups functioning as modifiers can often be made more compact. Look for any opportunities to reduce clauses to phrases or phrases to single words.

▶ We took a side trip to Monticello, ~~which was~~ the home of

Thomas Jefferson.

▶ In ~~the~~ essay*this*, ~~that follows,~~ I argue against Immanuel

Kant's claim *problematic* that we should not lie under any

circumstances, ~~which is a problematic claim.~~

EXERCISE 16–1   Edit the following sentences to reduce wordiness. Revisions of lettered sentences appear in the back of the book. Example:

The Wilsons moved into the house ~~in spite of the fact that~~ *even though*

the back door was only ten yards from the train tracks.

a.   Martin Luther King Jr. was a man who set a high standard for future leaders to meet.

b.   Alice has been deeply in love with cooking since she was little and could first peek over the edge of a big kitchen tabletop.

c.   In my opinion, Bloom's race for the governorship is a futile exercise.

d.   It is pretty important in being a successful graphic designer to have technical knowledge and at the same time an eye for color and balance.

e.   Your task will be the delivery of correspondence to all employees in the company.

1.   Seeing the barrels, the driver immediately slammed on his brakes.

2.   A really well-stocked bookshelf should have classical literature on it as well as important modern works of the current day.

3.   China's enormously huge workforce has an effect on the global world of high-tech manufacturing of things.

4.   A typical autocross course consists of at least two straightaways, and the rest of the course is made up of numerous slaloms and several sharp turns.

5.   At breakfast time, Mehrdad always started his day with cantaloupe, lemon yogurt, and black coffee.

EXERCISE 16–2   Edit the following business memo to reduce wordiness.

To: District managers
From: Margaret Davenport, Vice President
Subject: Customer database

It has recently been brought to my attention that a percentage of our sales representatives have been failing to log reports of their client calls in our customer database each and every day. I have also learned that some representatives are not checking the database on a routine basis.

Our clients sometimes receive a multiple number of sales calls from us when a sales representative is not cognizant of the fact that the client has been contacted at a previous time. Repeated telephone calls from our representatives annoy our customers. These repeated telephone calls also portray our company as one that is lacking in organization.

Effective as of immediately, direct your representatives to do the following:

- Record each and every customer contact in the customer database at the end of each day, without fail.
- Check the database at the very beginning of each day to ensure that telephone communications will not be initiated with clients who have already been called.

Let me extend my appreciation to you for cooperating in this important matter.

hackerhandbooks.com/bedhandbook > Grammar exercises > Word choice
> E-ex 16–3 to 16–6

17   Choose appropriate language.

Language is appropriate when it suits your subject, engages your audience, and blends naturally with your own voice.

To some extent, your choice of language will be governed by the conventions of the genre in which you are writing. When in doubt about the conventions of a particular genre—lab reports, informal essays, business memos, and so on—consult your instructor or look at models written by experts in the field.

17a Stay away from jargon.

Jargon is specialized language used among members of a trade, profession, or group. Use jargon only when readers will be familiar with it; even then, use it only when plain English will not do as well.

Sentences filled with jargon are likely to be long and lumpy. To revise such sentences, you must rewrite them, usually in fewer words.

JARGON   For years, the indigenous body politic of South Africa attempted to negotiate legal enfranchisement without result.

REVISED   For years, the indigenous people of South Africa negotiated unsuccessfully for the right to vote.

Though a political scientist might feel comfortable with the original version, jargon such as *body politic* and *legal enfranchisement* is needlessly complicated for most readers.

Broadly defined, jargon includes puffed-up language designed more to impress readers than to inform them. The following are common examples from business, government, higher education, and the military, with plain English alternatives in parentheses.

ameliorate (improve)   indicator (sign)
commence (begin)   optimal (best, most favorable)
components (parts)   parameters (boundaries, limits)
endeavor (try)   peruse (read, look over)
exit (leave)   prior to (before)
facilitate (help)   utilize (use)
impact (v.) (affect)   viable (workable)

Sentences filled with jargon are hard to read, and they are often wordy as well.

▶ All ~~employees functioning in the capacity of~~ work-study
       must prove that they are currently enrolled.
  students ~~are required to give evidence of current enrollment.~~
  ^

> The CEO should ~~dialogue~~ ^{talk} with investors about ~~partnering~~ ^{working}
> with clients to ~~purchase~~ ^{buy} land in ~~economically deprived zones.~~ ^{poor neighborhoods.}

17b Avoid pretentious language, most euphemisms, and "doublespeak."

Hoping to sound profound or poetic, some writers embroider their thoughts with large words and flowery phrases, language that in fact sounds pretentious. Pretentious language is so ornate and often so wordy that it obscures the thought that lies beneath.

> Taylor's ~~employment of multihued means of expression draws~~ ^{use of colorful language reveals that she has a}
> ~~back the curtains and lets slip the~~ nostalgic ~~vantage point~~ ^{view of}
> ~~from which she observes~~ American society ~~as well as her lack~~ ^{and does not}
> ~~of comprehension of~~ ^{understand} economic realities.

The writer of the original sentence had turned to a thesaurus (a dictionary of synonyms and antonyms) in an attempt to sound authoritative. When such a writer gains enough confidence to speak in his or her own voice, pretentious language disappears.

Related to pretentious language are euphemisms, nice-sounding words or phrases substituted for words thought to sound harsh or ugly. Like pretentious language, euphemisms are wordy and indirect. Unlike pretentious language, they are sometimes appropriate. It is our social custom, for example, to use euphemisms when speaking or writing about excretion (*I have to go to the bathroom*), sexual intercourse (*They did not sleep together until they were married*), and the like. We may also use euphemisms out of concern for someone's feelings. Telling parents, for example, that their daughter is "unmotivated" is more sensitive than saying she's lazy. Tact or politeness, then, can justify an occasional euphemism.

Most euphemisms, however, are needlessly evasive or even deceitful. Like pretentious language, they obscure the intended meaning.

EUPHEMISM	PLAIN ENGLISH
adult entertainment	pornography
preowned automobile	used car
economically deprived	poor
negative savings	debts
strategic withdrawal	retreat or defeat
revenue enhancers	taxes
chemical dependency	drug addiction
downsize	lay off, fire
correctional facility	prison

The term *doublespeak* applies to any deliberately evasive or deceptive language, including euphemisms. Doublespeak is especially common in politics and business. A military retreat is described as "tactical redeployment," "enhanced interrogation" is a euphemism for "torture," and "downsizing" really means "firing employees."

> **Grammar checkers** rarely identify jargon and only occasionally flag pretentious language, so you should be alert to your own use of jargon and pretentious language and simplify it whenever possible.

EXERCISE 17–1 Edit the following sentences to eliminate jargon, pretentious or flowery language, euphemisms, and doublespeak. You may need to make substantial changes in some sentences. Revisions of lettered sentences appear in the back of the book. Example:

After two weeks in the legal department, Sue has ~~worked~~ mastered

~~into~~ the routine, ~~of the office,~~ and her ~~functional and self-management skills have~~ office performance has exceeded all expectations.

a. In my youth, my family was under the constraints of difficult financial circumstances.

b. In order that I may increase my expertise in the area of delivery of services to clients, I feel that participation in this conference will be beneficial.

c. The prophetic meteorologist cautioned the general populace regarding the possible deleterious effects of the impending tempest.

d. Governmentally sanctioned investigations into the continued value of after-school programs indicate a perceived need in the public realm at large.

e. Passengers should endeavor to finalize the customs declaration form prior to exiting the aircraft.

1. We learned that the mayor had been engaging in a creative transfer of city employees' pension funds.

2. After a cursory examination of brand-new research findings on textiles, Patricia and the members of her team made the decision to engage in a series of visits to fashion manufacturers in the local vicinity.

3. The nurse announced that there had been a negative patient-care outcome due to a therapeutic misadventure on the part of the surgeon.

4. A generally leisurely pace at the onset of tai chi exercises can yield a variety of beneficial points within a short period of time.

5. The bottom line is that the company is experiencing a negative cash flow.

EXERCISE 17–2 Edit the following e-mail message to eliminate jargon.

Dear Ms. Jackson:

We members of the Nakamura Reyes team value our external partnering arrangements with Creative Software, and I look forward to seeing you next week at the trade show in Fresno. Per Mr. Reyes, please let me know when you'll have some downtime there so that he and I can conduct a strategizing session with you concerning our production schedule. It's crucial that we all be on the same page re our 2009–2010 product release dates.

Before we have some face time, however, I have some findings to share. Our customer-centric approach to the new products will necessitate that user testing periods trend upward. The enclosed data should help you effectuate any adjustments to your timeline; let me know ASAP if you require any additional information to facilitate the above.

Before we convene in Fresno, Mr. Reyes and I will agendize any further talking points. Thanks for your help.

Sincerely,

Sylvia Nakamura

hackerhandbooks.com/bedhandbook > Grammar exercises > Word choice
> E-ex 17–6

17c Avoid obsolete and invented words.

Although dictionaries list obsolete words such as *recomfort* and *reechy*, these words are not appropriate for current use. Invented words (called *neologisms*) are too recently created to be part of standard English. Many invented words fade out of use without becoming standard. *Bling* and *blogosphere* are neologisms that may not last. *Prequel* and *e-mail* are no longer neologisms; they have become standard English. Avoid using invented words in formal writing unless they are given in the dictionary as standard or unless no other word expresses your meaning.

17d In most contexts, avoid slang, regional expressions, and nonstandard English.

Slang is an informal and sometimes private vocabulary that expresses the solidarity of a group such as teenagers, rock musicians, or football fans; it is subject to more rapid change than standard English. For example, the slang teenagers use to express approval changes every few years; *cool, groovy, neat, awesome, phat,* and *sick* have replaced one another within the last three decades. Sometimes slang becomes so widespread that it is accepted as standard vocabulary. *Jazz,* for example, started out as slang but is now a standard term for a style of music.

Although slang has a certain vitality, it is a code that not everyone understands, and it is very informal. Therefore, it is inappropriate in most written work.

▶ When the server crashed unexpectedly, ~~three hours of~~ *we lost*

unsaved data. ~~went down the tubes.~~

▶ The government's "filth" guidelines for food will ~~gross you~~ *disgust you.*

~~out.~~

Regional expressions are common to a group in a geographic area. *Let's talk with the bark off* (for *Let's speak frankly*) is an expression in the southern United States, for example. Regional expressions have the same limitations as slang and are therefore inappropriate in most writing.

▶ John was four blocks from the house before he remembered
turn on
to ~~cut~~ the headlights. ~~on.~~

▶ Seamus wasn't ~~for~~ sure, but he thought the whales might

be migrating during his visit to Oregon.

Standard English is the language used in all academic, business, and professional fields. Nonstandard English is spoken by people with a common regional or social heritage. Although nonstandard English may be appropriate when spoken within a close group, it is out of place in most formal and informal writing.

doesn't
▶ The governor said he ~~don't~~ know if he will approve the

budget without the clean air provision.

If you speak a nonstandard dialect, try to identify the ways in which your dialect differs from standard English. Look especially for the following features of nonstandard English, which commonly cause problems in writing.

Misusing verb forms such as *began* and *begun* (See 27a.)

Leaving *-s* endings off verbs (See 27c.)

Leaving *-ed* endings off verbs (See 27d.)

Leaving out necessary verbs (See 27e.)

Using double negatives (See 26d.)

17e Choose an appropriate level of formality.

In deciding on a level of formality, consider both your subject and your audience. Does the subject demand a dignified treatment, or is a relaxed tone more suitable? Will readers be put off if you assume too close a relationship with them, or might you alienate them by seeming too distant?

For most college and professional writing, some degree of formality is appropriate. In a job application letter, for example, it is a mistake to sound too breezy and informal.

TOO INFORMAL I'd like to get that sales job you've got in the paper.

MORE FORMAL I would like to apply for the position of sales associate advertised in the *Peoria Journal Star*.

Informal writing is appropriate for private letters, personal e-mail and text messages, and business correspondence between close associates. Like spoken conversation, informal writing allows contractions (*don't, I'll*) and colloquial words (*kids, kinda*). Vocabulary and sentence structure are rarely complex.

In choosing a level of formality, above all be consistent. When a writer's voice shifts from one level of formality to another, readers receive mixed messages.

▶ Once a pitcher for the Blue Jays, Jorge shared with me the secrets of his trade. His lesson ~~commenced~~ *began* with his famous curveball, ~~implemented~~ *thrown* by tucking the little finger behind the ball. Next he ~~elucidated~~ *revealed* the mysteries of the sucker pitch, a slow ball coming behind a fast windup.

Words such as *commenced* and *elucidated* are inappropriate for the subject matter, and they clash with informal terms such as *sucker pitch* and *fast windup*.

> **Grammar checkers** rarely flag slang and informal language. They do, however, flag contractions. If your ear tells you that a contraction such as *isn't* or *doesn't* strikes the right tone, stay with it.

EXERCISE 17–3 Revise the following passage so that the level of formality is appropriate for a letter to the editor of a major newspaper.

> In pop culture, college grads who return home to live with the folks are seen as good-for-nothing losers who mooch off their families. And many older adults seem to feel that the trend of moving back home after school, which was rare in their day, is becoming too commonplace today. But society must realize that times have changed. Most young adults want to live on their own ASAP, but they graduate with heaps of debt and need some time to get back on their feet. College tuition and the cost of housing have increased way more than salary increases in the past fifty years. Also, the job market is tighter and more jobs require advanced degrees than in the past. So before people go off on college graduates who move back into their parents' house for a spell, they'd better consider all the facts.

17f Avoid sexist language.

Sexist language is language that stereotypes or demeans women or men. Using nonsexist language is a matter of courtesy—of respect for and sensitivity to the feelings of others.

Recognizing sexist language

Some sexist language is easy to recognize because it reflects genuine contempt for women: referring to a woman as a "chick," for example, or calling a lawyer a "lady lawyer."

Other forms of sexist language are less blatant. The following practices, while they may not result from conscious sexism, reflect stereotypical thinking: referring to members of one profession as exclusively male or exclusively female (teachers as women or computer engineers as men, for instance), using different conventions when naming or identifying women and men, or assuming that all of one's readers are men.

STEREOTYPICAL LANGUAGE

After a nursing student graduates, *she* must face a difficult state board examination. [Not all nursing students are women.]

Running for city council are Boris Stotsky, an attorney, and *Mrs.* Cynthia Jones, a professor of English and *mother of three*. [The title *Mrs.* and the phrase *mother of three* are irrelevant.]

All executives' *wives* are invited to the welcome dinner. [Not all executives are men.]

Still other forms of sexist language result from outdated traditions. The pronouns *he*, *him*, and *his*, for instance, were traditionally used to refer generically to persons of either sex. Nowadays, to avoid that sexist usage, some writers use *she*, *her*, and *hers* generically or substitute the female pronouns alternately with the male pronouns.

GENERIC PRONOUNS

A journalist is stimulated by *his* deadline.

A good interior designer treats *her* clients' ideas respectfully.

But both forms are sexist—for excluding one sex entirely and for making assumptions about the members of particular professions.

Similarly, the nouns *man* and *men* were once used to refer generically to persons of either sex. Current usage demands gender-neutral terms for references to both men and women.

INAPPROPRIATE	APPROPRIATE
chairman	chairperson, moderator, chair, head
clergyman	member of the clergy, minister, pastor
congressman	member of Congress, representative, legislator
fireman	firefighter
foreman	supervisor
mailman	mail carrier, postal worker, letter carrier
to man	to operate, to staff
mankind	people, humans
manpower	personnel, staff
policeman	police officer
salesman	salesperson, sales associate, salesclerk
weatherman	forecaster, meteorologist
workman	worker, laborer

> **Grammar checkers** are good at flagging obviously sexist terms, such as *mankind* and *fireman*, but they do not flag language that might be demeaning (*woman doctor*) or stereotypical. They also have no way of identifying the generic use of *he* or *she*. You must use your common sense to tell when a word or a construction is offensive.

Revising sexist language

When revising sexist language, you may be tempted to substitute *he or she* and *his or her*. These terms are inclusive but wordy; fine in small doses, they can become awkward when repeated throughout an essay. A better revision strategy is to write in the plural; yet another strategy is to recast the sentence so that the problem does not arise (see p. 214).

SEXIST

A journalist is stimulated by *his* deadline.

A good interior designer treats *her* clients' ideas respectfully.

ACCEPTABLE BUT WORDY

A journalist is stimulated by *his or her* deadline.

A good interior designer treats *his or her* clients' ideas respectfully.

BETTER: USING THE PLURAL

Journalists are stimulated by *their* deadlines.

Good interior designers treat *their* clients' ideas respectfully.

BETTER: RECASTING THE SENTENCE

A journalist is stimulated by *a* deadline.

A good interior designer treats clients' ideas respectfully.

For more examples of these revision strategies, see 22.

EXERCISE 17–4 Edit the following sentences to eliminate sexist language or sexist assumptions. Revisions of lettered sentences appear in the back of the book. Example:

> Scholarship athletes
> A scholarship athlete must be as concerned about his
>   they are   their
> academic performance as he is about his athletic
>
> performance.

a. Mrs. Geralyn Farmer, who is the mayor's wife, is the chief surgeon at University Hospital. Dr. Paul Green is her assistant.
b. Every applicant wants to know how much he will earn.
c. An elementary school teacher should understand the concept of nurturing if she intends to be effective.
d. An obstetrician needs to be available to his patients at all hours.
e. If man does not stop polluting his environment, mankind will perish.

1. A fireman must always be on call even when he is off duty.
2. The chairman for the new program in digital art is Ariana Tamlin, an accomplished portrait painter, computer programmer, and cookie baker.
3. In the governor's race, Lena Weiss, a defense lawyer and mother of two, easily defeated Harvey Tower, an architect.
4. Recent military history has shown that lady combat helicopter pilots are as skilled, reliable, and resourceful as men.
5. An emergency room head nurse must know how to use sophisticated digital equipment if she is to keep track of all her patients' data and guide her medical team.

EXERCISE 17–5 Eliminate sexist language or sexist assumptions in the following job posting for an elementary school teacher.

We are looking for qualified women for the position of elementary school teacher. The ideal candidate should have a bachelor's degree, a state teaching certificate, and one year of student teaching. She should be knowledgeable in all elementary subject areas, including science and math. While we want our new teacher to have a commanding presence in the classroom, we are also looking for motherly characteristics such as patience and trustworthiness. She must be able to both motivate an entire classroom and work with each student one-on-one to assess his individual needs. She must also be comfortable communicating with the parents of her students. For salary and benefits information, including maternity leave policy, please contact the Martin County School Board. Any qualified applicant should submit her résumé by March 15.

hackerhandbooks.com/bedhandbook > Grammar exercises > Word choice
> E-ex 17–7 and 17–8

17g Revise language that may offend groups of people.

Obviously it is impolite to use offensive terms such as *Polack* and *redneck*, but biased language can take more subtle forms. Because language evolves over time, names once thought acceptable may become offensive. When describing groups of people, choose names that the groups currently use to describe themselves.

▶ **North Dakota takes its name from the** ~~Indian~~ *Lakota* **word meaning "friend" or "ally."**

▶ **Many** ~~Oriental~~ *Asian* **immigrants have recently settled in our town.**

Negative stereotypes (such as "drives like a teenager" or "sour as a spinster") are of course offensive. But you should avoid stereotyping a person or a group even if you believe your generalization to be positive.

▶ It was no surprise that Greer, ~~a Chinese American,~~ was

an excellent math and science student,

selected for the honors chemistry program.

18   Find the exact words.

Two reference works (or their online equivalents) will help you find words to express your meaning exactly: a good dictionary, such as *The American Heritage Dictionary* or *Merriam-Webster's Collegiate Dictionary*, and a collection of synonyms and antonyms, such as *Roget's International Thesaurus*.

TIP: Do not turn to a thesaurus in search of flowery or impressive words. Look instead for words that exactly express your meaning.

Grammar checkers flag some nonstandard idioms but few clichés. They do not identify commonly confused words, such as *principal* and *principle*, or misused word forms, such as *significance* and *significant*. You must be alert for such words and use your dictionary if you are unsure of the correct form. Grammar checkers are of little help with the other problems discussed in 18.

18a Select words with appropriate connotations.

In addition to their strict dictionary meanings (or *denotations*), words have *connotations*, emotional colorings that affect how readers respond to them. The word *steel* denotes "commercial iron that contains carbon," but it also calls up a cluster of images associated with steel. These associations give the word its connotations—cold, hard, smooth, unbending.

   If the connotation of a word does not seem appropriate for your purpose, your audience, or your subject matter, you should change the word. When a more appropriate synonym does not come quickly to mind, consult a dictionary or a thesaurus.

▶ When American soldiers returned home after World War II,

        left

  many women ~~abandoned~~ their jobs in favor of marriage.

           ^

The word *abandoned* is too negative for the context.

                             sweat

▶ As I covered the boats with marsh grass, the ~~perspiration~~ I

                                  ^

  had worked up evaporated in the wind, and the cold

  morning air seemed even colder.

The term *perspiration* is too dainty for the context, which suggests vigorous exercise.

EXERCISE 18–1   Use a dictionary and a thesaurus to find at least four synonyms for each of the following words. Be prepared to explain any slight differences in meaning.

1. decay (verb)   3. hurry (verb)   5. secret (adjective)
2. difficult (adjective) 4. pleasure (noun)   6. talent (noun)

18b Prefer specific, concrete nouns.

Unlike general nouns, which refer to broad classes of things, specific nouns point to particular items. *Film*, for example, names a general class, *fantasy film* names a narrower class, and *The Golden Compass* is more specific still. Other examples: *team, football team, Denver Broncos*; *music, symphony, Beethoven's Ninth*.

Unlike abstract nouns, which refer to qualities and ideas (*justice, beauty, realism, dignity*), concrete nouns point to immediate, often sensory experience and to physical objects (*steeple, asphalt, lilac, stone, garlic*).

Specific, concrete nouns express meaning more vividly than general or abstract ones. Although general and abstract language is sometimes necessary to convey your meaning, use specific, concrete words whenever possible.

▶ **The senator spoke about the challenges of the future:**
pollution, dwindling resources, and terrorism.
~~the environment and world peace.~~
‸

Nouns such as *thing*, *area*, *aspect*, *factor*, and *individual* are especially dull and imprecise.

motherhood, and memory.
▶ **Toni Morrison's *Beloved* is about slavery,** ~~among other things.~~
‸

experienced technician.
▶ **Try pairing a trainee with an** ~~individual with technical~~
‸

~~experience.~~

18c Do not misuse words.

If a word is not in your active vocabulary, you may find your-self misusing it, sometimes with embarrassing consequences. When in doubt, check the dictionary.

climbing
▶ **The fans were** ~~migrating~~ **up the bleachers in search of seats.**
‸

permeated
▶ **The Internet has so** ~~diffused~~ **our culture that it touches all**
‸

segments of society.

Writing with sources

MLA-style citation

argues
▶ **Marie Winn** ~~quarrels~~ **that television viewing is bad for**
‸

families because it "serves to anesthetize parents into

accepting their family's diminished state" (357).

When you are introducing a quotation with a signal phrase, be sure to choose a verb that clearly reflects the source's intention. *Quarrel* suggests a heated or angry dispute; *argue* is a more neutral word. (Also see 52b on using signal phrases.)

Be especially alert for misused word forms—using a noun such as *absence*, *significance*, or *persistence*, for example, when your meaning requires the adjective *absent*, *significant*, or *persistent*.

▶ Most dieters are not ~~persistence~~ *persistent* enough to make a permanent

change in their eating habits.

EXERCISE 18–2 Edit the following sentences to correct misused words. Revisions of lettered sentences appear in the back of the book. Example:

These days the training required for a ballet dancer

is ~~all-absorbent.~~ *all-absorbing.*

a. We regret this delay; thank you for your patients.
b. Ada's plan is to require education and experience to prepare herself for a position as property manager.
c. Tiger Woods, the penultimate competitor, has earned millions of dollars just in endorsements.
d. Many people take for granite that public libraries have up-to-date computer systems.
e. The affect of Gao Xinjian's novels on Chinese exiles is hard to gauge.

1. Because Anne Tyler often writes about family loyalties, her illusions to *King Lear* are not surprising.
2. Designers of handheld devices understand that changes in ambience temperatures can damage the tiny circuit boards.
3. The Keweenaw Peninsula is surrounded on three sides by Lake Superior.
4. At the cooking school in Tuscany, I learned that rosemary is a perfect compliment to lamb.
5. The person who complained to the human resources manager wishes to remain unanimous.

hackerhandbooks.com/bedhandbook > Grammar exercises > Word choice > E-ex 18–5

18d Use standard idioms.

Idioms are speech forms that follow no easily specified rules. The English say "Bernice went *to hospital*," an idiom strange to American ears, which are accustomed to hearing *the* in front of *hospital*. Native speakers of a language seldom have problems with idioms, but prepositions (such as *with*, *to*, *at*, and *of*) sometimes cause trouble, especially when they follow certain verbs and adjectives. When in doubt, consult a dictionary.

UNIDIOMATIC	IDIOMATIC
abide with (a decision)	abide by (a decision)
according with	according to
agree to (an idea)	agree with (an idea)
angry at (a person)	angry with (a person)
capable to	capable of
comply to	comply with
desirous to	desirous of
different than (a person or thing)	different from (a person or thing)
intend on doing	intend to do
off of	off
plan on doing	plan to do
preferable than	preferable to
prior than	prior to
superior than	superior to
sure and	sure to
try and	try to
type of a	type of

ESL Because idioms follow no particular rules, you must learn them individually. You may find it helpful to keep a list of idioms that you frequently encounter in conversation and in reading.

EXERCISE 18–3 Edit the following sentences to eliminate errors in the use of idiomatic expressions. If a sentence is correct, write "correct" after it. Answers to lettered sentences appear in the back of the book. Example:

> We agreed to abide ~~with~~ by the decision of the judge.

a.   Queen Anne was so angry at Sarah Churchill that she refused to see her again.

b. Jean-Pierre's ambitious travel plans made it impossible for him to comply with the residency requirement for in-state tuition.
c. The parade moved off of the street and onto the beach.
d. The frightened refugees intend on making the dangerous trek across the mountains.
e. What type of a wedding are you planning?

1. Be sure and report on the danger of releasing genetically engineered bacteria into the atmosphere.
2. Why do you assume that embezzling bank assets is so different than robbing the bank?
3. The wilderness guide seemed capable to show us where the trail of petroglyphs was located.
4. In Evan's cautious mind, packing his own parachute seemed preferable to letting an indifferent teenager fold all that silk and cord into a small pack.
5. Andrea plans on joining the Peace Corps after graduation.

hackerhandbooks.com/bedhandbook > Grammar exercises > Word choice > E-ex 18–6

18e Do not rely heavily on clichés.

The pioneer who first announced that he had "slept like a log" no doubt amused his companions with a fresh and unlikely comparison. Today, however, that comparison is a cliché, a saying that has lost its dazzle from overuse. No longer can it surprise.

To see just how dully predictable clichés are, put your hand over the right-hand column in the following list and then finish the phrases on the left.

cool as a	cucumber
beat around	the bush
blind as a	bat
busy as a	bee, beaver
crystal	clear
dead as a	doornail
out of the frying pan and	into the fire
light as a	feather
like a bull	in a china shop

playing with	fire
nutty as a	fruitcake
selling like	hotcakes
starting out at the bottom	of the ladder
water under the	bridge
white as a	sheet, ghost
avoid clichés like the	plague

The solution for clichés is simple: Just delete them or rewrite them.

> **When I received a full scholarship from my second-choice**
>   felt squeezed to settle for second best.
>   **school, I** ~~found myself between a rock and a hard place.~~
>   ^

Sometimes you can write around a cliché by adding an element of surprise. One student, for example, who had written that she had butterflies in her stomach, revised her cliché like this:

> If all of the action in my stomach is caused by butterflies, there must be a horde of them, with horseshoes on.

The image of butterflies wearing horseshoes is fresh and unlikely, not predictable like the original cliché.

18f Use figures of speech with care.

A figure of speech is an expression that uses words imaginatively (rather than literally) to make abstract ideas concrete. Most often, figures of speech compare two seemingly unlike things to reveal surprising similarities.

In a *simile*, the writer makes the comparison explicitly, usually by introducing it with *like* or *as*: *By the time cotton had to be picked, Grandfather's neck was as red as the clay he plowed.* In a *metaphor*, the *like* or *as* is omitted, and the comparison is implied. For example, in the Old Testament Song of Solomon, a young woman compares the man she loves to a fruit tree: *With great delight I sat in his shadow, and his fruit was sweet to my taste.*

Although figures of speech are useful devices, writers sometimes use them without thinking through the images they evoke. The result is sometimes a *mixed metaphor*, the combination of two or more images that don't make sense together.

▶ Crossing Utah's salt flats in his new convertible, my father flew *at jet speed.*
~~under a full head of steam.~~
   ⌃

Flew suggests an airplane, whereas *under a full head of steam* suggests a steamboat or a train. To clarify the image, the writer should stick with one comparison or the other.

▶ Our business manager decided to put all controversial

issues ~~in a holding pattern~~ on a back burner until after the

annual meeting.

Here the writer is mixing airplanes and stoves. Simply deleting one of the images corrects the problem.

EXERCISE 18–4 Edit the following sentences to replace worn-out expressions and clarify mixed figures of speech. Revisions of lettered sentences appear in the back of the book. Example:

                         the color drained from his face.
When he heard about the accident, ~~he turned white as a~~
                           ⌃

~~sheet.~~

a. John stormed into the room like a bull in a china shop.
b. Some people insist that they'll always be there for you, even when they haven't been before.
c. The Cubs easily beat the Mets, who were in the soup early in the game today at Wrigley Field.
d. We ironed out the sticky spots in our relationship.
e. My mother accused me of beating around the bush when in fact I was just talking off the top of my head.

1. Priscilla was used to burning the candle at both ends to get her assignments done.

2. No matter how many books he reads, André can never seem to quench his thirst for knowledge.
3. In an era of cutbacks and outsourcing, the best tech-savvy workers discover that being a jack of all trades is a solid gold key to continued success.
4. Too many cooks are spoiling the broth at corporate headquarters.
5. Juanita told Kyle that keeping skeletons in the closet would be playing with fire.

hackerhandbooks.com/bedhandbook > Grammar exercises > Word choice > E-ex 18–7

Part V
Grammatical Sentences

225

19 Repair sentence fragments.

A sentence fragment is a word group that pretends to be a sentence. Sentence fragments are easy to recognize when they appear out of context, like these:

> When the cat leaped onto the table.
>
> Running for the bus.
>
> And immediately popped their flares and life vests.

When fragments appear next to related sentences, however, they are harder to spot.

> We had just sat down to dinner. When the cat leaped onto the table.
>
> I tripped and twisted my ankle. Running for the bus.
>
> The pilots ejected from the burning plane, landing in the water not far from the ship. And immediately popped their flares and life vests.

Recognizing sentence fragments

To be a sentence, a word group must consist of at least one full independent clause. An independent clause includes a subject and a verb, and it either stands alone or could stand alone.

To test whether a word group is a complete sentence or a fragment, use the flowchart on page 227. By using the flowchart, you can see exactly why *When the cat leaped onto the table* is a fragment: It has a subject (*cat*) and a verb (*leaped*), but it begins with a subordinating word (*When*). *Running for the bus* is a fragment because it lacks a subject and a verb (*Running* is a verbal, not a verb). *And immediately popped their flares and life vests* is a fragment because it lacks a subject. (See also 63b and 63e.)

Test for fragments

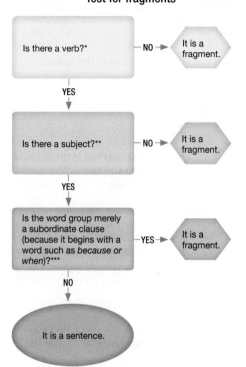

Is there a verb?* —NO→ It is a fragment.

↓ YES

Is there a subject?** —NO→ It is a fragment.

↓ YES

Is the word group merely a subordinate clause (because it begins with a word such as *because or when*)?*** —YES→ It is a fragment.

↓ NO

It is a sentence.

* Do not mistake verbals for verbs. A verbal is a verb form (such as *walking, to act*) that does not function as a verb of a clause. (See 63b.)

** The subject of a sentence may be *you*, understood but not present in the sentence. (See 62a.)

*** A sentence may open with a subordinate clause, but the sentence must also include an independent clause. (See 19a and 64a.)

If you find any fragments, try one of these methods of revision (see 19a–19c):

1. Attach the fragment to a nearby sentence.

2. Rewrite the fragment as a complete sentence.

> **ESL** Unlike some other languages, English requires a subject and
> a verb in every sentence (except in commands, where the subject *you*
> is understood but not present: *Sit down*). See 30a and 30b.
>
> It is
> ▶ ~~Is~~ often hot and humid during the summer.
>
> are
> ▶ Students usually very busy at the end of the semester.

> Grammar checkers can flag as many as half of the sentence frag-
> ments in a sample; but that means, of course, that they miss half
> or more of them. If you have trouble with fragments, you will still
> need to proofread for them.
>
> Sometimes the grammar checker will identify "false posi-
> tives," sentences that it flags but that are not fragments. When
> a program spots a possible fragment, you should check to see if
> the word group is really a fragment by using the flowchart on
> page 227.

Repairing sentence fragments

You can repair most fragments in one of two ways: Either pull
the fragment into a nearby sentence or rewrite the fragment as
a complete sentence.

when
▶ We had just sat down to dinner./ ~~When~~ the cat leaped onto
the table.

Running for the bus,
▶ I tripped and twisted my ankle. ~~Running for the bus.~~

▶ The pilots ejected from the burning plane, landing in the
They
water not far from the ship. ~~And~~ immediately popped their
flares and life vests.

19a Attach fragmented subordinate clauses or turn them into sentences.

A subordinate clause is patterned like a sentence, with both a subject and a verb, but it begins with a word that marks it as subordinate. The following words commonly introduce subordinate clauses.

after	before	so that	until	while
although	even though	than	when	who
as	how	that	where	whom
as if	if	though	whether	whose
because	since	unless	which	why

Subordinate clauses function within sentences as adjectives, as adverbs, or as nouns. They cannot stand alone. (See 63e.)

Most fragmented clauses beg to be pulled into a sentence nearby.

▶ Americans have come to fear the West Nile virus/~~Because~~ *because*

it is transmitted by the common mosquito.

Because introduces a subordinate clause, so it cannot stand alone. (For punctuation of subordinate clauses appearing at the end of a sentence, see 33f.)

▶ Although psychiatrist Peter Kramer expresses concerns

about Prozac/~~Many~~ *many* other doctors believe that the

benefits of antidepressants outweigh the risks.

Although introduces a subordinate clause, so it cannot stand alone. (For punctuation of subordinate clauses at the beginning of a sentence, see 32b.)

If a fragmented clause cannot be attached to a nearby sentence or if you feel that attaching it would be awkward, try turning the clause into a sentence. The simplest way to do this is to delete the opening word or words that mark it as subordinate.

▶ Population increases and uncontrolled development are

taking a deadly toll on the environment. ~~So that across~~ the
                                            Across

globe, fragile ecosystems are collapsing.

19b Attach fragmented phrases or turn them into sentences.

Like subordinate clauses, phrases function within sentences as adjectives, as adverbs, or as nouns. They cannot stand alone. Fragmented phrases are often prepositional or verbal phrases; sometimes they are appositives, words or word groups that re-name nouns or pronouns. (See 63a, 63b, and 63c.)

Often a fragmented phrase may simply be pulled into a nearby sentence.

▶ The archaeologists worked slowly, ~~Examining~~ and
                                    examining

labeling every pottery shard they uncovered.

The word group beginning with *Examining* is a verbal phrase.

▶ The patient displayed symptoms of ALS, A neuro-
                                         a

degenerative disease.

A neurodegenerative disease is an appositive renaming the noun *ALS*. (For punctuation of appositives, see 32e.)

If a fragmented phrase cannot be pulled into a nearby sentence effectively, turn the phrase into a sentence. You may need to add a subject, a verb, or both.

▶ In the training session, Jamie explained how to access our
                      She also taught us
new database. ~~Also~~ how to submit expense reports and

request vendor payments.

The revision turns the fragmented phrase into a sentence by add-ing a subject and a verb.

19c Attach other fragmented word groups or turn them into sentences.

Other word groups that are commonly fragmented include parts of compound predicates, lists, and examples introduced by *for example*, *in addition*, or similar expressions.

Parts of compound predicates

A predicate consists of a verb and its objects, complements, and modifiers (see 62b). A compound predicate includes two or more predicates joined with a coordinating conjunction such as *and*, *but*, or *or*. Because the parts of a compound predicate have the same subject, they should appear in the same sentence.

▶ The woodpecker finch of the Galápagos Islands carefully
  selects a twig of a certain size and shape/ ~~And~~ *and* then uses this
  tool to pry out grubs from trees.

> The subject is *finch*, and the compound predicate is *selects . . . and . . . uses*. (For punctuation of compound predicates, see 33a.)

Lists

To correct a fragmented list, often you can attach it to a nearby sentence with a colon or a dash. (See 35a and 39a.)

▶ It has been said that there are only three indigenous
  American art forms/: ~~Musical~~ *musical* comedy, jazz, and soap opera.

Sometimes terms like *especially*, *namely*, *like*, and *such as* introduce fragmented lists. Such fragments can usually be attached to the preceding sentence.

▶ In the twentieth century, the South produced some great
  American writers/, ~~Such~~ *such* as Flannery O'Connor, William
  Faulkner, Alice Walker, Tennessee Williams, and Thomas
  Wolfe.

Examples introduced by for example, in addition,
or similar expressions

Other expressions that introduce examples or explanations
can lead to unintentional fragments. Although you may begin
a sentence with some of the following words or phrases, make
sure that what follows has a subject and a verb.

also	for example	mainly
and	for instance	or
but	in addition	that is

Often the easiest solution is to turn the fragment into a
sentence.

▶ **In his memoir, Primo Levi describes the horrors of living**
                                    he worked
  in a concentration camp. For example, ~~working~~ without
    suffered
  food and ~~suffering~~ emotional abuse.

The writer corrected this fragment by adding a subject—*he*—and
substituting verbs for the verbals *working* and *suffering*.

▶ **Deborah Tannen's research reveals that men and women**

**Writing with
sources**

MLA-style
citation

  have different ideas about communication. For example,
  Tannen explains
  that a woman "expects her husband to be a new and

  improved version of her best friend" (441).

A quotation must be part of a complete sentence. *That a woman
"expects her husband to be a new and improved version of her best friend"*
is a fragment—a subordinate clause. In this case, adding a signal
phrase that includes a subject and a verb (*Tannen explains*) corrects
the fragment and clarifies that the quotation is from Tannen.

19d Exception: Occasionally a fragment may be used deliberately, for effect.

Skilled writers occasionally use sentence fragments for the following special purposes.

FOR EMPHASIS	Following the dramatic Americanization of their children, even my parents grew more publicly confident. *Especially my mother.*
	—Richard Rodriguez
TO ANSWER A QUESTION	Are these new drug tests 100 percent reliable? *Not in the opinion of most experts.*
TRANSITIONS	*And now the opposing arguments.*
EXCLAMATIONS	*Not again!*
IN ADVERTISING	*Fewer carbs. Improved taste.*

Although fragments are sometimes appropriate, writers and readers do not always agree on when they are appropriate. That's why you will find it safer to write in complete sentences.

EXERCISE 19–1   Repair any fragment by attaching it to a nearby sentence or by rewriting it as a complete sentence. If a word group is correct, write "correct" after it. Revisions of lettered sentences appear in the back of the book. Example:

> **One Greek island that should not be missed is Mykonos. A**
> **vacation spot for Europeans and a playground for the rich**
> **and famous.**

a.   Listening to the CD her sister had sent, Mia was overcome with a mix of emotions. Happiness, homesickness, nostalgia.

b.   Cortés and his soldiers were astonished when they looked down from the mountains and saw Tenochtitlán. The magnificent capital of the Aztecs.

c.   Although my spoken Spanish is not very good. I can read the language with ease.

d.   There are several reasons for not eating meat. One reason being that dangerous chemicals are used throughout the various stages of meat production.

e.   To learn how to sculpt beauty from everyday life. This is my intention in studying art and archaeology.

1. The panther lay motionless behind the rock. Waiting silently for its prey.
2. Aunt Mina loved to play all my favorite games. Cat's cradle, Uno, mancala, and even four square.
3. With machetes, the explorers cut their way through the tall grasses to the edge of the canyon. Then they began to lay out the tapes for the survey.
4. The owners of the online grocery store rented a warehouse in the Market district. An area catering to small businesses.
5. If a woman from the desert tribe showed anger toward her husband, she was whipped in front of the whole village. And shunned by the rest of the women.

EXERCISE 19–2 Repair each fragment in the following passage by attaching it to a sentence nearby or by rewriting it as a complete sentence.

Digital technology has revolutionized information delivery. Forever blurring the lines between information and entertainment. Yesterday's readers of books and newspapers are today's readers of e-books and news blogs. Countless readers have moved on from print information entirely. Choosing instead to point, click, and scroll their way through a text on their Amazon Kindle or in an online forum. Once a nation of people spoon-fed television commercials and the six o'clock evening news. We are now seemingly addicted to *YouTube*. Remember the family trip when Dad or Mom wrestled with a road map? On the way to St. Louis or Seattle? No wrestling is required with a slick GPS navigator by the driver's side. Unless it's Mom and Dad wrestling over who gets to program the address. Accessing information now seems to be America's favorite pastime. John Horrigan, associate director for research at the Pew Internet and American Life Project, reports that 31 percent of American adults are "elite" users of technology. Who are "highly engaged" with digital content. As a country, we embrace information and communication technologies. Which include iPods, cell phones, laptops, and handheld devices. Among children and adolescents, Internet and other personal technology use is on the rise. For activities like socializing, gaming, and information gathering.

hackerhandbooks.com/bedhandbook > Grammar exercises > Grammatical sentences > E-ex 19–3 to 19–6

20 Revise run-on sentences.

Run-on sentences are independent clauses that have not been joined correctly. An independent clause is a word group that can stand alone as a sentence. (See 64a.) When two independent clauses appear in one sentence, they must be joined in one of these ways:

- with a comma and a coordinating conjunction (*and, but, or, nor, for, so, yet*)
- with a semicolon (or occasionally with a colon or a dash)

Recognizing run-on sentences

There are two types of run-on sentences. When a writer puts no mark of punctuation and no coordinating conjunction between independent clauses, the result is called a *fused sentence.*

FUSED
┌──────── INDEPENDENT CLAUSE ────────┐ ┌──────
Air pollution poses risks to all humans it can be
┌──────── INDEPENDENT CLAUSE ────────┐
deadly for asthma sufferers.

A far more common type of run-on sentence is the *comma splice*—two or more independent clauses joined with a comma but without a coordinating conjunction. In some comma splices, the comma appears alone.

**COMMA
SPLICE**   Air pollution poses risks to all humans, it can be
deadly for asthma sufferers.

In other comma splices, the comma is accompanied by a joining word that is *not* a coordinating conjunction. There are only seven coordinating conjunctions in English: *and, but, or, nor, for, so,* and *yet.*

**COMMA
SPLICE**   Air pollution poses risks to all humans, however, it can
be deadly for asthma sufferers.

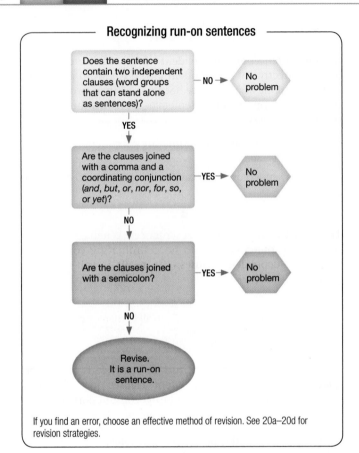

Recognizing run-on sentences

Does the sentence contain two independent clauses (word groups that can stand alone as sentences)? —NO→ No problem

YES ↓

Are the clauses joined with a comma and a coordinating conjunction (*and*, *but*, *or*, *nor*, *for*, *so*, or *yet*)? —YES→ No problem

NO ↓

Are the clauses joined with a semicolon? —YES→ No problem

NO ↓

Revise. It is a run-on sentence.

If you find an error, choose an effective method of revision. See 20a–20d for revision strategies.

Grammar checkers flag fewer than half the run-on sentences in a sample and may suggest inappropriate revision strategies. The flow-chart above can help you identify run-on sentences in your own writing.

However is a transitional expression, not a coordinating conjunction, and cannot be used with only a comma to join two independent clauses (see 20b).

Revising run-on sentences

To revise a run-on sentence, you have four choices.

1. Use a comma and a coordinating conjunction (*and*, *but*, *or*, *nor*, *for*, *so*, *yet*).

▶ Air pollution poses risks to all humans, _{but} it can be deadly for asthma sufferers.

2. Use a semicolon (or, if appropriate, a colon or a dash). A semicolon may be used alone; it can also be accompanied by a transitional expression.

▶ Air pollution poses risks to all humans/; it can be deadly for asthma sufferers.

▶ Air pollution poses risks to all humans/; _{however,} it can be deadly for asthma sufferers.

3. Make the clauses into separate sentences.

▶ Air pollution poses risks to all humans/. _{It} it can be deadly for asthma sufferers.

4. Restructure the sentence, perhaps by subordinating one of the clauses.

▶ _{Although air} Air pollution poses risks to all humans, it can be deadly for asthma sufferers.

One of these revision techniques usually works better than the others for a particular sentence. The fourth technique, the one requiring the most extensive revision, is often the most effective.

20a Consider separating the clauses with a comma and a coordinating conjunction.

There are seven coordinating conjunctions in English: *and*, *but*, *or*, *nor*, *for*, *so*, and *yet*. When a coordinating conjunction joins independent clauses, it is usually preceded by a comma. (See 32a.)

▶ Some lesson plans include exercises, *but* completing them

should not be the focus of all class periods.

▶ Many government officials privately admit that the poly-

graph is unreliable, ~~however,~~ *yet* they continue to use it as a

security measure.

> *However* is a transitional expression, not a coordinating conjunction, so it cannot be used with only a comma to join independent clauses. (See also 20b.)

20b Consider separating the clauses with a semicolon (or, if appropriate, with a colon or a dash).

When the independent clauses are closely related and their relation is clear without a coordinating conjunction, a semicolon is an acceptable method of revision. (See 34a.)

▶ Tragedy depicts the individual confronted with the fact

of death/; comedy depicts the adaptability of human

society.

A semicolon is required between independent clauses that have been linked with a transitional expression (such as *however, therefore, moreover, in fact,* or *for example*). For a longer list, see 34b.

▶ The timber wolf looks like a large German shepherd/; however, the wolf has longer legs, larger feet, and a wider head.

▶ In his film adaptation of the short story "Killings," director Todd Field changed key details of the plot/; as a matter of fact, he added whole scenes that do not appear in the story.

A colon or a dash may be more appropriate if the first independent clause introduces the second or if the second clause summarizes or explains the first. (See 35b and 39a.) In formal writing, the colon is usually preferred to the dash.

▶ Nuclear waste is hazardous: ~~this~~ This is an indisputable fact.

▶ The female black widow spider is often a widow of her own making/—she has been known to eat her partner after mating.

A colon is an appropriate method of revision if the first independent clause introduces a quoted sentence.

▶ Nobel Peace Prize winner Al Gore had this to say about climate change/: "The truth is that our circumstances are not only new; they are completely different than they have ever been in all of human history."

20c Consider making the clauses into separate sentences.

▶ Why should we spend money on expensive space
   exploration/? ~~we~~ We have enough underfunded programs here
   on Earth.

Since one independent clause is a question and the other is a statement, they should be separate sentences.

▶ Some studies have suggested that the sexual relationships

Writing with sources

APA-style citation

of bonobos set them apart from common chimpanzees/.
A
~~a~~according to Stanford (1998), these differences have been
exaggerated.

Using a comma to join two independent clauses creates a comma splice. In this example, an effective revision is to separate the first independent clause (*Some studies . . .*) from the second independent clause (*these differences . . .*) and to keep the signal phrase with the second clause. (See also 56c.)

NOTE: When two quoted independent clauses are divided by explanatory words, make each clause its own sentence.

▶ "It's always smart to learn from your mistakes," quipped my
   "It's
   supervisor/. "~~it's~~ even smarter to learn from the mistakes of
   others."

20d Consider restructuring the sentence, perhaps by subordinating one of the clauses.

If one of the independent clauses is less important than the other, turn it into a subordinate clause or phrase. (For more about subordination, see 14, especially the chart on p. 180.)

▶ One of the most famous advertising slogans is Wheaties

 cereal's "Breakfast of Champions," ~~it~~ *which* was penned in 1933.

 Although many
▶ ~~Many~~ scholars dismiss the abominable snowman of the

 Himalayas as a myth, others claim it may be a kind of ape.

▶ Mary McLeod Bethune, ~~was~~ the seventeenth child of former

 slaves, ~~she~~ founded the National Council of Negro Women

 in 1935.

 Minor ideas in these sentences are now expressed in subordinate
 clauses or phrases.

EXERCISE 20–1   Revise the following run-on sentences using the
method of revision suggested in brackets. Revisions of lettered sentences appear in the back of the book. Example:

 Because
 Orville had been obsessed with his weight as a teenager, he

 rarely ate anything sweet. [*Restructure the sentence.*]

a.   The city had one public swimming pool, it stayed packed with
     children all summer long. [*Restructure the sentence.*]
b.   The building is being renovated, therefore at times we have
     no heat, water, or electricity. [*Use a comma and a coordinating
     conjunction.*]
c.   The view was not what the travel agent had described, where
     were the rolling hills and the shimmering rivers? [*Make two
     sentences.*]
d.   All those gnarled equations looked like toxic insects, maybe I
     was going to have to rethink my major. [*Use a semicolon.*]
e.   City officials had good reason to fear a major earthquake, most
     of the business district was built on landfill. [*Use a colon.*]

1.   The car was hardly worth trading, the frame was twisted and
     the block was warped. [*Restructure the sentence.*]
2.   The next time an event is canceled because of bad weather, don't
     blame the meteorologist, blame nature. [*Make two sentences.*]

3. Ray was fluent in American Sign Language he could sign as easily as he could speak. [*Restructure the sentence.*]

4. Susanna arrived with a stack of her latest hats she hoped the gift shop would place a big winter order. [*Restructure the sentence.*]

5. There was one major reason for John's wealth, his grandfather had been a multimillionaire. [*Use a colon.*]

EXERCISE 20–2   Revise any run-on sentences using a technique that you find effective. If a sentence is correct, write "correct" after it. Revisions of lettered sentences appear in the back of the book. Example:

> Crossing so many time zones on an eight-hour flight, I knew
>
> I would be tired when I arrived, ~~however,~~ ^but^ I was too excited
>
> to sleep on the plane.

a. Wind power for the home is a supplementary source of energy, it can be combined with electricity, gas, or solar energy.

b. Aidan viewed Sofia Coppola's *Lost in Translation* three times and then wrote a paper describing the film as the work of a mysterious modern painter.

c. In the Middle Ages, the streets of London were dangerous places, it was safer to travel by boat along the Thames.

d. "He's not drunk," I said, "he's in a state of diabetic shock."

e. Are you able to endure extreme angle turns, high speeds, frequent jumps, and occasional crashes, then supermoto racing may be a sport for you.

1. Death Valley National Monument, located in southern California and Nevada, is one of the hottest places on Earth, temperatures there have soared as high as 134 degrees Fahrenheit.

2. Anamaria opened the boxes crammed with toys, out sprang griffins, dragons, and phoenixes.

3. Subatomic physics is filled with strange and marvelous particles, tiny bodies of matter that shiver, wobble, pulse, and flatten to no thickness at all.

4. As his first major project, Frederick Law Olmsted designed New York City's Central Park, one of the most beautiful urban spaces in the United States.

5. The neurosurgeon explained that the medication could have one side effect, it might cause me to experience temporary memory loss.

EXERCISE 20–3   In the following rough draft, revise any run-on sentences.

> Some parents and educators argue that requiring uniforms in public schools would improve student behavior and performance. They think that uniforms give students a more professional attitude toward school, moreover, they believe that uniforms help create a sense of community among students from diverse backgrounds. But parents and educators should consider the drawbacks to requiring uniforms in public schools.
>
> Uniforms do create a sense of community, they do this, however, by stamping out individuality. Youth is a time to express originality, it is a time to develop a sense of self. One important way young people express their identities is through the clothes they wear. The self-patrolled dress code of high school students may be stricter than any school-imposed code, nevertheless, trying to control dress habits from above will only lead to resentment or to mindless conformity.
>
> If children are going to act like adults, they need to be treated like adults, they need to be allowed to make their own choices. Telling young people what to wear to school merely prolongs their childhood. Requiring uniforms undermines the educational purpose of public schools, which is not just to teach facts and figures but to help young people grow into adults who are responsible for making their own choices.

hackerhandbooks.com/bedhandbook > Grammar exercises > Grammatical sentences
> E-ex 20–4 to 20–7

21   Make subjects and verbs agree.

In the present tense, verbs agree with their subjects in number (singular or plural) and in person (first, second, third): *I sing, you sing, he sings, she sings, we sing, they sing*. Even if your ear recognizes the standard subject-verb combinations presented in 21a, you will no doubt encounter tricky situations such as those described in 21b–21k.

21a Consult this section for standard subject-verb combinations.

This section describes the basic guidelines for making present-tense verbs agree with their subjects. The present-tense ending -*s* (or -*es*) is used on a verb if its subject is third-person singular (*he*, *she*, *it*, and singular nouns); otherwise the verb takes no ending. Consider, for example, the present-tense forms of the verbs *love* and *try*, given at the beginning of the chart on the following page.

The verb *be* varies from this pattern; unlike any other verb, it has special forms in *both* the present and the past tense. These forms appear at the end of the chart.

If you aren't confident that you know the standard forms, use the charts on pages 245 and 246 as you proofread for subject-verb agreement. You may also want to look at 27c on -*s* endings of regular and irregular verbs.

Grammar checkers are fairly good at flagging subject-verb agreement problems. But they occasionally flag a correct sentence, usually because they misidentify the subject, the verb, or both. Sometimes they miss an agreement problem because they don't recognize a pronoun's antecedent (see 21i).

21b Make the verb agree with its subject, not with a word that comes between.

Word groups often come between the subject and the verb. Such word groups, usually modifying the subject, may contain a noun that at first appears to be the subject. By mentally stripping away such modifiers, you can isolate the noun that is in fact the subject.

The *samples* on the tray in the lab *need* testing.

Subject-verb agreement at a glance

Present-tense forms of *love* and *try* (typical verbs)

	SINGULAR		PLURAL	
FIRST PERSON	I	love	we	love
SECOND PERSON	you	love	you	love
THIRD PERSON	he/she/it*	loves	they**	love

	SINGULAR		PLURAL	
FIRST PERSON	I	try	we	try
SECOND PERSON	you	try	you	try
THIRD PERSON	he/she/it*	tries	they**	try

Present-tense forms of *have*

	SINGULAR		PLURAL	
FIRST PERSON	I	have	we	have
SECOND PERSON	you	have	you	have
THIRD PERSON	he/she/it*	has	they**	have

Present-tense forms of *do* (including negative forms)

	SINGULAR		PLURAL	
FIRST PERSON	I	do/don't	we	do/don't
SECOND PERSON	you	do/don't	you	do/don't
THIRD PERSON	he/she/it*	does/doesn't	they**	do/don't

Present-tense and past-tense forms of *be*

	SINGULAR		PLURAL	
FIRST PERSON	I	am/was	we	are/were
SECOND PERSON	you	are/were	you	are/were
THIRD PERSON	he/she/it*	is/was	they**	are/were

*And singular nouns (*child*, *Roger*)
**And plural nouns (*children*, *the Mannings*)

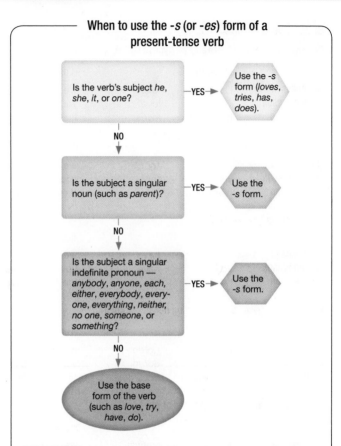

When to use the *-s* (or *-es*) form of a present-tense verb

Is the verb's subject *he, she, it,* or *one*? — **YES** → Use the *-s* form (*loves, tries, has, does*).

NO ↓

Is the subject a singular noun (such as *parent*)? — **YES** → Use the *-s* form.

NO ↓

Is the subject a singular indefinite pronoun — *anybody, anyone, each, either, everybody, everyone, everything, neither, no one, someone,* or *something*? — **YES** → Use the *-s* form.

NO ↓

Use the base form of the verb (such as *love, try, have, do*).

EXCEPTION: Choosing the correct present-tense form of *be* (*am, is,* or *are*) is not quite so simple. See the chart on the previous page for both present- and past-tense forms of *be*.

ESL TIP: Do not use the *-s* form of a verb if it follows a modal verb such as *can, must,* or *should* or another helping verb. (See 28b.)

▶ **High levels of air pollution causes damage to the respiratory**

tract.

> The subject is *levels*, not *pollution*. Strip away the phrase *of air pollution* to hear the correct verb: *levels cause.*

▶ **The slaughter of pandas for their pelts ~~have~~ caused the** *(has)*

panda population to decline drastically.

> The subject is *slaughter*, not *pandas* or *pelts.*

NOTE: Phrases beginning with the prepositions *as well as, in addition to, accompanied by, together with,* and *along with* do not make a singular subject plural.

▶ **The governor as well as his press secretary ~~were~~ on** *(was)*

the plane.

> To emphasize that two people were on the plane, the writer could use *and* instead: *The governor and his press secretary were on the plane.*

21c Treat most subjects joined with *and* as plural.

A subject with two or more parts is said to be compound. If the parts are connected with *and*, the subject is nearly always plural.

Leon and Jan often *jog* together.

▶ **The Supreme Court's willingness to hear the case and its**

affirmation of the original decision ~~has~~ set a new *(have)*

precedent.

EXCEPTIONS: When the parts of the subject form a single unit or when they refer to the same person or thing, treat the subject as singular.

> Strawberries and cream was a last-minute addition to the menu.

> Sue's friend and adviser was surprised by her decision.

When a compound subject is preceded by *each* or *every*, treat it as singular.

> Each tree, shrub, and vine needs to be sprayed.

> Every car, truck, and van is required to pass inspection.

This exception does not apply when a compound subject is followed by each: *Alan and Marcia each have different ideas.*

21d With subjects joined with *or* or *nor* (or with *either . . . or* or *neither . . . nor*), make the verb agree with the part of the subject nearer to the verb.

> A driver's *license* or credit *card is* required.

> A driver's *license* or two credit *cards are* required.

▶ If an infant or a child ~~are~~ _is_ having difficulty breathing, seek

medical attention immediately.

▶ Neither the chief financial officer nor the marketing

managers ~~was~~ _were_ able to convince the client to reconsider.

The verb must be matched with the part of the subject closer to it: *child is* in the first sentence, *managers were* in the second.

NOTE: If one part of the subject is singular and the other is plural, put the plural one last to avoid awkwardness.

21e Treat most indefinite pronouns as singular.

Indefinite pronouns are pronouns that do not refer to specific persons or things. The following commonly used indefinite pronouns are singular.

anybody	each	everyone	nobody	somebody
anyone	either	everything	no one	someone
anything	everybody	neither	nothing	something

Many of these words appear to have plural meanings, and they are often treated as such in casual speech. In formal written English, however, they are nearly always treated as singular.

Everyone on the team *supports* the coach.

▶ Each of the furrows ~~have~~ has been seeded.

▶ Nobody who participated in the clinical trials ~~were~~ was given a

placebo.

The subjects of these sentences are *Each* and *Nobody*. These indefinite pronouns are third-person singular, so the verbs must be *has* and *was*.

A few indefinite pronouns (*all, any, none, some*) may be singular or plural depending on the noun or pronoun they refer to.

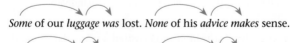

Some of our *luggage was* lost. *None* of his *advice makes* sense.

Some of the *rocks are* slippery. *None* of the *eggs were* broken.

NOTE: When the meaning of *none* is emphatically "not one," *none* may be treated as singular: *None* [meaning "Not one"] *of the eggs was broken.* However, some experts advise using *not one* instead: *Not one of the eggs was broken.*

21f Treat collective nouns as singular unless the meaning is clearly plural.

Collective nouns such as *jury, committee, audience, crowd, troop, family,* and *couple* name a class or a group. In American English, collective nouns are nearly always treated as singular: They emphasize the group as a unit. Occasionally, when there is some reason to draw attention to the individual members of the group, a collective noun may be treated as plural. (See also 22b.)

SINGULAR   The *class respects* the teacher.

PLURAL   The *class are* debating among themselves.

To underscore the notion of individuality in the second sentence, many writers would add a clearly plural noun.

PLURAL   The class *members are* debating among themselves.

▶ The board of trustees ~~meet~~ meets in Denver twice a year.

The board as a whole meets; there is no reason to draw attention to its individual members.

▶ A young couple ~~was~~ were arguing about politics while holding

hands.

The meaning is clearly plural. Only separate individuals can argue and hold hands.

NOTE: The phrase *the number* is treated as singular, *a number* as plural.

SINGULAR   *The number* of school-age children *is* declining.

PLURAL   *A number* of children *are* attending the wedding.

NOTE: In general, when fractions or units of measurement are used with a singular noun, treat them as singular; when they are used with a plural noun, treat them as plural.

SINGULAR   *Three-fourths* of the salad *has* been eaten.

SINGULAR   Twenty *inches* of wallboard *was* covered with mud.

PLURAL   *One-fourth* of the drivers *were* texting.

PLURAL   Two *pounds* of blueberries *were* used to make the pie.

21g Make the verb agree with its subject even when the subject follows the verb.

Verbs ordinarily follow subjects. When this normal order is reversed, it is easy to become confused. Sentences beginning with *there is* or *there are* (or *there was* or *there were*) are inverted; the subject follows the verb.

There *are* surprisingly few *children* in our neighborhood.

> There ~~was~~ a social worker and a neighbor at the scene of the

   ^{were}

   accident.

   The subject, *worker and neighbor*, is plural, so the verb must be *were*.

Occasionally you may decide to invert a sentence for variety or effect. When you do so, check to make sure that your subject and verb agree.

> Of particular concern ~~is~~ penicillin and tetracycline,

   ^{are}

   antibiotics used to make animals more resistant to disease.

   The subject, *penicillin and tetracycline*, is plural, so the verb must be *are*.

21h Make the verb agree with its subject, not with a subject complement.

One basic sentence pattern in English consists of a subject, a linking verb, and a subject complement: *Jack is a securities lawyer.* Because the subject complement (*lawyer*) names or describes the subject (*Jack*), it is sometimes mistaken for the subject. (See 62b on subject complements.)

These *exercises are* a way to test your ability to perform under pressure.

▶ A tent and a sleeping bag ~~is~~ ^{are} the required equipment for all

campers.

Tent and bag is the subject, not *equipment.*

▶ A major force in today's economy ~~are~~ ^{is} children—as

consumers, decision makers, and trend spotters.

Force is the subject, not *children*. If the corrected version seems too awkward, make *children* the subject: *Children are a major force in today's economy—as consumers, decision makers, and trend spotters.*

21i *Who*, *which*, and *that* take verbs that agree with their antecedents.

Like most pronouns, the relative pronouns *who*, *which*, and *that* have antecedents, nouns or pronouns to which they refer. Relative pronouns used as subjects of subordinate clauses take verbs that agree with their antecedents.

ANT   PN   V

Take a *course that prepares* you for classroom management.

One of the

Constructions such as *one of the students who* [or *one of the things that*] cause problems for writers. Do not assume that the antecedent must be *one*. Instead, consider the logic of the sentence.

▶ Our ability to use language is one of the things that sets us

  apart from animals.

The antecedent of *that* is *things*, not *one*. Several things set us apart from animals.

Only one of the

When the word *only* comes before *one*, you are safe in assuming that *one* is the antecedent of the relative pronoun.

▶ Veronica was the only one of the first-year Spanish
                          was
  students who ~~were~~ fluent enough to apply for the exchange

  program.

The antecedent of *who* is *one*, not *students*. Only one student was fluent enough.

21j Words such as *athletics, economics, mathematics, physics, politics, statistics, measles,* and *news* are usually singular, despite their plural form.

                is
▶ Politics ~~are~~ among my mother's favorite pastimes.

EXCEPTION: Occasionally some of these words, especially *economics, mathematics, politics,* and *statistics,* have plural meanings: *Office politics often sway decisions about hiring and promotion. The economics of the building plan are prohibitive.*

21k Titles of works, company names, words mentioned as words, and gerund phrases are singular.

▶ *Lost Cities* ~~describe~~ ^{describes} the discoveries of fifty ancient

civilizations.

▶ Delmonico Brothers ~~specialize~~ ^{specializes} in organic produce and

additive-free meats.

▶ *Controlled substances* ~~are~~ ^{is} a euphemism for illegal drugs.

A gerund phrase consists of an *-ing* verb form followed by any objects, complements, or modifiers (see 63b). Treat gerund phrases as singular.

▶ Encountering long hold times ~~make~~ ^{makes} customers impatient

with telephone tech support.

EXERCISE 21–1 For each sentence in the following passage, underline the subject (or compound subject) and then select the verb that agrees with it. (If you have trouble identifying the subject, consult 62a.)

Loggerhead sea turtles (migrate / migrates) thousands of miles before returning to their nesting location every two to three years. The nesting season for loggerhead turtles (span / spans) the hottest months of the summer. Although the habitat of Atlantic loggerheads (range / ranges) from Newfoundland to Argentina, nesting for these turtles (take / takes) place primarily along the southeastern coast of the United States. Female turtles that have reached sexual maturity (crawl / crawls) ashore at night to lay their eggs. The cavity that serves as a nest for the eggs (is / are) dug out with the female's strong flippers. Deposited into each nest (is / are) anywhere from fifty to two hundred spherical eggs, also known as a *clutch*. After a two-month incubation period, all eggs in the clutch (begin / begins) to hatch, and within a few days the young turtles attempt to make their way into the ocean. A major cause of the loggerhead's decreasing numbers (is / are) natural predators such as raccoons, birds, and crabs. Beach erosion and coastal development also (threaten / threatens) the turtles' survival. For example, a crowd of curious humans or lights from beachfront residences (is / are) enough to make the female abandon her nesting plans and return to the ocean. Since only one in one thousand loggerheads survives to adulthood, special care should be taken to protect this threatened species.

EXERCISE 21–2 Edit the following sentences to eliminate problems with subject-verb agreement. If a sentence is correct, write "correct" after it. Answers to lettered sentences appear in the back of the book. Example:

Jack's first days in the infantry ~~was~~ *were* grueling.

a. One of the main reasons for elephant poaching are the profits received from selling the ivory tusks.

b. Not until my interview with Dr. Hwang were other possibilities opened to me.

c. A number of students in the seminar was aware of the importance of joining the discussion.

d. Batik cloth from Bali, blue and white ceramics from Delft, and a bocce ball from Turin has made Angelie's room the talk of the dorm.

e. The board of directors, ignoring the wishes of the neighborhood, has voted to allow further development.

1. Measles is a contagious childhood disease.

2. Adorning a shelf in the lab is a Vietnamese figurine, a set of Korean clay gods, and an American plastic village.

3. The presence of certain bacteria in our bodies is one of the factors that determines our overall health.

4. Sheila is the only one of the many applicants who has the ability to step into this job.

5. Neither the explorer nor his companions was ever seen again.

22   Make pronouns and antecedents agree.

A pronoun is a word that substitutes for a noun. (See 61b.) Many pronouns have antecedents, nouns or pronouns to which they refer. A pronoun and its antecedent agree when they are both singular or both plural.

SINGULAR   *Dr. Ava Berto* finished *her* rounds.

PLURAL   The hospital *interns* finished *their* rounds.

ESL   The pronouns *he, his, she, her, it,* and *its* must agree in gender (masculine, feminine, or neuter) with their antecedents, not with the words they modify.

Steve visited *his* [not *her*] sister in Seattle.

Grammar checkers rarely flag problems with pronoun-antecedent agreement. It takes a human eye to see that a plural pronoun does not agree with a singular noun. When grammar checkers do flag agreement problems, they often suggest (correctly) substituting the singular phrase *his or her* for the plural pronoun *their*. For other revision strategies that avoid the wordy *his or her* construction, see the chart on page 259.

22a   Do not use plural pronouns to refer to singular antecedents.

Writers are frequently tempted to use plural pronouns to refer to two kinds of singular antecedents: indefinite pronouns and generic nouns.

Indefinite pronouns

Indefinite pronouns refer to nonspecific persons or things. Even though some of the following indefinite pronouns may seem to have plural meanings, treat them as singular in formal English.

anybody	each	everyone	nobody	somebody
anyone	either	everything	no one	someone
anything	everybody	neither	nothing	something

Everyone performs at *his or her* [not *their*] own fitness level.

When a plural pronoun refers mistakenly to a singular indefinite pronoun, you can usually choose one of three options for revision:

1. Replace the plural pronoun with *he or she* (or *his or her*).
2. Make the antecedent plural.
3. Rewrite the sentence so that no problem of agreement exists.

▶ When someone travels outside the United States for the
   first time, ~~they need~~ *he or she needs* to apply for a passport several months
   in advance.

▶ When ~~someone travels~~ *people travel* outside the United States for the
   first time, they need to apply for a passport several months
   in advance.

▶ ~~When someone~~ *Anyone who* travels outside the United States for the
   first time, ~~they need~~ *needs* to apply for a passport several months
   in advance.

Because the *he or she* construction is wordy, often the second or third revision strategy is more effective. Using *he* (or *his*) to refer to persons of either sex, while less wordy, is considered sexist, as is using *she* (or *her*) for all persons. Some writers alternate male and female pronouns throughout a text, but the result is often awkward. See 17f and the chart on page 259 for strategies that avoid sexist usage.

NOTE: If you change a pronoun from singular to plural (or vice versa), check to be sure that the verb agrees with the new pronoun (see 21e).

Generic nouns

A generic noun represents a typical member of a group, such as a typical student, or any member of a group, such as any lawyer. Although generic nouns may seem to have plural meanings, they are singular.

> Every *runner* must train rigorously if *he or she wants* [not *they want*] to excel.

When a plural pronoun refers mistakenly to a generic noun, you will usually have the same three revision options as mentioned on page 257 for indefinite pronouns.

▶ A medical student must study hard if ~~they want~~ to succeed.
     he or she wants

▶ ~~A medical student~~ must study hard if they want to succeed.
   Medical students

▶ A medical student must study hard ~~if they want~~ to succeed.

22b Treat collective nouns as singular unless the meaning is clearly plural.

Collective nouns such as *jury, committee, audience, crowd, class, troop, family, team,* and *couple* name a group. Ordinarily the group functions as a unit, so the noun should be treated as

Choosing a revision strategy that avoids sexist language

Because many readers object to sexist language, avoid using *he*, *him*, and *his* (or *she*, *her*, and *hers*) to refer to both men and women. Also try to avoid the wordy expressions *he or she* and *his or her*. More graceful alternatives are usually possible.

Use an occasional *he or she* (or *his or her*).

▶ In our office, everyone works at ~~their~~ own pace.
(his or her)

Make the antecedent plural.

▶ ~~An employee~~ on extended disability leave may continue their
(Employees)

life insurance.

Recast the sentence.

▶ The amount of vacation time a federal worker may

accrue depends on ~~their~~ length of service.

▶ ~~If a~~ child ~~is~~ born to parents who are both bipolar,/~~they~~
(A)   *(has)*

~~have~~ a high chance of being bipolar.

▶ A year later someone finally admitted ~~that they were~~
(to being)

involved in the kidnapping.

▶ In his autobiography, Benjamin Franklin suggests that anyone

can achieve success ~~as long as they live~~ a virtuous life and
(by living)

~~work~~ hard.
(working)

singular; if the members of the group function as individuals, however, the noun should be treated as plural. (See also 21f.)

AS A UNIT   The *committee* granted *its* permission to build.

AS INDIVIDUALS   The *committee* put *their* signatures on the document.

When treating a collective noun as plural, many writers prefer to add a clearly plural antecedent such as *members* to the sentence: *The members of the committee put their signatures on the document.*

▶ **Defense attorney Clarence Darrow surprisingly urged the jury to find his client, John Scopes, guilty so that he could appeal the case to a higher court. The jury complied, returning ~~their~~ verdict in only nine minutes.**
  its

There is no reason to draw attention to the individual members of the jury, so *jury* should be treated as singular.

22c Treat most compound antecedents joined with *and* as plural.

In 1987, *Reagan and Gorbachev* held a summit where *they* signed the Intermediate-Range Nuclear Forces Treaty.

22d With compound antecedents joined with *or* or *nor* (or with *either . . . or* or *neither . . . nor*), make the pronoun agree with the nearer antecedent.

Either *Bruce* or *Tom* should receive first prize for *his* poem.

Neither the *mouse* nor the *rats* could find *their* way through the maze.

NOTE: If one of the antecedents is singular and the other plural, as in the second example, put the plural one last to avoid awkwardness.

EXCEPTION: If one antecedent is male and the other female, do not follow the traditional rule. The sentence *Either Bruce or Elizabeth should receive first prize for her short story* makes no sense. The best solution is to recast the sentence: *The prize for best short story should go to either Bruce or Elizabeth.*

EXERCISE 22–1 Edit the following sentences to eliminate problems with pronoun-antecedent agreement. Most of the sentences can be revised in more than one way, so experiment before choosing a solution. If a sentence is correct, write "correct" after it. Revisions of lettered sentences appear in the back of the book. Example:

> Recruiters
> **~~The recruiter~~ may tell the truth, but there is much that they choose not to tell.**

a. Every presidential candidate must appeal to a wide variety of ethnic and social groups if they want to win the election.
b. David lent his motorcycle to someone who allowed their friend to use it.
c. The aerobics teacher motioned for everyone to move their arms in wide, slow circles.
d. The parade committee was unanimous in its decision to allow all groups and organizations to join the festivities.
e. The applicant should be bilingual if they want to qualify for this position.

1. If a driver refuses to take a blood or breath test, he or she will have their licenses suspended for six months.
2. Why should anyone learn a second language? One reason is to sharpen their minds.
3. The Department of Education issued guidelines for school security. They were trying to anticipate problems and avert disaster.
4. The logger in the Northwest relies on the old forest growth for their living.
5. If anyone notices any suspicious activity, they should report it to the police.

EXERCISE 22–2   Edit the following paragraph to eliminate problems with pronoun-antecedent agreement or sexist language.

> A common practice in businesses is to put each employee in their own cubicle. A typical cubicle resembles an office, but their walls don't reach the ceiling. Many office managers feel that a cubicle floor plan has its advantages. Cubicles make a large area feel spacious. In addition, they can be moved around so that each new employee can be accommodated in his own work area. Of course, the cubicle model also has problems. The typical employee is not as happy with a cubicle as they would be with a traditional office. Also, productivity can suffer. Neither a manager nor a frontline worker can ordinarily do their best work in a cubicle because of noise and lack of privacy. Each worker can hear his neighbors tapping on computer keyboards, making telephone calls, and muttering under their breath.

hackerhandbooks.com/bedhandbook > Grammar exercises > Grammatical sentences
> E-ex 22–3 to 22–5

23   Make pronoun references clear.

Pronouns substitute for nouns; they are a kind of shorthand. In a sentence like *After Andrew intercepted the ball, he kicked it as hard as he could,* the pronouns *he* and *it* substitute for the nouns *Andrew* and *ball.* The word a pronoun refers to is called its *antecedent.*

> Grammar checkers do not flag problems with faulty pronoun reference. Although a computer program can identify pronouns, it has no way of knowing which words, if any, they refer to. Only you can determine whether your readers will be confused.

23a Avoid ambiguous or remote pronoun reference.

Ambiguous pronoun reference occurs when a pronoun could refer to two possible antecedents.

> The pitcher broke when Gloria set it
> ▶ ~~When Gloria set the pitcher~~ on the glass-topped table~~. it broke.~~
> ^   ^

▶ Tom told James, ~~that he had~~ won the lottery." *"You have*

What broke—the pitcher or the table? Who won the lottery—Tom
or James? The revisions eliminate the ambiguity.

Remote pronoun reference occurs when a pronoun is too
far away from its antecedent for easy reading.

▶ After the court ordered my ex-husband to pay child support,

he refused. Approximately eight months later, we were back

in court. This time the judge ordered him to make payments

directly to the Support and Collections Unit, which would in

turn pay me. For the first six months, I received regular pay-

ments, but then they stopped. Again ~~he~~ was summoned to *my ex-husband*

appear in court; he did not respond.

The pronoun *he* was too distant from its antecedent, *ex-husband*,
which appeared several sentences earlier.

23b Generally, avoid broad reference of *this*, *that*, *which*, and *it*.

For clarity, the pronouns *this*, *that*, *which*, and *it* should ordinarily refer to specific antecedents rather than to whole ideas
or sentences. When a pronoun's reference is needlessly broad,
either replace the pronoun with a noun or supply an antecedent to which the pronoun clearly refers.

▶ By advertising on television, pharmaceutical companies

gain exposure for their prescription drugs. Patients

respond to ~~this~~ by requesting drugs they might not need. *the ads*

For clarity, the writer substituted the noun *ads* for the pronoun
this, which referred broadly to the idea expressed in the preceding
sentence.

▶ Romeo and Juliet were both too young to have acquired

 a fact

much wisdom, ~~and~~ that accounts for their rash actions.
            ^

The writer added an antecedent (*fact*) that the pronoun *that* clearly refers to.

EXCEPTION: Many writers view broad reference as acceptable when the pronoun refers clearly to the sense of an entire clause.

If you pick up a starving dog and make him prosperous, he will not bite you. *This* is the principal difference between a dog and a man.   —Mark Twain

23c Do not use a pronoun to refer to an implied antecedent.

A pronoun should refer to a specific antecedent, not to a word that is implied but not present in the sentence.

 the braids

▶ After braiding Ann's hair, Sue decorated ~~them~~ with ribbons.
                                    ^

The pronoun *them* referred to Ann's braids (implied by the term *braiding*), but the word *braids* did not appear in the sentence.

Modifiers, such as possessives, cannot serve as antecedents. A modifier may strongly imply the noun that a pronoun might logically refer to, but it is not itself that noun.

 Jamaica Kincaid

▶ In ~~Jamaica Kincaid's~~ "Girl," ~~she~~ describes the advice a
                              ^

mother gives her daughter, including the mysterious

warning not to be "the kind of woman who the baker won't

let near the bread" (454).

Writing with sources

MLA-style citation

Using the possessive form of an author's name to introduce a source leads to a problem later in this sentence: The pronoun *she* cannot refer logically to a possessive modifier (*Jamaica Kincaid's*). The revision substitutes the noun *Jamaica Kincaid* for the pronoun *she*, thereby eliminating the problem.

23d Avoid the indefinite use of *they*, *it*, and *you*.

Do not use the pronoun *they* to refer indefinitely to persons who have not been specifically mentioned. *They* should always refer to a specific antecedent.

▶ In 2001, ~~they~~ _{Congress} shut down all government agencies for more

than a month until the budget crisis was finally resolved.

The word *it* should not be used indefinitely in constructions such as *It is said on television . . .* or *In the article, it says that. . . .*

▶ ^{The} ~~In the~~ encyclopedia ~~it~~ states that male moths can smell

female moths from several miles away.

The pronoun *you* is appropriate only when the writer is addressing the reader directly: *Once you have kneaded the dough, let it rise in a warm place.* Except in informal contexts, however, *you* should not be used to mean "anyone in general." Use a noun instead. (See pp. 48–49.)

▶ Ms. Pickersgill's *Guide to Etiquette* stipulates that ~~you~~ ^{a guest}

should not arrive at a party too early or leave too late.

23e To refer to persons, use *who*, *whom*, or *whose*, not *which* or *that*.

In most contexts, use *who*, *whom*, or *whose* to refer to persons, *which* or *that* to refer to animals or things. *Which* is reserved only for animals or things, so it is impolite to use it to refer to persons.

▶ All thirty-two women in the study, half of ~~which~~ ^{whom} were

unemployed for more than six months, reported higher

self-esteem after job training.

Although *that* is sometimes used to refer to persons, many readers will find such references dehumanizing. It is more polite to use a form of *who*—a word reserved only for people.

▶ During the two-day festival El Día de los Muertos (Day of the

                                                               who

  Dead), Mexican families celebrate loved ones ~~that~~ have died.

NOTE: Occasionally *whose* may be used to refer to animals and things to avoid the awkward *of which* construction.

                whose

▶ A local school, ~~the name of which~~ will be in tomorrow's

  paper, has received the Governor's Gold Medal for out-

  standing community service.

EXERCISE 23–1 Edit the following sentences to correct errors in pronoun reference. In some cases, you will need to decide on an antecedent that the pronoun might logically refer to. Revisions of lettered sentences appear in the back of the book. Example:

  Although Apple makes the most widely recognized MP3

  player, other companies have gained a share of the market.

      The competition

  ~~This~~ has kept prices from skyrocketing.

a. They say that engineering students should have hands-on experience with dismantling and reassembling machines.

b. She had decorated her living room with posters from chamber music festivals. This led her date to believe that she was interested in classical music. Actually she preferred rock.

c. In my high school, you didn't need to get all A's to be considered a success; you just needed to work to your ability.

d. Marianne told Jenny that she was worried about her mother's illness.

e. Though Lewis cried for several minutes after scraping his knee, eventually it subsided.

1. Our German conversation group is made up of six people, three of which I had never met before.
2. Many people believe that the polygraph test is highly reliable if you employ a licensed examiner.
3. Parent involvement is high at Mission San Jose High School. They participate in many committees and activities that affect all aspects of school life.
4. Because of Paul Robeson's outspoken attitude toward fascism, he was labeled a Communist.
5. In the report, it points out that the bald eagle, after several decades of protection, was removed from the endangered species list in 1997.

EXERCISE 23–2 Edit the following passage to correct errors in pronoun reference. In some cases, you will need to decide on an antecedent that the pronoun might logically refer to.

Since the Internet's inception in the 1980s, it has grown to be one of the largest communications forums in the world. The Internet was created by a team of academics who were building on a platform that government scientists had started developing in the 1950s. They initially viewed it as a noncommercial enterprise that would serve only the needs of the academic and technical communities. But with the introduction of user-friendly browser technology in the 1990s, it expanded tremendously. By the late 1990s, many businesses were connecting to the Internet with high-speed broadband and fiber-optic connections, which is also true of many home users today. Accessing information, shopping, and communicating are easier than ever before. This, however, can lead to some possible downfalls. You can be bombarded with spam and pop-up ads or attacked by harmful viruses and worms. They say that the best way to protect home computers from harm is to keep antivirus protection programs up-to-date and to shut them down when not in use.

hackerhandbooks.com/bedhandbook > Grammar exercises > Grammatical sentences
> E-ex 23–3 to 23–5

24   Distinguish between pronouns such as *I* and *me*.

The personal pronouns in the following chart change what is known as *case form* according to their grammatical function in a sentence. Pronouns functioning as subjects or subject complements appear in the *subjective* case; those functioning as objects appear in the *objective* case; and those showing ownership appear in the *possessive* case.

	SUBJECTIVE CASE	OBJECTIVE CASE	POSSESSIVE CASE
SINGULAR	I	me	my
	you	you	your
	he/she/it	him/her/it	his/her/its
PLURAL	we	us	our
	you	you	your
	they	them	their

Pronouns in the subjective and objective cases are frequently confused. Most of the rules in this section specify when to use one or the other of these cases (*I* or *me*, *he* or *him*, and so on). Section 24g explains a special use of pronouns and nouns in the possessive case.

> Grammar checkers sometimes flag incorrect pronouns and suggest using the correct form. But they miss more incorrect pronouns than they catch, and their suggestions for revision are sometimes off the mark, especially with pronouns following *than* or *as* (see 24d).

24a Use the subjective case (*I*, *you*, *he*, *she*, *it*, *we*, *they*) for subjects and subject complements.

When personal pronouns are used as subjects, ordinarily your ear will tell you the correct pronoun. Problems sometimes arise, however, with compound word groups containing a pronoun, so it is not always safe to trust your ear.

▶ Joel ran away from home because his stepfather and ~~him~~ he had

quarreled.

His stepfather and he is the subject of the verb *had quarreled*. If we strip away the words *his stepfather and*, the correct pronoun becomes clear: *he had quarreled* (not *him had quarreled*).

When a pronoun is used as a subject complement (a word following a linking verb), your ear may mislead you, since the incorrect form is frequently heard in casual speech. (See "subject complement," 62b.)

▶ **During the Lindbergh trial, Bruno Hauptmann repeatedly**
denied that the kidnapper was ~~him~~ he.

If *kidnapper was he* seems too stilted, rewrite the sentence: *During the Lindbergh trial, Bruno Hauptmann repeatedly denied that he was the kidnapper.*

24b Use the objective case (*me, you, him, her, it, us, them*) for all objects.

When a personal pronoun is used as a direct object, an indirect object, or the object of a preposition, ordinarily your ear will lead you to the correct pronoun. When an object is compound, however, you may occasionally become confused.

▶ **Janice was indignant when she realized that the salesclerk**
was insulting her mother and ~~she~~ her.

Her mother and her is the direct object of the verb *was insulting*. Strip away the words *her mother and* to hear the correct pronoun: *was insulting her* (not *was insulting she*).

▶ **The most traumatic experience for her father and ~~I~~ me occurred**
long after her operation.

Her father and me is the object of the preposition *for*. Strip away the words *her father and* to test for the correct pronoun: *for me* (not *for I*).

When in doubt about the correct pronoun, some writers try to avoid making the choice by using a reflexive pronoun such as *myself.* Using a reflexive pronoun in such situations is nonstandard.

▶ The Indian cab driver gave my cousin and ~~myself~~ ^{me} some

good tips on traveling in New Delhi.

My cousin and me is the indirect object of the verb *gave.* For correct uses of *myself,* see the Glossary of Usage.

▶ The independent film company hired my sister and ~~myself~~ ^{me}

as marketing consultants.

My sister and me is the direct object of the verb *hired.* For correct uses of *myself,* see the Glossary of Usage.

24c Put an appositive and the word to which it refers in the same case.

Appositives are noun phrases that rename nouns or pronouns. A pronoun used as an appositive has the same function (usually subject or object) as the word(s) it renames.

▶ The chief strategists, Dr. Bell and ~~me,~~ ^{I,} could not agree on a

plan.

The appositive *Dr. Bell and I* renames the subject, *strategists.* Test: *I could not agree* (not *me could not agree*).

▶ The reporter interviewed only two witnesses, the bicyclist

and ~~I.~~ ^{me.}

The appositive *the bicyclist and me* renames the direct object, *witnesses.* Test: *interviewed me* (not *interviewed I*).

24d Following *than* or *as*, choose the pronoun that expresses your meaning.

When a comparison begins with *than* or *as*, your choice of a pronoun will depend on your intended meaning. Consider, for example, the difference in meaning between these sentences.

> My roommate likes football more than I.

> My roommate likes football more than me.

Finish each sentence mentally and its meaning becomes clear: *My roommate likes football more than I [do]. My roommate likes football more than [he likes] me.*

▶ In our position paper supporting nationalized health care

 in the United States, we argued that Canadians are much

 better off than ~~us.~~ ^{we.}

We is the subject of the verb *are*, which is understood: *Canadians are much better off than we [are].* If the correct English seems too formal, you can always add the verb.

▶ We respected no other candidate for the city council
 as much as ~~she.~~ ^{her.}

This sentence means that we respected no other candidate as much as *we respected her. Her* is the direct object of the understood verb *respected.*

24e For *we* or *us* before a noun, choose the pronoun that would be appropriate if the noun were omitted.

▶ ^{We} ~~Us~~ tenants would rather fight than move.

▶ Management is shortchanging ^{us} ~~we~~ tenants.

No one would say *Us would rather fight than move* or *Management is shortchanging we.*

24f Use the objective case for subjects and objects of infinitives.

An infinitive is the word *to* followed by the base form of a verb. (See 63b.) Subjects of infinitives are an exception to the rule that subjects must be in the subjective case. Whenever an infinitive has a subject, it must be in the objective case. Objects of infinitives also are in the objective case.

▶ Ms. Wilson asked John and ~~I~~ ^{me} to drive the senator and ~~she~~ ^{her} to

the airport.

John and me is the subject of the infinitive *to drive*; *senator and her* is the direct object of the infinitive.

24g Use the possessive case to modify a gerund.

A pronoun that modifies a gerund or a gerund phrase should be in the possessive case (*my, our, your, his, her, its, their*). A gerund is a verb form ending in *-ing* that functions as a noun. Gerunds frequently appear in phrases; when they do, the whole gerund phrase functions as a noun. (See 63b.)

▶ The chances of ~~you~~ ^{your} being hit by lightning are about two

million to one.

Your modifies the gerund phrase *being hit by lightning*.

Nouns as well as pronouns may modify gerunds. To form the possessive case of a noun, use an apostrophe and an *-s* (*victim's*) or just an apostrophe (*victims'*). (See 36a.)

▶ The old order in France paid a high price for the ~~aristocracy~~ ^{aristocracy's}

exploiting the lower classes.

The possessive noun *aristocracy's* modifies the gerund phrase *exploiting the lower classes*.

Gerund phrases should not be confused with participial phrases, which function as adjectives, not as nouns: *We saw him driving a yellow convertible.* Here *driving a yellow convertible* is a participial phrase modifying the pronoun *him*. (See 63b.)

The choice between the objective and the possessive case depends on your meaning; sometimes the distinction is subtle.

> We watched *them* dancing.
>
> We watched *their* dancing.

In the first sentence, the emphasis is on the people; we watched *them*, and they happened to be dancing. In the second sentence, the emphasis is on the dancing; we watched the *dancing*—a noun form modified by the possessive *their*.

NOTE: Do not use the possessive if it creates an awkward effect. Try to reword the sentence instead.

AWKWARD	The president agreed to the applications' being reviewed by a faculty committee.
REVISED	The president agreed that the applications could be reviewed by a faculty committee.
REVISED	The president agreed that a faculty committee could review the applications.

EXERCISE 24–1 Edit the following sentences to eliminate errors in pronoun case. If a sentence is correct, write "correct" after it. Answers to lettered sentences appear in the back of the book. Example:

> Grandfather cuts down trees for neighbors much younger
> than ~~him.~~ he.

a. Rick applied for the job even though he heard that other candidates were more experienced than he.
b. The volleyball team could not believe that the coach was she.
c. She appreciated him telling the truth in such a difficult situation.
d. The director has asked you and I to draft a proposal for a new recycling plan.

e. Five close friends and myself rented a station wagon, packed it with food, and drove two hundred miles to Mardi Gras.

1. The squawk of the brass horns nearly overwhelmed us oboe and bassoon players.

2. Ushio, the last rock climber up the wall, tossed Teri and she the remaining pitons and carabiners.

3. The programmer realized that her and the interface designers were creating an entirely new Web application.

4. My desire to understand classical music was aided by me working as an usher at Symphony Hall.

5. The shower of sinking bricks caused he and his diving partner to race away from the collapsing seawall.

EXERCISE 24–2 In the following paragraph, choose the correct pronoun in each set of parentheses.

We may blame television for the number of products based on characters in children's TV shows—from Big Bird to Sponge-Bob—but in fact merchandising that capitalizes on a character's popularity started long before television. Raggedy Ann began as a child's rag doll, and a few years later books about (she / her) and her brother, Raggedy Andy, were published. A cartoonist named Johnny Gruelle painted a cloth face on a family doll and applied for a patent in 1915. Later Gruelle began writing and illustrating stories about Raggedy Ann, and in 1918 (he / him) and a publisher teamed up to publish the books and sell the dolls. He was not the only one to try to sell products linked to children's stories. Beatrix Potter published the first of many Peter Rabbit picture books in 1902, and no one was better than (she / her) at making a living from spin-offs. After Peter Rabbit and Benjamin Bunny became popular, Potter began putting pictures of (they / them) and their little animal friends on merchandise. Potter had fans all over the world, and she understood (them / their) wanting to see Peter Rabbit not only in books but also on teapots and plates and lamps and other furnishings for the nursery. Potter and Gruelle, like countless others before and since, knew that entertaining children could be a profitable business.

hackerhandbooks.com/bedhandbook > Grammar exercises > Grammatical sentences
> E-ex 24–3 and 24–4
> E-ex 25–3 and 25–4 (pronoun review)

25 Distinguish between *who* and *whom*.

The choice between *who* and *whom* (or *whoever* and *whomever*) occurs primarily in subordinate clauses and in questions. *Who* and *whoever*, subjective-case pronouns, are used for subjects and subject complements. *Whom* and *whomever*, objective-case pronouns, are used for objects. (See 25a and 25b.)

An exception to this general rule occurs when the pronoun functions as the subject of an infinitive (see 25c). See also 24f.

Consult the chart on page 278 for a summary of the trouble spots with *who* and *whom*.

> **Grammar checkers** catch misuses of *who* and *whom* (or *whoever* and *whomever*) only about half the time. Pay special attention to sentences that include *who* or *whom* as you edit your writing.

25a In subordinate clauses, use *who* and *whoever* for subjects and subject complements, *whom* and *whomever* for all objects.

When *who* and *whom* (or *whoever* and *whomever*) introduce subordinate clauses, their case is determined by their function *within the clause they introduce*. To choose the correct pronoun, you must isolate the subordinate clause and then decide how the pronoun functions within it. (See "subordinate clauses," 63e.)

In the following two examples, the pronouns *who* and *whoever* function as the subjects of the clauses they introduce.

> ▶ First prize goes to the runner ~~whom~~ *who* earns the most
>
> points.

> The subordinate clause is *who earns the most points.* The verb of the clause is *earns,* and its subject is *who.*

▶ **Maya Angelou's *I Know Why the Caged Bird Sings* should be**
    whoever
read by ~~whomever~~ **is interested in the effects of racial**

prejudice on children.

The writer selected the pronoun *whomever*, thinking that it was
the object of the preposition *by*. However, the object of the preposition is the entire subordinate clause *whoever is interested in the
effects of racial prejudice on children*. The verb of the clause is *is*, and
the subject of the verb is *whoever*.

Who occasionally functions as a subject complement in a
subordinate clause. Subject complements occur with linking
verbs (usually *be*, *am*, *is*, *are*, *was*, *were*, *being*, and *been*). When
who is a subject complement, it appears in inverted order, before the subject and verb. (See 62b.)

▶ **From your social security number, anyone can find out**
    who
~~whom~~ **you are.**

The subordinate clause is *who you are*. Its subject is *you*, and its
subject complement is *who*.

When functioning as an object in a subordinate clause,
whom (or *whomever*) also appears out of order, before the subject and verb. To choose the correct pronoun, you can mentally restructure the clause.

                                           whom
▶ **You will work with our senior traders,** ~~who~~ **you will meet**

later.

The subordinate clause is *whom you will meet later*. The subject of
the clause is *you* and the verb is *will meet*. *Whom* is the direct object of the verb. The correct choice becomes clear if you mentally
restructure the clause: *you will meet whom*.

When functioning as the object of a preposition in
a subordinate clause, *whom* is often separated from its
preposition.

▶ The tutor ~~who~~ ^{whom} I was assigned to was very supportive.

> *Whom* is the object of the preposition *to*. In this sentence, the writer might choose to drop *whom*: *The tutor I was assigned to was very supportive.*

NOTE: Inserted expressions such as *they know*, *I think*, and *she says* should be ignored in determining whether to use *who* or *whom*.

▶ The speech pathologist reported a particularly difficult

  session with a stroke patient ~~whom~~ ^{who} she knew was suffering

  from aphasia.

> *Who* is the subject of *was suffering*, not the object of *knew*.

25b In questions, use *who* and *whoever* for subjects, *whom* and *whomever* for all objects.

When *who* and *whom* (or *whoever* and *whomever*) are used to open questions, their case is determined by their function within the question. In the following example, *who* functions as the subject of the question.

▶ ~~Whom~~ ^{Who} was responsible for creating that computer virus?

> *Who* is the subject of the verb *was*.

When *whom* functions as the object of a verb or the object of a preposition in a question, it appears out of normal order. To choose the correct pronoun, you can mentally restructure the question.

▶ ~~Who~~ ^{Whom} did the Democratic Party nominate in 2004?

> *Whom* is the direct object of the verb *did nominate*. This becomes clear if you restructure the question: *The Democratic Party did nominate whom in 2004?*

Checking for problems with *who* and *whom*

In subordinate clauses (25a)

Isolate the subordinate clause. Then read its subject, verb, and any objects, restructuring the clause if necessary. Some writers find it helpful to substitute *he* for *who* and *him* for *whom*.

Samuels hoped to become the business partner of (whoever/whomever) found the treasure.

TEST: . . . *whoever* found the treasure. [. . . *he* found the treasure.]

Ada always seemed to be bestowing a favor on (whoever/whomever) she worked for.

TEST: . . . she worked for *whomever*. [. . . she worked for *him*.]

In questions (25b)

Read the subject, verb, and any objects, rearranging the sentence structure if necessary.

(Who/Whom) conferred with Roosevelt and Stalin at Yalta in 1945?

TEST: *Who* conferred . . . ?

(Who/Whom) did the committee nominate?

TEST: The committee did nominate *whom*?

> Whom
> ► ~~Who~~ did you enter into the contract with?
>   ^

Whom is the object of the preposition *with,* as is clear if you recast the question: *You did enter into the contract with whom?*

25c Use *whom* for subjects or objects of infinitives.

An infinitive is the word *to* followed by the base form of a verb. (See 63b.) Subjects of infinitives are an exception to the rule that subjects must be in the subjective case. The subject of an infinitive must be in the objective case. Objects of infinitives also are in the objective case.

▶ When it comes to money, I know ~~who~~ *whom* to believe.

> The infinitive phrase *whom to believe* is the direct object of the verb *know*, and *whom* is the subject of the infinitive *to believe*.

NOTE: In spoken English, *who* is frequently used when the correct *whom* sounds too stuffy. Even educated speakers are likely to say *Who* [not *Whom*] *did Joe replace?* Although some readers will accept such constructions in informal written English, it is safer to use *whom* in formal English: *Whom did Joe replace?*

EXERCISE 25–1   Edit the following sentences to eliminate errors in the use of *who* and *whom* (or *whoever* and *whomever*). If a sentence is correct, write "correct" after it. Answers to lettered sentences appear in the back of the book. Example:

> What is the address of the artist ~~who~~ *whom* Antonio hired?

a. The roundtable featured scholars who I had never heard of.
b. Arriving late for rehearsal, we had no idea who was supposed to dance with whom.
c. Whom did you support for student government president?
d. Daniel always gives a holiday donation to whomever needs it.
e. So many singers came to the audition that Natalia had trouble deciding who to select for the choir.

1. My cousin Sylvie, who I am teaching to fly a kite, watches us every time we compete.
2. Who decided to research the history of Hungarians in New Brunswick?
3. According to Greek myth, the Sphinx devoured those who could not answer her riddles.
4. The people who ordered their medications from Canada were retirees whom don't have health insurance.
5. Who did the committee select?

hackerhandbooks.com/bedhandbook > Grammar exercises > Grammatical sentences
> E-ex 25–2
> E-ex 25–3 and 25–4 (pronoun review)

26   Choose adjectives and adverbs with care.

Adjectives modify nouns or pronouns. They usually come before the word they modify; occasionally they function as complements following the word they modify. Adverbs modify verbs, adjectives, or other adverbs. (See 61d and 61e.)

Many adverbs are formed by adding *-ly* to adjectives (*normal, normally; smooth, smoothly*). But don't assume that all words ending in *-ly* are adverbs or that all adverbs end in *-ly*. Some adjectives end in *-ly* (*lovely, friendly*), and some adverbs don't (*always, here, there*). When in doubt, consult a dictionary.

> **ESL**   Placement of adjectives and adverbs can be a tricky matter for multilingual writers. See 30f and 30h.

26a   Use adjectives to modify nouns.

Adjectives ordinarily precede the nouns they modify. But they can also function as subject complements or object complements, following the nouns they modify.

> **ESL**   In English, adjectives are not pluralized to agree with the words they modify: *The red* [not *reds*] *roses were a surprise.*

Subject complements

A subject complement follows a linking verb and completes the meaning of the subject. (See 62b.) When an adjective functions as a subject complement, it describes the subject.

Justice is *blind.*

Problems can arise with verbs such as *smell*, *taste*, *look*, and *feel*, which sometimes, but not always, function as linking verbs. If the word following one of these verbs describes the subject, use an adjective; if the word following the verb modifies the verb, use an adverb.

ADJECTIVE   The detective looked *cautious*.

ADVERB   The detective looked *cautiously* for fingerprints.

The adjective *cautious* describes the detective; the adverb *cautiously* modifies the verb *looked*.

Linking verbs suggest states of being, not actions. Notice, for example, the different meanings of *looked* in the preceding examples. To look cautious suggests the state of being cautious; to look cautiously is to perform an action in a cautious way.

▶ **The lilacs in our backyard smell especially ~~sweetly~~ this year.**
                                         sweet

The verb *smell* suggests a state of being, not an action. Therefore, it should be followed by an adjective, not an adverb.

▶ **The drawings looked ~~well~~ after the architect made a few**
                          good

   changes.

The verb *looked* is a linking verb suggesting a state of being, not an action. The adjective *good* is appropriate following the linking verb to describe *drawings*. (See also 26c.)

Object complements

An object complement follows a direct object and completes its meaning. (See 62b.) When an adjective functions as an object complement, it describes the direct object.

Sorrow makes *us wise*.

Object complements occur with verbs such as *call*, *consider*, *create*, *find*, *keep*, and *make*. When a modifier follows the direct object of one of these verbs, use an adjective to describe the direct object; use an adverb to modify the verb.

ADJECTIVE   The referee called the plays *perfect*.

ADVERB   The referee called the plays *perfectly*.

The first sentence means that the referee considered the plays to be perfect; the second means that the referee did an excellent job of calling the plays.

► **In terms of sharpness, Ray considers cheddar and Swiss**
equal.
~~equally.~~
∧

The adjective *equal* is an object complement describing the direct object *cheddar and Swiss*.

Grammar checkers sometimes flag problems with adjectives and adverbs: some misuses of *bad* or *badly* and *good* or *well*; some double comparisons, such as *more meaner*; some absolute comparisons, such as *most unique*; and some double negatives, such as *can't hardly*. However, the programs miss more problems than they find.

26b Use adverbs to modify verbs, adjectives, and other adverbs.

When adverbs modify verbs (or verbals), they nearly always answer the question When? Where? How? Why? Under what conditions? How often? or To what degree? When adverbs modify adjectives or other adverbs, they usually qualify or intensify the meaning of the word they modify. (See 61e.)

Adjectives are often used incorrectly in place of adverbs in casual or nonstandard speech.

► The transportation arrangement worked out ^{perfectly} ~~perfect~~ for
∧

everyone.

▶ The manager must see that the office runs ~~smooth~~ *smoothly* and
~~efficient.~~ *efficiently.*

The adverb *perfectly* modifies the verb *worked out*; the adverbs
smoothly and *efficiently* modify the verb *runs*.

▶ The chance of recovering any property lost in the fire looks
~~real~~ *really* slim.

Only adverbs can modify adjectives or other adverbs. *Really* intensifies
the meaning of the adjective *slim*.

26c Distinguish between *good* and *well*, *bad* and *badly*.

Good is an adjective (*good performance*). *Well* is an adverb when
it modifies a verb (*speak well*). The use of the adjective *good* in
place of the adverb *well* to modify a verb is nonstandard and
especially common in casual speech.

▶ We were glad that Sanya had done ~~good~~ *well* on the CPA exam.

The adverb *well* modifies the verb *had done*.

Confusion can arise because *well* is an adjective when it
modifies a noun or pronoun and means "healthy" or "satisfactory" (*The babies were well and warm*).

▶ Adrienne did not feel ~~good,~~ *well,* but she made her presentation

anyway.

As an adjective following the linking verb *did feel*, *well* describes
Adrienne's health.

Bad is always an adjective and should be used to describe a
noun; *badly* is always an adverb and should be used to modify
a verb. The adverb *badly* is often used inappropriately to describe a noun, especially following a linking verb.

> The sisters felt ~~badly~~ *bad* when they realized they had left their
>
> brother out of the planning.

The adjective *bad* is used after the linking verb *felt* to describe the noun *sisters*.

26d Use comparatives and superlatives with care.

Most adjectives and adverbs have three forms: the positive, the comparative, and the superlative.

POSITIVE	COMPARATIVE	SUPERLATIVE
soft	softer	softest
fast	faster	fastest
careful	more careful	most careful
bad	worse	worst
good	better	best

Comparative versus superlative

Use the comparative to compare two things, the superlative to compare three or more.

> Which of these two low-carb drinks is ~~best?~~ *better?*

> Though Shaw and Jackson are impressive, Hobbs is the
> ~~more~~ *most* qualified of the three candidates running for mayor.

Forming comparatives and superlatives

To form comparatives and superlatives of most one- and two-syllable adjectives, use the endings *-er* and *-est*: *smooth, smoother, smoothest; easy, easier, easiest.* With longer adjectives, use *more* and *most* (or *less* and *least* for downward comparisons): *exciting, more exciting, most exciting; helpful, less helpful, least helpful.*

Some one-syllable adverbs take the endings *-er* and *-est*
(*fast, faster, fastest*), but longer adverbs and all of those ending
in *-ly* form the comparative and superlative with *more* and *most*
(or *less* and *least*).

The comparative and superlative forms of some adjectives
and adverbs are irregular: *good, better, best; well, better, best; bad,
worse, worst; badly, worse, worst*.

► The Kirov is the ~~talentedest~~ ballet company we have seen.
  most talented

► According to our projections, sales at local businesses will

  be ~~worser~~ than those at the chain stores this winter.
  worse

Double comparatives or superlatives

Do not use double comparatives or superlatives. When you
have added *-er* or *-est* to an adjective or adverb, do not also use
more or *most* (or *less* or *least*).

► Of all her family, Julia is the ~~most~~ happiest about the move.

► All the polls indicated that Gore was more ~~likelier~~ to win
  likely

  than Bush.

Absolute concepts

Avoid expressions such as *more straight, less perfect, very round,*
and *most unique*. Either something is unique or it isn't. It is illogical to suggest that absolute concepts come in degrees.

► That is the most ~~unique~~ wedding gown I have ever seen.
  unusual

► The painting would have been even more ~~priceless~~ had it
  valuable

  been signed.

26e Avoid double negatives.

Standard English allows two negatives only if a positive meaning is intended: *The orchestra was not unhappy with its performance* (meaning that the orchestra was happy). Using a double negative to emphasize a negative meaning is nonstandard.

Negative modifiers such as *never, no,* and *not* should not be paired with other negative modifiers or with negative words such as *neither, none, no one, nobody,* and *nothing.*

▶ Management is not doing ~~nothing~~ anything to see that the trash is

picked up.

The double negative *not . . . nothing* is nonstandard.

The modifiers *hardly, barely,* and *scarcely* are considered negatives in standard English, so they should not be used with negatives such as *not, no one,* or *never.*

▶ Maxine is so weak that she ~~can't~~ can hardly climb stairs.

EXERCISE 26–1   Edit the following sentences to eliminate errors in the use of adjectives and adverbs. If a sentence is correct, write "correct" after it. Answers to lettered sentences appear in the back of the book. Example:

We weren't surprised by how ~~good~~ well the sidecar racing team

flowed through the tricky course.

a.   Did you do good on last week's chemistry exam?
b.   With the budget deadline approaching, our office hasn't hardly had time to handle routine correspondence.
c.   Some flowers smell surprisingly bad.

d.   The customer complained that he hadn't been treated nice.
e.   Of all my relatives, Uncle Roberto is the most cleverest.

1.   When you answer the phone, speak clear and courteous.
2.   Who was more upset about the loss? Was it the coach or the quarterback or the owner of the team?
3.   To a novice skateboarder, even the basic ollie seems real challenging.
4.   After checking how bad I had been hurt, my sister dialed 911.
5.   If the college's Web page had been updated more regular, students would have learned about the new course offerings.

EXERCISE 26–2   Edit the following passage to eliminate errors in the use of adjectives and adverbs.

Doctors recommend that to give skin the most fullest protection from ultraviolet rays, people should use plenty of sunscreen, limit sun exposure, and wear protective clothing. The commonest sunscreens today are known as "broad spectrum" because they block out both UVA and UVB rays. These lotions don't feel any differently on the skin from the old UVA-only types, but they work best at preventing premature aging and skin cancer. Many sunscreens claim to be waterproof, but they won't hardly provide adequate coverage after extended periods of swimming or perspiring. To protect good, even waterproof sunscreens should be reapplied liberal and often. All areas of exposed skin, including ears, backs of hands, and tops of feet, need to be coated good to avoid burning or damage. Some people's skin reacts bad to PABA, or para-aminobenzoic acid, so PABA-free (hypoallergenic) sunscreens are widely available. In addition to recommending sunscreen, doctors almost unanimously agree that people should stay out of the sun when rays are the most strongest—between 10:00 a.m. and 3:00 p.m.—and should limit time in the sun. They also suggest that people wear long-sleeved shirts, broad-brimmed hats, and long pants whenever possible.

hackerhandbooks.com/bedhandbook > Grammar exercises > Grammatical sentences
> E-ex 26–3 and 26–4

27 Choose appropriate verb forms, tenses, and moods in standard English.

In speech, some people use verb forms and tenses that match a home dialect or variety of English. In writing, use standard English verb forms unless you are quoting nonstandard speech or using alternative forms for literary effect. (See 17d.)

Except for the verb *be*, all verbs in English have five forms. The following list shows the five forms and provides a sample sentence in which each might appear.

BASE FORM	Usually I (*walk, ride*).
PAST TENSE	Yesterday I (*walked, rode*).
PAST PARTICIPLE	I have (*walked, ridden*) many times before.
PRESENT PARTICIPLE	I am (*walking, riding*) right now.
-S FORM	He/she/it (*walks, rides*) regularly.

Both the past-tense and past-participle forms of regular verbs end in *-ed* (*walked, walked*). Irregular verbs form the past tense and past participle in other ways (*rode, ridden*).

The verb *be* has eight forms instead of the usual five: *be, am, is, are, was, were, being, been.*

> Grammar checkers sometimes flag misused irregular verbs in sentences. But you cannot rely on grammar checkers to identify problems with irregular verbs—they miss about twice as many errors as they find.

27a Choose standard English forms of irregular verbs.

For all regular verbs, the past-tense and past-participle forms are the same (ending in *-ed* or *-d*), so there is no danger of confusion. This is not true, however, for irregular verbs, such as the following.

BASE FORM	PAST TENSE	PAST PARTICIPLE
go	went	gone
break	broke	broken
fly	flew	flown

The past-tense form always occurs alone, without a help-ing verb. It expresses action that occurred entirely in the past: *I rode to work yesterday. I walked to work last Tuesday.* The past participle is used with a helping verb. It forms the perfect tenses with *has*, *have*, or *had*; it forms the passive voice with *be*, *am*, *is*, *are*, *was*, *were*, *being*, or *been*. (See 61c for a com-plete list of helping verbs and 27f for a survey of tenses.)

PAST TENSE	Last July, we *went* to Paris.
HELPING VERB + PAST PARTICIPLE	We *have gone* to Paris twice.

The list of common irregular verbs beginning on the next page will help you distinguish between the past tense and the past participle. Choose the past-participle form if the verb in your sentence requires a helping verb; choose the past-tense form if the verb does not require a helping verb. (See verb tenses in 27f.)

▶ Yesterday we ~~seen~~ ^{saw} a documentary about Isabel Allende.

The past-tense *saw* is required because there is no helping verb.

▶ The truck was apparently ~~stole~~ ^{stolen} while the driver ate lunch.

▶ By Friday, the stock market had ~~fell~~ ^{fallen} two hundred points.

Because of the helping verbs *was* and *had*, the past-participle forms are required: *was stolen, had fallen*.

When in doubt about the standard English forms of irreg-ular verbs, consult the list on pages 290–92 or look up the base form of the verb in the dictionary, which also lists any irreg-ular forms. (If no additional forms are listed in the dictionary, the verb is regular, not irregular.)

Common irregular verbs

BASE FORM	PAST TENSE	PAST PARTICIPLE
arise	arose	arisen
awake	awoke, awaked	awaked, awoke, awoken
be	was, were	been
beat	beat	beaten, beat
become	became	become
begin	began	begun
bend	bent	bent
bite	bit	bitten, bit
blow	blew	blown
break	broke	broken
bring	brought	brought
build	built	built
burst	burst	burst
buy	bought	bought
catch	caught	caught
choose	chose	chosen
cling	clung	clung
come	came	come
cost	cost	cost
deal	dealt	dealt
dig	dug	dug
dive	dived, dove	dived
do	did	done
drag	dragged	dragged
draw	drew	drawn
dream	dreamed, dreamt	dreamed, dreamt
drink	drank	drunk
drive	drove	driven
eat	ate	eaten
fall	fell	fallen
fight	fought	fought
find	found	found
fly	flew	flown
forget	forgot	forgotten, forgot
freeze	froze	frozen
get	got	gotten, got
give	gave	given
go	went	gone

BASE FORM	PAST TENSE	PAST PARTICIPLE
grow	grew	grown
hang (execute)	hanged	hanged
hang (suspend)	hung	hung
have	had	had
hear	heard	heard
hide	hid	hidden
hurt	hurt	hurt
keep	kept	kept
know	knew	known
lay (put)	laid	laid
lead	led	led
lend	lent	lent
let (allow)	let	let
lie (recline)	lay	lain
lose	lost	lost
make	made	made
prove	proved	proved, proven
read	read	read
ride	rode	ridden
ring	rang	rung
rise (get up)	rose	risen
run	ran	run
say	said	said
see	saw	seen
send	sent	sent
set (place)	set	set
shake	shook	shaken
shoot	shot	shot
shrink	shrank	shrunk
sing	sang	sung
sink	sank	sunk
sit (be seated)	sat	sat
slay	slew	slain
sleep	slept	slept
speak	spoke	spoken
spin	spun	spun
spring	sprang	sprung
stand	stood	stood
steal	stole	stolen
sting	stung	stung

BASE FORM	PAST TENSE	PAST PARTICIPLE
strike	struck	struck, stricken
swear	swore	sworn
swim	swam	swum
swing	swung	swung
take	took	taken
teach	taught	taught
throw	threw	thrown
wake	woke, waked	waked, woken
wear	wore	worn
wring	wrung	wrung
write	wrote	written

27b Distinguish among the forms of *lie* and *lay*.

Writers and speakers frequently confuse the various forms of *lie* (meaning "to recline or rest on a surface") and *lay* (meaning "to put or place something"). *Lie* is an intransitive verb; it does not take a direct object: *The tax forms lie on the table.* The verb *lay* is transitive; it takes a direct object: *Please lay the tax forms on the table.* (See 62b.)

In addition to confusing the meaning of *lie* and *lay*, writers and speakers are often unfamiliar with the standard English forms of these verbs.

BASE FORM	PAST TENSE	PAST PARTICIPLE	PRESENT PARTICIPLE
lie ("recline")	lay	lain	lying
lay ("put")	laid	laid	laying

▶ Sue was so exhausted that she ~~laid~~ *lay* down for a nap.

The past-tense form of *lie* ("to recline") is *lay*.

▶ The patient had ~~laid~~ *lain* in an uncomfortable position all night.

The past-participle form of *lie* ("to recline") is *lain*. If the correct English seems too stilted, recast the sentence: *The patient had been lying in an uncomfortable position all night.*

► The prosecutor ~~lay~~ ^{laid} the pistol on a table close to the jurors.

The past-tense form of *lay* ("to place") is *laid*.

► Letters dating from the Civil War were ~~laying~~ ^{lying} in the corner of the chest.

The present participle of *lie* ("to rest on a surface") is *lying*.

EXERCISE 27–1   Edit the following sentences to eliminate problems with irregular verbs. If a sentence is correct, write "correct" after it. Answers to lettered sentences appear in the back of the book. Example:

The ranger ~~seen~~ ^{saw} the forest fire ten miles away.

a.   When I get the urge to exercise, I lay down until it passes.
b.   Grandmother had drove our new hybrid to the sunrise church service on Savage Mountain, so we were left with the station wagon.
c.   A pile of dirty rags was laying at the bottom of the stairs.
d.   How did the computer know that the gamer had went from the room with the blue ogre to the hall where the gold was heaped?
e.   Abraham Lincoln took good care of his legal clients; the contracts he drew for the Illinois Central Railroad could never be broke.

1.   The burglar must have gone immediately upstairs, grabbed what looked good, and took off.
2.   Have you ever dreamed that you were falling from a cliff or flying through the air?
3.   Tomás reached for the pen, signed the title page of his novel, and then laid the book on the table for the first customer in line.
4.   In her junior year, Cindy run the 440-yard dash in 51.1 seconds.
5.   Larry claimed that he had drank too much soda, but Esther suspected the truth.

hackerhandbooks.com/bedhandbook > Grammar exercises > Grammatical sentences
> E-ex 27–4 and 27–5

27c Use *-s* (or *-es*) endings on present-tense verbs that have third-person singular subjects.

All singular nouns (*child*, *tree*) and the pronouns *he*, *she*, and *it* are third-person singular; indefinite pronouns such as *everyone* and *neither* are also third-person singular. When the subject of a sentence is third-person singular, its verb takes an *-s* or *-es* ending in the present tense. (See also 21.)

	SINGULAR		**PLURAL**	
FIRST PERSON	I	know	we	know
SECOND PERSON	you	know	you	know
THIRD PERSON	he/she/it	knows	they	know
	child	knows	parents	know
	everyone	knows		

▶ My neighbor ~~drive~~ **drives** to Marco Island every weekend in the summer.

▶ Sulfur dioxide ~~turn~~ **turns** leaves yellow, ~~dissolve~~ **dissolves** marble, and ~~eat~~ **eats** away iron and steel.

The subjects *cousin* and *sulfur dioxide* are third-person singular, so the verbs must end in *-s*.

TIP: Do not add the *-s* ending to the verb if the subject is not third-person singular. The writers of the following sentences, knowing they sometimes dropped *-s* endings from verbs, over-corrected by adding the endings where they don't belong.

▶ I prepare~~s~~ program specifications and logic diagrams for every installation.

The writer mistakenly concluded that the *-s* ending belongs on present-tense verbs used with *all* singular subjects, not just *third-person* singular subjects. The pronoun *I* is first-person singular, so its verb does not require the *-s*.

▶ The dirt floors requires continual sweeping.

> The writer mistakenly thought that the verb needed an *-s* ending because of the plural subject. But the *-s* ending is used only on present-tense verbs with third-person *singular* subjects.

Has *versus* have

In the present tense, use *has* with third-person singular subjects; all other subjects require *have*.

	SINGULAR		PLURAL	
FIRST PERSON	I	have	we	have
SECOND PERSON	you	have	you	have
THIRD PERSON	he/she/it	has	they	have

▶ This respected musician almost always ~~have~~ *has* a message to

convey in his work.

▶ The retirement program ~~have~~ *has* finally been established.

> The subjects *musician* and *program* are third-person singular, so the verb should be *has* in each case.

TIP: Do not use *has* if the subject is not third-person singular.

▶ My law classes ~~has~~ *have* helped me understand contracts.

▶ I ~~has~~ *have* much to be thankful for.

> The subjects of these sentences—*classes* and *I*—are third-person plural and first-person singular, so standard English requires *have*. *Has* is used only with third-person singular subjects.

Does *versus* do *and* doesn't *versus* don't

In the present tense, use *does* and *doesn't* with third-person singular subjects; all other subjects require *do* and *don't*.

	SINGULAR		PLURAL	
FIRST PERSON	I	do/don't	we	do/don't
SECOND PERSON	you	do/don't	you	do/don't
THIRD PERSON	he/she/it	does/doesn't	they	do/don't

▶   Grandfather really ~~don't~~ *doesn't* have a place to call home.

▶   *Does* ~~Do~~ she know the correct procedure for setting up the

experiment?

Grandfather and *she* are third-person singular, so the verbs should
be *doesn't* and *Does*.

Am, is, *and* are; was *and* were

The verb *be* has three forms in the present tense (*am, is, are*) and
two in the past tense (*was, were*).

	SINGULAR		PLURAL	
FIRST PERSON	I	am/was	we	are/were
SECOND PERSON	you	are/were	you	are/were
THIRD PERSON	he/she/it	is/was	they	are/were

▶   Judy wanted to borrow Tim's notes, but she *was* ~~were~~ too shy to

ask for them.

The subject *she* is third-person singular, so the verb should be *was*.

▶   Did you think you *were* ~~was~~ going to drown?

The subject *you* is second-person singular, so the verb should be *were*.

Grammar checkers are fairly good at catching missing *-s* endings on
verbs and some misused *-s* forms of the verb. Also see the grammar
checker advice on page 244.

27d Do not omit *-ed* endings on verbs.

Speakers who do not fully pronounce *-ed* endings sometimes omit them unintentionally in writing. Failure to pronounce *-ed* endings is common in many dialects and in informal speech even in standard English. In the following frequently used words and phrases, for example, the *-ed* ending is not always fully pronounced.

advised	developed	prejudiced	supposed to
asked	fixed	pronounced	used to
concerned	frightened	stereotyped	

When a verb is regular, both the past tense and the past participle are formed by adding *-ed* (or *-d*) to the base form of the verb.

Past tense

Use an *-ed* or *-d* ending to express the past tense of regular verbs. The past tense is used when the action occurred entirely in the past.

▶ Over the weekend, Ed ~~fix~~ *fixed* his brother's skateboard and tuned up his mother's 1991 Fiat.

▶ Last summer, my counselor ~~advise~~ *advised* me to ask my chemistry instructor for help.

Past participles

Past participles are used in three ways: (1) following *have, has,* or *had* to form one of the perfect tenses; (2) following *be, am, is, are, was, were, being,* or *been* to form the passive voice; and (3) as adjectives modifying nouns or pronouns. The perfect tenses are listed on page 301, and the passive voice is discussed in 8a. For a discussion of participles as adjectives, see 63b.

▶ Robin has ~~ask~~ ^{asked} for more housing staff for next year.

> *Has asked* is present perfect tense (*have* or *has* followed by a past participle).

▶ Though it is not a new phenomenon, domestic violence is now ~~publicize~~ ^{publicized} more than ever.

> *Is publicized* is a verb in the passive voice (a form of *be* followed by a past participle).

▶ All aerobics classes end in a cool-down period to stretch ~~tighten~~ ^{tightened} muscles.

> The past participle *tightened* functions as an adjective modifying the noun *muscles*.

> **Grammar checkers** flag missing *-ed* endings on verbs more often than not. Unfortunately, they often suggest an *-ing* ending (*passing*) rather than the missing *-ed* ending (*passed*), when they encounter a sentence like this: *The law was pass last week.*

27e Do not omit needed verbs.

Although standard English allows some linking verbs and helping verbs to be contracted in informal contexts, it does not allow them to be omitted.

Linking verbs, used to link subjects to subject complements, are frequently a form of *be*: *be, am, is, are, was, were, being, been.* (See 62b.) Some of these forms may be contracted (*I'm, she's, we're, you're, they're*), but they should not be omitted altogether.

▶ When we ^{are} quiet in the evening, we can hear crickets in the woods.

▶ Sherman Alexie *is* a Native American author whose stories

have been made into a film.

   Helping verbs, used with main verbs, include forms of *be*, *do*, and *have* and the modal verbs *can*, *will*, *shall*, *could*, *would*, *should*, *may*, *might*, and *must*. (See 61c.) Some helping verbs may be contracted (*he's leaving*, *we'll celebrate*, *they've been told*), but they should not be omitted altogether.

▶ We *have* been in Chicago since last Thursday.

▶ Do you know someone who *would* be good for the job?

ESL   Some languages do not require a linking verb between a subject and its complement. English, however, requires a verb in every sentence. See 30a.

▶ Every night, I read a short book to my daughter. When I *am*

too busy, my husband reads to her.

Grammar checkers flag omitted verbs about half the time—but they often miss needed helping verbs. Proofread your work carefully to avoid leaving out helping verbs.

EXERCISE 27–2   Edit the following sentences to eliminate problems with -*s* and -*ed* verb forms and with omitted verbs. If a sentence is correct, write "correct" after it. Answers to lettered sentences appear in the back of the book. Example:

The Pell Grant sometimes ~~cover~~ *covers* the student's full tuition.

a.   The glass sculptures of the Swan Boats was prominent in the brightly lit lobby.

b. Visitors to the glass museum were not suppose to touch the exhibits.

c. Our church has all the latest technology, even a close-circuit television.

d. Christos didn't know about Marlo's promotion because he never listens. He always talking.

e. Most psychologists agree that no one performs well under stress.

1. Have there ever been a time in your life when you were too depressed to get out of bed?

2. My days in this department have taught me to do what I'm told without asking questions.

3. We have change our plan and are waiting out the storm before leaving.

4. Winter training for search-and-rescue divers consist of building up a tolerance to icy water temperatures.

5. How would you feel if a love one had been a victim of a crime like this?

hackerhandbooks.com/bedhandbook > Grammar exercises > Grammatical sentences > E-ex 27–6 and 27–7

27f Choose the appropriate verb tense.

Tenses indicate the time of an action in relation to the time of the speaking or writing about that action.

The most common problem with tenses — shifting confusingly from one tense to another — is discussed in section 13. Other problems with tenses are detailed in this section, after the following survey of tenses.

> **Grammar checkers** do not flag most problems with tense discussed in this section: special uses of the present tense, use of past versus past perfect tense, and sequence of tenses.

Survey of tenses

Tenses are classified as present, past, and future, with simple, perfect, and progressive forms for each.

Simple tenses   The simple tenses indicate relatively simple time relations. The *simple present* tense is used primarily for actions occurring at the same time they are being discussed or for actions occurring regularly. The *simple past* tense is used for actions completed in the past. The *simple future* tense is used for actions that will occur in the future. In the following table, the simple tenses are given for the regular verb *walk*, the irregular verb *ride*, and the highly irregular verb *be*.

SIMPLE PRESENT

SINGULAR		PLURAL	
I	walk, ride, am	we	walk, ride, are
you	walk, ride, are	you	walk, ride, are
he/she/it	walks, rides, is	they	walk, ride, are

SIMPLE PAST

SINGULAR		PLURAL	
I	walked, rode, was	we	walked, rode, were
you	walked, rode, were	you	walked, rode, were
he/she/it	walked, rode, was	they	walked, rode, were

SIMPLE FUTURE

I, you, he/she/it, we, they	will walk, ride, be

Perfect tenses   More complex time relations are indicated by the perfect tenses. A verb in one of the perfect tenses (a form of *have* plus the past participle) expresses an action that was or will be completed at the time of another action.

PRESENT PERFECT

I, you, we, they	have walked, ridden, been
he/she/it	has walked, ridden, been

PAST PERFECT

I, you, he/she/it, we, they	had walked, ridden, been

FUTURE PERFECT

I, you, he/she/it, we, they	will have walked, ridden, been

Progressive forms The simple and perfect tenses have progressive forms that describe actions in progress. A progressive verb consists of a form of *be* followed by a present participle. The progressive forms are not normally used with certain verbs, such as *believe, know, hear, seem,* and *think.*

PRESENT PROGRESSIVE

I	am walking, riding, being
he/she/it	is walking, riding, being
you, we, they	are walking, riding, being

PAST PROGRESSIVE

I, he/she/it	was walking, riding, being
you, we, they	were walking, riding, being

FUTURE PROGRESSIVE

I, you, he/she/it, we, they	will be walking, riding, being

PRESENT PERFECT PROGRESSIVE

I, you, we, they	have been walking, riding, being
he/she/it	has been walking, riding, being

PAST PERFECT PROGRESSIVE

I, you, he/she/it, we, they	had been walking, riding, being

FUTURE PERFECT PROGRESSIVE

I, you, he/she/it, we, they	will have been walking, riding, being

> **ESL** See 28a for more specific examples of verb tenses that can be challenging for multilingual writers.

Special uses of the present tense

Use the present tense when expressing general truths, when writing about literature, and when quoting, summarizing, or paraphrasing an author's views.

General truths or scientific principles should appear in the present tense unless such principles have been disproved.

> *revolves*
> ▶ Galileo taught that the earth ~~revolved~~ around the sun.

Because Galileo's teaching has not been discredited, the verb should be in the present tense. The following sentence, however, is acceptable: *Ptolemy taught that the sun revolved around the earth.*

When writing about a work of literature, you may be tempted to use the past tense. The convention, however, is to describe fictional events in the present tense.

> *reaches*
> ▶ In Masuji Ibuse's *Black Rain*, a child ~~reached~~ for a
>
> pomegranate in his mother's garden, and a moment later
>
> *is*
> he ~~was~~ dead, killed by the blast of the atomic bomb.

When you are quoting, summarizing, or paraphrasing the author of a nonliterary work, use present-tense verbs such as *writes*, *reports*, *asserts*, and so on to introduce the source. This convention is usually followed even when the author is dead (unless a date or the context specifies the time of writing).

> *argues*
> ▶ Dr. Jerome Groopman ~~argued~~ that doctors are
>
> "susceptible to the subtle and not so subtle efforts of the
>
> pharmaceutical industry to sculpt our thinking" (9).

Writing with sources
MLA-style citation

In MLA style, signal phrases are written in the present tense, not the past tense. (See also 52b.)

APA NOTE: When you are documenting a paper with the APA (American Psychological Association) style of in-text citations, use past tense verbs such as *reported* or *demonstrated* or present perfect verbs such as *has reported* or *has demonstrated* to introduce the source.

> E. Wilson (1994) reported that positive reinforcement alone was a less effective teaching technique than a mixture of positive reinforcement and constructive criticism.

The past perfect tense

The past perfect tense consists of a past participle preceded by *had* (*had worked, had gone*). This tense is used for an action already completed by the time of another past action or for an action already completed at some specific past time.

> Everyone *had spoken* by the time I arrived.

> I pleaded my case, but Paula *had made up* her mind.

Writers sometimes use the simple past tense when they should use the past perfect.

▶ We built our cabin high on a pine knoll, forty feet above an
abandoned quarry that ~~was~~ flooded in 1920 to create a lake.
(had been)

The building of the cabin and the flooding of the quarry both occurred in the past, but the flooding was completed before the time of building.

▶ By the time dinner was served, the guest of honor left.
(had)

The past perfect tense is needed because the action of leaving was already completed at a specific past time (when dinner was served).

Some writers tend to overuse the past perfect tense. Do not use the past perfect if two past actions occurred at the same time.

▶ When Ernest Hemingway lived in Cuba, he ~~had written~~
(wrote)

For Whom the Bell Tolls.

Sequence of tenses with infinitives and participles

An infinitive is the base form of a verb preceded by *to*. (See 63b.) Use the present infinitive to show action at the same time as or later than the action of the verb in the sentence.

▶ The club had hoped to ~~have raised~~ a thousand dollars by *raise*

April 1.

The action expressed in the infinitive (*to raise*) occurred later than the action of the sentence's verb (*had hoped*).

Use the perfect form of an infinitive (*to have* followed by the past participle) for an action occurring earlier than that of the verb in the sentence.

▶ Dan would like to ~~join~~ the navy, but he did not pass the *have joined*

physical.

The liking occurs in the present; the joining would have occurred in the past.

Like the tense of an infinitive, the tense of a participle is governed by the tense of the sentence's verb. Use the present participle (ending in *-ing*) for an action occurring at the same time as that of the sentence's verb.

Hiking the Appalachian Trail in early spring, we spotted many wildflowers.

Use the past participle (such as *given* or *helped*) or the present perfect participle (*having* plus the past participle) for an action occurring before that of the verb.

Discovered off the coast of Florida, the Spanish galleon yielded many treasures.

Having worked her way through college, Lee graduated debt-free.

27g Use the subjunctive mood in the few contexts that require it.

There are three moods in English: the *indicative*, used for facts, opinions, and questions; the *imperative*, used for orders or advice; and the *subjunctive*, used in certain contexts to express wishes, requests, or conditions contrary to fact. For many writers, the subjunctive causes the most problems.

Forms of the subjunctive

In the subjunctive mood, present-tense verbs do not change form to indicate the number and person of the subject (see 21). Instead, the subjunctive uses the base form of the verb (*be*, *drive*, *employ*) with all subjects.

> It is important that you *be* [not *are*] prepared for the interview.

> We asked that she *drive* [not *drives*] more slowly.

Also, in the subjunctive mood, there is only one past-tense form of *be*: *were* (never *was*).

> If I *were* [not *was*] you, I'd proceed more cautiously.

Uses of the subjunctive

The subjunctive mood appears only in a few contexts: in contrary-to-fact clauses beginning with *if* or expressing a wish; in *that* clauses following verbs such as *ask*, *insist*, *recommend*, *request*, and *suggest*; and in certain set expressions.

In contrary-to-fact clauses beginning with *if* When a subordinate clause beginning with *if* expresses a condition contrary to fact, use the subjunctive *were* in place of *was*.

▶ If I ~~was~~ a member of Congress, I would vote for that bill.
   were

▶ The astronomers would be able to see the moons of Jupiter
   tonight if the weather ~~was~~ clearer.
   were

The verbs in these sentences express conditions that do not exist: The writer is not a member of Congress, and the weather is not clear.

Do not use the subjunctive mood in *if* clauses expressing conditions that exist or may exist.

> If Dana *wins* the contest, she will leave for Barcelona in June.

In contrary-to-fact clauses expressing a wish In formal English, use the subjunctive *were* in clauses expressing a wish or desire. While use of the indicative is common in informal speech, it is not appropriate in academic writing.

INFORMAL   I wish that Dr. Vaughn *was* my professor.

FORMAL   I wish that Dr. Vaughn *were* my professor.

In *that* clauses following verbs such as *ask, insist, request,* and *suggest* Because requests have not yet become reality, they are expressed in the subjunctive mood.

▶ Professor Moore insists that her students ~~are~~ ^be^ on time.

▶ We recommend that Lambert ~~files~~ ^file^ form 1050 soon.

In certain set expressions The subjunctive mood, once more widely used, remains in certain set expressions: *Be that as it may, as it were, far be it from me,* and so on.

> **Grammar checkers** only sometimes flag problems with the subjunctive mood. What they catch is very spotty, so you must be alert to the correct uses of the subjunctive in your own writing.

EXERCISE 27–3 Edit the following sentences to eliminate errors in verb tense or mood. If a sentence is correct, write "correct" after it. Answers to lettered sentences appear in the back of the book. Example:

After the path ~~was~~ ^had been^ plowed, we were able to walk through the park.

a. The palace of Knossos in Crete is believed to have been destroyed by fire around 1375 BCE.

b. Watson and Crick discovered the mechanism that controlled inheritance in all life: the workings of the DNA molecule.

c. When city planners proposed rezoning the waterfront, did they know that the mayor promised to curb development in that neighborhood?

d. Tonight's concert begins at 9:30. If it were earlier, I'd consider going.

e. As soon as my aunt applied for the position of pastor, the post was filled by an inexperienced seminary graduate who had been so hastily snatched that his mortarboard was still in midair.

1. Don Quixote, in Cervantes's novel, was an idealist ill suited for life in the real world.

2. Visiting the technology museum inspired the high school seniors and had reminded them that science could be fun.

3. I would like to have been on the *Mayflower* but not to have experienced the first winter.

4. When the director yelled "Action!" I forgot my lines, even though I practiced my part every waking hour for three days.

5. If midday naps were a regular practice in American workplaces, employees would be far more productive.

hackerhandbooks.com/bedhandbook > Grammar exercises > Grammar
> E-ex 27–8 and 27–9

Part VI
Challenges for ESL and Multilingual Writers

Part VI of *The Bedford Handbook* is primarily for multilingual writers. You may find this section helpful if you learned English as a second language (ESL) or if you speak a language other than English with your friends and family.

hackerhandbooks.com/bedhandbook > ESL help
> Charts and study help
> Sample student paper (draft and final)
> Exercises
> Links to online resources

28 **Verbs**

Both native and nonnative speakers of English encounter challenges with verbs. Section 28 focuses on specific challenges that multilingual writers sometimes face. You can find more help with verbs in other sections in the book:

making subjects and verbs agree (21)

using irregular verb forms (27a, 27b)

leaving off verb endings (27c, 27d)

choosing the correct verb tense (27f)

avoiding inappropriate uses of the passive voice (8a)

28a Use the appropriate verb form and tense.

This section offers a brief review of English verb forms and tenses.

Basic verb forms

Every main verb in English has five forms, which are used to create all of the verb tenses in standard English. The chart at the top of page 311 shows these forms for the regular verb *help* and the irregular verbs *give* and *be*. See 27a for the forms of other common irregular verbs.

Basic verb forms

	REGULAR VERB *HELP*	IRREGULAR VERB *GIVE*	IRREGULAR VERB *BE**
BASE FORM	help	give	be
PAST TENSE	helped	gave	was, were
PAST PARTICIPLE	helped	given	been
PRESENT PARTICIPLE	helping	giving	being
-S FORM	helps	gives	is

*Be also has the forms *am* and *are*, which are used in the present tense.

Verb tenses

Section 27f describes all the verb tenses in English, showing the forms of a regular verb, an irregular verb, and the verb *be* in each tense. The following chart provides more details about the tenses commonly used in the active voice in writing; the chart beginning on page 318 gives details about tenses commonly used in the passive voice.

Verb tenses commonly used in the active voice

For descriptions and examples of all verb tenses, see 27f. For verb tenses commonly used in the passive voice, see the chart on pages 318–19.

Simple tenses
For general facts, states of being, habitual actions

Simple present	**Base form or *-s* form**
• general facts	College students often *study* late at night.
• states of being	Water *becomes* steam at 100° centigrade.
• habitual, repetitive actions	We *donate* to a different charity each year.
• scheduled future events	The train *arrives* tomorrow at 6:30 p.m.

NOTE: For uses of the present tense in writing about literature, see page 303.

→

Verb tenses commonly used in the active voice, *continued*

Simple past

Base form + *-ed* or *-d* or irregular form

- completed actions at a specific time in the past

  The storm *destroyed* their property. She *drove* to Montana three years ago.

- facts or states of being in the past

  When I *was* young, I usually *walked* to school with my sister.

Simple future

***will* + base form**

- future actions, promises, or predictions

  I *will exercise* tomorrow. The snowfall *will begin* around midnight.

Simple progressive forms
For continuing actions

Present progressive

***am, is, are* + present participle**

- actions in progress at the present time, not continuing indefinitely

  The students *are taking* an exam in Room 105. The valet *is parking* the car.

- future actions (with *leave, go, come, move,* etc.)

  I *am leaving* tomorrow morning.

Past progressive

***was, were* + present participle**

- actions in progress at a specific time in the past

  They *were swimming* when the storm struck.

- *was going to, were going to* for past plans that did not happen

  We *were going to* drive to Florida for spring break, but the car broke down.

NOTE: Some verbs are not normally used in the progressive: *appear, believe, belong, contain, have, hear, know, like, need, see, seem, taste, understand,* and *want.*

>   want
> ▸ I ~~am wanting~~ to see August Wilson's *Radio Golf*.

→

Perfect tenses
For actions that happened or will happen before another time

Present perfect	***has, have* + past participle**
• repetitive or constant actions that began in the past and continue to the present	I *have loved* cats since I was a child. Alicia *has worked* in Kenya for ten years.
• actions that happened at an unknown or unspecific time in the past	Stephen *has visited* Wales three times.

Past perfect	***had* + past participle**
• actions that began or occurred before another time in the past	She *had* just *crossed* the street when the runaway car crashed into the building.

NOTE: For more discussion of uses of the past perfect, see 27f. For uses of the past perfect in conditional sentences, see 28e.

Perfect progressive forms
For continuous past actions before another time

Present perfect progressive	***has, have* + *been* + present participle**
• continuous actions that began in the past and continue to the present	Yolanda *has been trying* to get a job in Boston for five years.

Past perfect progressive	***had* + *been* + present participle**
• actions that began and continued in the past until some other past action	By the time I moved to Georgia, I *had been supporting* myself for five years.

EXERCISE 28–1 Revise the following sentences to correct errors in verb forms and verb tenses. You may need to look at 27a for the correct form of some irregular verbs and at 27f for help with tenses. Answers to lettered sentences appear in the back of the book. Example:

> begins
> The meeting ~~begin~~ tonight at 7:30.
> ^

a. In the past, tobacco companies deny any connection between smoking and health problems.
b. There is nothing in the world that TV has not touch on.
c. I am wanting to register for a summer tutoring session.
d. By the end of the year, the state will have test 139 birds for avian flu.
e. The benefits of eating fruits and vegetables have been promoting by health care providers.

1. By the time he was twelve years old, Mozart had compose an entire opera.
2. A serious accident was happened at the corner of Main Street and First Avenue last night.
3. My family has been gone to Sam's restaurant ever since we moved to this neighborhood.
4. I have ate Thai food only once before.
5. The bear is appearing to be sedated.

hackerhandbooks.com/bedhandbook > Grammar exercises > ESL challenges > E-ex 28–5

28b Use the base form of the verb after a modal.

The modal verbs are *can, could, may, might, must, shall, should, will,* and *would*. (*Ought to* is also considered a modal verb.) The modals are used with the base form of a verb to show certainty, necessity, or possibility.

Modals and the verbs that follow them do not change form to indicate tense. For a summary of modals and their meanings, see the chart on pages 316–17. (See also 27e.)

> launch
> ▶ The art museum will ~~launches~~ its fundraising campaign
> ^
>
> next month.

The modal *will* must be followed by the base form *launch,* not the present tense *launches.*

▶ The translator could s̶p̶o̶k̶e̶ ^speak^ many languages, so the ambassador hired her for the European tour.

The modal *could* must be followed by the base form *speak,* not the past tense *spoke.*

TIP: Do not use *to* in front of a main verb that follows a modal.

▶ Gina can t̶o̶ drive us home if we miss the last train.

For the use of modals in conditional sentences, see 28e.

EXERCISE 28–2   Edit the following sentences to correct errors in the use of verb forms with modals. You may find it helpful to consult the chart on pages 316–17. If a sentence is correct, write "correct" after it. Answers to lettered sentences appear in the back of the book. Example:

> We should t̶o̶ order pizza for dinner.

a.   A major league pitcher can to throw a baseball more than ninety-five miles per hour.

b.   The writing center tutor will helps you revise your essay.

c.   A reptile must adjusted its body temperature to its environment.

d.   In some states, individuals may renew a driver's license online or in person.

e.   My uncle, a cartoonist, could sketched a face in less than two minutes.

1.   Working more than twelve hours a day might to contribute to insomnia, according to researchers.

2.   A wasp will carry its immobilized prey back to the nest.

3.   Hikers should not wandered too far from the trail.

4.   Should we continued to submit hard copies of our essays?

5.   Physical therapy may to help people after heart surgery.

Modals and their meanings

can

- general ability (present)

Ants *can survive* anywhere, even in space. Jorge *can run* a marathon faster than his brother.

- informal requests or permission

Can you *tell* me where the light is? Sandy *can borrow* my calculator.

could

- general ability (past)

Lea *could read* when she was only three years old.

- polite, informal requests or permission

Could you *give* me that pen?

may

- formal requests or permission

May I *see* the report? Students *may park* only in the yellow zone.

- possibility

I *may try* to finish my homework tonight, or I *may wake up* early and *finish* it tomorrow.

might

- possibility

The population of New Delhi *might reach* thirteen million by 2013.

NOTE: *Might* usually expresses a stronger possibility than *may*.

must

- necessity (present or future)

To be effective, welfare-to-work programs *must provide* access to job training.

- strong probability

Amy *must be* sick. [She is probably sick.]

- near certainty (present or past)

I *must have left* my wallet at home. [I almost certainly left my wallet at home.]

should

- suggestions or advice

Diabetics *should drink* plenty of water every day.

- obligations or duties

The government *should protect* citizens' rights.

- expectations

The books *should arrive* soon. [We expect the books to arrive soon.]

→

will	
• certainty	If you don't leave now, you *will be* late.
• requests	*Will* you *help* me study for my test?
• promises and offers	Jonah *will arrange* the carpool.

would	
• polite requests	*Would* you *help* me carry these books? I *would like* some coffee. [*Would like* is more polite than *want*.]
• habitual or repeated actions (past)	Whenever Elena needed help with sewing, she *would call* her aunt.

28c To write a verb in the passive voice, use a form
of *be* with the past participle.

When a sentence is written in the passive voice, the subject
receives the action instead of doing it. (See 62c.)

> The solution *was measured* by the lab assistant.

> Melissa *was taken* to the hospital.

To form the passive voice, use a form of *be*—*am, is, are,
was, were, being, be,* or *been*—followed by the past participle of
the main verb: *was chosen, are remembered.* (Sometimes a form
of *be* follows another helping verb: *will be stopped, could have
been broken.*)

> ▶ *Dreaming in Cuban* was ~~writing~~ by Cristina García.

written above *writing*

In the passive voice, the past participle *written*, not the present
participle *writing*, must follow *was* (the past tense of *be*).

> ▶ Senator Dixon will defeated.

be above the space before *defeated*

The passive voice requires a form of *be* before the past participle.

Verb tenses commonly used in the passive voice

For details about verb tenses in the active voice, see pages 311–13.

Simple tenses (passive voice)

Simple present   *am, is, are* + past participle

- general facts   Meals *are served* by students in the hotel management program.

- habitual, repetitive actions   The receipts *are counted* every night.

Simple past   *was, were* + past participle

- completed past actions   He *was punished* for being late.

Simple future   *will be* + past participle

- future actions, promises, or predictions   The decision *will be made* by the committee next week.

Simple progressive forms (passive voice)

Present progressive   *am, is, are* + *being* + past participle

- actions in progress at the present time   The new stadium *is being built* with private money.

- future actions (with *leave*, *go*, *come*, *move*, etc.)   Jo *is being moved* to a new class next month.

Past progressive   *was, were* + *being* + past participle

- actions in progress at a specific time in the past   We thought we *were being followed*.

Perfect tenses (passive voice)

Present perfect   *has, have* + *been* + past participle

- actions that began in the past and continue to the present   The flight *has been delayed* because of violent storms in the Midwest.

- actions that happened at an unknown or unspecific time in the past   Wars *have been fought* throughout history.

→

Past perfect	***had* + *been* + past participle**
• actions that began or occurred before another time in the past	He *had been given* all the hints he needed to complete the puzzle.

NOTE: Future progressive, future perfect, and perfect progressive forms are not used in the passive voice.

▶ The child was being ~~tease.~~ teased.

The past participle *teased*, not the base form *tease*, must be used with *was being* to form the passive voice.

For details on forming the passive in various tenses, consult the chart beginning on page 318. (For appropriate uses of the passive voice, see 8a.)

NOTE: Only transitive verbs, those that take direct objects, may be used in the passive voice. Intransitive verbs such as *occur, happen, sleep, die, become,* and *fall* are not used in the passive. (See 62b.)

▶ The accident ~~was~~ happened suddenly.

▶ Stock prices ~~were fallen~~ fell all week.

28d To make negative verb forms, add *not* in the appropriate place.

If the verb is the simple present or past tense of *be* (*am, is, are, was, were*), add *not* after the verb.

Mario *is not* a member of the club.

For simple present-tense verbs other than *be*, use *do* or *does* plus *not* before the base form of the verb. (For the correct forms of *do* and *does*, see the chart in 21a.)

▶ Mariko ~~no~~ want more dessert.
  does not

▶ Mariko does not ~~wants~~ more dessert.

For simple past-tense verbs other than *be*, use *did* plus *not* before the base form of the verb.

▶ They did not ~~planted~~ corn this year.
  plant

In a verb phrase consisting of one or more helping verbs and a present or past participle (*is watching*, *were living*, *has played*, *could have been driven*), use the word *not* after the first helping verb.

▶ Inna should have ~~not~~ gone dancing last night.
  not

▶ Bonnie is ~~no~~ singing this weekend.
  not

NOTE: English allows only one negative in an independent clause to express a negative idea; using more than one is an error known as a *double negative* (see 26e).

▶ We could not find ~~no~~ books about the history of our
  any

school.

28e In a conditional sentence, choose verb tenses according to the type of condition expressed in the sentence.

Conditional sentences contain two clauses: a subordinate clause (usually starting with *if*, *when*, or *unless*) and an independent clause. The subordinate clause (sometimes called the *if* or *unless* clause) states the condition or cause; the independent clause states the result or effect. In each example in this section, the subordinate clause (*if* clause) is marked SUB, and the independent clause is marked IND. (See 63e on clauses.)

Factual

Factual conditional sentences express factual relationships. If the relationship is a scientific truth, use the present tense in both clauses.

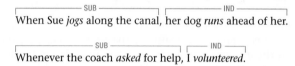

────── SUB ────── ── IND ──
If water *cools* to 32° Fahrenheit, it *freezes.*

If the sentence describes a condition that is (or was) habitually true, use the same tense in both clauses.

────────── SUB ────────── ────────── IND ──────────
When Sue *jogs* along the canal, her dog *runs* ahead of her.

────────── SUB ────────── ──── IND ────
Whenever the coach *asked* for help, I *volunteered.*

Predictive

Predictive conditional sentences are used to predict the future or to express future plans or possibilities. To form a predictive sentence, use a present-tense verb in the subordinate clause; in the independent clause, use the modal *will, can, may, should,* or *might* plus the base form of the verb.

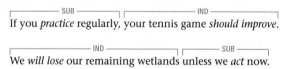

──── SUB ──── ────────── IND ──────────
If you *practice* regularly, your tennis game *should improve.*

──── IND ──── ──── SUB ────
We *will lose* our remaining wetlands unless we *act* now.

TIP: In all types of conditional sentences (factual, predictive, and speculative), *if* or *unless* clauses do not use the modal verb *will.*

        passes
▶ **If Jenna ~~will pass~~ her history test, she will graduate this year.**

Speculative

Speculative conditional sentences express unlikely, contrary-to-fact, or impossible conditions. English uses the past or past perfect tense in the *if* clause, even for conditions in the present or the future.

Unlikely possibilities If the condition is possible but unlikely in the present or the future, use the past tense in the subordinate clause; in the independent clause, use *would*, *could*, or *might* plus the base form of the verb.

> ┌──── SUB ────┐ ┌──── IND ────┐
> If I *won* the lottery, I *would travel* to Egypt.

The writer does not expect to win the lottery. Because this is a possible but unlikely present or future situation, the subordinate clause uses the past tense.

Conditions contrary to fact In conditions that are currently unreal or contrary to fact, use the past-tense verb *were* (not *was*) in the *if* clause for all subjects. (See also 27g, on the subjunctive mood.)

>   were
> ▶ If I ~~was~~ president, I would make children's issues a priority.
>   ⌃

The writer is not president, so *were* is correct in the *if* clause.

Events that did not happen In a conditional sentence that speculates about an event that did not happen or was impossible in the past, use the past perfect tense in the *if* clause; in the independent clause, use *would have*, *could have*, or *might have* with the past participle. (See also past perfect tense, p. 313.)

> ┌──── SUB ────┐ ┌──── IND ────┐
> If I *had saved* more money, I *would have visited* Laos last year.

The writer did not save more money and did not travel to Laos. This sentence shows a possibility that did not happen.

> ┌──────── SUB ────────┐ ┌── IND ──┐
> If Aunt Grace *had been* alive for your graduation, she *would*
> ┌──────────────┐
> *have been* very proud.

Aunt Grace was not alive at the time of the graduation. This sentence shows an impossible situation in the past.

EXERCISE 28–3   Edit the following conditional sentences to correct problems with verbs. In some cases, more than one revision is possible. Suggested revisions of lettered sentences appear in the back of the book. Example:

>   *had*
> If I ~~have~~ time, I would study both French and Russian next
>   ^
> semester.

a. The electrician might have discovered the broken circuit if she went through the modules one at a time.

b. If Verena wins a scholarship, she would go to graduate school.

c. Whenever there is a fire in our neighborhood, everybody came out to watch.

d. Sarah will take the paralegal job unless she would get a better offer.

e. If I live in Budapest with my cousin Szusza, she would teach me Hungarian cooking.

1. If the science fiction festival starts Monday, we wouldn't need to plan entertainment for our visitors.

2. If everyone has voted in the last election, the results would have been very different.

3. The tenants will not pay the rent unless the landlord fixed the furnace.

4. When dark gray clouds appeared on a hot summer afternoon, a thunderstorm often follows.

5. Our daughter would have drowned if Officer Blake didn't risk his life to save her.

hackerhandbooks.com/bedhandbook > Grammar exercises > ESL challenges
> E-ex 28–7

28f Become familiar with verbs that may be followed by gerunds or infinitives.

A gerund is a verb form that ends in *-ing* and is used as a noun: *sleeping, dreaming.* (See 63b.) An infinitive is the word *to* plus the base form of the verb: *to sleep, to dream.* (The word *to* is an infinitive marker, not a preposition, in this use.)

A few verbs may be followed by either a gerund or an infinitive; others may be followed by a gerund but not by an infinitive; still others may be followed by an infinitive but not by a gerund.

Verb + gerund or infinitive (no change in meaning)

The following commonly used verbs may be followed by a gerund or an infinitive, with little or no difference in meaning:

begin	hate	love
continue	like	start

I love *skiing*. I love *to ski*.

Verb + gerund or infinitive (change in meaning)

With a few verbs, the choice of a gerund or an infinitive changes the meaning dramatically:

forget	remember	stop	try

She stopped *speaking* to Lucia. [She no longer spoke to Lucia.]

She stopped *to speak* to Lucia. [She paused so that she could speak to Lucia.]

Verb + gerund

These verbs may be followed by a gerund but not by an infinitive:

admit	enjoy	postpone	resist
appreciate	escape	practice	risk
avoid	finish	put off	suggest
deny	imagine	quit	tolerate
discuss	miss	recall	

Bill enjoys *playing* [not *to play*] the piano.

Jamie quit *smoking*.

Verb + infinitive

These verbs may be followed by an infinitive but not by a gerund:

agree	expect	need	refuse
ask	help	offer	wait
beg	hope	plan	want
claim	manage	pretend	wish
decide	mean	promise	would like

Jill has offered *to water* [not *watering*] the plants while we are away.

Joe finally managed *to find* a parking space.

The man refused *to join* the rebellion.

A few of these verbs may be followed either by an infinitive directly or by a noun or pronoun plus an infinitive:

ask	help	promise	would like
expect	need	want	

We asked *to speak* to the congregation.

We asked *Rabbi Abrams to speak* to our congregation.

Alex expected *to get* the lead in the play.

Ira expected *Alex to get* the lead in the play.

Verb + noun or pronoun + infinitive

With certain verbs in the active voice, a noun or pronoun must come between the verb and the infinitive that follows it. The noun or pronoun usually names a person who is affected by the action of the verb.

advise	convince	order	tell
allow	encourage	persuade	urge
cause	have ("own")	remind	warn
command	instruct	require	

The class encouraged Luis to tell the story of his escape.

The counselor *advised Haley to take* four courses instead of five.

Professor Howlett *instructed us to write* our names on the left side of the paper.

Verb + noun or pronoun + unmarked infinitive

An unmarked infinitive is an infinitive without *to*. A few verbs (often called *causative verbs*) may be followed by a noun or pronoun and an unmarked infinitive.

have ("cause")   let ("allow")

help   make ("force")

Jorge *had the valet park* his car.

▶ Please let me ~~to~~ pay for the tickets.

▶ Frank made me ~~to~~ carry his book for him.

NOTE: *Help* can be followed by a noun or pronoun and either an unmarked or a marked infinitive.

Emma *helped Brian wash* the dishes.

Emma *helped Brian to wash* the dishes.

EXERCISE 28–4   Form sentences by adding gerund or infinitive constructions to the following sentence openings. In some cases, more than one kind of construction is possible. Possible answers to lettered items appear in the back of the book. Example:

Please remind your sister to call me.

a.   I enjoy
b.   The tutor told Samantha
c.   The team hopes
d.   Ricardo and his brothers miss
e.   The babysitter let

1.   Pollen makes
2.   The club president asked
3.   Next summer we plan
4.   My supervisor intends
5.   Please stop

29 Articles

Articles (*a, an, the*) are part of a category of words known as *noun markers* or *determiners*.

29a Be familiar with articles and other noun markers.

Standard English uses noun markers to help identify the nouns that follow. In addition to articles (*a, an,* and *the*), noun markers include

- possessive nouns, such as *Elena's* (See 36a.)
- possessive pronoun/adjectives: *my, your, his, her, its, our, their* (See 61b.)
- demonstrative pronoun/adjectives: *this, that, these, those* (See 61b.)
- quantifiers: *all, any, each, either, every, few, many, more, most, much, neither, several, some,* and so on (See 29d.)
- numbers: *one, twenty-three,* and so on

Using articles and other noun markers

Articles and other noun markers always appear before nouns; sometimes other modifiers, such as adjectives, come between a noun marker and a noun.

>   ART N
> Felix is reading a book about mythology.

>   ART   ADJ   N
> We took an exciting trip to Alaska last summer.

> NOUN
> MARKER ADV   ADJ   N
> That very delicious meal was expensive.

In most cases, do not use an article with another noun marker.

▶ ~~The~~ Natalie's older brother lives in Wisconsin.

Expressions like *a few, the most,* and *all the* are exceptions: *a few potatoes, all the rain.* See also 29d.

Types of articles and types of nouns

To choose an appropriate article for a noun, you must first determine whether the noun is *common* or *proper*, *count* or *noncount*, *singular* or *plural*, and *specific* or *general*. The chart on pages 329–30 describes the types of nouns.

Articles are classified as *indefinite* and *definite*. The indefinite articles, *a* and *an*, are used with general nouns. The definite article, *the*, is used with specific nouns. (The last section of the chart on p. 330 explains general and specific nouns.)

A and *an* both mean "one" or "one among many." Use *a* before a consonant sound: *a banana, a tree, a picture, a happy child, a united family.* Use *an* before a vowel sound: *an eggplant, an occasion, an uncle, an honorable person.* (See also *a, an* in the Glossary of Usage.)

The shows that a noun is specific; use *the* with one or more than one specific thing: *the newspaper, the soldiers.*

29b Use *the* with most specific common nouns.

The definite article, *the*, is used with most nouns—both count and noncount—that the reader can identify specifically. Usually the identity will be clear to the reader for one of the following reasons. (See also the chart on p. 332.)

1. The noun has been previously mentioned.

▶ A truck cut in front of our van. When ^the^ truck skidded a few

seconds later, we almost crashed into it.

The article *A* is used before *truck* when the noun is first mentioned. When the noun is mentioned again, it needs the article *the* because readers can now identify which truck skidded—the one that cut in front of the van.

2. A phrase or clause following the noun restricts its identity.

▶ Bryce warned me that ^the^ computer on his desk had just crashed.

The phrase *on his desk* identifies the specific computer.

Types of nouns

Common or proper

Common nouns
- name general
  persons, places,
  things, or ideas
- begin with lowercase

Examples

religion	beauty
knowledge	student
rain	country

Proper nouns
- name specific
  persons, places,
  things, or ideas
- begin with capital letter

Examples

Hinduism	President Adams
Philip	Washington Monument
Vietnam	Renaissance

Count or noncount (common nouns only)

Count nouns
- name persons, places,
  things, or ideas that
  can be counted
- have plural forms

Examples

girl, girls
city, cities
goose, geese
philosophy, philosophies

Noncount nouns
- name things or
  abstract ideas that
  cannot be counted
- cannot be made plural

Examples

water	patience
silver	knowledge
furniture	air

NOTE: See the chart on page 333 for commonly used noncount nouns.

Singular or plural (both common and proper)

Singular nouns
(count and noncount)
- represent one person,
  place, thing, or idea

Examples

backpack	rain
country	beauty
woman	Nile River
achievement	Block Island

Types of nouns, *continued*

Plural nouns
(count only)

	Examples	
• represent more than one person, place, thing, or idea	backpacks countries women	Ural Mountains Falkland Islands achievements
• must be count nouns		

Specific (definite) or general (indefinite) (count and noncount)

Specific nouns

Examples

• name persons, places, things, or ideas that can be identified within a group of the same type

The students in Professor Martin's *class* should study.

The airplane carrying *the senator* was late.

The furniture in *the truck* was damaged.

General nouns

Examples

• name categories of persons, places, things, or ideas (often plural)

Students should study.

Books bridge *gaps* between *cultures*.

The airplane has made commuting between cities easy.

NOTE: Descriptive adjectives do not necessarily make a noun specific. A specific noun is one that readers can identify within a group of nouns of the same type.

> If I win the lottery, I will buy ~~the~~ *a* brand-new bright red
>
> sports car.

The reader cannot identify which specific brand-new bright red sports car the writer will buy. Even though *car* has many adjectives in front of it, it is a general noun in this sentence.

3. A superlative adjective such as *best* or *most intelligent* makes the noun's identity specific. (See also 26d on comparatives and superlatives.)

▶ Our petite daughter dated *the* tallest boy in her class.

> The superlative *tallest* makes the noun *boy* specific. Although there might be several tall boys, only one boy can be the tallest.

4. The noun describes a unique person, place, or thing.

▶ During an eclipse, one should not look directly at *the* sun.

> There is only one sun in our solar system, so its identity is clear.

5. The context or situation makes the noun's identity clear.

▶ Please don't slam *the* door when you leave.

> Both the speaker and the listener know which door is meant.

6. The noun is singular and refers to a scientific class or category of items (most often animals, musical instruments, and inventions).

▶ ~~Microchip~~ *The microchip* has transformed nearly everyone's life.

> The writer is referring to the microchip as an invention.

29c Use *a* (or *an*) with common singular count nouns that refer to "one" or "any."

If a count noun refers to one unspecific item (not a whole category), use the indefinite article, *a* or *an*. *A* and *an* usually mean "one among many" but can also mean "any one." (See the chart on p. 332.)

▶ My English professor asked me to bring *a* dictionary to class.

> The noun *dictionary* refers to "one unspecific dictionary" or "any dictionary."

Choosing articles for common nouns

Use *the*

* if the reader has enough information to identify the noun specifically

COUNT: Please turn on *the lights*. We're going to *the lake* tomorrow.

NONCOUNT: *The food* in Italy is excellent.

Use *a* or *an*

* if the noun refers to one item

and

* if the item is singular but not specific

COUNT: Bring *a pencil* to class. Charles wrote *an essay* about his first job.

NOTE: Do not use *a* or *an* with plural or noncount nouns.

Use a quantifier (*enough*, *many*, *some*, etc.)

* if the noun represents an unspecified amount of something
* if the amount is more than one but not all items in a category

COUNT (plural): Amir showed us *some photos* of India. *Many turtles* return to the same nesting site each year.

NONCOUNT: We expect *some rain* this evening.

NOTE: Sometimes no article conveys an unspecified amount: *Amir showed us photos of India*.

Use no article

* if the noun represents all items in a category
* if the noun represents a category in general

COUNT (plural): *Students* can attend the show for free.

NONCOUNT: *Coal* is a natural resource.

NOTE: *The* is occasionally used when a singular count noun refers to all items in a class or a specific category: *The bald eagle is no longer endangered in the United States*.

Commonly used noncount nouns

Food and drink

beef, bread, butter, candy, cereal, cheese, cream, meat, milk, pasta, rice, salt, sugar, water, wine

Nonfood substances

air, cement, coal, dirt, gasoline, gold, paper, petroleum, plastic, rain, silver, snow, soap, steel, wood, wool

Abstract nouns

advice, anger, beauty, confidence, courage, employment, fun, happiness, health, honesty, information, intelligence, knowledge, love, poverty, satisfaction, wealth

Other

biology (and other areas of study), clothing, equipment, furniture, homework, jewelry, luggage, machinery, mail, money, news, poetry, pollution, research, scenery, traffic, transportation, violence, weather, work

NOTE: A few noncount nouns (such as *love*) can also be used as count nouns: *He had two loves: music and archery.*

>   *an*
> We want to rent ⌃apartment close to the lake.

The noun *apartment* refers to "any apartment close to the lake," not a specific apartment.

29d Use a quantifier such as *some* or *more*, not *a* or *an*, with a noncount noun to express an approximate amount.

Do not use *a* or *an* with noncount nouns. Also do not use numbers or words such as *several* or *many* because they must be used with plural nouns, and noncount nouns do not have plural forms. (See the chart on p. 333 for a list of commonly used noncount nouns.)

▶ Dr. Snyder gave us ~~an~~ information about the Peace Corps.

▶ Do you have ~~many~~ money with you?

You can use quantifiers such as *enough*, *less*, and *some* to suggest approximate amounts or nonspecific quantities of noncount nouns: *a little salt, any homework, enough wood, less information, much pollution.*

▶ Vincent's mother told him that she had ~~a~~ ^some^ news that

would surprise him.

29e Do not use articles with nouns that refer to all of something or something in general.

When a noncount noun refers to all of its type or to a concept in general, it is not marked with an article.

▶ ~~The~~ ^Kindness^ ~~kindness~~ is a virtue.

The noun represents kindness in general; it does not represent a specific type of kindness.

▶ In some parts of the world, ~~the~~ rice is preferred to all other

grains.

The noun *rice* represents rice in general, not a specific type or serving of rice.

In most cases, when you use a count noun to represent a general category, make the noun plural. Do not use unmarked singular count nouns to represent whole categories.

▶ ~~Fountain is~~ ^Fountains are^ an expensive element of landscape design.

Fountains is a count noun that represents fountains in general.

EXCEPTION: In some cases, *the* can be used with singular count nouns to represent a class or specific category: *The Chinese alligator is smaller than the American alligator.* See also number 6 in 29b.

29f Do not use articles with most singular proper nouns. Use *the* with most plural proper nouns.

Since singular proper nouns are already specific, they typically do not need an article: *Prime Minister Brown, Jamaica, Lake Huron, Mount Etna.*

There are, however, many exceptions. In most cases, if the proper noun consists of a common noun with modifiers (adjectives or an *of* phrase), use *the* with the proper noun.

▶ We visited ^the^ Great Wall of China last year.

▶ Rob wants to be a translator for ^the^ Central Intelligence Agency.

The is used with most plural proper nouns: *the McGregors, the Bahamas, the Finger Lakes, the United States.*

Geographic names create problems because there are so many exceptions to the rules. When in doubt, consult the chart on page 336, check a dictionary, or ask a native speaker.

EXERCISE 29–1 Edit the following sentences for proper use of articles and nouns. If a sentence is correct, write "correct" after it. Answers to lettered sentences appear in the back of the book. Example:

~~The~~ Josefina's dance routine was flawless.

a. Doing volunteer work often brings a satisfaction.
b. As I looked out the window of the plane, I could see the Cape Cod.
c. Melina likes to drink her coffees with lots of cream.
d. Recovering from abdominal surgery requires patience.
e. I completed the my homework assignment quickly.

1. The attorney argued that her client should receive a money for emotional suffering.

Using *the* with geographic nouns

When to omit *the*

streets, squares, parks	Ivy Street, Union Square, Denali National Park
cities, states, counties	Miami, New Mexico, Bee County
most countries, continents	Italy, Nigeria, China, South America, Africa
bays, single lakes	Tampa Bay, Lake Geneva
single mountains, islands	Mount Everest, Crete

When to use *the*

country names with *of* phrase	the United States (of America), the People's Republic of China
large regions, deserts	the East Coast, the Sahara
peninsulas	the Baja Peninsula, the Sinai Peninsula
oceans, seas, gulfs	the Pacific Ocean, the Dead Sea, the Persian Gulf
canals and rivers	the Panama Canal, the Amazon
mountain ranges	the Rocky Mountains, the Alps
groups of islands	the Solomon Islands

2. Please check to see if there is a mail in the mailbox.
3. The Times Square in New York City is known for its billboards and theaters.
4. A cement is one of the components of concrete.
5. I took all the boys on the roller coaster after lunch.

EXERCISE 29–2 Articles have been omitted from the following description of winter weather. Insert the articles *a, an,* and *the* where English requires them and be prepared to explain the reasons for your choices.

> Many people confuse terms *hail, sleet,* and *freezing rain.* Hail normally occurs in thunderstorm and is caused by strong updrafts that lift growing chunks of ice into clouds. When

chunks of ice, called hailstones, become too heavy to be carried by updrafts, they fall to ground. Hailstones can cause damage to crops, windshields, and people. Sleet occurs during winter storms and is caused by snowflakes falling from layer of cold air into warm layer, where they become raindrops, and then into another cold layer. As they fall through last layer of cold air, raindrops freeze and become small ice pellets, forming sleet. When it hits car windshield or windows of house, sleet can make annoying racket. Driving and walking can be hazardous when sleet accumulates on roads and sidewalks. Freezing rain is basically rain that falls onto ground and then freezes after it hits ground. It causes icy glaze on trees and any surface that is below freezing.

hackerhandbooks.com/bedhandbook > Grammar exercises > ESL challenges
> E-ex 29–3 to 29–5

30 Sentence structure

Although their structure can vary widely, sentences in English generally flow from subject to verb to object or complement: *Bears eat fish.* This section focuses on the major challenges that multilingual students face when writing sentences in English. For more details on the parts of speech and the elements of sentences, consult sections 61–64.

30a Use a linking verb between a subject and its complement.

Some languages, such as Russian and Turkish, do not use linking verbs (*is, are, was, were*) between subjects and complements (nouns or adjectives that rename or describe the subject). Every English sentence, however, must include a verb. For more on linking verbs, see 27e.

▶ Jim *is* intelligent.

▶ Many streets in San Francisco *are* very steep.

30b Include a subject in every sentence.

Some languages, such as Spanish and Japanese, do not require a subject in every sentence. Every English sentence, however, needs a subject. Commands are an exception: The subject *you* is understood but not present (*Give me the book*).

▶ Your aunt is very energetic. ~~Seems~~ *She seems* young for her age.

The word *it* is used as the subject of a sentence describing the weather or temperature, stating the time, indicating distance, or suggesting an environmental fact.

▶ *It is* ~~Is~~ raining in the valley and snowing in the mountains.

▶ In July, *it* is very hot in Arizona.

▶ *It is* ~~Is~~ 9:15 a.m.

In most English sentences, the subject appears before the verb. Some sentences, however, are inverted: The subject comes after the verb. In these sentences, a placeholder called an *expletive* (*there* or *it*) often comes before the verb.

    EXP   V   ⌐——— S ———⌐   ⌐——— S ——⌐   V
There are many people here today. (Many people are here today.)

▶ *There is* ~~Is~~ an apple in the refrigerator.

▶ As you know, *there are* many religious sects in India.

Notice that the verb agrees with the subject that follows it: *apple is*, *sects are*. (See 21g.)

Sometimes an inverted sentence has an infinitive (*to work*)
or a noun clause (*that she is intelligent*) as the subject. In such
sentences, the placeholder *it* is needed before the verb. (Also
see 63b and 63c.)

EXP V ⎯S⎯ ⎯S⎯ V
It is important to study daily. (To study daily is important.)

▶ Because the road is flooded, *it* is necessary to change our route.

TIP: The words *here* and *there* are not used as subjects. When
they mean "in this place" (*here*) or "in that place" (*there*), they
are adverbs, not nouns.

▶ I just returned from a vacation in Japan. ~~There~~ *It* is very
beautiful/ *there*.

▶ ~~Here~~ *This school* offers a master's degree in physical therapy; ~~there~~ *that school* has
only a bachelor's program.

> **Grammar checkers** can flag some sentences with a missing exple-
> tive, or placeholder (*there* or *it*), as in the sentence *Are many stores
> on Main Street.* But they often misdiagnose the problem because
> they cannot tell whether the sentence needs an expletive to make a
> statement (*There are many stores on Main Street*) or to ask a question
> (*Are there many stores on Main Street?*).

30c Do not use both a noun and a pronoun to perform the same grammatical function in a sentence.

English does not allow a subject to be repeated in its own clause.

▶ The doctor ~~she~~ advised me to cut down on salt.

The pronoun *she* cannot repeat the subject, *doctor*.

Do not add a pronoun even when a word group comes between the subject and the verb.

▶ **The watch that I lost on vacation i̶t̶ was in my**

backpack.

The pronoun *it* cannot repeat the subject, *watch*.

Some languages allow "topic fronting," placing a word or phrase (a "topic") at the beginning of a sentence and following it with an independent clause that explains something about the topic. This form is not allowed in English because the sentence seems to start with one subject but then introduces a new subject in an independent clause.

┌─ TOPIC ─┐ ┌────── IND CLAUSE ──────┐
INCORRECT   The seeds I planted them last fall.

The sentence can be corrected by bringing the topic (*seeds*) into the independent clause.

                        the seeds
▶ ~~The seeds~~ I planted t̶h̶e̶m̶ last fall.
                        ^

30d Do not repeat an object or an adverb in an adjective clause.

Adjective clauses begin with relative pronouns (*who, whom, whose, which, that*) or relative adverbs (*when, where*). Relative pronouns usually serve as subjects or objects in the clauses they introduce; another word in the clause cannot serve the same function. Relative adverbs should not be repeated by other adverbs later in the clause.

                          ┌──────── ADJ CLAUSE ────────┐
The cat ran under the car that was parked on the street.

▶ **The cat ran under the car that i̶t̶ was parked on the street.**

The relative pronoun *that* is the subject of the adjective clause, so the pronoun *it* cannot be added as a subject.

▶ **Myrna enjoyed the investment seminars that she attended**

~~**them**~~ **last week.**

The relative pronoun *that* is the object of the verb *attended*. The pronoun *them* cannot also serve as an object.

Sometimes the relative pronoun is understood but not present in the sentence. In such cases, do not add another word with the same function as the omitted pronoun.

▶ **Myrna enjoyed the investment seminars she attended** ~~**them**~~

last week.

The relative pronoun *that* is understood after *seminars* even though it is not present in the sentence.

If the clause begins with a relative adverb, do not use another adverb with the same meaning later in the clause.

▶ **The office where I work** ~~**there**~~ **is one hour from the city.**

The adverb *there* cannot repeat the relative adverb *where*.

Grammar checkers are not much help with repeated subjects or objects. If they flag them at all, the programs often identify the problems incorrectly.

EXERCISE 30–1 In the following sentences, add needed subjects or expletives and delete any repeated subjects, objects, or adverbs. Answers to lettered sentences appear in the back of the book. Example:

The new geology professor is the one whom we saw ~~**him**~~ **on**

TV this morning.

a. Are some cartons of ice cream in the freezer.
b. I don't use the subway because am afraid.
c. The prime minister she is the most popular leader in my country.

   d.   We tried to get in touch with the same manager whom we spoke to him earlier.

   e.   Recently have been a number of earthquakes in Turkey.

1. We visited an island where several ancient ruins are being excavated there.
2. In this city is difficult to find a high-paying job.
3. Beginning knitters they are often surprised that their fingers are sore at first.
4. Is a banyan tree in our backyard.
5. The CD that teaches Italian for opera lovers it was stolen from my backpack.

hackerhandbooks.com/bedhandbook > Grammar exercises > ESL challenges
> E-ex 30–5

30e Avoid mixed constructions beginning with *although* or *because*.

A word group that begins with *although* cannot be linked to a word group that begins with *but* or *however*. The result is an error called a *mixed construction* (see also 11a). Similarly, a word group that begins with *because* cannot be linked to a word group that begins with *so* or *therefore*.

If you want to keep *although* or *because*, drop the other linking word.

▶ Although Nikki Giovanni is best known for her poetry for

  adults, ~~but~~ she has written several books for children.

▶ Because finance laws are not always enforced, ~~therefore~~

  investing in the former Soviet Union can be risky.

If you want to keep the other linking word, omit *although* or *because*.

▶ ~~Although~~ Nikki Giovanni is best known for her poetry for

  adults, but she has written several books for children.

▶ ~~Because finance~~ *Finance* laws are not always enforced~~/~~; therefore,
investing in the former Soviet Union can be risky.

For advice about using commas and semicolons with linking words, see 32a and 34b.

30f Do not place an adverb between a verb and its direct object.

Adverbs modifying verbs can appear in various positions: at the beginning or end of a sentence, before or after a verb, or between a helping verb and its main verb.

Slowly, we drove along the rain-slick road.

Mia handled the teapot *very carefully*.

Martin *always* wins our tennis matches.

Christina is *rarely* late for our lunch dates.

My daughter has *often* spoken of you.

The election results were being *closely* followed by analysts.

However, an adverb cannot appear between a verb and its direct object.

▶ Mother wrapped *carefully* ~~carefully~~ the gift.

The adverb *carefully* cannot appear between the verb, *wrapped*, and its direct object, *the gift*.

EXERCISE 30–2 Edit the following sentences for proper sentence structure. If a sentence is correct, write "correct" after it. Answers to lettered sentences appear in the back of the book. Example:

She peeled ~~slowly~~ the banana/ *slowly.*

a. Although freshwater freezes at 32 degrees Fahrenheit, however ocean water freezes at 28 degrees Fahrenheit.

b. Because we switched cable packages, so our channel lineup has changed.

c. The competitor mounted confidently his skateboard.

d. My sister performs well the *legong*, a Balinese dance.

e. Because product development is behind schedule, we will have to launch the product next spring.

1. The teller counted methodically the stack of one-dollar bills.

2. I gasped when I saw lightning strike repeatedly the barn.

3. Although hockey is traditionally a winter sport, but many towns offer skills programs all year long.

4. Because salmon can survive in both freshwater and salt water, so they are classified as anadromous fish.

5. A surveyor determines precisely the boundaries of a piece of property.

hackerhandbooks.com/bedhandbook > Grammar exercises > ESL challenges > E-ex 30–6

30g Distinguish between present participles and past participles used as adjectives.

Both present and past participles may be used as adjectives. The present participle always ends in *-ing*. Past participles usually end in *-ed*, *-d*, *-en*, *-n*, or *-t*. (See 27a.)

PRESENT PARTICIPLES confusing, speaking, boring

PAST PARTICIPLES confused, spoken, bored

Like all other adjectives, participles can come before nouns; they also can follow linking verbs, in which case they describe the subject of the sentence. (See 62b.)

Use a present participle to describe a person or thing *causing or stimulating an experience*.

The *boring lecture* put us to sleep. [The lecture caused boredom.]

Use a past participle to describe a person or thing *undergoing an experience*.

The *audience* was *bored* by the lecture. [The audience experienced boredom.]

Participles that describe emotions or mental states often cause the most confusion.

annoying/annoyed	exhausting/exhausted
boring/bored	fascinating/fascinated
confusing/confused	frightening/frightened
depressing/depressed	satisfying/satisfied
exciting/excited	surprising/surprised

▶ Our hike was ~~exhausted.~~ *exhausting.*

Exhausting suggests that the hike caused exhaustion.

▶ The ~~exhausting~~ *exhausted* hikers reached the campground at sunset.

Exhausted describes how the hikers felt.

Grammar checkers do not flag problems with present and past participles used as adjectives. Not surprisingly, the programs have no way of knowing the meaning a writer intends.

EXERCISE 30–3 Edit the following sentences for proper use of present and past participles. If a sentence is correct, write "correct" after it. Answers to lettered sentences appear in the back of the book. Example:

Danielle and Monica were very ~~exciting~~ *excited* to be going to a Broadway show for the first time.

a. Listening to everyone's complaints all day was irritated.
b. The long flight to Singapore was exhausted.
c. His skill at chess is amazing.
d. After a great deal of research, the scientist made a fascinated discovery.
e. That blackout was one of the most frightened experiences I've ever had.

1. I couldn't concentrate on my homework because I was distracted.
2. The directions to the new board game seem extremely complicating.
3. How interested are you in visiting Civil War battlefields?
4. The aerial view of the devastated villages was depressing.
5. Even after the lecturer went over the main points again, the students were still confusing.

hackerhandbooks.com/bedhandbook > Grammar exercises > ESL challenges > E-ex 30–7

30h Place cumulative adjectives in an appropriate order.

Adjectives usually come before the nouns they modify and may also come after linking verbs. (See 61d and 62b.)

          ADJ   N   V   ADJ

Janine wore a new necklace. Janine's necklace was new.

Cumulative adjectives, which cannot be joined by the word *and* or separated by commas, must come in a particular order. If you use cumulative adjectives before a noun, see the chart on page 347. The chart is only a guide; don't be surprised if you encounter exceptions. (See also 33d.)

▶ My dorm room has only a small desk and a ~~plastic red smelly~~ *smelly red plastic*

   chair.

▶ Nice weather, ~~blue clear~~ *clear blue* water, and ancient monuments

   attract many people to Italy.

EXERCISE 30–4   Using the chart on page 347, arrange the following modifiers and nouns in their proper order. Answers to lettered items appear in the back of the book. Example:

   two new French racing bicycles
new, French, two, bicycles, racing

a. woman, young, an, Vietnamese, attractive
b. dedicated, a, priest, Catholic
c. old, her, sweater, blue, wool
d. delicious, Joe's, Scandinavian, bread
e. many, boxes, jewelry, antique, beautiful

1. oval, nine, brass, lamps, miniature
2. several, yellow, tulips, tiny
3. the, tree, gingko, yellow, ancient, Mongolian
4. courtyard, a, square, small, brick
5. charming, restaurants, Latvian, several

hackerhandbooks.com/bedhandbook > Grammar exercises > ESL challenges
> E-ex 30–8

Order of cumulative adjectives

FIRST **ARTICLE OR OTHER NOUN MARKER** a, an, the, her, Joe's, two, many, some

EVALUATIVE WORD attractive, dedicated, delicious, ugly, disgusting

SIZE large, enormous, small, little

LENGTH OR SHAPE long, short, round, square

AGE new, old, young, antique

COLOR yellow, blue, crimson

NATIONALITY French, Peruvian, Vietnamese

RELIGION Catholic, Protestant, Jewish, Muslim

MATERIAL silver, walnut, wool, marble

LAST **NOUN/ADJECTIVE** tree (as in *tree* house), kitchen (as in *kitchen* table)

THE NOUN MODIFIED house, sweater, bicycle, bread, woman, priest

My long green wool coat is in the attic.

Ana's collection includes *four small antique silver* coins.

31   Prepositions and idiomatic expressions

31a   Become familiar with prepositions that show time and place.

The most frequently used prepositions in English are *at, by, for, from, in, of, on, to,* and *with.* Prepositions can be difficult to master because the differences among them are subtle and idiomatic. The chart on page 349 is limited to three troublesome prepositions that show time and place: *at, on,* and *in.*

Not every possible use is listed in the chart, so don't be surprised when you encounter exceptions and idiomatic uses that you must learn one at a time. For example, in English a person rides *in* a car but *on* a bus, plane, train, or subway.

▶ My first class starts ~~on~~ *at* 8:00 a.m.

▶ The farmers go to market ~~in~~ *on* Wednesday.

▶ I want to work at one of the biggest companies ~~on~~ *in* the world.

EXERCISE 31–1   In the following sentences, replace prepositions that are not used correctly. If a sentence is correct, write "correct" after it. Answers to lettered sentences appear in the back of the book. Example:

The play begins ~~on~~ *at* 7:20 p.m.

a.   Whenever we eat at the Centerville Café, we sit at a small table on the corner of the room.

b.   At the beginning of the dot-com wave, students created new businesses in record numbers.

c.   In Thursday, Nancy will attend her first home repair class at the community center.

d.   Alex began looking for her lost mitten in another location.

e.   We decided to go to a restaurant because there was no fresh food on the refrigerator.

1. I like walking at my neighborhood in night.
2. If the train is on time, it will arrive on six o'clock at the morning.
3. In the corner of the room is a large bookcase with a pair of small Russian dolls standing at the top shelf.
4. She licked the stamp, stuck it in the envelope, put the envelope on her pocket, and walked to the nearest mailbox.
5. The mailbox was in the intersection of Laidlaw Avenue and Williams Street.

hackerhandbooks.com/bedhandbook > Grammar exercises > ESL challenges
> E-ex 31–1

At, on, *and* in *to show time and place*

Showing time

AT *at* a specific time: *at* 7:20, *at* dawn, *at* dinner

ON *on* a specific day or date: *on* Tuesday, *on* June 4

IN *in* a part of a 24-hour period: *in* the afternoon, *in* the daytime [but *at* night]

   in a year or month: *in* 1999, *in* July

   in a period of time: finished *in* three hours

Showing place

AT *at* a meeting place or location: *at* home, *at* the club

   at the edge of something: sitting *at* the desk

   at the corner of something: turning *at* the intersection

   at a target: throwing the snowball *at* Lucy

ON *on* a surface: placed *on* the table, hanging *on* the wall

   on a street: the house *on* Spring Street

   on an electronic medium: *on* television, *on* the Internet

IN *in* an enclosed space: *in* the garage, *in* an envelope

   in a geographic location: *in* San Diego, *in* Texas

   in a print medium: *in* a book, *in* a magazine

31b Use nouns (including *-ing* forms) after prepositions.

In a prepositional phrase, use a noun (not a verb) after the preposition. Sometimes the noun will be a gerund, the *-ing* verb form that functions as a noun (see 63b).

▶ Our student government is good at ~~save~~ money.
                               saving

Distinguish between the preposition *to* and the infinitive marker *to*. If *to* is a preposition, it should be followed by a noun or a gerund.

▶ We are dedicated to ~~help~~ the poor.
                     helping

If *to* is an infinitive marker, it should be followed by the base form of the verb.

▶ We want to ~~helping~~ the poor.
               help

To test whether *to* is a preposition or an infinitive marker, insert a word that you know is a noun after the word *to*. If the noun makes sense in that position, *to* is a preposition.

> Zoe is addicted *to* _____.

> They are planning *to* _____.

In the first case, a noun (such as *magazines*) makes sense after *to*, so *to* is a preposition and should be followed by a noun or a gerund.

> Zoe is addicted *to magazines*.

> Zoe is addicted *to reading*.

In the second case, a noun (such as *village*) does not make sense after *to*, so *to* is an infinitive marker and must be followed by the base form of the verb.

> They are planning *to build* a new school.

31c Become familiar with common adjective + preposition combinations.

Some adjectives appear only with certain prepositions. These expressions are idiomatic and may be different from the combinations used in your native language.

▶ Paula is married ~~with~~ *to* Jon.

Check an ESL dictionary for combinations that are not listed in the chart at the bottom of this page.

31d Become familiar with common verb + preposition combinations.

Many verbs and prepositions appear together in idiomatic phrases. Pay special attention to the combinations that are different from the combinations used in your native language.

▶ Your success depends ~~of~~ *on* your effort.

Check an ESL dictionary for combinations that are not listed in the chart on page 352.

Adjective + preposition combinations

accustomed to	connected to	guilty of	preferable to
addicted to	covered with	interested in	proud of
afraid of	dedicated to	involved in	responsible for
angry with	devoted to	involved with	satisfied with
ashamed of	different from	known as	scared of
aware of	engaged to (*or*	known for	similar to
committed to	engaged in)	made of (*or*	tired of
concerned	excited about	made from)	worried about
about	familiar with	married to	
concerned with	full of	opposed to	

Verb + preposition combinations

agree with	compare with	forget about	speak to (*or*
apply to	concentrate on	happen to	speak with)
approve of	consist of	hope for	stare at
arrive at	count on	insist on	succeed at
arrive in	decide on	listen to	succeed in
ask for	depend on	participate in	take advantage of
believe in	differ from	rely on	take care of
belong to	disagree with	reply to	think about
care about	dream about	respond to	think of
care for	dream of	result in	wait for
compare to	feel like	search for	wait on

Part VII
Punctuation

353

32   The comma

The comma was invented to help readers. Without it, sentence parts can collide into one another unexpectedly, causing misreadings.

CONFUSING   If you cook Elmer will do the dishes.

CONFUSING   While we were eating a rattlesnake approached our campsite.

Add commas in the logical places (after *cook* and *eating*), and suddenly all is clear. No longer is Elmer being cooked, the rattlesnake being eaten.

Various rules have evolved to prevent such misreadings and to speed readers along through complex grammatical structures. Those rules are detailed in this section. (Section 33 explains when not to use commas.)

> Grammar checkers rarely flag missing or misused commas. They sometimes recognize that a comma belongs before a *which* clause but not before a *that* clause (see 32e). For all other uses of the comma covered in section 32, they are unreliable.

32a Use a comma before a coordinating conjunction joining independent clauses.

When a coordinating conjunction connects two or more independent clauses—word groups that could stand alone as separate sentences—a comma must precede it. There are seven coordinating conjunctions in English: *and, but, or, nor, for, so,* and *yet.*

A comma tells readers that one independent clause has come to a close and that another is about to begin.

▶ The department sponsored a seminar on college survival

skills during fall orientation‿and it also hosted a barbecue

to make new students feel at home.

EXCEPTION: If the two independent clauses are short and there is no danger of misreading, the comma may be omitted.

The plane took off and we were on our way.

TIP: As a rule, do *not* use a comma to separate coordinate word groups that are not independent clauses. (See 33a.)

▶ A good money manager controls expenses/and invests

surplus dollars to meet future needs.

The word group following *and* is not an independent clause; it is the second half of a compound predicate (*controls* . . . and *invests*).

32b Use a comma after an introductory clause or phrase.

The most common introductory word groups are clauses and phrases functioning as adverbs. Such word groups usually tell when, where, how, why, or under what conditions the main action of the sentence occurred. (See 63a, 63b, and 63e.)

A comma tells readers that the introductory clause or phrase has come to a close and that the main part of the sentence is about to begin.

▶ When Irwin was ready to iron‚ his cat tripped on the

cord.

Without the comma, readers may have Irwin ironing his cat. The comma signals that *his cat* is the subject of a new clause, not part of the introductory one.

▶ Near a small stream at the bottom of the canyon‚ the park

rangers discovered an abandoned mine.

The comma tells readers that the introductory prepositional phrase has come to a close.

EXCEPTION: The comma may be omitted after a short adverb clause or phrase if there is no danger of misreading.

In no time we were at 2,800 feet.

Sentences also frequently begin with participial phrases describing the noun or pronoun immediately following them. The comma tells readers that they are about to learn the identity of the person or thing described; therefore, the comma is usually required even when the phrase is short. (See 63b.)

▶ Thinking his motorcade drive through Dallas was routine,

President Kennedy smiled and waved at the crowds.

▶ Buried under layers of younger rocks, the earth's oldest

rocks contain no fossils.

NOTE: Other introductory word groups include transitional expressions and absolute phrases (see 32f).

EXERCISE 32–1 Add or delete commas where necessary in the following sentences. If a sentence is correct, write "correct" after it. Answers to lettered sentences appear in the back of the book. Example:

Because we had been saving molding for a few weeks, we

had enough wood to frame all thirty paintings.

a. Alisa brought the injured bird home, and fashioned a splint out of Popsicle sticks for its wing.

b. Considered a classic of early animation *The Adventures of Prince Achmed* used hand-cut silhouettes against colored backgrounds.

c. If you complete the enclosed evaluation form and return it within two weeks you will receive a free breakfast during your next stay.

d. After retiring from the New York City Ballet in 1965, legendary dancer Maria Tallchief went on to found the Chicago City Ballet.

e.   Roger had always wanted a handmade violin but he couldn't afford one.

1.   While I was driving a huge delivery truck ran through a red light.
2.   He pushed the car beyond the tollgate, and poured a bucket of water on the smoking hood.
3.   Lit by bright halogen lamps hundreds of origami birds sparkled like diamonds in sunlight.
4.   As the first chord sounded, Aileen knew that her spirits were about to rise.
5.   Many musicians of Bach's time played several instruments but few mastered them as early or played with as much expression as Bach.

EXERCISE 32–2   Add or delete commas where necessary in the following sentences. If a sentence is correct, write "correct" after it. Answers to lettered sentences appear in the back of the book. Example:

The car had been sitting idle for a month, so the battery

was completely dead.

a.   J. R. R. Tolkien finished writing his draft of *The Lord of the Rings* trilogy in 1949 but the first book in the series wasn't published until 1954.
b.   In the first two minutes of its ascent the space shuttle had broken the sound barrier and reached a height of over twenty-five miles.
c.   German shepherds can be gentle guide dogs or they can be fierce attack dogs.
d.   Some former professional cyclists claim that the use of performance-enhancing drugs is widespread in cycling and they argue that no rider can be competitive without doping.
e.   As an intern, I learned most aspects of the broadcasting industry but I never learned about fundraising.

1.   To be considered for the position candidates must demonstrate initiative and strong communication skills.
2.   The cinematic lighting effect known as *chiaroscuro* was first used in German Expressionist filmmaking, and was later seen in American film noir.

3. Reptiles are cold-blooded and they are covered with scales.
4. Using a variety of techniques, advertisers grab the audience's attention and imprint their messages onto consumers' minds.
5. By the end of the first quarter the operating budget will be available online.

32c Use a comma between all items in a series.

When three or more items are presented in a series, those items should be separated from one another with commas. Items in a series may be single words, phrases, or clauses.

▶ Bubbles of air, leaves, ferns, bits of wood, and insects are

often found trapped in amber.

▶ Langston Hughes's poetry is concerned with racial pride,

social justice, and the diversity of the African American

experience.

Although some writers view the comma between the last two items as optional, most experts advise using the comma because its omission can result in ambiguity or misreading.

▶ Uncle David willed me all of his property, houses, and

warehouses.

Did Uncle David will his property *and* houses *and* warehouses—or simply his property, consisting of houses and warehouses? If the former meaning is intended, a comma is necessary to prevent ambiguity.

▶ The activities include touring the White House, visiting

the Air and Space Museum, attending a lecture about the

Founding Fathers, and kayaking on the Potomac River.

Without the comma, the activities might seem to include a lecture about kayaking, not participating in kayaking. The comma makes it clear that *kayaking on the Potomac River* is a separate item in the series.

32d Use a comma between coordinate adjectives not joined with *and*. Do not use a comma between cumulative adjectives.

When two or more adjectives each modify a noun separately, they are coordinate.

> Roberto is a *warm, gentle, affectionate* father.

TEST: If the adjectives can be joined with *and*, the adjectives are coordinate, so you should use commas: *warm* and *gentle* and *affectionate* (*warm, gentle, affectionate*).

> Adjectives that do not modify the noun separately are cumulative.

> *Three large gray* shapes moved slowly toward us.

Beginning with the adjective closest to the noun *shapes*, these modifiers lean on one another, piggyback style, with each modifying a larger word group. *Gray* modifies *shapes*, *large* modifies *gray shapes*, and *three* modifies *large gray shapes*. Cumulative adjectives cannot be joined with *and* (not *three* and *large* and *gray shapes*).

COORDINATE ADJECTIVES

▶ Should patients with severe‚ irreversible brain damage

be put on life support systems?

> Adjectives are coordinate if they can be connected with *and*: *severe and irreversible*.

CUMULATIVE ADJECTIVES

▶ Ira ordered a rich/chocolate/layer cake.

> Ira didn't order a cake that was rich and chocolate and layer: He ordered a *layer cake* that was *chocolate*, a *chocolate layer cake* that was *rich*.

EXERCISE 32–3 Add or delete commas where necessary in the following sentences. If a sentence is correct, write "correct" after it. Answers to lettered sentences appear in the back of the book. Example:

> **We gathered our essentials, took off for the great outdoors,**
>
> **and ignored the fact that it was Friday the 13th.**

a.   The cold impersonal atmosphere of the university was unbearable.

b.   An ambulance threaded its way through police cars, fire trucks and irate citizens.

c.   The *1812 Overture* is a stirring, magnificent piece of music.

d.   After two broken arms, three cracked ribs and one concussion, Ken quit the varsity football team.

e.   My cat's pupils had constricted to small black shining slits.

1.   We prefer our staff to be orderly, prompt and efficient.

2.   For breakfast the children ordered cornflakes, English muffins with peanut butter and cherry Cokes.

3.   It was a small, unimportant part, but I was happy to have it.

4.   Cyril was clad in a luminous orange rain suit and a brilliant white helmet.

5.   Animation master Hironobu Sakaguchi makes computer-generated scenes look realistic, vivid and seductive.

EXERCISE 32–4 Add or delete commas where necessary in the following sentences. If a sentence is correct, write "correct" after it. Answers to lettered sentences appear in the back of the book. Example:

> **Good social workers excel in patience, diplomacy, and**
>
> **positive thinking.**

a.   NASA's rovers on Mars are equipped with special cameras that can take close-up high-resolution pictures of the terrain.

b.   A baseball player achieves the triple crown by having the highest batting average, the most home runs, and the most runs batted in during the regular season.

c.   If it does not get enough sunlight, a healthy green lawn can turn into a shriveled brown mess within a matter of days.

d.   Love, vengeance, greed and betrayal are common themes in Western literature.

e.   Many experts believe that shark attacks on surfers are a result of the sharks' mistaking surfboards for small, injured seals.

1.   In Sherman's march to the sea, the Union army set fire to all crops, killed all livestock and destroyed all roads and bridges in its path.

2.   Milk that comes from grass-fed steroid-free cows has been gaining market share.

3.   The film makes three main points about global warming: It is real, it is the result of human activity, and it should not be ignored.

4.   The three, handmade, turquoise bracelets brought in the most money at the charity auction.

5.   Matisse is well known for vibrant colorful prints that have been reproduced extensively on greeting cards and posters.

32e Use commas to set off nonrestrictive elements. Do not use commas to set off restrictive elements.

Certain word groups that modify nouns or pronouns can be restrictive or nonrestrictive—that is, essential or not essential to the meaning of a sentence. These word groups are usually adjective clauses, adjective phrases, or appositives.

Restrictive elements

A restrictive element defines or limits the meaning of the word it modifies; it is therefore essential to the meaning of the sentence and is not set off with commas. If you remove a restrictive modifier from a sentence, the meaning changes significantly, becoming more general than you intended.

RESTRICTIVE (NO COMMAS)

The campers need clothes *that are durable*.

Scientists *who study the earth's structure* are called geologists.

The writer of the first sentence does not mean that the campers need clothes in general. The intended meaning is more limited: The campers need durable clothes. The writer of the second sentence does not mean that scientists in general are called geologists; those scientists who specifically study the earth's structure are called geologists. The italicized word groups are essential and are therefore not set off with commas.

Nonrestrictive elements

A nonrestrictive modifier describes a noun or pronoun whose meaning has already been clearly defined or limited. Because the modifier contains nonessential or parenthetical information, it is set off with commas. If you remove a nonrestrictive element from a sentence, the meaning does not change dramatically. Some meaning is lost, to be sure, but the defining characteristics of the person or thing described remain the same.

> **NONRESTRICTIVE (WITH COMMAS)**
>
> The campers need sturdy shoes, *which are expensive.*
>
> The scientists, *who represented eight different universities*, met to review applications for the prestigious O'Hara Award.

In the first sentence, the campers need sturdy shoes, and the shoes happen to be expensive. In the second sentence, the scientists met to review applications for the O'Hara Award; that they represented eight different universities is informative but not critical to the meaning of the sentence. The nonessential information in both sentences is enclosed in commas.

NOTE: Often it is difficult to tell whether a word group is restrictive or nonrestrictive without seeing it in context and considering the writer's meaning. Both of the following sentences are grammatically correct, but their meaning is slightly different.

> The dessert made with fresh raspberries was delicious.
>
> The dessert, made with fresh raspberries, was delicious.

In the first example, the phrase *made with fresh raspberries* tells readers which of two or more desserts the writer is referring to. In the example with commas, the phrase merely adds information about the dessert.

Adjective clauses

Adjective clauses are patterned like sentences, containing subjects and verbs, but they function within sentences as modifiers of nouns or pronouns. They always follow the word they modify, usually immediately. Adjective clauses begin with a relative pronoun (*who, whom, whose, which, that*) or with a relative adverb (*where, when*).

Nonrestrictive adjective clauses are set off with commas; restrictive adjective clauses are not.

NONRESTRICTIVE CLAUSE (WITH COMMAS)

▶ **Ed's house‚ which is located on thirteen acres‚ was completely furnished with bats in the rafters and mice in the kitchen.**

The adjective clause *which is located on thirteen acres* does not restrict the meaning of *Ed's house*; the information is nonessential and is therefore enclosed in commas.

RESTRICTIVE CLAUSE (NO COMMAS)

▶ **The giant panda⁄that was born at the San Diego Zoo in 2003⁄was sent to China in 2007.**

Because the adjective clause *that was born at the San Diego Zoo in 2003* identifies one particular panda out of many, the information is essential and is therefore not enclosed in commas.

NOTE: Use *that* only with restrictive (essential) clauses. Many writers prefer to use *which* only with nonrestrictive (nonessential) clauses, but usage varies.

Adjective phrases

Prepositional or verbal phrases functioning as adjectives may be restrictive or nonrestrictive. Nonrestrictive phrases are set off with commas; restrictive phrases are not.

NONRESTRICTIVE PHRASE (WITH COMMAS)

▶ The helicopter, with its million-candlepower spotlight illuminating the area, circled above.

The *with* phrase is nonessential because its purpose is not to specify which of two or more helicopters is being discussed. The phrase is not required for readers to understand the meaning of the sentence.

RESTRICTIVE PHRASE (NO COMMAS)

▶ One corner of the attic was filled with newspapers/dating from the early 1900s.

Dating from the early 1900s restricts the meaning of *newspapers*, so the comma should be omitted.

▶ The bill/proposed by the Illinois representative/would lower taxes and provide services for middle-income families.

Proposed by the Illinois representative identifies exactly which bill is meant.

Appositives

An appositive is a noun or noun phrase that renames a nearby noun. Nonrestrictive appositives are set off with commas; restrictive appositives are not.

NONRESTRICTIVE APPOSITIVE (WITH COMMAS)

▶ Darwin's most important book, *On the Origin of Species,* was the result of many years of research.

Most important restricts the meaning to one book, so the appositive *On the Origin of Species* is nonrestrictive and should be set off with commas.

RESTRICTIVE APPOSITIVE (NO COMMAS)

▶ The song⁄ "Viva la Vida⁄" was blasted out of huge amplifiers

at the concert.

Once they've read *song*, readers still don't know precisely which song the writer means. The appositive following *song* restricts its meaning, so the appositive should not be enclosed in commas.

EXERCISE 32–5 Add or delete commas where necessary in the following sentences. If a sentence is correct, write "correct" after it. Answers to lettered sentences appear in the back of the book. Example:

My youngest sister‸ who plays left wing on the soccer

team‸ now lives at The Sands‸ a beach house near

Los Angeles.

a. Choreographer Alvin Ailey's best-known work *Revelations* is more than just a crowd-pleaser.
b. Twyla Tharp's contemporary ballet *Push Comes to Shove* was made famous by the Russian dancer Baryshnikov. [Tharp has written more than one contemporary ballet.]
c. The glass sculptor sifting through hot red sand explained her technique to the other glassmakers. [There is more than one glass sculptor.]
d. A member of an organization, that provides job training for teens, was also appointed to the education commission.
e. Brian Eno who began his career as a rock musician turned to meditative compositions in the late seventies.

1. I had the pleasure of talking to a woman who had just returned from India where she had lived for ten years.
2. Patrick's oldest sister Fiona graduated from MIT with a degree in aerospace engineering.
3. The artist painting a portrait of Aung San Suu Kyi, the Burmese civil rights leader, was once a political prisoner himself.

4. *Jumanji,* the 1982 Caldecott Medal winner, is my nephew's favorite book.
5. The flame crawled up a few blades of grass to reach a low-hanging palmetto branch which quickly ignited.

32f Use commas to set off transitional and parenthetical expressions, absolute phrases, and elements expressing contrast.

Transitional expressions

Transitional expressions serve as bridges between sentences or parts of sentences. They include conjunctive adverbs such as *however, therefore,* and *moreover* and transitional phrases such as *for example, as a matter of fact,* and *in other words.* (For complete lists of these expressions, see 34b.)

When a transitional expression appears between independent clauses in a compound sentence, it is preceded by a semicolon and is usually followed by a comma. (See 34b.)

▶ Minh did not understand our language; moreover, he was

unfamiliar with our customs.

When a transitional expression appears at the beginning of a sentence or in the middle of an independent clause, it is usually set off with commas.

▶ As a matter of fact, American football was established

by fans who wanted to play a more organized game of

rugby.

▶ Natural foods are not always salt free; celery, for example,

contains more sodium than most people would imagine.

EXCEPTION: If a transitional expression blends smoothly with the rest of the sentence, calling for little or no pause in reading, it does not need to be set off with a comma. Expressions such as *also, at least, certainly, consequently, indeed, of course, moreover, no doubt, perhaps, then,* and *therefore* do not always call for a pause.

> Alice's bicycle is broken; *therefore* you will need to borrow Sue's.

NOTE: The conjunctive adverb *however* always calls for a pause. It should not be confused with the adverb *however* meaning "no matter how," which does not require a pause or a comma: *However hard Bill tried, he could not match his previous record.*

Parenthetical expressions

Expressions that are distinctly parenthetical, providing only supplemental information, should be set off with commas. They interrupt the flow of a sentence or appear at the end as afterthoughts.

▶ **Evolution, as far as we know, doesn't work this way.**

▶ **The bass weighed about twelve pounds, give or take a few ounces.**

Absolute phrases

An absolute phrase, which modifies the whole sentence, usually consists of a noun followed by a participle or participial phrase. (See 63d.) Absolute phrases may appear at the beginning or at the end of a sentence. Wherever they appear, they should be set off with commas.

```
┌────────── ABSOLUTE PHRASE ──────────┐
  N     PARTICIPLE
```
The sun appearing for the first time in a week, we were at last able to begin the archaeological dig.

▶ **Elvis Presley made music industry history in the 1950s, his records having sold more than ten million copies.**

NOTE: Do not insert a comma between the noun and the participle in an absolute construction.

▶ The next contestant/being five years old, the emcee

adjusted the height of the microphone.

Contrasted elements

Sharp contrasts beginning with words such as *not, never,* and *unlike* are set off with commas.

▶ The Epicurean philosophers sought mental‚ not bodily‚

pleasures.

▶ Unlike Robert‚ Celia loved dance contests.

32g Use commas to set off nouns of direct address, the words *yes* and *no*, interrogative tags, and mild interjections.

▶ Forgive me‚ Angela‚ for forgetting your birthday.

▶ Yes‚ the loan will probably be approved.

▶ The film was faithful to the book‚ wasn't it?

▶ Well‚ cases like these are difficult to decide.

32h Use commas with expressions such as *he said* to set off direct quotations. (See also 37f.)

▶ In his "Letter from Birmingham Jail," Martin Luther King

Jr. wrote‚ "We know through painful experience that

freedom is never voluntarily given by the oppressor; it must

be demanded by the oppressed" (225).

▶ "Happiness in marriage is entirely a matter of chance,"

says Charlotte Lucas in *Pride and Prejudice*, a novel that

ends with two happy marriages (ch. 6; 69).

See pages 528–29 on citing literary sources in MLA style.

32i Use commas with dates, addresses, titles, and numbers.

Dates

In dates, the year is set off from the rest of the sentence with a pair of commas.

▶ On December 12, 1890, orders were sent out for the arrest of

Sitting Bull.

EXCEPTIONS: Commas are not needed if the date is inverted or if only the month and year are given.

The security alert system went into effect on 15 April 2009.

January 2008 was an extremely cold month.

Addresses

The elements of an address or a place name are separated with commas. A zip code, however, is not preceded by a comma.

▶ John Lennon was born in Liverpool, England, in 1940.

▶ Please send the package to Greg Tarvin at 708 Spring Street,

Washington, IL 61571.

Titles

If a title follows a name, separate the title from the rest of the sentence with a pair of commas.

▶ Sandra Belinsky, MD, has been appointed to the board
                   ^   ^

of trustees.

Numbers

In numbers more than four digits long, use commas to separate the numbers into groups of three, starting from the right.
In numbers four digits long, a comma is optional.

> 3,500 [*or* 3500]
>
> 100,000
>
> 5,000,000

EXCEPTIONS: Do not use commas in street numbers, zip codes,
telephone numbers, or years with four or fewer digits.

32j Use a comma to prevent confusion.

In certain contexts, a comma is necessary to prevent confusion. If the writer has omitted a word or phrase, for example,
a comma may be needed to signal the omission.

▶ To err is human; to forgive, divine.
                          ^

If two words in a row echo each other, a comma may be
needed for ease of reading.

▶ All of the catastrophes that we had feared might happen,
                                                          ^

happened.

Sometimes a comma is needed to prevent readers from
grouping words in ways that do not match the writer's
intention.

▶ Patients who can, walk up and down the halls several
                  ^

times a day.

EXERCISE 32–6 This exercise covers the major uses of the comma described in 32a–32e. Add or delete commas where necessary. If a sentence is correct, write "correct" after it. Answers to lettered sentences appear in the back of the book. Example:

> **Even though Pavel had studied Nigella Lawson's recipes for a week, he underestimated how long it would take to juice two hundred lemons.**

a. Cricket which originated in England is also popular in Australia, South Africa and India.
b. At the sound of the starting pistol the horses surged forward toward the first obstacle, a sharp incline three feet high.
c. After seeing an exhibition of Western art Gerhard Richter escaped from East Berlin, and smuggled out many of his notebooks.
d. Corrie's new wet suit has an intricate, blue pattern.
e. The cookies will keep for two weeks in sturdy airtight containers.

1. Research on Andean condors has shown that high levels of the pesticide chlorinated hydrocarbon can cause the thinning of eggshells.
2. Founded in 1868 Hampton University was one of the first colleges for African Americans.
3. Aunt Emilia was an impossible demanding guest.
4. The French Mirage, a high-tech fighter, is an astonishing machine to fly.
5. At the bottom of the ship's rusty hold sat several, well-preserved trunks, reminders of a bygone era of sea travel.

EXERCISE 32–7 This exercise covers all uses of the comma. Add or delete commas where necessary in the following sentences. If a sentence is correct, write "correct" after it. Answers to lettered sentences appear in the back of the book. Example:

> **"Yes, dear, you can have dessert," my mother said.**

a. On January 15, 2008 our office moved to 29 Commonwealth Avenue, Mechanicsville VA 23111.
b. The coach having bawled us out thoroughly, we left the locker room with his harsh words ringing in our ears.

c. Ms. Carlson you are a valued customer whose satisfaction is very important to us.

d. Mr. Mundy was born on July 22, 1939 in Arkansas, where his family had lived for four generations.

e. Her board poised at the edge of the half-pipe, Nina waited her turn to drop in.

1. President Lincoln's original intention was to save the Union, not to destroy slavery.

2. For centuries people believed that Greek culture had developed in isolation from the world. Today however scholars are acknowledging the contributions made by Egypt and the Middle East.

3. Putting together a successful fundraiser, Patricia discovered, requires creativity and good timing.

4. Fortunately science is creating many alternatives to research performed on animals.

5. While the machine was printing the oversize paper jammed.

hackerhandbooks.com/bedhandbook > Grammar exercises > Punctuation
> E-ex 32–8 to 32–10

33   Unnecessary commas

Many common misuses of the comma result from an incomplete understanding of the major comma rules presented in 32. In particular, writers frequently form misconceptions about rules 32a–32e, either extending the rules inappropriately or misinterpreting them. Such misconceptions can lead to the errors described in 33a–33e; rules 33f–33h list other common misuses of the comma.

33a Do not use a comma between compound elements that are not independent clauses.

Though a comma should be used before a coordinating conjunction joining independent clauses (see 32a), this rule should not be extended to other compound word groups.

▶ Marie Curie discovered radium/and later applied her work

on radioactivity to medicine.

And links two verbs in a compound predicate: *discovered* and *applied*.

▶ Jake told us that his illness is serious/but that changes in

his lifestyle can improve his chances for survival.

The coordinating conjunction *but* links two subordinate clauses,
each beginning with *that*: *that his illness is serious* and *that changes
in his lifestyle*. . . .

33b Do not use a comma after a phrase that begins an inverted sentence.

Though a comma belongs after most introductory phrases
(see 32b), it does not belong after phrases that begin an inverted sentence. In an inverted sentence, the subject follows
the verb, and a phrase that ordinarily would follow the verb is
moved to the beginning (see 62c).

▶ At the bottom of the hill/sat the stubborn mule.

33c Do not use a comma before the first or after the last item in a series.

Though commas are required between items in a series (32c),
do not place them either before or after the whole series.

▶ Other causes of asthmatic attacks are/stress, change in

temperature, and cold air.

▶ Ironically, even novels that focus on horror, evil, and

alienation/often have themes of spiritual renewal and

redemption as well.

33d Do not use a comma between cumulative adjectives, between an adjective and a noun, or between an adverb and an adjective.

Commas are required between coordinate adjectives (those that can be joined with *and*), but they do not belong between cumulative adjectives (those that cannot be joined with *and*). (For a full discussion, see 32d.)

▶ In the corner of the closet we found an old/maroon hatbox

from Sears.

A comma should never be used between an adjective and the noun that follows it.

▶ It was a senseless, dangerous/mission.

Nor should a comma be used between an adverb and an adjective that follows it.

▶ The Hillside is a good home for severely/disturbed youths.

33e Do not use commas to set off restrictive or mildly parenthetical elements.

Restrictive elements are modifiers or appositives that restrict the meaning of the nouns they follow. Because they are essential to the meaning of the sentence, they are not set off with commas. (For a full discussion of restrictive and nonrestrictive elements, see 32e.)

▶ Drivers/who think they own the road/make cycling a

dangerous sport.

The modifier *who think they own the road* restricts the meaning of *Drivers* and is therefore essential to the meaning of the sentence. Putting commas around the *who* clause falsely suggests that all drivers think they own the road.

▶ Margaret Mead's book/*Coming of Age in Samoa*/stirred

up considerable controversy when it was published in 1928.

Since Mead wrote more than one book, the appositive contains
information essential to the meaning of the sentence.

Although commas should be used with distinctly parenthetical expressions (see 32f), do not use them to set off elements that are only mildly parenthetical.

▶ Texting has/essentially/replaced e-mail for casual

communication.

33f Do not use a comma to set off a concluding adverb clause that is essential to the meaning of the sentence.

When adverb clauses introduce a sentence, they are nearly always followed by a comma (see 32b). When they conclude a
sentence, however, they are not set off by commas if their content is essential to the meaning of the earlier part of the sentence. Adverb clauses beginning with *after, as soon as, because,
before, if, since, unless, until,* and *when* are usually essential.

▶ Don't visit Paris at the height of the tourist season/unless

you have booked hotel reservations.

Without the *unless* clause, the meaning of the sentence might at
first seem broader than the writer intended.

When a concluding adverb clause is nonessential, it should
be preceded by a comma. Clauses beginning with *although,
even though, though,* and *whereas* are usually nonessential.

▶ The lecture seemed to last only a short time, although the

clock said it had gone on for more than an hour.

33g Do not use a comma to separate a verb from its subject or object.

A sentence should flow from subject to verb to object without unnecessary pauses. Commas may appear between these major sentence elements only when a specific rule calls for them.

▶ **Zoos large enough to give the animals freedom to roam/are**

becoming more popular.

> The comma should not separate the subject, *Zoos*, from the verb, *are becoming*.

▶ **The director explained to the board/that she was resigning**

because of a conflict of interest.

> The comma should not separate the verb, *explained*, from its object, the subordinate clause *that she was resigning because of a conflict of interest*.

▶ **Maxine Hong Kingston writes/that many Chinese**

American families struggle "to figure out how the invisible

world the emigrants built around our childhoods fits in

solid America" (107).

> The comma should not separate the verb, *writes*, from its object, the subordinate clause beginning with *that*. A signal phrase ending in a word like *writes* or *says* is followed by a comma only when a direct quotation immediately follows: *Kingston writes, "Those of us in the first American generations have had to figure out how the invisible world . . ." (107).* (See also 37f.)

Writing with sources
MLA-style citation

33h Avoid other common misuses of the comma.

Do not use a comma in the following situations.

AFTER A COORDINATING CONJUNCTION (*AND, BUT, OR, NOR, FOR, SO, YET*)

▶ **Occasionally TV talk shows are performed live, but/more**

often they are taped.

AFTER *SUCH AS* OR *LIKE*

▶ Shade-loving plants such as⁄begonias, impatiens, and

coleus can add color to a shady garden.

BEFORE *THAN*

▶ Touring Crete was more thrilling for us⁄than visiting the

Greek islands frequented by the rich.

AFTER *ALTHOUGH*

▶ Although⁄the air was balmy, the water was too cold for

swimming.

BEFORE A PARENTHESIS

▶ At InterComm, Sylvia began at the bottom⁄(with only

three and a half walls and a swivel chair), but within three

years she had been promoted to supervisor.

TO SET OFF AN INDIRECT (REPORTED) QUOTATION

▶ Samuel Goldwyn once said⁄that a verbal contract isn't

worth the paper it's written on.

WITH A QUESTION MARK OR AN EXCLAMATION POINT

▶ "Why don't you try it?⁄" she coaxed. "You can't do any

worse than the rest of us."

EXERCISE 33–1   Delete commas where necessary in the following
sentences. If a sentence is correct, write "correct" after it. Answers to
lettered sentences appear in the back of the book. Example:

In his Silk Road Project, Yo-Yo Ma incorporates work by

musicians such as⁄Kayhan Kahlor and Richard Danielpour.

a. After the morning rains cease, the swimmers emerge from their cottages.

b. Tricia's first artwork was a bright, blue, clay dolphin.

c. Some modern musicians, (trumpeter John Hassell is an example) blend several cultural traditions into a unique sound.

d. Myra liked hot, spicy foods such as, chili, kung pao chicken, and buffalo wings.

e. On the display screen, was a soothing pattern of light and shadow.

1. Mesquite, the hardest of the softwoods, grows primarily in the Southwest.

2. Jolie's parents encouraged independent thinking, but required respect for others' opinions.

3. The border guards told their sergeant, that their heat-sensing equipment was malfunctioning.

4. The streets that three hours later would be bumper to bumper with commuters, were quiet and empty except for a few prowling cats.

5. Some first-year architecture students, expect to design intricate structures immediately.

EXERCISE 33–2 Delete commas where necessary in the following passage.

Each spring since 1970, New Orleans has hosted the Jazz and Heritage Festival, an event that celebrates the music, food, and culture, of the region. Although, it is often referred to as "Jazz Fest," the festival typically includes a wide variety of musical styles such as, gospel, Cajun, blues, zydeco, and, rock and roll. Famous musicians who have appeared regularly at Jazz Fest, include Dr. John, B. B. King, and Aretha Franklin. Large stages are set up throughout the fairgrounds in a way, that allows up to ten bands to play simultaneously without any sound overlap. Food tents are located throughout the festival, and offer popular, local dishes like crawfish Monica, jambalaya, and fried, green tomatoes. In 2009, Jazz Fest marked its fortieth anniversary. Fans, who could not attend the festival, still enjoyed the music by downloading MP3 files, and watching performances online.

34 The semicolon

The semicolon is used to connect major sentence elements of equal grammatical rank.

> Grammar checkers flag some, but not all, misused semicolons (34d). In addition, they can alert you to some run-on sentences (34a). However, they miss more run-on sentences than they identify, and they sometimes flag correct sentences as possible run-ons.

34a Use a semicolon between closely related independent clauses not joined with a coordinating conjunction.

When related independent clauses appear in one sentence, they are ordinarily linked with a comma and a coordinating conjunction (*and*, *but*, *or*, *nor*, *for*, *so*, *yet*). The coordinating conjunction signals the relation between the clauses. If the clauses are closely related and the relation is clear without a conjunction, they may be linked with a semicolon instead.

> In film, a low-angle shot makes the subject look powerful; a high-angle shot does just the opposite.

A semicolon must be used whenever a coordinating conjunction has been omitted between independent clauses. To use merely a comma creates a type of run-on sentence known as a *comma splice*. (See 20.)

▶ In 1800, a traveler needed six weeks to get from New York

City to Chicago⌃; in 1860, the trip by railroad took only

two days.

TIP: Do not overuse the semicolon as a means of revising run-on sentences. For other revision strategies, see 20a, 20c, and 20d.

34b Use a semicolon between independent clauses linked with a transitional expression.

Transitional expressions include conjunctive adverbs and transitional phrases.

CONJUNCTIVE ADVERBS

accordingly	furthermore	moreover	still
also	hence	nevertheless	subsequently
anyway	however	next	then
besides	incidentally	nonetheless	therefore
certainly	indeed	now	thus
consequently	instead	otherwise	
conversely	likewise	similarly	
finally	meanwhile	specifically	

TRANSITIONAL PHRASES

after all	even so	in fact
as a matter of fact	for example	in other words
as a result	for instance	in the first place
at any rate	in addition	on the contrary
at the same time	in conclusion	on the other hand

When a transitional expression appears between independent clauses, it is preceded by a semicolon and usually followed by a comma.

▶ Many corals grow very gradually/; in fact, the creation of a

coral reef can take centuries.

When a transitional expression appears in the middle or at the end of the second independent clause, the semicolon goes *between the clauses*.

▶ Biologists have observed laughter in primates other than

humans/; chimpanzees, however, sound more like they are

panting than laughing.

Transitional expressions should not be confused with the coordinating conjunctions *and, but, or, nor, for, so,* and *yet,* which are preceded by a comma when they link independent clauses. (See 32a.)

34c Use a semicolon between items in a series containing internal punctuation.

▶ Classic science fiction sagas are *Star Trek*, with Mr. Spock/;

Battlestar Galactica, with its Cylons/; and *Star Wars,*

with Han Solo, Luke Skywalker, and Darth Vader.

Without the semicolons, the reader would have to sort out the major groupings, distinguishing between important and less important pauses according to the logic of the sentence. By inserting semicolons at the major breaks, the writer does this work for the reader.

34d Avoid common misuses of the semicolon.

Do not use a semicolon in the following situations.

BETWEEN A SUBORDINATE CLAUSE AND THE REST OF THE SENTENCE

▶ Although children's literature was added to the National

Book Awards in 1969/, it has had its own award, the Newbery

Medal, since 1922.

BETWEEN AN APPOSITIVE AND THE WORD IT REFERS TO

▶ The scientists were fascinated by the species *Argyroneta*

aquatica/, a spider that lives underwater.

TO INTRODUCE A LIST

▶ Some of my favorite celebrities have their own blogs/:
Lindsay Lohan, Rosie O'Donnell, and Zach Braff.

BETWEEN INDEPENDENT CLAUSES JOINED BY *AND*, *BUT*, *OR*, *NOR*, *FOR*, *SO*, OR *YET*

▶ Five of the applicants had worked with spreadsheets ;

but only one was familiar with database management.

EXCEPTIONS: If at least one of the independent clauses contains internal punctuation, you may use a semicolon even though the clauses are joined with a coordinating conjunction.

> As a vehicle [the model T] was hard-working, commonplace, and heroic; and it often seemed to transmit those qualities to the person who rode in it.   —E. B. White

Although a comma would also be correct in this sentence, the semicolon is more effective, for it indicates the relative weights of the pauses.

Occasionally, a semicolon may be used to emphasize a sharp contrast or a firm distinction between clauses joined with a coordinating conjunction.

> We hate some persons because we do not know them; and we will not know them because we hate them.
>   —Charles Caleb Colton

EXERCISE 34–1 Add commas or semicolons where needed in the following well-known quotations. If a sentence is correct, write "correct" after it. Answers to lettered sentences appear in the back of the book. Example:

> **If an animal does something , we call it instinct ; if we do**
>
> **the same thing , we call it intelligence.**   —Will Cuppy

a.   Do not ask me to be kind just ask me to act as though I were.
                                        —Jules Renard

b.   When men talk about defense they always claim to be protect-ing women and children but they never ask the women and children what they think.   —Pat Schroeder

c.   When I get a little money I buy books if any is left I buy food and clothes.   —Desiderius Erasmus

d. America is a country that doesn't know where it is going but is determined to set a speed record getting there.
                                                        —Lawrence J. Peter

e. Wit has truth in it wisecracking is simply calisthenics with words.   —Dorothy Parker

1. Standing in the middle of the road is very dangerous you get knocked down by the traffic from both sides.
                                                        —Margaret Thatcher

2. I do not believe in an afterlife, although I am bringing a change of underwear.   —Woody Allen

3. Once the children were in the house the air became more vivid and more heated every object in the house grew more alive.
                                                        —Mary Gordon

4. We don't know what we want but we are ready to bite someone to get it.   —Will Rogers

5. I've been rich and I've been poor rich is better.
                                                        —Sophie Tucker

EXERCISE 34–2 Edit the following sentences to correct errors in the use of the comma and the semicolon. If a sentence is correct, write "correct" after it. Answers to lettered sentences appear in the back of the book. Example:

   Love is blind; envy has its eyes wide open.

a. Strong black coffee will not sober you up, the truth is that time is the only way to get alcohol out of your system.

b. Margaret was not surprised to see hail and vivid lightning, conditions had been right for violent weather all day.

c. There is often a fine line between right and wrong; good and bad; truth and deception.

d. My mother always says that you can't learn common sense; either you're born with it or you're not.

e. Severe, unremitting pain is a ravaging force; especially when the patient tries to hide it from others.

1. Another delicious dish is the chef's special; a roasted duck rubbed with spices and stuffed with wild rice.

2. Martin Luther King Jr. had not always intended to be a preacher, initially, he had planned to become a lawyer.

3. We all assumed that the thief had been Jean's boyfriend; even though we had seen him only from the back.

4. The Victorians avoided the subject of sex but were obsessed with death, a hundred years later, people were obsessed with sex but avoided thinking about death.

5. Some educators believe that African American history should be taught in separate courses, others prefer to see it integrated into survey courses.

hackerhandbooks.com/bedhandbook > Grammar exercises > Punctuation
> E-ex 34–3 and 34–4

35   The colon

The colon is used primarily to call attention to the words that follow it. In addition, the colon has some conventional uses.

> **Grammar checkers** are fairly good at flagging colons that incorrectly follow a verb (*The office work includes: typing, filing, and answering the phone*). They also point out semicolons used where colons are needed, although they don't suggest revisions.

35a Use a colon after an independent clause to direct attention to a list, an appositive, or a quotation.

A LIST

The daily routine should include at least the following: twenty knee bends, fifty sit-ups, fifteen leg lifts, and five minutes of running in place.

AN APPOSITIVE

My roommate is guilty of two of the seven deadly sins: gluttony and sloth.

A QUOTATION

Consider the words of Benjamin Franklin: "There never was a good war or a bad peace."

For other ways of introducing quotations, see "Introducing quoted material" on pages 396–97.

35b Use a colon between independent clauses if the second summarizes or explains the first.

Faith is like love: It cannot be forced.

NOTE: When an independent clause follows a colon, it may begin with a capital or a lowercase letter (see 45f).

35c Use a colon after the salutation in a formal letter, to indicate hours and minutes, to show proportions, between a title and subtitle, and between city and publisher in bibliographic entries.

Dear Sir or Madam:

5:30 p.m.

The ratio of women to men was 2:1.

The Glory of Hera: Greek Mythology and the Greek Family

Boston: Bedford, 2009

NOTE: In biblical references, a colon is ordinarily used between chapter and verse (Luke 2:14). The Modern Language Association (MLA) recommends a period instead (Luke 2.14).

35d Avoid common misuses of the colon.

A colon must be preceded by a full independent clause. Therefore, avoid using it in the following situations.

BETWEEN A VERB AND ITS OBJECT OR COMPLEMENT

▶ Some important vitamins found in vegetables are: vitamin A,

thiamine, niacin, and vitamin C.

BETWEEN A PREPOSITION AND ITS OBJECT

▶ The heart's two pumps each consist of⟋ an upper chamber,

or atrium, and a lower chamber, or ventricle.

AFTER *SUCH AS*, *INCLUDING*, OR *FOR EXAMPLE*

▶ The NCAA regulates college athletic teams, including⟋

basketball, baseball, softball, and football.

EXERCISE 35–1   Edit the following sentences to correct errors in the use of the comma, the semicolon, or the colon. If a sentence is correct, write "correct" after it. Answers to lettered sentences appear in the back of the book. Example:

> Lifting the cover gently, Luca found the source of the odd
>
> sound⟋: a marble in the gears.
>   ^

a. We always looked forward to Thanksgiving in Vermont: It was our only chance to see our Grady cousins.

b. If we have come to fight, we are far too few, if we have come to die, we are far too many.

c. The travel package includes: a round-trip ticket to Athens, a cruise through the Cyclades, and all hotel accommodations.

d. The news article portrays the land use proposal as reckless; although 62 percent of the town's residents support it.

e. Psychologists Kindlon and Thompson (2000) offer parents a simple starting point for raising male children, "Teach boys that there are many ways to be a man" (p. 256).

1. Harry Potter prevails against pain and evil for one reason, his heart is pure.

2. While traveling through France, Rose visited: the Loire Valley, Chartres, the Louvre, and the McDonald's stand at the foot of the Eiffel Tower.

3. There are three types of leave; annual leave, used for vacations, sick leave, used for medical appointments and illness, and personal leave, used for a variety of personal reasons.

4. American poet Carl Sandburg once asked these three questions,
    "Who paid for my freedom? What was the price? And am I
    somehow beholden?"
5. Amelie had four goals: to be encouraging, to be effective, to be
    efficient, and to be elegant.

hackerhandbooks.com/bedhandbook > Grammar exercises > Punctuation
                                      > E-ex 35–2

36   The apostrophe

> Grammar checkers flag only some missing or misused apostrophes.
> They catch missing apostrophes in contractions, such as *don't*.
> They also flag problems with possessives (*sled dogs feet, a babys
> eyes*), although they miss as many problems as they identify. Only
> you can decide when to add an apostrophe and whether to put it
> before or after the -*s* in possessives.

36a Use an apostrophe to indicate that a noun is possessive.

Possessive nouns usually indicate ownership, as in *Tim's hat,
the lawyer's desk*, or *someone's glove*. Frequently, however,
ownership is only loosely implied: *the tree's roots, a day's
work*. If you are not sure whether a noun is possessive, try
turning it into an *of* phrase: *the roots of the tree, the work of
a day*.

When to add -'s

1. If the noun does not end in -*s*, add -'*s*.

    Luck often propels a rock musician's career.

    The Children's Defense Fund is a nonprofit organization that
    supports programs for poor and minority children.

2. If the noun is singular and ends in *-s* or an *s* sound,
    add *-'s*.

> Lois's sister spent last year in India.

> Her article presents an overview of Marx's teachings.

NOTE: To avoid potentially awkward pronunciation, some writers use only the apostrophe with a singular noun ending in *-s*:
Sophocles'.

When to add only an apostrophe

If the noun is plural and ends in *-s*, add only an apostrophe.

> Both diplomats' briefcases were searched by guards.

Joint possession

To show joint possession, use *-'s* or (*-s'*) with the last noun only;
to show individual possession, make all nouns possessive.

> Have you seen Joyce and Greg's new camper?

> John's and Marie's expectations of marriage couldn't have
> been more different.

Joyce and Greg jointly own one camper. John and Marie individually have different expectations.

Compound nouns

If a noun is compound, use *-'s* (or *-s'*) with the last element.

> My father-in-law's memoir about his childhood in Sri Lanka
> was published in October.

36b Use an apostrophe and -s to indicate that an indefinite pronoun is possessive.

Indefinite pronouns refer to no specific person or thing: *everyone, someone, no one, something*. (See 61b.)

> Someone's raincoat has been left behind.

36c Use an apostrophe to mark omissions in contractions and numbers.

In a contraction, the apostrophe takes the place of one or more missing letters.

> It's a shame that Frank can't go on the tour.

It's stands for *it is,* *can't* for *cannot.*

> The apostrophe is also used to mark the omission of the first two digits of a year (*the class of '08*) or years (*the '60s generation*).

36d Do not use an apostrophe to form the plural of numbers, letters, abbreviations, and words mentioned as words.

An apostrophe typically is not used to pluralize numbers, letters, abbreviations, and words mentioned as words. Note the few exceptions and be consistent throughout your paper.

Plural numbers   Omit the apostrophe in the plural of all numbers, including decades.

> Oksana skated nearly perfect figure 8s.

> The 1920s are known as the Jazz Age.

Plural letters   Italicize the letter and use roman (regular) font style for the *-s* ending. Do not italicize academic grades.

> Two large *J*s were painted on the door.

> He received two Ds for the first time in his life.

EXCEPTIONS: To avoid misreading, use an apostrophe to form the plural of lowercase letters and the capital letters *A* and *I*: *p*'s, *A*'s.

> Beginning readers often confuse *b*'s and *d*'s.

MLA NOTE: The Modern Language Association recommends using an apostrophe for the plural of both capital and lowercase letters: *J*'s, *p*'s.

Plural abbreviations   Do not use an apostrophe to pluralize an abbreviation.

> Harriet has thirty DVDs on her desk.

> Marco earned two PhDs before his thirtieth birthday.

Plural of words mentioned as words   Generally, omit the apostrophe to form the plural of words mentioned as words. If the word is italicized, the *-s* ending appears in roman (regular) type.

> We've heard enough *maybe*s.

Words mentioned as words may also appear in quotation marks. When you choose this option, use the apostrophe.

> We've heard enough "maybe's."

36e Avoid common misuses of the apostrophe.

Do not use an apostrophe in the following situations.

WITH NOUNS THAT ARE NOT POSSESSIVE

>   *outpatients*
> ▶ Some ~~outpatient's~~ have special parking permits.

IN THE POSSESSIVE PRONOUNS *ITS*, *WHOSE*, *HIS*, *HERS*, *OURS*, *YOURS*, AND *THEIRS*

>   *its*
> ▶ Each area has ~~it's~~ own conference room.

It's means "it is." The possessive pronoun *its* contains no apostrophe despite the fact that it is possessive.

> ▶ *The House on Mango Street* was written by Sandra Cisneros,
>   *whose*
> ~~who's~~ work focuses on the Latino community in the
> United States.

Who's means "who is." The possessive pronoun is *whose*.

EXERCISE 36–1   Edit the following sentences to correct errors in the use of the apostrophe. If a sentence is correct, write "correct" after it. Answers to lettered sentences appear in the back of the book. Example:

> We rented an art studio above a barbecue restaurant, Poor
> ~~Richards~~ Ribs.   *Richard's*

a.   This diet will improve almost anyone's health.
b.   The innovative shoe fastener was inspired by the designers young son.
c.   Each days menu features a different European country's dish.
d.   Sue worked overtime to increase her families earnings.
e.   Ms. Jacobs is unwilling to listen to students complaints about computer failures.

1.   Siddhartha sat by the river and listened to its many voices.
2.   Three teenage son's can devour about as much food as four full-grown field hands. The only difference is that they dont do half as much work.
3.   We handle contracts with NASA and many other government agency's.
4.   Patience and humor are key tools in a travelers survival kit.
5.   My sister-in-law's quilts are being shown at the Fendrick Gallery.

EXERCISE 36–2   Edit the following passage to correct errors in the use of the apostrophe.

Its never too soon to start holiday shopping. In fact, some people choose to start shopping as early as January, when last seasons leftover's are priced at their lowest. Many stores try to lure customers in with promise's of savings up to 90 percent. Their main objective, of course, is to make way for next years inventory. The big problem with postholiday shopping, though, is that there isn't much left to choose from. Store's shelves have been picked over by last-minute shoppers desperately searching for gifts. The other problem is that its hard to know what to buy so far in advance. Next year's hot items are anyones guess. But proper timing, mixed with lot's of luck and determination, can lead to good purchases at great price's.

37   Quotation marks

> **Grammar checkers** are no help with quotation marks. They do not recognize direct and indirect quotations, they fail to identify quotation marks used incorrectly inside periods and commas, and they do not point out a missing quotation mark in a pair.

37a Use quotation marks to enclose direct quotations.

Direct quotations of a person's words, whether spoken or written, must be in quotation marks.

> "The contract negotiations are stalled," the airline executive told reporters, "but I am prepared to work night and day to bring both sides together."

Do not use quotation marks around indirect quotations. An indirect quotation reports someone's ideas without using that person's exact words.

> The airline executive told reporters that although contract negotiations were at a standstill, she was prepared to work hard with both labor and management to bring about a settlement.

NOTE: In academic writing, indirect quotation is called *paraphrase* or *summary*. See 48c.

In dialogue, begin a new paragraph to mark a change in speaker.

> "Mom, his name is Willie, not William. A thousand times I've told you, it's *Willie*."
> "Willie is a derivative of William, Lester. Surely his birth certificate doesn't have Willie on it, and I like calling people by their proper names."
> "Yes, it does, ma'am. My mother named me Willie K. Mason."   —Gloria Naylor

with direct quotations • with exact
language • not with long, indented quotations
" " **37b**   **393**

If a single speaker utters more than one paragraph, introduce each paragraph with quotation marks, but do not use closing quotation marks until the end of the speech.

37b Set off long quotations of prose or poetry by indenting.

The guidelines in this section are those of the Modern Language Association (MLA). The American Psychological Association (APA) and *The Chicago Manual of Style* have slightly different guidelines (see pp. 631–32 and 695–96).

When a quotation of prose runs to more than four typed lines in your paper, set it off by indenting one inch from the left margin. Quotation marks are not required because the indented format tells readers that the quotation is taken word-for-word from a source. Long quotations are ordinarily introduced by a sentence ending with a colon.

> After making an exhaustive study of the historical record, James Horan evaluates Billy the Kid like this:
>
> > The portrait that emerges of [the Kid] from the thousands of pages of affidavits, reports, trial transcripts, his letters, and his testimony is neither the mythical Robin Hood nor the stereotyped adenoidal moron and pathological killer. Rather Billy appears as a disturbed, lonely young man, honest, loyal to his friends, dedicated to his beliefs, and betrayed by our institutions and the corrupt, ambitious, and compromising politicians in his time. (158)

The number in parentheses is a citation handled according to MLA style. (See 53a.)

NOTE: When you quote two or more paragraphs from the source, indent the first line of each paragraph an additional one-quarter inch.

When you quote more than three lines of a poem, indent the quoted lines one inch from the left margin. Use no quotation marks unless they appear in the poem itself. (To quote two or three lines of poetry, see 39e.)

> Although many anthologizers "modernize" her punctuation, Emily Dickinson relied heavily on dashes, using them, perhaps, as a musical device. Here, for example, is the original version of the opening of one poem:
>> A narrow Fellow in the Grass
>> Occasionally rides —
>> You may have met Him — did you not
>> His notice sudden is — (1-4)

37c Use single quotation marks to enclose a quotation within a quotation.

> Megan Marshall notes that what Elizabeth Peabody "hoped to accomplish in her school was not merely 'teaching' but 'educating children morally and spiritually as well as intellectually from the first'" (107).

37d Use quotation marks around the titles of short works.

Short works include newspaper and magazine articles, poems, short stories, songs, episodes of television and radio programs, and chapters or subdivisions of books.

> James Baldwin's story "Sonny's Blues" tells the story of two brothers who come to understand each other's suffering.

NOTE: Titles of books, plays, Web sites, television and radio programs, films, magazines, and newspapers are put in italics.

37e Quotation marks may be used to set off words used as words.

Although words used as words are ordinarily italicized (see 42d), quotation marks are also acceptable. Be consistent throughout your paper.

The words "accept" and "except" are frequently confused.

The words *accept* and *except* are frequently confused.

37f Use punctuation with quotation marks according to convention.

This section describes the conventions used by American publishers in placing various marks of punctuation inside or outside quotation marks. It also explains how to punctuate when introducing quoted material.

Periods and commas

Place periods and commas inside quotation marks.

> "I'm here as part of my service-learning project," I told the classroom teacher. "I'm hoping to become a reading specialist."

This rule applies to single quotation marks as well as double quotation marks. (See 37c.) It also applies to all uses of quotation marks: for quoted material, for titles of works, and for words used as words.

EXCEPTION: In the Modern Language Association's style of parenthetical in-text citations (see 53a), the period follows the citation in parentheses.

> James M. McPherson comments, approvingly, that the Whigs "were not averse to extending the blessings of American liberty, even to Mexicans and Indians" (48).

Colons and semicolons

Put colons and semicolons outside quotation marks.

> Harold wrote, "I regret that I am unable to attend the fundraiser for AIDS research"; his letter, however, came with a substantial contribution.

Question marks and exclamation points

Put question marks and exclamation points inside quotation marks unless they apply to the whole sentence.

> Contrary to tradition, bedtime at my house is marked by "Mommy, can I tell you a story now?"

> Have you heard the old proverb "Do not climb the hill until you reach it"?

In the first sentence, the question mark applies only to the quoted question. In the second sentence, the question mark applies to the whole sentence.

NOTE: In MLA style for a quotation that ends with a question mark or an exclamation point, the parenthetical citation and a period should follow the entire quotation.

> Rosie Thomas asks, "Is nothing in life ever straight and clear, the way children see it?"(77).

Introducing quoted material

After a word group introducing a quotation, choose a colon, a comma, or no punctuation at all, whichever is appropriate in context.

Formal introduction   If a quotation is formally introduced, a colon is appropriate. A formal introduction is a full independent clause, not just an expression such as *he said* or *she remarked*.

> Thomas Friedman provides a challenging yet optimistic view of the future: "We need to get back to work on our country and on our planet. The hour is late, the stakes couldn't be higher, the project couldn't be harder, the payoff couldn't be greater" (25).

Expression such as *he said*   If a quotation is introduced with an expression such as *he said* or *she remarked*—or if it is followed by such an expression—a comma is needed.

> About New England's weather, Mark Twain once declared, "In the spring I have counted one hundred and thirty-six different kinds of weather within four and twenty hours" (55).

"Unless another war is prevented it is likely to bring destruction on a scale never before held possible and even now hardly conceived," Albert Einstein wrote in the aftermath of the atomic bomb (29).

Blended quotation When a quotation is blended into the writer's own sentence, either a comma or no punctuation is appropriate, depending on the way in which the quotation fits into the sentence structure.

> The future champion could, as he put it, "float like a butterfly and sting like a bee."

> Virginia Woolf wrote in 1928 that "a woman must have money and a room of her own if she is to write fiction; and that, as you will see, leaves the great problem of the true nature of woman and the true nature of fiction unsolved" (4).

Beginning of sentence If a quotation appears at the beginning of a sentence, set it off with a comma unless the quotation ends with a question mark or an exclamation point.

> "I've always thought of myself as a reporter," claimed American poet Gwendolyn Brooks (162).

> "What is it?" she asked, bracing herself.

Interrupted quotation If a quoted sentence is interrupted by explanatory words, use commas to set off the explanatory words.

> "With regard to air travel," Stephen Ambrose notes, "Jefferson was a full century ahead of the curve" (53).

If two successive quoted sentences from the same source are interrupted by explanatory words, use a comma before the explanatory words and a period after them.

> "Everyone agrees journalists must tell the truth," Bill Kovach and Tom Rosenstiel write. "Yet people are befuddled about what 'the truth' means" (37).

37g Avoid common misuses of quotation marks.

Do not use quotation marks to draw attention to familiar slang, to disown trite expressions, or to justify an attempt at humor.

▶ The economist estimated that single-family home prices

would decline another 5 percent by the end of the year,

emphasizing that this was only a ~~"~~ballpark figure.~~"~~

Do not use quotation marks around indirect quotations. (See also 37a.)

▶ After leaving the scene of the domestic quarrel, the officer

said that ~~"~~he was due for a coffee break.~~"~~

Do not use quotation marks around the title of your own essay.

EXERCISE 37–1 Add or delete quotation marks as needed and make any other necessary changes in punctuation in the following sentences. If a sentence is correct, write "correct" after it. Answers to lettered sentences appear in the back of the book. Example:

Gandhi once said, "An eye for an eye only ends up making

the whole world blind."

a. As for the advertisement "Sailors have more fun", if you consider chipping paint and swabbing decks fun, then you will have plenty of it.
b. Even after forty minutes of discussion, our class could not agree on an interpretation of Robert Frost's poem "The Road Not Taken."
c. After winning the lottery, Juanita said that "she would give half the money to charity."
d. After the movie, Vicki said, "The reviewer called this flick "trash of the first order." I guess you can't believe everything you read."

e. "Cleaning your house while your kids are still growing,"
    said Phyllis Diller, "is like shoveling the walk before it stops
    snowing."

1. "That's the most beautiful seashell I've ever seen!", shouted
    Alexa.
2. "Get your head in the game, and the rest will come" advised
    the coach just before the whistle.
3. Gloria Steinem once twisted an old proverb like this, "A woman
    without a man is like a fish without a bicycle."
4. "Even when freshly washed and relieved of all obvious confec-
    tions," says Fran Lebowitz, "children tend to be sticky."
5. Have you heard the Cowboy Junkies' cover of Hank Williams's
    "I'm So Lonesome I Could Cry?"

EXERCISE 37–2   Add or delete quotation marks as needed and make
any other necessary changes in punctuation in the following passage. Citations should conform to MLA style (see 53a).

In his article The Moment of Truth, former vice president
Al Gore argues that global warming is a genuine threat to life
on Earth and that we must act now to avoid catastrophe. Gore
calls our situation a "true *planetary emergency*" and cites scientific evidence of the greenhouse effect and its consequences
(170-71). "What is at stake, Gore insists, is the survival of our
civilization and the habitability of the Earth (197)." With such
a grim predicament at hand, Gore questions why so many political and economic leaders are reluctant to act. "Is it simply
more convenient to ignore the warnings," he asks (171)?

The crisis, of course, will not go away if we just pretend it
isn't there. Gore points out that in Chinese two symbols form
the character for the word crisis. The first of those symbols
means "danger", and the second means "opportunity." The
danger we face, he claims, is accompanied by "unprecedented
opportunity." (172) Gore contends that throughout history we
have won battles against seemingly unbeatable evils such as
slavery and fascism and that we did so by facing the truth and
choosing the moral high ground. Gore's final appeal is to our
humanity:

"Ultimately, [the fight to end global warming] is not
about any scientific discussion or political dialogue; it

is about who we are as human beings. It is about our
capacity to transcend our limitations, to rise to this new
occasion. To see with our hearts, as well as our heads, the
response that is now called for." (244)

Gore feels that the fate of our world rests in our own hands,
and his hope is that we will make the choice to save the
planet.

Quotations are from Al Gore, "The Moment of Truth,"
Vanity Fair May 2006: 170+; print.

hackerhandbooks.com/bedhandbook > Grammar exercises > Punctuation
> E-ex 37–3 and 37–4

38 End punctuation

> **Grammar checkers** occasionally flag sentences beginning with
> words like *Why* or *Are* and suggest that a question mark may be
> needed. On the whole, however, grammar checkers are of little
> help with end punctuation. Most notably, they neglect to tell you
> when your sentence is missing end punctuation.

38a The period

Use a period to end all sentences except direct questions or genuine exclamations. Also use periods in abbreviations according
to convention.

To end sentences

Most sentences should end with a period. Problems sometimes
arise when a writer must choose between a period and a question mark or between a period and an exclamation point.

If a sentence reports a question instead of asking it directly, it should end with a period, not a question mark.

▶ **The professor asked whether talk therapy was more**

beneficial than antidepressants?.

to end a sentence •
periods in abbreviations • question mark
.?! **38b** 401

If a sentence is not a genuine exclamation, it should end with a period, not an exclamation point. (See also 38c.)

▶ **After years of working her way through school, Geeta finally**

graduated with high honors̸.
　　　　　　　　　　　　　　　^

In abbreviations

A period is conventionally used in abbreviations of titles and Latin words or phrases, including the time designations for morning and afternoon.

Mr.	i.e.	a.m. (or AM)
Ms.	e.g.	p.m. (or PM)
Dr.	etc.	

NOTE: If a sentence ends with a period marking an abbreviation, do not add a second period.

Do not use a period with US Postal Service abbreviations for states: MD, TX, CA.

Current usage is to omit the period in abbreviations of organization names, academic degrees, and designations for eras.

NATO	UNESCO	UCLA	BS	BC
IRS	AFL-CIO	NIH	PhD	AD
USA	NAACP	SEC	RN	BCE

38b The question mark

A direct question should be followed by a question mark.

What is the horsepower of a 777 engine?

If a polite request is written in the form of a question, it may be followed by a period.

Would you please send me your catalog of lilies.

TIP: Do not use a question mark after an indirect question, one that is reported rather than asked directly. Use a period instead.

▶ He asked me who was teaching the mythology course

this year?.

NOTE: Questions in a series may be followed by question marks even when they are not complete sentences.

> We wondered where Calamity had hidden this time. Under the sink? Behind the furnace? On top of the bookcase?

38c The exclamation point.

Use an exclamation point after a word group or sentence to express exceptional feeling or to provide special emphasis. The exclamation point is rarely appropriate in academic writing.

> When Gloria entered the room, I switched on the lights, and we all yelled, "Surprise!"

TIP: Do not overuse the exclamation point.

▶ In the fisherman's memory the fish lives on, increasing in

length and weight with each passing year, until at last it is

big enough to shade a fishing boat!.

This sentence doesn't need to be pumped up with an exclamation point. It is emphatic enough without it.

▶ Whenever I see my favorite hitter, Derek Lee, up at bat,

I dream of making it to the big leagues!. My team would

win every time!

The first exclamation point should be deleted so that the second one will have more force.

EXERCISE 38–1 Add appropriate end punctuation in the following paragraph.

> Although I am generally rational, I am superstitious I never walk under ladders or put shoes on the table If I spill

the salt, I go into frenzied calisthenics picking up the grains and tossing them over my left shoulder As a result of these curious activities, I've always wondered whether knowing the roots of superstitions would quell my irrational responses Superstition has it, for example, that one should never place a hat on the bed This superstition arises from a time when head lice were common and placing a guest's hat on the bed stood a good chance of spreading lice through the host's bed Doesn't this make good sense And doesn't it stand to reason that if I know that my guests don't have lice I shouldn't care where their hats go Of course it does It is fair to ask, then, whether I have changed my ways and place hats on beds Are you kidding I wouldn't put a hat on a bed if my life depended on it

39   Other punctuation marks: the dash, parentheses, brackets, the ellipsis mark, the slash

Grammar checkers rarely flag problems with the punctuation marks in this section: the dash, parentheses, brackets, the ellipsis mark, and the slash.

39a The dash

When typing, use two hyphens to form a dash (--). Do not put spaces before or after the dash. If your word processing program has what is known as an "em-dash" (—), you may use it instead, with no space before or after it. Dashes are used for the following purposes.

To set off parenthetical material that deserves emphasis

Everything that went wrong—from the peeping Tom at her window last night to my head-on collision today—we blamed on our move.

To set off appositives that contain commas

An appositive is a noun or noun phrase that renames a nearby noun. Ordinarily most appositives are set off with commas (32e), but when the appositive itself contains commas, a pair of dashes helps readers see the relative importance of all the pauses.

> In my hometown, the basic needs of people—food, clothing, and shelter—are less costly than in a big city like Los Angeles.

To prepare for a list, a restatement, an amplification, or a dramatic shift in tone or thought

> Along the wall are the bulk liquids—sesame seed oil, honey, safflower oil, and that half-liquid "peanuts only" peanut butter.

> In his last semester, Peter tried to pay more attention to his priorities—applying to graduate school and getting financial aid.

> Everywhere we looked there were little kids—a box of Cracker Jacks in one hand and mommy or daddy's sleeve in the other.

> Kiere took a few steps back, came running full speed, kicked a mighty kick—and missed the ball.

In the first two examples, the writer could also use a colon. (See 35a.) The colon is more formal than the dash and not quite as dramatic.

TIP: Unless there is a specific reason for using the dash, avoid it. Unnecessary dashes create a choppy effect.

> ▶ Insisting that students use computers as instructional tools—for information retrieval—makes good sense. Herding them—sheeplike—into computer technology does not.

39b Parentheses

Use parentheses to enclose supplemental material, minor digressions, and afterthoughts.

Nurses record patients' vital signs (temperature, pulse, and blood pressure) several times a day.

Use parentheses to enclose letters or numbers labeling items in a series.

Regulations stipulated that only the following equipment could be used on the survival mission: (1) a knife, (2) thirty feet of parachute line, (3) a book of matches, (4) two ponchos, (5) an E tool, and (6) a signal flare.

TIP: Do not overuse parentheses. Rough drafts are likely to contain more afterthoughts than necessary. As writers head into a sentence, they often think of additional details, occasionally working them in as best they can with parentheses. Usually such sentences should be revised so that the additional details no longer seem to be afterthoughts.

▶ Researchers have said that seventeen ~~million (estimates run~~ *from* ~~as high as~~ twenty-three million) Americans have diabetes. *to*

39c Brackets

Use brackets to enclose any words or phrases that you have inserted into an otherwise word-for-word quotation.

Audubon reports that "if there are not enough young to balance deaths, the end of the species [California condor] is inevitable."

The sentence quoted from the *Audubon* article did not contain the words *California condor* (since the context of the full article made clear what species was meant), so the writer needed to add the name in brackets.

The Latin word "sic" in brackets indicates that an error in a quoted sentence appears in the original source.

According to the review, Nelly Furtado's performance was brilliant, "exceeding [sic] the expectations of even her most loyal fans."

Do not overuse "sic," however, since calling attention to others' mistakes can appear snobbish. The preceding quotation, for example, might have been paraphrased instead: *According to the review, even Nelly Furtado's most loyal fans were surprised by the brilliance of her performance.*

39d The ellipsis mark

The ellipsis mark consists of three spaced periods. Use an ellipsis mark to indicate that you have deleted words from an otherwise word-for-word quotation.

> Reuben reports that "when the amount of cholesterol circulating in the blood rises over . . . 300 milligrams per 100, the chances of a heart attack increase dramatically."

If you delete a full sentence or more in the middle of a quoted passage, use a period before the three ellipsis dots.

> "Most of our efforts," writes Dave Erikson, "are directed toward saving the bald eagle's wintering habitat along the Mississippi River. . . . It's important that the wintering birds have a place to roost, where they can get out of the cold wind."

TIP: Ordinarily, do not use the ellipsis mark at the beginning or at the end of a quotation. Readers will understand that the quoted material is taken from a longer passage. If you have cut some words from the end of the final quoted sentence, however, MLA requires an ellipsis mark, as in the second example on page 407.

In quoted poetry, use a full line of ellipsis dots to indicate that you have dropped a line or more from the poem, as in this example from "To His Coy Mistress" by Andrew Marvell:

> Had we but world enough, and time,
> This coyness, lady, were no crime.
> . . . .
> But at my back I always hear
> Time's wingèd chariot hurrying near; (1-2, 21-22)

The ellipsis mark may also be used to indicate a hesitation or an interruption in speech or to suggest unfinished thoughts.

> "The apartment building next door . . . it's going up in flames!" yelled Marcia.

> Before falling into a coma, the victim whispered, "It was a man with a tattoo on his . . . "

39e The slash

Use the slash to separate two or three lines of poetry that have been run into your text. Add a space both before and after the slash.

> In the opening lines of "Jordan," George Herbert pokes gentle fun at popular poems of his time: "Who says that fictions only and false hair / Become a verse? Is there in truth no beauty?" (1-2).

More than three lines of poetry should be handled as an indented quotation. (See 37b.)

The slash may occasionally be used to separate paired terms such as *pass/fail* and *producer/director*. Do not use a space before or after the slash. Be sparing in this use of the slash. In particular, avoid the use of *and/or*, *he/she*, and *his/her*. Instead of using *he/she* and *his/her* to solve sexist language problems, you can usually find more graceful alternatives. (See 17f and 22a.)

EXERCISE 39–1 Edit the following sentences to correct errors in punctuation, focusing especially on appropriate use of the dash, parentheses, brackets, ellipsis mark, and slash. If a sentence is correct, write "correct" after it. Answers to lettered sentences appear in the back of the book. Example:

> Social insects/– bees, for example/– are able to
>
> communicate complicated messages to one another.

a. A client has left his/her cell phone in our conference room.
b. The films we made of Kilauea—on our trip to Hawaii Volcanoes National Park—illustrate a typical spatter cone eruption.

c. Greg selected the pass/fail option for Chemistry 101.
d. Masahiro poked through his backpack—laptop, digital camera, guidebook—to make sure he was ready for a day's study at the Ryoanji Temple garden.
e. Of three engineering fields, chemical, mechanical, and materials, Keegan chose materials engineering for its application to toy manufacturing.

1. The old Valentine verse we used to chant says it all: "Sugar is sweet, / And so are you."
2. In studies in which mothers gazed down at their infants in their cribs but remained facially unresponsive, for example, not smiling, laughing, or showing any change of expression, the infants responded with intense weariness and eventual withdrawal.
3. There are three points of etiquette in poker: 1. always allow someone else to cut the cards, 2. don't forget to ante up, and 3. never stack your chips.
4. In *Lifeboat*, Alfred Hitchcock appears [some say without his knowledge] in a newspaper advertisement for weight loss.
5. The writer Chitra Divakaruni explained her work with other Indian American immigrants: "Many women who came to Maitri [a women's support group in San Francisco] needed to know simple things like opening a bank account or getting citizenship. . . . Many women in Maitri spoke English, but their English was functional rather than emotional. They needed someone who understands their problems and speaks their language."

hackerhandbooks.com/bedhandbook > **Grammar exercises** > **Punctuation** > **E-ex 39–2**

Part VIII
Mechanics

40 Abbreviations

> Grammar checkers can flag a few inappropriate abbreviations, such as *Xmas* and e.g., but do not assume that a program will catch all problems with abbreviations.

40a Use standard abbreviations for titles immediately before and after proper names.

TITLES BEFORE PROPER NAMES	TITLES AFTER PROPER NAMES
Mr. Rafael Zabala	William Albert Sr.
Ms. Nancy Linehan	Thomas Hines Jr.
Mrs. Edward Horn	Anita Lor, PhD
Dr. Margaret Simmons	Robert Simkowski, MD
Rev. John Stone	Margaret Chin, LLD
Prof. James Russo	Polly Stein, DDS

Do not abbreviate a title if it is not used with a proper name.

>   professor
> ▶ My history ~~prof.~~ is an expert on race relations in South Africa.

Avoid redundant titles such as *Dr. Amy Day, MD*. Choose one title or the other: *Dr. Amy Day* or *Amy Day, MD*.

40b Use abbreviations only when you are sure your readers will understand them.

Familiar abbreviations, written without periods, are acceptable.

CIA	FBI	MD	NAACP
NBA	NEA	PhD	CD-ROM
YMCA	CBS	USA	ESL

Talk show host Conan O'Brien is a Harvard graduate with a BA in history.

The YMCA has opened a new gym close to my office.

NOTE: When using an unfamiliar abbreviation (such as NASW for National Association of Social Workers) throughout a paper, write the full name followed by the abbreviation in parentheses at the first mention of the name. Then use just the abbreviation throughout the rest of the paper.

40c Use *BC*, *AD*, *a.m.*, *p.m.*, *No.*, and *$* only with specific dates, times, numbers, and amounts.

The abbreviation BC ("before Christ") follows a date, and AD ("*anno Domini*") precedes a date. Acceptable alternatives are BCE ("before the common era") and CE ("common era"), both of which follow a date.

40 BC (or 40 BCE)	4:00 a.m. (or AM)	No. 12 (or no. 12)
AD 44 (or 44 CE)	6:00 p.m. (or PM)	$150

Avoid using *a.m.*, *p.m.*, *No.*, or *$* when not accompanied by a specific figure.

▶ The governor argued that the new sales tax would raise
much-needed $ for the state.
      money

40d Be sparing in your use of Latin abbreviations.

Latin abbreviations are acceptable in footnotes and bibliographies and in informal writing for comments in parentheses.

> cf. (Latin *confer*, "compare")
> e.g. (Latin *exempli gratia*, "for example")
> et al. (Latin *et alia*, "and others")
> etc. (Latin *et cetera*, "and so forth")
> i.e. (Latin *id est*, "that is")
> N.B. (Latin *nota bene*, "note well")
>
> Harold Simms et al., *The Race for Space*
>
> Alfred Hitchcock directed many classic thrillers (e.g., *Psycho*, *Rear Window*, and *Vertigo*).

In formal writing, use the appropriate English phrases.

▶ Many obsolete laws remain on the books. A law in

Vermont, ~~e.g.,~~ *for example,* forbids an unmarried man and woman to

sit closer than six inches apart on a park bench.

40e Avoid inappropriate abbreviations.

In formal writing, abbreviations for the following are not commonly accepted: personal names, units of measurement, days of the week, holidays, months, courses of study, divisions of written works, states, and countries (except in complete addresses and except Washington, DC). Do not abbreviate *Company* and *Incorporated* unless their abbreviated forms are part of an official name.

PERSONAL NAMES Charles (not Chas.)

UNITS OF MEASUREMENT feet (not ft.)

DAYS OF THE WEEK Monday (not Mon.)

HOLIDAYS Christmas (not Xmas)

MONTHS January, February, March (not Jan., Feb., Mar.)

COURSES OF STUDY political science (not poli. sci.)

DIVISIONS OF WRITTEN WORKS chapter, page (not ch., p.)

STATES AND COUNTRIES Massachusetts (not MA or Mass.)

PARTS OF A BUSINESS NAME Adams Lighting Company (not Adams Lighting Co.); Kim and Brothers (not Kim and Bros.)

▶ The American Red Cross requires that blood donors be at

least seventeen ~~yrs.~~ *years* old, weigh at least 110 ~~lb.,~~ *pounds,* and not

have given blood in the past eight ~~wks.~~ *weeks.*

EXERCISE 40–1 Edit the following sentences to correct errors in abbreviations. If a sentence is correct, write "correct" after it. Answers to lettered sentences appear in the back of the book. Example:

This year ~~Xmas~~ will fall on a ~~Tues.~~
(above Xmas: Christmas) (above Tues.: Tuesday.)

a. Since its inception, the BBC has maintained a consistently high standard of radio and television broadcasting.
b. Some combat soldiers are trained by govt. diplomats to be sensitive to issues of culture, history, and religion.
c. Mahatma Gandhi has inspired many modern leaders, including Martin Luther King Jr.
d. How many lb. have you lost since you began running four miles a day?
e. Denzil spent all night studying for his psych. exam.

1. My favorite prof., Dr. Barker, is on sabbatical this semester.
2. When we visited NYU in early September, we were charmed by the lull of summer crickets in Washington Square Park.
3. Some historians think that the New Testament was completed by AD 100.
4. My mother's birthday was on Fri. the 13th this year.
5. Some first-time Flash users panic before the complex menus— i.e., they develop a blank stare and the tingling of a migraine.

hackerhandbooks.com/bedhandbook > Grammar exercises > Mechanics > E-ex 40–2

41   Numbers

> **Grammar checkers** can tell you to spell out certain numbers, such as _thirty-three_ and numbers that begin a sentence, but they won't help you understand when it is acceptable to use numerals.

41a Follow the conventions in your discipline for spelling out or using numerals to express numbers.

In the humanities, which generally follow either Modern Language Association (MLA) style or _The Chicago Manual of Style_, use numerals only for specific numbers above one hundred: _353, 1,020._ Spell out numbers one hundred and below and large round numbers: _eleven, thirty-five, sixty, fifteen million._

The social sciences and sciences, which follow American Psychological Association (APA) style or Council of Science Editors (CSE) style, use numerals for all but the numbers one through nine.

In all fields, treat related numbers in a passage consistently: *The survey found that 89 of 157 respondents had not taken any courses related to alcohol use.*

When one number immediately follows another, spelling out one number and using numerals for the other is usually effective: *three 100-meter events, 25 four-poster beds.*

▶ It's been 8̲ years since I visited Peru.
        eight

▶ Enrollment in the charter school in its first year will be limited to ~~three hundred forty~~ students.
                                        340

If a sentence begins with a number, spell out the number or rewrite the sentence.

▶ ~~150~~ children in our program need expensive dental treatment.
   One hundred fifty

Rewriting the sentence will also correct the error and may be less awkward if the number is long: *In our program, 150 children need expensive dental treatment.*

41b Use numerals according to convention in dates, addresses, and so on.

DATES   July 4, 1776; 56 BC; AD 30

ADDRESSES   77 Latches Lane, 519 West 42nd Street

PERCENTAGES   55 percent (or 55%)

FRACTIONS, DECIMALS $\frac{1}{2}$, 0.047

SCORES   7 to 3, 21–18

STATISTICS   average age 37, average weight 180

SURVEYS   4 out of 5

EXACT AMOUNTS OF MONEY $105.37, $106,000

DIVISIONS OF BOOKS volume 3, chapter 4, page 189

DIVISIONS OF PLAYS act 3, scene 3 (or act III, scene iii)

IDENTIFICATION NUMBERS serial number 10988675

TIME OF DAY 4:00 p.m., 1:30 a.m.

$430,000
► The foundation raised ~~four hundred thirty thousand~~
                        ^
~~dollars~~ for cancer research.

NOTE: When not using *a.m.* or *p.m.*, write out the time in words
(*two o'clock in the afternoon, twelve noon, seven in the morning*).

EXERCISE 41–1 Edit the following sentences to correct errors in
the use of numbers. If a sentence is correct, write "correct" after
it. Answers to lettered sentences appear in the back of the book.
Example:

$3.06
By the end of the evening, Ashanti had only ~~three dollars~~
                                            ^
~~and six cents~~ left.

a.   The carpenters located 3 maple timbers, 21 sheets of cherry,
     and 10 oblongs of polished ebony for the theater set.
b.   The program's cost is well over one billion dollars.
c.   The score was tied at 5–5 when the momentum shifted and car-
     ried the Standards to a decisive 12–5 win.
d.   8 students in the class had been labeled "learning disabled."
e.   The Vietnam Veterans Memorial in Washington, DC, had fifty-
     eight thousand one hundred thirty-two names inscribed on it
     when it was dedicated in 1982.

1.   One of my favorite scenes in Shakespeare is the property divi-
     sion scene in act 1 of *King Lear*.
2.   The botany lecture will begin at precisely 3:30 p.m.
3.   40 percent of all gamers in the United States are women.
4.   In two thousand twelve, the world population may reach
     7 billion.
5.   On a normal day, I spend at least 4 to 5 hours surfing the Internet.

42   Italics

This section describes conventional uses for italics. While italics is accepted by all three style guides covered in this handbook (MLA, APA, and *Chicago*), some instructors may prefer underlining in student papers. If that is the case in your course, simply substitute underlining for italics in the examples in this section.

Some computer and online applications do not allow for italics. To indicate words that should be italicized, you can use underscore marks or asterisks before and after the italic words.

I am planning to write my senior thesis on _Memoirs of a Geisha_.

NOTE: Excessive use of italics to emphasize words or ideas, especially in academic writing, is distracting and should be avoided.

42a Italicize the titles of works according to convention.

Titles of the following types of works, including electronic works, should be italicized.

TITLES OF BOOKS *The Color Purple, Middlesex, Encarta*

MAGAZINES *Time, Scientific American, Salon.com*

NEWSPAPERS the *Baltimore Sun,* the *Orlando Sentinel Online*

PAMPHLETS *Common Sense, Facts about Marijuana*

LONG POEMS *The Waste Land, Paradise Lost*

PLAYS *'Night Mother, Wicked*

FILMS *Casablanca, Do the Right Thing*

TELEVISION PROGRAMS *American Idol, Frontline*

RADIO PROGRAMS *All Things Considered*

MUSICAL COMPOSITIONS *Porgy and Bess*

CHOREOGRAPHIC WORKS *Brief Fling*

WORKS OF VISUAL ART *American Gothic*

ELECTRONIC DATABASES *InfoTrac*

WEB SITES *ZDNet, Google*

ELECTRONIC GAMES *Everquest, Guitar Hero*

The titles of other works, such as short stories, essays, episodes of radio and television programs, songs, and short poems, are enclosed in quotation marks. (See 37d.)

NOTE: Do not use italics when referring to the Bible, titles of books in the Bible (Genesis, not *Genesis*), or titles of legal documents (the Constitution, not the *Constitution*). Do not italicize the titles of computer software (Keynote, Photoshop). Do not italicize the title of your own paper.

42b Italicize the names of specific ships, spacecraft, and aircraft.

Queen Mary 2, Challenger, Spirit of St. Louis

The success of the Soviets' *Sputnik* energized the US space program.

42c Italicize foreign words used in an English sentence.

Shakespeare's Falstaff is a comic character known for both his excessive drinking and his general *joie de vivre*.

EXCEPTION: Do not italicize foreign words that have become a standard part of the English language—"laissez-faire," "fait accompli," "modus operandi," and "per diem," for example.

42d Italicize words mentioned as words, letters mentioned as letters, and numbers mentioned as numbers.

Tomás assured us that the chemicals could probably be safely mixed, but his *probably* stuck in our minds.

Some toddlers have trouble pronouncing the letter *s*.

A big *3* was painted on the stage door.

NOTE: Quotation marks may be used instead of italics to set off words mentioned as words. (See 37e.)

EXERCISE 42–1 Edit the following sentences to correct errors in the use of italics. If a sentence is correct, write "correct" after it. Answers to lettered sentences appear in the back of the book. Example:

> **We had a lively discussion about Gini Alhadeff's memoir**
>
> ***The Sun at Midday.*** Correct

a. Howard Hughes commissioned the Spruce Goose, a beautifully built but thoroughly impractical wooden aircraft.

b. The old man *screamed* his anger, *shouting* to all of us, "I will not leave my money to you worthless layabouts!"

c. I learned the Latin term ad infinitum from an old nursery rhyme about fleas: "Great fleas have little fleas upon their back to bite 'em, / Little fleas have lesser fleas and so on ad infinitum."

d. Cinema audiences once gasped at hearing the word *damn* in *Gone with the Wind*.

e. Neve Campbell's lifelong interest in ballet inspired her involvement in the film "The Company," which portrays a season with the Joffrey Ballet.

1. Yasmina spent a year painting white flowers in imitation of Georgia O'Keeffe's Calla Lilies.

2. On the monastery walls are murals depicting scenes from the book of Kings and the book of Proverbs.

3. My per diem allowance was two hundred dollars.

4. Cecily watched in amazement as the tattoo artist made angles and swooping loops into the Gothic letter G.

5. The blend of poetic lyrics and progressive instruments on Seal's "Human Being" makes it one of my favorite CDs.

hackerhandbooks.com/bedhandbook > Grammar exercises > Mechanics
> E-ex 42–2

43 Spelling

You learned to spell from repeated experience with words in both reading and writing, but especially writing. Words have a look, a sound, and even a feel to them as the hand moves across the page. As you proofread, you can probably tell if a word doesn't look quite right. In such cases, the solution is simple: Look up the word in the dictionary.

> **Spell checkers** are useful alternatives to a dictionary, but only to a point. A spell checker will not tell you how to spell words not listed in its dictionary; nor will it help you catch words commonly confused, such as *accept* and *except*, or some typographical errors, such as *own* for *won*. You will still need to proofread, and for some words you may need to turn to the dictionary.

43a Become familiar with your dictionary.

A good dictionary, whether print or online—such as *The American Heritage Dictionary of the English Language, The Random House College Dictionary*, or *Merriam-Webster's Collegiate Dictionary*—is an indispensable writer's aid.

A sample print dictionary entry, taken from *The American Heritage Dictionary*, appears on page 420. Labels show where various kinds of information about a word can be found in that dictionary.

A sample online dictionary entry, taken from *Merriam-Webster Online*, appears on page 421.

Spelling, word division, pronunciation

The main entry (*re•gard* in the sample entries) shows the correct spelling of the word. When there are two correct spellings of a word (as in *collectible, collectable*, for example), both are given, with the preferred spelling usually appearing first.

The main entry also shows how the word is divided into syllables. The dot between *re* and *gard* separates the two syllables and indicates where the word should be divided if it can't fit at the end of a line of type (see 44f). When a word is compound, the main entry shows how to write it: as one word (*crossroad*), as a hyphenated word (*cross-stitch*), or as two words (*cross section*).

The word's pronunciation is given just after the main entry. The accents indicate which syllables are stressed; the other marks are explained in the dictionary's pronunciation key. In print dictionaries, this key usually appears at the

PRINT DICTIONARY ENTRY

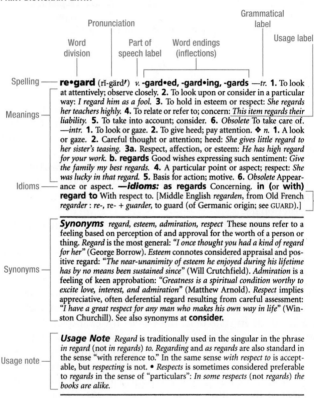

Pronunciation

Word division

Part of speech label

Word endings (inflections)

Grammatical label

Usage label

Spelling —— **re•gard** (rǐ-gärd′) *v.* **-gard•ed, -gard•ing, -gards** —*tr.* **1.** To look at attentively; observe closely. **2.** To look upon or consider in a particular way: *I regard him as a fool.* **3.** To hold in esteem or respect: *She regards her teachers highly.* **4.** To relate or refer to; concern: *This item regards their liability.* **5.** To take into account; consider. **6.** *Obsolete* To take care of. —*intr.* **1.** To look or gaze. **2.** To give heed; pay attention. ❖ *n.* **1.** A look or gaze. **2.** Careful thought or attention; heed: *She gives little regard to her sister's teasing.* **3a.** Respect, affection, or esteem: *He has high regard for your work.* **b. regards** Good wishes expressing such sentiment: *Give the family my best regards.* **4.** A particular point or aspect; respect: *She was lucky in that regard.* **5.** Basis for action; motive. **6.** *Obsolete* Appearance or aspect. —**idioms: as regards** Concerning. **in** (or **with**) **regard to** With respect to. [Middle English *regarden,* from Old French *regarder* : *re-,* re- + *guarder,* to guard (of Germanic origin; see GUARD.)]

Synonyms *regard, esteem, admiration, respect* These nouns refer to a feeling based on perception of and approval for the worth of a person or thing. *Regard* is the most general: *"I once thought you had a kind of regard for her"* (George Borrow). *Esteem* connotes considered appraisal and positive regard: *"The near-unanimity of esteem he enjoyed during his lifetime has by no means been sustained since"* (Will Crutchfield). *Admiration* is a feeling of keen approbation: *"Greatness is a spiritual condition worthy to excite love, interest, and admiration"* (Matthew Arnold). *Respect* implies appreciative, often deferential regard resulting from careful assessment: *"I have a great respect for any man who makes his own way in life"* (Winston Churchill). See also synonyms at **consider.**

Usage Note *Regard* is traditionally used in the singular in the phrase *in regard* (not *in regards*) *to. Regarding* and *as regards* are also standard in the sense "with reference to." In the same sense *with respect to* is acceptable, but *respecting* is not. • *Respects* is sometimes considered preferable to *regards* in the sense of "particulars": *In some respects* (not *regards*) *the books are alike.*

Meanings

Idioms

Synonyms

Usage note

Word origin (etymology)

bottom of every page or every other page. Many online entries include an audio link to a person's voice pronouncing the word. And most online dictionaries have an audio pronunciation guide.

ONLINE DICTIONARY ENTRY

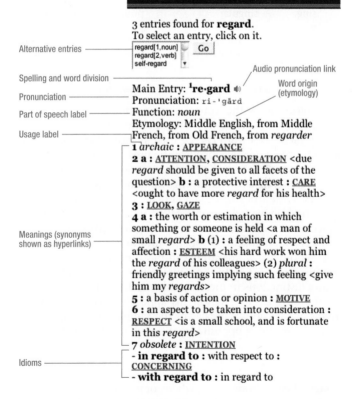

Merriam-Webster Online Dictionary

3 entries found for **regard**.
To select an entry, click on it.

Alternative entries — | regard[1,noun]
regard[2,verb]
self-regard | Go |

Spelling and word division ——————————————— Audio pronunciation link

Word origin (etymology)

Pronunciation ———— Main Entry: ¹re·gard ◄»)
Pronunciation: ri-'gärd
Part of speech label ———— Function: *noun*
Etymology: Middle English, from Middle
Usage label ———— French, from Old French, from *regarder*
1 *archaic* : APPEARANCE
2 a : ATTENTION, CONSIDERATION <due *regard* should be given to all facets of the question> **b** : a protective interest : CARE <ought to have more *regard* for his health>
3 : LOOK, GAZE
4 a : the worth or estimation in which something or someone is held <a man of small *regard*> **b** (1) : a feeling of respect and affection : ESTEEM <his hard work won him the *regard* of his colleagues> (2) *plural* : friendly greetings implying such feeling <give him my *regards*>
5 : a basis of action or opinion : MOTIVE
6 : an aspect to be taken into consideration : RESPECT <is a small school, and is fortunate in this *regard*>
7 *obsolete* : INTENTION

Meanings (synonyms shown as hyperlinks)

Idioms ———— - **in regard to** : with respect to : CONCERNING
- **with regard to** : in regard to

Word endings and grammatical labels

When a word takes endings to indicate grammatical functions (called *inflections*), the endings are listed in boldface, as with *-garded*, *-garding*, and *-gards* in the sample print entry (p. 420).

Labels for the parts of speech and for other grammatical terms are sometimes abbreviated, as they are in the print entry. The most commonly used abbreviations are these:

n.	noun	adj.	adjective
pl.	plural	adv.	adverb
sing.	singular	pron.	pronoun
v.	verb	prep.	preposition
tr.	transitive verb	conj.	conjunction
intr.	intransitive verb	interj.	interjection

Meanings, word origin, synonyms, and antonyms

Each meaning for the word is given a number. Occasionally a word's use is illustrated in a quoted sentence.

Sometimes a word can be used as more than one part of speech (*regard*, for instance, can be used as either a verb or a noun). In such a case, all the meanings for one part of speech are given before all the meanings for another, as in the sample entries. The entries also give idiomatic uses of the word.

The origin of the word, called its *etymology*, appears in brackets after all the meanings in the print version; in the on-line version, it appears before the meanings.

Synonyms, words similar in meaning to the main entry, are frequently listed. In the sample print entry, the dictionary draws distinctions in meaning among the various synonyms. In the online entry, synonyms appear as hyperlinks. Antonyms, which do not appear in the sample entries, are words having a meaning opposite from that of the main entry.

Usage

Usage labels indicate when, where, or under what conditions a particular meaning for a word is appropriately used. Common labels are *informal* (or *colloquial*), *slang*, *archaic*, *poetic*, *nonstandard*, *dialect*, *obsolete*, and *British*. In the sample print entry (p. 420), two meanings of *regard* are labeled *obsolete* because they are no longer in use. The sample online entry (p. 421) has meanings labeled both *archaic* and *obsolete*.

Dictionaries sometimes include usage notes as well. In the sample print entry, the dictionary offers advice on several uses of *regard* not specifically covered by the meanings. Such advice is based on the opinions of many experts and on actual usage in current magazines, newspapers, and books.

43b Discriminate between words that sound alike but have different meanings.

Words that sound alike or nearly alike but have different meanings and spellings are called *homophones*. The following sets of words are so commonly confused that a careful writer will double-check their every use.

> affect (verb: to exert an influence)
> effect (verb: to accomplish; noun: result)
>
> its (possessive pronoun: of or belonging to it)
> it's (contraction of *it is* or *it has*)
>
> loose (adjective: free, not securely attached)
> lose (verb: to fail to keep, to be deprived of)
>
> principal (adjective: most important; noun: head of a school)
> principle (noun: a fundamental guideline or truth)
>
> their (possessive pronoun: belonging to them)
> they're (contraction of *they are*)
> there (adverb: that place or position)
>
> who's (contraction of *who is* or *who has*)
> whose (possessive form of *who*)
>
> your (possessive pronoun: belonging to you)
> you're (contraction of *you are*)

To check for correct use of these and other commonly confused words, see the Glossary of Usage (p. 789).

43c Become familiar with the major spelling rules.

i before e except after c

Use *i* before *e* except after *c* or when sounded like *ay*, as in *neighbor* and *weigh*.

I BEFORE *E*	relieve, believe, sieve, niece, fierce, frieze
E BEFORE *I*	receive, deceive, sleigh, freight, eight
EXCEPTIONS	seize, either, weird, height, foreign, leisure

Suffixes

Final silent *-e*   Generally, drop a final silent *-e* when adding a suffix that begins with a vowel. Keep the final *-e* if the suffix begins with a consonant.

combine, combination	achieve, achievement
desire, desiring	care, careful
prude, prudish	entire, entirety
remove, removable	gentle, gentleness

Words such as *changeable*, *judgment*, *argument*, and *truly* are exceptions.

Final *-y*   When adding *-s* or *-d* to words ending in *-y*, ordinarily change *-y* to *-ie* when the *-y* is preceded by a consonant but not when it is preceded by a vowel.

comedy, comedies	monkey, monkeys
dry, dried	play, played

With proper names ending in *-y*, however, do not change the *-y* to *-ie* even if it is preceded by a consonant: *the Dougherty family*, *the Doughertys*.

Final consonants   If a final consonant is preceded by a single vowel *and* the consonant ends a one-syllable word or a

stressed syllable, double the consonant when adding a suffix
beginning with a vowel.

bet, betting	occur, occurrence
commit, committed	

Plurals

-s or -es   Add *-s* to form the plural of most nouns; add *-es* to
singular nouns ending in *-s, -sh, -ch*, and *-x*.

table, tables	church, churches
paper, papers	dish, dishes

Ordinarily add *-s* to nouns ending in *-o* when the *-o* is preceded by a vowel. Add *-es* when it is preceded by a consonant.

radio, radios	hero, heroes
video, videos	tomato, tomatoes

ESL   Spelling varies slightly among English-speaking countries.
This can prove particularly confusing for multilingual students in
the United States, who may have learned British English. Following
is a list of some common words spelled differently in American and
British English. Consult a dictionary for others.

AMERICAN	BRITISH
canceled, traveled	cancelled, travelled
color, humor	colour, humour
judgment	judgement
check	cheque
realize, apologize	realise, apologise
defense	defence
anemia, anesthetic	anaemia, anaesthetic
theater, center	theatre, centre
fetus	foetus
mold, smolder	mould, smoulder
civilization	civilisation
connection, inflection	connexion, inflexion
licorice	liquorice

Other plurals To form the plural of a hyphenated compound word, add -s to the chief word even if it does not appear at the end.

mother-in-law, mothers-in-law

English words derived from other languages such as Latin or French sometimes form the plural as they would in their original language.

medium, media   chateau, chateaux
criterion, criteria

43d Be alert to commonly misspelled words.

absence	benefited	eligible	independence
academic	bureau	embarrass	indispensable
accidentally	business	emphasize	inevitable
accommodate	calendar	entirely	intelligence
achievement	candidate	environment	irrelevant
acknowledge	cemetery	especially	irresistible
acquaintance	changeable	exaggerated	knowledge
acquire	column	exercise	library
address	commitment	exhaust	license
all right	committed	existence	lightning
amateur	committee	extraordinary	loneliness
analyze	competitive	extremely	maintenance
answer	completely	familiar	maneuver
apparently	conceivable	fascinate	marriage
appearance	conscience	February	mathematics
arctic	conscientious	foreign	mischievous
argument	conscious	forty	necessary
arithmetic	criticism	fourth	noticeable
arrangement	criticize	friend	occasion
ascend	decision	government	occurred
athlete	definitely	grammar	occurrence
athletics	descendant	guard	pamphlet
attendance	desperate	harass	parallel
basically	dictionary	height	particularly
beautiful	different	humorous	pastime
beginning	disastrous	incidentally	permanent
believe	eighth	incredible	permissible

perseverance	professor	schedule	tomorrow
phenomenon	pronunciation	seize	tragedy
physically	publicly	separate	transferred
playwright	quiet	sergeant	tries
practically	quite	siege	truly
precede	quizzes	similar	unnecessarily
preference	receive	sincerely	usually
preferred	recognize	sophomore	vacuum
prejudice	referred	strictly	vengeance
presence	restaurant	subtly	villain
prevalent	rhythm	succeed	weird
privilege	roommate	surprise	whether
proceed	sandwich	thorough	writing

EXERCISE 43–1 The following memo has been run through a spell checker. Proofread it carefully, editing the spelling and typographical errors that remain.

November 3, 2009

To: Patricia Wise
From: Constance Mayhew
Subject: Express Tours annual report

Thank you for agreeing to draft the annual report for Express Tours. Before you begin you're work, let me outline the initial steps.

First, its essential for you to include brief profiles of top management. Early next week, I'll provide profiles for all manages accept Samuel Heath, who's biographical information is being revised. You should edit these profiles carefully and than format them according to the enclosed instructions. We may ask you to include other employee's profiles at some point.

Second, you should arrange to get complete financial information for fiscal year 2009 from our comptroller, Richard Chang. (Helen Boyes, to, can provide the necessary figures.) When you get this information, precede according tot he plans we discuss in yesterday's meeting. By the way, you will notice from the figures that the sale of our Charterhouse division did not significantly effect net profits.

Third, you should submit first draft of the report by December 15. I assume that you won a laser printer, but if you don't, you can e-mail a file and we'll print out a draft here. Of coarse, you should proofread you writing.

I am quiet pleased that you can take on this project. If I can answers questions, don't hesitate to call.

44 The hyphen

> Spell checkers can flag some, but not all, missing or misused hyphens. For example, the programs can often tell you that a hyphen is needed in compound numbers, such as *sixty-four*. They can also tell you how to spell certain compound words, such as *breakup* (not *break-up*).

44a Consult the dictionary to determine how to treat a compound word.

The dictionary will tell you whether to treat a compound word as a hyphenated compound (*water-repellent*), one word (*waterproof*), or two words (*water table*). If the compound word is not in the dictionary, treat it as two words.

▶ The prosecutor chose not to cross-examine any witnesses.

▶ All students are expected to record their data in a small

note book.

▶ Alice walked through the looking-glass into a backward

world.

44b Use a hyphen to connect two or more words functioning together as an adjective before a noun.

▶ Mrs. Douglas gave Toshiko a seashell and some newspaper-

wrapped fish to take home to her mother.

▶ Richa Gupta is not yet a well-known candidate.

Newspaper-wrapped and *well-known* are adjectives used before the nouns *fish* and *candidate*.

Generally, do not use a hyphen when such compounds follow the noun.

▶ After our television campaign, Richa Gupta will be well-

known.

Do not use a hyphen to connect *-ly* adverbs to the words they modify.

▶ A slowly-moving truck tied up traffic.

NOTE: When two or more hyphenated adjectives in a row modify the same noun, you can suspend the hyphens.

Do you prefer first-, second-, or third-class tickets?

44c Hyphenate the written form of fractions and of compound numbers from twenty-one to ninety-nine.

▶ One-fourth of my income goes to pay my child care

expenses.

44d Use a hyphen with the prefixes *all-*, *ex-* (meaning "former"), and *self-* and with the suffix *-elect*.

▶ The private foundation is funneling more money into

self-help projects.

▶ The Student Senate bylaws require the president-elect to

attend all senate meetings between the election and the

official transfer of office.

44e Use a hyphen in certain words to avoid ambiguity or to separate awkward double or triple letters.

Without the hyphen, there would be no way to distinguish between words such as *re-creation* and *recreation*.

> Bicycling in the city is my favorite form of recreation.

> The film was praised for its astonishing re-creation of nineteenth-century London.

Hyphens are sometimes used to separate awkward double or triple letters in compound words (*anti-intellectual, cross-stitch*). Always check a dictionary for the standard form of the word.

44f Check for correct word breaks when words must be divided at the end of a line.

Some word processing programs and other computer applications automatically generate word breaks at the ends of lines. When you're writing an academic paper, it's best to set your computer application not to hyphenate automatically. Some hyphenation is inevitable, however, so you should be familiar with the following hyphenation conventions.

1. Words must be divided between syllables, and one-syllable words should not be divided.

> When I returned from my semester overseas, I didn't ~~reco-~~ rec-
> ~~ognize~~ ognize
> ~~gnize~~ one face on the magazine covers.

> He didn't have the courage or the ~~stren-~~ strength
> ~~gth~~ to open the door.

2. A single letter should not stand alone at the end of a line, and no fewer than three letters should begin a line.

> She'll bring her brother with her when she comes ~~a-~~ again.
> ~~gain.~~

▶ As audience to the play *The Mousetrap*, Hamlet is a ~~watch-~~
  watcher
  ~~er~~ watching watchers.
  ^

3. Compound words should either be divided between the words that form the compound or not be divided at all.

▶ My niece Marielena is determined to become a long-~~dis-~~
  distance
  ~~tance~~ runner when she grows up.
  ^

NOTE: E-mail addresses and URLs need special attention when they occur at the end of a line of text. You can't rely on your computer application to divide these terms correctly, so you must make a decision in each case. Do not insert a hyphen to divide e-mail addresses and URLs. Instead, break an e-mail address after the @ symbol or before a period. Break a URL after a slash or a double slash or before any other punctuation mark.

> I repeatedly e-mailed Janine at janine.r.rose@dunbaracademy .org before I gave up and called her cell phone.

> To find a zip code quickly, I always use the United States Postal Service Web site at http://zip4.usps.com/zip4/ welcome.jsp.

For breaks in URLs in MLA, APA, and *Chicago* documentation styles, see 54a, 56e, and 57e, respectively.

EXERCISE 44–1   Edit the following sentences to correct errors in hyphenation. If a sentence is correct, write "correct" after it. Answers to lettered sentences appear in the back of the book. Example:

Zola's first readers were scandalized by his slice–of–life novels.
                                                       ^   ^

a. Gold is the seventy-ninth element in the periodic table.
b. The swiftly-moving tugboat pulled alongside the barge and directed it away from the oil spill in the harbor.
c. The Moche were a pre-Columbian people who established a sophisticated culture in ancient Peru.
d. Your dog is well-known in our neighborhood.
e. Road-blocks were set up along all the major highways leading out of the city.

1. We knew we were driving too fast when our tires skidded on the rain slick surface.
2. The Black Death reduced the population of some medieval villages by two thirds.
3. Sewing forty-eight sequined tutus for the ballet recital nearly made Karyn cross-eyed.
4. Olivia had hoped to find a pay as you go plan to finance the construction of her observatory.
5. Gail Sheehy writes that at age twenty five many people assume that the choices they make are irrevocable.

hackerhandbooks.com/bedhandbook > Grammar exercises > Mechanics
> E-ex 44–2

45 Capitalization

In addition to the rules in this section, a good dictionary can tell you when to use capital letters.

> **Grammar checkers** remind you that sentences should begin with capital letters and that some words, such as *Cherokee*, are proper nouns. Many words, however, should be capitalized only in certain contexts, and you must determine when to do so.

45a Capitalize proper nouns and words derived from them; do not capitalize common nouns.

Proper nouns are the names of specific persons, places, and things. All other nouns are common nouns. The following types of words are usually capitalized: names of deities, religions, religious followers, sacred books; words of family relationship used as names; particular places; nationalities and their languages, races, tribes; educational institutions, departments, degrees, particular courses; government departments, organizations, political parties; historical movements, periods, events, documents; specific electronic sources; and trade names.

PROPER NOUNS	COMMON NOUNS
God (used as a name)	a god
Book of Common Prayer	a sacred book
Uncle Pedro	my uncle
Father (used as a name)	my father
Lake Superior	a picturesque lake
the Capital Center	a center for advanced studies
the South	a southern state
Wrigley Field	a baseball stadium
University of Wisconsin	a state university
Geology 101	geology
Environmental Protection Agency	a federal agency
Phi Kappa Psi	a fraternity
a Democrat	an independent
the Enlightenment	the eighteenth century
the Treaty of Versailles	a treaty
the World Wide Web, the Web	a home page
the Internet, the Net	a computer network
Advil	a painkiller

Months, holidays, and days of the week are treated as proper nouns; the seasons and numbers of the days of the month are not.

> Our academic year begins on a Tuesday in early September, right after Labor Day.

> Graduation is in early summer, on the second of June.

EXCEPTION: Capitalize Fourth of July (or July Fourth) when referring to the holiday.

Names of school subjects are capitalized only if they are names of languages. Names of particular courses are capitalized.

> This semester Austin is taking math, geography, geology, French, and English.

> Professor Obembe offers Modern American Fiction 501 to graduate students.

CAUTION: Do not capitalize common nouns to make them seem important: *Our company is currently hiring computer programmers* (not *Company, Computer Programmers*).

45b Capitalize titles of persons when used as part of a proper name but usually not when used alone.

> Professor Margaret Barnes; Dr. Sinyee Sein; John Scott Williams Jr.
>
> District Attorney Marshall was reprimanded for badgering the witness.
>
> The district attorney was elected for a two-year term.

Usage varies when the title of an important public figure is used alone: *The president* [or *President*] *vetoed the bill.*

45c Capitalize the first, last, and all major words in titles and subtitles of works such as books, articles, songs, and online documents.

In both titles and subtitles, major words such as nouns, pronouns, verbs, adjectives, and adverbs should be capitalized. Minor words such as articles, prepositions, and coordinating conjunctions are not capitalized unless they are the first or last word of a title or subtitle. Capitalize the second part of a hyphenated term in a title if it is a major word but not if it is a minor word. Capitalize chapter titles and the titles of other major divisions of a work following the same guidelines used for titles of complete works.

> *Seizing the Enigma: The Race to Break the German U-Boat Codes*
> *A River Runs through It*
> "I Want to Hold Your Hand"
> *The Canadian Green Page*

To see why some of the titles in the list are italicized and some are put in quotation marks, see 42a and 37d.

45d Capitalize the first word of a sentence.

The first word of a sentence should be capitalized. When a sentence appears within parentheses, capitalize its first word unless the parentheses appear within another sentence.

> Early detection of breast cancer significantly increases survival rates. (See table 2.)

Early detection of breast cancer significantly increases survival rates (see table 2).

45e Capitalize the first word of a quoted sentence but not a quoted phrase.

Robert Hughes writes, "There are only about sixty Watteau paintings on whose authenticity all experts agree" (102).

Russell Baker has written that in our country, sports are "the opiate of the masses" (46).

If a quoted sentence is interrupted by explanatory words, do not capitalize the first word after the interruption. (See 37f.)

"If you want to go out," he said, "tell me now."

When quoting poetry, copy the poet's capitalization exactly. Many poets capitalize the first word of every line of poetry; a few contemporary poets dismiss capitalization altogether.

it was the week   that
i felt the city's narrow breezes rush about
me   —Don L. Lee

45f Capitalize the first word after a colon if it begins an independent clause.

If a group of words following a colon could stand on its own as a complete sentence, capitalize the first word.

Clinical trials called into question the safety profile of the drug: A high percentage of participants reported hypertension and kidney problems.

Preferences vary among academic disciplines. See 54c, 56f, and 57f for MLA, APA, and *Chicago* style, respectively.

Always use lowercase for a list or an appositive that follows a colon.

Students were divided into two groups: residents and commuters.

45g Capitalize abbreviations according to convention.

Abbreviations for government agencies and other organizations as well as call numbers for radio and television stations are capitalized.

EPA, FBI, OPEC, IBM, WCRB, KNBC-TV

EXERCISE 45–1 Edit the following sentences to correct errors in capitalization. If a sentence is correct, write "correct" after it. Answers to lettered sentences appear in the back of the book. Example:

On our trip to the West, we visited the grand ¢anyon and the
great ¢alt ¢esert.

a. Assistant dean Shirin Ahmadi recommended offering more world language courses.

b. We went to the Mark Taper Forum to see a production of *Angels in America*.

c. Kalindi has an ambitious semester, studying differential calculus, classical hebrew, brochure design, and greek literature.

d. Lydia's Aunt and Uncle make modular houses as beautiful as modernist works of art.

e. We amused ourselves on the long flight by discussing how Spring in Kyoto stacks up against Summer in London.

1. When the Ducati will not start, I try a few tricks with the ignition key: Jiggling it to the left, pulling it out a quarter of an inch, and gently pulling down on it.

2. When you slowly bake a clove of garlic, the most amazing thing happens: It loses its bitter tang and becomes sweet and buttery.

3. After World War II, aunt Helena left Poland to study in Italy.

4. When we drove through the south last year, we enjoyed stopping at the peanut stands along the road.

5. Following in his sister's footsteps, Leonid is pursuing a degree in Marketing Research.

hackerhandbooks.com/bedhandbook > Grammar exercises > Mechanics > E-ex 45–2

Part IX
Researched Writing

46 Conducting research

College research assignments ask you to pose a question worth exploring, to read widely in search of possible answers, to interpret what you read, to draw reasoned conclusions, and to support those conclusions with valid and well-documented evidence.

The process takes time: time for researching and time for drafting, revising, and documenting the paper in the style recommended by your instructor (see 49). Before beginning a research project, set a realistic schedule of deadlines. Think about how much time you might need for each step on the way to your final draft.

SAMPLE STEPS IN A RESEARCH ASSIGNMENT

Receive and analyze the assignment.

Pose questions you might explore.

Talk with a reference librarian and plan a search strategy.

Settle on a topic.

Locate sources.

Read and take notes.

Draft a working thesis and an outline.

Draft the paper.

Visit the writing center to discuss a revision plan.

Do additional research if needed.

Revise the paper; if necessary, revise the thesis.

Prepare a list of works cited.

Proofread the final draft.

Submit the final draft.

One student created a calendar to map out her tasks for a research paper assigned on October 3 and due October 31, keeping in mind that some tasks might overlap or need to be repeated. Notice that she has budgeted more than a week for

SAMPLE CALENDAR FOR A RESEARCH ASSIGNMENT

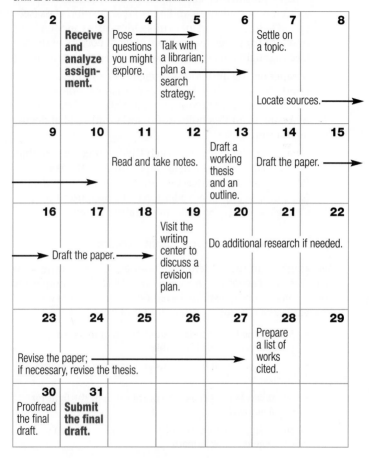

drafting and revising the paper. It's easy to spend too much time gathering sources; make sure you allow a significant portion of your schedule for drafting and revising your work.

Sections 46 and 47 include examples related to three sample student research papers:

- A paper on Internet surveillance in the workplace, written by a student in an English composition class (see pp. 583–88). The student, Anna Orlov, uses the MLA (Modern Language Association) style of documentation. (See highlights of Orlov's research process on pp. 573–82.)

- A paper on the limitations of medications to treat childhood obesity, written by a student in a psychology class (see pp. 674–83). The student, Luisa Mirano, uses the APA (American Psychological Association) style of documentation.

- A paper on the extent to which Civil War general Nathan Bedford Forrest can be held responsible for the Fort Pillow massacre, written by a student in a history class (see pp. 718–26). The student, Ned Bishop, uses the *Chicago Manual of Style* documentation system.

46a Pose questions you might explore.

Working within the guidelines of your assignment, pose a few questions that seem worth researching. Here, for example, are some preliminary questions jotted down by students enrolled in a variety of courses in different disciplines.

- Should the FCC broaden its definition of indecent programming to include violence?

- Which geological formations are the safest repositories for nuclear waste?

- What was Marcus Garvey's contribution to the fight for racial equality?

- How can governments and zoos help preserve Asia's endangered snow leopard?

- Why was amateur archaeologist Heinrich Schliemann such a controversial figure in his own time?

As you think about possible questions, make sure that they are appropriate lines of inquiry for a research paper. Choose questions that are narrow (not too broad), challenging (not too bland), and grounded (not too speculative).

Choosing a narrow question

If your initial question is too broad, given the length of the paper you plan to write, look for ways to restrict your focus (see the chart on p. 5). Here, for example, is how three students narrowed their initial questions.

TOO BROAD	NARROWER
What are the hazards of fad diets?	Why are low-carbohydrate diets hazardous?
What are the benefits of stricter auto emissions standards?	How will stricter auto emissions standards create new, more competitive auto industry jobs?
What causes depression?	How has the widespread use of antidepressant drugs affected teenage suicide rates?

Choosing a challenging question

Your research paper will be more interesting to both you and your audience if you base it on an intellectually challenging line of inquiry. Avoid bland questions that fail to provoke thought or engage readers in a debate.

TOO BLAND	CHALLENGING
What is obsessive-compulsive disorder?	Why is obsessive-compulsive disorder so difficult to treat?
Where is wind energy being used?	What makes wind farms economically viable?
How does DNA testing work?	How reliable is DNA testing?

You may need to address a bland question in the course of answering a more challenging one. For example, if you were writing about promising treatments for obsessive-compulsive disorder, you would no doubt answer the question "What is obsessive-compulsive disorder?" at some point in your paper. It would be a mistake, however, to use the bland question as the focus for the whole paper.

Choosing a grounded question

Finally, you will want to make sure that your research question is grounded, not too speculative. Although speculative questions—such as those that address philosophical, ethical, or religious issues—are worth asking and may receive some attention in a research paper, they are inappropriate central questions. The central argument of a research paper should be grounded in facts; it should not be based entirely on beliefs.

TOO SPECULATIVE	GROUNDED
Is it wrong to share music files on the Internet?	How has Internet file sharing affected the earning potential of musicians?
Do medical scientists have the right to experiment on animals?	How have technical breakthroughs made medical experiments on animals increasingly unnecessary?
Are youth sports too dangerous?	Why should school districts fund cardiac screening for all student athletes?

hackerhandbooks.com/bedhandbook > Research exercises > Researching > E-ex 46–1

46b Map out a search strategy.

A search strategy is a systematic plan for tracking down sources. To create a search strategy appropriate for your research question, consult a reference librarian and take a look at your library's Web site, which will give you an overview of available resources.

Getting started

Reference librarians are information specialists who can save you time by steering you toward relevant and reliable sources. With the help of an expert, you can make the best use of electronic databases, Web search engines, your library's catalog, and other reference tools.

Before you ask a reference librarian for help, be sure you have thought through the following questions:

- What is your assignment?
- In which academic discipline are you writing?
- What is your tentative research question?
- How long will the paper be?
- How much time can you spend on the project?

It's a good idea to bring a copy of the assignment with you.

In addition to speaking with a reference librarian, take some time to explore your library's Web site. You will typically find links to the library's catalog and to a variety of databases and electronic sources that you can access from any networked computer. You may also find resources listed by subject, research guides, information about interlibrary loans, and links to Web sites selected by librarians for their quality. Many libraries offer online reference assistance to help you locate information and refine your search strategy.

NOTE FOR DISTANCE LEARNERS: Even if you are unable to visit the library, as an enrolled student you can still use its resources. Most libraries offer chat reference services and access to online databases, though you may have to follow special procedures to use them. Check your library's Web site for information for distance learners.

Including the library in your plan

You may be tempted to ignore your library's resources, but using them can save you time and money in the end. Libraries weed out questionable sources and make a wide range of quality materials readily available.

While a general Internet search might seem quick and convenient, it is often more time-consuming and can be less reliable than a search in a library's databases. Initial searches may generate thousands of results. Figuring out which of these

LIBRARY HOME PAGE

are credible, relevant, and worth further investigation can require many additional steps:

- Refining search terms to generate fewer results (See the chart on refining keyword searches on p. 449.)
- Narrowing the domain to include only .org, .gov, or .edu sites
- Weeding out any advertisements associated with results
- Determining which sites might present useful arguments by scanning their titles and, in some cases, viewing their content
- Visiting sites that seem promising to determine their currency and relevance
- Combing through sites to determine the credibility of their authors

Starting with your library's collection of databases to run the same search can save you time and effort. Library database searches will turn up a manageable number of results, most of which are relevant, even if your initial search is broader than it should be. Because these searches are limited to only academic databases, you can count on finding reliable sources. Not all of the results will be worth examining in detail, but most library searches automatically sort them into subject categories that allow you to view narrowed results with just one click.

Using library databases can also save money. Most college assignments will require using at least some books and scholarly journal articles. Internet search engines can help you locate such sources, but the published texts are often not free online. *Google Scholar*, for example, provides scholarly results, but often you have to pay a fee or purchase a subscription to access the full texts. Most libraries subscribe to databases that will give you unlimited access to many of these materials as well as scholarly resources that might not turn up outside of a database. You will be able to do some of your work from any computer that can connect to the campus network.

Choosing an appropriate search strategy

No single search strategy works for every topic. For some topics, it may be appropriate to search for information in newspapers, magazines, and Web sites. For others, the best sources might be found in scholarly journals and books and specialized reference works. Still other topics might be enhanced by field research — interviews, surveys, or direct observation.

With the help of a reference librarian, each of the students mentioned on page 440 constructed a search strategy appropriate for his or her research question.

Anna Orlov   Anna Orlov's topic, Internet surveillance in the workplace, was current and influenced by technological changes, so she relied heavily on recent sources, especially those online. To find information on her topic, Orlov decided to

- search her library's general database for articles in magazines, newspapers, and journals
- check the library's catalog for recently published books
- use Web search engines, such as *Google*, to locate articles and government publications that might not show up in a database search

Luisa Mirano Luisa Mirano's topic, the limitations of medications for childhood obesity, is the subject of psychological studies as well as articles in the popular press (newspapers and magazines aimed at the general public). Thinking that both scholarly and popular works would be appropriate, Mirano decided to

- locate books through her library's catalog
- check a specialized encyclopedia, *Encyclopedia of Psychology*
- search a specialized database, *PsycINFO*, for scholarly articles
- search her library's general database for popular articles

Ned Bishop Ned Bishop's topic, Nathan Bedford Forrest's role in the Fort Pillow massacre, has been investigated and debated by professional historians. Given the nature of his historical topic, Bishop decided to

- locate books through his library's catalog
- locate scholarly articles by searching a specialized database, *America: History and Life*
- locate newspaper articles from 1864 by searching the historical archive at the *New York Times* Web site
- search the Web for other historical primary sources

46c To locate articles, search a database or consult a print index.

Libraries subscribe to a variety of electronic databases (sometimes called *periodical databases*) that give students access to articles and other materials without charge. Because many databases are limited to recent works, you may need to consult a print index as well.

What databases offer

Your library has access to databases that can lead you to articles in periodicals such as newspapers, magazines, and scholarly or technical journals. Some databases cover several subject areas; others cover one subject area in depth. Your library might subscribe to some of the following databases.

General databases   College libraries typically subscribe to one or more general databases. The information in those databases is not restricted to a specific discipline or subject area. You may find searching a general database helpful in the early stages of your research process.

> *Academic Search Premier.* An interdisciplinary database that indexes thousands of popular and scholarly journals on all subjects, offering many articles in full text.
>
> *Expanded Academic ASAP.* An interdisciplinary database that indexes the contents of magazines, newspapers, and scholarly journals in all subject areas. It also includes many full-text articles.
>
> *JSTOR.* A full-text archive of scholarly journals from many disciplines; unlike most databases, it includes articles published decades ago but does not include articles from the most recent issues of publications.
>
> *LexisNexis.* A database that is particularly strong in coverage of news, business, legal, and political topics. Nearly all of the material is available in full text.
>
> *ProQuest.* A database of periodical articles, many in full text. Through *ProQuest*, your library may subscribe to databases in subjects such as nursing, biology, and psychology.

Subject-specific databases   Libraries have dozens of specialized databases covering many different subjects. Your library's

Web site will guide you to what's available. The following are examples of subject-specific databases.

ERIC. A database offering education-related documents and abstracts of articles published in education journals.

MLA Bibliography. A database of literary criticism, with citations to help researchers find articles, books, and dissertations.

PsycINFO. A comprehensive database of psychology research, including abstracts of articles in journals and books.

PubMed. A database offering millions of abstracts of medical research studies.

Many databases include the full text of at least some articles; others list only citations or citations with short summaries called *abstracts*. In the case of full-text articles, you may have the option to print an article, save it, or e-mail it to yourself.

When full text is not available, the citation will give you enough information to track down an article. Your library's Web site will help you determine which articles are available in your library, either in print or in electronic form. If the library does not own the item you want, you can usually request a copy through interlibrary loan; check with a librarian to find out how long it may take for the source to arrive.

Making the most of your handbook

Freewriting, listing, and clustering can help you come up with additional search terms.

▶ Exploring your subject: 1b

How to search a database

To find articles on your topic in a database, start with a keyword search. If the first keyword you try results in too few or no matches, experiment with synonyms or ask a librarian for suggestions. For example, if you're searching for sources on a

Refining keyword searches in databases and search engines

Although command terms and characters vary among electronic databases and Web search engines, some of the most commonly used functions are listed here.

- Use quotation marks around words that are part of a phrase: "gateway drug".

- Use AND to connect words that must appear in a document: hyperactivity AND children. In some search engines—*Google*, for example—*and* is assumed, so typing it is unnecessary. Other search engines require a plus sign instead: Ireland +peace.

- Use NOT in front of words that must not appear in a document: shepherd NOT dog. Some search engines require a minus sign (hyphen) instead: shepherd -dog.

- Use OR if only one of the terms must appear in a document: "mountain lion" OR cougar.

- Use an asterisk as a substitute for letters that might vary: "marine biolog*" (to find *marine biology* or *marine biologist*, for example).

- Use parentheses to group a search expression and combine it with another: (standard OR student OR test*) AND reform.

NOTE: Many search engines and databases offer an advanced search option that makes it easy to refine your search.

topic related to education, you might also try the terms *teaching*, *learning*, *pedagogy*, and *curriculum*. If your keyword search results in too many matches, narrow it by using one of the strategies in the chart on this page.

For her paper on Internet surveillance in the workplace, Anna Orlov conducted a keyword search in a general periodical database. She typed *"internet use"* and *employee* and *surveillance* (see the database screen on p. 450). This search brought up twenty possible articles, some of which looked promising.

DATABASE SCREEN: KEYWORD SEARCH

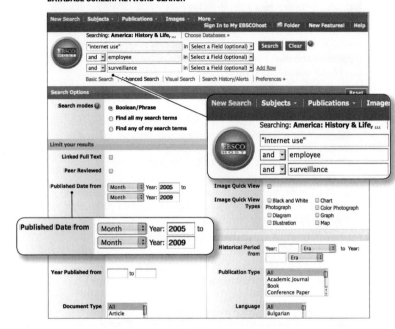

(See pp. 575–76 to view Orlov's annotated list of search results.) Orlov e-mailed several full-text articles to herself and printed citations to others so that she could locate them in the library.

When to use a print index

A print index to periodical articles is a useful tool when you are researching a historical topic, especially from the early to mid-twentieth century. The *Readers' Guide to Periodical Literature* or *Poole's Index to Periodical Literature* indexes magazine articles beginning around 1900, many of which are too old to appear in electronic databases. You can usually access the print articles themselves in your library's shelves, on microfilm or microfiche, or by interlibrary loan.

46d To locate books, consult the library's catalog.

The books your library owns are listed in its catalog, along with other resources such as videos. You can search the catalog by author, title, or subject keywords.

If your first search calls up too few results, try different keywords or search for books on broader topics. If your search gives you too many results, use the strategies in the chart on page 449 or try an advanced search tool to combine concepts and limit your results. If those strategies don't work, ask a librarian for suggestions.

When Luisa Mirano, whose topic was childhood obesity, entered the term *obesity* into the library's catalog, she was faced with an unmanageable number of hits. She narrowed her search by adding two specific terms to *obesity*: *child** (to include the terms *child*, *children*, and *childhood*) and *treatment*. When she still got too many results, she limited the first two terms to subject searches to find books with obesity in children as their primary subject. Mirano's advanced search and the seven records she retrieved are illustrated in screens 1 and 2.

**LIBRARY CATALOG SCREEN 1:
ADVANCED SEARCH**

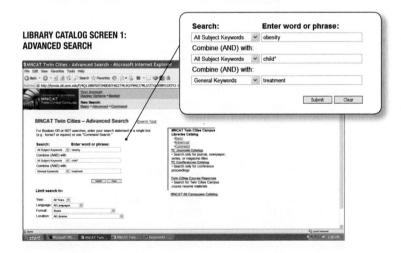

LIBRARY CATALOG SCREEN 2: SEARCH RESULTS

MNCAT Twin Cities
Results for : All Subjects KW= (obesity) AND All Subjects KW= (child*) AND General Key
Sort options : ▸Author/Year(d)▸ Year(d)/Author ▸Author/Title ▸Title/Year(d) ▸Year(d)/Title

Records 1 - 7 of 7

#	Title	Author
1 ☐	Treatment of overweight children and adolescents : a needs assessment of health practitioners.	
2 ☐	Body image, eating disorders, and obesity in youth : assessment, prevention, and treatment /	Thompson, J. Kevin.
3 ☐	Childhood and adolescent obesity /	Styne, Dennis M.
4 ☐	Obesity : impact on cardiovascular disease /	Fletcher, Gerald F., 1935-
5 ☐	Obesity in childhood and adolescence : assessment, prevention and treatment : papers emanating from a conference held in Minneapolis, Minnesota, USA, May, 1997 /	Himes, J. H. (John H.)
6 ☐	Prevention and treatment of childhood obesity /	Williams, Christine L., 1943-
7 ☐	Treating childhood and adolescent obesity /	Kirschenbaum, Daniel S.,

---

LIBRARY CATALOG SCREEN 3: COMPLETE RECORD FOR A BOOK

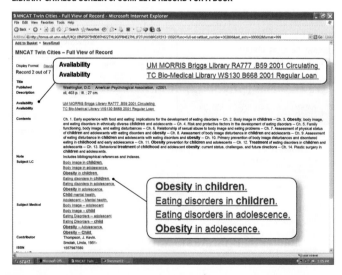

Once you have narrowed your search to a list of relevant sources, you can display or save the complete record for each source, which includes its bibliographic information (author, title, publication information) and a call number. Screen 3 shows the complete record for the second title on the list generated by Mirano's search. The call number, listed beside *Availability*, is the book's address on the library shelf. When you're retrieving a book from the shelf, take the time to scan other books in the area since they are likely to be on the same topic.

LIBRARIAN'S TIP: The catalog record for a book lists related subject headings. These headings are a good way to locate other books on your subject. For example, the record in screen 3 lists the terms *obesity in children* and *obesity in adolescence* as related subject headings. By clicking on these new terms, Mirano found a few more books on her subject. Subject headings can be useful terms for a database search as well.

46e To locate other sources, use a variety of online tools.

You can find a variety of reliable sources using online tools beyond those offered by your library. For example, most government agencies post information on their Web sites, and federal and state governments use Web sites to communicate with citizens. The sites of many private organizations, such as Doctors without Borders and the Sierra Club, contain useful information about current issues. Museums and libraries often post digital versions of primary sources, such as photographs, political speeches, and classic literary texts.

Although the Internet at large can be a rich source of information, some of which can't be found anywhere else, it lacks quality control. The material on many sites has not necessarily been reviewed by experts. So when you're not working with your library's tools to locate online sources, carefully evaluate what you find (see 47e).

This section describes the following general Web resources: search engines, directories, digital archives, government and news sites, blogs, and wikis.

hackerhandbooks.com/bedhandbook > Additional resources > Links Library
> Conducting research

Search engines

When using a search engine, such as *Google* or *Ask.com,* focus your search as narrowly as possible. You can refine your search by using many of the tips in the chart on page 449 or by using the search engine's advanced search form. For her paper on Internet surveillance in the workplace, Anna Orlov had difficulty restricting the number of hits. When she typed the words *internet, surveillance, workplace,* and *privacy* into a search engine, she got more than 80,000 matches. After examining the first page of results and viewing some that looked promising, Orlov grouped her search terms into the phrases "*internet surveillance*" and "*workplace privacy*" and added the term *employee* to narrow the focus. The result was 422 matches. To refine her search further, Orlov clicked on Advanced Search and restricted her search to sites with URLs ending in *.org* and to those updated in the last three months. (See the results screen on p. 455.)

Directories

If you want to find good resources on topics too broad for a search engine, try a directory. Unlike search engines, directories are put together by information specialists who choose reputable sites and arrange them by topic: education, health, politics, and so on.

Some directories are particularly useful for research. For example, links included in the *Internet Scout Project* are selected by an expert research team and include annotations that both describe and evaluate each site.

SEARCH ENGINE SCREEN: RESULTS OF AN ADVANCED SEARCH

Web Results 1 - 5 of about 9 over the past 3 months for "Internet surveillance" employee "workplace privacy"

Web Results 1 - 5 of about 9 over the past 3 months for "Internet surveillance" employee "workplace privacy" site:.org (0.44 seconds)

Tip: Try removing quotes from your search to get more results.

EPIC/PI - Privacy & Human Rights 2000
Now the supervision of **employee**'s performance, behavior and... [89]Information and
Privacy Commissioner/Ontario, **Workplace Privacy**: The Need for a..
www.privacyinternational.org/survey/phr2000/threats.html - 131k Cached - Similar pages

Privacy and Human Rights 2003: Threats to Privacy
Other issues that raise **workplace privacy** concerns are employer requirements that
employees complete medical tests, questionnaires, and polygraph tests..
www.privacyinternational.org/survey/phr2003/threats.htm - 279k Cached - Similar pages
[More results from www.privacyinternational.org]

[PDF] Monitoring **Employee** E-Mail And Internet Usage: Avoiding The..
File Format: PDF/Adobe Acrobat - View as HTML
Internet surveillance by employers in the American workplace. At present, US **employees**
in the private workplace have no constitutional, common law or statu
lsr.nellco.org/cgi/viewcontent.cgi?article=1006&context=suffolk/ip - Similar pages

Previous EPIC Top News
The agencies plan to use RFID to track **employees**' movements and in ID cards... For more
information on **workplace privacy**, see the EPIC **Workplace Privacy** ...
www.epic.org/news/2005.html - 163k Cached - Similar pages

The following directories are especially useful for scholarly research:

Internet Scout Project <http://scout.wisc.edu/Archives>

Librarian's Internet Index <http://lii.org>

Open Directory Project <http://dmoz.org>

WWW Virtual Library <http://vlib.org>

Digital archives

Archives are a good place to find primary sources. They may contain the texts of poems, books, speeches, and historically significant documents; photographs; and political cartoons.

The materials in these sites are usually limited to official documents and older works because of copyright laws. The following online archives are impressive collections:

American Memory <http://memory.loc.gov>

Avalon Project <http://yale.edu/lawweb/avalon/avalon.htm>

Eurodocs <http://eudocs.lib.byu.edu>

Google Books <http:// books.google.com>

Google Scholar <http://scholar.google.com>

The Making of America <http://quod.lib.umich.edu/m/moagrp>

Online Books Page <http://onlinebooks.library.upenn.edu>

Government and news sites

For current topics, both government and news sites can prove useful. Many government agencies at every level provide on-line information. Government-maintained sites include resources such as legal texts, facts and statistics, government reports, and searchable reference databases. Here are just a few government sites:

Fedstats <http://www.fedstats.gov>

GPO Access <http://www.gpoaccess.gov>

United Nations <http://www.un.org>

University of Michigan Documents Center <http://www.lib.umich.edu/govdocs>

US Census Bureau <http://www.census.gov>

NOTE: You can access a state's Web site by putting the two-letter state abbreviation into a standard URL: <http://www.state.ga.us>. Substitute any state's two-letter abbreviation for the letters *ga*, which in this case stand for Georgia.

Many news organizations offer up-to-date information on the Web. Some require registration and may charge fees for some articles. Check with your library to see if it subscribes to online newspapers that you can access at no charge. The following are some free news sites:

BBC <http://www.bbc.co.uk>

Google News <http://news.google.com>

Kidon Media-Link <http://www.kidon.com/media-link>

New York Times <http://nytimes.com>

Blogs

A blog (short for *Weblog*) is a site that contains dated text or multimedia entries usually written and maintained by one person, with comments contributed by readers. Though some blogs are personal diaries and others are devoted to partisan politics, many journalists and academics maintain blogs that cover topics of interest to researchers. Some blogs feature short essays that provide useful insights or analysis; others point to new developments in an area of interest. Because blogs are frequently updated, you may want to subscribe to especially useful ones. The following Web sites can lead you to a wide range of blogs:

Academic Blog Portal <http://academicblogs.org>

Google Blog Search <http://www.google.com/blogsearch>

Science Blogs <http://scienceblogs.com>

Technorati <http://technorati.com>

Wikis

A wiki is a collaborative Web site with many contributors and with content that may change frequently. *Wikipedia*, the collaborative online encyclopedia, is one of the most frequently consulted wikis.

In general, *Wikipedia* may be helpful if you're checking for something that is common knowledge (facts available in multiple sources, such as dates and well-known historical events) or looking for very current information about a topic in contemporary culture that isn't covered elsewhere. However, many scholars do not consider *Wikipedia* and wikis in general to be appropriate sources for college research. Authorship is open to anyone, not limited to experts; articles may be written by enthusiastic amateurs who are not well informed. And because the articles can be changed by anyone, controversial texts are often altered to reflect a particular perspective and are especially susceptible to bias. When possible, locate and cite another, more reliable source for any useful information you find in a wiki. (Sometimes a wiki's own citations can lead you to such credible sources.) If you cannot find a second source, check with your instructor before integrating ideas from a wiki into your researched writing.

46f Use other search tools.

In addition to articles, books, and online sources, you may want to consult references such as encyclopedias and almanacs. Citations in scholarly works can also lead you to additional sources.

Reference works

The reference section of the library holds both general and specialized encyclopedias, dictionaries, almanacs, atlases, and biographical references, some available in electronic form through the library's Web site. Such works often provide a good overview of your subject and include references to the most significant works on a topic. Check with a reference librarian to see which works are most appropriate for your project.

General reference works General reference works are good places to check facts and get basic information. Here are a few frequently used general references:

American National Biography

National Geographic Atlas of the World

The New Encyclopaedia Britannica

The Oxford English Dictionary

Statistical Abstract of the United States

Although general encyclopedias are often a good place to find background about your topic, you should rarely use them in your final paper. Most instructors expect you to rely on more specialized sources.

Specialized reference works Specialized reference works often explore a topic in depth, usually in the form of articles written by leading authorities. They offer a quick way to gain an expert's overview of a complex topic. Many specialized works are available, including these:

Contemporary Authors

Encyclopedia of Bioethics

Encyclopedia of Crime and Justice

Encyclopedia of Psychology

Encyclopedia of World Environmental History

International Encyclopedia of Communication

New Encyclopedia of Africa

Check with a reference librarian to see what specialized references are available for your topic.

hackerhandbooks.com/bedhandbook > Research and Documentation Online
> Finding sources

Bibliographies and scholarly citations as shortcuts

Scholarly books and articles list the works the author has cited, usually at the end. These lists are useful shortcuts to additional reliable sources on your topic. For example, most of the scholarly articles Luisa Mirano consulted contained citations to related research studies, selected by experts in the field; through these citations, she quickly located other sources related to her topic, treatments for childhood obesity. If you need help using an author's citations to find additional sources, ask a reference librarian.

46g Conduct field research, if appropriate.

Your own field research can enhance or be the focus of a writing project. For a composition class, for example, you might want to interview a local politician about a current issue, such as the use of alternative energy sources. For a sociology class, you might decide to conduct a survey regarding campus trends in community service. At work, you might need to learn how food industry executives have responded to reports that their products are contributing to health problems.

NOTE: Colleges and universities often require researchers to submit projects to an institutional review board (IRB) if the research involves human subjects outside of a classroom setting. Before administering a survey or conducting other fieldwork, check with your instructor to see if IRB approval is required.

Interviewing

Interviews can often shed new light on a topic. Look for an expert who has firsthand knowledge of the subject or seek out someone whose personal experience provides a valuable perspective on your topic.

When asking for an interview, be clear about who you are, what the purpose of the interview is, and how you would prefer to conduct it: via e-mail, over the phone, or in person. Plan for the interview by writing down a series of questions. Try to avoid questions with yes or no answers or those that encourage vague rambling. Instead, ask questions that lead to facts, anecdotes, and opinions that will add a meaningful dimension to your paper.

INEFFECTIVE INTERVIEW QUESTIONS

How many years have you spent studying childhood obesity?

Is your work interesting?

EFFECTIVE INTERVIEW QUESTIONS

What are some current interpretations of the causes of child-hood obesity?

What treatments have you found to be most effective? Why do you think they work?

When quoting your source in your paper, be as accurate and fair as possible. To ensure accuracy, you might want to ask permission to record the interview; if you cannot record it, take careful notes or conduct it by e-mail.

Surveying opinion

For some topics, you may find it useful to survey opinions through written questionnaires, telephone or e-mail polls, or questions posted on a Web forum. Many people are reluctant to fill out long questionnaires or answer long-winded telephone pollsters, so if you want a good response rate, you will need to limit your questions and frame them carefully.

When possible, ask yes/no questions or give multiple-choice options. Surveys with such queries can be completed quickly, and they are easy to tabulate.

SAMPLE YES/NO QUESTION

Do you favor the use of Internet surveillance in the work-place?

You may also want to ask a few open-ended questions to elicit more individual responses, some of which may be worth quoting in your paper.

SAMPLE OPEN-ENDED QUESTION

What, if any, experiences have you had with Internet surveillance in the workplace?

Some online survey companies such as SurveyMonkey <http://www.surveymonkey.com> and Zoomerang <http://zoomerang.com> host Web-based surveys and provide for a limited number of questions and responses for free. They allow you to create easy-to-take online surveys and collate the results. See the note on page 460 if you intend to survey students on your campus.

Visiting and observing

Your firsthand observations of significant places, people, or events can enhance a paper in a variety of disciplines. For example, while researching trends in contemporary American folk art, a student in New York City went to an exhibit on folk art at the Museum of Modern Art. To gather information for a paper on nineteenth-century utopian experiments, a student in Peoria, Illinois, drove to nearby Bishop Hill, a commune founded in 1846 by Swedish refugees seeking religious freedom. For his political science paper on civic participation, a student in Salt Lake City attended a local school board meeting.

Contacting organizations

Many organizations, both public and private, have information on their Web sites and may provide literature in response to a phone call, an e-mail, or a letter. Although this literature sometimes contains up-to-date information, use it judiciously. Groups tend to promote their own interests; you can't always count on them to present a balanced view.

The Encyclopedia of Associations (available electronically and in print) lists groups by their concerns, such as the environment or health care, and provides addresses and phone numbers.

47   Evaluating sources

With electronic search tools, you can often locate dozens or even hundreds of potential sources for your topic—far more than you will have time to read. Your challenge will be to determine what kinds of sources you need and to zero in on a reasonable number of quality sources, those truly worth your time and attention.

Later, once you have decided on some sources worth consulting, your challenge will be to read them with an open mind and a critical eye.

47a Think about how sources might contribute to your writing.

How you plan to use sources will affect how you evaluate them. Not every source must directly support your thesis; sources can have other functions in a paper:

- provide background information or context for your topic
- explain terms or concepts that your readers might not understand
- provide evidence for your argument
- lend authority to your argument
- offer counterevidence and alternative interpretations to your argument

One student, for example, wrote an essay arguing that public funding for the arts should be granted on artistic merit alone and not on so-called decency standards. She used a 1998 Supreme Court decision (*National Endowment for the Arts v. Finley*) and the text of the First Amendment to provide background on the decency debate in the arts and to set her argument in context. She used published interviews given by controversial artists Karen Finley and Tim Miller to lend authority to her argument. She also used passages from a profile of conservative North Carolina senator Jesse Helms to represent an alternative point of view in the debate. With her overall purpose in mind, the student judged each source according to the specific role it would play in her argument. For more examples of how student writers use sources for a variety of purposes, see 50c, 56a, 57a, and page 574.

47b Select sources worth your time and attention.

Section 46 shows how to refine your searches in databases, in the library's book catalog, and in search engines. This section explains how to scan through the results for the most promising sources and how to preview them—without actually reading them—to see whether they are likely to live up to your expectations and meet your needs.

Scanning search results

As you scan through a list of search results, watch for clues indicating whether a source might be useful for your purposes or not worth pursuing. (For an annotated list of one student's search results, see pp. 575–76.) You will need to use somewhat different strategies when scanning search results from a database, a book catalog, and a Web search engine.

Databases   Most databases, such as *Expanded Academic ASAP*, list at least the following information, which can help you decide if a source is relevant, current, scholarly enough (see the chart on p. 468), and a suitable length for your purposes.

> Title and brief description (How relevant?)
>
> Date (How current?)
>
> Name of periodical (How scholarly?)
>
> Length (How extensive in coverage?)

On the following page are just a few of the hits Ned Bishop came up with when he consulted a general database for articles on the Fort Pillow massacre, using the search term *Fort Pillow*.

Many databases allow you to sort your list of results by relevance or date; sorting may help you scan the information more efficiently. By scanning the titles in his search results, Bishop saw that only one contained the words *Fort Pillow*. The name of the periodical in which it appeared, *Journal of American History*, suggested that the source was scholarly. The

EVALUATING SEARCH RESULTS: LIBRARY DATABASE

☐ **Black, blue and gray: the other Civil War; African-American soldiers, sailors and spies were the**
Mark **unsung heroes.** *Ebony* Feb 1991 v46 n4 p96(6)
     View <u>text and retrieval choices</u>

Popular magazine.
Not relevant.

☐ **The Civil War.** (movie reviews) Lewis Cole. *The Nation* Dec 3, 1990 v251 n19 p694(5)
Mark View <u>text and retrieval choices</u>

Movie review. Not
relevant.

☐ **The hard fight was getting into the fight at all.** (black soldiers in the Civil War) Jack Fincher.
Mark *Smithsonian* Oct 1990 v21 n7 p46(13)
     View <u>text and retrieval choices</u>

Subject too broad.

☑ **The Fort Pillow massacre: a statistical note.** John Cimprich, Robert C. Mainfort Jr.. *Journal of Ameri*
Mark *History* Dec 1989 v76 n3 p830(8)
     View <u>extended citation and retrieval choices</u>

Brief scholarly
article. Matches
the student's topic.
Promising.

1989 publication date was not a problem, since currency is
not necessarily a key issue for historical topics. The article's
length (eight pages) is given in parentheses at the end of the
citation. While the article may seem short, the topic—a statistical note—is narrow enough to ensure adequate depth of
coverage. Bishop decided that the article was worth consulting. Because the other sources were irrelevant or too broad, he
decided not to consult them.

Book catalogs   The library's book catalog usually lists basic
information about books, enough for a first impression (see
also p. 452). A book's title and date of publication will often
be your first clues about whether the book is worth consulting.
Be cautious about books that were published ten or more years
ago; depending on the topic, they may be outdated. If a title
looks interesting, you can click on it for information about the
book's subject matter and its length. The table of contents may
also be available, offering a glimpse of what's inside.

Web search engines   Because anyone can publish a Web site,
legitimate sources and unreliable sources live side-by-side
online. As you scan through search results, look for the following clues about the probable relevance, currency, and reliability of a site—but be aware that the clues are by no means
foolproof.

The title, keywords, and lead-in text (How relevant?)

A date (How current?)

An indication of the site's sponsor or purpose (How reliable?)

The URL, especially the domain name extension: for example, .com, .edu, .gov, or .org (How relevant? How reliable?)

At the bottom of this page are a few of the results that Luisa Mirano retrieved after typing the keywords *childhood obesity* into a search engine; she limited her search to works with those words in the title.

Mirano found the first site, sponsored by a research-based organization, promising enough to explore for her paper. The second and fourth sites held less promise because they seemed to offer popular rather than scholarly information. In addition, the *KidSource* site was populated by distracting commercial advertisements. Mirano rejected the third source not because she doubted its reliability—in fact, research from the National Institutes of Health was what she hoped to find—but because a quick skim of its contents revealed that the information was too general for her purposes.

EVALUATING SEARCH RESULTS: INTERNET SEARCH ENGINE

Content from a research-based organization. Promising.

American **Obesity** Association - **Childhood Obesity**
Childhood Obesity. **Obesity** in **children** ... Note: The term "**childhood obesity**" may refer to both **children** and adolescents. In general, we ...
www.**obesity**.org/subs/**childhood**/ - 17k - Jan 8, 2005 - Cached - Similar pages

Popular rather than scholarly source. Not relevant.

Childhood Obesity
KS Logo, **Childhood Obesity**. advertisement. Source. ERIC Clearinghouse on Teaching and Teacher Education. Contents. ... Back to the Top Causes of **Childhood Obesity**. ...
www.kidsource.com/kidsource/content2/**obesity**.html - 18k - Cached - Similar pages

Content too general. Not relevant.

Childhood Obesity, June 2002 Word on Health - National Institutes ...
Childhood Obesity on the Rise, an article in the June 2002 edition of The NIH Word on Health - Consumer Information Based on Research from the National ...
www.nih.gov/news/WordonHealth/ jun2002/**childhoodobesity**.htm - 22k -
Cached - Similar pages

Popular and too general. Not relevant.

MayoClinic.com - **Childhood obesity**: Parenting advice
... **Childhood obesity**: Parenting advice By Mayo Clinic staff. ... Here are some other tips to help your **obese child** — and yourself: Be a positive role model. ...
www.mayoclinic.com/invoke.cfm?id=FL00058 - 42k - Jan 8, 2005 - Cached - Similar pages

Previewing sources

Once you have decided that a source looks promising, preview it quickly to see whether it lives up to its promise. If you can reject irrelevant or unreliable sources before actually reading them, you will save yourself time. Techniques for previewing an article from your library's subscription database or a book are relatively simple; strategies for investigating the likely worth of a Web site are more complicated.

Previewing an article The techniques for previewing an article are fairly straightforward. In researching her paper on childhood obesity, Luisa Mirano spent no more than a few minutes scanning an article before deciding whether it was worth her time.

Here are a few strategies for previewing an article:

- Consider the publication in which the article is printed. Is it a scholarly journal (see the chart on p. 468)? A popular magazine? A newspaper with a national reputation?

- For a magazine or journal article, look for an abstract or a statement of purpose at the beginning; also look for a summary at the end.

- For a newspaper article, focus on the headline and the opening paragraphs, known as the *lead*.

- Skim any headings and look at any visuals—charts, graphs, diagrams, or illustrations—that might indicate the article's focus and scope.

Previewing a book As you preview a book, keep in mind that even if the entire book is not worth your time, parts of it may prove useful. For example, by using the indexes of several books on Civil War history, Ned Bishop quickly located useful passages describing the Fort Pillow massacre.

Try any or all of the following techniques to preview a book:

- Glance through the table of contents, keeping your research question in mind.

- Skim the preface in search of a statement of the author's purposes.
- Use the index to look up a few words related to your topic.
- If a chapter looks useful, read its opening and closing paragraphs and skim any headings.
- Consider the author's style and approach. Does the style suggest enough intellectual depth, or is the book too specialized for your purposes? Does the author present ideas in an unbiased way?

Previewing a Web site   It is a fairly quick and easy job to track down numerous potentially useful sources on the Web, but evaluating those sources can require some detective work.

Determining if a source is scholarly

For many college assignments, you will be asked to use scholarly sources. These are written by experts for a knowledgeable audience and usually go into more depth than books and articles written for a general audience. (Scholarly sources are sometimes called *refereed* or *peer-reviewed* because the work is evaluated by experts in the field before publication.) To determine if a source is scholarly, you should look for the following:

- Formal language and presentation
- Authors who are academics or scientists
- Footnotes or a bibliography documenting the works cited by the author in the source
- Original research and interpretation (rather than a summary of other people's work)
- Quotations from and analysis of primary sources (in humanities disciplines such as literature, history, and philosophy)
- A description of research methods or a review of related research (in the sciences and social sciences)

NOTE: In some databases, searches can be limited to refereed or peer-reviewed journals.

Web sites can be created by anyone, and their authors and purposes are not always apparent. In addition, there are no required standards for the design of Web sites, so you may need to do a fair amount of clicking and scrolling before you locate clues about a site's reliability. In researching her paper on Internet surveillance in the workplace, Anna Orlov spent considerable time previewing Web sites, many of which she rejected (see pp. 476–77).

As you preview a Web site, check for relevance, reliability, and currency:

- Browse the home page. Do its contents and links seem relevant to your research question?

- Ask yourself what the site is trying to do: Sell a product? Promote an idea? Inform the public? Is the site's purpose consistent with your research?

- Look for the name of an author or a Webmaster and, if possible, review his or her credentials. Often a site's author is named at the bottom of the home page. If you have landed on an internal page of a site and no author is evident, try navigating to the home page, either through a link or by truncating the URL (see the tip on p. 474).

- Check for a sponsor name, and consider possible motives the organization might have for sponsoring the site. Is the group likely to look at only one side of an issue?

- Find out when the site was created or last updated. Is it current enough for your purposes?

TIP: When conducting academic research, do not rely on sites that give very little information about authors or sponsors.

Distinguishing between primary and secondary sources

As you begin assessing evidence in a source, determine whether you are reading a primary or a secondary source. Primary sources are original documents such as letters, diaries, legislative bills, laboratory studies, field research reports, and eyewitness accounts.

Secondary sources are commentaries on primary sources—another writer's opinions about or interpretation of a primary source. A primary source for Ned Bishop was Nathan Bedford Forrest's official report on the battle at Fort Pillow. Bishop also consulted a number of secondary sources, some of which relied heavily on primary sources such as letters.

Although a primary source is not necessarily more reliable than a secondary source, it has the advantage of being a first-hand account. Naturally, you can better evaluate what a secondary source says if you have first read any primary sources it discusses.

47c Select appropriate versions of online sources.

An online source may appear as an abstract, an excerpt, or a full-text article or book. It is important to distinguish among these versions of sources and to use a complete version of a source, preferably one with page numbers, for your research.

Abstracts and excerpts are shortened versions of complete works. An abstract—a summary of a work's contents—might appear in a database record for a periodical article (see p. 471) and can give you clues about the usefulness of an article for your paper. Abstracts are brief (usually fewer than five hundred words) and usually do not contain enough information to function alone as sources in a research paper. Reading the complete article is the best way to understand the author's argument before referring to it in your own writing. When you determine that the full article is worth reading, scroll through the record to find a link to the complete text in your library's databases. If you cannot access the complete article from a database, see if the library has a print copy on the shelves. Ask a librarian for assistance if you are unsure whether your library keeps the periodical.

An excerpt is the first few sentences or paragraphs of a newspaper or magazine article and sometimes appears in a list of hits in an online search (see p. 472). From an excerpt, you can often determine whether the complete article would be useful for your paper. Sometimes, however, the thesis or topic sentence of the article is buried deeper in the article than the excerpt reveals. In these cases, the headline might be a clue to the relevance of the complete article. Be sure to retrieve and read the full text of any article you might want to cite. If you are working with an Internet search engine such as *Google*, you may find that your results lead to articles available only for a fee. Before paying a fee, see if you can get the article through your library system.

A full-text work may appear online as a PDF (portable document format) file or as an HTML file (sometimes called a *text file*). A PDF file is usually an exact copy of the pages of a periodical article as they appeared in print, including the page numbers. Some corporate and government reports are presented online as PDF files, and they are usually paginated. A full-text document that appears as an HTML or a text file is not paginated. If your source is available in both formats, choose the PDF file for your research because you will be able to cite specific page numbers.

DATABASE RECORD WITH AN ABSTRACT

LINCC, Library Information Network for Community Colleges
Expanded Academic ASAP

—— Article 1 of 2 —— ▶

☐
Mark
Civil War History, June 1996 v42 n2 p116(17)

"These devils are not fit to live on God's earth": war crimes and the Committee on the Conduct of the War, 1864-1865. *Bruce Tap*.

Abstract: The Committee on the Conduct of the War's report on the April 1864 Fort Pillow massacre of black Union soldiers by Confederate forces influenced public opinion against the atrocities of the Confederate troops and accelerated the reconstruction program. Hostility against blacks and abolition in the South prompted the Confederates to target black troops and deny them prisoner of war status. Investigation exposed the barbaric act and the Northern prisoners' suffering in Southern prisons. The report helped the inclusion of black troops in the prisoner exchange program.

Article A18749078

SEARCH RESULT WITH AN EXCERPT

▾ BOSTON GLOBE ARCHIVES

Your search for ((fort AND pillow AND massacre)) returned **1** article(s) matching your terms.
To purchase the full-text of an article, follow the link that says "Click for complete article."

| Perform a new search |

Your search results:

TALES OF BLACKS IN THE CIVIL WAR, FOR ALL AGES
Published on March 23, 1998
Author(s):   Scott Alarik, Globe Correspondent

For African Americans, the Civil War was always two wars. It was, of course, the war to save the
union and destroy slavery, but for the nearly 180,000 black soldiers who served in the Union
Army, it was also a war to establish their rights as citizens and human beings in the United
States. Their role in defeating the Confederacy is grandly chronicled in two new books, the
massively complete "Like Men of War" and the superbly readable children's book "Black, Blue"
and
Click for complete article *(782 words)*

47d Read with an open mind and a critical eye.

As you begin reading the sources you have chosen, keep an
open mind. Do not let your personal beliefs prevent you from
listening to new ideas and opposing viewpoints. Your research
question—not a snap judgment about the question—should
guide your reading.

When you read critically, you are not necessarily judging
an author's work harshly; you are simply examining its assumptions, assessing its evidence, and weighing its conclusions. (To
see one student's careful reading of a source text, see p. 577.)

> **Academic English**   When you research on the Web, it is easy to ignore
> views different from your own. Web pages that appeal to you will often
> link to other pages that support the same viewpoint. If your sources all
> seem to agree with you—and with one another—try to find sources
> with opposing views and evaluate them with an open mind.

Being alert for signs of bias

Both in print and online, some sources are more objective
than others. If you were exploring the conspiracy theories surrounding John F. Kennedy's assassination, for example, you

wouldn't look to a supermarket tabloid for answers. Even publications that are considered reputable can be editorially biased. For example, *USA Today*, *National Review*, and *Ms.* are all credible sources that are likely to interpret events quite differently from one another. If you are uncertain about a periodical's special interests, consult *Magazines for Libraries*. To check for bias in a book, see what book reviewers have written about it. A reference librarian can help you locate reviews and assess the credibility of both the book and the reviewers.

Like publishers, some authors are more objective than others. If you have reason to believe that a writer is particularly

---

Evaluating all sources

Checking for signs of bias

- Does the author or publisher endorse political or religious views that could affect objectivity?

- Is the author or publisher associated with a special-interest group, such as Greenpeace or the National Rifle Association, that might present only one side of an issue?

- Are alternative views presented and addressed? How fairly does the author treat opposing views? (See 6c.)

- Does the author's language show signs of bias? (See 6b.)

Assessing an argument

- What is the author's central claim or thesis?

- How does the author support this claim—with relevant and sufficient evidence or with just a few anecdotes or emotional examples?

- Are statistics consistent with those you encounter in other sources? Have they been used fairly? Does the author explain where the statistics come from? (It is possible to "lie" with statistics by using them selectively or by omitting mathematical details.)

- Are any of the author's assumptions questionable?

- Does the author consider opposing arguments and refute them persuasively? (See 6c.)

- Does the author fall prey to any logical fallacies? (See 6a.)

biased, you will want to assess his or her arguments with special care. For a list of questions worth asking, see the chart on page 473.

Assessing the author's argument

In nearly all subjects worth writing about, there is some element of argument, so don't be surprised to encounter experts who disagree. When you find areas of disagreement, you will want to read each source's arguments with special care, testing them with your own critical intelligence. The questions in the chart on page 473 can help you weigh the strengths and weaknesses of each author's arguments.

Making the most of your handbook

Good college writers read critically.

▶ Judging whether a source is reasonable: 6a

▶ Judging whether a source is fair: 6c

47e Assess Web sources with special care.

Web sources can provide valuable information, but verifying their credibility may take time. Before using a Web source in your paper, make sure you know who created the material and for what purpose.

TIP: If both the sponsorship and the authorship of a site are unclear, think twice about using the site for your research. To discover a site's sponsor, you may have to shorten the full URL to its domain name.

> **FULL URL:** http://www.bankofamerica.com/environment/dex .cfm?template=env_reports_speeches&context=smartgrowth
>
> **DOMAIN NAME:** http://www.bankofamerica.com
>
> **SPONSOR:** Bank of America

Many sophisticated-looking sites contain questionable information. Even a well-designed hate site may at first appear unbiased and informative. Sites with reliable information, however, can stand up to careful scrutiny. For a checklist on evaluating Web sources, see the chart on page 475.

Evaluating Web sources

Authorship

- Does the Web site or document have an author? You may
  need to do some clicking and scrolling to find the author's
  name. If you have landed directly on an internal page of a
  site, for example, you may need to navigate to the home
  page or find an "about this site" link to learn the name of the
  author.

- If there is an author, can you tell whether he or she is
  knowledgeable and credible? When the author's qualifications
  aren't listed on the site itself, look for links to the author's home
  page, which may provide evidence of his or her interests and
  expertise.

Sponsorship

- Who, if anyone, sponsors the site? The sponsor of a site is often
  named and described on the home page.

- What does the URL tell you? The domain name extension
  often indicates the type of group hosting the site: commercial
  (.com), educational (.edu), nonprofit (.org), governmental
  (.gov), military (.mil), or network (.net). URLs may also indicate
  a country of origin: .uk (United Kingdom) or .jp (Japan), for
  instance.

Purpose and audience

- Why was the site created: To argue a position? To sell a product?
  To inform readers?

- Who is the site's intended audience?

Currency

- How current is the site? Check for the date of publication or the
  latest update, often located at the bottom of the home page or
  at the beginning or end of an internal page.

- How current are the site's links? If many of the links no longer
  work, the site may be too dated for your purposes.

Ned Bishop came across unreliable Web sources while researching his topic, the Fort Pillow massacre. This topic is of great interest to Civil War buffs, who might not have scholarly backgrounds. One impressive-looking site turned out to have been created by a high school junior—an intelligent young man, no doubt, but by no means an authority on the subject.

In researching Internet surveillance and workplace privacy, Anna Orlov encountered sites that raised her suspicions.

EVALUATING A WEB SITE: CHECKING RELIABILITY

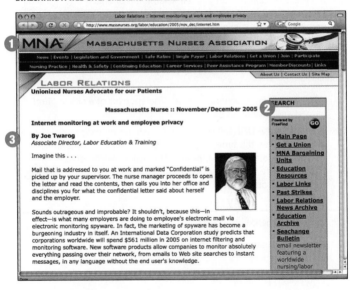

1 This article on Internet monitoring is on a site sponsored by the Massachusetts Nurses Association, a professional health care association and union whose staff and members advocate for nurses in the workplace. The URL ending .org marks this sponsor as a nonprofit organization.

2 Clear dates of publication show currency.

3 The author is a credible expert whose credentials can be verified.

In particular, some sites were authored by surveillance software companies, which have an obvious interest in focusing on the benefits of such software to company management.

Knowing that the creator of a site is an amateur or could be biased is not sufficient reason, however, to reject the site's information out of hand. For example, the surveillance software companies' Web sites provided some insight into why company management would want to monitor employees, and the high

EVALUATING A WEB SITE: CHECKING PURPOSE

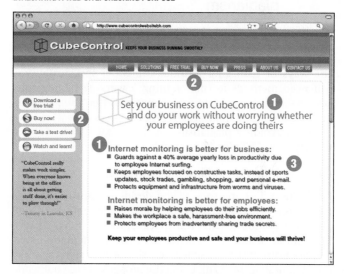

1   The site is sponsored by a company that specializes in employee monitoring software.

2   Repeated links for trial downloads and purchase suggest the site's intended audience: consumers seeking to purchase software (probably not researchers seeking detailed information about employees' use of the Internet in the workplace).

3   The site appears to provide information and even shows statistics from studies, but ultimately the purpose of the site is to sell a product.

school junior had intelligent things to say about the Fort Pillow massacre. Nevertheless, when you know something about the creator of a site and have a sense of a site's purpose, you will be in a good position to evaluate the likely worth of its information. Consider, for example, the two sites pictured on pages 476 and 477. Anna Orlov decided that the first Web site would be more useful for her project than sites like the second.

48 Managing information; avoiding plagiarism

An effective researcher is a good record keeper. Whether you decide to keep records on paper or on your computer—or both—your challenge as a researcher will be to find systematic ways of managing information. More specifically, you will need methods for maintaining a working bibliography (see 48a), keeping track of source materials (see 48b), and taking notes without plagiarizing your sources (see 48c). (For more on avoiding plagiarism, see 51 for MLA style, 56b for APA style, and 57b for *Chicago* style.)

48a Maintain a working bibliography.

Keep a record of any sources you decide to consult. You will need this record, called a *working bibliography*, when you compile the list of sources that will appear at the end of your paper. The format of this list depends on the documentation style you are using (for MLA style, see 53b; for APA style, see 56d; for *Chicago* style, see 57d). Using the proper style in your working bibliography will ensure that you have all the information you need to correctly cite any sources you use. Your working bibliography will probably contain more sources than you will actually include in the list of works cited in your final paper.

Most researchers save bibliographic information from the library's computer catalog, its periodical databases, and the Web. The information you need to collect is given in the chart on pages 480–81. If you download a visual, you must gather the same information as for a print source.

For Web sources, some bibliographic information may not be available, but spend time looking for it before assuming that it doesn't exist. When information isn't available on the home page, you may have to drill into the site, following links to interior pages. Look especially for the author's name, the date of publication (or latest update), and the name of any sponsoring organization. Do not omit such information unless it is genuinely unavailable.

Once you have created a working bibliography, you can annotate it. Writing several brief sentences summarizing key points of a source will help you identify how it relates to your argument and to your other sources. Clarifying the source's ideas at this stage will help you separate them from your own and avoid plagiarizing them later. Though annotated bibliographies can be informal writing in preparation for an essay, some instructors may require that you submit an annotated bibliography as a formal writing assignment.

SAMPLE ANNOTATED BIBLIOGRAPHY ENTRY (MLA STYLE)

Gonsalves, Chris. "Wasting Away on the Web." *eWeek.com*. Ziff Davis
Enterprise Holdings, 8 Aug. 2005. Web. 16 Feb. 2009.

Summarize the source.

In this editorial, Gonsalves considers the implications of several surveys, including one in which 61% of respondents said that their companies have the right to spy on them. The author agrees with this majority, claiming that it's fine if his company chooses to monitor him as long as the company discloses its monitoring practices. He adds that he would prefer not to know the extent of the monitoring.

Annotations should be three to seven sentences long.

Interpret the relationship between this source and others in the bibliography.

This article, though not entirely objective, offers an employee's perspective on Internet surveillance in the workplace. It also contradicts some of my other sources, which claim that employees want to know and should know all the details of their company's monitoring procedures.

Evaluate the source for bias and relevance.

hackerhandbooks.com/bedhandbook > **Model papers**
> MLA annotated bibliography: Orlov
> APA annotated bibliography: Haddad

48b Keep track of source materials.

The best way to keep track of source materials is to save a copy of each one. Many database subscription services will allow you to e-mail, save, or print citations or full texts of articles, and you can easily download, copy, or take screen shots of information from the Web.

Working with photocopies, printouts, and electronic files—as opposed to relying on memory or hastily written notes—has several benefits. You save time spent in the library. You can highlight key passages, perhaps even color-coding them to reflect topics in your outline. You can annotate the source in the margins by hand or with your word processing program's comment fields and get a head start on note taking (for an example, see the annotated article on p. 577). Finally, you reduce the chances of unintentional plagiarism, since you will be able to compare your use of a source in your paper with the actual source, not just with your notes (see 48c).

NOTE: It's especially important to keep print or electronic copies of Web sources, which may change or even become

---

Information for a working bibliography

For an entire book

- All authors; any editors or translators
- Title and subtitle
- Edition (if not the first)
- Publication information: city, publisher, and date

For a periodical article

- All authors of the article
- Title and subtitle of the article
- Title of the magazine, journal, or newspaper
- Date; volume, issue, and page numbers

→

**For a periodical article retrieved from a database
(in addition to preceding information)**

- Name of the database
- Name of the subscription service
- URL of the subscription service (for an online database)
- Accession number or other number assigned by the database
- Digital object identifier (DOI), if there is one
- Date you retrieved the source

NOTE: Use particular care when printing or saving articles in PDF files. The files themselves may not include some of the elements you need to cite the electronic source properly. You may need to record additional information from the database or Web site where you retrieved the PDF file.

For a Web source (including visuals)

- All authors, editors, or creators of the source
- Editor or compiler of the Web site, if there is one
- Title and subtitle of the source
- Title of the longer work, if applicable
- Title of the site
- Publication information for the source, if available
- Page or paragraph numbers, if any
- Date of online publication (or latest update)
- Sponsor of the site
- Date you accessed the source
- The site's URL

NOTE: For the exact bibliographic format to use in your working bibliography and in the final paper, see 53b (MLA), 56d (APA), or 57d (*Chicago*).

inaccessible over time. Make sure that your copy includes the site's URL and your date of access.

TIP: Your school may provide citation software, which allows researchers to download references directly from databases, import saved searches, or type in citations. Similarly, many databases format citations with a mouse click, and Web sites offer fill-in-the-blank forms for generating formatted citations. You must proofread these results carefully, however, because the programs sometimes provide incorrect results.

48c As you take notes, avoid unintentional plagiarism.

When you take notes and jot down ideas, be very careful not to borrow language from your sources. Even if you half-copy the author's sentences—either by mixing the author's phrases with your own without using quotation marks or by plugging your synonyms into the author's sentence structure—you are committing plagiarism, a serious academic offense. (For examples of this kind of plagiarism, see 51b, 56b, and 57b.)

To prevent unintentional borrowing, resist the temptation to look at the source as you take notes—except when you are quoting. Keep the source close by so you can check for accuracy, but don't try to put ideas in your own words with the source's sentences in front of you. When you need to quote the exact words of a source, make sure you copy the words precisely and put quotation marks around them.

For strategies for avoiding Internet plagiarism, see pages 485–87.

TIP: Be especially careful when using copy and paste functions in electronic files. Some researchers have unwittingly plagiarized their sources because they lost track of which words came from sources and which were their own. To prevent unintentional plagiarism, put quotation marks around any text that you plan to insert into your own work.

> **Academic English**   Even in the early stages of note taking, it is important to keep in mind that in the United States written texts are considered an author's property. (This "property" isn't a physical object, so it is often referred to as *intellectual property*.) The author (or publisher) owns the language as well as any original ideas contained in the writing, whether the source is published in print or electronic form. When you use another author's property in your own writing, you are required to follow certain conventions for citing the material, or you risk committing *plagiarism*.

There are three kinds of note taking: summarizing, paraphrasing, and quoting. Be sure to include exact page references for all three types of notes; you will need the page numbers later if you use the information in your paper.

Summarizing without plagiarizing

A summary condenses information, perhaps reducing a chapter to a short paragraph or a paragraph to a single sentence. A summary should be written in your own words; if you use phrases from the source, put them in quotation marks.

Here is a passage from a source about mountain lions. Following the passage is the student's summary. (The bibliographic information is recorded in MLA style.)

ORIGINAL SOURCE

In some respects, the increasing frequency of mountain lion encounters in California has as much to do with a growing *human* population as it does with rising mountain lion numbers. The scenic solitude of the western ranges is prime cougar habitat, and it is falling swiftly to the developer's spade. Meanwhile, with their ideal habitat already at its carrying capacity, mountain lions are forcing younger cats into less suitable terrain, including residential areas. Add that cougars have generally grown bolder under a lengthy ban on their being hunted, and an unsettling scenario begins to emerge.

    —Rychnovsky, Ray. "Clawing into Controversy." *Outdoor Life* Jan. 1995: 38-42. Print. [p. 40]

SUMMARY

Source: Rychnovsky, Ray. "Clawing into Controversy." *Outdoor Life* Jan.
1995: 38-42. Print. [p. 40]

Encounters between mountain lions and humans are on the rise in
California because increasing numbers of lions are competing for a
shrinking habitat. As the lions' wild habitat shrinks, older lions force
younger lions into residential areas. These lions have lost some of their
fear of humans because of a ban on hunting.

See page 579 for additional sample summaries in MLA style.

Paraphrasing without plagiarizing

Like a summary, a paraphrase is written in your own words;
but whereas a summary reports significant information in
fewer words than the source, a paraphrase retells the information in roughly the same number of words. If you retain occasional choice phrases from the source, use quotation marks so
that later you will know which phrases are not your own.

As you read the following paraphrase of the original
source (see p. 483), notice that the language is significantly
different from that in the original.

PARAPHRASE

Source: Rychnovsky, Ray. "Clawing into Controversy." *Outdoor Life* Jan.
1995: 38-42. Print. [p. 40]

Californians are encountering mountain lions more frequently because
increasing numbers of humans and a rising population of lions are
competing for the same territory. Humans have moved into
mountainous regions once dominated by the lions, and the wild
habitat that is left cannot sustain the current lion population.
Therefore, the older lions are forcing younger lions into residential
areas. And because of a ban on hunting, these younger lions have
become bolder—less fearful of encounters with humans.

See page 580 for an additional sample paraphrase in MLA style.

Using quotation marks to avoid plagiarizing

A quotation consists of the exact words from a source. In your notes, put all quoted material in quotation marks; do not assume that you will remember later which words, phrases, and passages you have quoted and which are your own. When you quote, be sure to copy the words of your source exactly, including punctuation and capitalization.

QUOTATION

Source: Rychnovsky, Ray. "Clawing into Controversy." *Outdoor Life* Jan.
  1995: 38-42. Print. [p. 40]

Rychnovsky explains that as humans expand residential areas into
mountain ranges, the cougar's natural habitat "is falling swiftly to the
developer's spade" (40).

See page 581 for an additional sample quotation in MLA style.

Avoiding Internet plagiarism

Understand what plagiarism is. When you use another author's intellectual property—language, visuals, or ideas—in your own writing without giving proper credit, you commit a kind of academic theft called *plagiarism.*

Treat Web sources the same way you treat print sources. Any language that you find on the Internet must be carefully cited, even if the material is in the public domain or is publicly accessible on free sites. When you use material from Web sites sponsored by federal, state, or municipal governments (.gov sites) or by nonprofit organizations (.org sites), you must acknowledge that material, too, as intellectual property owned by those agencies.

Keep track of which words come from sources and which are your own. To prevent unintentional plagiarism when you copy and paste passages from Web sources to an electronic

Integrating and citing sources to avoid plagiarism

Source text

Our language is constantly changing. Like the Mississippi, it keeps forging new channels and abandoning old ones, picking up debris, depositing unwanted silt, and frequently bursting its banks. In every generation, there are people who deplore changes in the language and many who wish to stop the flow. But if our language stopped changing it would mean that American society had ceased to be dynamic, innovative, pulsing with life—that the river had frozen up.

—Robert MacNeil and William Cran,
Do You Speak American? p. 1

Avoiding plagiarism

If you are using an exact sentence from a source, with no changes at all . . .	→	. . . put quotation marks around the sentence. Use a signal phrase and include a page number in parentheses.

MacNeil and Cran write, "Our language is constantly changing" (1).

"Our language," according to MacNeil and Cran, "is constantly changing" (1).

If you are using a few exact words from the source but not an entire sentence . . .	→	. . . put quotation marks around the exact words that you have used from the source. Use a signal phrase and include a page number in parentheses.

The English language, according to MacNeil and Cran, is "like the Mississippi" (1).

If you are using near-exact words from the source but changing some word forms (*I* to *she*, *walk* to *walked*) or adding words to	→	. . . put quotation marks around the quoted words and put brackets around the changes you have introduced. Use a signal phrase and include a page number in parentheses.

MacNeil and Cran compare the English language to the Mississippi River, which "forg[es] new channels and abandon[s] old ones" (1).

→

clarify and make the quotation flow with your own text . . .

"In every generation, there are people who deplore changes in the [English] language and many who wish to stop the flow," write MacNeil and Cran (1).

If you are paraphrasing or summarizing the source, using the author's ideas but not any of the author's exact words . . .

→ . . . introduce the ideas with a signal phrase and put the page number at the end of your sentence. Do not use quotation marks. (See 51, 56b, and 57b.)

MacNeil and Cran argue that changes in the English language are natural and that they represent cultural progress (1).

If you have used the source's sentence structure but substituted a few synonyms for the author's words . . .

→ STOP! This is a form of plagiarism even if you use a signal phrase and a page number. Change your sentence by using one of the techniques given in this chart or in 52, 56c, or 57c.

PLAGIARIZED

MacNeil and Cran claim that, like a river, English creates new waterways and discards old ones.

INTEGRATED AND CITED CORRECTLY

MacNeil and Cran claim, "Like the Mississippi, [English] keeps forging new channels and abandoning old ones" (1).

NOTE: The examples in this chart follow MLA style (see 53). For information on APA and *Chicago* styles, see 56d and 57d, respectively.

file, put quotation marks around any text that you have inserted into your own work. In addition, during note taking and drafting, you might use a different color font or your word processing program's highlighting feature to draw attention to text taken from sources—so that material from articles, Web sites, and other sources stands out unmistakably as someone else's words.

Avoid Web sites that bill themselves as "research services" and sell essays. When you use Web search engines to research a topic, you will often see links to sites that appear to offer legitimate writing support but that actually sell college essays. Of course, submitting a paper that you have purchased is cheating, but even using material from such a paper is considered plagiarism.

For details on avoiding plagiarism while working with sources, see 51 (MLA style), 56b (APA style), and 57b (*Chicago* style).

49 Choosing a documentation style

The various academic disciplines use their own style for citing sources and for listing the works that are cited in a paper. *The Bedford Handbook* describes three commonly used styles:

> Modern Language Association (MLA) in section 53
>
> American Psychological Association (APA) in section 56d
>
> *Chicago Manual of Style* (CMS) in section 57d

In researched writing, sources are cited for several reasons. First, it is important to acknowledge the contributions of others. If you fail to credit sources properly, you commit plagiarism, a serious academic offense. Second, choosing appropriate sources will add credibility to your work; in a sense, you are calling on authorities to serve as expert witnesses. The more care you have taken in choosing reliable sources, the stronger your argument will be. Finally—and most importantly—you are engaging in a scholarly conversation and showing readers where they can pursue your topic in greater depth.

All of the academic disciplines cite sources for these same reasons. However, the different styles for citing sources are based on the values and intellectual goals of scholars in different disciplines.

MLA and APA in-text citations

MLA style and APA style both use citations in the text of a paper that refer to a list of works at the end of the paper. The systems work somewhat differently, however, because MLA style was created for scholars in English composition and literature and APA style was created for researchers in the social sciences.

MLA IN-TEXT CITATION

Brandon Conran argues that the story is written from "a bifocal point of view" (111).

APA IN-TEXT CITATION

As researchers Yanovski and Yanovski (2002) have explained, obesity was once considered "either a moral failing or evidence of underlying psychopathology" (p. 592).

While MLA and APA styles work in a similar way, some basic disciplinary differences show up in these key elements:

author's name

date of publication

page numbers

verb tense in signal phrases

MLA style gives the author's full name on first mention, emphasizing authorship and interpretation. APA style, which uses last names only, gives a date after the author's name, reflecting the social scientist's concern with the currency of study findings. MLA style places the date in the works cited list but omits it in the text. While currency is important, what someone had to say a century ago may be as significant as the latest contribution to the field.

Both styles include page numbers for quotations. MLA style requires page numbers for summaries and paraphrases as well; with a page number, readers can easily find the original passage that has been summarized or paraphrased. While APA does not require page numbers for summaries and paraphrases, it recommends that writers use a page number if doing so would help readers find the passage in a longer work.

Finally, MLA style uses the present tense (such as *argues*) to introduce cited material (see 52b), whereas APA style uses the past or present perfect tense (such as *argued* or *has argued*) in signal phrases (see 56c). The present tense evokes the timelessness of a literary text; the past or present perfect tense emphasizes that research or experimentation occurred in the past.

Chicago-*style footnotes or endnotes*

Most historians and many scholars in the humanities use the style of footnotes or endnotes recommended by *The Chicago Manual of Style* (CMS). Historians base their work on a wide variety of primary and secondary sources, all of which must be cited. The *Chicago* note system has the virtue of being relatively unobtrusive; even when a paper or an article is thick with citations, readers will not be overwhelmed. In the text of the paper, only a raised number appears. Readers who are interested can consult the accompanying numbered note, which is given either at the foot of the page or at the end of the paper.

TEXT

Historian Albert Castel quotes several eyewitnesses on both the Union and the Confederate sides as saying that Forrest ordered his men to stop firing.[7]

NOTE

     7. Albert Castel, "The Fort Pillow Massacre: A Fresh Examination of the Evidence," *Civil War History* 4, no. 1 (1958): 44-45.

The *Chicago* system gives as much information as the MLA or APA system, but less of that information appears in the text of the paper.

hackerhandbooks.com/bedhandbook > Additional resources > List of style manuals

Writing MLA papers

Brief directory

Most English instructors and some humanities instructors will ask you to document your sources with the Modern Language Association (MLA) system of citations described in section 53.

    When writing an MLA paper that is based on sources, you face three main challenges: (1) supporting a thesis, (2) citing your sources and avoiding plagiarism, and (3) integrating quotations and other source material.

    Examples in sections 50–52 are drawn from a student's research related to online monitoring of employees' computer use. Anna Orlov's research paper, which argues that electronic surveillance in the workplace threatens employees' privacy, appears on pages 583–88. (See highlights of Anna Orlov's research process on pp. 573–82.)

If you are writing an MLA paper about literature (a short story, novel, play, film, or poem), see section 55.

NOTE: For advice on finding and evaluating sources and on managing information in all your college courses, see sections 46–49.

50   Supporting a thesis

Most research assignments ask you to form a thesis, or main idea, and to support that thesis with well-organized evidence. (See also 1c.) Remain flexible as you draft because you may need to revise your approach later. Writing about a subject is a way of learning about it; as you write, your understanding of your subject will almost certainly deepen.

50a Form a working thesis.

Once you have read a variety of sources and considered your issue from different perspectives, you are ready to form a working thesis: a one-sentence (or occasionally a two-sentence) statement of your central idea. (See also 1e and 50d.) Because it is a working, or tentative, thesis, it is flexible enough to change as your ideas develop. Ultimately, the thesis expresses not just your opinion but your informed, reasoned judgment.

In a research paper, your thesis will answer the central research question that you posed earlier (see 46a). Here, for example, are Anna Orlov's research question and working thesis.

RESEARCH QUESTION

Should employers monitor their employees' online activities in the workplace?

WORKING THESIS

Employers should not monitor their employees' online activities because electronic surveillance can compromise workers' privacy.

After you have written a rough draft and perhaps done more reading, you may decide to revise your thesis, as Orlov did.

REVISED THESIS

Although companies often have legitimate concerns that lead them to monitor employees' Internet usage—from expensive security breaches to reduced productivity—the benefits of electronic surveillance are outweighed by its costs to employees' privacy and autonomy.

The thesis usually appears at the end of the introductory paragraph. To read Anna Orlov's thesis in the context of her introduction, see page 583.

50b Organize ideas with a rough outline.

The body of your paper will consist of evidence in support of your thesis. Instead of getting tangled up in a complex, formal outline, sketch an informal plan that organizes your ideas in bold strokes. Anna Orlov, for example, used this simple plan to outline the structure of her argument:

- Compared with older types of surveillance, electronic surveillance allows employers to monitor workers more efficiently.
- Some experts argue that companies have important financial and legal reasons to monitor employees' Internet usage.
- But monitoring employees' Internet usage may lower worker productivity when the threat to privacy creates distrust.

Making the most of your handbook

It's helpful to start off with a working thesis and a rough outline—especially when writing from sources.

▶ Draft a working thesis: 1c

▶ Sketch a plan: 1d

- Current laws do little to protect employees' privacy rights, so
  employees and employers have to negotiate the potential risks and
  benefits of electronic surveillance.

After you have written a rough draft, a more formal outline can
be a useful way to shape the complexities of your argument.

hackerhandbooks.com/bedhandbook > Research exercises > MLA
> E-ex 50–1 and 50–2

50c Use sources to inform and support your argument.

Used thoughtfully, the source materials you have gathered
will make your argument more complex and convincing for
readers. Sources can play several different roles as you develop
your points.

Providing background information or context

You can use facts and statistics to support generalizations or to
establish the importance of your topic, as student writer Anna
Orlov does in her introduction.

> As the Internet has become an integral tool of businesses,
> company policies on Internet usage have become as common as
> policies regarding vacation days or sexual harassment. A 2005 study by
> the American Management Association and ePolicy Institute found that
> 76% of companies monitor employees' use of the Web, and the number
> of companies that block employees' access to certain Web sites has
> increased 27% since 2001 (1).

Explaining terms or concepts

If readers are unlikely to be familiar with a word or an idea
important to your topic, you must explain it for them. Quoting or paraphrasing a source can help you define terms and
concepts in accessible language.

One popular monitoring method is keystroke logging, which is done by
means of an undetectable program on employees' computers. . . . As
Lane explains, these programs record every key entered into the
computer in hidden directories that can later be accessed or uploaded
by supervisors; the programs can even scan for keywords tailored to
individual companies (128-29).

Supporting your claims

As you draft your argument, make sure to back up your assertions with facts, examples, and other evidence from your
research. (See also 5e.) Orlov, for example, uses an anecdote
from one of her sources to support her claim that limiting
computer access causes resentment among a company's staff.

Monitoring online activities can have the unintended effect
of making employees resentful. . . . Kesan warns that "prohibiting
personal use can seem extremely arbitrary and can seriously harm
morale. . . . Imagine a concerned parent who is prohibited from
checking on a sick child by a draconian company policy" (315-16).
As this analysis indicates, employees can become disgruntled when
Internet usage policies are enforced to their full extent.

Lending authority to your argument

Expert opinion can give weight to your argument. (See also
5e.) But don't rely on experts to make your arguments for
you. Construct your argument in your own words and, when
appropriate, cite the judgment of an authority in the field to
support your position.

Additionally, many experts disagree with employers' assumption
that online monitoring can increase productivity. Employment law
attorney Joseph Schmitt argues that, particularly for employees who
are paid a salary rather than an hourly wage, "a company shouldn't care
whether employees spend one or 10 hours on the Internet as long as
they are getting their jobs done—and provided that they are not
accessing inappropriate sites" (qtd. in Verespej).

Anticipating and countering objections

Do not ignore sources that seem contrary to your position or that offer arguments different from your own. Instead, use them to give voice to opposing points of view and to state potential objections to your argument before you counter them (see 5f). Readers often have opposing points of view in mind already, whether or not they agree with you. Anna Orlov, for example, cites conflicting evidence to acknowledge that some readers may feel that unlimited Internet access in the workplace hinders productivity. In doing so, she creates an opportunity to counter that objection and persuade those readers.

> **Making the most of your handbook**
>
> Seeing how other writers use sources can help you think about your own writing.
>
> ▶ Highlights of one student's research process: 54b

> On the one hand, computers and Internet access give employees powerful tools to carry out their jobs; on the other hand, the same technology offers constant temptations to avoid work. As a 2005 study by *Salary.com* and *America Online* indicates, the Internet ranked as the top choice among employees for ways of wasting time on the job; it beat talking with co-workers—the second most popular method—by a margin of nearly two to one (Frauenheim).

50d Draft an introduction for your thesis.

In a research paper, readers are accustomed to seeing the thesis statement—the paper's main point—at the end of the first or second paragraph. The advantage of putting it in the first paragraph is that readers can immediately grasp your point. The advantage of delaying the thesis until the second paragraph is that you can provide a fuller context for your point.

As you draft your introduction, you may change your preliminary thesis, either because you have refined your thinking or because new wording fits more smoothly into the context you have provided for it.

In addition to stating your thesis and establishing a context for it, an introduction should hook readers (see 1e). For example, in your first sentence or two you might connect your topic to a recent news item or point to emerging trends in an academic discipline. Other strategies are to pose a puzzling problem or to cite a startling statistic. Anna Orlov begins her paper by using results from a recent study to show a significant trend in companies' electronic surveillance of employees (see p. 583).

50e Provide organizational cues.

Even if you are working with a good outline, your paper will appear disorganized unless you provide organizational cues: topic sentences, transitions between major sections of the paper, and perhaps headings. Anna Orlov's paper is easy to follow because she begins paragraphs with clear topic sentences and uses transitions to help readers move from one idea to the next (see pp. 583–88). For more about topic sentences, transitions, and headings, see 3a, 3d, and 58b.

50f Draft the paper in an appropriate voice.

A chatty, breezy voice is usually not appropriate in a research paper, but neither is a stuffy, pretentious style or a timid, unsure one.

TOO CHATTY

What's up with companies snooping around when their employees are surfing the Net? Employers who constantly spy on their workers' Internet habits are messing with people's rights.

MORE FORMAL

Although companies often have legitimate concerns that lead them to monitor employees' Internet usage, the benefits of electronic surveillance are outweighed by its costs to employees' privacy and autonomy.

TOO STUFFY

It has been concluded that an evident majority of companies undertake the monitoring of employees' utilization of the Internet.

MORE DIRECT

A recent study found that 76% of companies monitor employees' Internet use.

TOO TIMID

I may not be an expert, but it seems to me that monitoring online activities maybe has the unintended effect of making employees resentful.

MORE AUTHORITATIVE

Monitoring online activities can have the unintended effect of making employees resentful.

51 Citing sources; avoiding plagiarism

In a research paper, you will draw on the work of other writers, and you must document their contributions by citing your sources. Sources are cited for two reasons:

1. to tell readers where your information comes from—so that they can assess its reliability and, if interested, find and read the original source
2. to give credit to the writers from whom you have borrowed words and ideas

Borrowing another writer's language, sentence structures, or ideas without proper acknowledgment is a form of dishonesty known as *plagiarism*.

You must include a citation when you quote from a source, when you summarize or paraphrase, and when you borrow facts that are not common knowledge (see also 51b).

51a For most English papers, use the MLA system for citing sources.

Most English professors and some humanities professors require the MLA (Modern Language Association) system of in-text citations. Here, briefly, is how the MLA citation system usually works. (See 53 for more details and model citations.)

1. The source is introduced by a signal phrase that names its author.
2. The material being cited is followed by a page number in parentheses.
3. At the end of the paper, a list of works cited (arranged alphabetically by authors' last names) gives complete publication information for the source.

IN-TEXT CITATION

Legal scholar Jay Kesan points out that the law holds employers liable for employees' actions such as violations of copyright laws, the distribution of offensive or graphic sexual material, and illegal disclosure of confidential information (312).

ENTRY IN THE LIST OF WORKS CITED

Kesan, Jay P. "Cyber-Working or Cyber-Shirking? A First Principles Examination of Electronic Privacy in the Workplace." *Florida Law Review* 54.2 (2002): 289-332. Print.

This basic MLA format varies for different types of sources. For a detailed discussion and other models, see 53.

51b Avoid plagiarism when quoting, summarizing, and paraphrasing sources.

Your research paper is a collaboration between you and your sources. To be fair and ethical, you must acknowledge your debt to the writers of those sources. If you don't, you commit plagiarism, a serious academic offense. (See also 48c and 54b.)

In general, these three acts are considered plagiarism: (1) failing to cite quotations and borrowed ideas, (2) failing to enclose borrowed language in quotation marks, and (3) failing to put summaries and paraphrases in your own words. Definitions of plagiarism may vary; it's a good idea to find out how your school defines academic dishonesty.

Citing quotations and borrowed ideas

You must cite all direct quotations. You must also cite any ideas borrowed from a source: summaries and paraphrases; statistics and other specific facts; and visuals such as cartoons, graphs, and diagrams.

The only exception is common knowledge—information your readers could easily find in any number of general sources. For example, most encyclopedias will tell readers that Alfred Hitchcock directed *Notorious* in 1946 and that Emily Dickinson published only a handful of her many poems during her lifetime.

As a rule, when you have seen information repeatedly in your reading, you don't need to cite it. However, when information has appeared in only one or two sources, when it is highly specific (as with statistics), or when it is controversial, you should cite the source. If a topic is new to you and you are not sure what is considered common knowledge or what is controversial, ask your instructor or someone else with expertise. When in doubt, cite the source. (See 53 for details.)

Enclosing borrowed language in quotation marks

Making the most of your handbook

When you use exact language from a source, you need to show that it is a quotation.

▶ Quotation marks for direct quotations: 37a

▶ Setting off long quotations: 37b

To indicate that you are using a source's exact phrases or sentences, you must enclose them in quotation marks unless they have been set off from the text by indenting (see p. 506). To omit the quotation marks is to claim—falsely—that the language is your own. Such an omission is plagiarism even if you have cited the source.

ORIGINAL SOURCE

Without adequate discipline, the World Wide Web can be
a tremendous time sink; no other medium comes close to
matching the Internet's depth of materials, interactivity, and
sheer distractive potential.

        —Frederick Lane, *The Naked Employee*, p. 142

PLAGIARISM

Frederick Lane points out that if people do not have adequate
discipline, the World Wide Web can be a tremendous time sink; no other
medium comes close to matching the Internet's depth of materials,
interactivity, and sheer distractive potential (142).

BORROWED LANGUAGE IN QUOTATION MARKS

Frederick Lane points out that for those not exercising self-control,
"the World Wide Web can be a tremendous time sink; no other medium
comes close to matching the Internet's depth of materials, interactivity,
and sheer distractive potential" (142).

Putting summaries and paraphrases in your own words

Summaries and paraphrases are written in your own words.
A summary condenses information from a source; a paraphrase uses roughly the same number of words as the original
source to convey the information. When you summarize or
paraphrase, it is not enough to name the source; you must
restate the source's meaning using your own language. (See
also 48c.) You commit plagiarism if you half-copy the author's
sentences—either by mixing the author's phrases with your
own without using quotation marks or by plugging your synonyms into the author's sentence structure.

The first paraphrase of the following source is plagiarized—even though the source is cited—because too much
of its language is borrowed from the original. The underlined
strings of words have been copied exactly (without quotation
marks). In addition, the writer has closely echoed the sentence
structure of the source, merely substituting some synonyms
(*restricted* for *limited*, *modern era* for *computer age*, *monitoring* for
surveillance, and *inexpensive* for *cheap*).

Revising with comments | Your words?

Understanding the comment

When a teacher or tutor asks "Your words?" the comment often signals that it's unclear whether certain words you've used are your own or those of your sources.

> Internet technology has made it possible for extremist groups to recruit and train members and carry out terrorist activity. The membership of these groups reaches beyond local geographic areas because of the Web. The world has become a cacophony of parochialisms where individuals seek association with coreligionists in a mystique of participation. Combating the influences of these groups is now harder than ever.

Your words?

One student wrote this body paragraph in a research paper on the Internet's role in facilitating terrorism.

Part of this paragraph doesn't sound like the student's voice. To revise, the student must determine which words are his own and which come from sources he consulted. If he chooses to include words or ideas from a source, he'll need to decide if he wants to quote, summarize, or paraphrase the source. He'll also need to properly cite the source in his paper.

Similar comments: source? • quotation? • who's talking here?

Revising when *your* readers wonder whose words they're reading

1. *Reread your sentences* to see if you have clearly marked the boundaries between your source material and your own words. Is every word your own? Or have you borrowed words from sources without properly acknowledging them?

2. *Use signal phrases* to introduce each source and provide context. Doing so prepares readers for a source's words.

3. *Use quotation marks* to enclose language that you borrow word-for-word from a source, and follow each quotation with a parenthetical citation.

4. *Put summaries and paraphrases in your own words* and always cite your sources.

More advice on citing quotations, paraphrases, and summaries: **51** (MLA); **56b** (APA); and **57b** (*Chicago*)

ORIGINAL SOURCE

In earlier times, surveillance was limited to the information that a supervisor could observe and record firsthand and to primitive counting devices. In the computer age surveillance can be instantaneous, unblinking, cheap, and, maybe most importantly, easy.

— Carl Botan and Mihaela Vorvoreanu,
"What Do Employees Think about
Electronic Surveillance at Work?" p. 126

PLAGIARISM: UNACCEPTABLE BORROWING

Scholars Carl Botan and Mihaela Vorvoreanu argue that in earlier times monitoring of employees was restricted to the information that a supervisor could observe and record firsthand. In the modern era, monitoring can be instantaneous, inexpensive, and, most importantly, easy.

To avoid plagiarizing an author's language, resist the temptation to look at the source while you are summarizing or paraphrasing. After you have read the passage you want to paraphrase, set the source aside. Ask yourself, "What is the author's meaning?" In your own words, state your understanding of the author's basic point. Return to the source and check that you haven't used the author's language or sentence structure or misrepresented the author's ideas. Following these steps will help you avoid plagiarizing the source. When you fully understand another writer's meaning, you can more easily and accurately represent those ideas in your own words.

ACCEPTABLE PARAPHRASE

Scholars Carl Botan and Mihaela Vorvoreanu claim that the nature of workplace surveillance has changed over time. Before the arrival of computers, managers could collect only small amounts of information about their employees based on what they saw or heard. Now, because computers are standard workplace technology, employers can monitor employees efficiently (126).

For more discussion of summary and paraphrase, see 48c and 54b.

hackerhandbooks.com/bedhandbook > **Research exercises** > MLA > E-ex 51–1 to 51–6

Integrating sources

Quotations, summaries, paraphrases, and facts will help you develop your argument, but they cannot speak for you. You can use several strategies to integrate information from research sources into your paper while maintaining your own voice.

NOTE: If you are integrating quotations from a literary source, such as a poem or a short story, see 55f.

52a Use quotations appropriately.

In your academic writing, keep the emphasis on your ideas and your language; use your own words to summarize and to paraphrase your sources and to explain your points. Sometimes, however, quotations can be the most effective way to integrate a source's ideas.

WHEN TO USE QUOTATIONS

- When language is especially vivid or expressive
- When exact wording is needed for technical accuracy
- When it is important to let the debaters of an issue explain their positions in their own words
- When the words of an authority lend weight to an argument
- When the language of a source is the topic of your discussion (as in an analysis or interpretation)

Limiting your use of quotations

Although it is tempting to insert many quotations in your paper and to use your own words only for connecting passages, do not quote excessively. It is almost impossible to integrate numerous quotations smoothly into your own text.

It is not always necessary to quote full sentences from a source. To reduce your reliance on the words of others, you can often integrate language from a source into your own sentence structure.

> Kizza and Ssanyu observe that technology in the workplace has been accompanied by "an array of problems that needed quick answers," such as electronic monitoring to prevent security breaches (4).

Using the ellipsis mark and brackets

Two useful marks of punctuation, the ellipsis mark and brackets, allow you to keep quoted material to a minimum and to integrate it smoothly into your text.

The ellipsis mark   To condense a quoted passage, you can use the ellipsis mark (three periods, with spaces between) to indicate that you have left words out. What remains must be grammatically complete.

> Lane acknowledges the legitimate reasons that many companies have for monitoring their employees' online activities, particularly management's concern about preventing "the theft of information that can be downloaded to a . . . disk, e-mailed to oneself . . . , or even posted to a Web page for the entire world to see" (12).

The writer has omitted from the source the words *floppy or Zip* before *disk* and *or a confederate* after *oneself.*

On the rare occasions when you want to leave out one or more full sentences, use a period before the three ellipsis dots.

> Charles Lewis, director of the Center for Public Integrity, points out that "by 1987, employers were administering nearly 2,000,000 polygraph tests a year to job applicants and employees. . . . Millions of workers were required to produce urine samples under observation for drug testing . . ." (22).

Ordinarily, do not use an ellipsis mark at the beginning or at the end of a quotation. Your readers will understand that the quoted material is taken from a longer passage, so such marks are not necessary. The only exception occurs when you have dropped words at the end of the final quoted sentence. In such cases, put three ellipsis dots before the closing quotation mark and parenthetical reference, as in the previous example.

Make sure omissions and ellipsis marks do not distort the meaning of your source.

Brackets　Brackets allow you to insert your own words into quoted material. You can insert words in brackets to clarify a confusing reference or to keep a sentence grammatical in your context. You also use brackets to indicate that you are changing a letter from capital to lowercase (or vice versa) to fit into your sentence.

> Legal scholar Jay Kesan notes that "[a] decade ago, losses [from employees' computer crimes] were already mounting to five billion dollars annually" (311).

This quotation began *A decade ago* . . . in the source, so the writer indicated the change to lowercase with brackets and inserted words in brackets to clarify the meaning of *losses*.

To indicate an error such as a misspelling in a quotation, insert the word "sic" in brackets right after the error.

> Johnson argues that "while online monitoring is often imagined as harmles [sic], the practice may well threaten employees' rights to privacy" (14).

Do not overuse "sic" to call attention to errors in a source. Sometimes paraphrasing is a better option. (See 39c.)

Setting off long quotations

When you quote more than four typed lines of prose or more than three lines of poetry, set off the quotation by indenting it one inch from the left margin.

Long quotations should be introduced by an informative sentence, usually followed by a colon. Quotation marks are

Revising with comments | Cite your sources

Understanding the comment

When a teacher or tutor responds "Cite your sources," the comment often signals that you need to acknowledge and give proper credit to the contributions of others.

> At the story's end, Edna Pontellier is described as a "naked . . . new-born creature" who, in the act of ending her own life, is experiencing a kind of re-birth. *Cite your sources*

One student wrote this sentence in an essay interpreting Kate Chopin's novel *The Awakening*.

The student has borrowed language from both a primary source and a secondary source without proper citation. To revise, she needs to consult her notes or return to the novel to locate the exact page number for the quotation she uses. In addition, she needs to include quotation marks around the words "a kind of re-birth," which come from a secondary source, and to provide a parenthetical citation.

Similar comments: *cite this* • *documentation* • *source?*

Revising when *you* need to cite your sources

1. *Reread your sentence and ask questions.* Have you properly acknowledged all the contributions—words, ideas, or facts—that you use as evidence? Have you given credit to the sources you quote, summarize, or paraphrase? Have you made it clear to readers how to locate the source if they want to consult it?

2. *Ask your instructor* which documentation style you are required to use—MLA, APA, or *Chicago*.

3. *Read your notes* or check the source itself to find the exact words. Make sure you have the author's name, the title, the date of publication, and the page number for each source you cite.

4. *Revise* by including an in-text citation for any words, ideas, or facts that you used as evidence—and by including quotation marks around any language borrowed word-for-word from a source.

More on citing sources: **53a** (MLA), **56d** (APA), and **57d** (*Chicago*)

unnecessary because the indented format tells readers that the passage is taken word-for-word from the source.

> Botan and Vorvoreanu examine the role of gender in company practices of electronic surveillance:
>> There has never been accurate documentation of the extent of gender differences in surveillance, but by the middle 1990s, estimates of the proportion of surveilled employees that were women ranged from 75% to 85%. . . . Ironically, this gender imbalance in workplace surveillance may be evening out today because advances in surveillance technology are making surveillance of traditionally male dominated fields, such as long-distance truck driving, cheap, easy, and frequently unobtrusive. (127)

Notice that at the end of an indented quotation the parenthetical citation goes outside the final mark of punctuation. (When a quotation is run into your text, the opposite is true. See the sample citations on p. 505.)

52b Use signal phrases to integrate sources.

Whenever you include a paraphrase, summary, or direct quotation of another writer in your paper, prepare your readers for it with introductory words called a *signal phrase*. A signal phrase usually names the author of the source and often provides some context for the source material. (See also 52c and 54b.)

When you write a signal phrase, choose a verb that is appropriate for the way you are using the source (see 50c). Are you providing background, explaining a concept, supporting a claim, lending authority, or refuting a belief? See the chart on page 509 for a list of verbs commonly used in signal phrases.

Note that MLA style calls for verbs in the present or present perfect tense (*argues, has argued*) to introduce source material unless you include a date that specifies the time of the original author's writing.

Using signal phrases in MLA papers

To avoid monotony, try to vary both the language and the placement of your signal phrases.

Model signal phrases

In the words of researchers Greenfield and Davis, ". . ."

As legal scholar Jay Kesan has noted, ". . ."

The ePolicy Institute, an organization that advises companies about reducing risks from technology, reports that ". . ."

". . . ," writes Daniel Tynan, ". . ."

". . . ," attorney Schmitt claims.

Kizza and Ssanyu offer a persuasive counterargument: ". . ."

Verbs in signal phrases

acknowledges	comments	endorses	reasons
adds	compares	grants	refutes
admits	confirms	illustrates	rejects
agrees	contends	implies	reports
argues	declares	insists	responds
asserts	denies	notes	suggests
believes	disputes	observes	thinks
claims	emphasizes	points out	writes

Marking boundaries

Readers need to move from your words to the words of a source without feeling a jolt. Avoid dropping quotations into the text without warning. Instead, provide clear signal phrases, including at least the author's name, to indicate the boundary between your words and the source's words. (The signal phrase is underlined in the second example.)

DROPPED QUOTATION

Some experts have argued that a range of legitimate concerns justifies employer monitoring of employee Internet usage. "Employees could

accidentally (or deliberately) spill confidential corporate information . . .
or allow worms to spread throughout a corporate network" (Tynan).

QUOTATION WITH SIGNAL PHRASE

Some experts have argued that a range of legitimate concerns
justifies employer monitoring of employee Internet usage. As *PC World*
columnist Daniel Tynan points out, "Employees could accidentally
(or deliberately) spill confidential corporate information . . . or allow
worms to spread throughout a corporate network."

NOTE: Because this quotation is from an unpaginated Web source,
no page number appears in parentheses after the quotation. See
item 4 on page 520.

Establishing authority

Good research writing uses evidence from reliable sources. The
first time you mention a source, include in the signal phrase
the author's title, credentials, or experience—anything that
would help your readers recognize the source's authority. (Signal phrases are underlined in the next two examples.)

SOURCE WITH NO CREDENTIALS

Jay Kesan points out that the law holds employers liable for employees'
actions such as violations of copyright laws, the distribution of
offensive or graphic sexual material, and illegal disclosure of
confidential information (312).

SOURCE WITH CREDENTIALS

Legal scholar Jay Kesan points out that the law holds employers liable
for employees' actions such as violations of copyright laws, the
distribution of offensive or graphic sexual material, and illegal
disclosure of confidential information (312).

When you establish your source's authority, as with the phrase
Legal scholar in the previous example, you also signal to readers your own credibility as a responsible researcher who has
located reliable sources.

Introducing summaries and paraphrases

Introduce most summaries and paraphrases with a signal phrase that names the author and places the material in the context of your argument. (See also 52c and 54b.) Readers will then understand that everything between the signal phrase and the parenthetical citation summarizes or paraphrases the cited source.

Without the signal phrase (underlined) in the following example, readers might think that only the quotation at the end is being cited, when in fact the whole paragraph is based on the source.

> <u>Frederick Lane believes</u> that the personal computer has posed new challenges for employers worried about workplace productivity. Whereas early desktop computers were primitive enough to prevent employees from using them to waste time, the machines have become so sophisticated that they now make non-work-related computer activities easy and inviting. Many employees spend considerable company time customizing features and playing games on their computers. But perhaps most problematic from the employer's point of view, Lane asserts, is giving employees access to the Internet, "roughly the equivalent of installing a gazillion-channel television set for each employee" (15-16).

There are times when a summary or a paraphrase does not require a signal phrase. When the context makes clear where the cited material begins, you may omit the signal phrase and include the author's last name in parentheses.

Using signal phrases with statistics and other facts

When you are citing a statistic or another specific fact, a signal phrase is often not necessary. In most cases, readers will understand that the citation refers to the statistic or fact (not the whole paragraph).

> Roughly 60% of responding companies reported disciplining employees who had used the Internet in ways the companies deemed inappropriate; 30% had fired their employees for those transgressions (Greenfield and Davis 347).

There is nothing wrong, however, with using a signal phrase to introduce a statistic or fact.

Putting source material in context

Readers should not have to guess why source material appears in your paper. A signal phrase can help you make the connection between your own ideas and those of another writer by clarifying how the source will contribute to your paper (see 47a).

If you use another writer's words, you must explain how they relate to your point. It's a good idea to embed a quotation between sentences of your own. In addition to introducing it with a signal phrase, follow it with interpretive comments that link the quotation to your paper's argument (see also 52c).

QUOTATION WITH EFFECTIVE CONTEXT

The difference, Lane argues, between old methods of data gathering and electronic surveillance involves quantity:

> Technology makes it possible for employers to gather enormous amounts of data about employees, often far beyond what is necessary to satisfy safety or productivity concerns. And the trends that drive technology—faster, smaller, cheaper—make it possible for larger and larger numbers of employers to gather ever-greater amounts of personal data. (3-4)

In an age when employers can collect data whenever employees use their computers—when they send e-mail, surf the Web, or even arrive at or depart from their workstations—the challenge for both employers and employees is to determine how much is too much.

52c Synthesize sources.

When you synthesize multiple sources in a research paper, you create a conversation about your research topic. You show readers that your argument is based on your active analysis

and integration of ideas, not just a list of quotations and paraphrases. Your synthesis will show how your sources relate to
one another; one source may support, extend, or counter the
ideas of another. Not every source has to "speak" to another
in a research paper, but readers should be able to see how each
one functions in your argument (see 47a).

Considering how sources relate to your argument

Before you integrate sources and show readers how they relate to one another, consider how each one might contribute
to your own argument. As student writer Anna Orlov became
more informed through her research about Internet surveillance in the workplace, she asked herself these questions:
*What do I think about monitoring employees online? Which sources
might support my ideas? Which sources might help extend or illustrate the points I want to make? What common or compelling
counterarguments do I need to address to strengthen my position?*
She annotated a passage from an *eWeek* article that challenged
the case she was building against Internet surveillance in the
workplace.

STUDENT NOTES ON THE ORIGINAL SOURCE

*Catchy
language—a
good quotation.*

*Common
examples—
readers can
relate.*

While bosses can easily detect and interrupt water-
cooler chatter, the employee who is shopping at
Lands' End or IMing with fellow fantasy baseball
managers may actually appear to be working.
Thwarting the activity is a technology challenge,
and it's one that more and more enterprises are
taking seriously, despite resistance from privacy
advocates and some employees themselves.
            —Chris Gonsalves, "Wasting Away on the Web"

*Strong case for
surveillance, but
I'm not convinced.
Counter with use-
ful workplace Web
surfing?*

Because Orlov felt that the Gonsalves article would convince many readers that Internet surveillance was good for
workplace productivity, she knew she needed to present and
counter his argument. The author's memorable language and

clear illustration seemed worth quoting, but she wanted to keep the emphasis on her own argument. So she quoted the passage from Gonsalves and then analyzed it, discussing and countering his view in her own writing. She also found other sources to support and extend her counterargument.

Placing sources in conversation

You can show readers how the ideas of one source relate to those of another by connecting and analyzing the ideas in your own voice. After all, you've done the research and thought through the issues, so you should control the conversation. When you effectively synthesize sources, the emphasis is still on your own writing; the thread of your argument should be easy to identify and to understand, with or without your sources.

SAMPLE SYNTHESIS (DRAFT)

Student writer Anna Orlov begins with a claim that needs support.

Signal phrases indicate how sources contribute to Orlov's paper and show that the ideas that follow are not her own.

Student writer

Productivity is not easily measured in the wired workplace. As a result, employers find it difficult to determine how much freedom to allow their employees. On the one hand, computers and Internet access give employees powerful tools to carry out their jobs; on the other hand, the same technology offers constant temptations to avoid work. As a 2005 study by *Salary.com* and *America Online* indicates, the Internet ranked as the top choice among employees for ways of wasting time on the job (Frauenheim). Chris Gonsalves, an editor for *eWeek.com*, argues that technology has changed the terms between employers and employees: "While bosses can easily detect and interrupt water-cooler chatter," he writes, "the employee who is shopping at Lands' End or IMing with fellow fantasy baseball managers may actually appear to be working." The gap between observable behaviors and actual online activities has motivated some employers to invest in surveillance programs.

Source 1

Source 2

Student writer

Orlov presents a counterposition to extend her argument.

Many experts, however, disagree with employers' assumption that online monitoring can increase productivity. Employment law attorney Joseph Schmitt argues that, particularly for salaried employees, "a company shouldn't care whether employees spend one or 10 hours on the Internet as long as they are getting their jobs done—and provided that they are not accessing inappropriate sites" (qtd. in Verespej). Other experts even argue that time spent on personal Internet browsing can actually be productive for companies. According to Bill Coleman, an executive at *Salary.com*, "Personal Internet use and casual office conversations often turn into new business ideas or suggestions for gaining operating efficiencies" (qtd. in Frauenheim). Employers, in other words, may benefit from showing more faith in their employees' ability to exercise their autonomy.

Student writer

Source 3

Orlov builds her case—each quoted passage offers a more detailed claim or example in support of her larger claim.

Student writer

Source 4

Student writer

In this draft, Orlov uses her own analyses to shape the conversation among her sources. She does not simply string quotations together or allow them to overwhelm her writing. The final sentence, written in her own voice, gives her an opportunity to explain to readers how the various sources support her argument.

When synthesizing sources in your own writing, ask yourself the following questions:

- Which sources inform, support, or extend your argument?
- Do you vary the functions of sources—to provide background information, explain terms or concepts, lend authority to your argument, and anticipate counterarguments?
- Do you explain to readers how your sources support your argument?
- Do you connect and analyze sources in your own voice?
- Is your own argument easy to identify and to understand, with or without your sources?

hackerhandbooks.com/bedhandbook > Research exercises > MLA > E-ex 52–1 to 52–4

Reviewing an MLA paper: Use of sources

Use of quotations

- Is quoted material enclosed in quotation marks (unless it has been set off from the text)? (See 51b and p. 508.)

- Is quoted language word-for-word accurate? If not, do brackets or ellipsis marks indicate the changes or omissions? (See pp. 505–06.)

- Does a clear signal phrase (usually naming the author) prepare readers for each quotation and for the purpose the quotation serves? (See 52b.)

- Does a parenthetical citation follow each quotation? (See 53a.)

- Is each quotation put in context? (See 52c.)

Use of summaries and paraphrases

- Are summaries and paraphrases free of plagiarized wording—not copied or half-copied from the source? (See 51b.)

- Are summaries and paraphrases documented with parenthetical citations? (See 51b and 53a.)

- Do readers know where the cited material begins? In other words, does a signal phrase mark the boundary between your words and the summary or paraphrase? Or does the context alone make clear exactly what you are citing? (See 52b.)

- Does a signal phrase prepare readers for the purpose the summary or paraphrase has in your argument?

Use of statistics and other facts

- Are statistics and facts (other than common knowledge) documented with parenthetical citations? (See 51b and 53a.)

- If there is no signal phrase, will readers understand exactly which facts are being cited? (See 52b.)

53 MLA documentation style

In English and other humanities classes, you may be asked to use the MLA (Modern Language Association) system for documenting sources, which is set forth in the *MLA Handbook for Writers of Research Papers*, 7th ed. (New York: MLA, 2009).

MLA recommends in-text citations that refer readers to a list of works cited. An in-text citation names the author of the source, often in a signal phrase, and gives a page number in parentheses. At the end of the paper, a list of works cited provides publication information about the source; the list is alphabetized by authors' last names (or by titles for works without authors). There is a direct connection between the in-text citation and the alphabetical listing. In the following example, that connection is highlighted in orange.

IN-TEXT CITATION

Jay Kesan notes that even though many companies now routinely monitor employees through electronic means, "there may exist less intrusive safeguards for employers" (293).

ENTRY IN THE LIST OF WORKS CITED

Kesan, Jay P. "Cyber-Working or Cyber-Shirking? A First Principles Examination of Electronic Privacy in the Workplace." *Florida Law Review* 54.2 (2002): 289-332. Print.

For a list of works cited that includes this entry, see page 588.

53a MLA in-text citations

MLA in-text citations are made with a combination of signal phrases and parenthetical references. A signal phrase introduces information taken from a source (a quotation, summary, paraphrase, or fact); usually the signal phrase includes the author's name. The parenthetical reference comes after the cited material, often at the end of the sentence. It includes at least a page number (except for unpaginated sources, such as those found online). In the models in 53a, the elements of the in-text citation are highlighted in color.

IN-TEXT CITATION

Kwon points out that the Fourth Amendment does not give employees any protections from employers' "unreasonable searches and seizures" (6).

Readers can look up the author's last name in the alphabetized list of works cited, where they will learn the work's title and other publication information. If readers decide to consult the source, the page number will take them straight to the passage that has been cited.

Basic rules for print and online sources

The MLA system of in-text citations, which depends heavily on authors' names and page numbers, was created with print sources in mind. Although many online sources have unclear authorship and lack page numbers, the basic rules are the same for both print and online sources.

The models in this section (items 1–5) show how the MLA system usually works and explain what to do if your source has no author or page numbers.

1. Author named in a signal phrase   Ordinarily, introduce the material being cited with a signal phrase that includes the author's name. In addition to preparing readers for the source, the signal phrase allows you to keep the parenthetical citation brief.

Frederick Lane reports that employers do not necessarily have to use software to monitor how their employees use the Web: employers can "use a hidden video camera pointed at an employee's monitor" and even position a camera "so that a number of monitors [can] be viewed at the same time" (147).

The signal phrase—*Frederick Lane reports*—names the author; the parenthetical citation gives the page number of the book in which the quoted words may be found.

Notice that the period follows the parenthetical citation. When a quotation ends with a question mark or an exclamation point, leave the end punctuation inside the quotation mark and add a period at the end of your sentence: ". . . ?" (8). (See also the note on p. 396.)

2. Author named in parentheses   If a signal phrase does not name the author, put the author's last name in parentheses along with the page number. Use no punctuation between the name and the page number.

> Companies can monitor employees' every keystroke without legal penalty,
> but they may have to combat low morale as a result (Lane 129).

3. Author unknown Either use the complete title in a signal phrase or use a short form of the title in parentheses. Titles of books are italicized; titles of articles are put in quotation marks.

> A popular keystroke logging program operates invisibly on workers'
> computers yet provides supervisors with details of the workers' online
> activities ("Automatically").

TIP: Before assuming that a Web source has no author, do some detective work. Often the author's name is available but is not easy to find. For example, it may appear at the end of the page, in tiny print. Or it may appear on another page of the site, such as the home page.

NOTE: If a source has no author and is sponsored by a corporation or government agency, name the corporation or agency as the author (see items 8 and 17 on pp. 522 and 525, respectively).

4. Page number unknown Do not include the page number if a work lacks page numbers, as is the case with many Web sources. Even if a printout from a Web site shows page numbers, treat the source as unpaginated in the in-text citation because not all printouts give the same page numbers. (When the pages of a Web source are stable, as in PDF files, supply a page number in your in-text citation.)

> As a 2005 study by *Salary.com* and *America Online* indicates, the
> Internet ranked as the top choice among employees for ways of
> wasting time on the job; it beat talking with co-workers—the
> second most popular method—by a margin of nearly two to one
> (Frauenheim).

If a source has numbered paragraphs or sections, use "par." (or "pars.") or "sec." (or "secs.") in the parentheses: (Smith, par. 4). Notice that a comma follows the author's name in this case.

5. One-page source   If the source is one page long, MLA allows (but does not require) you to omit the page number. Many instructors will want you to supply the page number because without it readers may not know where your citation ends or, worse, may not realize that you have provided a citation at all.

NO PAGE NUMBER IN CITATION

Anush Yegyazarian reports that in 2000 the National Labor Relations Board's Office of the General Counsel helped win restitution for two workers who had been dismissed because their employers were displeased by the employees' e-mails about work-related issues. The case points to the ongoing struggle to define what constitutes protected speech in the workplace.

PAGE NUMBER IN CITATION

Anush Yegyazarian reports that in 2000 the National Labor Relations Board's Office of the General Counsel helped win restitution for two workers who had been dismissed because their employers were displeased by the employees' e-mails about work-related issues (62). The case points to the ongoing struggle to define what constitutes protected speech in the workplace.

Variations on the basic rules

This section describes the MLA guidelines for handling a variety of situations not covered by the basic rules in items 1–5. These rules for in-text citations are the same for both print and online sources.

6. Two or three authors   Name the authors in a signal phrase, as in the following example, or include their last names in the parenthetical reference: (Kizza and Ssanyu 2).

Kizza and Ssanyu note that "employee monitoring is a dependable, capable, and very affordable process of electronically or otherwise recording all employee activities at work" and elsewhere (2).

When three authors are named in the parentheses, separate the names with commas: (Alton, Davies, and Rice 56).

7. Four or more authors Name all of the authors or include only the first author's name followed by "et al." (Latin for "and others"). The format you use should match the format in your works cited entry (see item 3 on p. 533).

> The study was extended for two years, and only after results were reviewed by an independent panel did the researchers publish their findings (Blaine et al. 35).

8. Organization as author When the author is a corporation or an organization, name that author either in the signal phrase or in the parentheses. (For a government agency as author, see item 17 on p. 525.)

> According to a 2001 survey of human resources managers by the American Management Association, more than three-quarters of the responding companies reported disciplining employees for "misuse or personal use of office telecommunications equipment" (2).

In the list of works cited, the American Management Association is treated as the author and alphabetized under *A*. When you give the organization name in parentheses, abbreviate common words in the name: "Assn.," "Dept.," "Natl.," "Soc.," and so on.

> In a 2001 survey of human resources managers, more than three-quarters of the responding companies reported disciplining employees for "misuse of personal use of office telecommunications equipment" (Amer. Management Assn. 2).

9. Authors with the same last name If your list of works cited includes works by two or more authors with the same last name, include the author's first name in the signal phrase or first initial in the parentheses.

> Estimates of the frequency with which employers monitor employees' use of the Internet each day vary widely (A. Jones 15).

10. Two or more works by the same author   Mention the title
of the work in the signal phrase or include a short version of
the title in the parentheses.

> The American Management Association and ePolicy Institute have
> tracked employers' practices in monitoring employees' e-mail use. The
> groups' 2003 survey found that one-third of companies had a policy of
> keeping and reviewing employees' e-mail messages ("2003 E-mail" 2);
> in 2005, more than 55% of companies engaged in e-mail monitoring
> ("2005 Electronic" 1).

Titles of articles and other short works are placed in quotation
marks; titles of books are italicized.

In the rare case when both the author's name and a
short title must be given in parentheses, separate them with a
comma.

> A 2004 survey found that 20% of employers responding had
> employees' e-mail "subpoenaed in the course of a lawsuit or regulatory
> investigation," up 7% from the previous year (Amer. Management Assn.
> and ePolicy Inst., "2004 Workplace" 1).

11. Two or more works in one citation   To cite more than one
source in the parentheses, give the citations in alphabetical
order and separate them with a semicolon.

> The effects of sleep deprivation among college students have been well
> documented (Cahill 42; Leduc 114; Vasquez 73).

Multiple citations can be distracting, so you should not overuse the technique. If you want to alert readers to several
sources that discuss a particular topic, consider using an information note instead (see 53c).

12. Repeated citations from the same source   When you are
writing about a single work of fiction, you do not need to include the author's name each time you quote from or paraphrase the work. After you mention the author's name at the

beginning of your paper, you may include just the page number in your parenthetical citations. (For specific guidelines for citing novels, plays, and poems, see 55f.)

> In Susan Glaspell's short story "A Jury of Her Peers," two women accompany their husbands and a county attorney to an isolated house where a farmer named John Wright has been choked to death in his bed with a rope. The chief suspect is Wright's wife, Minnie, who is in jail awaiting trial. The sheriff's wife, Mrs. Peters, has come along to gather some personal items for Minnie, and Mrs. Hale has joined her. Early in the story, Mrs. Hale sympathizes with Minnie and objects to the way the male investigators are "snoopin' round and criticizin'" her kitchen (200). In contrast, Mrs. Peters shows respect for the law, saying that the men are doing "no more than their duty" (201).

In a second citation from the same nonfiction source in one paragraph, you may omit the author's name in the signal phrase as long as it is clear that you are still referring to the same source.

13. Encyclopedia or dictionary entry   Unless an encyclopedia or a dictionary has an author, it will be alphabetized in the list of works cited under the word or entry that you consulted (see item 18 on p. 539). Either in your text or in your parenthetical citation, mention the word or entry. No page number is required, since readers can easily look up the word or entry.

> The word *crocodile* has a surprisingly complex etymology ("Crocodile").

14. Multivolume work   If your paper cites more than one volume of a multivolume work, indicate in the parentheses the volume you are referring to, followed by a colon and the page number.

> In his studies of gifted children, Terman describes a pattern of accelerated language acquisition (2: 279).

If you cite only one volume of a multivolume work, you will include the volume number in the list of works cited and will not need to include it in the parentheses. (See the second example in item 17 on p. 539.)

15. Entire work   Use the author's name in a signal phrase or a parenthetical citation. There is no need to use a page number.

Lane explores the evolution of surveillance in the workplace.

16. Selection in an anthology   Put the name of the author of the selection (not the editor of the anthology) in the signal phrase or the parentheses.

In "Love Is a Fallacy," the narrator's logical teachings disintegrate when Polly declares that she should date Petey because "[h]e's got a raccoon coat" (Shulman 379).

In the list of works cited, the work is alphabetized under *Shulman*, not under the name of the editor of the anthology.

Shulman, Max. "Love Is a Fallacy." *Current Issues and Enduring
    Questions*. Ed. Sylvan Barnet and Hugo Bedau. 8th ed.
    Boston: Bedford, 2008. 371-79. Print.

17. Government document   When a government agency is the author, you will alphabetize it in the list of works cited under the name of the government, such as *United States* or *Great Britain* (see item 73 on p. 563). For this reason, you must name the government as well as the agency in your in-text citation.

Online monitoring by the United States Department of the
Interior over a one-week period found that employees' use of
"sexually explicit and gambling websites . . . accounted for over
24 hours of Internet use" and that "computer users spent over
2,004 hours accessing game and auction sites" during the same
period (3).

18. Historical document For a historical document, such as the United States Constitution or the Canadian Charter of Rights and Freedoms, provide the document title, neither italicized nor in quotation marks, along with relevant article and section numbers. In parenthetical citations, use common abbreviations such as "art." and "sec." and abbreviations of well-known titles (US Const., art. 1, sec. 2).

> While the United States Constitution provides for the formation of
> new states (art. 4, sec. 3), it does not explicitly allow or prohibit
> the secession of states.

For other historical documents, cite as you would any other work, by the first element in the works cited entry (see item 74 on p. 564).

19. Legal source For legislative acts (laws) and court cases, name the act or case either in a signal phrase or in parentheses. Italicize the names of cases but not the names of acts.

> The Jones Act of 1917 granted US citizenship to Puerto Ricans.

> In 1857, Chief Justice Roger B. Taney declared in *Dred Scott v. Sandford*
> that blacks, whether enslaved or free, could not be citizens of the
> United States.

20. Visual such as a photograph, map, or chart To cite a visual that has a figure number in the source, use the abbreviation "fig." and the number in place of a page number in your parenthetical citation: (Manning, fig. 4). Spell out the word "figure" if you refer to it in your text.

To cite a visual that does not have a figure number in a print source, use the visual's title or a general description in your text and cite the author and page number as for any other source.

For a visual that is not contained in a source such as a book or periodical, identify the visual in your text and then cite it using the first element in the works cited entry: the photographer's or artist's name or the title of the work. (See item 69 on p. 562.)

> Photographs such as *Woman Aircraft Worker* (Bransby) and *Women Welders* (Parks) demonstrate the US government's attempt to document the contributions of women on the home front during World War II.

21. E-mail, letter, or personal interview   Cite e-mail messages, personal letters, and personal interviews by the name listed in the works cited entry, as you would for any other source. Identify the type of source in your text if you feel it is necessary. (See item 53 on p. 557 and items 83 and 84 on p. 567.)

22. Web site or other electronic source   Your in-text citation for an electronic source should follow the same guidelines as for other sources. If the source lacks page numbers but has numbered paragraphs, sections, or divisions, use those numbers with the appropriate abbreviation in your in-text citation: "par.," "sec.," "ch.," "pt.," and so on. Do not add such numbers if the source itself does not use them. In that case, simply give the author or title in your in-text citation.

> Julian Hawthorne points out profound differences between his father and Ralph Waldo Emerson but concludes that, in their lives and their writing, "together they met the needs of nearly all that is worthy in human nature" (ch. 4).

23. Indirect source (source quoted in another source)   When a writer's or a speaker's quoted words appear in a source written by someone else, begin the parenthetical citation with the abbreviation "qtd. in."

> Researchers Botan and McCreadie point out that "workers are objects of information collection without participating in the process of exchanging the information . . ." (qtd. in Kizza and Ssanyu 14).

Literary works and sacred texts

Literary works and sacred texts are usually available in a variety of editions. Your list of works cited will specify which edition you are using, and your in-text citation will usually consist of a page number from the edition you consulted (see item 24). When possible, give enough information—such as book parts, play divisions, or line numbers—so that readers can locate the cited passage in any edition of the work (see items 25–27).

24. Literary work without parts or line numbers   Many literary works, such as most short stories and many novels and plays, do not have parts or line numbers. In such cases, simply cite the page number.

> At the end of Kate Chopin's "The Story of an Hour," Mrs. Mallard drops dead upon learning that her husband is alive. In the final irony of the story, doctors report that she has died of a "joy that kills" (25).

25. Verse play or poem   For verse plays, give act, scene, and line numbers that can be located in any edition of the work. Use arabic numerals and separate the numbers with periods.

> In Shakespeare's *King Lear*, Gloucester, blinded for suspected treason, learns a profound lesson from his tragic experience: "A man may see how this world goes / with no eyes" (4.2.148-49).

For a poem, cite the part, stanza, and line numbers, if it has them, separated by periods.

> The Green Knight claims to approach King Arthur's court "because the praise of you, prince, is puffed so high, / And your manor and your men are considered so magnificent" (1.12.258-59).

For poems that are not divided into numbered parts or stanzas, use line numbers. For a first reference, use the word "lines": (lines 5-8). Thereafter use just the numbers: (12-13).

26. Novel with numbered divisions   When a novel has numbered divisions, put the page number first, followed by a semicolon, and then the book, part, or chapter in which the passage may be found. Use abbreviations such as "pt." and "ch."

One of Kingsolver's narrators, teenager Rachel, pushes her vocabulary
beyond its limits. For example, Rachel complains that being forced to
live in the Congo with her missionary family is "a sheer tapestry of
justice" because her chances of finding a boyfriend are "dull and void"
(117; bk. 2, ch. 10).

27. Sacred text   When citing a sacred text such as the Bible
or the Qur'an, name the edition you are using in your works
cited entry (see item 19 on p. 542). In your parenthetical citation, give the book, chapter, and verse (or their equivalent),
separated by periods. Common abbreviations for books of the
Bible are acceptable.

Consider the words of Solomon: "If your enemy is hungry, give him
bread to eat; and if he is thirsty, give him water to drink" (*Oxford
Annotated Bible*, Prov. 25.21).

The title of a sacred work is italicized when it refers to a
specific edition of the work, as in the preceding example. If
you refer to the book in a general sense in your text, neither
italicize it nor put it in quotation marks: "The Bible and the
Qur'an provide allegories that help readers understand how to
lead a moral life."

hackerhandbooks.com/bedhandbook > Research exercises > MLA > E-ex 53–1 to 53–3

53b MLA list of works cited

An alphabetized list of works cited, which appears at the end
of your research paper, gives publication information for each
of the sources you have cited in the paper. Include only sources
that you have quoted, summarized, or paraphrased. (For information about preparing the list, see pp. 571–72; for a sample
list of works cited, see p. 588.)

General guidelines for works cited in MLA style

In an MLA works cited entry, the first author's name is inverted (the last name comes first, followed by a comma and

Directory to MLA works cited models

the first name), and all other names are in normal order. In titles of works, all words are capitalized except articles (*a, an, the*), prepositions (*to, from, between,* and so on), coordinating conjunctions (*and, but, or, nor, for, so, yet*), and the *to* in infinitives—unless they are the first or last word of the title or subtitle. Titles of periodical articles and other short works, such as brief documents from Web sites, are put in quotation marks; titles of books and other long works, such as entire Web sites, are italicized.

The city of publication is given without a state name. Publishers' names are shortened, usually to the first principal word ("Wiley" for "John Wiley and Sons," for instance), and "University" and "Press" are abbreviated "U" and "P" in the names of university publishers: UP of Florida. The date of publication is the date on the title page or the most recent date on the copyright page.

All works cited entries must include the medium in which a work was published, produced, or delivered. The medium usually appears at the end of the entry, capitalized but neither italicized nor in quotation marks. Typical designations for the medium are "Print," "Web," "Radio," "Television," "CD," "Audiocassette," "Film," "Videocassette," "DVD," "Photograph," "Performance," "Lecture," "MP3 file," and "PDF file." (See specific items throughout this section.)

Listing authors (print and online)

Alphabetize entries in the list of works cited by authors' last names (or by title if a work has no author). The author's name is important because citations in the text of the paper refer to it and readers will be looking for it at the beginning of an entry in the alphabetized list.

NAME CITED IN TEXT

According to Nancy Flynn, . . .

BEGINNING OF WORKS CITED ENTRY

Flynn, Nancy.

1. Single author

author: last
name first — title (book) — city of publication — publisher — date — medium

Wood, James. *How Fiction Works*. New York: Farrar, 2008. Print.

2. Two or three authors

first author:
last name first — second author: in normal order — title (book) — city of publication

Gourevitch, Philip, and Errol Morris. *Standard Operating Procedure*. New York:

publisher — date — medium

Penguin, 2008. Print.

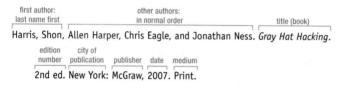

first author:
last name first | other authors:
in normal order | title (newspaper article)

Farmer, John, John Azzarello, and Miles Kara. "Real Heroes, Fake Stories."

newspaper title | date of
publication | page | medium

New York Times 14 Sept. 2008: WK10. Print.

3. Four or more authors Name all the authors or name the first author followed by "et al." (Latin for "and others"). In an in-text citation, use the same form for the authors' names as you use in the works cited entry. See item 7 on page 522.

first author:
last name first | other authors:
in normal order | title (book)

Harris, Shon, Allen Harper, Chris Eagle, and Jonathan Ness. *Gray Hat Hacking.*

edition
number | city of
publication | publisher | date | medium

2nd ed. New York: McGraw, 2007. Print.

4. Organization as author

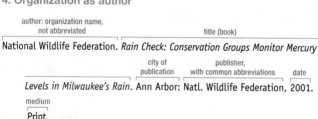

author: organization name,
not abbreviated | title (book)

National Wildlife Federation. *Rain Check: Conservation Groups Monitor Mercury*

city of
publication | publisher,
with common abbreviations | date

Levels in Milwaukee's Rain. Ann Arbor: Natl. Wildlife Federation, 2001.

medium

Print.

For a publication by a government agency, see item 73. Your in-text citation should also treat the organization as the author (see item 8 on p. 522).

5. Unknown author

Article or other short work

title (newspaper article) | label | newspaper title | date of publication | page

"Poverty, by Outdated Numbers." Editorial. *Boston Globe* 20 Sept. 2008: A16.

medium

Print.

title (TV episode) title (TV program)   producer   network   city of station broadcast   date of broadcast

"Heat." *Frontline*. Prod. Martin Smith. PBS. KTWU,Topeka. 21 Oct. 2008.

medium
Television.

For other examples of an article with no author and a television program, see items 31 and 65, respectively.

Book, entire Web site, or other long work

title (book)   city of publication   publisher   date   medium

New Concise World Atlas. New York: Oxford UP, 2007. Print.

title (Web site)
Women of Protest: Photographs from the Records of the National Woman's Party.

sponsor of site   no date   medium   date of access
Lib. of Cong., n.d. Web. 29 Sept. 2008.

Before concluding that the author of an online source is unknown, check carefully (see the tip on p. 520). Also remember that an organization or a government may be the author (see items 4 and 73).

6. Two or more works by the same author   If your list of works cited includes two or more works by the same author, first alphabetize the works by title (ignoring the article *A*, *An*, or *The* at the beginning of a title). Use the author's name for the first entry only; for subsequent entries, use three hyphens followed by a period. The three hyphens must stand for exactly the same name or names as in the first entry.

Knopp, Lisa. *Field of Vision*. Iowa City: U of Iowa P, 1996. Print.

---. *The Nature of Home: A Lexicon and Essays*. Lincoln: U of Nebraska P, 2002. Print.

Books (print)

Items 7–24 apply to print books. For online books, see items 41 and 42. For an illustrated citation of a print book, see page 536.

7. Basic format for a book

author: last
name first   book title   city of
publication   publisher

Sacks, Oliver. *Musicophilia: Tales of Music and the Brain*. New York: Knopf,

    date   medium

    2007. Print.

Take the information about the book from its title page and copyright page. Use a short form of the publisher's name; omit terms such as "Press," "Inc.," and "Co." except when naming university presses ("Harvard UP," for example). If the copyright page lists more than one date, use the most recent one.

8. Book with an author and an editor

author: last
name first   book title   editor's name:
in normal order   city of
publication

Plath, Sylvia. *The Unabridged Journals of Sylvia Plath*. Ed. Karen V. Kukil. New York:

   imprint-publisher   date   medium

   Anchor-Doubleday, 2000. Print.

The abbreviation "Ed." means "Edited by," so it is the same for one or multiple editors.

9. Book with an author and a translator

"Trans." means "Translated by," so it is the same for one or multiple translators.

Scirocco, Alfonso. *Garibaldi: Citizen of the World*. Trans. Allan Cameron.

    Princeton: Princeton UP, 2007. Print.

10. Book with an editor

Begin with the editor's name. For one editor, use "ed." (for "editor") after the name; for multiple editors, use "eds." (for "editors"). See the example on page 537.

Citation at a glance | Book (MLA)

To cite a print book in MLA style, include the following elements:

1 Author
2 Title and subtitle
3 City of publication
4 Publisher
5 Date of publication
6 Medium

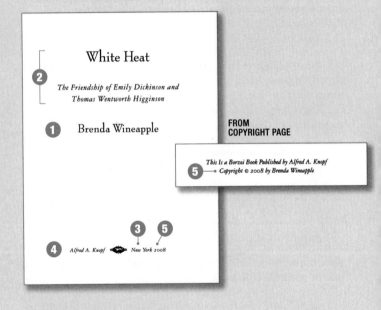

White Heat

2 The Friendship of Emily Dickinson and
Thomas Wentworth Higginson

1 Brenda Wineapple

FROM COPYRIGHT PAGE

This Is a Borzoi Book Published by Alfred A. Knopf
5 Copyright © 2008 by Brenda Wineapple

4 Alfred A. Knopf **3** New York **5** 2008

WORKS CITED ENTRY FOR A PRINT BOOK

```
┌──── 1 ────┐ ┌────────── 2 ──────────
```
Wineapple, Brenda. *White Heat: The Friendship of Emily Dickinson and*

```
                              ┌── 3 ──┐ ┌ 4 ┐ ┌ 5 ┐ ┌ 6 ┐
```
Thomas Wentworth Higginson. New York: Knopf, 2008. Print.

For more on citing print books in MLA style, see pages 535–43.

Lago, Mary, Linda K. Hughes, and Elizabeth MacLeod Walls, eds. *The BBC Talks of E. M. Forster, 1929-1960*. Columbia: U of Missouri P, 2008. Print.

11. Graphic narrative or illustrated book For a book that combines text and illustrations, begin your citation with the person you wish to emphasize (writer, illustrator, artist) and list any other contributors after the title of the book. Use the abbreviation "illus." and other common labels to identify contributors. If the writer and illustrator are the same person, cite the work as you would a book, with no labels.

Weaver, Dustin, illus. *The Tenth Circle*. By Jodi Picoult. New York: Washington Square, 2006. Print.

Moore, Alan. *V for Vendetta*. Illus. David Lloyd. New York: Vertigo-DC Comics, 2008. Print.

Thompson, Craig. *Blankets*. Marietta: Top Shelf, 2005.

12. Book with an author using a pseudonym Give the author's name as it appears on the title page (the pseudonym), and follow it with the author's real name in brackets.

Dinesen, Isak [Karen Blixen]. *Winter's Tales*. 1942. New York: Vintage, 1993. Print.

13. Book in a language other than English If your readers are not familiar with the language of the book, include a translation of the title in brackets. Capitalize the title according to the conventions of the book's language, and give the original publication information.

Nemtsov, Boris, and Vladimir Milov. *Putin. Itogi. Nezavisimyi Ekspertnyi Doklad* [*Putin. The Results: An Independent Expert Report*]. Moscow: Novaya Gazeta, 2008. Print.

14. Entire anthology An anthology is a collection of works on a common theme, often with different authors for the selections and usually with an editor for the entire volume. The abbreviation "eds." is for multiple editors. If the book has only one editor, use the singular "ed." after the editor's name.

Dumanis, Michael, and Cate Marvin, eds. *Legitimate Dangers: American Poets of the New Century*. Louisville: Sarabande, 2006. Print.

15. One or more selections from an anthology

One selection from anthology

author of selection:
last name first   title of selection   title of anthology

Brouwer, Joel. "The Spots." *Legitimate Dangers: American Poets of the*

                editor(s) of anthology: city of
                name(s) in normal order   publication   publisher

New Century. Ed. Michael Dumanis and Cate Marvin. Louisville: Sarabande,

           pages of
date   selection   medium

2006. 51-52. Print.

The abbreviation "Ed." means "Edited by," so it is the same for one or multiple editors. For an illustrated citation of a selection from an anthology, see pages 540–41.

If you use two or more works from the same anthology in your paper, provide an entry for the entire anthology (see item 14) and give a shortened entry for each selection. Cross-reference the editor(s) of the anthology and give the page number(s) on which the selection appears. Use the medium only in the entry for the complete anthology. Alphabetize the entries in the list of works cited by authors' or editors' last names, as shown here.

Two or more selections, with separate anthology entry

                         editor(s) of anthology: pages
author of selection   title of selection   last name(s) only   of selection

Brouwer, Joel. "Aesthetics." Dumanis and Marvin 51-52.

      editor(s) of anthology   title of anthology

Dumanis, Michael, and Cate Marvin, eds. *Legitimate Dangers: American Poets of the*

          city of
          publication   publisher   date   medium

New Century. Louisville: Sarabande, 2006. Print.

author of
selection · title of selection · editor(s) of anthology:
last name(s) only · pages of
selection
Keith, Sally. "Orphean Song." Dumanis and Marvin 195-96.

16. Edition other than the first   Include the number of the
edition (1st, 2nd, 3rd, and so on). If the book has a translator
or an editor in addition to the author, give the name of the
translator or editor after the edition number, using the abbreviation "Trans." for "Translated by" (see item 9) or "Ed." for
"Edited by" (see item 10).

Auletta, Ken. *The Underclass*. 2nd ed. Woodstock: Overlook, 2000. Print.

17. Multivolume work   Include the total number of volumes
before the city and publisher, using the abbreviation "vols."
If the volumes were published over several years, give the inclusive dates of publication. The abbreviation "Ed." means
"Edited by," so it is the same for one or multiple editors.

author: last
name first · title · editor's name:
in normal order · total
volumes · city of
publication · publisher
Stark, Freya. *Letters*. Ed. Lucy Moorehead. 8 vols. Salisbury: Compton,

inclusive
dates · medium
1974-82. Print.

If you cite only one of the volumes in your paper, include
the volume number before the city and publisher and give the
date of publication for that volume. After the date, give the medium of publication followed by the total number of volumes.

author: last
name first · title · editor: in
normal order · volume
cited · city of
publication · publisher · date of
volume
Stark, Freya. *Letters*. Ed. Lucy Moorehead. Vol. 5. Salisbury: Compton, 1978.

total
medium volumes
Print. 8 vols.

18. Encyclopedia or dictionary entry   List the author of the
entry (if there is one), the title of the entry, the title of the reference work, the edition number (if any), the date of the

Citation at a glance | Selection from an anthology (MLA)

To cite a selection from an anthology in MLA style, include the following elements:

1 Author of selection
2 Title of selection
3 Title and subtitle of anthology
4 Editor(s) of anthology
5 City of publication
6 Publisher
7 Date of publication
8 Page numbers of selection
9 Medium

3 ASIAN-AMERICAN LITERATURE

An Anthology

FROM COPYRIGHT PAGE

Published by NTC/Contemporary Publishing Group, Inc.
4255 West Touhy Avenue, Lincolnwood (Chicago), Illinois 60646-1975 U.S.A.
7 ©2000 NTC/Contemporary Publishing Group, Inc.

4 Shirley Geok-lin Lim
University of California, Santa Barbara

6
NTC Publishing Group
a division of NTC/Contemporary Publishing Company
Lincolnwood, Illinois USA

5 Lincolnwood, Illinois USA

FIRST PAGE OF SELECTION

GUILTY ON BOTH COUNTS **151**

GUILTY ON BOTH COUNTS **151**

2 GUILTY ON BOTH COUNTS

1 *Mitsuye Yamada*

Born in Kyushu, Japan, in 1923 and raised in Seattle, Washington, Mitsuye Yamada earned a bachelor's degree from New York University and a master's degree from the University of Chicago. She is an emeritus professor of English at Cypress College, where she taught for twenty years.

Yamada is the founder of Multi-Cultural Women Writers of Orange County, and she coedited an anthology of the organization's work entitled *Sowing Ti Leaves: Writings by Multi-Cultural Women* (1990). She and poet Nellie Wong are the focus of *Mitsuye and Nellie: Asian American Poets*, a documentary film that came out in 1981. Yamada was also a board member of Amnesty International, U.S.A., and has served on Amnesty International's Committee on International Development. The poetic pieces in Yamada's *Camp Notes and Other Poems* (1976) recount her experiences in an internment camp in Idaho during World War II.

In the following selection from *Desert Run: Poems and Stories* (1988), the American speaker, revisiting her birthplace in Japan after forty years, learns some ironic lessons about the perception of guilt and the gulf between cultures. (J.I.)

I glide in by Bullet Train
to my birthplace in Kyushu
after forty years
only the elevated tracks
that dwarf the village scene
jangle my framed memory.

8

WORKS CITED ENTRY FOR A SELECTION FROM AN ANTHOLOGY

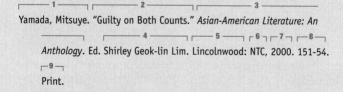

Yamada, Mitsuye. "Guilty on Both Counts." *Asian-American Literature: An Anthology.* Ed. Shirley Geok-lin Lim. Lincolnwood: NTC, 2000. 151–54. Print.

For more on citing selections from anthologies in MLA style, see pages 537–39.

edition, and the medium. Volume and page numbers are not necessary because the entries in the source are arranged alphabetically and are therefore easy to locate.

Posner, Rebecca. "Romance Languages." *The Encyclopaedia Britannica: Macropaedia*. 15th ed. 1987. Print.

"Sonata." *The American Heritage Dictionary of the English Language*. 4th ed. 2000. Print.

19. Sacred text Give the title of the edition of the sacred text (taken from the title page), italicized; the editor's or translator's name (if any); publication information; and the medium. Add the name of the version, if there is one.

The Oxford Annotated Bible with the Apocrypha. Ed. Herbert G. May and Bruce M. Metzger. New York: Oxford UP, 1965. Print. Rev. Standard Vers.

The Qur'an: Translation. Trans. Abdullah Yusuf Ali. Elmhurst: Tahrike, 2000. Print.

20. Foreword, introduction, preface, or afterword

author of foreword:
last name first   book part   book title

Bennett, Hal Zina. Foreword. *Shimmering Images: A Handy Little Guide to Writing*

            author of book: city of
            in normal order   publication   imprint-publisher   date

   Memoir. By Lisa Dale Norton. New York: Griffin-St. Martin's, 2008.

pages of
foreword   medium

   xiii-xvi. Print.

If the book part has a title, include it in quotation marks immediately after the author's name and before the label for the book part.

Ozick, Cynthia. "Portrait of the Essay as a Warm Body." Introduction. *The Best American Essays 1998*. Ed. Ozick. Boston: Houghton, 1998. xv-xxi. Print.

21. Book with a title in its title   If the book title contains a title normally italicized, neither italicize the internal title nor place it in quotation marks.

Woodson, Jon. *A Study of Joseph Heller's* Catch-22: Going Around Twice.
New York: Lang, 2001. Print.

If the title within the title is normally put in quotation marks, retain the quotation marks and italicize the entire book title.

Millás, Juan José. *"Personality Disorders" and Other Stories*. Trans. Gregory
B. Kaplan. New York: MLA, 2007. Print. MLA Texts and Trans.

22. Book in a series   After the publication information, give the medium of publication and then the series name as it appears on the title page, followed by the series number, if any.

Douglas, Dan. *Assessing Languages for Specific Purposes*. Cambridge:
Cambridge UP, 2000. Print. Cambridge Applied Linguistics Ser.

23. Republished book   After the title of the book, give the original publication date, followed by the current publication information. If the republished book contains new material, such as an introduction or afterword, include information about the new material after the original date.

Trilling, Lionel. *The Liberal Imagination*. 1950. Introd. Louis Menand.
New York: New York Review of Books, 2008. Print.

24. Publisher's imprint   If a book was published by an imprint (a division) of a publishing company, give the name of the imprint, a hyphen, and the name of the publisher.

Ackroyd, Peter. *The Fall of Troy*. New York: Talese-Doubleday, 2007. Print.

Articles in periodicals (print)

This section shows how to prepare works cited entries for articles in print magazines, journals, and newspapers. See "General guidelines" and "Listing authors" on pages 529 and 532 for how to handle basic parts of the entries. See also "Online sources" on page 548 for articles from Web sites and articles accessed through a library's database.

For articles appearing on consecutive pages, provide the range of pages (see items 25 and 26). When an article does not appear on consecutive pages, give the number of the first page followed by a plus sign: 32+. For dates requiring a month, abbreviate all but May, June, and July. For an illustrated citation of an article in a periodical, see pages 546–47.

25. Article in a journal (paginated by volume or by issue)

author: last name first   article title

Blackburn, Robin. "Economic Democracy: Meaningful, Desirable, Feasible?"

journal title | volume, issue | year | page range | medium

Daedalus 136.3 (2007): 36-45. Print.

26. Article in a monthly magazine

author: last name first   article title   magazine title   date: month(s) + year

Lanting, Frans. "Life: A Journey through Time." *Audubon* Nov.-Dec. 2006:

page range | medium

48-52. Print.

27. Article in a weekly magazine

author: last name first   article title   magazine title   date: day + month + year   page range   medium

von Drehle, David. "The Ghosts of Memphis." *Time* 7 Apr. 2008: 34-37. Print.

28. Article in a daily newspaper

Give the page range of the article. If the article does not appear on consecutive pages, use a plus sign (+) after the first page number. If the city of publication is not obvious from the title of the newspaper, include the city in brackets after the name of the newspaper.

If sections are identified by letter, include the section letter as part of the page number. If sections are numbered, include the section number between the date and the page number, using the abbreviation "sec.": 14 Sept. 2008, sec. 2: 21.

Page number with section letter

Include the section letter as part of the page number.

author: last name first	article title	newspaper title	date: day + month + year

McKenna, Phil. "It Takes Just One Village." *New York Times* 23 Sept. 2008,

name of edition	page	medium

    New England ed.: D1. Print.

Page number with section number

Include the section number immediately after the date, using
the abbreviation "sec."

author, last name first	article title	newspaper title	city of publication

Knox, David Blake. "Lord Archer, Storyteller." *Sunday Independent* [Dublin]

date: inverted	section	page medium

    14 Sept. 2008, sec. 2: 9. Print.

29. Abstract of a journal article   Include the word "Abstract"
after the title of the article.

Walker, Joyce. "Narratives in the Database: Memorializing September 11th
    Online." Abstract. *Computers and Composition* 24.2 (2007): 121. Print.

30. Article with a title in its title   Use single quotation marks
around a title or another quoted term that appears in an
article title. Italicize a title or term normally italicized.

Shen, Min. "'Quite a Moon!' The Archetypal Feminine in *Our Town*." *American
    Drama* 16.2 (2007): 1-14. Print.

31. Editorial or other unsigned article   Begin with the article
title and alphabetize the entry by title in the list of works cited.

"Getting the Message: Communicating Electronically with Doctors Can Spur
    Honesty from Young Patients." Editorial. *Columbus* [OH] *Dispatch* 19
    June 2008: 10A. Print.

32. Letter to the editor

Morris, David. "Fiercely Proud." Letter. *Progressive* Feb. 2008: 6. Print.

Citation at a glance | Article in a periodical (MLA)

To cite an article in a print periodical in MLA style, include the following elements:

1 Author of article
2 Title and subtitle of article
3 Title of periodical
4 Volume and issue number (for scholarly journal)
5 Date or year of publication
6 Page numbers of article
7 Medium

Volume 41   Issue 3   2008

The Journal of Popular Culture

Editor
GARY HOPPENSTAND
Michigan State University

Book Review Editor
PETER C. HOLLORAN
Worcester State College

Managing Editor
Kathryn Edney

Technology Director
Jeff Johnson

Editorial Assistants
Adam Capitanio
Joseph Darowski
Jennifer DeFore
Yuya Kiuchi

Editorial Consultant
Christine Birdwell

Please visit the *JPC* Editorial Office at www.msu.edu/~tjpc

Published by Blackwell Publishing, Inc.

The Journal of Popular Culture, the official journal of the Popular Culture Association, was founded in 1967 by Ray Browne.

FIRST PAGE OF ARTICLE

For the Love of Joe: The Language of
Starbucks

CONSTANCE M. RUZICH

E ASY CHAIRS, QUIET JAZZ, AND CAFFE LATTES: STARBUCKS' COFFEE SHOPS
have become America's public living and dining rooms, or as
company founder Howard Schultz describes his stores, "an extension of people's front porch" (Serwer and Bonamici). As of January
2004, there were over 7,500 Starbucks locations in 28 countries
(Serwer and Bonamici), and based on company predictions, some believe that "The number of Starbucks locations worldwide could some-
day rival the total of McDonald's' restaurants" (Bishop). This paper will
examine the ways in which Starbucks' use of language appeals to more
than our craving for caffeine. In his book *Bobos in Paradise*, David
Brooks argues that the dominant tone of American culture has been set
by America's new educated elite, or "bobos," a term meshing bohe-
mians with bourgeois (11). Brooks notes that bobos have "combined
the counter-cultural sixties and the achieving eighties into one social
ethos . . ."

turn ideas and em...
associated coffee...
and philanthropic...
crafted to appear...
as a steamed latte, and as socially conscious as the Fair Trade coffee
offered for sale in their stores.

The history of coffee production, consumption, and advertising has
less to do with love, however, than with conspiracy, colonialism, and
capitalism. The drink appears to have been brewed first in Ethiopia,
and achieved widespread popularity in the Islamic world during the

The Journal of Popular Culture, Vol. 41, No. 3, 2008
© 2008, Copyright the Authors
Journal compilation © 2008, Blackwell Publishing, Inc.

The Journal of Popular Culture, Vol. 41, No. 3, 2008
© 2008, Copyright the Authors
Journal compilation © 2008, Blackwell Publishing, Inc.

428

WORKS CITED ENTRY FOR AN ARTICLE IN A PRINT PERIODICAL

Ruzich, Constance M. "For the Love of Joe: The Language of Starbucks."

Journal of Popular Culture 41.3 (2008): 428-42. Print.

For more on citing print periodical articles in MLA style, see pages 543–48.

33. Book or film review   Name the reviewer and the title of the review, if any, followed by "Rev. of" and the title and author or director of the work reviewed. Add the publication information for the periodical in which the review appears. If the review has no author and no title, begin with "Rev. of" and alphabetize the entry by the first principal word in the title of the work reviewed.

Dodge, Chris. Rev. of *The Radical Jack London: Writings on War and*
> *Revolution*, ed. Jonah Raskni. *Utne Reader* Sept.-Oct. 2008: 35.
> Print.

Lane, Anthony. "Dream On." Rev. of *The Science of Sleep* and *Renaissance*, dir.
> Michel Gondry. *New Yorker* 25 Sept. 2006: 155-57. Print.

Online sources

MLA guidelines assume that readers can locate most online sources by entering the author, title, or other identifying information in a search engine or a database. Consequently, the *MLA Handbook* does not require a Web address (URL) in citations for online sources. Some instructors may require a URL; for an example, see the note at the end of item 34.

MLA style calls for a sponsor or a publisher for most online sources. If a source has no sponsor or publisher, use the abbreviation "N.p." (for "No publisher") in the sponsor position. If there is no date of publication or update, use "n.d." (for "no date") after the sponsor. For an article in an online journal or an article from a database, give page numbers if they are available; if they are not, use the abbreviation "n. pag." (See item 37.)

34. Entire Web site

Web site with author

| author: last name first | title of Web site | sponsor of site (personal page) | update | medium |

Peterson, Susan Lynn. *The Life of Martin Luther*. Susan Lynn Peterson, 2005. Web.

| date of access: inverted |

24 Jan. 2009.

Web site with organization (group) as author

```
         organization name:                                       sponsor:
          not abbreviated              title of Web site          abbreviated
```
American Library Association. *American Library Association*. ALA,

```
                       date of access:
       update medium    inverted
```
   2008. Web. 14 Jan. 2009.

Web site with no author

```
        title of Web site                 sponsor of site            update        medium
```
Margaret Sanger Papers Project. History Dept., New York U, 18 Oct. 2000. Web.

```
        date of access:
         inverted
```
   6 Jan. 2009.

Web site with editor
See item 10 (p. 535) for listing the name(s) of editor(s).

Halsall, Paul, ed. *Internet Modern History Sourcebook*. Fordham U, 22 Sept.

   2001. Web. 19 Jan. 2009.

Web site with no title
Use the label "Home page" or another appropriate description
in place of a title.

Yoon, Mina. Home page. Oak Ridge Natl. Laboratory, 28 Dec. 2006. Web.

   12 Jan. 2009.

NOTE: If your instructor requires a URL for Web sources, include
the URL, enclosed in angle brackets, at the end of the entry.
When a URL in a works cited entry must be divided at the end
of a line, break it after a slash. Do not insert a hyphen.

Peterson, Susan Lynn. *The Life of Martin Luther*. Susan Lynn Peterson, 2005.

   Web. 24 Jan. 2009. <http://www.susanlynnpeterson.com/index_files/

   luther.htm>.

35. Short work from a Web site Short works include articles,
poems, and other documents that are not book length or that
appear as internal pages on a Web site. For an illustrated citation of a short work from a Web site, see page 550.

Citation at a glance | Short work from a Web site (MLA)

To cite a short work from a Web site in MLA style, include the following elements:

1   Author of short work (if any)
2   Title of short work
3   Title of Web site
4   Sponsor of Web site ("N.p." if none)
5   Update date ("n.d." if none)
6   Medium
7   Date of access

INTERNAL PAGE OF WEB SITE

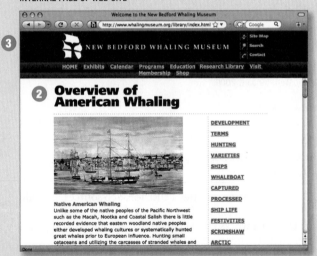

FOOTER ON HOME PAGE

the local area. It houses the most extensive collection of art, artifacts, and manuscripts pertaining to American whaling in the age of sail - late eighteenth century to the early twentieth, when sailing ships dominated merchant trade and whaling.

18 Johnny Cake Hill | New Bedford, MA | 02740-6398 | Tel. (508) 997-0046
Fax: (508) 997-0018 | Library Fax: (508) 207-1064

©Copyright 2006 Old Dartmouth Historical Society / New Bedford Whaling Museum

WORKS CITED ENTRY FOR A SHORT WORK FROM A WEB SITE

```
          2                            3
"Overview of American Whaling." New Bedford Whaling Museum. Old
                    4                        5      6
    Dartmouth Hist. Soc./New Bedford Whaling Museum, 2006. Web.
          7
    27 Oct. 2008.
```

For more on citing sources from Web sites in MLA style, see pages 548–49 and 551–58.

Short work with author

```
    author: last                          title of          no update
    name first      title of short work   Web site   sponsor   date
Shiva, Vandana. "Bioethics: A Third World Issue." NativeWeb. NativeWeb, n.d.
              date of access:
    medium    inverted
    Web. 22 Jan. 2007.
```

Short work with no author

```
    title of        title of                                  date of access:
  short work        Web site     sponsor of site  update  medium   inverted
"Sister Aimee." American Experience. PBS Online, 2 Apr. 2007. Web. 30 Oct. 2008.
```

36. Web site with an author using a pseudonym   Begin the entry with the pseudonym and add the author's or creator's real name, if known, in brackets. Follow with the information required for a Web site or a short work from a Web site (see item 34 or 35).

Grammar Girl [Mignon Fogarty]. "What Is the Plural of 'Mouse'?" *Grammar Girl:*
    Quick and Dirty Tips for Better Writing. Holtzbrinck, 16 Sept. 2008. Web.
    10 Nov. 2008.

Citation at a glance | Article from a database (MLA)

To cite an article from a database in MLA style, include the following elements:

1 Author of article
2 Title of article
3 Title of periodical
4 Volume and issue numbers (for scholarly journal)
5 Date or year of publication

6 Page numbers of article ("n. pag." if there are none)
7 Name of database
8 Medium
9 Date of access

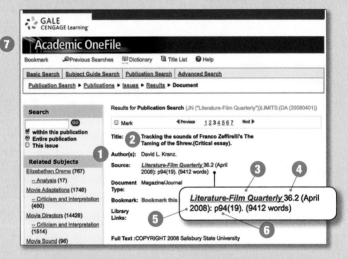

WORKS CITED ENTRY FOR AN ARTICLE FROM A DATABASE

Kranz, David L. "Tracking the Sounds of Franco Zeffirelli's *The Taming of the Shrew*." *Literature-Film Quarterly* 36.2 (2008): 94-112. *Academic OneFile*. Web. 28 Oct. 2008.

For more on citing articles from a database in MLA style, see pages 553–54.

37. Article in an online scholarly journal

author: last name first   article title

Mason, John Edwin. "'Mannenberg': Notes on the Making of an Icon and Anthem."

| | volume, | | not | date of access: |
| journal title | issue | year | paginated medium | inverted |

African Studies Quarterly 9.4 (2007): n. pag. Web. 23 Sept. 2008.

38. Article in an online magazine   Give the author; the title of the article, in quotation marks; the title of the magazine, italicized; the sponsor or publisher of the site (use "N.p." if there is none); the date of publication; the medium; and your date of access.

Burton, Robert. "The Certainty Epidemic." *Salon.com*. Salon Media Group,

29 Feb. 2008. Web. 18 Jan. 2009.

39. Article in an online newspaper   Give the author, the title of the article, in quotation marks; the title of the newspaper, italicized; the sponsor or publisher of the site (use "N.p." if there is none); the date of publication; the medium; and your date of access.

Smith, Andrew D. "Poll: More than 70% of US Workers Use Internet on the

Job." *Dallasnews.com*. Dallas Morning News, 25 Sept. 2008. Web.

29 Sept. 2008.

40. Work from a database   For a source retrieved from a library's subscription database, first list the publication information for the source (see items 25–33) and then provide information about the database. For an illustrated citation of an article from a database, see page 552.

| author of source: | title of | | volume, | | page |
| last name first | article | journal title | issue | year | numbers |

Heyen, William. "Sunlight." *American Poetry Review* 36.2 (2007): 55-56. *Expanded*

| | | date of access: |
| database name | medium | inverted |

Academic ASAP. Web. 24 Sept. 2008.

Barrera, Rebeca María. "A Case for Bilingual Education." *Scholastic Parent and*

Child Nov.-Dec. 2004: 72-73. *Academic Search Premier*. Web. 1 Feb. 2009.

Williams, Jeffrey J. "Why Today's Publishing World Is Reprising the Past."

  Chronicle of Higher Education 13 June 2008: 8+. *LexisNexis Academic*.

  Web. 29 Sept. 2008.

41. Online book-length work   Cite a book or a book-length work, such as a play or a long poem, as you would a short work from a Web site (see item 35), but italicize the title of the work.

author: last
name first · title of long poem · title of Web site · sponsor of site · update

Milton, John. *Paradise Lost: Book I*. *Poetryfoundation.org*. Poetry Foundation, 2008.

medium · date of access: inverted

  Web. 14 Dec. 2008.

Give the print publication information for the work, if available (see items 7–24), followed by the title of the Web site, the medium, and your date of access.

author: last
name first · book title

Jacobs, Harriet A. *Incidents in the Life of a Slave Girl: Written by Herself*. Ed.

editor of original book · city of publication · year · title of Web site · medium

  L. Maria Child. Boston, 1861. *Documenting the American South*. Web.

date of access: inverted

  3 Feb. 2009.

42. Part of an online book   Begin as for a part of a print book (see item 20 on p. 542). If the online book part has no page numbers, use "N. pag." following the publication information. End with the Web site on which the work is found, the medium, and your date of access.

Adams, Henry. "Diplomacy." *The Education of Henry Adams*. Boston: Houghton,

  1918. N. pag. *Bartleby.com: Great Books Online*. Web. 8 Jan. 2009.

43. Digital archives   Digital archives are online collections of documents or records—books, letters, photographs, data—that have been converted to digital form. Cite publication information for the original document, if it is available, using the models throughout section 53b. Then give the location of the document, if any, neither italicized nor in quotation marks; the name of the archive, italicized; the medium ("Web"); and your date of access.

Fiore, Mark. *Shockwaves*. 18 Oct. 2001. *September 11 Digital Archive*. Web.

    3 Apr. 2009.

Oblinger, Maggie. Letter to Charlie Thomas. 31 Mar. 1895. Nebraska State

    Hist. Soc. *Prairie Settlement: Nebraska Photographs and Family Letters,*

    1862-1912. Web. 3 Apr. 2009.

WPA Household Census for 1047 W. 50th Street, Los Angeles County. 1939. USC

    Lib. Spec. Collections. *USC Libraries Digital Archive*. Web. 12 Mar. 2009.

44. Entry in an online reference work Give the title of the entry, in quotation marks; the title of the site; the sponsor and update date (use "n.d." if there is none); the medium; and your date of access.

"Native American Church." *Britannica*. Encyclopaedia Britannica, 2008. Web.

    29 Jan. 2009.

45. Online poem Cite as you would a short work from a Web site and an online book-length work (you may need to combine elements from items 35 and 42).

Bell, Acton [Anne Brontë]. "Mementos." *Poems by Currer, Ellis, and Acton Bell*.

    London, 1846. N. pag. *A Celebration of Women Writers*. Web. 18 Sept.

    2008.

46. Entire Weblog (blog) Cite a blog as you would an entire Web site (see item 34).

Gristmill. Grist Magazine, 2008. Web. 19 Jan. 2009.

47. Entry or comment in a Weblog (blog) Cite an entry or a comment (a response to an entry) in a blog as you would a short work from a Web site (see item 35). If the comment or entry has no title, use the label "Weblog entry" or "Weblog comment." Follow with the remaining information as for an entire blog in item 46.

"Social Media: Facebook and MySpace as University Curricula." *Open
   Education*. Open Education.net, n.d. Web. 19 Sept. 2008.

Cindy. Weblog comment. *Open Education*. Open Education.net, 5 Sept. 2008.
   Web. 14 Aug. 2009.

48. Academic course or department home page Cite as a short work from a Web site (see item 35). For a course home page, begin with the name of the instructor and the title of the course or title of the page (use "Course home page" if there is no other title). For a department home page, begin with the name of the department and the label "Dept. home page."

Marrone, Carole. "355:301: College Writing and Research." *Rutgers*. Rutgers U,
   2008. Web. 19 Sept. 2008.

Comparative Media Studies. Dept. home page. *Massachusetts Institute of
   Technology*. MIT, 2006. Web. 6 Oct. 2009.

49. Online video clip Cite as you would a short work from a Web site (see item 34).

author: last   title of
name first   video title   Web site   sponsor   update
Murphy, Beth. "Tips for a Good Profile Piece." *YouTube*. YouTube, 7 Sept. 2008.

            date of access:
medium   inverted
   Web. 19 Apr. 2009.

50. Online abstract Cite as you would an abstract of a journal article (see item 29), giving whatever print information is available, followed by the medium and your date of access. If you found the abstract in an online periodical database, include the name of the database after the print publication information (see item 40).

Turner, Fred. "Romantic Automatism: Art, Technology, and Collaborative Labor
     in Cold War America." Abstract. *Journal of Visual Culture* 7.1 (2008): 5.
     Web. 25 Oct. 2008.

51. Online editorial or letter to the editor   Cite as you would
an editorial or a letter to the editor in a print publication (see
item 31 or 32), adding information for a short work from a
Web site (see item 35).

"Compromise Is Key with Religion at Work." Editorial. *StarTribune.com*. Star
     Tribune, 18 June 2008. Web. 25 June 2008.

52. Online review   Begin the entry as you would for a review
in a magazine or newspaper (see item 33). If the review is
published in print as well as online, add publication information as for an article in a periodical (see items 25–28),
the Web site on which the review appears, the medium, and
your date of access. If the review is published only on the
Web, add information as for a short work from a Web site
(see item 35). If you found the review in a database, cite as
in item 40.

Greer, W. R. "Who's the Fairest One of All?" Rev. of *Mirror, Mirror*, by Gregory
     Maguire. *Reviewsofbooks.com*. Reviewsofbooks.com, 2003. Web. 26 Oct.
     2008.

53. E-mail message   Begin with the writer's name and the
subject line. Then write "Message to" followed by the name
of the recipient. End with the date of the message and the
medium ("E-mail").

Lowe, Walter. "Review Questions." Message to the author. 15 Mar. 2009. E-mail.

54. Posting to an online discussion list   When possible, cite
archived versions of postings. If you cannot locate an archived version, keep a copy of the posting for your records.
Begin with the author's name, followed by the title or subject
line, in quotation marks (use the label "Online posting" if the

posting has no title). Then proceed as for a short work from a Web site (see item 35).

Fainton, Peter. "Re: Backlash against New Labour." *Media Lens Message
     Board*. Media Lens, 7 May 2008. Web. 2 June 2008.

55. Entry in a wiki   A wiki is an online reference that is openly edited by its users. Treat an entry in a wiki as you would a short work from a Web site (see item 35). Because wiki content is, by definition, collectively edited and can be updated frequently, do not include an author. Give the title of the entry; the name of the wiki, italicized; the sponsor or publisher of the wiki (use "N.p." if there is none); the date of the last update; the medium; and your date of access.

"Hip Hop Music." *Wikipedia*. Wikimedia Foundation, 26 Sept. 2008. Web.
     18 Mar. 2009.

"Negation in Languages." *UniLang.org*. UniLang, 25 Oct. 2004. Web.
     9 June 2009.

Audio and visual sources (including online versions)

56. Digital file   A digital file is any document or image that exists in digital form, independent of a Web site. To cite a digital file, begin with information required for the source (such as a photograph, a report, a sound recording, or a radio program), following the guidelines throughout 53b. Then for the medium, indicate the type of file: "JPEG file," "PDF file," "MP3 file," and so on.

| | | date of | |
| photographer | photograph title | composition | location of photograph |

Hine, Lewis W. *Girl in Cherryville Mill*. 1908. Prints and Photographs Div., Lib. of

| |
| medium: file type |

Cong. JPEG file.

"Scenes from a Recession." *This American Life*. Narr. Ira Glass. NPR, 30 Mar.
     2009. MP3 file.

National Institute of Mental Health. *What Rescue Workers Can Do*.

Washington: US Dept. of Health and Human Services, 2006. PDF file.

57. Podcast   If you view or listen to a podcast online, cite it as you would a short work from a Web site (see item 35). If you download the podcast and view or listen to it on a computer or portable player, cite it as a digital file (see item 56).

Podcast online

"Calculating the Demand for Charter Schools." Narr. David Guenthner. *Texas PolicyCast*. Texas Public Policy Foundation, 28 Aug. 2008. Web. 10 Jan. 2009.

Podcast downloaded as digital file

"Calculating the Demand for Charter Schools." Narr. David Guenthner. *Texas PolicyCast*. Texas Public Policy Foundation, 28 Aug. 2008. MP3 file.

58. Musical score   For both print and online versions, begin with the composer's name; the title of the work, italicized (unless it is named by form, number, and key); and the date of composition. For a print source, give the place of publication; the name of the publisher and date of publication; and the medium. For an online source, give the title of the Web site; the publisher or sponsor of the site; the date of Web publication; the medium; and your date of access.

Handel, G. F. *Messiah: An Oratorio*. N.d. *CCARH Publications: Scores and Parts*. Center for Computer Assisted Research in the Humanities, 2003. Web. 5 Jan. 2009.

59. Sound recording   Begin with the name of the person you want to emphasize: the composer, conductor ("Cond."), or performer ("Perf."). For a long work, give the title, italicized (unless it is named by form, number, and key); the names of pertinent artists (such as performers, readers, or musicians); and the orchestra and conductor, if relevant. End with the manufacturer, the date, and the medium ("CD," "Audiocassette").

Bizet, Georges. *Carmen*. Perf. Jennifer Laramore, Thomas Moser, Angela Gheorghiu, and Samuel Ramey. Bavarian State Orch. and Chorus. Cond. Giuseppe Sinopoli. Warner, 1996. CD.

For a song, put the title in quotation marks. If you include the name of the album or CD, italicize it.

Blige, Mary J. "Be without You." *The Breakthrough*. Geffen, 2005. CD.

60. Film Begin with the title, italicized. Then give the director and the lead actors ("Perf.") or narrator ("Narr."); the distributor; the year of the film's release; and the medium ("Film," "Videocassette"). If your paper emphasizes a person or category of people involved with the film, you may begin with those names and titles (see item 61).

movie title   director   major performers
Frozen River. Dir. Courtney Hunt. Perf. Melissa Leo, Charlie McDermott, and Misty

release
distributor date medium
Upham. Sony, 2008. Film.

61. DVD For a film on DVD, cite as you would a film (see item 60), giving "DVD" as the medium.

Forster, Marc, dir. *Finding Neverland*. Perf. Johnny Depp, Kate Winslet, Julie
    Christie, Radha Mitchell, and Dustin Hoffman. Miramax, 2004. DVD.

For any other work on DVD, such as an educational work or a game, cite as you would a film, giving whatever information is available about the author, director, distributor, and so on.

Across the Drafts: Students and Teachers Talk about Feedback. Harvard
    Expository Writing Program, 2005. DVD.

62. Special feature on a DVD Begin with the title of the feature, in quotation marks, and the names of any important contributors, as for films or DVDs (item 60 or 61). End with information about the DVD, as in item 61.

"Sweeney's London." Prod. Eric Young. *Sweeney Todd: The Demon Barber of
    Fleet Street*. Dir. Tim Burton. DreamWorks, 2007. DVD. Disc 2.

63. CD-ROM   Treat a CD-ROM as you would any other source, but add the medium ("CD-ROM").

"Pimpernel." *The American Heritage Dictionary of the English Language*.
    4th ed. Boston: Houghton, 2000. CD-ROM.

64. Computer software or video game   List the developer or author of the software (if any); the title, italicized; the distributor and date of publication; and the platform or medium.

Firaxis Games. *Sid Meier's Civilization Revolution*. Take-Two Interactive, 2008.
    Xbox 360.

65. Radio or television program   Begin with the title of the radio segment or television episode (if there is one), in quotation marks. Then give the title of the program or series, italicized; relevant information about the program, such as the writer ("By"), director ("Dir."), performers ("Perf."), or narrator ("Narr."); the network; the local station (if any) and location; the date of broadcast; and the medium ("Television," "Radio"). For a program you accessed online, after the information about the program give the network, the original broadcast date, the title of the Web site, the medium ("Web"), and your date of access.

"Machines of the Gods." *Ancient Discoveries*. History Channel. 14 Oct. 2008.
    Television.

"Elif Shafak: Writing under a Watchful Eye." *Fresh Air*. Narr. Terry Gross. Natl.
    Public Radio, 6 Feb. 2007. *NPR.org*. Web. 22 Feb. 2009.

66. Radio or television interview   Begin with the name of the person who was interviewed, followed by the word "Interview" and the interviewer's name, if relevant. End with information about the program as in item 65.

De Niro, Robert, Barry Levinson, and Art Linson. Interview by Charlie Rose.
    Charlie Rose. PBS. WGBH, Boston, 13 Oct. 2008. Television.

67. Live performance   For a live performance of a concert, a play, a ballet, or an opera, begin with the title of the work performed, italicized. Then give the author or composer of the work ("By"); relevant information such as the director ("Dir."), the choreographer ("Chor."), the conductor ("Cond."), or the major performers ("Perf."); the theater, ballet, or opera company, if any; the theater and location; the date of the performance; and the label "Performance."

The Brothers Size. By Tarell Alvin McCraney. Dir. Bijan Sheibani. Young Vic
    Theatre, London. 15 Oct. 2008. Performance.

Symphony no. 4 in G. By Gustav Mahler. Cond. Mark Wigglesworth. Perf.
    Juliane Banse and Boston Symphony Orch. Symphony Hall, Boston.
    17 Apr. 2009. Performance.

68. Lecture or public address   Begin with the speaker's name, followed by the title of the lecture (if any), in quotation marks; the organization sponsoring the lecture; the location; the date; and a label such as "Lecture" or "Address."

Wellbery, David E. "On a Sentence of Franz Kafka." Franke Inst. for the
    Humanities. Gleacher Center, Chicago. 1 Feb. 2006. Lecture.

69. Work of art   Cite the artist's name; the title of the artwork, italicized; the date of composition; the medium of composition (for instance, "Lithograph on paper," "Photograph," "Charcoal on paper"); and the institution and city in which the artwork is located. For artworks found online, omit the medium of composition and include the title of the Web site, the medium ("Web"), and your date of access.

Constable, John. *Dedham Vale*. 1802. Oil on canvas. Victoria and Albert
    Museum, London.

Hessing, Valjean. *Caddo Myth*. 1976. Joslyn Art Museum, Omaha. *Joslyn Art
    Museum*. Web. 19 Apr. 2009.

70. Cartoon   Give the cartoonist's name; the title of the cartoon, if it has one, in quotation marks; the label "Cartoon"

or "Comic strip"; publication information; and the medium.
To cite an online cartoon, instead of publication information
give the title of the Web site, the sponsor or publisher, the
medium, and your date of access.

Keefe, Mike. "Content of Character." Cartoon. *Denverpost.com*. Denver Post,

28 Aug. 2008. Web. 12 Dec. 2008.

71. Advertisement   Name the product or company being advertised, followed by the word "Advertisement." Give publication information for the source in which the advertisement
appears.

Truth by Calvin Klein. Advertisement. *Vogue* Dec. 2000: 95-98. Print.

Arbella Insurance. Advertisement. *Boston.com*. NY Times, n.d. Web. 3 June

2008.

72. Map or chart   Cite a map or a chart as you would a book
or a short work within a longer work. Use the word "Map" or
"Chart" following the title. Add the medium and, for an online source, the sponsor or publisher and the date of access.

Joseph, Lori, and Bob Laird. "Driving While Phoning Is Dangerous." Chart.

USA Today 16 Feb. 2001: 1A. Print.

"Serbia." Map. *Syrena Maps*. Syrena, 2 Feb. 2001. Web. 17 Mar. 2009.

Other sources (including online versions)

This section includes a variety of sources not covered elsewhere. For online sources, consult the appropriate model in
this section and also see items 34–55.

73. Government document   Treat the government agency as
the author, giving the name of the government followed by
the name of the department and the agency, if any. For print
sources, add the medium at the end of the entry. For online
sources, follow the model for an entire Web site (item 34) or a
short work from a Web site (item 35).

government   department   agency

United States. Dept. of the Interior. Office of Inspector General. "Excessive

document title

Indulgences: Personal Use of the Internet at the Department of the Interior."

Web site title   publisher/sponsor   publication date   medium

Office of Inspector General. Dept. of the Interior, Sept. 1999. Web.

date of access: inverted

20 May 2009.

Canada. Minister of Indian Affairs and Northern Dev. *Gathering Strength:*
    Canada's Aboriginal Action Plan. Ottawa: Minister of Public Works and
    Govt. Services Can., 2000. Print.

74. Historical document   To cite a historical document, such
as the US Constitution or the Canadian Charter of Rights and
Freedoms, begin with the document author, if it has one, and
then give the document title, neither italicized nor in quotation marks, and the document date. For a print version, continue as for a selection in an anthology (see item 15) or for a
book (with the title not italicized). For an online version, cite
as a short work from a Web site (see item 35).

Jefferson, Thomas. First Inaugural Address. 1801. *The American Reader*.
    Ed. Diane Ravitch. New York: Harper, 1990. 42-44. Print.

The Virginia Declaration of Rights. 1776. *A Chronology of US*
    Historical Documents. U of Oklahoma Coll. of Law, 2008. Web.
    23 Feb. 2009.

75. Legal source

Legislative act (law)
Begin with the name of the act, neither italicized nor in quotation marks. Then provide the act's Public Law number; its
Statutes at Large volume and page numbers; its date of enact-
ment; and the medium of publication.

Electronic Freedom of Information Act Amendments of 1996. Pub. L.

104-231. 110 Stat. 3048. 2 Oct. 1996. Print.

Court case

Name the first plaintiff and the first defendant. Then give the
volume, name, and page number of the law report; the court
name; the year of the decision; and publication information.
Do not italicize the name of the case. (In the text of the paper,
the name of the case is italicized; see item 19 on p. 526.)

Utah v. Evans. 536 US 452. Supreme Court of the US. 2002. *Supreme Court
Collection*. Legal Information Inst., Cornell U Law School, n.d. Web.
30 Apr. 2008.

76. Pamphlet or brochure   Cite as you would a book (see items
7–24).

Commonwealth of Massachusetts. Dept. of Jury Commissioner. *A Few Facts
about Jury Duty*. Boston: Commonwealth of Massachusetts, 2004.
Print.

77. Unpublished dissertation   Begin with the author's name,
followed by the dissertation title in quotation marks; the abbreviation "Diss."; the name of the institution; the year the dissertation was accepted; and the medium of the dissertation.

Jackson, Shelley. "Writing Whiteness: Contemporary Southern Literature in
Black and White." Diss. U of Maryland, 2000. Print.

78. Published dissertation   For dissertations that have been
published in book form, italicize the title. After the title and
before the book's publication information, give the abbreviation "Diss.," the name of the institution, and the year the dissertation was accepted. Add the medium of publication at the
end.

Damberg, Cheryl L. *Healthcare Reform: Distributional Consequences of an
Employer Mandate for Workers in Small Firms*. Diss. Rand Graduate
School, 1995. Santa Monica: Rand, 1996. Print.

79. Abstract of a dissertation   Cite an abstract as you would an unpublished dissertation. After the dissertation date, give the abbreviation *DA* or *DAI* (for *Dissertation Abstracts* or *Dissertation Abstracts International*), followed by the volume and issue numbers; the year of publication; inclusive page numbers or, if the abstract is not numbered, the item number; and the medium of publication. For an abstract accessed in an online database, give the item number in place of the page number, followed by the name of the database, the medium, and your date of access.

Chen, Shu-Ling. "Mothers and Daughters in Morrison, Tan, Marshall, and
     Kincaid." Diss. U of Washington, 2000. *DAI* 61.6 (2000): ATT9975963.
     ProQuest Dissertations and Theses. Web. 22 Feb. 2009.

80. Published proceedings of a conference   Cite as you would a book, adding the name, date, and location of the conference after the title.

Urgo, Joseph R., and Ann J. Abadie, eds. *Faulkner and Material Culture*.
     Proc. of Faulkner and Yoknapatawpha Conf., 25-29 July 2004, U of
     Mississippi. Jackson: UP of Mississippi, 2007. Print.

81. Paper in conference proceedings   Cite as you would a selection in an anthology (see item 15), giving information about the conference after the title and editors of the conference proceedings (see item 80).

Henninger, Katherine R. "Faulkner, Photography, and a Regional Ethics of
     Form." *Faulkner and Material Culture*. Ed. Joseph R. Urgo and Ann
     J. Abadie. Proc. of Faulkner and Yoknapatawpha Conf., 25-29 July
     2004, U of Mississippi. Jackson: UP of Mississippi, 2007. 121-38.
     Print.

82. Published interview   Name the person interviewed, followed by the title of the interview (if there is one). If the interview does not have a title, include the word "Interview" after the interviewee's name. Give publication information for the work in which the interview was published.

Armstrong, Lance. "Lance in France." *Sports Illustrated* 28 June 2004: 46+.
Print.

If the name of the interviewer is relevant, include it after the name of the interviewee.

Prince. Interview by Bilge Ebiri. *Yahoo! Internet Life* 7.6 (2001): 82-85.
Print.

83. Personal interview   To cite an interview that you conducted, begin with the name of the person interviewed. Then write "Personal interview" or "Telephone interview," followed by the date of the interview.

Akufo, Dautey. Personal interview. 11 Apr. 2009.

84. Personal letter   To cite a letter that you received, begin with the writer's name and add the phrase "Letter to the author," followed by the date. Add the medium ("MS" for "manuscript," or a handwritten letter; "TS" for "typescript," or a typed letter).

Primak, Shoshana. Letter to the author. 6 May 2009. TS.

85. Published letter   Begin with the writer of the letter, the words "Letter to" and the recipient, and the date of the letter (use "N.d." if the letter is undated). Then add the title of the collection and proceed as for a selection in an anthology (see item 15).

Wharton, Edith. Letter to Henry James. 28 Feb. 1915. *Henry James and Edith
Wharton: Letters, 1900-1915*. Ed. Lyall H. Powers. New York: Scribner's,
1990. 323-26. Print.

86. Manuscript   Give the author, a title or a description of the manuscript, and the date of composition, followed by the abbreviation "MS" for "manuscript" (handwritten) or "TS" for "typescript." Add the name and location of the institution housing the material. For a manuscript found online, give the preceding information but omit "MS" or "TS." Then list the title of the Web site, the medium ("Web"), and your date of access.

Arendt, Hannah. *Between Past and Present*. N.d. 1st draft. Hannah Arendt
    Papers. MS Div., Lib. of Cong. *Manuscript Division, Library of Congress*.
    Web. 24 Apr. 2009.

hackerhandbooks.com/bedhandbook > **Research exercises** > **MLA** > **E-ex 53–4 to 53–8**

53c MLA information notes (optional)

Researchers who use the MLA system of parenthetical documentation may also use information notes for one of two purposes:

1. to provide additional material that is important but might interrupt the flow of the paper
2. to refer to several sources or to provide comments on sources

Information notes may be either footnotes or endnotes. Footnotes appear at the foot of the page; endnotes appear on a separate page at the end of the paper, just before the list of works cited. For either style, the notes are numbered consecutively throughout the paper. The text of the paper contains a raised arabic numeral that corresponds to the number of the note.

TEXT

In the past several years, employees have filed a number of lawsuits against employers because of online monitoring practices.[1]

NOTE

    1. For a discussion of federal law applicable to electronic surveillance in the workplace, see Kesan 293.

54   MLA manuscript format; student research process and sample paper

The following guidelines are consistent with advice given in the *MLA Handbook for Writers of Research Papers*, 7th ed. (New York: MLA, 2009), and with typical requirements for student papers. For a sample MLA paper, see pages 583–88.

54a MLA manuscript format

Formatting the paper

Papers written in MLA style should be formatted as follows.

Materials and font   Use good-quality 8½″ × 11″ white paper. Avoid a font that is unusual or hard to read.

Title and identification   MLA does not require a title page. On the first page of your paper, place your name, your instructor's name, the course title, and the date on separate lines against the left margin. Then center your title. (See p. 583 for a sample first page.)

    If your instructor requires a title page, ask for formatting guidelines. A format similar to the one on page 674 may be acceptable.

Pagination   Put the page number preceded by your last name in the upper right corner of each page, one-half inch below the top edge. Use arabic numerals (1, 2, 3, and so on).

Margins, line spacing, and paragraph indents Leave margins of one inch on all sides of the page. Left-align the text.

Double-space throughout the paper. Do not add extra space above or below the title of the paper or between paragraphs.

Indent the first line of each paragraph one-half inch from the left margin.

Capitalization and italics In titles of works, capitalize all words except articles (*a*, *an*, *the*), prepositions (*to*, *from*, *between*, and so on), coordinating conjunctions (*and*, *but*, *or*, *nor*, *for*, *so*, *yet*), and the *to* in infinitives—unless they are the first or last word of the title or subtitle. Follow these guidelines in your paper even if the title appears in all capital or all lowercase letters in the source.

In the text of an MLA paper, when a complete sentence follows a colon, lowercase the first word following the colon unless the sentence is a well-known expression or principle.

Italicize the titles of books and other long works, such as Web sites. Use quotation marks around the titles of periodical articles, short stories, poems, and other short works. (Some instructors may prefer underlining for the titles of long works. Be consistent throughout your paper.)

Long quotations When a quotation is longer than four typed lines of prose or three lines of verse, set it off from the text by indenting the entire quotation one inch from the left margin. Double-space the indented quotation, and do not add extra space above or below it.

Quotation marks are not needed when a quotation has been set off from the text by indenting. See page 584 for an example.

Web addresses When a Web address (URL) mentioned in the text of your paper must be divided at the end of a line, break it only after a slash and do not insert a hyphen. For MLA rules on dividing Web addresses in your list of works cited, see page 572.

Headings MLA neither encourages nor discourages the use of headings and provides no guidelines for their use. If you would like to insert headings in a long essay or research paper, check first with your instructor.

Visuals MLA classifies visuals as tables and figures (figures include graphs, charts, maps, photographs, and drawings). Label each table with an arabic numeral ("Table 1," "Table 2," and so on) and provide a clear caption that identifies the subject. Capitalize the caption as you would a title (see 45c); do not italicize the label and caption or place them in quotation marks. The label and caption should appear on separate lines above the table, flush with the left margin.

For a table that you have borrowed or adapted, give the source below the table in a note like the following:

Source: David N. Greenfield and Richard A. Davis; "Lost in Cyberspace: The Web @ Work"; *CyberPsychology and Behavior* 5.4 (2002): 349; print.

For each figure, place the figure number (using the abbreviation "Fig.") and a caption below the figure, flush left. Capitalize the caption as you would a sentence; include source information following the caption. (When referring to the figure in your paper, use the abbreviation "fig." in parenthetical citations; otherwise spell out the word.) See page 586 for an example of a figure in a paper.

Place visuals in the text, as close as possible to the sentences that relate to them, unless your instructor prefers them in an appendix.

Preparing the list of works cited

Begin the list of works cited on a new page at the end of the paper. Center the title Works Cited about one inch from the top of the page. Double-space throughout. See page 588 for a sample list of works cited.

Alphabetizing the list Alphabetize the list by the last names of the authors (or editors); if a work has no author or editor, alphabetize by the first word of the title other than *A*, *An*, or *The*.

If your list includes two or more works by the same author, use the author's name for the first entry only. For subsequent entries, use three hyphens followed by a period. List the titles in alphabetical order. (See item 6 on page 534.)

Indenting Do not indent the first line of each works cited entry, but indent any additional lines one-half inch. This technique highlights the names of the authors, making it easy for readers to scan the alphabetized list. See page 588.

Web addresses If you need to include a Web address (URL) in a works cited entry, do not insert a hyphen when dividing it at the end of a line. Break the URL only after a slash. Insert angle brackets around the URL. (See the note following item 34 on p. 549.) If your word processing program automatically turns Web addresses into links (by underlining them and changing the color), turn off this feature.

54b Highlights of one student's research process

The following pages describe key steps in student writer Anna Orlov's research process, from selecting a research question to documenting sources. At each step, cross-references in the margins point to more discussion and examples elsewhere in the handbook. Samples from Orlov's process illustrate strategies and skills she used to create an accurate and effective essay. See pages 583–88 for Orlov's final paper.

Making the most of your handbook
Highlights of one student's research process (MLA style)

Anna Orlov, a student in a composition class, was assigned a research essay related to technology and the American workplace. The assignment called for her to use a variety of print and electronic sources and to follow MLA style. Orlov immediately thought of her summer internship at an insurance company and her surprise at the strict employee Internet use policy in place there. As she thought about how to turn her experience into a research project, she developed some questions and strategies to guide her research and writing.

"How do I begin a research paper?"

Before getting started, Orlov worked with a writing tutor to break her research plan into several stages. (Section numbers in blue refer to relevant discussions throughout the book.)

- Ask worthwhile questions about my topic.   1b, 46a
- Talk with a reference librarian about useful types of sources and where to find them.   46b
- Consider how each source can contribute to my paper.   47a
- Decide which search results are worth a closer look.   47b
- Evaluate the sources.   47d, 47e
- Take notes and keep track of the sources.   48
- Write a working thesis.   1c, 50a
- Write a draft and integrate sources.   1e–1g, 52, 53a
- Document sources.   49, 53b

Orlov began by jotting down the research question she wanted to investigate: *Is Internet surveillance in the workplace fair or unfair to employees?* She thought the practice might be unfair but knew that she needed to consider all sides of the issue. Her instructor had explained that sources uncovered in the research process would both support and challenge her ideas and ultimately help shape the paper. Orlov knew she would have to be

1b and 46a: Posing questions for a research paper

open-minded and flexible and revisit her main ideas as she examined the information and arguments in her sources.

"What sources do I need, and where should I look for them?"

47a: Roles sources can play in a paper

Orlov planned to consider a variety of sources to help her focus her argument. Some sources might provide background information and context; others might provide evidence to help shape and support her developing ideas; still others might offer counterevidence and alternative interpretations that she would address when she built her argument. Orlov worked with a reference librarian to develop a search strategy.

Finding articles in journals, magazines, and newspapers with the library's online databases. Because her topic was current, Orlov wanted to search for up-to-date information. She turned to her library's subscription databases for trustworthy, scholarly writing. There she hoped to find recent articles with concrete examples of workplace Internet surveillance.

46b: Working with reference librarians

Searching the library's book catalog. For reliable sources covering legal, business, and labor issues, Orlov looked for recently published books in the library catalog. Books could offer in-depth context, including the history of online monitoring and the laws governing workplace surveillance. Orlov noticed that one book on the topic had the subject heading "electronic monitoring in the workplace." Using that heading as a search term, she found a more focused list of books. One book that provided a solid overview helped her identify issues and terms for further searches in databases and on the Web. She also found references to other sources that looked promising.

46c–46e: Searching databases, library catalogs, and the Web

Locating relevant sites, online articles, and government publications on the Web. Orlov decided to search for online articles and relevant Web sites as well, particularly those that might specialize in digital issues. She hoped to find explanations of the software used by employers and opinions held by those who use the Internet and e-mail in the workplace, including supervisors, employers, and employees who might disagree with her.

"What search terms should I use?"

Orlov thought that searches on her controversial topic might generate too many results if she started with an Internet search engine like *Google*. To save time, she asked a librarian to help her conduct a narrower search with her library's general periodical database. She could count on the database for fewer, more reliable results than an Internet search could provide.

Anna's search terms	Date restrictions
employee	Past four years
internet use	**Number of results**
surveillance	20

46c and p. 449: Refining keyword searches, selecting search terms

"How do I select sources from my search results?"

Orlov used several criteria to decide which results of her general database search were worth a closer look. Would a source

- be relevant to her topic?
- provide authoritative support?
- provide background information?
- offer a range of views or evidence that Orlov could address when forming her argument?

47: Evaluating sources

DATABASE SCREEN: SEARCH RESULTS

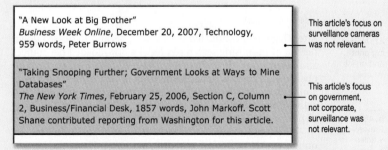

"A New Look at Big Brother"
Business Week Online, December 20, 2007, Technology, 959 words, Peter Burrows

This article's focus on surveillance cameras was not relevant.

"Taking Snooping Further; Government Looks at Ways to Mine Databases"
The New York Times, February 25, 2006, Section C, Column 2, Business/Financial Desk, 1857 words, John Markoff. Scott Shane contributed reporting from Washington for this article.

This article's focus on government, not corporate, surveillance was not relevant.

Orlov would want to respond to this survey if she argued that Internet surveillance is unfair.

"Wasting Away on the Web; More Employers Are Taking Workers' Web Use Seriously"
eWeek, August 8, 2005, 692 words, Chris Gonsalves

The *Wall Street Journal* is widely respected and might offer background for Orlov's topic.

"Snooping E-Mail by Software Is Now a Workplace Norm"
The Wall Street Journal Online, March 9, 2005, Pui-Wing Tam et al.

Orlov wondered if the *Progressive* had a political slant. She made a note to check for bias.

"Snooping Bosses; Electronic Surveillance Program"
The Progressive, February 1, 2006: 14, Barbara Ehrenreich.

Reviewed by legal experts, a law review article could provide legal context and lend credibility.

"Cyber-Working or Cyber-Shirking? A First Principles Examination of Electronic Privacy in the Workplace"
Florida Law Review 54.2 (2002): 289-332, Jay P. Kesan

"Should I consider using a blog?"

46e: Using blogs

Orlov was intrigued by a blog called *Today's Workplace*, which was critical of workplace surveillance. She remembered her instructor's caution about using blogs, since their credibility is difficult to establish. But her librarian had suggested that blogs can provide useful links to studies and to articles in reputable magazines and newspapers as well as compelling arguments of their own. Orlov knew that if the blog looked like a helpful source, she could check with her instructor before using it.

"How do I evaluate my sources?"

47: Assessing print and online sources

After Orlov had conducted several searches and narrowed down her list of promising search results, she downloaded her sources and began evaluating them. As she read, she tried to keep an open mind, knowing that some sources might make her reexamine her own views. Orlov wanted to see what evidence and claims she would need to address to strengthen her argument in progress.

p. 467: Previewing articles

She looked carefully at an article she found in *eWeek*, an online weekly business computing magazine. It was the kind of

ORLOV'S NOTES ON PASSAGES FROM AN ARTICLE

Wasting Away on the Web
Opinion: More employers are taking workers' Web use seriously.

Writer is sympathetic to employers?

By Chris Gonsalves
2005-08-08

SECTION: OPINION; Pg. 26

The issue of IT surveillance was driven home last month when
Salary.com and America Online released a survey of 10,000 American
workers, many of whom admitted that goofing off on the Internet was
their primary method of frittering away the workday. In a sign of the
times, it beat out socializing with co-workers, 45 percent to 23 percent.

Consider statistics. Is using work time for personal Internet use so bad?

While bosses can easily detect and interrupt water-cooler chatter, the
employee who is shopping at **Lands'** End or IMing with fellow fantasy
baseball managers may actually appear to be working. Thwarting the
activity is a technology challenge, and it's one that more and more
enterprises are taking seriously, despite resistance from privacy
advocates and some employees themselves.

Does the AMA side with employers? Survey results—good for background and counter-argument.

According to the American Management Association, 78 percent of large
U.S. employers are regularly checking workers' e-mail messages,
Internet use, computer files and phone calls. Nearly half of such
employers store employee e-mail messages for review. The AMA also
found that 65 percent of enterprises had disciplined employees for
misuse of e-mail or the Internet at work, and 27 percent had actually
fired someone over such offenses.

According to a recent poll of workers in technology-related fields
published by the executive recruiting company FPC, 61 percent said
they felt their bosses had the right to cyber-spy on them, but only with
consent. Just 28 percent felt IT had the right to monitor their activity
without consent, and only 1 percent said an employer never has the
right to monitor Internet use.

Employees want employers to be up-front about monitoring.

"It's not surprising that companies want to assure that their employees'
time is predominantly spent on work-related computer usage," said FPC
President Ron Herzog. "The majority of employees . . . would like to be
informed, so it is always in the company's best interest to have an
Internet usage policy clearly outlining the company's expectations,
which all employees sign upon hiring."

When is workplace surveillance unfair and when not?

As the stakes grow beyond a few wasted man-hours and some
misappropriated bandwidth, it grows increasingly important for IT to let
everyone in the company know they might be watched.

An extreme case. Does it justify Big Brother in the workplace?

Nowhere was that more evident than at the storied New York printing
company Bowne & Co. In June, Robert Johnson, the high-profile CEO of
Bowne and the former publisher of Newsday, was arrested and charged
with downloading child pornography to company PCs and laptops,
according to published reports. The case, which reportedly involved IT
tipping off Johnson to the investigation and ultimately resulted in the
dismissal of Bowne's CIO, illustrates the need for diligence in keeping
tabs on company computer use right up to the highest levels.

*Executive Editor/News Chris Gonsalves can be contacted at
chris_gonsalves@ziffdavis.com.*
LOAD-DATE: August 8, 2005
LANGUAGE: English

up-to-date, specialized publication that Orlov wanted to check for in-depth background information.

48a–48c:
Managing
your
information

So that she would remember her thoughts about the author's text while drafting her argument, she made notes in the margins as she read. Taking good notes would help her to begin forming her own lines of argument and avoid plagiarism.

"How do I integrate my sources into my paper?"

1c and 50a:
Writing a
working
thesis

1d–1g:
Planning and
drafting

After reading and evaluating a number of sources, Orlov wrote down her working thesis: *Though companies may have legitimate reasons to monitor employees' Internet usage, electronic surveillance is more unfair than beneficial to employees since it threatens their privacy.* She then sketched an informal plan to organize her ideas and began writing a rough draft. As she wrote and revised, she tried to integrate sources from her research that she had found useful.

For example, Orlov had selected a book on electronic surveillance in the workplace, written by Frederick Lane III. Because the American Management Association was the publisher, Orlov thought the book might be biased in favor of management's use of electronic surveillance. But by skimming the introduction, she saw that the author took the side of employees.

pp. 467–68:
Previewing
books

Orlov looked through the table of contents and selected a few chapters that seemed relevant to her working thesis. She read the chapters for ideas and information that she could paraphrase, summarize, or quote to provide background, support her argument, and help her counter the kind of pro-surveillance position that Chris Gonsalves takes in his *eWeek* article.

Summarizing a source

48c and 52b:
Summariz-
ing and
paraphrasing

Orlov turned to Lane's text for an authoritative explanation of how surveillance software typically works. Some passages contained more details than she could use, so she decided to summarize what she needed from the source.

ORIGINAL SOURCE PASSAGE (LANE, *THE NAKED EMPLOYEE*, 128-29)

> relay chat, or instant messenger session that takes place on the computer.
>
> *Investigator* could be monitoring activity on your office computer right now, but chances are, you'd never know if it's running or not. Eaton designed the program to be hidden in plain sight: An icon may appear in the system tray, but the various modules that make the program operate periodically change their name to make them more difficult to find. Similarly, the files that are used to hold the data that *Investigator* collects are given arbitrary names and dates so that they can't be easily located.
>
> Even if you know that *Investigator* is running on your office computer system, you may not realize the extent to which it is actively reporting on your activities. *Investigator* can be configured to surreptitiously send its collected data by e-mail to your boss on a regular basis or wait until it discovers certain preset keywords ("boss," "pornography," "kill," or the name of an unreleased product).

Concrete example of monitoring software. Too much detail. Summarize?

Use key points about what software tells supervisors.

FIRST ATTEMPT AT SUMMARY

These programs record on-screen activity in the computer in hidden directories that can later be accessed or uploaded by supervisors; the programs can even scan for keywords tailored to individual companies and have employees receive warning e-mails from their bosses (128-29).

Orlov condenses the original source passage in her own words.

This summary misrepresents the source.

A signal phrase credits the author with the explanation.

REVISED SUMMARY

As Lane explains, these programs record on-screen activity in the computer in hidden directories that can later be accessed or uploaded by supervisors; the programs can even scan for keywords tailored to individual companies (128-29).

To avoid misrepresenting the source, Orlov removes the comment about e-mail warnings.

The page number and signal phrase show the boundaries of the source material.

Paraphrasing a source

48c and 51b:
Avoiding
plagiarism
when taking
notes and
paraphrasing

Orlov had photocopied the following passage from Lane's book because it contained broader claims about electronic surveillance in the workplace. To keep most of her paper in her own voice, she tried to paraphrase important ideas. She used quotations only when integrating especially effective language from Lane's writing.

ORIGINAL SOURCE PASSAGE (LANE, *THE NAKED EMPLOYEE*, 3-4)

*Advanced
technology
= increased
surveillance.*

*Good
quotation,
but too much?
Paraphrase
this point and
quote last
sentence?*

> particularly as an employee, our cloak is at its thinnest and most revealing.
>
> As we'll see in this chapter, there are a number of reasons—some of them quite compelling—for surveillance of employees. A major problem, however, is that technology makes it possible for employers to gather enormous amounts of data about employees, often far beyond what is necessary to satisfy safety or productivity concerns. And the trends that drive technology—faster, smaller, cheaper—make it possible for larger and larger numbers of employers to gather ever-greater amounts of personal data.
>
> To date, the nation's legislatures and courts have made occasional efforts to reweave some threads of the privacy

Signal phrase shows where
Lane's idea begins.

ORLOV'S PARAPHRASE

Orlov uses her
own words,
avoiding Lane's
terms, phrasing,
and structure.

Lane notes that employers can use Internet surveillance technology to collect significantly more information from workers than they need (3-4).

The citation shows where to find this
information in Lane's book.

Selecting and integrating a quotation

52: Integrat-
ing sources

In the same photocopied passage, Orlov noted phrases that were striking and worth quoting.

ORIGINAL SOURCE PASSAGE (LANE, *THE NAKED EMPLOYEE*, 3-4)

particularly as an employee, our cloak is at its thinnest and most revealing.

As we'll see in this chapter, there are a number of reasons — some of them quite compelling — for surveillance of employees. A major problem, however, is that technology makes it possible for employers to gather enormous amounts of data about employees, often far beyond what is necessary to satisfy safety or productivity concerns. And the trends that drive technology — faster, smaller, cheaper — make it possible for larger and larger numbers of employers to gather ever-greater amounts of personal data.

> Surveillance can go too far. "Faster, smaller, cheaper" — strong, surprising language for invasion of employee privacy.

ORLOV'S INTEGRATED QUOTATION

While surveillance of employees is not a new phenomenon, electronic surveillance allows employers to monitor workers with unprecedented efficiency. In his book *The Naked Employee*, Frederick Lane describes offline ways in which employers have been permitted to intrude on employees' privacy for decades, such as drug testing, background checks, psychological exams, lie detector tests, and in-store video surveillance. The difference, Lane argues, between these old methods of data gathering and electronic surveillance involves quantity. He notes that employers can use this technology to collect significantly more information from workers than they need. Lane also contends that "the trends that drive technology — faster, smaller, cheaper — make it possible for larger and larger numbers of employers to gather ever-greater amounts of personal data" (3-4).

- The signal phrase shows that the idea that follows is not Orlov's.
- Orlov uses the source to provide background information.
- Orlov's summary points out a key contrast in Lane's argument.
- Lane's striking and succinct language is worth quoting.

The citation shows where this passage can be found in the source.

Orlov was careful not to let her sources overwhelm her writing. To keep the emphasis on her ideas, she used her own analyses to shape the conversation among the sources she summarized, paraphrased, and quoted, creating an effective synthesis.

52c: Synthesizing and placing sources in conversation

"How do I document my sources?"

Throughout her research process, Orlov took careful notes about publication information and page numbers for source material she planned to use in her paper. Because she kept good records, she didn't need to hunt down information as she cited her sources. Managing her information also helped her avoid unintentional plagiarism.

48b: Keeping track of source materials

When it came time for her to document her sources in the paper, she followed the MLA (Modern Language Association) system. In addition to using in-text parenthetical citations, Orlov prepared an alphabetized list of works cited at the end of her paper. Entries in the works cited list gave publication information for the sources Orlov used in her paper and cited with page numbers in parentheses.

ENTRY IN WORKS CITED LIST

49 and 53a–53b: Documenting sources in MLA style

Lane, Frederick S., III. *The Naked Employee: How Technology Is Compromising Workplace Privacy*. New York: Amer. Management Assn., 2003. Print.

1 Author
2 Title and subtitle
3 City of publication
4 Publisher
5 Date of publication
6 Medium

54c Sample MLA research paper

On the following pages is a research paper on the topic of electronic surveillance in the workplace, written by Anna Orlov, a student in a composition class. Orlov's paper is documented with in-text citations and a list of works cited in MLA style. Annotations in the margins of the paper draw your attention to Orlov's use of MLA style and her effective writing. For highlights of Anna Orlov's research process, see pages 573–82.

hackerhandbooks.com/bedhandbook > Model papers
> MLA papers: Orlov; Daly; Levi
> MLA annotated bibliography: Orlov

Orlov 1

Anna Orlov

Professor Willis

English 101

17 March 2009

Online Monitoring:

A Threat to Employee Privacy in the Wired Workplace

As the Internet has become an integral tool of businesses,
company policies on Internet usage have become as common as
policies regarding vacation days or sexual harassment. A 2005 study by
the American Management Association and ePolicy Institute found that
76% of companies monitor employees' use of the Web, and the number
of companies that block employees' access to certain Web sites has
increased 27% since 2001 (1). Unlike other company rules, however,
Internet usage policies often include language authorizing companies
to secretly monitor their employees, a practice that raises questions
about rights in the workplace. Although companies often have
legitimate concerns that lead them to monitor employees' Internet
usage—from expensive security breaches to reduced productivity—the
benefits of electronic surveillance are outweighed by its costs to
employees' privacy and autonomy.

While surveillance of employees is not a new phenomenon,
electronic surveillance allows employers to monitor workers with
unprecedented efficiency. In his book *The Naked Employee*, Frederick
Lane describes offline ways in which employers have been permitted
to intrude on employees' privacy for decades, such as drug testing,
background checks, psychological exams, lie detector tests, and in-store
video surveillance. The difference, Lane argues, between these old
methods of data gathering and electronic surveillance involves quantity:

Title is centered.

*Opening sentences
provide background
for thesis.*

*Thesis asserts Orlov's
main point.*

*Summary and
long quotation are
introduced with a
signal phrase naming
the author.*

Marginal annotations indicate MLA-style formatting and effective writing.

Orlov 2

Technology makes it possible for employers to gather

enormous amounts of data about employees, often far

beyond what is necessary to satisfy safety or productivity

concerns. And the trends that drive technology—faster,

smaller, cheaper—make it possible for larger and larger

numbers of employers to gather ever-greater amounts of

personal data. (3-4)

Long quotation is set off from the text; quotation marks are omitted.

Page number is given in parentheses after the final period.

In an age when employers can collect data whenever employees use
their computers—when they send e-mail, surf the Web, or even arrive
at or depart from their workstations—the challenge for both employers
and employees is to determine how much is too much.

Clear topic sentences, like this one, are used throughout the paper.

Another key difference between traditional surveillance and
electronic surveillance is that employers can monitor workers' computer
use secretly. One popular monitoring method is keystroke logging, which is
done by means of an undetectable program on employees' computers. The
Web site of a vendor for Spector Pro, a popular keystroke logging program,
explains that the software can be installed to operate in "Stealth" mode
so that it "does not show up as an icon, does not appear in the Windows
system tray, . . . [and] cannot be uninstalled without the Spector Pro
password which YOU specify" ("Automatically"). As Lane explains, these
programs record every key entered into the computer in hidden directories
that can later be accessed or uploaded by supervisors; the programs can
even scan for keywords tailored to individual companies (128-29).

Source with an unknown author is cited by a shortened title.

Some experts have argued that a range of legitimate concerns
justifies employer monitoring of employee Internet usage. As *PC World*
columnist Daniel Tynan points out, companies that don't monitor
network traffic can be penalized for their ignorance: "Employees could
accidentally (or deliberately) spill confidential information . . . or allow
worms to spread throughout a corporate network." The ePolicy
Institute, an organization that advises companies about reducing risks

Orlov anticipates objections and provides sources for opposing views.

Orlov 3

from technology, reported that breaches in computer security cost institutions $100 million in 1999 alone (Flynn). Companies also are held legally accountable for many of the transactions conducted on their networks and with their technology. Legal scholar Jay Kesan points out that the law holds employers liable for employees' actions such as violations of copyright laws, the distribution of offensive or graphic sexual material, and illegal disclosure of confidential information (312).

These kinds of concerns should give employers, in certain instances, the right to monitor employee behavior. But employers rushing to adopt surveillance programs might not be adequately weighing the effect such programs can have on employee morale. Employers must consider the possibility that employees will perceive surveillance as a breach of trust that can make them feel like disobedient children, not responsible adults who wish to perform their jobs professionally and autonomously.

Yet determining how much autonomy workers should be given is complicated by the ambiguous nature of productivity in the wired workplace. On the one hand, computers and Internet access give employees powerful tools to carry out their jobs; on the other hand, the same technology offers constant temptations to avoid work. As a 2005 study by *Salary.com* and *America Online* indicates, the Internet ranked as the top choice among employees for ways of wasting time on the job; it beat talking with co-workers—the second most popular method—by a margin of nearly two to one (Frauenheim). Chris Gonsalves, an editor for *eWeek.com*, argues that the technology has changed the terms between employers and employees: "While bosses can easily detect and interrupt water-cooler chatter," he writes, "the employee who is shopping at Lands' End or IMing with fellow fantasy baseball managers may actually appear to be working." The gap

Transition helps readers move from one paragraph to the next.

Orlov treats both sides fairly; she provides a transition to her own argument.

No page number is available for this Web source.

Orlov 4

Illustration has figure number, caption, and source information.

Fig. 1. This "Dilbert" comic strip suggests that personal Internet usage is widespread in the workplace (Adams 106).

between behaviors that are observable to managers and the employee's actual activities when sitting behind a computer has created additional motivations for employers to invest in surveillance programs. "Dilbert," a popular cartoon that spoofs office culture, aptly captures how rampant recreational Internet use has become in the workplace (see fig. 1).

Orlov counters opposing views and provides support for her argument.

But monitoring online activities can have the unintended effect of making employees resentful. As many workers would be quick to point out, Web surfing and other personal uses of the Internet can provide needed outlets in the stressful work environment; many scholars have argued that limiting and policing these outlets can exacerbate tensions between employees

Orlov uses a brief signal phrase to move from her argument to the words of a source.

and managers. Kesan warns that "prohibiting personal use can seem extremely arbitrary and can seriously harm morale. . . . Imagine a concerned parent who is prohibited from checking on a sick child by a draconian company policy" (315-16). As this analysis indicates, employees can become disgruntled when Internet usage policies are enforced to their full extent.

Additionally, many experts disagree with employers' assumption that online monitoring can increase productivity. Employment law attorney Joseph Schmitt argues that, particularly for employees who

Orlov 5

are paid a salary rather than an hourly wage, "a company shouldn't
care whether employees spend one or 10 hours on the Internet
as long as they are getting their jobs done—and provided that
they are not accessing inappropriate sites" (qtd. in Verespej).
Other experts even argue that time spent on personal Internet
browsing can actually be productive for companies. According to
Bill Coleman, an executive at *Salary.com*, "Personal Internet use
and casual office conversations often turn into new business
ideas or suggestions for gaining operating efficiencies" (qtd.
in Frauenheim). Employers, in other words, may benefit from
showing more faith in their employees' ability to exercise their
autonomy.

Orlov cites an indirect source: words quoted in another source.

Employees' right to privacy and autonomy in the workplace,
however, remains a murky area of the law. Although evaluating
where to draw the line between employee rights and employer
powers is often a duty that falls to the judicial system, the courts
have shown little willingness to intrude on employers' exercise of
control over their computer networks. Federal law provides few
guidelines related to online monitoring of employees, and only
Connecticut and Delaware require companies to disclose this type
of surveillance to employees (Tam et al.). "It is unlikely that
we will see a legally guaranteed zone of privacy in the American
workplace," predicts Kesan (293). This reality leaves employees
and employers to sort the potential risks and benefits of
technology in contract agreements and terms of employment. With
continuing advances in technology, protecting both employers and
employees will require greater awareness of these programs, better
disclosure to employees, and a more public discussion about what
types of protections are necessary to guard individual freedoms in
the wired workplace.

Orlov sums up her argument and suggests a course of action.

Orlov 6

Heading is centered.

Works Cited

Adams, Scott. *Dilbert and the Way of the Weasel*. New York: Harper,
2002. Print.

American Management Association and ePolicy Institute. "2005
Electronic Monitoring and Surveillance Survey." *American
Management Association*. Amer. Management Assn., 2005. Web.
15 Feb. 2009.

"Automatically Record Everything They Do Online! Spector Pro 5.0
FAQ's." *Netbus.org*. Netbus.Org, n.d. Web. 17 Feb. 2009.

Flynn, Nancy. "Internet Policies." *ePolicy Institute*. ePolicy Inst., n.d.
Web. 15 Feb. 2009.

Frauenheim, Ed. "Stop Reading This Headline and Get Back to Work."
CNET News.com. CNET Networks, 11 July 2005. Web. 17 Feb.
2009.

Gonsalves, Chris. "Wasting Away on the Web." *eWeek.com*. Ziff Davis
Enterprise Holdings, 8 Aug. 2005. Web. 16 Feb. 2009.

Kesan, Jay P. "Cyber-Working or Cyber-Shirking? A First Principles
Examination of Electronic Privacy in the Workplace." *Florida Law
Review* 54.2 (2002): 289-332. Print.

Lane, Frederick S., III. *The Naked Employee: How Technology Is
Compromising Workplace Privacy*. New York: Amer. Management
Assn., 2003. Print.

Tam, Pui-Wing, et al. "Snooping E-mail by Software Is Now a
Workplace Norm." *Wall Street Journal* 9 Mar. 2005: B1+. Print.

Tynan, Daniel. "Your Boss Is Watching." *PC World*. PC World
Communications, 6 Oct. 2004. Web. 17 Feb. 2009.

Verespej, Michael A. "Inappropriate Internet Surfing." *Industry Week*.
Penton Media, 7 Feb. 2000. Web. 16 Feb. 2009.

List is alphabetized by authors' last names (or by title when a work has no author).

Abbreviation "n.d." indicates that the online source has no update date.

First line of each entry is at the left margin; extra lines are indented ½".

Double-spacing is used throughout.

A work with four authors is listed by the first author's name and the abbreviation "et al." (for "and others").

55 Writing about literature

All good writing about literature attempts to answer a question, spoken or unspoken, about the text: "Why doesn't Hamlet kill his uncle sooner?" "How does street language function in Gwendolyn Brooks's 'We Real Cool'?" "What does Orwell's 'Shooting an Elephant' imply about the role the British played in imperial India?" "How do rhyme and meter support the meaning of Blake's 'The Tyger'?" "In what ways does Louise Erdrich's *Love Medicine* draw on oral narrative traditions?" The goal of a literature paper should be to answer such questions with a meaningful interpretation, presented forcefully and persuasively.

55a Get involved in the work; be an active reader.

Read the work closely and carefully. Think of the work as speaking to you: What is it telling you? Asking you? Trying to make you feel? If the work provides an introduction and footnotes, read them attentively. They may be a source of important information. Use the dictionary to look up words unfamiliar to you or words with subtle nuances that may affect the work's meaning.

Rereading is a central part of the process. You should read short works several times, first to get an overall impression and then again to focus on meaningful details. With longer works, such as novels or plays, read the most important chapters or scenes more than once while keeping in mind the work as a whole.

As you read and reread, interact with the work by posing questions and looking for answers. The chart on pages 594–95 suggests some questions about literature that may help you consider the composition and context of your reading. The chart on page 87 suggests strategies for active reading. The conclusions you draw in response to such questions shape and support your overall interpretation of the work (see 55b).

Annotating the work

Annotating the work is a way to focus your reading. The first time through, you may want to pencil a check mark next to passages you find especially significant. On a more careful rereading, pay particular attention to those passages and jot down your ideas and reactions in a notebook or (if you own the book) in the margins of the page.

Here is one student's annotation of a poem by Shakespeare:

Shall I compare thee to a summer's day? ———— Who? (Must be a loved one.)

Thou art more lovely and more temperate:

Rough winds do shake the darling buds of May, ——— Pleasant-natured (like pleasant weather)?

And summer's lease hath all too short a date.

Rhyming pattern of sonnet

Sometime too hot the eye of heaven shines,

And often is his gold complexion dimmed; ——— Summer is fleeting and not always perfect. (But lover is perfect?)

And every fair from fair sometimes declines,

By chance, or nature's changing course, untrimmed.

Fair = beauty, or more than beauty?

But thy eternal summer shall not fade,

Nor lose possession of that fair thou ow'st

Nor shall death brag thou wand'rest in his shade, —— Death would be proud to claim the lover but can't?

When in eternal lines to time thou grow'st.

What are "eternal lines to time"? Ask in class?

So long as men can breathe or eyes can see,

So long lives this, and this gives life to thee.

Final couplet seems to signal a shift in thought.

This = the poem? (Art, like the writer's love, is eternal.)

Taking notes

Note taking is also an important part of rereading a work of literature. In your notes, you can try out ideas and develop your perspective on the work. Here are some notes one student took on a short story, "Chrysanthemums," by John Steinbeck. Notice that some of these notes pose questions for further thought. Such notes are the raw material out of which you will build an interpretation.

TAKING NOTES ON A LITERARY WORK

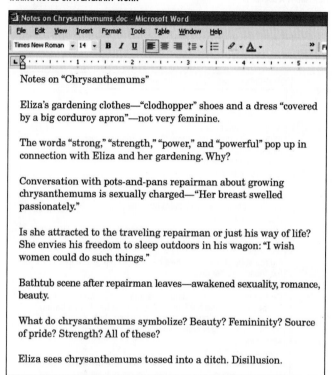

Notes on "Chrysanthemums"

Eliza's gardening clothes—"clodhopper" shoes and a dress "covered by a big corduroy apron"—not very feminine.

The words "strong," "strength," "power," and "powerful" pop up in connection with Eliza and her gardening. Why?

Conversation with pots-and-pans repairman about growing chrysanthemums is sexually charged—"Her breast swelled passionately."

Is she attracted to the traveling repairman or just his way of life? She envies his freedom to sleep outdoors in his wagon: "I wish women could do such things."

Bathtub scene after repairman leaves—awakened sexuality, romance, beauty.

What do chrysanthemums symbolize? Beauty? Femininity? Source of pride? Strength? All of these?

Eliza sees chrysanthemums tossed into a ditch. Disillusion.

Discussing the work

As you have no doubt discovered, class discussions can lead to interesting insights about a literary work, perhaps by calling attention to details in the work that you failed to notice on a first reading. Discussions don't always need to occur face-to-face. Many literature instructors encourage online discussion groups, where the class can post topics and explore ideas. Here, for example, is a series of postings about a character in Joyce Carol Oates's short story "Where Are You Going, Where Have You Been?"

CONVERSATION ABOUT A SUBJECT

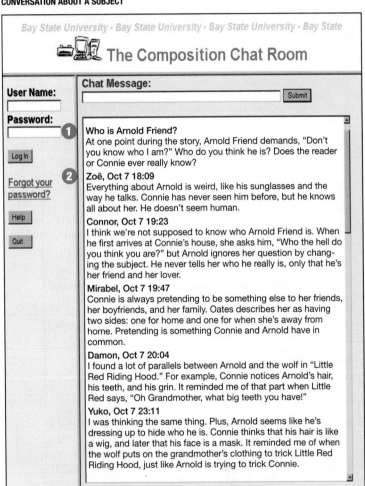

The Composition Chat Room

User Name:

Password:

Log In

Forgot your password?

Help

Quit

Chat Message:

Submit

Who is Arnold Friend?
At one point during the story, Arnold Friend demands, "Don't you know who I am?" Who do you think he is? Does the reader or Connie ever really know?

Zoë, Oct 7 18:09
Everything about Arnold is weird, like his sunglasses and the way he talks. Connie has never seen him before, but he knows all about her. He doesn't seem human.

Connor, Oct 7 19:23
I think we're not supposed to know who Arnold Friend is. When he first arrives at Connie's house, she asks him, "Who the hell do you think you are?" but Arnold ignores her question by changing the subject. He never tells her who he really is, only that he's her friend and her lover.

Mirabel, Oct 7 19:47
Connie is always pretending to be something else to her friends, her boyfriends, and her family. Oates describes her as having two sides: one for home and one for when she's away from home. Pretending is something Connie and Arnold have in common.

Damon, Oct 7 20:04
I found a lot of parallels between Arnold and the wolf in "Little Red Riding Hood." For example, Connie notices Arnold's hair, his teeth, and his grin. It reminded me of that part when Little Red says, "Oh Grandmother, what big teeth you have!"

Yuko, Oct 7 23:11
I was thinking the same thing. Plus, Arnold seems like he's dressing up to hide who he is. Connie thinks that his hair is like a wig, and later that his face is a mask. It reminded me of when the wolf puts on the grandmother's clothing to trick Little Red Riding Hood, just like Arnold is trying to trick Connie.

1 Instructor's prompt

2 A series of students' responses to the prompt

55b Form an interpretation.

After rereading, jotting notes, and perhaps discussing the work, you are ready to start forming an interpretation. At this stage, try to focus on a single aspect of the work. Look through your notes and annotations for recurring questions and insights related to the aspect you have chosen.

Focusing on a central issue

In forming an interpretation, avoid trying to do everything at once. You may think, for example, that *Huckleberry Finn* is a great book because it contains brilliant descriptions of scenery, has many humorous moments, but also tells a serious story of one boy's development. These are legitimate responses to the work, but your job in writing an essay will be to close in on one issue that you can develop into a sustained, in-depth interpretation. For example, you might focus on how the runaway slave Jim uses humor to preserve his dignity. Or you might focus on ironic discrepancies between what Huck says and what his heart tells him.

Asking questions that lead to an interpretation

Think of your interpretation as answering a question about the work. Some interpretations answer questions about literary techniques, such as the writer's handling of plot, setting, or character. Others focus on questions about social context: what a work reveals about the time and culture in which it was written. You can find examples of both types of questions in the chart on pages 594–95.

Frequently you will find yourself writing about both technique and social context. For example, Margaret Peel, a student who wrote an essay on Langston Hughes's poem "Ballad of the Landlord" (see pp. 611–13), addressed the following question, which touches on both language and race:

> How does the poem's language—through its four voices—dramatize the experience of a black man in a society dominated by whites?

Questions to ask about literature

Questions about technique

Plot: What central conflicts drive the plot? Are they internal (within a character) or external (between characters or between a character and a force)? How are conflicts resolved? Why are events revealed in a particular order?

Setting: Does the setting (time and place) create an atmosphere, offer insight into a character, suggest symbolic meanings, or hint at the theme of the work?

Character: What seems to motivate the central characters? Do any characters change significantly? If so, what—if anything—have they learned from their experiences? Do sharp contrasts between characters highlight important themes?

Point of view: Does the point of view—the perspective from which the story is narrated or the poem is spoken—affect the reader's understanding of events? Does the narration reveal character traits of the speaker, or does the speaker merely observe others? Is the narrator innocent, naive, or deceitful? Is the story told by multiple narrators?

Theme: Does the work have an overall theme (a central insight about people or a truth about life)? If so, how do details in the work illuminate this theme?

Language: Does language—such as formal or informal, standard or dialect, prosaic or poetic, cool or passionate—reveal the character of speakers? How do metaphors, similes, and sensory images contribute to the work? How do recurring images enrich the work and hint at its meaning? To what extent do sentence rhythms and sounds underscore the writer's meaning?

Questions about social context

Historical context: What does the work reveal about the time and place in which it was written? Does the work appear to promote or undermine a philosophy that was popular in its time, such as social Darwinism in the late nineteenth century or globalization in the late twentieth century?

Class: How does membership in a social class affect the characters' choices and their successes or failures? How does →

class affect the way characters view—or are viewed by—others? What do economic struggles reveal about power relationships in the society being depicted?

Race and culture: Are any characters portrayed as being caught between cultures: between the cultures of home and work, for example, or between a traditional and an emerging culture? Are any characters struggling against society because of their race or ethnic background? To what extent does the work celebrate a specific culture and its traditions?

Gender: Are any characters' choices restricted because of gender? What are the power relationships between the sexes, and do these change during the course of the work? Do any characters resist the gender roles that society has assigned to them? Do other characters choose to conform to those roles?

Archetypes: Does a character, an image, or a plot fit a pattern—an archetype—that has been repeated in stories throughout history and across cultures? (For example, nearly every culture has stories about heroes, quests, redemption, and revenge.) How does an archetypal character, image, or plot line correspond to or differ from others like it?

In the introduction of your paper, you will usually announce your interpretation in a one- or two-sentence thesis. The thesis answers the central question that you posed. Here, for example, is Margaret Peel's two-sentence thesis:

> Langston Hughes's "Ballad of the Landlord" is narrated through four voices, each with its own perspective on the poem's action. These opposing voices—of a tenant, a landlord, the police, and the press—dramatize a black man's experience in a society dominated by whites.

55c Draft a thesis and organize your ideas.

A thesis, which nearly always appears in the introduction, announces an essay's main point (see also 1c and 50a). In a literature paper, your thesis will answer the central question that you have asked about the work. Putting your draft thesis and notes into an informal outline can help you organize your ideas.

Drafting a thesis

In drafting your thesis, aim for a strong, assertive summary of your interpretation. Here, for example, are two successful thesis statements taken from student essays, together with the central question each student had posed.

QUESTION

What does Stephen Crane's short story "The Open Boat" reveal about the relation between humans and nature?

THESIS

In Stephen Crane's gripping tale "The Open Boat," four men lost at sea discover not only that nature is indifferent to their fate but also that their own particular talents make little difference as they struggle for survival.

QUESTION

In the Greek tragedy *Electra*, by Euripides, how do Electra and her mother, Clytemnestra, respond to the limitations society has placed on women?

THESIS

The experience of powerlessness has taught Electra and her mother two very different lessons: Electra has learned the value of traditional, conservative sex roles for women, but Clytemnestra has learned just the opposite.

As in other college papers, the thesis of a literature paper should not be too factual, too broad, or too vague (see 1e). For an essay on Mark Twain's *Huckleberry Finn*, the first three examples would all make poor thesis statements.

TOO FACTUAL

As a runaway slave, Jim is in danger from the law.

TOO BROAD

In *Huckleberry Finn*, Mark Twain criticizes mid-nineteenth-century American society.

TOO VAGUE

Huckleberry Finn is Twain's most exciting work.

The following thesis statement is sharply focused and presents a central idea that requires discussion and support.

ACCEPTABLE THESIS

Because Huckleberry Finn is a naive narrator, his comments on conventional religion are ironic at every turn, allowing Twain to poke fun at empty piety.

hackerhandbooks.com/bedhandbook > **Research exercises** > E-ex 55–1

Sketching an outline

Your thesis may strongly suggest a method of organization, in which case you will have little difficulty jotting down your essay's key points. Consider, for example, the following informal outline, based on a thesis that leads naturally to a three-part organization.

Thesis: George Bernard Shaw's *Major Barbara* depicts the ways in which three "religions" address the problem of poverty. The Established Church ignores poverty, the Salvation Army tries rather ineffectually to alleviate it, and a form of utopianism based on guns and money promises to eliminate it—but at a terrible cost.

- The Established Church (Lady Britomart)
- The Salvation Army (Major Barbara)
- Utopianism based on guns and money (Undershaft)

If your thesis does not by itself suggest a method of organization, turn to your notes and begin putting them into categories that relate to the thesis. For example, one student who was writing about Euripides's play *Medea* constructed the following formal outline from her notes.

Thesis: Although Medea professes great love for her children, Euripides gives us reason to suspect her sincerity: Medea does not hesitate to use the children as weapons in her bloody battle with Jason, and from the outset she displays little real concern for their fate.

I. From the very beginning of the play, Medea is a less than ideal mother.
   A. Her first words about the children are hostile.
   B. Her first actions suggest indifference.
II. In three scenes, Medea appears to be a loving mother, but in each of these scenes we have reason to doubt her sincerity.
III. Throughout the play, as Medea plots her revenge, her overriding concern is not her children but her reputation.
   A. Fearing ridicule, she is proud of her reputation as one who can "help her friends and hurt her enemies."
   B. Her obsession with reputation may stem from the Greek view of reputation as a means of immortality.
IV. After she kills her children, Medea reveals her real concern.
   A. She shows no remorse.
   B. She revels in Jason's agony over their death.

Whether to use a formal or an informal outline is to some extent a matter of personal preference. For most purposes, you will probably find that an informal outline is sufficient, perhaps even preferable. (See 1d.)

Drafting an introduction that announces your interpretation

The introduction to a literature paper is usually one paragraph long—and often begins with a few sentences that provide context for your thesis. The opening paragraph typically ends with your thesis, a single sentence that sums up your interpretation. Here, for example, is an introductory paragraph announcing one student's interpretation of one aspect of the play *Electra*. The first four sentences provide context for the thesis (underlined).

> In *Electra*, Euripides depicts two women who have had too little control over their lives. Electra, ignored by her mother, Clytemnestra, has been married off to a farmer and treated more or less like a slave. Clytemnestra has fared even worse. Her husband, Agamemnon, has slashed the throat of their daughter Iphigenia as a sacrifice to the gods. <u>The experience of powerlessness has taught Electra and her</u>

mother two very different lessons: Electra has learned the value of
traditional, conservative sex roles for women, but Clytemnestra has
learned just the opposite.

55d Support your interpretation with evidence from the work; avoid plot summary.

Your thesis and preliminary outline will point you toward details
in the work relevant to your interpretation. As you begin drafting the body of your paper, make good use of those details.

Supporting your interpretation

As a rule, the topic sentence of each paragraph in the body of
your paper should focus on some aspect of your overall interpretation. The rest of the paragraph should present details and
perhaps quotations from the work that back up your interpretation. In the following paragraph, which develops part of the organization sketched on page 597, the topic sentence comes first.
It sums up the religious views represented by Lady Britomart, a
character in George Bernard Shaw's play *Major Barbara*.

> Lady Britomart, a member of the Established Church of England,
> reveals her superficial attitude toward religion in a scene that takes
> place in her fashionable London townhouse. Religion, according to
> Lady Britomart, is a morbid topic of conversation. She admonishes
> her daughter Barbara: "Really, Barbara, you go on as if religion were a
> pleasant subject. Do have some sense of propriety" (1.686-87). Religion
> is an unpleasant subject to Lady Britomart because, unlike Barbara, she
> finds no joy or humor within her religion. It is not simply that she is a
> humorless person, for she frequently displays a sharp wit. But in Lady
> Britomart's upper-class world, religion has its proper place—a serious
> place bound by convention and cut off from the real world. When
> Undershaft suggests, for example, that religion can be a pleasant and
> profoundly important subject, Lady Britomart replies, "Well if you are
> determined to have it [religion], then I insist on having it in a proper
> and respectable way. Charles: ring for prayers" (1.690-93).

Notice that the writer has quoted dialogue from the play to lend both flavor and substance to her interpretation (quotations are cited with the act and line numbers and are enclosed in quotation marks). Notice too that the writer is *interpreting* the work: She is not merely summarizing the plot.

Avoiding plot summary

In a literature paper, it is tempting to rely heavily on plot summary and avoid interpretation. You can resist this temptation by paying special attention to your topic sentences.

The following rough-draft topic sentence, for instance, led to a plot summary rather than an interpretation.

> As they drift down the river on a raft, Huck and the runaway slave Jim have many philosophical discussions.

The student's revised topic sentence announces an interpretation.

> The theme of dawning moral awareness is reinforced by the many philosophical discussions between Huck and Jim, the runaway slave, as they drift down the river on a raft.

Usually a little effort can make the difference between a plot summary that cannot be developed and a focused, forceful interpretation. As with all forms of writing, revision is key. To avoid simple plot summary, keep the following strategies in mind as you write.

- When you write for an academic audience, you can assume that readers have read the work. They don't need a summary but are interested instead in your ideas about the work.

- Pose questions that lead to an interpretation or judgment of the work rather than to a summary. The questions in the chart on pages 594–95 can help steer you away from summary and toward interpretation.

- Read your essay out loud. If you hear yourself listing events from the work, stop and revise.

- If organizing your paper according to the work's sequence of events is getting in the way of your own ideas, look again at your outline and consider other ways of arranging your material.

55e Observe the conventions of literature papers.

The academic discipline of English literature has certain conventions, or standard practices, that scholars in the field use when writing about literature. In your literature paper, it is important that you observe the conventions so that your readers' attention will be focused on your interpretation, not on the details of your presentation.

Referring to authors, titles, and characters according to convention

When referring to the author of a literary work or secondary source, such as a critical essay, you should give the author's full name the first time you mention it; in subsequent references, you may use the last name only. As a rule, do not use personal titles such as *Mr.* or *Ms.* or *Dr.* when referring to authors.

When you mention the title of a short story, an essay, or a short or medium-length poem, put the title in quotation marks (see 37d). Italicize the titles of novels, nonfiction books, plays, and long poems (see 42a).

Refer to each character by the name most often used for him or her in the work. If, for instance, a character's name is Lambert Strether and he is always referred to as "Strether," do not call him "Lambert" or "Mr. Strether." Similarly, write "Lady Macbeth," not "Mrs. Macbeth."

Using the present tense to describe fictional events

Perhaps because fictional events have not actually occurred in the past, the literary convention is to describe them in the present tense. Until you become used to this convention, you may find yourself shifting between present and past tense. As you revise your draft, make sure that you have used the present tense consistently.

INCONSISTENT USE OF TENSES

Octavia <u>demands</u> blind obedience from James and from all of her children. When James and Ty <u>caught</u> two redbirds in their trap, they <u>wanted</u> to play with them; Octavia, however, <u>had</u> other plans for the birds (89-90).

CONSISTENT USE OF THE PRESENT TENSE

Octavia <u>demands</u> blind obedience from James and from all of her children. When James and Ty <u>catch</u> two redbirds in their trap, they <u>want</u> to play with them; Octavia, however, <u>has</u> other plans for the birds (89-90).

NOTE: Also see pages 604–05 on avoiding shifts in tenses when you integrate quotations from a work into your own text.

55f Integrate quotations from the work.

Integrating quotations from a literary work can lend vivid support to your argument, but keep most quotations fairly short. Excessive use of long quotations interrupts the flow of your interpretation and can bore readers.

Integrating quotations smoothly into your own text can present a challenge. Because of the complexities of literature, do not be surprised to find yourself puzzling over the most graceful way to tuck in a short phrase or the clearest way to introduce a more extended passage from the work.

Using MLA style to cite and format passages quoted from the work

Unless your instructor suggests otherwise, use MLA (Modern Language Association) style for citing and formatting passages quoted from literary works.

MLA style typically requires that you name the author of the work quoted and give a page number for the exact location of the passage in the work. When writing about nonfiction articles and books, introduce a quotation with a signal phrase naming the author (*John Smith points out . . .*) or place the author's name and page number in parentheses at the end of the quoted passage: *. . . for all time" (Smith 22).*

When writing about a single work of fiction, you do not need to include the author's name each time you quote from the work. You will name the author in the introduction to your paper. Then, when you are quoting from the work, include just the page number in parentheses following the quotation (see the second example on p. 604). You may, of course, use the author's name in a signal phrase to highlight the author's role or technique, but you are not required to do so.

MLA guidelines for handling citations in the text of your paper differ somewhat for short stories or novels, poems, and plays, each of which is discussed in this section (see pp. 605–08). (If your instructor requires a works cited page, see p. 620.)

Introducing literary quotations

When introducing quotations from a literary work, make sure that you don't confuse the author with the narrator of a story, the speaker of a poem, or a character in a story or play. Instead of naming the author, you can refer to the narrator or speaker—or to the work itself.

INAPPROPRIATE

Poet Andrew Marvell describes his fear of death like this: "But at my back I always hear / Time's wingèd chariot hurrying near" (21-22).

APPROPRIATE

Addressing his beloved in an attempt to win her sexual favors, the speaker of the poem argues that death gives them no time to waste: "But at my back I always hear / Time's wingèd chariot hurrying near" (21-22).

APPROPRIATE

The poem "To His Coy Mistress" says as much about fleeting time and death as it does about sexual passion. Its most powerful lines are "But at my back I always hear / Time's wingèd chariot hurrying near" (21-22).

In the last example, you could mention the author as well: *Marvell's poem "To His Coy Mistress" says as much. . . .* Although the author is mentioned, readers will not confuse him with the speaker of the poem.

Providing context for quotations

When you quote the words of a narrator, speaker, or character in a literary work, you should name who is speaking and provide a context for the quoted words. In the following examples, the quoted dialogue is from Tennessee Williams's play *The Glass Menagerie* and Shirley Jackson's short story "The Lottery."

> Laura is so completely under Amanda's spell that when urged to make a wish on the moon, she asks, "What shall I wish for, Mother?" (1.5.140).

> When a neighbor suggests that the lottery should be abandoned, Old Man Warner responds, "There's *always* been a lottery" (284).

Avoiding shifts in tense when quoting

Because it is conventional to write about literature in the present tense (see pp. 601–02) and because literary works often use other tenses, you will need to exercise some care when weaving quotations into your own writing. A first-draft attempt may result in an awkward shift between your words and the quoted text, as it did for one student who was writing about Nadine Gordimer's short story "Friday's Footprint."

> **TENSE SHIFT**
>
> When Rita sees Johnny's relaxed attitude, "she blushed, like a wave of illness" (159).

To avoid the distracting shift from present to past tense, the writer had two choices: to paraphrase the reference to Rita's blushing and reduce the length of the quotation or to change the verb in the quotation to the present tense, using brackets to indicate the change.

REVISED

When Rita sees Johnny's relaxed attitude, she is overcome with
embarrassment, "like a wave of illness" (159).

REVISED

When Rita sees Johnny's relaxed attitude, "she blushe[s], like a wave of
illness" (159).

Using brackets around just one letter of a word can seem
fussy, so the writer chose the first revision. (For advice on
using brackets to indicate changes in a quotation, see 39c.)

Using quotations within quotations

In writing about literature, you may sometimes want to use a
quotation that has another quotation embedded in it—when
you are integrating dialogue from a novel, for example. In
such cases, set off the main quotation with double quotation
marks, as you usually would, and set off the embedded quotation with single quotation marks. (See also 37c.) The following example from a student paper integrates lines from Amy
Tan's novel *The Hundred Secret Senses*.

Early in the novel the narrator's half-sister Kwan sees—or thinks she
sees—ghosts: "'Libby-ah,' she'll say to me. 'Guess who I see yesterday,
you guess.' And I don't have to guess that she's talking about someone
dead" (3).

Formatting quotations

MLA guidelines for formatting quotations differ somewhat for
short stories or novels, poems, and plays.

Short stories or novels   To cite a passage from a short story or a
novel, use a page number in parentheses after the quoted words.

The narrator of Eudora Welty's "Why I Live at the P.O.," known to us only
as "Sister," makes many catty remarks about her enemies. For example,
she calls Mr. Whitaker "this photographer with the pop-eyes" (46).

If a novel has numbered divisions, give the page number and a semicolon; then indicate the book, part, or chapter in which the passage is found. Use abbreviations such as "bk." and "ch."

> White relies on past authors to help retell the legend of King Arthur. The narrator does not provide specifics about Lancelot's tournament at Corbin, instead telling readers, "If you want to read about the Corbin tournament, Malory has it" (489; bk. 3, ch. 39).

When a quotation from a work of fiction takes up four or fewer typed lines, put it in quotation marks and run it into the text of your essay, as in the two previous examples. When a quotation is five lines or longer, set it off from the text by indenting one inch from the left margin; when you set a quotation off from the text, do not use quotation marks. Put the parenthetical citation after the final mark of punctuation.

> Sister's tale begins with "I," and she makes every event revolve around herself, even her sister's marriage:
>
>> I was getting along fine with Mama, Papa-Daddy, and Uncle Rondo until my sister Stella-Rondo just separated from her husband and came back home again. Mr. Whitaker! Of course I went with Mr. Whitaker first, when he first appeared here in China Grove, taking "Pose Yourself" photos, and Stella-Rondo broke us up. (46)

Poems To cite lines from a poem, use line numbers in parentheses at the end of the quotation. For the first reference, use the word "lines": (lines 1-2). Thereafter use just the numbers: (12-13).

> The opening lines of Frost's "Fire and Ice" strike a conversational tone: "Some say the world will end in fire, / Some say in ice" (1-2).

Enclose quotations of three or fewer lines of poetry in quotation marks within your text, and indicate line breaks with a slash, as in the example just given. (See also 39e and item 25 on p. 528.)

When you quote four or more lines of poetry, set the quotation off from the text by indenting one inch and omit the quotation marks. Put the line numbers in parentheses after the final mark of punctuation.

> In the second stanza of "A Noiseless Patient Spider," Whitman turns the spider's weaving into a metaphor for the activity of the human soul:
>
>> And you O my soul where you stand,
>>
>> Surrounded, detached, in measureless oceans of space,
>>
>> Ceaselessly musing, venturing, throwing, seeking the spheres
>>> to connect them,
>>
>> Till the bridge you will need be form'd, till the ductile anchor
>>> hold,
>>
>> Till the gossamer thread you fling catch somewhere, O my
>>> soul. (6-10)

NOTE: If any line of the poem takes up more than one line of your paper, carry the extra words to the next line of the paper and indent them an additional one-quarter inch, as in the previous example. Alternatively, you may indent the entire poem a little less than one inch to fit the long line.

Plays To cite lines from a play, include the act number, scene number, and line numbers (as many of these as are available) in parentheses at the end of the quotation. Separate the numbers with periods, and use arabic numerals unless your instructor prefers roman numerals.

> Two attendants silently watch as the sleepwalking Lady Macbeth subconsciously struggles with her guilt: "Here's the smell of the blood still. All the perfumes of Arabia will not sweeten this little hand" (5.1.50-51).

If no act, scene, or line numbers are available, use a page number.

When a quotation from a play takes up four or fewer typed lines in your paper and is spoken by only one character, put quotation marks around it and run it into the text of your essay, as in the previous example. If the quotation consists of two or three lines from a verse play, use a slash for line breaks, as for poetry (see p. 606). When a dramatic quotation by a single character is five typed lines or longer (or more than three lines in a verse play), indent it one inch from the left margin and omit quotation marks. Include the citation in parentheses after the final mark of punctuation.

> Speaking to Electra, Clytemnestra complains about the sexual double standard that has allowed her husband to justify sacrificing her other daughter, Iphigenia, to the gods. She asks what would have happened if Menelaus, and not his wife Helen, had been seized by the Trojans:
>> If Menelaus had been raped from home on the sly, should I have had to kill Orestes so my sister's husband could be rescued? You think your father would have borne it? He would have killed me. Then why was it fair for him to kill what belonged to me and not be killed? (1041-45)

When quoting dialogue between two or more characters in a play, no matter how many lines you use, set the quotation off from the text. Type each character's name in all capital letters at a one-inch indent from the left margin. Indent subsequent lines under the character's name an additional one-quarter inch.

> Throughout *The Importance of Being Earnest*, Algernon criticizes romance and the institution of marriage, as in the scene when he learns of Jack's intention to marry Gwendolen:
>> ALGERNON. My dear fellow, the way you flirt with Gwendolen is perfectly disgraceful. It is almost as bad as the way Gwendolen flirts with you.
>> JACK. I am in love with Gwendolen. I have come up to town expressly to propose to her.
>> ALGERNON. I thought you had come up for pleasure? — I call that business. (act 1)

55g If you use secondary sources, document them appropriately and avoid plagiarism.

Many literature papers rely wholly on primary sources—the literary text under discussion. (For an example of an essay with only a primary source, see pp. 611–13.)

Other literature papers use some ideas from secondary sources, such as articles or books of literary criticism, biographies of the author, the author's own essays and autobiography, or histories of the era in which the work was written. (For an example of a paper that uses secondary sources, see pp. 615–20.) Even if you use secondary sources, your main goal should always be to develop your own understanding and interpretation of the literary work.

Whenever you use secondary sources, you must document them, and you must avoid plagiarism. Plagiarism is unacknowledged borrowing—whether intentional or unintentional—of a source's words or ideas. (See 51b.)

Documenting secondary sources

Most literature papers use the documentation system recommended by the Modern Language Association (MLA). This system of documentation is discussed in detail in 53.

MLA recommends in-text citations that refer readers to a list of works cited. An in-text citation names the author of the source, often in a signal phrase, and gives the page number in parentheses. At the end of the paper, a list of works cited provides publication information about the sources used in the paper.

SAMPLE MLA IN-TEXT CITATION

Arguing that fate has little to do with the tragedy that befalls Oedipus, Bernard Knox writes that "the catastrophe of Oedipus is that he discovers his own identity; and for his discovery he is first and last responsible" (6).

The signal phrase names the author of the secondary source; the number in parentheses is the page on which the quoted words appear.

Anyone interested in knowing additional information about the secondary source can consult the list of works cited at the end of the paper. Here, for example, is the works cited entry for the work referred to in the sample in-text citation.

SAMPLE ENTRY IN THE LIST OF WORKS CITED

Knox, Bernard. *Oedipus at Thebes: Sophocles' Tragic Hero and His Time*.
　　　New York: Norton, 1971. Print.

As you document secondary sources with in-text citations, consult 53a; as you construct your list of works cited, consult 53b.

Avoiding plagiarism

The rules about plagiarism are the same for literary papers as for other research writing (see 48c and 51 for important details). To be fair and ethical, you must acknowledge your debt to the writers of any sources you use. If an interpretation was suggested to you by another critic's work or if an obscure point was clarified by someone else's research, it is your responsibility to cite the source. If you have borrowed any phrases or sentences from your source, you must put them in quotation marks and credit the author.

55h Sample literature papers

Following are two sample essays. The first, by Margaret Peel, has no secondary sources. (Its primary source, Langston Hughes's "Ballad of the Landlord," appears on p. 614.) The second sample paper, by Dan Larson, uses secondary sources.

hackerhandbooks.com/bedhandbook > Model papers
　　　　　　　　　　　　　　　　　　　> MLA papers: Peel
　　　　　　　　　　　　　　　　　　　> MLA papers: Larson

Peel 1

Margaret Peel

Professor Lin

English 102

20 April 2005

Opposing Voices in "Ballad of the Landlord"

Langston Hughes's "Ballad of the Landlord" is narrated through

four voices, each with its own perspective on the poem's action. These

opposing voices—of a tenant, a landlord, the police, and the press—

dramatize a black man's experience in a society dominated by whites.

The main voice in the poem is that of the tenant, who, as the

last line tells us, is black. The tenant is characterized by his informal,

nonstandard speech. He uses slang ("Ten Bucks"), contracted words

(*'member, more'n*), and nonstandard grammar ("These steps is broken

down"). This colloquial English suggests the tenant's separation from

the world of convention, represented by the formal voices of the police

and the press, which appear later in the poem.

Although the tenant uses nonstandard English, his argument

is organized and logical. He begins with a reasonable complaint and

a gentle reminder that the complaint is already a week old: "My roof

has sprung a leak. / Don't you 'member I told you about it / Way last

week?" (lines 2-4). In the second stanza, he appeals diplomatically to

the landlord's self-interest: "These steps is broken down. / When you

come up yourself / It's a wonder you don't fall down" (6-8). In the

third stanza, when the landlord has responded to his complaints with

a demand for rent money, the tenant becomes more forceful, but his

voice is still reasonable: "Ten Bucks you say is due? / Well, that's Ten

Bucks more'n I'll pay you / Till you fix this house up new" (10-12).

The fourth stanza marks a shift in the tone of the argument.

At this point the tenant responds more emotionally, in reaction to

Marginal annotations (right column):

Thesis states Peel's main idea.

Details from the poem illustrate Peel's point.

The first citation of lines of the poem includes the word "lines." Subsequent citations from the poem are cited with line numbers alone.

Topic sentence focuses on an interpretation.

Peel 2

the landlord's threats to evict him. By the fifth stanza, the tenant
has unleashed his anger: "Um-huh! You talking high and mighty"
(17). Hughes uses an exclamation point for the first time; the tenant
is raising his voice at last. As the argument gets more heated, the
tenant finally resorts to the language of violence: "You ain't gonna
be able to say a word / If I land my fist on you" (19-20).

These are the last words the tenant speaks in the poem. Perhaps
Hughes wants to show how black people who threaten violence are
silenced. When a new voice is introduced—the landlord's—the poem
shifts to a frantic tone:

> *Police! Police!*
> *Come and get this man!*
> *He's trying to ruin the government*
> *And overturn the land!* (21-24)

This response is clearly an overreaction to a small threat. Instead
of dealing with the tenant directly, the landlord shouts for the police.
His hysterical voice—marked by repetitions and punctuated with
exclamation points—reveals his disproportionate fear and outrage.
And his conclusions are equally excessive: this black man, he claims,
is out to "ruin the government" and "overturn the land." Although the
landlord's overreaction is humorous, it is sinister as well, because the
landlord knows that, no matter how excessive his claims are, he has
the police and the law on his side.

In line 25, the regular meter and rhyme of the poem break
down, perhaps showing how an arrest disrupts everyday life. The
"voice" in lines 25-29 has two parts: the clanging sound of the
police ("Copper's whistle! / Patrol bell!") and, in sharp contrast,
the unemotional, factual tone of a police report ("Arrest. / Precinct
Station. / Iron cell.").

Transition prepares readers for the next topic.

Peel interprets the landlord's response.

Peel shows how meter and rhyme support the poem's meaning.

Peel 3

The last voice in the poem is the voice of the press, represented in newspaper headlines: "MAN THREATENS LANDLORD/ TENANT HELD NO BAIL / JUDGE GIVES NEGRO 90 DAYS IN COUNTY JAIL" (31-33). Meter and rhyme return here, as if to show that once the tenant is arrested, life can go on as usual. The language of the press, like that of the police, is cold and distant, and it gives the tenant less and less status. In line 31, he is a "man"; in line 32, he has been demoted to a "tenant"; and in line 33, he has become a "Negro," or just another statistic.

Peel sums up her interpretation.

By using four opposing voices in "Ballad of the Landlord," Hughes effectively dramatizes different views of minority assertiveness. To the tenant, assertiveness is informal and natural, as his language shows; to the landlord, it is a dangerous threat, as his hysterical response suggests. The police response is, like the language that describes it, short and sharp. Finally, the press's view of events, represented by the headlines, is distant and unsympathetic.

By the end of the poem, we understand the predicament of the black man. Exploited by the landlord, politically oppressed by those who think he's out "to ruin the government," physically restrained by the police and the judicial system, and denied his individuality by the press, he is saved only by his own sense of humor. The very title of the poem suggests his—and Hughes's—sense of humor. The tenant is singing a *ballad* to his oppressors, but this ballad is no love song. It portrays the oppressors, through their own voices, in an unflattering light: the landlord as cowardly and ridiculous, the police and press as dull and soulless. The tenant may lack political power, but he speaks with vitality, and no one can say he lacks dignity or the spirit to survive.

Peel concludes with an analysis of the poem's political significance.

Ballad of the Landlord

LANGSTON HUGHES

Landlord, landlord,
My roof has sprung a leak.
Don't you 'member I told you about it
Way last week?

Landlord, landlord,
These steps is broken down.
When you come up yourself
It's a wonder you don't fall down.

Ten Bucks you say I owe you?
Ten Bucks you say is due?
Well, that's Ten Bucks more'n I'll pay you
Till you fix this house up new.

What? You gonna get eviction orders?
You gonna cut off my heat?
You gonna take my furniture and
Throw it in the street?

Um-huh! You talking high and mighty.
Talk on—till you get through.
You ain't gonna be able to say a word
If I land my fist on you.

Police! Police!
Come and get this man!
He's trying to ruin the government
And overturn the land!

Copper's whistle!
Patrol bell!
Arrest.

Precinct Station.
Iron cell.
Headlines in press:

MAN THREATENS LANDLORD
TENANT HELD NO BAIL
JUDGE GIVES NEGRO 90 DAYS IN COUNTY JAIL

Dan Larson

Professor Duncan

English 102

18 April 2005

The Transformation of Mrs. Peters:

An Analysis of "A Jury of Her Peers"

In Susan Glaspell's 1917 short story "A Jury of Her Peers," two women accompany their husbands and a county attorney to an isolated house where a farmer named John Wright has been choked to death in his bed with a rope. The chief suspect is Wright's wife, Minnie, who is in jail awaiting trial. The sheriff's wife, Mrs. Peters, has come along to gather some personal items for Minnie, and Mrs. Hale has joined her. Early in the story, Mrs. Hale sympathizes with Minnie and objects to the way the male investigators are "snoopin' round and criticizin'" her kitchen (200). In contrast, Mrs. Peters shows respect for the law, saying that the men are doing "no more than their duty" (201). By the end of the story, however, Mrs. Peters has joined Mrs. Hale in a conspiracy of silence, lied to the men, and committed a crime—hiding key evidence. What causes this dramatic change?

One critic, Leonard Mustazza, argues that Mrs. Hale recruits Mrs. Peters "as a fellow 'juror' in the case, moving the sheriff's wife away from her sympathy for her husband's position and towards identification with the accused woman" (494). While this is true, Mrs. Peters also reaches insights on her own. Her observations in the kitchen lead her to understand Minnie's grim and lonely plight as the wife of an abusive farmer, and her identification with both Minnie and Mrs. Hale is strengthened as the men conducting the investigation trivialize the lives of women.

The opening lines name the story and establish context.

Present tense is used to describe details from the story.

Quotations from the story are cited with page numbers in parentheses.

The opening paragraph ends with Larson's research question.

The thesis asserts Larson's main point.

Marginal annotations indicate MLA-style formatting and effective writing.

Larson 2

The first evidence that Mrs. Peters reaches understanding on her own surfaces in the following passage:

> The sheriff's wife had looked from the stove to the sink—to the pail of water which had been carried in from outside. . . . That look of seeing into things, of seeing through a thing to something else, was in the eyes of the sheriff's wife now. (203)

A long quotation is set off by indenting with no quotation marks. Ellipsis dots indicate a sentence omitted from the source.

Something about the stove, the sink, and the pail of water connects with her own experience, giving Mrs. Peters a glimpse into the life of Minnie Wright. The details resonate with meaning.

Larson summarizes ideas from a secondary source and then quotes from that source; he names the author in a signal phrase and gives a page number in parentheses.

Social historian Elaine Hedges argues that such details, which evoke the drudgery of a farm woman's work, would not have been lost upon Glaspell's readers in 1917. Hedges tells us what the pail and the stove, along with another detail from the story—a dirty towel on a roller—would have meant to women of the time. Laundry was a dreaded all-day affair. Water had to be pumped, hauled, and boiled; then the wash was rubbed, rinsed, wrung through a wringer, carried outside, and hung on a line to dry. "What the women see, beyond the pail and the stove," writes Hedges, "are the hours of work it took Minnie to produce that one clean towel" (56).

Topic sentences focus on Larson's interpretation.

On her own, Mrs. Peters discovers clues about the motive for the murder. Her curiosity leads her to pick up a sewing basket filled with quilt pieces and then to notice something strange: a sudden row of badly sewn stitches. "What do you suppose she was so—nervous about?" asks Mrs. Peters (204). A short time later, Mrs. Peters spots another clue, an empty birdcage. Again she observes details on her own, in this case a broken door and hinge, suggesting that the cage has been roughly handled.

In addition to noticing details, both women draw conclusions from them and speculate on their significance. When Mrs. Hale finds the dead canary beneath a quilt patch, for example, the women conclude that its neck has been wrung and understand who must have wrung it.

As the women speculate on the significance of the dead canary, each connects the bird with her own experience. Mrs. Hale knows that Minnie once sang in the church choir, an activity that Mr. Wright put a stop to, just as he put a stop to the bird's singing. Also, as a farmer's wife, Mrs. Hale understands the desolation and loneliness of life on the prairie. She sees that the bird was both a thing of beauty and a companion. "If there had been years and years of—nothing, then a bird to sing to you," says Mrs. Hale, "it would be awful—still—after the bird was still" (208). To Mrs. Peters, the stillness of the canary evokes memories of the time when she and her husband homesteaded in the northern plains. "I know what stillness is," she says, as she recalls the death of her first child, with no one around to console her (208).

Elaine Hedges has written movingly of the isolation that women experienced on late-nineteenth- and early-twentieth-century farms of the West and Midwest:

> Women themselves reported that it was not unusual to
> spend five months in a log cabin without seeing another
> woman . . . or to spend one and a half years after arriving
> before being able to take a trip to town. . . . (54)

To combat loneliness and monotony, says Hedges, many women bought canaries and hung the cages outside their sod huts. The canaries provided music and color, a spot of beauty that "might spell the difference between sanity and madness" (60).

Mrs. Peters and Mrs. Hale understand—and Glaspell's readers in 1917 would have understood—what the killing of the bird means to Minnie. For Mrs. Peters, in fact, the act has a special significance. When she was a child, a boy axed her kitten to death and, as she says, "If they hadn't held me back I would have . . . hurt him" (207).

Details from the story provide evidence for the interpretation.

Ellipsis dots indicate omitted words within the sentence and at the end of the sentence.

Larson 4

She has little difficulty comprehending Minnie's murderous rage, for she has felt it herself.

Although Mrs. Peters's growing empathy for Minnie stems largely from her observations, it is also prompted by her negative reaction to the patronizing comments of the male investigators. At several points in the story, her body language reveals her feelings. For example, when Mr. Hale remarks that "women are used to worrying over trifles," both women move closer together and remain silent. When the county attorney asks, "for all their worries, what would we do without the ladies?" the women do not speak, nor do they "unbend" (199). The fact that the women respond in exactly the same way reveals the extent to which they are bonding.

Both women are annoyed at the way in which the men criticize and trivialize the world of women. The men question the difficulty of women's work. For example, when the county attorney points to the dirty towel on the rack as evidence that Minnie wasn't much of a housekeeper, Mrs. Hale replies, "There's a great deal of work to be done on a farm" (199). Even the importance of women's work is questioned. The men kid the women for trying to decide if Minnie was going to quilt or knot patches together for a quilt and laugh about such trivial concerns. Those very quilts, of course, kept the men warm at night and cost them nothing beyond the price of thread.

The men also question the women's wisdom and intelligence. For example, when the county attorney tells the women to keep their eyes out for clues, Mr. Hale replies, "But would the women know a clue if they did come upon it?" (200). The women's response is to stand motionless and silent. The irony is that the men don't see the household clues that are right in front of them.

By the end of the story, Mrs. Peters has been so transformed that she risks lying to the men. When the district attorney walks into the kitchen and notices the birdcage the women have found, he asks

Transition serves as a bridge from one section of the paper to the next.

Larson gives evidence that Mrs. Peters has been transformed.

Larson 5

about the whereabouts of the bird. Mrs. Hale replies, "We think the cat got it," even though she knows from Mrs. Peters that Minnie was afraid of cats and would not have owned one. Instead of correcting the lie, Mrs. Peters elaborates on it, saying of cats, "They're superstitious, you know; they leave" (207). Clearly Mrs. Hale is willing to risk lying because she is confident that Mrs. Peters won't contradict her.

The Mrs. Peters character may have been based on a real sheriff's wife. Seventeen years before writing "A Jury of Her Peers," Susan Glaspell covered a murder case for the *Des Moines Daily News*. A farmer's wife, Margaret Hossack, was accused of murdering her sleeping husband with two axe blows to the head. In one of her newspaper reports, Glaspell wrote that the sheriff's wife sat next to Mrs. Hossack and "frequently applied her handkerchief to her eyes" (qtd. in Ben-Zvi 30).

> Larson draws on a secondary source that gives background on Glaspell's life.

We do not know from the short story the ultimate fate of Minnie Wright, but Margaret Hossack, whose case inspired the story, was found guilty, though the case was later thrown out by the Iowa Supreme Court. However, as Linda Ben-Zvi points out, the women's guilt or innocence is not the issue:

> Whether Margaret Hossack or Minnie Wright committed murder is moot; what is incontrovertible is the brutality of their lives, the lack of options they had to redress grievances or to escape abusive husbands, and the complete disregard of their plight by the courts and by society. (38)

These are the issues that Susan Glaspell wished to stress in "A Jury of Her Peers."

These are also the issues that Mrs. Peters comes to understand as the story unfolds, with her understanding deepening as she identifies with Minnie and Mrs. Hale and is repulsed by male attitudes. Her transformation becomes complete when the men joke that she is "married to the law" and she responds by violating the law: hiding key evidence, the dead canary.

> Larson's conclusion echoes his main point without dully repeating it.

Works Cited

Ben-Zvi, Linda. "'Murder, She Wrote': The Genesis of Susan Glaspell's
        Trifles." *Theatre Journal* 44.2 (1992): 141-62. Rpt. in *Susan
        Glaspell: Essays on Her Theater and Fiction*. Ed. Ben-Zvi. Ann
        Arbor: U of Michigan P, 1995. 19-48. Print.

Glaspell, Susan. "A Jury of Her Peers." *Literature and Its Writers: A
        Compact Introduction to Fiction, Poetry, and Drama*. Ed. Ann
        Charters and Samuel Charters. 3rd ed. Boston: Bedford, 2004.
        194-210. Print.

Hedges, Elaine. "Small Things Reconsidered: 'A Jury of Her Peers.'"
        Women's Studies 12.1 (1986): 89-110. Rpt. in *Susan Glaspell:
        Essays on Her Theater and Fiction*. Ed. Linda Ben-Zvi. Ann Arbor:
        U of Michigan P, 1995. 49-69. Print.

Mustazza, Leonard. "Generic Translation and Thematic Shift in Susan
        Glaspell's *Trifles* and 'A Jury of Her Peers.'" *Studies in Short
        Fiction* 26.4 (1989): 489-96. Print.

The works cited page lists the primary source (Glaspell's story) and secondary sources.

Writing APA papers

56 APA papers

Many writing assignments in the social sciences are either reports of original research or reviews of the literature written about a research topic. Often an original research report contains a "review of the literature" section that places the writer's project in the context of previous research.

Most social science instructors will ask you to document your sources with the American Psychological Association (APA) system of in-text citations and references described in 56d. You face three main challenges when writing a social science paper that draws on sources: (1) supporting a thesis, (2) citing your sources and avoiding plagiarism, and (3) integrating quotations and other source material.

Examples in this section are drawn from one student's research for a review of the literature on treatments for childhood obesity. Luisa Mirano's paper appears on pages 674–83.

56a Supporting a thesis

Most assignments ask you to form a thesis, or main idea, and to support that thesis with well-organized evidence. (See also 1c.) In a paper reviewing the literature on a topic, the thesis analyzes the often competing conclusions drawn by a variety of researchers. Remain flexible as you draft because you may need to revise your approach later. Writing about a subject is a way of learning about it; as you write, your understanding of your subject will almost certainly deepen.

Forming a working thesis

Once you have read a variety of sources and considered your issue from different perspectives, you are ready to form a working thesis: a one-sentence (or occasionally a two-sentence) statement of your central idea. (See also 1c.) You will be reading articles and other sources that address the central research question you posed earlier (see 46c). Ultimately, your thesis will express not just your opinion but your informed, reasoned answer to that question, given the current state of research in the field. Here, for example, is a research question posed by Luisa Mirano, a student in a psychology class, followed by a thesis that answers the question.

RESEARCH QUESTION

Is medication the right treatment for the escalating problem of childhood obesity?

WORKING THESIS

Treating cases of childhood obesity with medication alone is too narrow an approach for this growing problem.

Notice that the thesis expresses a view on a debatable issue — an issue about which intelligent, well-meaning people might disagree. The writer's job is to convince such readers that this view is worth taking seriously.

Organizing your ideas

The American Psychological Association encourages the use of headings to help readers follow the organization of a paper. For an original research report, the major headings often

thesis • organizing ideas • how sources
work in a paper • supporting arguments
APA 56a 623

follow a standard model: Method, Results, Discussion. The introduction is not given a heading; it consists of the material between the title of the paper and the first heading.

For a literature review, headings will vary. The student who wrote about treatments for childhood obesity used four questions to focus her research; the questions then became headings in her paper (see pp. 674–83).

Making the most of your handbook

When writing from sources, it helps to start with a working thesis and a rough outline.

▶ Draft a working thesis: 1c
▶ Sketch a plan: 1d

hackerhandbooks.com/bedhandbook > Research exercises > APA > E-ex 56–1 and 56–2

Using sources to inform and support your argument

Used thoughtfully, your source materials will make your argument more complex and convincing for readers. Sources can play several different roles as you develop your points.

Providing background information or context   You can use facts and statistics to support generalizations or to establish the importance of your topic, as student writer Luisa Mirano does in her introduction.

> In March 2004, U.S. Surgeon General Richard Carmona called
> attention to a health problem in the United States that, until
> recently, has been overlooked: childhood obesity. Carmona said that
> the "astounding" 15% child obesity rate constitutes an "epidemic."
> Since the early 1980s, that rate has "doubled in children and tripled
> in adolescents." Now more than nine million children are classified
> as obese.

Explaining terms or concepts   If readers are unlikely to be familiar with a word or an idea important to your topic, you must explain it for them. Quoting or paraphrasing a source can help you define terms and concepts in accessible language. Luisa Mirano uses a footnote in her paper to define the familiar word *obesity* in the technical sense used by researchers.

Obesity is measured in terms of body-mass index (BMI): weight in kilograms divided by square of height in meters. A child or an adolescent with a BMI in the 95th percentile for his or her age and gender is considered obese.

Supporting your claims As you draft your argument, make sure to back up your assertions with facts, examples, and other evidence from your research (see also 5e). Luisa Mirano, for example, uses one source's findings to support her central idea that the medical treatment of childhood obesity has limitations.

As journalist Greg Critser (2003) noted in his book *Fat Land*, use of weight-loss drugs is unlikely to have an effect without the proper "support system"—one that includes doctors, facilities, time, and money (p. 3).

Lending authority to your argument Including expert opinion can add credibility to your argument. (See also 5e.) But don't rely on experts to make your argument for you. Construct your argument in your own words and, when appropriate, cite the judgment of an authority in the field for support.

Both medical experts and policymakers recognize that solutions might come not only from a laboratory but also from policy, education, and advocacy. A handbook designed to educate doctors on obesity called for "major changes in some aspects of western culture" (Hoppin & Taveras, 2004, Conclusion section, para. 1).

Anticipating and countering alternative interpretations Do not ignore sources that seem contrary to your position or that offer interpretations different from your own. Instead, use them to give voice to opposing points of view before you counter them (see 5f). Readers often have objections in mind already, whether or not they agree with you. Mirano uses a source to acknowledge value in her opponents' position that medication alone can successfully treat childhood obesity.

As researchers Yanovski and Yanovski (2002) have explained, obesity was once considered "either a moral failing or evidence of underlying psychopathology" (p. 592). But this view has shifted: Many medical professionals now consider obesity a biomedical rather than a moral condition, influenced by both genetic and environmental factors. Yanovski and Yanovski have further noted that the development of weight-loss medications in the early 1990s showed that "obesity should be treated in the same manner as any other chronic disease . . . through the long-term use of medication" (p. 592).

56b Citing sources; avoiding plagiarism

In a research paper, you will draw on the work of other writers, and you must document their contributions by citing your sources. Sources are cited for two reasons:

- to tell readers where your information comes from—so that they can assess its reliability and, if interested, find and read the original source
- to give credit to the writers from whom you have borrowed words and ideas

Borrowing another writer's language, sentence structures, or ideas without proper acknowledgment is a form of dishonesty known as *plagiarism.*

You must include a citation when you quote from a source, when you summarize or paraphrase a source, and when you borrow facts that are not common knowledge. (See also "Avoiding plagiarism," p. 626.)

Using the APA system for citing sources

The American Psychological Association recommends an author-date style of citations. The following is a brief description of how the author-date system often works. (See 56d for more details and model citations.)

1. The source is introduced by a signal phrase that includes the last name of the author followed by the date of publication in parentheses.

2. The material being cited is followed by a page number in parentheses.

3. At the end of the paper, an alphabetized list of references gives complete publication information for the source.

IN-TEXT CITATION

As researchers Yanovski and Yanovski (2002) have explained, obesity was once considered "either a moral failing or evidence of underlying psychopathology" (p. 592).

ENTRY IN THE LIST OF REFERENCES

Yanovski, S. Z., & Yanovski, J. A. (2002). Drug therapy: Obesity. *The New England Journal of Medicine, 346,* 591-602.

This basic APA format varies for different types of sources. For a detailed discussion and other models, see 56d.

Avoiding plagiarism

Your research paper is a collaboration between you and your sources. To be fair and ethical, you must acknowledge your debt to the writers of those sources. If you don't, you commit plagiarism, a serious academic offense. (See also 48c.)

In general, these three acts are considered plagiarism: (1) failing to cite quotations and borrowed ideas, (2) failing to enclose borrowed language in quotation marks, and (3) failing to put summaries and paraphrases in your own words. Definitions of plagiarism may vary; it's a good idea to find out how your school defines academic dishonesty.

Citing quotations and borrowed ideas   You must cite all direct quotations. You must also cite any ideas borrowed from a source: summaries and paraphrases; statistics and other specific facts; and visuals such as cartoons, graphs, and diagrams.

The only exception is common knowledge—information that your readers may know or could easily locate in any number of reference sources. For example, most general encyclopedias will tell readers that Sigmund Freud wrote *The Interpretation of Dreams* and that chimpanzees can learn American Sign Language.

As a rule, when you have seen certain information repeatedly in your reading, you don't need to cite it. However, when information has appeared in only a few sources, when it is highly specific (as with statistics), or when it is controversial, you should cite the source. If a topic is new to you and you are not sure what is considered common knowledge and what is considered controversial, ask your instructor or someone else with expertise. When in doubt, cite the source.

Enclosing borrowed language in quotation marks   To indicate that you are using a source's exact phrases or sentences, you must enclose them in quotation marks unless they have been set off from the text by indenting (see p. 631). To omit the quotation marks is to claim—falsely—that the language is your own. Such an omission is plagiarism even if you have cited the source.

ORIGINAL SOURCE

In an effort to seek the causes of this disturbing trend, experts have pointed to a range of important potential contributors to the rise in childhood obesity that are unrelated to media: a reduction in physical education classes and after-school athletic programs, an increase in the availability of sodas and snacks in public schools, the growth in the number of fast-food outlets across the country, the trend toward "super-sizing" food portions in restaurants, and the increasing number of highly processed high-calorie and high-fat grocery products.

—Henry J. Kaiser Family Foundation, "The Role of Media in Childhood Obesity" (2004), p. 1

PLAGIARISM

According to the Henry J. Kaiser Family Foundation (2004), experts have pointed to a range of important potential contributors to the rise in childhood obesity that are unrelated to media (p. 1).

BORROWED LANGUAGE IN QUOTATION MARKS

According to the Henry J. Kaiser Family Foundation (2004), "experts have pointed to a range of important potential contributors to the rise in childhood obesity that are unrelated to media" (p. 1).

Putting summaries and paraphrases in your own words   Summaries and paraphrases are written in your own words. A summary condenses information; a paraphrase uses roughly the same number of words as the original source to convey the information. When you summarize or paraphrase, it is not enough to name the source; you must restate the source's meaning using your own language. (See also 48c.) You commit plagiarism if you half-copy the author's sentences—either by mixing the author's phrases with your own without using quotation marks or by plugging your own synonyms into the author's sentence structure. The following paraphrases are plagiarized—even though the source is cited—because their language and sentence structure are too close to those of the source.

ORIGINAL SOURCE

In an effort to seek the causes of this disturbing trend, experts have pointed to a range of important potential contributors to the rise in childhood obesity that are unrelated to media.
—Henry J. Kaiser Family Foundation, "The Role of Media in Childhood Obesity" (2004), p. 1

UNACCEPTABLE BORROWING OF PHRASES

According to the Henry J. Kaiser Family Foundation (2004), experts have indicated a range of significant potential contributors to the rise in childhood obesity that are not linked to media (p. 1).

UNACCEPTABLE BORROWING OF STRUCTURE

According to the Henry J. Kaiser Family Foundation (2004), experts have identified a variety of significant factors causing a rise in childhood obesity, factors that are not linked to media (p. 1).

To avoid plagiarizing an author's language, resist the temptation to look at the source while you are summarizing or paraphrasing. After you have read the passage you want to paraphrase, set the source aside. Ask yourself, "What is the author's meaning?" In your own words, state your understanding of the author's basic point. Return to the source and check that you haven't used the author's language or sentence structure or misrepresented the author's ideas. When you fully understand another writer's meaning, you can more easily and accurately represent those ideas in your own words.

ACCEPTABLE PARAPHRASE

A report by the Henry J. Kaiser Family Foundation (2004) described causes other than media for the childhood obesity crisis.

hackerhandbooks.com/bedhandbook > **Research exercises** > APA > E-ex 56–3 to 56–7

56c Integrating sources

Quotations, summaries, paraphrases, and facts will help you develop your argument, but they cannot speak for you. You can use several strategies to integrate information from sources into your paper while maintaining your own voice.

Using quotations appropriately

In your academic writing, keep the emphasis on your ideas and your language; use your own words to summarize and to paraphrase your sources and to explain your points. Sometimes, however, quotations can be the most effective way to integrate a source.

WHEN TO USE QUOTATIONS

- When language is especially vivid or expressive
- When exact wording is needed for technical accuracy
- When it is important to let the debaters of an issue explain their positions in their own words
- When the words of an authority lend weight to an argument
- When the language of a source is the topic of your discussion (as in an analysis or interpretation)

Limiting your use of quotations Although it is tempting to insert many quotations in your paper and to use your own words only for connecting passages, do not quote excessively. It is almost impossible to integrate numerous quotations smoothly into your own text.

It is not always necessary to quote full sentences from a source. To reduce your reliance on the words of others, you can often integrate language from a source into your own sentence structure.

> Carmona (2004) advised the subcommittee that the situation constitutes an "epidemic" and that the skyrocketing statistics are "astounding."

> As researchers continue to face a number of unknowns about obesity, it may be helpful to envision treating the disorder, as Yanovski and Yanovski (2002) suggested, "in the same manner as any other chronic disease" (p. 592).

Using the ellipsis mark To condense a quoted passage, you can use the ellipsis mark (three periods, with spaces between) to indicate that you have left words out. What remains must be grammatically complete.

> Roman (2003) reported that "social factors are nearly as significant as individual metabolism in the formation of . . . dietary habits of adolescents" (p. 345).

The writer has omitted the words *both healthy and unhealthy* from the source.

When you want to leave out one or more full sentences, use a period before the three ellipsis dots.

> According to Sothern and Gordon (2003), "Environmental factors may contribute as much as 80% to the causes of childhood obesity. . . . Research suggests that obese children demonstrate decreased levels of physical activity and increased psychosocial problems" (p. 104).

Ordinarily, do not use an ellipsis mark at the beginning or at the end of a quotation. Readers will understand that you

using quotations • ellipsis mark (dots) •
brackets • long quotations
APA 56c 631

have taken the quoted material from a longer passage, so such marks are not necessary. The only exception occurs when you have dropped words at the end of the final quoted sentence. In such cases, put three ellipsis dots before the closing quotation mark.

Make sure omissions and ellipsis marks do not distort the meaning of your source.

Using brackets Brackets allow you to insert your own words into quoted material. You can insert words in brackets to clarify a confusing reference or to keep a sentence grammatical in your context.

> The cost of treating obesity currently totals $117 billion per year—a price, according to the surgeon general, "second only to the cost of [treating] tobacco use" (Carmona, 2004).

To indicate an error in a quotation, insert the word *sic* in brackets right after the error. Do not overuse *sic* to call attention to errors in a source. Sometimes paraphrasing is a better option. (See 39c.)

Setting off long quotations

When you quote forty or more words from a source, set off the quotation by indenting it one-half inch from the left margin. Use the normal right margin and do not single-space the quotation.

Long quotations should be introduced by an informative sentence, usually followed by a colon. Quotation marks are unnecessary because the indented format tells readers that the passage is taken word-for-word from the source.

> Yanovski and Yanovski (2002) have described earlier treatments for obesity that focused on behavior modification:
>
>> With the advent of behavioral treatments for obesity in the 1960s, hope arose that modification of maladaptive eating and exercise habits would lead to sustained weight loss, and that

> time-limited programs would produce permanent changes in weight. Medications for the treatment of obesity were proposed as short-term adjuncts for patients, who would presumably then acquire the skills necessary to continue to lose weight, reach "ideal body weight," and maintain a reduced weight indefinitely. (p. 592)

Notice that at the end of an indented quotation the parenthetical citation goes outside the final mark of punctuation. (When a quotation is run into your text, the opposite is true. See the sample citations on p. 630.)

Using signal phrases to integrate sources

Whenever you include a paraphrase, summary, or direct quotation of another writer in your paper, prepare your readers for it with introductory words called a *signal phrase.* A signal phrase usually names the author of the source and gives the publication year in parentheses and often provides context for the source material (see also p. 635).

When you write a signal phrase, choose a verb that is appropriate for the way you are using the source (see p. 623). Are you providing background, explaining a concept, supporting a claim, lending authority, or refuting a belief? By choosing an appropriate verb, you can make your source's role clear. See the chart on page 633 for a list of verbs commonly used in signal phrases.

APA requires using verbs in the past tense or present perfect tense (*noted* or *has noted*) to introduce quotations and other source material. Use the present tense only for discussing the results of an experiment (*the results show*) or knowledge that has clearly been established (*researchers agree*).

It is generally acceptable in the social sciences to call authors by their last name only, even on first mention. If your paper refers to two authors with same last name, use initials as well.

Marking boundaries Readers need to move from your words to the words of a source without feeling a jolt. Avoid dropping direct quotations into your text without warning. Instead, provide clear signal phrases, including at least the author's name and the date of publication. Signal phrases mark the boundaries between source material and your own words; they can also tell readers why a source is worth quoting. (The signal phrase is underlined in the second example.)

DROPPED QUOTATION

Obesity was once considered in a very different light. "For many years, obesity was approached as if it were either a moral failing or evidence of underlying psychopathology" (Yanovski & Yanovski, 2002, p. 592).

QUOTATION WITH SIGNAL PHRASE

Obesity was once considered in a very different light. <u>As researchers Yanovski and Yanovski (2002) have explained</u>, obesity was widely thought of as "either a moral failing or evidence of underlying psychopathology" (p. 592).

Using signal phrases with summaries and paraphrases   As with quotations, you should introduce most summaries and paraphrases with a signal phrase that mentions the author and the year and places the material in the context of your argument. Readers will then understand where the summary or paraphrase begins.

Without the signal phrase (underlined) in the following example, readers might think that only the last sentence is being cited, when in fact the whole paragraph is based on the source.

<u>Carmona (2004) advised a Senate subcommittee</u> that the problem of childhood obesity is dire and that the skyrocketing statistics—which put the child obesity rate at 15%—are cause for alarm. More than 9 million children, double the number in the early 1980s, are classified as obese. Carmona warned that obesity can cause myriad physical problems that only worsen as children grow older.

There are times, however, when a summary or a paraphrase does not require a signal phrase naming the author. When the context makes clear where the cited material begins, you may omit the signal phrase and include the author's

Using signal phrases in APA papers

To avoid monotony, try to vary both the language and the placement of your signal phrases.

Model signal phrases

In the words of Carmona (2004), ". . ."

As Yanovski and Yanovski (2002) have noted, ". . ."

Hoppin and Taveras (2004), medical researchers, pointed out that ". . ."

". . .," claimed Critser (2003).

". . .," wrote Duenwald (2004), ". . ."

Researchers McDuffie et al. (2003) have offered a compelling argument for this view: ". . ."

Hilts (2002) answered objections with the following analysis: ". . ."

Verbs in signal phrases

admitted	compared	insisted	rejected
agreed	confirmed	noted	reported
argued	contended	observed	responded
asserted	declared	pointed out	suggested
believed	denied	reasoned	thought
claimed	emphasized	refuted	wrote

name and the date in the parentheses. Unless the work is short, also include the page number in the parentheses.

Integrating statistics and other facts When you are citing a statistic or another specific fact, a signal phrase is often not necessary. In most cases, readers will understand that the citation refers to the statistic or fact (not the whole paragraph).

> In purely financial terms, the drugs cost more than $3 a day on average (Duenwald, 2004).

There is nothing wrong, however, with using a signal phrase to introduce a statistic or fact.

> Duenwald (2004) reported that the drugs cost more than $3 a day on average.

Putting source material in context   Readers should not have to guess why source material appears in your paper. A signal phrase can help you make the connection between your own ideas and those of another writer by clarifying how the source will contribute to your paper (see 47a).

If you use another writer's words, you must explain how they relate to your point. It's a good idea to embed a quotation between sentences of your own. In addition to introducing it with a signal phrase, follow it with interpretive comments that link the quotation to your paper's argument. (See also "Synthesizing sources," below.)

QUOTATION WITH EFFECTIVE CONTEXT

> A report by the Henry J. Kaiser Family Foundation (2004) outlined trends that may have contributed to the childhood obesity crisis, including food advertising for children as well as
>
> > a reduction in physical education classes . . . , an increase in the availability of sodas and snacks in public schools, the growth in the number of fast-food outlets . . . , and the increasing number of highly processed high-calorie and high-fat grocery products. (p. 1)
>
> Addressing each of these areas requires more than a doctor armed with a prescription pad; it requires a broad mobilization not just of doctors and concerned parents but of educators, food industry executives, advertisers, and media representatives.

hackerhandbooks.com/bedhandbook > **Research exercises** > **APA** > **E-ex 56–8 to 56–11**

Synthesizing sources

When you synthesize multiple sources in a research paper, you create a conversation about your research topic. You show readers that your argument is based on your active analysis and integration of ideas, not just a list of quotations and paraphrases. Your synthesis will show how your sources relate to one another. What one of your sources says may support, extend, or counter the ideas of another. Not every source has to "speak" to another in a research paper, but readers should be able to see how each one functions in your argument (see 47a).

Considering how sources relate to your argument Before you integrate sources and show readers how they relate to one another, consider how each one might contribute to your own argument. As student writer Luisa Mirano became more informed through her research about treatments for childhood obesity, she asked herself these questions: *What do I think about the various treatments for childhood obesity? Which sources might support my ideas? Which sources might help extend or illustrate the points I want to make? What common or compelling counterarguments do I need to address to strengthen my position?* She annotated a passage by journalist Greg Critser supporting her view that medication alone could not win the fight against childhood obesity.

STUDENT NOTES ON THE ORIGINAL SOURCE

> Yet the more I contemplated my success [at losing weight], the more I came to see it not as a triumph of will, but as a triumph of my economic and social class. The weight loss medication Meridia, for example, had been effective not because it is such a good drug; even its purveyors freely admit it is far from effective for most people. What had made the drug work for me was the (upper-middle-class support system) that I had brought to it: a good physician who insisted on seeing me every two weeks, access to a safe park where I could walk and jog, friends who shared the value of becoming slender, healthy home-cooked food consumed with my wife, books about health, and medical journals about the latest nutritional breakthroughs. And money. And time.
>
> —Greg Critser, *Fat Land*, pp. 2–3

Concrete examples—useful context.

No easy fix for obesity. Critser had economic, educational, and medical support.

Catchy term—good to quote

What about people without money and time? Even broader solution needed?

Critser's term *support system* offered Mirano a concise, visual way of referring to the extensive resources needed to fight obesity. His experience provided context and was a good choice for summary. Mirano planned to keep the emphasis on her own argument by analyzing Critser's text, discussing and expanding on his view in her own writing. She also looked for sources to support her view that larger-scale social and political change was needed to fight such a complex and widespread problem.

Placing sources in conversation You can show readers how the ideas of one source relate to those of another by connecting and analyzing the ideas in your own voice. After all, you've done the research and thought through the issues, so you should control the conversation. When you synthesize sources, the emphasis is still on your own writing; the thread of your argument should be easy to identify and to understand, with or without your sources.

SAMPLE SYNTHESIS (DRAFT)

Student writer Luisa Mirano begins with a claim that needs support.

Signal phrases indicate how sources contribute to Mirano's paper and show that the ideas that follow are not her own.

Mirano interprets and connects sources. Each paragraph ends with her own thoughts.

Medical treatments have clear costs for individual patients, including unpleasant side effects, little information about long-term use, and uncertainty that they will yield significant weight loss. The financial burden is heavy as well; the drugs cost more than $3 a day on average (Duenwald, 2004). In each of the clinical trials, use of medication was accompanied by expensive behavioral therapies, including counseling, nutrition education, fitness advising, and monitoring. As Critser (2003) noted in his book *Fat Land*, use of weight-loss drugs is unlikely to have an effect without the proper "support system"—one that includes doctors, facilities, time, and money (p. 3). For many families, this level of care is prohibitively expensive.

Both medical experts and policymakers recognize that solutions might come not only from a laboratory but also from policy, education, and advocacy. A handbook designed to educate doctors on obesity called for "major changes in some aspects of western culture" (Hoppin & Taveras, 2004, Conclusion section, para. 1). Solving the childhood obesity problem will require broad mobilization of doctors and concerned parents and also of educators, food industry executives, advertisers, and media representatives.

Student writer

Source 1

Student writer

Source 2

Student writer

Source 3

Student writer

In this draft, Mirano uses her own analyses to shape the conversation among her quoted sources. She does not simply string quotations together or allow them to overwhelm her writing. The final sentence, written in her own voice, gives her an opportunity to explain to readers how the various sources support and extend her argument.

When synthesizing sources in your own writing, ask yourself the following questions:

- Which sources inform, support, or extend your argument?
- Do you vary the functions of sources—to provide background information, explain terms or concepts, lend authority to your argument, and anticipate counterarguments?
- Do you explain to readers how your sources support your argument?
- Do you control the conversation by connecting and analyzing sources in your own voice?
- Is your own argument easy to identify and to understand, with or without your sources?

56d APA documentation style

In most social science classes, you will be asked to use the APA system for documenting sources, which is set forth in the *Publication Manual of the American Psychological Association*, 6th ed. (Washington: APA, 2010). APA recommends in-text citations that refer readers to a list of references.

An in-text citation gives the author of the source (often in a signal phrase), the year of publication, and at times a page number in parentheses. At the end of the paper, a list of references provides publication information about the source (see p. 683 for a sample list of references). The direct link between the in-text citation and the entry in the reference list is highlighted in the following example.

IN-TEXT CITATION

Yanovski and Yanovski (2002) reported that "the current state of the treatment for obesity is similar to the state of the treatment of hypertension several decades ago" (p. 600).

ENTRY IN THE LIST OF REFERENCES

Yanovski, S. Z., & Yanovski, J. A. (2002). Drug therapy: Obesity. *The New England Journal of Medicine, 346*, 591-602.

For a reference list that includes this entry, see page 683.

APA in-text citations

APA's in-text citations provide at least the author's last name and the year of publication. For direct quotations and some paraphrases, a page number is given as well.

NOTE: APA style requires the use of the past tense or the present perfect tense in signal phrases introducing cited material: *Smith (2005) reported, Smith (2005) has argued.*

1. Basic format for a quotation   Ordinarily, introduce the quotation with a signal phrase that includes the author's last name followed by the year of publication in parentheses. Put the page number (preceded by "p.") in parentheses after the quotation.

Critser (2003) noted that despite growing numbers of overweight Americans, many health care providers still "remain either in ignorance or outright denial about the health danger to the poor and the young" (p. 5).

If the author is not named in the signal phrase, place the author's name, the year, and the page number in parentheses after the quotation: (Critser, 2003, p. 5).

NOTE: APA style requires the year of publication in an in-text citation. Do not include a month, even if the entry in the reference list includes the month.

2. Basic format for a summary or a paraphrase Include the author's last name and the year either in a signal phrase introducing the material or in parentheses following it. A page number is not required for a summary or a paraphrase, but include one if it would help readers find the passage in a long work. (For the use of other locators, such as paragraph numbers or section names in online sources, see pp. 643–44.)

Yanovski and Yanovski (2002) explained that sibutramine suppresses appetite by blocking the reuptake of the neurotransmitters serotonin and norepinephrine in the brain (p. 594).

Sibutramine suppresses appetite by blocking the reuptake of the neurotransmitters serotonin and norepinephrine in the brain (Yanovski & Yanovski, 2002, p. 594).

3. Work with two authors Name both authors in the signal phrase or the parentheses each time you cite the work. In the parentheses, use "&" between the authors' names; in the signal phrase, use "and."

According to Sothern and Gordon (2003), "Environmental factors may contribute as much as 80% to the causes of childhood obesity" (p. 104).

Obese children often engage in limited physical activity (Sothern & Gordon, 2003, p. 104).

4. Work with three to five authors Identify all authors in the
signal phrase or the parentheses the first time you cite the
source.

In 2003, Berkowitz, Wadden, Tershakovec, and Cronquist concluded,
"Sibutramine . . . must be carefully monitored in adolescents, as in
adults, to control increases in [blood pressure] and pulse rate" (p. 1811).

In subsequent citations, use the first author's name followed
by "et al." in either the signal phrase or the parentheses.

As Berkowitz et al. (2003) advised, "Until more extensive safety and
efficacy data are available, . . . weight-loss medications should be used
only on an experimental basis for adolescents" (p. 1811).

5. Work with six or more authors Use the first author's name
followed by "et al." in the signal phrase or the parentheses.

McDuffie et al. (2002) tested 20 adolescents, aged 12-16, over a
three-month period and found that orlistat, combined with behavioral
therapy, produced an average weight loss of 4.4 kg, or 9.7 pounds (p. 646).

6. Work with unknown author If the author is unknown,
mention the work's title in the signal phrase or give the first
word or two of the title in the parenthetical citation. Titles
of articles and chapters are put in quotation marks; titles of
books and reports are italicized. (For online sources with no
author, see item 12 on p. 643.)

Children struggling to control their weight must also struggle with the
pressures of television advertising that, on the one hand, encourages
the consumption of junk food and, on the other, celebrates thin
celebrities ("Television," 2002).

NOTE: In the rare case when "Anonymous" is specified as the
author, treat it as if it were a real name: (Anonymous, 2001). In
the list of references, also use the name Anonymous as author.

7. Organization as author If the author is a government
agency or another organization, name the organization in

the signal phrase or in the parenthetical citation the first time
you cite the source.

> Obesity puts children at risk for a number of medical complications,
> including type 2 diabetes, hypertension, sleep apnea, and orthopedic
> problems (Henry J. Kaiser Family Foundation, 2004, p. 1).

If the organization has a familiar abbreviation, you may
include it in brackets the first time you cite the source and use
the abbreviation alone in later citations.

FIRST CITATION   (Centers for Disease Control and Prevention
                       [CDC], 2009)

LATER CITATIONS   (CDC, 2009)

8. Authors with the same last name   To avoid confusion, use
initials with the last names if your reference list includes two
or more authors with the same last name.

> Research by E. Smith (1989) revealed that . . .

**9. Two or more works by the same author in the same
year**   When your list of references includes more than one
work by the same author in the same year, use lowercase letters ("a," "b," and so on) with the year to order the entries in
the reference list. (See item 6 on p. 648.) Use those same letters with the year in the in-text citation.

> Research by Durgin (2003b) has yielded new findings about the role of
> counseling in treating childhood obesity.

10. Two or more works in the same parentheses   When your
parenthetical citation names two or more works, put them
in the same order that they appear in the reference list, separated with semicolons.

> Researchers have indicated that studies of pharmacological treatments
> for childhood obesity are inconclusive (Berkowitz et al., 2003; McDuffie
> et al., 2003).

11. Personal communication   Personal interviews, memos, letters, e-mail, and similar unpublished communications should

be cited in the text only, not in the reference list. (Use the first initial with the last name in parentheses.)

> One of Atkinson's colleagues, who has studied the effect of the
> media on children's eating habits, has contended that advertisers
> for snack foods will need to design ads responsibly for their younger
> viewers (F. Johnson, personal communication, October 20, 2009).

12. Electronic source   When possible, cite electronic sources, including online sources, as you would any other source, giving the author and the year.

> Atkinson (2001) found that children who spent at least four hours a
> day watching TV were less likely to engage in adequate physical activity
> during the week.

Electronic sources sometimes lack authors' names, dates, or page numbers.

Unknown author
If no author is named, mention the title of the source in the signal phrase or give the first word or two of the title in the parentheses (see also item 6). (If an organization serves as the author, see item 7.)

> The body's basal metabolic rate, or BMR, is a measure of its at-rest
> energy requirement ("Exercise," 2003).

Unknown date
When the date is unknown, use the abbreviation "n.d." (for "no date").

> Attempts to establish a definitive link between television programming
> and children's eating habits have been problematic (Magnus, n.d.).

No page numbers
APA ordinarily requires page numbers for quotations, and it recommends them for summaries and paraphrases from long sources. When an electronic source lacks stable numbered pages, your citation should include information that will help readers locate the particular passage being cited.

If the source has numbered paragraphs, use the paragraph number preceded by the abbreviation "para.": (Hall, 2008, para. 5). If the source contains headings, cite the appropriate heading in parentheses; you may also indicate the paragraph under the heading that you are referring to, even if the paragraphs are not numbered.

> Hoppin and Taveras (2004) pointed out that several other medications were classified by the Drug Enforcement Administration as having the "potential for abuse" (Weight-Loss Drugs section, para. 6).

NOTE: Electronic files in portable document format (PDF) often have stable page numbers. For such sources, give the page number in the parenthetical citation.

13. Indirect source   If you use a source that was cited in another source (a secondary source), name the original source in your signal phrase. List the secondary source in your reference list and include it in your parenthetical citation, preceded by the words "as cited in." In the following example, Satcher is the original source, and Critser is the secondary source, given in the reference list.

> Former surgeon general Dr. David Satcher described "a nation of young people seriously at risk of starting out obese and dooming themselves to the difficult task of overcoming a tough illness" (as cited in Critser, 2003, p. 4).

14. Sacred or classical text   Identify the text, the version or edition you used, and the relevant part (chapter, verse, line). It is not necessary to include the source in the reference list.

> Peace activists have long cited the biblical prophet's vision of a world without war: "And they shall beat their swords into plowshares, and their spears into pruning hooks; nation shall not lift up sword against nation, neither shall they learn war any more" (Isaiah 2:4, Revised Standard Version).

APA list of references

In APA style, the alphabetical list of works cited, which appears at the end of the paper, is titled "References." For advice on preparing the reference list, see pages 672–73. For a sample reference list, see page 683.

Alphabetize entries in the list of references by authors' last names; if a work has no author, alphabetize it by its title. The first element of each entry is important because citations in the text of the paper refer to it and readers will be looking for it in the alphabetized list. The date of publication appears immediately after the first element of the citation.

In APA style, titles of books are italicized; titles of articles are neither italicized nor put in quotation marks. (For rules on capitalization of titles, see p. 670.)

General guidelines for listing authors (print and online)

In APA style, all authors' names are inverted (the last name comes first), and initials only are used for all first and middle names.

NAME AND DATE CITED IN TEXT

Duncan (2008) has reported that . . .

BEGINNING OF ENTRY IN THE LIST OF REFERENCES

Duncan, B. (2008).

1. Single author

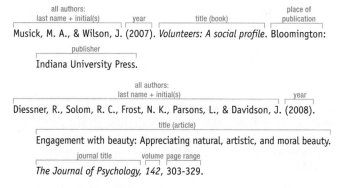

author: last name
+ initial(s)   year   title (book)

Egeland, J. (2008). *A billion lives: An eyewitness report from the frontlines of*

place of
publication   publisher

humanity. New York, NY: Simon & Schuster.

2. Multiple authors   List up to seven authors by last names followed by initials. Use an ampersand (&) before the name of the last author. If there are more than seven authors, list the first six followed by three ellipsis dots and the last author's name. (See pp. 640–41 for citing works with multiple authors in your paper.)

Two to seven authors

all authors:
last name + initial(s)   year   title (book)   place of
publication

Musick, M. A., & Wilson, J. (2007). *Volunteers: A social profile*. Bloomington:

publisher

Indiana University Press.

all authors:
last name + initial(s)   year

Diessner, R., Solom, R. C., Frost, N. K., Parsons, L., & Davidson, J. (2008).

title (article)

Engagement with beauty: Appreciating natural, artistic, and moral beauty.

journal title   volume page range

The Journal of Psychology, 142, 303-329.

Eight or more authors

Mulvaney, S. A., Mudasiru, E., Schlundt, D. G., Baughman, C. L., Fleming, M.,
VanderWoude, A., . . . Rothman, R. (2008). Self-management in Type 2
diabetes: The adolescent perspective. *The Diabetes Educator, 34*, 118–127.

3. Organization as author

author:
organization name — year — title (book)

American Psychiatric Association. (1994). *Diagnostic and statistical manual of*

edition number — place of publication — organization as author and publisher

mental disorders (4th ed.). Washington, DC: Author.

If the publisher is not the same as the author, give the publisher's name as you would for any other source.

4. Unknown author   Begin the entry with the work's title.

title (book) — year — place of publication — publisher

New concise world atlas. (2007). New York, NY: Oxford University Press.

title (article) — year + date (for weekly publication) — journal title — volume, issue — page range

Order in the jungle. (2008, March 15). *The Economist, 386*(8571), 83-85.

5. Two or more works by the same author   Use the author's name for all entries. List the entries by year, the earliest first.

Barry, P. (2007, December 8). Putting tumors on pause. *Science News, 172*,
365.

Barry, P. (2008, August 2). Finding the golden genes. *Science News, 174*,
16-21.

6. Two or more works by the same author in the same year   List the works alphabetically by title. In the parentheses, following the year add "a," "b," and so on. Use these same letters when giving the year in the in-text citation. (See also p. 672.)

Elkind, D. (2008a, Spring). Can we play? *Greater Good, 4*(4), 14-17.

Elkind, D. (2008b, June 27). The price of hurrying children [Web log
message]. Retrieved from http://blogs.psychologytoday.com/blog
/digital-children

Articles in periodicals (print)

Periodicals include scholarly journals, magazines, and newspapers. For a journal or a magazine, give only the volume number if the publication is paginated continuously through each volume; give the volume and issue numbers if each issue of the volume begins on page 1. Italicize the volume number and put the issue number, not italicized, in parentheses.

For all periodicals, when an article appears on consecutive pages, provide the range of pages. When an article does not appear on consecutive pages, give all page numbers: A1, A17. (See also "Online sources" beginning on p. 656 for online articles and articles accessed through a library's database.) For an illustrated citation of an article in a periodical, see page 650.

7. Article in a journal

author: last name
   + initial(s)   year   article title

Zhang, L.-F. (2008). Teachers' styles of thinking: An exploratory study. *The Journal*

                           page
   journal title   volume   range

     of Psychology, 142, 37-55.

8. Article in a magazine

Cite as a journal article, but give the year and the month for monthly magazines; add the day for weekly magazines.

McKibben, B. (2007, October). Carbon's new math. *National Geographic,*
     212(4), 32-37.

9. Article in a newspaper

author: last name   year + month + day
   + initial(s)   (for daily publication)   article title

Svoboda, E. (2008, October 21). Deep in the rain forest, stalking the next

                             page
          newspaper title   number

     pandemic. *The New York Times*, p. D5.

Citation at a glance | Article in a periodical (APA)

To cite an article in a print periodical in APA style, include the following elements:

1. Author
2. Year of publication
3. Title of article
4. Name of periodical
5. Volume number; issue number, if required (see p. 649)
6. Page numbers of article

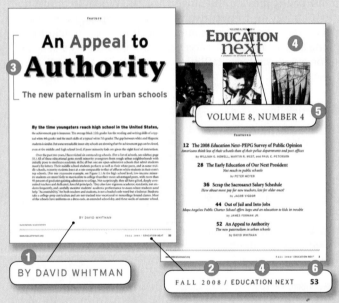

REFERENCE LIST ENTRY FOR AN ARTICLE IN A PRINT PERIODICAL

Whitman, D. (2008). An appeal to authority: The new paternalism in urban

schools. *Education Next, 8*(4), 53-58.

For variations on citing articles in print periodicals in APA style, see pages 649–52.

Give the year, month, and day for daily and weekly newspapers. Use "p." or "pp." before page numbers.

10. Article with three to seven authors

Ungar, M., Brown, M., Liebenberg, L., Othman, R., Kwong, W. M., Armstrong,
M., & Gilgun, J. (2007). Unique pathways to resilience across cultures.
Adolescence, 42, 287-310.

11. Article with eight or more authors
List the first six authors followed by three ellipsis dots and the last author.

Krippner, G., Granovetter, M., Block, F., Biggart, N., Beamish, T., Hsing, Y.,
. . . O'Riain, S. (2004). Polanyi Symposium: A conversation on
embeddedness. *Socio-Economic Review, 2*, 109-135.

12. Abstract of a journal article

Lahm, K. (2008). Inmate-on-inmate assault: A multilevel examination of
prison violence [Abstract]. *Criminal Justice and Behavior, 35*(1),
120-137.

13. Letter to the editor
Letters to the editor appear in journals, magazines, and newspapers. Follow the appropriate model (see items 7–9), and insert the words "Letter to the editor" in brackets after the title of the letter. If the letter has no title, use the bracketed words as the title.

Park, T. (2008, August). Defining the line [Letter to the editor]. *Scientific
American, 299*(2), 10.

14. Editorial or other unsigned article

The global justice movement [Editorial]. (2005). *Multinational Monitor,
26*(7/8), 6.

15. Newsletter article

Setting the stage for remembering. (2006, September). *Mind, Mood, and
Memory, 2*(9), 4-5.

16. Review Give the author and title of the review (if any); in brackets, indicate the type of work being reviewed (book, motion picture) and the title of the work. If the review has no author or title, use the material in brackets as the title.

Applebaum, A. (2008, February 14). A movie that matters [Review of the motion picture *Katyn*, 2007]. *The New York Review of Books, 55*(2), 13-15.

Agents of change. (2008, February 2). [Review of the book *The power of unreasonable people: How social entrepreneurs create markets that change the world,* by J. Elkington & P. Hartigan]. *The Economist, 386*(8565), 94.

Books (print)

Items 17–29 apply to print books. For online books, see items 36 and 37. For an illustrated citation of a print book, see page 653.

Take the information about a book from its title page and copyright page. If more than one place of publication is listed, use only the first. Give the state (abbreviated) or the country for all cities. Do not give a state abbreviation if the publisher's name includes the state (as in many university presses, for example).

17. Basic format for a book

author: last   year of
name + initial(s)   publication   book title

McKenzie, F. R. (2008). *Theory and practice with adolescents: An applied approach.*

place of
publication   publisher

Chicago, IL: Lyceum Books.

18. Book with an editor

all editors: year of
last name + initial(s)   publication   book title

Aronson, J., & Aronson, E. (Eds.). (2008). *Readings about the social animal*

edition   place of
number   publication   publisher

(10th ed.). New York, NY: Worth.

The abbreviation "Eds." is for multiple editors. If the book has one editor, use "Ed."

19. Book with an author and an editor

author: last name
\+ initial(s)   year of publication   book title   name(s) of editor(s): in normal order

McLuhan, M. (2003). *Understanding me: Lectures and interviews* (S. McLuhan

           place of publication (city, country)   publisher

    & D. Staine, Eds.). Toronto, Canada: McClelland & Stewart.

The abbreviation "Eds." is for multiple editors. If the book has one editor, use "Ed."

20. Book with an author and a translator
After the title, name the translator, followed by "Trans.," in parentheses. Add the original date of publication at the end of the entry.

Steinberg, M. D. (2003). *Voices of revolution, 1917* (M. Schwartz, Trans.). New
    Haven, CT: Yale University Press. (Original work published 2001)

21. Edition other than the first

O'Brien, J. A. (Ed.). (2006). *The production of reality: Essays and readings on
    social interaction* (4th ed.). Thousand Oaks, CA: Pine Forge Press.

22. Article or chapter in an edited book or an anthology

author of chapter:
last name + initial(s)   year of publication   title of chapter

Denton, N. A. (2006). Segregation and discrimination in housing. In R. G.

     book editor(s): in normal order   book title

    Bratt, M. E. Stone, & C. Hartman (Eds.), *A right to housing: Foundation of*

             page range for chapter   place of publication   publisher

    a new social agenda (pp. 61-81). Philadelphia, PA: Temple University Press.

The abbreviation "Eds." is for multiple editors. If the book has one editor, use "Ed."

Citation at a glance | Book (APA)

To cite a print book in APA style, include the following
elements:

1 Author
2 Year of publication
3 Title and subtitle
4 Place of publication
5 Publisher

Farrar, Straus and Giroux
18 West 18th Street, New York 10011

Copyright © 2008 by Thomas L. Friedman
All rights reserved
Distributed in Canada by Douglas & McIntyre Ltd.
Printed in the United States of America
First edition, 2008

2 Copyright © 2008 by Thomas L. Friedman

Library of Congress Control Number: 2008930589
ISBN-13: 978-0-374-16685-4
ISBN-10: 0-374-16685-4

Designed by Jonathan D. Lippincott

www.fsgbooks.com

1 3 5 7 9 10 8 6 4 2

FSC
Mixed Sources

This book was printed on text paper containing
30 percent post-consumer recycled content.

1 THOMAS L. FRIEDMAN

Hot, Flat, and Crowded
3 WHY WE NEED A GREEN REVOLUTION—
AND HOW IT CAN RENEW AMERICA

5 FARRAR, STRAUS AND GIROUX
4 NEW YORK

FARRAR, STRAUS AND GIROUX
NEW YORK

REFERENCE LIST ENTRY FOR A PRINT BOOK

1 —— 2 —— 3 ——

Friedman, T. L. (2008). *Hot, flat, and crowded: Why we need a green revolution—*

—— 4 —— 5 ——

And how it can renew America. New York, NY: Farrar, Straus & Giroux.

For more on citing print books in APA style, see pages 652–55.

23. Multivolume work   Give the number of volumes after the title.

Luo, J. (Ed.). (2005). *China today: An encyclopedia of life in the People's Republic* (Vols. 1-2). Westport, CT: Greenwood Press.

24. Introduction, preface, foreword, or afterword

Gore, A. (2000). Foreword. In B. Katz (Ed.), *Reflections on regionalism* (pp. ix-x). Washington, DC: Brookings Institution Press.

25. Dictionary or other reference work

Leong, F. T. L. (Ed.). (2008). *Encyclopedia of counseling* (Vols. 1-4). Thousand Oaks, CA: Sage.

26. Article in a reference work

Konijn, E. A. (2008). Affects and media exposure. In W. Donsbach (Ed.), *The international encyclopedia of communication* (Vol. 1, pp. 123-129). Malden, MA: Blackwell.

27. Republished book

Mailer, N. (2008). *Miami and the siege of Chicago: An informal history of the Republican and Democratic conventions of 1968*. New York, NY: New York Review Books. (Original work published 1968)

28. Book with a title in its title   If the book title contains another book title or an article title, neither italicize the internal title nor place it in quotation marks.

Marcus, L. (Ed.). (1999). *Sigmund Freud's* The interpretation of dreams*: New interdisciplinary essays*. Manchester, England: Manchester University Press.

29. Sacred or classical text   It is not necessary to list sacred works such as the Bible or the Qur'an or classical Greek and Roman works in your reference list. See item 14 on page 644 for how to cite these sources in the text of your paper.

Online sources

When citing an online article, include publication information as for a print periodical (see items 7–16) and add information about the online version (see items 30–35).

Online articles and books sometimes include a DOI (digital object identifier). APA uses the DOI, when available, in place of a URL in reference list entries.

Use a retrieval date for an online source only if the content is likely to change. Most of the examples in this section do not show a retrieval date because the content of the sources is stable; if you are unsure about whether to use a retrieval date, include the date or consult your instructor.

If you must break a DOI or a URL at the end of a line, break it after a double slash or before any other mark of punctuation; do not add a hyphen. Do not put a period at the end of the entry.

30. Article in an online journal

author: last name + initial(s) — year of publication — article title — journal title
Whitmeyer, J. M. (2000). Power through appointment. *Social Science Research,*

volume page range — DOI
29, 535-555. doi:10.1006/ssre.2000.0680

If there is no DOI, include the URL for the article or for the journal's home page.

Ashe, D. D., & McCutcheon, L. E. (2001). Shyness, loneliness, and attitude
toward celebrities. *Current Research in Social Psychology, 6*, 124-133.
Retrieved from http://www.uiowa.edu/~grpproc/crisp/crisp.html

31. Article in an online magazine   Treat as an article in a print magazine (see item 8), and add the URL for the magazine's home page.

Shelburne, E. C. (2008, September). The great disruption. *The Atlantic, 302*(2).
Retrieved from http://www.theatlantic.com/

32. Article in an online newspaper   Treat as an article in a print newspaper (see item 9), adding the URL for the newspaper's home page.

Watson, P. (2008, October 19). Biofuel boom endangers orangutan habitat.
   Los Angeles Times. Retrieved from http://www.latimes.com/

33. Article published only online   If an article in a journal, magazine, or newspaper appears only online, give whatever publication information is available in the source and add the description "Supplemental material" in brackets following the article title.

Samuel, T. (2009, March 27). Mind the wage gap [Supplemental material].
   The American Prospect. Retrieved from http://www.prospect.org/

34. Article from a database   Start with the publication information for the source (see items 7–16). If the database entry gives a DOI for the article, use that number at the end and do not include the database name. For an illustrated citation of a work from a database, see page 658.

all authors:
last name + initial(s)   year   article title
Eskritt, M., & McLeod, K. (2008). Children's note taking as a mnemonic tool.

                                                 volume,   page
              journal title   issue   range   DOI
     Journal of Experimental Child Psychology, 101, 52-74. doi:10.1016

/jecp.2008.05.007

If there is no DOI, include the URL for the home page of the journal.

Howard, K. R. (2007). Childhood overweight: Parental perceptions and
   readiness for change. *The Journal of School Nursing, 23*, 73-79.
   Retrieved from http://jsn.sagepub.com/

Citation at a glance | Article from a database (APA)

To cite an article from a database in APA style, include the following elements:

1 Author(s)
2 Date of publication
3 Title of article
4 Name of periodical
5 Volume number; issue number, if required (see p. 649)
6 Page range
7 DOI (digital object identifier)
8 URL for journal's home page (if there is no DOI)

ON-SCREEN VIEW OF DATABASE RECORD

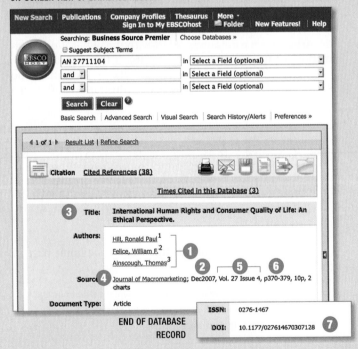

END OF DATABASE RECORD

REFERENCE LIST ENTRY FOR AN ARTICLE FROM A DATABASE

Hill, R. P., Felice, W. F., & Ainscough, T. (2007). International human rights

and consumer quality of life: An ethical perspective. *Journal of*

Macromarketing, 27, 370-379. doi:10.1177/027614670307128

For more on citing articles from a database in APA style, see item 34.

35. Abstract for an online article

Brockerhoff, E. G., Jactel, H., Parrotta, J. A., Quine, C. P., & Sayer, J. (2008).
    Plantation forests and biodiversity: Oxymoron or opportunity? [Abstract].
    Biodiversity and Conservation, 17, 925-951. doi:10.1007/s10531-008
    -9380-x

36. Online book

Adams, B. (2004). *The theory of social revolutions*. Retrieved from
    http://www.gutenberg.org/catalog/world/readfile?fk_files=44092
    (Original work published 1913)

37. Chapter in an online book

Clinton, S. J. (1999). What can be done to prevent childhood obesity? In
    Understanding childhood obesity (pp. 81-98). Retrieved from http://
    www.questia.com/

38. Online reference work

Swain, C. M. (2004). Sociology of affirmative action. In N. J. Smelser
    & P. B. Baltes (Eds.), *International encyclopedia of the social and
    behavioral sciences*. Retrieved from http://www.sciencedirect.com
    /science/referenceworks/9780080430768

Use a retrieval date only if the content of the work is likely to change.

39. Document from a Web site List as many of the following elements as are available: author's name, publication date (or "n.d." if there is no date), title (in italics), and URL. Give your retrieval date only if the content of the source is likely to change.

Source with date

all authors:
last name + initial(s)   online publication
date: year + month   document title

Cain, A., & Burris, M. (1999, April). *Investigation of the use of mobile*

URL

phones while driving. Retrieved from http://www.cutr.eng.usf.edu/its

/mobile_phone_text.htm

Source with no date

Archer, D. (n.d.). *Exploring nonverbal communication*. Retrieved from http://

nonverbal.ucsc.edu

Source with no author

If a source has no author, begin with the title and follow it with the date in parentheses.

What causes Alzheimer's disease. (2008). Retrieved from http://

www.memorystudy.org/alzheimers_causes.htm

40. Section in a Web document

author (organization)   year   title of section

National Institute on Media and the Family. (2009). Mobile networking.

title of Web document

In *Guide to social networking: Risks*. Retrieved from http://www

URL

.mediafamily.org/network_pdf/MediaWise_Guide_to_Social

_Networking_Risks_09.pdf

For an illustrated citation of a section in a Web document, see page 662.

41. Document from a university Web site or government agency Name the organization or agency in your retrieval statement.

Cosmides, L., & Tooby, J. (1997). *Evolutionary psychology: A primer.*
Retrieved from University of California, Santa Barbara, Center for
Evolutionary Psychology website: http://www.psych.ucsb.edu
/research/cep/primer.html

42. Article in an online newsletter Cite as an online article (see items 30–32), giving the title of the newsletter and whatever other information is available, including volume and issue numbers.

In the face of extinction. (2008, May). *NSF Current.* Retrieved from http://
www.nsf.gov/news/newsletter/may_08/index.jsp

43. Podcast

organization as producer   date of posting
National Academies (Producer). (2007, June 6). Progress in preventing

     podcast title   descriptive label
childhood obesity: How do we measure up? [Audio podcast].

     series title   URL
The sounds of science podcast. Retrieved from http://media.nap.edu

/podcasts/

writer/
presenter   date of posting   podcast title
Chesney, M. (2007, September 13). Gender differences in the use of

     podcast number   descriptive label
complementary and alternative medicine (No. 12827) [Audio podcast].

     Web site hosting podcast
Retrieved from University of California Television website:

     URL
http://www.uctv.tv/ondemand

Citation at a glance | Section in a Web document (APA)

To cite a section in a Web document in APA style, include the following elements:

1 Author
2 Date of publication or most recent update
3 Title of section
4 Title of document
5 URL of section

BROWSER PRINTOUT OF WEB SITE

2003 Minnesota Health Statistics Annual Summary - Minneso.. https://www.health.state.mn.us/divs/chs/03annsum/index.html

 Minnesota Department of Health
Protecting, maintaining and improving the health of all Minnesotans

MDH

Minnesota Center for Health Statistics
- Home
- General statistics
  - Minnesota Vital Statistics Interactive Queries
  - Minnesota Vital Signs
  - Minnesota County Health Tables
  - Mini Profiles
  - Minnesota Health Statistics Annual Summary
  - Population Health Assessment Quarterly
- Topic-specific statistics
  - Induced Abortions in Minnesota Reports
  - Populations of Color Health Status Report
  - Tobacco Reports

2003 Minnesota Health Statistics Annual Summary

The Minnesota "Annual Summary" or "Minnesota Health Statistics" is a report published yearly. The most recent version of this report is *2003 Minnesota Health Statistics*, published February 2005. This report provides statistical data on the following seven subjects for the state of Minnesota.

 published February 2005.

To view the PDF files, you will need Adobe Acrobat Reader or for screen reader accessibility Adobe Acrobat Access (free downloads from Adobe's Web site).

- **Overview of 2003 Annual Summary (PDF: 251KB/11 pages)**
- **Live Births (PDF: 608KB/21 pages)**
- **Fertility (PDF: 80KB/2 pages)** ● ──── 3
- **Infant Mortality and Fetal Deaths (PDF: 414KB/15 pages)**
- **General Mortality (PDF: 581KB/40 pages)**
- **Marriage (PDF: 83KB/4 pages)**
- **Divorce (PDF: 62KB/3 pages)**
- **Population (PDF: 29KB/12 pages)**

Note: Induced abortion statistics previously reported in this publication are now published separately.
See > Report to the Legislature: Induced Abortions in Minnesota

See also> Minnesota Health Statistics Annual Summary Main Page

1of3   6/28/05 5:14 PM

ON-SCREEN VIEW OF DOCUMENT

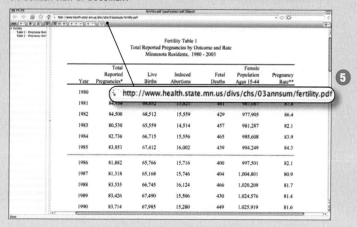

REFERENCE LIST ENTRY FOR A SECTION IN A WEB DOCUMENT

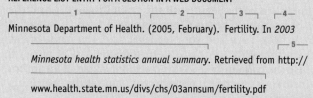

Minnesota Department of Health. (2005, February). Fertility. In *2003*

Minnesota health statistics annual summary. Retrieved from http://

www.health.state.mn.us/divs/chs/03annsum/fertility.pdf

For more on citing documents from Web sites in APA style, see pages 660–65.

44. Weblog (blog) post   Give the writer's name, the date of the post, and the title or subject of the post. Follow with the words "Message posted to" and the URL.

Kellermann, M. (2007, May 23). Disclosing clinical trials [Web log
      message]. Retrieved from http://www.iq.harvard.edu/blog/sss
      /archives/2007/05

45. Online audio or video file   Give the medium or a description of the source file in brackets following the title.

Chomsky, N. (n.d.). The new imperialism [Audio file]. Retrieved from http://
      www.rhapsody.com/noamchomsky

Zakaria, F. (Host), & McCullough, C. (Writer). (2007, March 6). In focus:
      American teens, Rwandan truths [Video file]. Retrieved from http://
      www.pulitzercenter.org/showproject.cfm?id=26

46. Entry in a wiki   Begin with the title of the entry and the date of posting, if there is one (use "n.d." for "no date" if there is not). Then add your retrieval date, the name of the wiki, and the URL for the wiki. Include the date of retrieval because the content of a wiki is often not stable. If an author or an editor is identified, include that name at the beginning of the entry.

Ethnomethodology. (n.d.). Retrieved August 22, 2008, from http://
      en.stswiki.org/index.php/Ethnomethodology

47. Data set or graphic representation   Give information about the type of source in brackets following the title. If there is no title, give a brief description of the content of the source in brackets in place of the title.

U.S. Department of Agriculture, Economic Research Service. (2009). *Eating
      and health module (ATUS): 2007 data* [Data set]. Retrieved from http://
      www.ers.usda.gov/Data/ATUS/Data/2007/2007data.htm

Gallup. (2008, October 23). *No increase in proportion of first-time voters*
[Graphs]. Retrieved from http://www.gallup.com/poll/111331
/No-Increase-Proportion-First-Time-Voters.aspx

48. Conference hearing

Carmona, R. H. (2004, March 2). *The growing epidemic of childhood obesity*.
Testimony before the Subcommittee on Competition, Foreign Commerce,
and Infrastructure of the U.S. Senate Committee on Commerce, Science,
and Transportation. Retrieved from http://www.hhs.gov/asl/testify
/t040302.html

49. E-mail   E-mail messages, letters, and other personal communications are not included in the list of references. (See
p. 642 for citing these sources in the text of your paper.)

50. Online posting   If an online posting is not archived, cite
it as a personal communication in the text of your paper and
do not include it in the list of references. If the posting is archived, give the URL and the name of the discussion list if it
is not part of the URL.

McKinney, J. (2006, December 19). Adult education-healthcare
partnerships [Electronic mailing list message]. Retrieved from http://
www.nifl.gov/pipermail/healthliteracy/2006/000524.html

Other sources (including online versions)

51. Dissertation from a database

Hymel, K. M. (2009). *Essays in urban economics* (Doctoral dissertation). Available
from ProQuest Dissertations and Theses database. (AAT 3355930)

52. Unpublished dissertation

Mitchell, R. D. (2007). *The Wesleyan Quadrilateral: Relocating the conversation*
(Unpublished doctoral dissertation). Claremont School of Theology,
Claremont, CA.

53. Government document

U.S. Census Bureau. (2006). *Statistical abstract of the United States*. Washington, DC: Government Printing Office.

U.S. Census Bureau, Bureau of Economic Analysis. (2008, August). *U.S. international trade in goods and services* (Report No. CB08-121, BEA08-37, FT-900). Retrieved from http://www.census.gov /foreign-trade/Press-Release/2008pr/06/ftdpress.pdf

54. Report from a private organization If the publisher and the author are the same, begin with the publisher. For a print source, use "Author" as the publisher at the end of the entry (see item 3 on p. 648); for an online source, give the URL. If the report has a number, put it in parentheses following the title.

Ford Foundation. (n.d.). *Helping citizens to understand and influence state budgets*. Retrieved December 15, 2008, from http://www.fordfound.org /pdfs/impact/evaluations/state_fiscal_initiative.pdf

55. Legal source

Sweatt v. Painter, 339 U.S. 629 (1950). Retrieved from Cornell University Law School, Legal Information Institute website: http://www.law.cornell .edu/supct/html/historics/USSC_CR_0339_0629_ZS.html

56. Conference proceedings

Stahl, G. (Ed.). (2002). *Proceedings of CSCL '02: Computer support for collaborative learning*. Hillsdale, NJ: Erlbaum.

57. Paper presented at a meeting or symposium (unpublished)

Anderson, D. N. (2008, May). *Cab-hailing and the micropolitics of gesture*. Paper presented at the Arizona Linguistics and Anthropology Symposium, Tucson, AZ.

58. Poster session at a conference

Wang, Z., & Keogh, T. (2008, June). *A click away: Student response to clickers*. Poster session presented at the annual conference of the American Library Association, Anaheim, CA.

59. Map or chart

Ukraine [Map]. (2008). Retrieved from the University of Texas at Austin
      Perry-Castañeda Library Map Collection website: http://www.lib.utexas
      .edu/maps/cia08/ukraine_sm_2008.gif

60. Advertisement

Xbox 360 [Advertisement]. (2007, February). *Wired, 15*(2), 71.

61. Published interview

Murphy, C. (2007, June 22). As the Romans did [Interview by G. Hahn].
      Retrieved from http://www.theatlantic.com/

62. Lecture, speech, or address

Fox, V. (2008, March 5). *Economic growth, poverty, and democracy in Latin
      America: A president's perspective.* Address at the Freeman Spogli
      Institute, Stanford University, Stanford, CA.

63. Work of art or photograph

Weber, J. (1992). *Toward freedom* [Outdoor mural]. Sherman Oaks, CA.

Newkirk, K. (2006). *Gainer (part II)*. Museum of Contemporary Art, Chicago,
      IL.

64. Brochure, pamphlet, or fact sheet

National Council of State Boards of Nursing. (n.d.). *Professional boundaries*
      [Brochure]. Retrieved October 24, 2008, from https://www.ncsbn.org
      /Professional_Boundaries_2007_Web.pdf

World Health Organization. (2007, October). *Health of indigenous peoples*
      (No. 326) [Fact sheet]. Retrieved from http://www.who.int/mediacentre
      /factsheets/fs326/en/index.html

65. Presentation slides

Boeninger, C. F. (2008, August). *Web 2.0 tools for reference and
      instructional services* [Presentation slides]. Retrieved from http://
      libraryvoice.com/archives/2008/08/04/opal-20-conference
      -presentation-slides/

66. Film or video (motion picture) Give the director, producer, and other relevant contributors, followed by the year of the film's release, the title, the description "Motion picture" in brackets, the country where the film was made, and the studio. If you viewed the film on videocassette or DVD, indicate that medium in brackets in place of "Motion picture." If the original release date and the date of the DVD or videocassette are different, add "Original release" and that date in parentheses at the end of the entry. If the motion picture would be difficult for your readers to find, include instead the name and address of its distributor.

Guggenheim, D. (Director), & Bender, L. (Producer). (2006). *An inconvenient truth* [DVD]. United States: Paramount Home Entertainment.

Spurlock, M. (Director). (2004). *Super size me* [Motion picture].
Available from IDP Films, 1133 Broadway, Suite 926, New York,
NY 10010

67. Television program List the producer and the date the program was aired. Give the title, followed by "Television broadcast" in brackets, the city, and the television network or service.

Pratt, C. (Executive producer). (2008, October 5). *Face the nation* [Television broadcast]. Washington, DC: CBS News.

For a television series, use the year in which the series was produced, and follow the title with "Television series" in brackets. For an episode in a series, list the writer and director and the year. After the episode title, put "Television series episode" in brackets. Follow with information about the series.

Fanning, D. (Executive producer). (2008). *Frontline* [Television series].
Boston, MA: WGBH.

Smith, M. (Writer/producer). (2008). Heat [Television series episode]. In
D. Fanning (Executive producer), *Frontline*. Boston, MA: WGBH.

68. Sound recording

Thomas, G. (1996). Breath. On *Didgeridoo: Ancient sound of the future* [CD]. Oxnard, CA: Aquarius International Music.

69. Computer software or video game   Add the words "Computer software" (neither italicized nor in quotation marks) in brackets after the title of the program.

Sims 2 [Computer software]. (2005). New York, NY: Maxis.

hackerhandbooks.com/bedhandbook > Research exercises > APA > E-ex 56–15 to 56–19

56e APA manuscript format

The American Psychological Association makes a number of recommendations for formatting a paper and preparing a list of references. The following guidelines are consistent with advice given in the *Publication Manual of the American Psychological Association*, 6th ed. (Washington: APA, 2010), and typical requirements for undergraduate papers.

Formatting the paper

Many instructors in the social sciences require students to follow APA guidelines for formatting a paper.

NOTE ON APA GUIDELINES FOR STUDENT PAPERS: The APA manual provides guidelines for papers prepared for publication in a scholarly journal; it does not provide specific guidelines for papers prepared for undergraduate classes. The formatting guidelines in this section and the sample paper on pages 674–83 are consistent with typical requirements for undergraduate writing. The samples on page 684 show APA formatting for a paper prepared for publication. If you are in doubt about which format is preferred or required in your course, ask your instructor.

Materials and font   Use good-quality 8½" × 11" white paper. Avoid a font that is unusual or hard to read.

Title page   The APA manual provides few guidelines for formatting the title page of an undergraduate paper, but most instructors expect students to include one. See the sample on page 674; see also the note on page 669.

Page numbers and running head   For a student paper, number all pages with arabic numerals (1, 2, 3, and so on), including the title page. In the upper right-hand corner of each page, type a short version of your title, capitalizing all words of four letters or more, followed by one space and the page number. See pages 674–83. For a paper submitted for publication, in the upper left-hand corner of every page place the words "Running head," a colon, and a short form of the title in all capital letters. On the same line in the right-hand corner, place the page number, beginning with 1 on the title page. See page 684.

Margins, line spacing, and paragraph indents   Use margins of one inch on all sides of the page. Left-align the text.

Double-space throughout the paper, but single-space footnotes. Indent the first line of each paragraph one-half inch.

Capitalization, italics, and quotation marks   Capitalize all words of four letters or more in titles of works and in headings that appear in the text of the paper. Capitalize the first word after a colon if the word begins a complete sentence.

Italicize the titles of books and other long works, such as Web sites. Use quotation marks around the titles of periodical articles, short stories, poems, and other short works.

NOTE: APA has different requirements for titles in the reference list. See page 673.

Long quotations and footnotes   When a quotation is longer than forty words, set it off from the text by indenting it one-half inch from the left margin. Double-space the quotation. Do not use quotation marks around a quotation that has been set off from the text. See page 682 for an example.

Place each footnote, if any, at the bottom of the page on which the text reference occurs. Double-space between the last line of text on the page and the footnote. Indent the first line of the footnote one-half inch. Begin the note with the superscript arabic numeral that corresponds to the number in the text. See page 676 for an example.

Abstract   If your instructor requires an abstract, include it immediately after the title page. Center the word Abstract one inch from the top of the page; double-space the abstract as you do the body of your paper.

An abstract is a 100-to-150-word paragraph that provides readers with a quick overview of your essay. It should express your main idea and your key points; it might also briefly suggest any implications or applications of the research you discuss in the paper. See page 675 for an example.

Headings   Although headings are not always necessary, their use is encouraged in the social sciences. For most undergraduate papers, one level of heading will usually be sufficient.

In APA style, major headings are centered and boldface. Capitalize the first word of the heading, along with all words except articles, short prepositions, and coordinating conjunctions. See the sample paper on pages 674–83.

Visuals   APA classifies visuals as tables and figures (figures include graphs, charts, drawings, and photographs). Keep visuals as simple as possible.

Label each table with an arabic numeral (Table 1, Table 2, and so on) and provide a clear title. The label and title should appear on separate lines above the table, flush left and single-spaced.

Below the table, give its source in a note. If any data in the table require an explanatory footnote, use a superscript lowercase letter in the body of the table and in a footnote following the source note. Single-space source notes and footnotes and do not indent the first line of each note. See page 679 for an example of a table in a model paper.

For each figure, place a label and a caption below the figure, flush left and single-spaced. The label and caption need not appear on separate lines.

In the text of your paper, discuss the most significant features of each visual. Place the visual as close as possible to the sentences that relate to it unless your instructor prefers it in an appendix.

Preparing the list of references

Begin your list of references on a new page at the end of the paper. Center the title References one inch from the top of the page. Double-space throughout. For a sample reference list, see page 683.

Indenting entries   Use a hanging indent in the reference list: Type the first line of each entry flush left and indent any additional lines one-half inch, as shown on page 683.

Alphabetizing the list   Alphabetize the reference list by the last names of the authors (or editors); when a work has no author or editor, alphabetize by the first word of the title other than *A, An,* or *The.*

If your list includes two or more works by the same author, arrange the entries by year, the earliest first. If your list includes two or more works by the same author in the same year, arrange the works alphabetically by title. Add the letters "a," "b," and so on within the parentheses after the year. Use only the year and the letter for articles in journals: (2002a). Use the full date and the letter for articles in magazines and newspapers in the reference list: (2005a, July 7). Use only the year and the letter in the in-text citation.

Authors' names   Invert all authors' names and use initials instead of first names. With two or more authors, use an ampersand (&) before the last author's name. Separate the names with commas. Include names for the first seven authors;

if there are eight or more authors, give the first six authors, three ellipsis dots, and the last author (see p. 647).

Titles of books and articles   Italicize the titles and subtitles of books. Do not use quotation marks around the titles of articles. Capitalize only the first word of the title and subtitle (and all proper nouns) of books and articles. Capitalize names of periodicals as you would capitalize them normally (see 45c).

Abbreviations for page numbers   Abbreviations for "page" and "pages" ("p." and "pp.") are used before page numbers of newspaper articles and articles in edited books (see item 9 on p. 649 and item 22 on p. 654) but not before page numbers of articles in magazines and scholarly journals (see items 7 and 8 on p. 649).

Breaking a URL   When a URL or a DOI (digital object identifier) must be divided, break it after a double slash or before any other mark of punctuation. Do not insert a hyphen, and do not add a period at the end.

For information about the exact format of each entry in your list, consult the models on pages 647–69.

56f Sample APA research paper

On the following pages is a research paper on the effectiveness of treatments for childhood obesity, written by Luisa Mirano, a student in a psychology class. Mirano's assignment was to write a literature review paper documented with APA-style citations and references.

See the note on page 669 for a discussion of formatting differences in APA-style student papers and papers prepared for scholarly publication.

hackerhandbooks.com/bedhandbook > Model papers
　　　　　　　　　　　　　　　　 > APA papers: Mirano; Shaw
　　　　　　　　　　　　　　　　 > APA annotated bibliography: Haddad

Short title and page number for student papers. (See p. 684 for a title page of a paper prepared for publication.)

Full title, centered.

Can Medication Cure Obesity in Children?

A Review of the Literature

Writer's name, course, instructor's name, and date, all centered.

Luisa Mirano

Psychology 108, Section B

Professor Kang

October 31, 2004

Marginal annotations indicate APA-style formatting **and** effective writing.

Obesity in Children 2

Abstract

In recent years, policymakers and medical experts have expressed
alarm about the growing problem of childhood obesity in the United
States. While most agree that the issue deserves attention, consensus
dissolves around how to respond to the problem. This literature review
examines one approach to treating childhood obesity: medication. The
paper compares the effectiveness for adolescents of the only two drugs
approved by the Food and Drug Administration (FDA) for long-term
treatment of obesity, sibutramine and orlistat. This examination of
pharmacological treatments for obesity points out the limitations of
medication and suggests the need for a comprehensive solution that
combines medical, social, behavioral, and political approaches to this
complex problem.

Abstract appears on
a separate page.

Can Medication Cure Obesity in Children?

A Review of the Literature

In March 2004, U.S. Surgeon General Richard Carmona called attention to a health problem in the United States that, until recently, has been overlooked: childhood obesity. Carmona said that the "astounding" 15% child obesity rate constitutes an "epidemic." Since the early 1980s, that rate has "doubled in children and tripled in adolescents." Now more than nine million children are classified as obese.[1] While the traditional response to a medical epidemic is to hunt for a vaccine or a cure-all pill, childhood obesity has proven more elusive. The lack of success of recent initiatives suggests that medication might not be the answer for the escalating problem. This literature review considers whether the use of medication is a promising approach for solving the childhood obesity problem by responding to the following questions:

1. What are the implications of childhood obesity?

2. Is medication effective at treating childhood obesity?

3. Is medication safe for children?

4. Is medication the best solution?

Understanding the limitations of medical treatments for children highlights the complexity of the childhood obesity problem in the United States and underscores the need for physicians, advocacy groups, and policymakers to search for other solutions.

What Are the Implications of Childhood Obesity?

Obesity can be a devastating problem from both an individual and a societal perspective. Obesity puts children at risk for a number of

---

[1] Obesity is measured in terms of body-mass index (BMI): weight in kilograms divided by square of height in meters. A child or an adolescent with a BMI in the 95th percentile for his or her age and gender is considered obese.

Margin notes:

Full title, centered.

Mirano sets up her organization by posing four questions.

Mirano states her thesis.

Headings, centered, help readers follow the organization.

Mirano uses a footnote to define an essential term that would be cumbersome to define within the text.

Obesity in Children 4

medical complications, including type 2 diabetes, hypertension, sleep apnea, and orthopedic problems (Henry J. Kaiser Family Foundation, 2004, p. 1). Researchers Hoppin and Taveras (2004) have noted that obesity is often associated with psychological issues such as depression, anxiety, and binge eating (Table 4).

In a signal phrase, the word "and" links the names of two authors; the date is given in parentheses.

Obesity also poses serious problems for a society struggling to cope with rising health care costs. The cost of treating obesity currently totals $117 billion per year—a price, according to the surgeon general, "second only to the cost of [treating] tobacco use" (Carmona, 2004). And as the number of children who suffer from obesity grows, long-term costs will only increase.

Because the author (Carmona) is not named in the signal phrase, his name and the date appear in parentheses.

Is Medication Effective at Treating Childhood Obesity?

The widening scope of the obesity problem has prompted medical professionals to rethink old conceptions of the disorder and its causes. As researchers Yanovski and Yanovski (2002) have explained, obesity was once considered "either a moral failing or evidence of underlying psychopathology" (p. 592). But this view has shifted: Many medical professionals now consider obesity a biomedical rather than a moral condition, influenced by both genetic and environmental factors. Yanovski and Yanovski have further noted that the development of weight-loss medications in the early 1990s showed that "obesity should be treated in the same manner as any other chronic disease . . . through the long-term use of medication" (p. 592).

Ellipsis mark indicates omitted words.

The search for the right long-term medication has been complicated. Many of the drugs authorized by the Food and Drug Administration (FDA) in the early 1990s proved to be a disappointment. Two of the medications—fenfluramine and dexfenfluramine—were withdrawn from the market because of severe side effects (Yanovski & Yanovski, 2002, p. 592), and several others

Obesity in Children 5

were classified by the Drug Enforcement Administration as having the

"potential for abuse" (Hoppin & Taveras, 2004, Weight-Loss Drugs
section, para. 6). Currently only two medications have been approved
by the FDA for long-term treatment of obesity: sibutramine (marketed
as Meridia) and orlistat (marketed as Xenical). This section compares
studies on the effectiveness of each.

Sibutramine suppresses appetite by blocking the reuptake of
the neurotransmitters serotonin and norepinephrine in the brain
(Yanovski & Yanovski, 2002, p. 594). Though the drug won FDA
approval in 1998, experiments to test its effectiveness for younger
patients came considerably later. In 2003, University of Pennsylvania
researchers Berkowitz, Wadden, Tershakovec, and Cronquist released
the first double-blind placebo study testing the effect of sibutramine
on adolescents, aged 13-17, over a 12-month period. Their findings
are summarized in Table 1.

After 6 months, the group receiving medication had lost
4.6 kg (about 10 pounds) more than the control group. But during
the second half of the study, when both groups received sibutramine,
the results were more ambiguous. In months 6-12, the group that
continued to take sibutramine gained an average of 0.8 kg, or
roughly 2 pounds; the control group, which switched from placebo to
sibutramine, lost 1.3 kg, or roughly 3 pounds (p. 1808). Both groups
received behavioral therapy covering diet, exercise, and mental health.

These results paint a murky picture of the effectiveness of the
medication: While initial data seemed promising, the results after
one year raised questions about whether medication-induced weight
loss could be sustained over time. As Berkowitz et al. (2003) advised,
"Until more extensive safety and efficacy data are available, . . .
weight-loss medications should be used only on an experimental
basis for adolescents" (p. 1811).

Obesity in Children 6

Table 1

Effectiveness of Sibutramine and Orlistat in Adolescents

Mirano uses a table to summarize the findings presented in two sources.

Medication	Subjects	Treatment[a]	Side effects	Average weight loss/gain
Sibutramine	Control	0-6 mos.: placebo 6-12 mos.: sibutramine	Mos. 6-12: increased blood pressure; increased pulse rate	After 6 mos.: loss of 3.2 kg (7 lb) After 12 mos.: loss of 4.5 kg (9.9 lb)
	Medicated	0-12 mos.: sibutramine	Increased blood pressure; increased pulse rate	After 6 mos.: loss of 7.8 kg (17.2 lb) After 12 mos.: loss of 7.0 kg (15.4 lb)
Orlistat	Control	0-12 mos.: placebo	None	Gain of 0.67 kg (1.5 lb)
	Medicated	0-12 mos.: orlistat	Oily spotting; flatulence; abdominal discomfort	Loss of 1.3 kg (2.9 lb)

Note. The data on sibutramine are adapted from "Behavior Therapy and Sibutramine for the Treatment of Adolescent Obesity," by R. I. Berkowitz, T. A. Wadden, A. M. Tershakovec, & J. L. Cronquist, 2003, *Journal of the American Medical Association, 289*, pp. 1807-1809. The data on orlistat are adapted from *Xenical (Orlistat) Capsules: Complete Product Information*, by Roche Laboratories, December 2003, retrieved from http://www.rocheusa.com/products/xenical/pi.pdf

[a]The medication and/or placebo were combined with behavioral therapy in all groups over all time periods.

A note gives the source of the data.

A content note explains data common to all subjects.

Obesity in Children 7

A study testing the effectiveness of orlistat in adolescents showed similarly ambiguous results. The FDA approved orlistat in 1999 but did not authorize it for adolescents until December 2003. Roche Laboratories (2003), maker of orlistat, released results of a one-year study testing the drug on 539 obese adolescents, aged 12-16. The drug, which promotes weight loss by blocking fat absorption in the large intestine, showed some effectiveness in adolescents: an average loss of 1.3 kg, or roughly 3 pounds, for subjects taking orlistat for one year, as opposed to an average gain of 0.67 kg, or 1.5 pounds, for the control group (pp. 8-9). See Table 1.

Short-term studies of orlistat have shown slightly more dramatic results. Researchers at the National Institute of Child Health and Human Development tested 20 adolescents, aged 12-16, over a three-month period and found that orlistat, combined with behavioral therapy, produced an average weight loss of 4.4 kg, or 9.7 pounds (McDuffie et al., 2002, p. 646). The study was not controlled against a placebo group; therefore, the relative effectiveness of orlistat in this case remains unclear.

Is Medication Safe for Children?

While modest weight loss has been documented for both medications, each carries risks of certain side effects. Sibutramine has been observed to increase blood pressure and pulse rate. In 2002, a consumer group claimed that the medication was related to the deaths of 19 people and filed a petition with the Department of Health and Human Services to ban the medication (Hilts, 2002). The sibutramine study by Berkowitz et al. (2003) noted elevated blood pressure as a side effect, and dosages had to be reduced or the medication discontinued in 19 of the 43 subjects in the first six months (p. 1809).

The main side effects associated with orlistat were abdominal discomfort, oily spotting, fecal incontinence, and nausea (Roche

For a source with six or more authors, the first author's surname followed by "et al." is used for the first and subsequent references.

When this article was first cited, all four authors were named. In subsequent citations of a work with three to five authors, "et al." is used after the first author's name.

Obesity in Children 8

Laboratories, 2003, p. 13). More serious for long-term health is the concern that orlistat, being a fat-blocker, would affect absorption of fat-soluble vitamins, such as vitamin D. However, the study found that this side effect can be minimized or eliminated if patients take vitamin supplements two hours before or after administration of orlistat (p. 10). With close monitoring of patients taking the medication, many of the risks can be reduced.

Is Medication the Best Solution?

The data on the safety and efficacy of pharmacological treatments of childhood obesity raise the question of whether medication is the best solution for the problem. The treatments have clear costs for individual patients, including unpleasant side effects, little information about long-term use, and uncertainty that they will yield significant weight loss.

In purely financial terms, the drugs cost more than $3 a day on average (Duenwald, 2004). In each of the clinical trials, use of medication was accompanied by an expensive regime of behavioral therapies, including counseling, nutritional education, fitness advising, and monitoring. As journalist Greg Critser (2003) noted in his book *Fat Land*, use of weight-loss drugs is unlikely to have an effect without the proper "support system"—one that includes doctors, facilities, time, and money (p. 3). For some, this level of care is prohibitively expensive.

A third complication is that the studies focused on adolescents aged 12-16, but obesity can begin at a much younger age. Little data exist to establish the safety or efficacy of medication for treating very young children.

While the scientific data on the concrete effects of these medications in children remain somewhat unclear, medication is not the only avenue for addressing the crisis. Both medical experts and

Mirano develops the paper's thesis.

Obesity in Children 9

policymakers recognize that solutions might come not only from a laboratory but also from policy, education, and advocacy. A handbook designed to educate doctors on obesity called for "major changes in some aspects of western culture" (Hoppin & Taveras, 2004, Conclusion section, para. 1). Cultural change may not be the typical realm of medical professionals, but the handbook urged doctors to be proactive and "focus [their] energy on public policies and interventions" (Conclusion section, para. 1).

Brackets indicate a word not in the original source.

The solutions proposed by a number of advocacy groups underscore this interest in political and cultural change. A report by the Henry J. Kaiser Family Foundation (2004) outlined trends that may have contributed to the childhood obesity crisis, including food advertising for children as well as

A quotation longer than forty words is indented without quotation marks.

> a reduction in physical education classes and after-school athletic programs, an increase in the availability of sodas and snacks in public schools, the growth in the number of fast-food outlets . . . , and the increasing number of highly processed high-calorie and high-fat grocery products. (p. 1)

Mirano interprets the evidence; she doesn't just report it.

Addressing each of these areas requires more than a doctor armed with a prescription pad; it requires a broad mobilization not just of doctors and concerned parents but of educators, food industry executives, advertisers, and media representatives.

The tone of the conclusion is objective.

The barrage of possible approaches to combating childhood obesity—from scientific research to political lobbying—indicates both the severity and the complexity of the problem. While none of the medications currently available is a miracle drug for curing the nation's 9 million obese children, research has illuminated some of the underlying factors that affect obesity and has shown the need for a comprehensive approach to the problem that includes behavioral, medical, social, and political change.

Obesity in Children 10

References

Berkowitz, R. I., Wadden, T. A., Tershakovec, A. M., & Cronquist, J. L.
  (2003). Behavior therapy and sibutramine for the treatment of
  adolescent obesity. *Journal of the American Medical Association*,
  289, 1805-1812.

Carmona, R. H. (2004, March 2). *The growing epidemic of childhood
  obesity*. Testimony before the Subcommittee on Competition,
  Foreign Commerce, and Infrastructure of the U.S. Senate
  Committee on Commerce, Science, and Transportation. Retrieved
  from http://www.hhs.gov/asl/testify/t040302.html

Critser, G. (2003). *Fat land*. Boston: Houghton Mifflin.

Duenwald, M. (2004, January 6). Slim pickings: Looking beyond ephedra.
  The New York Times, p. F1. Retrieved from http://nytimes.com/

Henry J. Kaiser Family Foundation. (2004, February). *The role of media
  in childhood obesity*. Retrieved from http://www.kff.org
  /entmedia/7030.cfm

Hilts, P. J. (2002, March 20). Petition asks for removal of diet drug
  from market. *The New York Times*, p. A26. Retrieved from http://
  nytimes.com/

Hoppin, A. G., & Taveras, E. M. (2004, June 25). Assessment and
  management of childhood and adolescent obesity. *Clinical Update*.
  Retrieved from http://www.medscape.com/viewarticle/481633

McDuffie, J. R., Calis, K. A., Uwaifo, G. I., Sebring, N. G., Fallon, E. M.,
  Hubbard, V. S., et al. (2003). Three-month tolerability of orlistat
  in adolescents with obesity-related comorbid conditions. *Obesity
  Research*, *10*, 642-650.

Roche Laboratories. (2003, December). *Xenical (orlistat) capsules:
  Complete product information*. Retrieved from http://www
  .rocheusa.com/products/xenical/pi.pdf

Yanovski, S. Z., & Yanovski, J. A. (2002). Drug therapy: Obesity. *The New
  England Journal of Medicine*, *346*, 591-602.

List of references
begins on a new page.
Heading is centered.

List is alphabetized by
authors' last names.
All authors' names are
inverted.

The first line of an
entry is at the left
margin; subsequent
lines indent ½".

Double-spacing is
used throughout.

APA TITLE PAGE: PAPER FOR PUBLICATION (see note on p. 669)

A running head, which will be used in the printed journal article, consists of a shortened title in all capital letters preceded by the label "Running head." Page numbers appear in the upper right corner.

Running head: CAN MEDICATION CURE OBESITY IN CHILDREN?   1

Full title, writer's name, and school name are centered halfway down the page.

Can Medication Cure Obesity in Children?

A Review of the Literature

Luisa Mirano

Northwest-Shoals Community College

An author's note lists specific information about the course or department and can provide acknowledgments and contact information.

Author Note

This paper was prepared for Psychology 108, Section B, taught by Professor Kang.

APA SAMPLE PAGE: PAPER FOR PUBLICATION

The running head, in the upper left corner, and the page number, in the upper right corner, are repeated on each page of the paper.

Running head: CAN MEDICATION CURE OBESITY IN CHILDREN?   3

were classified by the Drug Enforcement Administration as having the "potential for abuse" (Hoppin & Taveras, 2004, Weight-Loss Drugs section, para. 6). Currently only two medications have been approved by the FDA for long-term treatment of obesity: sibutramine (marketed

Marginal annotations indicate APA-style formatting.

Writing *Chicago* papers

57   *Chicago* papers

Most history instructors and some humanities instructors require you to document sources with footnotes or endnotes based on *The Chicago Manual of Style,* 15th ed. (Chicago: U of Chicago P, 2003). (See 57f.)

When you write a paper using sources, you face three main challenges: (1) supporting a thesis, (2) citing your sources and avoiding plagiarism, and (3) integrating quotations and other source material.

57a Supporting a thesis

Most research assignments ask you to form a thesis, or main idea, and to support that thesis with well-organized evidence. (See also 1c.) Remain flexible as you draft because you may need to revise your approach later. Writing about a subject is a way of learning about it; as you write, your understanding of your subject will almost certainly deepen.

Forming a working thesis

Once you have read a variety of sources and considered your issue from different perspectives, you are ready to form a working thesis: a one-sentence (or occasionally a two-sentence) statement of your central idea. (See also 1e.) Because it is a working, or tentative, thesis, it is flexible enough to change as your ideas develop. Ultimately, the thesis expresses not just your opinion but your informed, reasoned judgment.

> **Making the most of your handbook**
>
> When writing from sources, it helps to start with a working thesis and a rough outline.
>
> ▶ Draft a working thesis: 1c
> ▶ Sketch a plan: 1d

In a research paper, your thesis will answer the central research question that you posed earlier (see 46a). Here, for example, are student writer Ned Bishop's research question and working thesis statement.

RESEARCH QUESTION

To what extent was Confederate Major General Nathan Bedford Forrest responsible for the massacre of Union troops at Fort Pillow?

WORKING THESIS

By encouraging racism among his troops, Nathan Bedford Forrest was directly responsible for the massacre of Union troops at Fort Pillow.

Notice that the thesis expresses a view on a debatable issue—an issue about which intelligent, well-meaning people might disagree. The writer's job is to convince such readers that this view is worth taking seriously.

The thesis usually appears at the end of the introductory paragraph. To read Ned Bishop's thesis in the context of his introduction, see page 719.

Organizing your ideas

The body of your paper will consist of evidence in support of your thesis. Instead of getting tangled up in a complex, formal outline, sketch an informal plan that organizes your evidence in bold strokes. Ned Bishop, for example, used a simple outline to structure his ideas. In the paper itself, these points became headings that helped readers follow his line of argument.

> What happened at Fort Pillow?
>
> Did Forrest order the massacre?
>
> Can Forrest be held responsible for the massacre?

hackerhandbooks.com/bedhandbook > **Research exercises**
> *Chicago* > E-ex 57–1 and 57–2

Using sources to inform and support your argument

Used thoughtfully, the source materials you have gathered will make your argument more complex and convincing for readers. Sources can play several different roles as you develop your points.

Providing background information or context   You can use facts and statistics to support generalizations or to establish the importance of your topic, as student writer Ned Bishop does early in his paper.

> Fort Pillow, Tennessee, which sat on a bluff overlooking the Mississippi River, had been held by the Union for two years. It was garrisoned by 580 men, 292 of them from United States Colored Heavy and Light Artillery regiments, 285 from the white Thirteenth Tennessee Cavalry. Nathan Bedford Forrest commanded about 1,500 troops.[1]

Explaining terms or concepts   If readers are unlikely to be familiar with a word or an idea important to your topic, you must explain it for them. Quoting or paraphrasing a source can help you define terms and concepts clearly and concisely.

> The Civil War practice of giving no quarter to an enemy—in other words, "denying [an enemy] the right of survival"—defied Lincoln's mandate for humane and merciful treatment of prisoners.[9]

Supporting your claims As you draft your argument, make sure to back up your assertions with facts, examples, and other evidence from your research. (See also 5e.) Ned Bishop, for example, uses an eyewitness report of the racially motivated violence perpetrated by Nathan Bedford Forrest's troops.

> The slaughter at Fort Pillow was no doubt driven in large part by racial hatred. . . . A Southern reporter traveling with Forrest makes clear that the discrimination was deliberate: "Our troops maddened by the excitement, shot down the ret[r]eating Yankees, and not until they had attained t[h]e water's edge and turned to beg for mercy, did any prisoners fall in [t]o our hands— Thus the whites received quarter, but the negroes were shown no mercy."[19]

Lending authority to your argument Expert opinion can give weight to your argument. (See also 5e.) But don't rely on experts to make your argument for you. Construct your argument in your own words and, when appropriate, cite the judgment of an authority in the field to support your position.

> Fort Pillow is not the only instance of a massacre or threatened massacre of black soldiers by troops under Forrest's command. Biographer Brian Steel Wills points out that at Brice's Cross Roads in June 1864, "black soldiers suffered inordinately" as Forrest looked the other way and Confederate soldiers deliberately sought out those they termed "the damned negroes."[21]

Anticipating and countering objections Do not ignore sources that seem contrary to your position or that offer arguments different from your own. Instead, use them to give voice to opposing points of view and to state potential objections to your arguments before you counter them (see 5f). Readers often have opposing points of view in mind already, whether or not they agree with you. Ned Bishop, for example, presents conflicting evidence to acknowledge that some readers may credit Nathan Bedford Forrest with stopping the massacre. In doing so, Bishop creates an opportunity to counter that objection and persuade those readers that Forrest can be held accountable.

> Hurst suggests that the temperamental Forrest "may have ragingly ordered a massacre and even intended to carry it out— until he rode inside the fort and viewed the horrifying result" and ordered it stopped.[15] While this is an intriguing interpretation of events, even Hurst would probably admit that it is merely speculation.

57b Citing sources; avoiding plagiarism

In a research paper, you will draw on the work of other writers, and you must document their contributions by citing your sources. Sources are cited for two reasons:

- to tell readers where your information comes from—so that they can assess its reliability and, if interested, find and read the original source
- to give credit to the writers from whom you have borrowed words and ideas

Borrowing another writer's language, sentence structures, or ideas without proper acknowledgment is a form of dishonesty known as *plagiarism*.

Using the Chicago system for citing sources

You must include a citation when you quote from a source, when you summarize or paraphrase a source, and when you borrow facts that are not common knowledge. (See also "Avoiding plagiarism" on p. 690.)

Chicago citations consist of superscript numbers in the text of the paper that refer readers to notes with corresponding numbers either at the foot of the page (footnotes) or at the end of the paper (endnotes).

TEXT

Governor John Andrew was not allowed to recruit black soldiers from out of state. "Ostensibly," writes Peter Burchard, "no recruiting was done outside Massachusetts, but it was an open secret that Andrew's agents were working far and wide."[1]

NOTE

    1. Peter Burchard, *One Gallant Rush: Robert Gould Shaw and His Brave Black Regiment* (New York: St. Martin's, 1965), 85.

For detailed advice on using *Chicago*-style notes, see 57d. When you use footnotes or endnotes, you will usually need to provide a bibliography as well (see p. 716).

Avoiding plagiarism

Your research paper is a collaboration between you and your sources. To be fair and ethical, you must acknowledge your debt to the writers of those sources. If you don't, you commit plagiarism, a serious academic offense. (See also 48c.)

    In general, these three acts are considered plagiarism: (1) failing to cite quotations and borrowed ideas, (2) failing to enclose borrowed language in quotation marks, and (3) failing to put summaries and paraphrases in your own words. Definitions of plagiarism may vary; it's a good idea to find out how your school defines academic dishonesty.

Citing quotations and borrowed ideas You must cite all direct quotations. You must also cite any ideas you borrow from a source: summaries and paraphrases; statistics and other specific facts; and visuals such as cartoons, graphs, and diagrams.

    The only exception is common knowledge—information your readers could easily find in any number of general sources. For example, most encyclopedias will tell readers that the Korean War ended in 1953 and that President Theodore Roosevelt was the first American to receive the Nobel Prize.

As a rule, when you have seen certain general information repeatedly in your reading, you don't need to cite it. However, when information has appeared in only a few sources, when it is highly specific (as with statistics), or when it is controversial, you should cite the source. If a topic is new to you and you are not sure what is considered common knowledge or what is controversial, ask your instructor or someone else with expertise. When in doubt, cite the source. (See 57d for details.)

Enclosing borrowed language in quotation marks   To indicate that you are using a source's exact phrases or sentences, you must enclose them in quotation marks unless they have been set off from the text by indenting (see p. 695). To omit the quotation marks is to claim—falsely—that the language is your own. Such an omission is plagiarism even if you have cited the source.

> **ORIGINAL SOURCE**
> For many Southerners it was psychologically impossible to see a black man bearing arms as anything but an incipient slave uprising complete with arson, murder, pillage, and rapine.
> —Dudley Taylor Cornish, *The Sable Arm*, p. 158

> **PLAGIARISM**
> According to Civil War historian Dudley Taylor Cornish, for many Southerners it was psychologically impossible to see a black man bearing arms as anything but an incipient slave uprising complete with arson, murder, pillage, and rapine.[2]

> **BORROWED LANGUAGE IN QUOTATION MARKS**
> According to Civil War historian Dudley Taylor Cornish, "For many Southerners it was psychologically impossible to see a black man bearing arms as anything but an incipient slave uprising complete with arson, murder, pillage, and rapine."[2]

Putting summaries and paraphrases in your own words   Summaries and paraphrases are written in your own words. A summary condenses information; a paraphrase uses roughly the same number of words as the original source to convey the information. When you summarize or paraphrase, it is not enough to name the source; you must restate the source's meaning using your own language. (See also 48c.) You commit plagiarism if you half-copy the author's sentences—either by mixing the author's phrases with your own without using quotation marks or by plugging your own synonyms into the author's sentence structure.

The first paraphrase of the following source is plagiarized—even though the source is cited—because too much of its language is borrowed from the original. The underlined strings of words have been copied exactly (without quotation marks). In addition, the writer has closely followed the sentence structure of the original source, merely making a few substitutions (such as *Fifty percent* for *Half* and *angered and perhaps frightened* for *enraged and perhaps terrified*).

ORIGINAL SOURCE

Half of the force holding Fort Pillow were Negroes, former slaves now enrolled in the Union Army. Toward them Forrest's troops had the fierce, bitter animosity of men who had been educated to regard the colored race as inferior and who for the first time had encountered that race armed and fighting against white men. The sight enraged and perhaps terrified many of the Confederates and aroused in them the ugly spirit of a lynching mob.

　　　—Albert Castel, "The Fort Pillow Massacre," pp. 46–47

PLAGIARISM: UNACCEPTABLE BORROWING

Albert Castel suggests that much of the brutality at Fort Pillow can be traced to racial attitudes. Fifty percent of the troops holding Fort Pillow were Negroes, former slaves who had joined the Union Army. Toward them Forrest's soldiers displayed the savage hatred of men who had been taught the inferiority of blacks and who for the first time had confronted them armed and fighting against white men. The vision angered and perhaps frightened the Confederates and aroused in them the ugly spirit of a lynching mob.[3]

To avoid plagiarizing an author's language, resist the temptation to look at the source while you are summarizing or paraphrasing. After you have read the passage you want to paraphrase, set the source aside. Ask yourself, "What is the author's meaning?" In your own words, state your understanding of the author's basic point. Return to the source and check that you haven't used the author's language or sentence structure or misrepresented the author's ideas. Following these steps will help you avoid plagiarizing the source. When you fully understand another writer's meaning, you can more easily and accurately represent those ideas in your own words.

ACCEPTABLE PARAPHRASE

Albert Castel suggests that much of the brutality at Fort Pillow can be traced to racial attitudes. Fifty percent of the Union troops were blacks, men whom the Confederates had been raised to consider their inferiors. The shock and perhaps fear of facing armed ex-slaves in battle may well have unleashed the fury that led to the massacre.[3]

hackerhandbooks.com/bedhandbook > **Research exercises**
> *Chicago* > E-ex 57–3 to 57–7

57c Integrating sources

Quotations, summaries, paraphrases, and facts will support your argument, but they cannot speak for you. You can use several strategies to integrate information from research sources into your paper while maintaining your own voice.

Using quotations appropriately

In your academic writing, keep the emphasis on your ideas and your language; use your own words to summarize and to paraphrase your sources and to explain your points. Sometimes, however, quotations can be the most effective way to integrate a source.

WHEN TO USE QUOTATIONS

- When language is especially vivid or expressive
- When exact wording is needed for technical accuracy

- When it is important to let the debaters of an issue explain their positions in their own words
- When the words of an authority lend weight to an argument
- When the language of a source is the topic of your discussion (as in an analysis or interpretation)

Limiting your use of quotations   Although it is tempting to insert many quotations in your paper and to use your own words only for connecting passages, do not quote excessively. It is almost impossible to integrate numerous quotations smoothly into your own text.

It is not always necessary to quote full sentences from a source. To reduce your reliance on the words of others, you can often integrate language from a source into your own sentence structure.

> As Hurst has pointed out, until "an outcry erupted in the Northern press," even the Confederates did not deny that there had been a massacre at Fort Pillow.[4]

> Union surgeon Dr. Charles Fitch testified that after he was in custody he "saw" Confederate soldiers "kill every negro that made his appearance dressed in Federal uniform."[20]

Using the ellipsis mark   To condense a quoted passage, you can use the ellipsis mark (three periods, with spaces between) to indicate that you have left words out. What remains must be grammatically complete.

> Union surgeon Fitch's testimony that all women and children had been evacuated from Fort Pillow before the attack conflicts with Forrest's report: "We captured . . . about 40 negro women and children."[6]

The writer has omitted several words not relevant to the issue at hand: *164 Federals, 75 negro troops, and.*

When you want to leave out one or more full sentences, use a period before the three ellipsis dots. For an example, see the long quotation at the bottom of page 695.

Ordinarily, do not use the ellipsis mark at the beginning or at the end of a quotation. Readers will understand that the quoted material is taken from a longer passage, so such marks are not necessary. The only exception occurs when you have dropped words at the end of the final quoted sentence. In such cases, put three ellipsis dots before the closing quotation mark.

Make sure omissions and ellipsis marks do not distort the meaning of your source.

Using brackets   Brackets allow you to insert words of your own into quoted material to clarify a confusing reference or to keep a sentence grammatical in your context.

> According to Albert Castel, "It can be reasonably argued that he [Forrest] was justified in believing that the approaching steamships intended to aid the garrison [at Fort Pillow]."[7]

NOTE: Use the word *sic* in brackets to indicate that an error in a quoted sentence appears in the original source. (An example appears on p. 696.) Do not overuse *sic* to call attention to errors in a source. Sometimes paraphrasing is a better option. (See 39c.)

Setting off long quotations   *Chicago* style allows you some leeway in deciding whether to set off a long quotation or run it into your text. For emphasis, you may want to set off a quotation of more than four or five typed lines of text; almost certainly you should set off quotations of ten or more lines. To set off a quotation, indent it one-half inch from the left margin and use the normal right margin. Double-space the indented quotation.

Long quotations should be introduced by an informative sentence, usually followed by a colon. Quotation marks are unnecessary because the indented format tells readers that the passage is taken word-for-word from the source.

> In a letter home, Confederate officer Achilles V. Clark recounted what happened at Fort Pillow:
>
> > Words cannot describe the scene. The poor deluded negroes would run up to our men fall upon their knees and with uplifted hands

scream for mercy but they were ordered to their feet and then
shot down. The whitte [*sic*] men fared but little better. . . . I with
several others tried to stop the butchery and at one time had
partially succeeded[,] but Gen. Forrest ordered them shot down like
dogs[,] and the carnage continued.[8]

Using signal phrases to integrate sources

Whenever you include a paraphrase, summary, or direct quotation of another writer in your paper, prepare your readers for it with introductory words called a *signal phrase*. A signal phrase names the author of the source and often provides some context for the source material.

When you write a signal phrase, choose a verb that is appropriate for the way you are using the source (see p. 687). Are you providing background, explaining a concept, supporting a claim, lending authority, or refuting a belief? By choosing an appropriate verb, you can make your source's role clear. See the chart on page 697 for a list of verbs commonly used in signal phrases.

Note that *Chicago* style calls for verbs in the present or present perfect tense (*points out, has pointed out*) to introduce source material unless you include a date that specifies the time of the original author's writing.

The first time you mention an author, use the full name: *Shelby Foote argues*. . . . When you refer to the author again, you may use the last name only: *Foote raises an important question.*

Marking boundaries   Readers should be able to move from your own words to the words you quote from a source without feeling a jolt. Avoid dropping quotations into the text without warning. Instead, provide clear signal phrases, usually including the author's name, to indicate the boundary between your words and the source's words. (The signal phrase is underlined in the second example.)

Using signal phrases in *Chicago* papers

To avoid monotony, try to vary both the language and the placement of your signal phrases.

Model signal phrases

In the words of historian James M. McPherson, ". . ."[1]

As Dudley Taylor Cornish has argued, ". . ."[2]

In a letter to his wife, a Confederate soldier who witnessed the massacre wrote that ". . ."[3]

". . . ," claims Benjamin Quarles.[4]

". . . ," writes Albert Castel, ". . ."[5]

Shelby Foote offers an intriguing interpretation: ". . ."[6]

Verbs in signal phrases

admits	compares	insists	rejects
agrees	confirms	notes	reports
argues	contends	observes	responds
asserts	declares	points out	suggests
believes	denies	reasons	thinks
claims	emphasizes	refutes	writes

DROPPED QUOTATION

Not surprisingly, those testifying on the Union and Confederate sides recalled events at Fort Pillow quite differently. Unionists claimed that their troops had abandoned their arms and were in full retreat. "The Confederates, however, all agreed that the Union troops retreated to the river with arms in their hands."[9]

QUOTATION WITH SIGNAL PHRASE

Not surprisingly, those testifying on the Union and Confederate sides recalled events at Fort Pillow quite differently. Unionists claimed that their troops had abandoned their arms and were in full retreat. "The Confederates, however," writes historian Albert Castel,

"all agreed that the Union troops retreated to the river with arms
in their hands."[9]

Using signal phrases with summaries and paraphrases   Introduce most summaries and paraphrases with a signal phrase
that mentions the author and places the material in the context of your argument. Readers will then understand where
the summary or paraphrase begins.

Without the signal phrase (underlined) in the following
example, readers might think that only the last sentence is
being cited, when in fact the whole paragraph is based on the
source.

> <u>According to Jack Hurst</u>, official Confederate policy was that black
> soldiers were to be treated as runaway slaves; in addition, the
> Confederate Congress decreed that white Union officers commanding
> black troops be killed. Confederate Lieutenant General Kirby Smith
> went one step further, declaring that he would kill all captured black
> troops. Smith's policy never met with strong opposition from the
> Richmond government.[10]

Integrating statistics and other facts   When you are citing a
statistic or another specific fact, a signal phrase is often not necessary. In most cases, readers will understand that the citation
refers to the statistic or fact (not the whole paragraph).

> Of the 295 white troops garrisoned at Fort Pillow, 168 were taken
> prisoner. Black troops fared worse, with only 58 of 262 captured and
> most of the rest presumably killed or wounded.[12]

There is nothing wrong, however, with using a signal phrase
to introduce a statistic or another fact.

Putting source material in context   Readers should not have
to guess why source material appears in your paper. A signal
phrase can help you make the connection between your own
ideas and those of another writer by setting up how a source
will contribute to your paper (see 47a).

If you use another writer's words, you must explain how they relate to your point. It's a good idea to embed a quotation between sentences of your own. In addition to introducing it with a signal phrase, follow it with interpretive comments that link the source material to your paper's argument.

QUOTATION WITH EFFECTIVE CONTEXT

In a respected biography of Nathan Bedford Forrest, Hurst suggests that the temperamental Forrest "may have ragingly ordered a massacre and even intended to carry it out—until he rode inside the fort and viewed the horrifying result" and ordered it stopped.[15] While this is an intriguing interpretation of events, even Hurst would probably admit that it is merely speculation.

NOTE: When you bring other sources into a conversation about your research topic, you are synthesizing. For more on synthesis, see 52c.

hackerhandbooks.com/bedhandbook > Research exercises
> *Chicago* > E-ex 57–8 to 57–11

57d *Chicago* documentation style

In history and some humanities courses, you may be asked to use the documentation system set forth in *The Chicago Manual of Style*, 15th ed. (Chicago: U of Chicago P, 2003). In *Chicago* style, superscript numbers in the text of the paper refer readers to notes with corresponding numbers either at the foot of the page (footnotes) or at the end of the paper (endnotes). A bibliography is often required as well; it appears at the end of the paper and gives publication information for all the works cited in the notes.

TEXT

A Union soldier, Jacob Thompson, claimed to have seen Forrest order the killing, but when asked to describe the six-foot-two general, he called him "a little bit of a man."[12]

FOOTNOTE OR ENDNOTE

    12. Brian Steel Wills, *A Battle from the Start: The Life of Nathan Bedford Forrest* (New York: HarperCollins, 1992), 187.

BIBLIOGRAPHY ENTRY

Wills, Brian Steel. *A Battle from the Start: The Life of Nathan Bedford Forrest*. New York: HarperCollins, 1992.

First and subsequent notes for a source

The first time you cite a source, the note should include publication information for that work as well as the page number on which the passage being cited may be found.

    1. Peter Burchard, *One Gallant Rush: Robert Gould Shaw and His Brave Black Regiment* (New York: St. Martin's, 1965), 85.

For subsequent references to a source you have already cited, you may simply give the author's last name, a short form of the title, and the page or pages cited. A short form of the title of a book is italicized; a short form of the title of an article is put in quotation marks.

    4. Burchard, *One Gallant Rush*, 31.

When you have two consecutive notes from the same source, you may use "Ibid." (meaning "in the same place") and the page number for the second note. Use "Ibid." alone if the page number is the same.

    5. Jack Hurst, *Nathan Bedford Forrest: A Biography* (New York: Knopf, 1993), 8.

    6. Ibid., 174.

Chicago-*style bibliography*

A bibliography, which appears at the end of your paper, lists every work you have cited in your notes; in addition, it may include works that you consulted but did not cite. For advice on constructing the list, see page 716. A sample bibliography appears on page 726.

NOTE: If you include a bibliography, *The Chicago Manual of Style* suggests that you shorten all notes, including the first reference to a source, as described on page 700. Check with your instructor, however, to see whether using an abbreviated note for a first reference to a source is acceptable.

Model notes and bibliography entries

The following models are consistent with guidelines set forth in *The Chicago Manual of Style*, 15th ed. For each type of source, a model note appears first, followed by a model bibliography entry. The note shows the format you should use when citing a source for the first time. For subsequent citations of a source, use shortened notes (see p. 700).

Some online sources, typically periodical articles, use a permanent locator called a digital object identifier (DOI). Use the DOI, when it is available, in place of page numbers in your citations of online sources.

When a Web address (URL) must break across lines, do not insert a hyphen or break at a hyphen if the URL contains one. Instead, break the URL after a slash or a double slash or before any other mark of punctuation.

Books (print and online)

1. Basic format for a print book

1. William H. Rehnquist, *The Supreme Court: A History* (New York: Knopf, 2001), 204.

Rehnquist, William H. *The Supreme Court: A History*. New York: Knopf, 2001.

2. Basic format for an online book

2. Heinz Kramer, *A Changing Turkey: The Challenge to Europe and the United States* (Washington, DC: Brookings Press, 2000), 85, http://brookings.nap.edu/books/0815750234/html/R1.html.

Kramer, Heinz. *A Changing Turkey: The Challenge to Europe and the United States*. Washington, DC: Brookings Press, 2000. http://brookings.nap .edu/books/0815750234/html/R1.html.

3. Two or three authors

    3. Michael D. Coe and Mark Van Stone, *Reading the Maya Glyphs* (London: Thames and Hudson, 2002), 129-30.

Coe, Michael D., and Mark Van Stone. *Reading the Maya Glyphs*. London: Thames and Hudson, 2002.

4. Four or more authors

    4. Lynn Hunt and others, *The Making of the West: Peoples and Cultures*, 3rd ed. (Boston: Bedford/St. Martin's, 2009), 541.

Hunt, Lynn, Thomas R. Martin, Barbara H. Rosenwein, R. Po-chia Hsia, and Bonnie G. Smith. *The Making of the West: Peoples and Cultures*. 3rd ed. Boston: Bedford/St. Martin's, 2009.

5. Organization as author

    5. Dormont Historical Society, *Images of America: Dormont* (Charleston, SC: Arcadia Publishing, 2008), 24.

Dormont Historical Society. *Images of America: Dormont*. Charleston, SC: Arcadia Publishing, 2008.

6. Unknown author

    6. *The Men's League Handbook on Women's Suffrage* (London, 1912), 23.

The Men's League Handbook on Women's Suffrage. London, 1912.

7. Multiple works by the same author In the bibliography, use three hyphens in place of the author's name in the second and subsequent entries. Arrange the entries alphabetically by title or by date; be consistent throughout the bibliography.

Harper, Raymond L. *A History of Chesapeake, Virginia*. Charleston, SC: History Press, 2008.

---. *South Norfolk, Virginia, 1661-2005*. Charleston, SC: History Press, 2005.

8. Edited work without an author

    8. Jack Beatty, ed., *Colossus: How the Corporation Changed America* (New York: Broadway Books, 2001), 127.

Directory to *Chicago*-style notes and bibliography entries

Beatty, Jack, ed. *Colossus: How the Corporation Changed America*. New York: Broadway Books, 2001.

9. Edited work with an author

9. Ted Poston, *A First Draft of History,* ed. Kathleen A. Hauke (Athens: University of Georgia Press, 2000), 46.

Poston, Ted. *A First Draft of History*. Edited by Kathleen A. Hauke. Athens: University of Georgia Press, 2000.

10. Translated work

10. Tonino Guerra, *Abandoned Places*, trans. Adria Bernardi (Barcelona: Guernica, 1999), 71.

Guerra, Tonino. *Abandoned Places*. Translated by Adria Bernardi. Barcelona: Guernica, 1999.

11. Edition other than the first

11. Andrew F. Rolle, *California: A History*, 5th ed. (Wheeling, IL: Harlan Davidson, 1998), 243.

Rolle, Andrew F. *California: A History*. 5th ed. Wheeling, IL: Harlan Davidson, 1998.

12. Volume in a multivolume work

12. *The New Encyclopedia of Southern Culture*, vol. 4, *Myth, Manner, and Memory*, ed. Charles Reagan Wilson (Chapel Hill: University of North Carolina Press, 2006), 198.

The New Encyclopedia of Southern Culture. Vol. 4, *Myth, Manner, and Memory*, edited by Charles Reagan Wilson. Chapel Hill: University of North Carolina Press, 2006.

13. Work in an anthology

13. Zora Neale Hurston, "From *Dust Tracks on a Road*," in *The Norton Book of American Autobiography*, ed. Jay Parini (New York: Norton, 1999), 336.

Hurston, Zora Neale. "From *Dust Tracks on a Road*." In *The Norton Book of American Autobiography*, edited by Jay Parini, 333-43. New York: Norton, 1999.

14. Introduction, preface, foreword, or afterword

14. Nelson DeMille, foreword to *Flag: An American Biography*, by Marc Leepson (New York: Thomas Dunne, 2005), xii.

DeMille, Nelson. Foreword to *Flag: An American Biography*, by Marc Leepson, xi-xiv. New York: Thomas Dunne, 2005.

15. Republished book

15. Garry Wills, *Inventing America: Jefferson's Declaration of Independence* (1978; repr., Boston: Houghton Mifflin, 2002), 86.

Wills, Garry. *Inventing America: Jefferson's Declaration of Independence*. 1978. Reprint, Boston: Houghton Mifflin, 2002.

16. Work with a title in its title

16. Gary Schmidgall, ed., *Conserving Walt Whitman's Fame: Selections from Horace Traubel's "Conservator," 1890-1919* (Iowa City: University of Iowa Press, 2006), 165.

Schmidgall, Gary, ed. *Conserving Walt Whitman's Fame: Selections from Horace Traubel's "Conservator," 1890-1919*. Iowa City: University of Iowa Press, 2006.

17. Letter in a published collection

17. Thomas Gainsborough to Elizabeth Rasse, 1753, in *The Letters of Thomas Gainsborough*, ed. John Hayes (New Haven: Yale University Press, 2001), 5.

Gainsborough, Thomas. Letter to Elizabeth Rasse, 1753. In *The Letters of Thomas Gainsborough*, edited by John Hayes, 5. New Haven: Yale University Press, 2001.

18. Work in a series

18. R. Keith Schoppa, *The Columbia Guide to Modern Chinese History*, Columbia Guides to Asian History (New York: Columbia University Press, 2000), 256-58.

Schoppa, R. Keith. *The Columbia Guide to Modern Chinese History*. Columbia Guides to Asian History. New York: Columbia University Press, 2000.

19. Encyclopedia or dictionary entry

19. *Encyclopaedia Britannica*, 15th ed., s.v. "Monroe Doctrine."

19. Bryan A. Garner, *Garner's Modern American Usage* (Oxford: Oxford University Press, 2003), s.v. "brideprice."

Garner, Bryan A. *Garner's Modern American Usage*. Oxford: Oxford University Press, 2003.

The abbreviation "s.v." is for the Latin *sub verbo* ("under the word").

Well-known reference works such as encyclopedias do not require publication information and are usually not included in the bibliography.

20. Sacred text

20. Matt. 20:4-9 (Revised Standard Version).

20. Qur'an 18:1-3.

Sacred texts are usually not included in the bibliography.

21. Source quoted in another source

21. Ron Grossman and Charles Leroux, "A Local Outpost of Democracy," *Chicago Tribune*, March 5, 1996, quoted in William Julius Wilson and Richard P. Taub, *There Goes the Neighborhood: Racial, Ethnic, and Class Tensions in Four Chicago Neighborhoods and Their Meaning for America* (New York: Knopf, 2006), 18.

Grossman, Ron, and Charles Leroux. "A Local Outpost of Democracy." *Chicago Tribune*, March 5, 1996. Quoted in William Julius Wilson and Richard P. Taub, *There Goes the Neighborhood: Racial, Ethnic, and Class Tensions in Four Chicago Neighborhoods and Their Meaning for America* (New York: Knopf, 2006), 18.

Articles in periodicals (print and online)

22. Article in a print journal Include the volume and issue numbers and the date; end the bibliography entry with the page range of the article.

22. Jonathan Zimmerman, "Ethnicity and the History Wars in the 1920s," *Journal of American History* 87, no. 1 (2000): 101.

Zimmerman, Jonathan. "Ethnicity and the History Wars in the 1920s."
    Journal of American History 87, no. 1 (2000): 92-111.

23. Article in an online journal   For unpaginated online articles, you may include in your note a locator, such as a numbered paragraph or a heading from the article.

   23. Linda Belau, "Trauma and the Material Signifier," *Postmodern
Culture* 11, no. 2 (2001): par. 6, http://www.iath.virginia.edu/pmc/text-only/
issue.101/11.2belau.txt.

Belau, Linda. "Trauma and the Material Signifier." *Postmodern Culture*
    11, no. 2 (2001). http://www.iath.virginia.edu/pmc/text-only/
    issue.101/11.2belau.txt.

24. Journal article from a database   Include the URL for the
database. If the article is paginated, give a page number in the
note and a page range in the bibliography.

   24. Eugene F. Provenzo Jr., "Time Exposure," *Educational Studies* 34,
no. 2 (2003): 266, http://search.epnet.com/.

Provenzo, Eugene F., Jr. "Time Exposure." *Educational Studies* 34, no. 2
    (2003): 266-67. http://search.epnet.com/.

25. Article in a print magazine   Provide a page number in the
note and a page range in the bibliography.

   25. Tom Bissell, "Improvised, Explosive, and Divisive," *Harper's*, January
2006, 42.

   Bissell, Tom. "Improvised, Explosive, and Divisive." *Harper's*, January
2006, 41-54.

26. Article in an online magazine   Include the URL for the article. If the article is paginated, give a page number in the
note and a page range in the bibliography.

   26. Katharine Mieszkowski, "A Deluge Waiting to Happen," *Salon*,
July 3, 2008, http://www.salon.com/news/feature/2008/07/03/floods/
index.html.

Mieszkowski, Katharine. "A Deluge Waiting to Happen." *Salon*, July 3, 2008. http://www.salon.com/news/feature/2008/07/03/floods/index.html.

27. Magazine article from a database   Include the URL for the database. If the article is paginated, give a page number in the note and a page range in the bibliography.

   27. David Pryce-Jones, "The Great Sorting Out: Postwar Iraq," *National Review*, May 5, 2003, 17, http://newfirstsearch.oclc.org/.

Pryce-Jones, David. "The Great Sorting Out: Postwar Iraq." *National Review*, May 5, 2003, 17-18. http://newfirstsearch.oclc.org/.

28. Article in a print newspaper   Page numbers are not necessary; a section letter or number, if available, is sufficient.

   28. Randal C. Archibold, "These Neighbors Are Good Ones without a New Fence," *New York Times*, October 22, 2008, sec. A.

Archibold, Randal C. "These Neighbors Are Good Ones without a New Fence." *New York Times*, October 22, 2008, sec. A.

29. Article in an online newspaper   Include the URL for the article; omit page numbers, even if the source provides them.

   29. Phil Willon, "Ready or Not," *Los Angeles Times*, December 2, 2001, http://www.latimes.com/news/la-foster-special.special/.

Willon, Phil. "Ready or Not." *Los Angeles Times*, December 2, 2001. http://www.latimes.com/news/la-foster-special.special/.

30. Newspaper article from a database   Include the URL for the database; omit page numbers, even if the source provides them.

   30. Gina Kolata, "Scientists Debating Future of Hormone Replacement," *New York Times*, October 23, 2002, http://www.proquest.com/.

Kolata, Gina. "Scientists Debating Future of Hormone Replacement." *New York Times*, October 23, 2002. http://www.proquest.com/.

31. Unsigned article   When the author of a periodical article is unknown, treat the periodical itself as the author.

31. *Boston Globe*, "Renewable Energy Rules," August 11, 2003, sec. A.

Boston Globe. "Renewable Energy Rules." August 11, 2003, sec. A.

32. Book review

32. Nancy Gabin, review of *The Other Feminists: Activists in the Liberal Establishment*, by Susan M. Hartman, *Journal of Women's History* 12, no. 3 (2000): 230.

Gabin, Nancy. Review of *The Other Feminists: Activists in the Liberal Establishment*, by Susan M. Hartman. *Journal of Women's History* 12, no. 3 (2000): 227-34.

33. Letter to the editor   Do not use the letter's title, even if the publication gives one.

33. David Harlan, letter to the editor, *New York Review of Books*, October 9, 2008.

Harlan, David. Letter to the editor. *New York Review of Books*, October 9, 2008.

Online sources

34. Web site   Include as much of the following information as is available: author, title of the site, sponsor of the site, and the site's URL. When no author is named, treat the sponsor as the author.

34. Kevin Rayburn, *The 1920s*, http://www.louisville.edu/~kprayb01/1920s.html.

Rayburn, Kevin. *The 1920s*. http://www.louisville.edu/~kprayb01/1920s.html.

NOTE: *Chicago* does not advise including the date you accessed a Web source, but you may provide an access date after the URL if the cited material is time-sensitive or if your instructor requires one: for example, http://www.historychannel.com/today (accessed October 24, 2008).

35. Short work from a Web site   Include as many of the following elements as are available: author's name, title of the short work, title of the site, sponsor of the site, and the URL. When no author is named, treat the site's sponsor as the author.

   35. Sheila Connor, "Historical Background," *Garden and Forest*, Library of Congress, http://lcweb.loc.gov/preserv/prd/gardfor/historygf.html.

Connor, Sheila. "Historical Background." *Garden and Forest*. Library of Congress. http://lcweb.loc.gov/preserv/prd/gardfor/historygf.html.

   35. PBS Online, "Heat," *Frontline*, http://www.pbs.org/wgbh/pages/frontline/heat/.

PBS Online. "Heat." *Frontline*. http://www.pbs.org/wgbh/pages/frontline/heat/.

36. Online posting or e-mail   If an online posting has been archived, include a URL. E-mails that are not part of an online discussion are treated as personal communications (see item 42). Online postings and e-mails are not included in the bibliography.

   36. Janice Klein, posting to State Museum Association discussion list, June 19, 2003, http://listserv.nmmnh-abq.mus.nm.us/scripts/wa.exe?A2=ind0306c&L=sma-l&F=lf&S=&P=81.

37. Weblog (blog) post   Treat as a short document from a Web site, including the following, as available: the author's name; the title of the post; the title of the blog; the sponsor, if any; and the URL.

   37. Miland Brown, "The Flawed Montevideo Convention of 1933," *World History Blog*, http://www.worldhistoryblog.com/2008/05/flawed-montevideo-convention-of-1933.html.

Brown, Miland. "The Flawed Montevideo Convention of 1933." *World History Blog*. http://www.worldhistoryblog.com/2008/05/flawed-montevideo-convention-of-1933.html.

38. Podcast   Treat as a short work from a Web site (see item 35), including the following, if available: the author's (or speaker's) name; the title of the podcast, in quotation marks; the title of the site on which it appears; the sponsor of the site; and the URL. If the podcast is a downloadable file, identify the file format or medium before the URL.

38. Clay S. Jenkinson, "Prejudice and Parties," Show 734, *Thomas Jefferson Hour*, New Enlightenment Radio Network, Makoché Recording, and Prairie Public Radio, MP3 audio file, http://www .jeffersonhour.org/.

Jenkinson, Clay S. "Prejudice and Parties." Show 734. *Thomas Jefferson Hour*. New Enlightenment Radio Network, Makoché Recording, and Prairie Public Radio. MP3 audio file. http://www.jeffersonhour.org/.

39. Online audio or visual source   Cite as a short work from a Web site (see item 35). If the source is a downloadable file, identify the file format or medium before the URL (see item 38).

39. Richard B. Freeman, "Conversations with History," Institute of International Studies, University of California at Berkeley, http://www .youtube.com/watch?v=cgNCFsXGUa0.

Freeman, Richard B. "Conversations with History." Institute of International Studies, University of California at Berkeley. http://www.youtube.com/ watch?v=cgNCFsXGUa0.

Other sources (including online versions)

40. Government document

40. U.S. Department of State, *Foreign Relations of the United States: Diplomatic Papers, 1943* (Washington, DC: GPO, 1965), 562.

U.S. Department of State. *Foreign Relations of the United States: Diplomatic Papers, 1943*. Washington, DC: GPO, 1965.

41. Unpublished dissertation

41. Stephanie Lynn Budin, "The Origins of Aphrodite (Greece)" (PhD diss., University of Pennsylvania, 2000), 301-2.

Budin, Stephanie Lynn. "The Origins of Aphrodite (Greece)." PhD diss., University of Pennsylvania, 2000.

42. Personal communication

42. Sara Lehman, e-mail message to author, August 13, 2003.

Personal communications are not included in the bibliography.

43. Published or broadcast interview

43. Ron Haviv, interview by Charlie Rose, *The Charlie Rose Show*, PBS, February 12, 2001.

Haviv, Ron. Interview by Charlie Rose. *The Charlie Rose Show*, PBS, February 12, 2001.

44. Published proceedings of a conference

44. Julie Kimber, Peter Love, and Phillip Deery, eds., *Labour Traditions: Proceedings of the Tenth National Labour History Conference*, University of Melbourne, Carlton, Victoria, Australia, July 4-6, 2007 (Melbourne: Australian Society for the Study of Labour History, 2007), 5.

Kimber, Julie, Peter Love, and Phillip Deery, eds. *Labour Traditions: Proceedings of the Tenth National Labour History Conference*. University of Melbourne, Carlton, Victoria, Australia, July 4-6, 2007. Melbourne: Australian Society for the Study of Labour History, 2007.

45. Video or DVD

45. *The Secret of Roan Inish*, DVD, directed by John Sayles (1993; Culver City, CA: Columbia TriStar Home Video, 2000).

The Secret of Roan Inish. DVD. Directed by John Sayles. 1993; Culver City, CA: Columbia TriStar Home Video, 2000.

46. Sound recording

46. Gustav Holst, *The Planets*, Royal Philharmonic, André Previn, Telarc compact disc 80133.

Holst, Gustav. *The Planets*. Royal Philharmonic. André Previn. Telarc compact disc 80133.

47. Musical score or composition

47. Antonio Vivaldi, *L'Estro armonico*, op. 3, ed. Eleanor Selfridge-Field (Mineola, NY: Dover, 1999).

Vivaldi, Antonio. *L'Estro armonico*, op. 3. Edited by Eleanor Selfridge-Field. Mineola, NY: Dover, 1999.

48. Work of art For an original work, give the artist, the title (italicized), the medium, the date of composition, and the institution or collection housing the work. To cite a reproduction, omit the medium and location and give publication information for the source.

48. Aaron Siskind, *Untitled (The Most Crowded Block)*, gelatin silver print, 1939, Kemper Museum of Contemporary Art, Kansas City, MO.

Siskind, Aaron. *Untitled (The Most Crowded Block)*. Gelatin silver print, 1939. Kemper Museum of Contemporary Art, Kansas City, MO.

48. Edward Hopper, *August in the City*, in *Edward Hopper: The Art and the Artist*, by Gail Levin (New York: Whitney Museum of American Art, 1980), 197.

Hopper, Edward. *August in the City*. In *Edward Hopper: The Art and the Artist*, by Gail Levin, 197. New York: Whitney Museum of American Art, 1980.

49. Performance

49. Robert Schenkkan, *The Kentucky Cycle*, directed by Richard Elliott, Willows Theatre, Concord, CA, August 31, 2007.

Schenkkan, Robert. *The Kentucky Cycle*. Directed by Richard Elliott. Willows Theatre, Concord, CA, August 31, 2007.

hackerhandbooks.com/bedhandbook > Research exercises
> *Chicago* > E-ex 57–12 to 57–19

57e *Chicago* manuscript format

The following guidelines for formatting a *Chicago*-style paper and preparing its endnotes and bibliography are based on *The Chicago Manual of Style*, 15th ed. (Chicago: U of Chicago P, 2003). For a sample paper, see 57f.

Formatting the paper

Chicago manuscript guidelines are fairly generic because they were not created with a specific type of writing in mind.

Materials and font   Use good-quality 8½″ × 11″ white paper. Avoid a font that is unusual or hard to read.

Title page   Include the full title of your paper, your name, the course title, the instructor's name, and the date. See page 718 for a sample title page.

Pagination   Using arabic numerals, number the pages in the upper right corner. Do not number the title page but count it in the manuscript numbering; that is, the first page of the text will be numbered 2. Depending on your instructor's preference, you may also use a short title or your last name before the page numbers to help identify pages.

Margins and line spacing   Leave margins of at least one inch at the top, bottom, and sides of the page. Double-space the body of the paper, including long quotations that have been set off from the text. (For line spacing in notes and the bibliography, see p. 716.) Left-align the text.

Capitalization and italics   In titles of works, capitalize all words except articles (*a*, *an*, *the*), prepositions (*at*, *from*, *between*, and so on), coordinating conjunctions (*and*, *but*, *or*, *nor*, *for*, *so*, *yet*), and *to* and *as*—unless one of these words is first or last in the title or subtitle. Follow these guidelines in your paper even if the title is styled differently in the source.

Lowercase the first word following a colon even if the word begins a complete sentence. When the colon introduces a series of sentences or questions, capitalize all sentences in the series, including the first.

Italicize the titles of books and other long works, such as entire Web sites. Use quotation marks around the titles of periodical articles, short stories, poems, and other short works.

Long quotations   You can choose to set off a long quotation of five to ten typed lines by indenting the entire quotation one-half inch from the left margin. (You should always set off quotations of ten or more lines.) Double-space the quotation; do not use quotation marks. (See pp. 720 and 722 for a long quotation in the text of a paper; also see p. 695.)

Visuals   *Chicago* classifies visuals as tables and illustrations (illustrations, or figures, include drawings, photographs, maps, and charts). Keep visuals as simple as possible. Label each table with an arabic numeral (Table 1, Table 2, and so on) and provide a clear title that identifies the table's subject. The label and the title should appear on separate lines above the table, flush left. Below the table, give its source in a note like this one:

> *Source:* Edna Bonacich and Richard P. Appelbaum, *Behind the Label* (Berkeley: University of California Press, 2000), 145.

For each figure, place a label and a caption below the figure, flush left. The label and caption need not appear on separate lines. The word "Figure" may be abbreviated to "Fig."

In the text of your paper, discuss the most significant features of each visual. Place visuals as close as possible to the sentences that relate to them unless your instructor prefers visuals in an appendix.

Web addresses (URLs)   When a URL must break across lines, do not insert a hyphen or break at a hyphen if the URL contains one. Instead, break the URL after a slash or a double slash or before any other mark of punctuation. If your word processing program automatically turns Web addresses into links (by underlining them and changing the color), turn off this feature.

Headings   *Chicago* does not provide guidelines for the use of headings in student papers. If you would like to insert headings in a long essay or research paper, check first with your instructor. See the sample *Chicago*-style paper on pages 718–26 for typical placement and formatting of headings.

Preparing the endnotes

Begin the endnotes on a new page at the end of the paper. Center the title Notes about one inch from the top of the page, and number the pages consecutively with the rest of the manuscript. See page 724 for an example.

Indenting and numbering Indent the first line of each note one-half inch from the left margin; do not indent additional lines in the note. Begin the note with the arabic numeral that corresponds to the number in the text. Put a period after the number.

Line spacing Single-space each note and double-space between notes (unless your instructor prefers double-spacing throughout).

Preparing the bibliography

Typically, the notes in *Chicago*-style papers are followed by a bibliography, an alphabetically arranged list of all the works cited or consulted. Center the title Bibliography about one inch from the top of the page. Number bibliography pages consecutively with the rest of the paper. See page 726 for a sample bibliography.

Alphabetizing the list Alphabetize the bibliography by the last names of the authors (or editors); when a work has no author or editor, alphabetize it by the first word of the title other than *A, An,* or *The.*

If your list includes two or more works by the same author, use three hyphens instead of the author's name in all entries after the first. You may arrange the entries alphabetically by title or by date; be consistent throughout the bibliography.

Indenting and line spacing Begin each entry at the left margin, and indent any additional lines one-half inch. Single-space each entry and double-space between entries (unless your instructor prefers double-spacing throughout).

57f Sample *Chicago* research paper

Following is a research paper by Ned Bishop, a student in a history class. Bishop was asked to document his paper using *Chicago*-style endnotes and bibliography. In preparing his manuscript, Bishop also followed *Chicago* guidelines.

hackerhandbooks.com/bedhandbook > Model papers > *Chicago* paper: Bishop

Title of paper.

The Massacre at Fort Pillow:

Holding Nathan Bedford Forrest Accountable

Writer's name.

Ned Bishop

Title of course,
instructor's name,
and date.

History 214

Professor Citro

March 22, 2001

Marginal annotations indicate *Chicago*-style formatting and effective writing.

Bishop 2

Although Northern newspapers of the time no doubt exaggerated
some of the Confederate atrocities at Fort Pillow, most modern sources
agree that a massacre of Union troops took place there on April 12,
1864. It seems clear that Union soldiers, particularly black soldiers,
were killed after they had stopped fighting or had surrendered or were
being held prisoner. Less clear is the role played by Major General
Nathan Bedford Forrest in leading his troops. Although we will never
know whether Forrest directly ordered the massacre, evidence suggests
that he was responsible for it.

Thesis asserts Bishop's main point.

What happened at Fort Pillow?

Fort Pillow, Tennessee, which sat on a bluff overlooking the
Mississippi River, had been held by the Union for two years. It was
garrisoned by 580 men, 292 of them from United States Colored
Heavy and Light Artillery regiments, 285 from the white Thirteenth
Tennessee Cavalry. Nathan Bedford Forrest commanded about 1,500
troops.[1]

Headings, centered, help readers follow the organization.

Statistics are cited with an endnote.

The Confederates attacked Fort Pillow on April 12, 1864, and
had virtually surrounded the fort by the time Forrest arrived on the
battlefield. At 3:30 p.m., Forrest demanded the surrender of the Union
forces, sending in a message of the sort he had used before: "The
conduct of the officers and men garrisoning Fort Pillow has been such
as to entitle them to being treated as prisoners of war. . . . Should
my demand be refused, I cannot be responsible for the fate of your
command."[2] Union Major William Bradford, who had replaced Major
Booth, killed earlier by sharpshooters, asked for an hour to consider
the demand. Forrest, worried that vessels in the river were bringing
in more troops, "shortened the time to twenty minutes."[3] Bradford
refused to surrender, and Forrest quickly ordered the attack.

Quotation is cited with an endnote.

The Confederates charged to the fort, scaled the parapet, and
fired on the forces within. Victory came quickly, with the Union forces

Bishop 3

running toward the river or surrendering. Shelby Foote describes the scene like this:

> Some kept going, right on into the river, where a number drowned and the swimmers became targets for marksmen on the bluff. Others, dropping their guns in terror, ran back toward the Confederates with their hands up, and of these some were spared as prisoners, while others were shot down in the act of surrender.[4]

In his own official report, Forrest makes no mention of the massacre. He does make much of the fact that the Union flag was not lowered by the Union forces, saying that if his own men had not taken down the flag, "few, if any, would have survived unhurt another volley."[5] However, as Jack Hurst points out and Forrest must have known, in this twenty-minute battle, "Federals running for their lives had little time to concern themselves with a flag."[6]

The federal congressional report on Fort Pillow, which charged the Confederates with appalling atrocities, was strongly criticized by Southerners. Respected writer Shelby Foote, while agreeing that the report was "largely" fabrication, points out that the "casualty figures . . . indicated strongly that unnecessary killing had occurred."[7] In an important article, John Cimprich and Robert C. Mainfort Jr. argue that the most trustworthy evidence is that written within about ten days of the battle, before word of the congressional hearings circulated and Southerners realized the extent of Northern outrage. The article reprints a group of letters and newspaper sources written before April 22 and thus "untainted by the political overtones the controversy later assumed."[8] Cimprich and Mainfort conclude that these sources "support the case for the occurrence of a massacre" but that Forrest's role remains "clouded" because of inconsistencies in testimony.[9]

Marginal annotations:

Long quotation is set off from text by indenting. Quotation marks are omitted.

Bishop uses a primary source as well as secondary sources.

Quotation is introduced with a signal phrase.

Bishop draws attention to an article that reprints primary sources.

Bishop 4

Did Forrest order the massacre?

We will never really know whether Forrest directly ordered the massacre, but it seems unlikely. True, Confederate soldier Achilles Clark, who had no reason to lie, wrote to his sisters that "I with several others tried to stop the butchery . . . but Gen. Forrest ordered them [Negro and white Union troops] shot down like dogs[,] and the carnage continued."[10] But it is not clear whether Clark heard Forrest giving the orders or was just reporting hearsay. Many Confederates had been shouting "No quarter! No quarter!" and, as Shelby Foote points out, these shouts were "thought by some to be at Forrest's command."[11] A Union soldier, Jacob Thompson, claimed to have seen Forrest order the killing, but when asked to describe the six-foot-two general, he called him "a little bit of a man."[12]

Perhaps the most convincing evidence that Forrest did not order the massacre is that he tried to stop it once it had begun. Historian Albert Castel quotes several eyewitnesses on both the Union and Confederate sides as saying that Forrest ordered his men to stop firing.[13] In a letter to his wife three days after the battle, Confederate soldier Samuel Caldwell wrote that "if General Forrest had not run between our men & the Yanks with his pistol and sabre drawn not a man would have been spared."[14]

In a respected biography of Nathan Bedford Forrest, Hurst suggests that the temperamental Forrest "may have ragingly ordered a massacre and even intended to carry it out—until he rode inside the fort and viewed the horrifying result" and ordered it stopped.[15] While this is an intriguing interpretation of events, even Hurst would probably admit that it is merely speculation.

Can Forrest be held responsible for the massacre?

Even assuming that Forrest did not order the massacre, he can still be held accountable for it. That is because he created an

---

Topic sentence states the main idea for this section.

Writer presents a balanced view of the evidence.

Topic sentence for this section reinforces the thesis.

atmosphere ripe for the possibility of atrocities and did nothing to ensure that it wouldn't happen. Throughout his career Forrest repeatedly threatened "no quarter," particularly with respect to black soldiers, so Confederate troops had good reason to think that in massacring the enemy they were carrying out his orders. As Hurst writes, "About all he had to do to produce a massacre was issue no order against one."[16] Dudley Taylor Cornish agrees:

> It has been asserted again and again that Forrest did not order a massacre. He did not need to. He had sought to terrify the Fort Pillow garrison by a threat of no quarter, as he had done at Union City and at Paducah in the days just before he turned on Pillow. If his men did enter the fort shouting "Give them no quarter; kill them; kill them; it is General Forrest's orders," he should not have been surprised.[17]

The slaughter at Fort Pillow was no doubt driven in large part by racial hatred. Numbers alone suggest this: Of 295 white troops, 168 were taken prisoner, but of 262 black troops, only 58 were taken into custody, with the rest either dead or too badly wounded to walk.[18] A Southern reporter traveling with Forrest makes clear that the discrimination was deliberate: "Our troops maddened by the excitement, shot down the ret[r]eating Yankees, and not until they had attained t[h]e water's edge and turned to beg for mercy, did any prisoners fall in [t]o our hands—Thus the whites received quarter, but the negroes were shown no mercy."[19] Union surgeon Dr. Charles Fitch, who was taken prisoner by Forrest, testified that after he was in custody he "saw" Confederate soldiers "kill every negro that made his appearance dressed in Federal uniform."[20]

Fort Pillow is not the only instance of a massacre or threatened massacre of black soldiers by troops under Forrest's command.

Transition sentence links new material to old.

Bishop 6

Biographer Brian Steel Wills points out that at Brice's Cross Roads in June 1864, "black soldiers suffered inordinately" as Forrest looked the other way and Confederate soldiers deliberately sought out those they termed "the damned negroes."[21] Just a day after Fort Pillow, on April 13, 1864, one of Forrest's generals, Abraham Buford, after consulting with Forrest, demanded that the federal garrison in Columbus, Kentucky, surrender. The demand stated that if an attack became necessary, "no quarter will be shown to the negro troops whatever; the white troops will be treated as prisoners of war."[22]

Nathan Bedford Forrest, a crude man who had made his fortune as a slave trader, was noted for both his violence and his hatred of blacks. In the words of historian James M. McPherson, "Forrest possessed a killer instinct toward . . . blacks in any capacity other than slave."[23] Forrest's battle successes were largely due to his brazen tactics—tactics that Hurst says would not have occurred to the "aristocratic, well-educated Confederate military hierarchy." [24] Some Southerners, in fact, found Forrest's leadership style distasteful. As one Mississippi aristocrat put it, "Forrest may be, and no doubt is, the best cavalry officer in the West, but I object to a tyrannical [*sic*], hot-headed vulgarian's commanding me."[25]

> Ellipsis mark indicates that words have been omitted.

Because he was so crudely racist, Forrest surely understood the rage that his troops felt toward the very idea of blacks as soldiers. Further, he must have known that his standard threats of "No quarter" would fuel the Confederate soldiers' rage. Although Forrest may have tried to prevent the massacre once it was under way, he can still be held accountable for it. That is because he created the conditions that led to the massacre (especially of black troops) and with full knowledge of those conditions took no steps to prevent what was a nearly inevitable bloodbath.

> Conclusion supports the writer's central argument.

Notes begin on a new page.

Notes

First line of each note is indented ½".

1. John Cimprich and Robert C. Mainfort Jr., eds., "Fort Pillow Revisited: New Evidence about an Old Controversy," *Civil War History* 28, no. 4 (1982): 293-94.

Note number is not raised and is followed by a period.

2. Quoted in Brian Steel Wills, *A Battle from the Start: The Life of Nathan Bedford Forrest* (New York: HarperCollins, 1992), 182.

3. Ibid., 183.

4. Shelby Foote, *The Civil War, a Narrative: Red River to Appomattox* (New York: Vintage, 1986), 110.

Authors' names are not inverted.

5. Nathan Bedford Forrest, "Report of Maj. Gen. Nathan B. Forrest, C. S. Army, Commanding Cavalry, of the Capture of Fort Pillow," *Shotgun's Home of the American Civil War*, http://www.civilwarhome.com/forrest.htm.

6. Jack Hurst, *Nathan Bedford Forrest: A Biography* (New York: Knopf, 1993), 174.

Last name and title refer to an earlier note by the same author.

7. Foote, *Civil War*, 111.

8. Cimprich and Mainfort, "Fort Pillow," 305.

9. Ibid., 305.

10. Ibid., 299.

11. Foote, *Civil War*, 110.

12. Quoted in Wills, *Battle from the Start*, 187.

Notes are single-spaced, with double-spacing between notes. (Some instructors may prefer double-spacing throughout.)

13. Albert Castel, "The Fort Pillow Massacre: A Fresh Examination of the Evidence," *Civil War History* 4, no. 1 (1958): 44-45.

14. Cimprich and Mainfort, "Fort Pillow," 300.

15. Hurst, *Nathan Bedford Forrest*, 177.

16. Ibid.

Bishop 8

17. Dudley Taylor Cornish, *The Sable Arm: Black Troops in the Union Army, 1861-1865* (Lawrence, KS: University Press of Kansas, 1987), 175.

18. Foote, *Civil War*, 111.

19. Cimprich and Mainfort, "Fort Pillow," 304.

20. Quoted in Wills, *Battle from the Start*, 189.

21. Ibid., 215.

22. Quoted in Hurst, *Nathan Bedford Forrest*, 177.

23. Quoted in James M. McPherson, *Battle Cry of Freedom: The Civil War Era* (New York: Oxford University Press, 1988), 402.

24. Hurst, *Nathan Bedford Forrest*, 74.

25. Quoted in Foote, *Civil War*, 106.

Bibliography begins on a new page.

Bibliography

Entries are alphabetized by authors' last names.

Castel, Albert. "The Fort Pillow Massacre: A Fresh Examination of the Evidence." *Civil War History* 4, no. 1 (1958): 37-50.

Cimprich, John, and Robert C. Mainfort Jr., eds. "Fort Pillow Revisited: New Evidence about an Old Controversy." *Civil War History* 28, no. 4 (1982): 293-306.

Cornish, Dudley Taylor. *The Sable Arm: Black Troops in the Union Army, 1861-1865*. Lawrence: University Press of Kansas, 1987.

Foote, Shelby. *The Civil War, a Narrative: Red River to Appomattox*. New York: Vintage, 1986.

Forrest, Nathan Bedford. "Report of Maj. Gen. Nathan B. Forrest, C. S. Army, Commanding Cavalry, of the Capture of Fort Pillow." *Shotgun's Home of the American Civil War*. http://www.civilwarhome.com/forrest.htm.

Hurst, Jack. *Nathan Bedford Forrest: A Biography*. New York: Knopf, 1993.

McPherson, James M. *Battle Cry of Freedom: The Civil War Era*. New York: Oxford University Press, 1988.

Wills, Brian Steel. *A Battle from the Start: The Life of Nathan Bedford Forrest*. New York: HarperCollins, 1992.

First line of entry is at left margin; additional lines are indented ½".

Entries are single-spaced, with double-spacing between entries. (Some instructors may prefer double-spacing throughout.)

Part X
Document Design

The term *document* is broad enough to describe anything you might write in a college class, in the business world, and in everyday life. How you design a document (format it for the printed page or for a computer screen) will affect how readers respond to it.

58 Become familiar with the principles of document design.

Good document design promotes readability, but what *readability* means depends on your purpose and audience and perhaps on other elements of your writing situation, such as your subject, length restrictions, or any other specific requirements (see the checklist on p. 9). All of your design choices—formatting options, headings, and lists—should be made with your writing situation in mind. Likewise, different types of visuals—tables, charts, and images—can support your writing if they are used appropriately.

58a Select appropriate format options.

Similar types of documents share similar design features. Taken together, these features—layout, margins and line spacing, alignment, fonts, and font styles—form an appearance that helps to guide readers.

Layout

Most readers have set ideas about how different kinds of documents should look. Advertisements, for example, have a distinctive appearance, as do newsletters and brochures. Instructors have expectations about how a college paper should look (see 59). Employers too expect documents such as letters, résumés, memos, and e-mail messages to be presented in standard ways (see 60).

Unless you have a compelling reason to stray from convention, it's best to choose a document layout that conforms to your readers' expectations. If you're not sure what readers expect, look at examples of the kind of document you are producing.

Margins, line spacing, and alignment

Margins help control the look of a page. For most academic and business documents, leave a margin of one to one and a half inches on all sides. These margins create a visual frame for the text and provide room for annotations, such as an instructor's comments or an editor's suggestions. Tight margins generally make a page crowded and difficult to read.

Most manuscripts in progress are double-spaced to allow room for editing. Final copy is often double-spaced as well, since single-spaced text is less inviting to read. If you are unsure about margin and spacing requirements for your document, check with your instructor or consult documents similar to the one you are writing.

At times, the advantages of wide margins and double-spaced lines are offset by other considerations. For example, most business and technical documents are single-spaced, with double-spacing between paragraphs, to save paper and promote quick scanning. Keep your purpose and audience in mind as you determine appropriate margins and line spacing for your document.

SINGLE-SPACED, UNFORMATTED   **DOUBLE-SPACED, FORMATTED**

Word processing programs allow you to align text and visuals on a page in four ways:

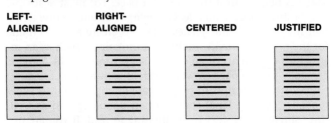

LEFT-ALIGNED   **RIGHT-ALIGNED**   **CENTERED**   **JUSTIFIED**

Most academic and business documents are left-aligned for easy reading.

Fonts

If you have a choice, select a font that fits your writing situation in an easy-to-read size (usually 10 to 12 points). Although offbeat fonts may seem attractive, they slow readers down and can distract them from your ideas. For example, using Comic Sans, a font with a handwritten, childish feel, can make an essay seem too informal or unpolished, regardless of how well it's written. Fonts that are easy to read and appropriate for college and workplace documents include the following: Arial, Courier, Georgia, Times New Roman, and Verdana. Check with your instructor; he or she may expect or prefer a particular font.

Font styles

Font styles—such as **boldface**, *italics*, and <u>underlining</u>—can be useful for calling attention to parts of a document. On the whole, it is best to use restraint when selecting styles. Applying too many different styles within a document can result in busy-looking pages and may confuse readers.

TIP: Never write a document in all capital or all lowercase letters. Doing so can frustrate or annoy readers. Although some readers have become accustomed to instant messages and e-mails that omit capital letters entirely, their absence makes a piece of writing difficult to read.

58b Use headings to guide readers.

You will have little need for headings in short essays, especially if you use paragraphing and clear topic sentences to guide readers. In more complex documents, however, such as longer essays, research papers, business reports, and Web sites, headings can be a useful visual cue for readers.

Headings help readers see at a glance the organization of a document. If more than one level of heading is used, the headings also indicate the hierarchy of ideas—as they do throughout this book.

Headings serve a number of functions, depending on the needs of different readers. When readers are simply looking up information, headings will help them find it quickly. When readers are scanning, hoping to pick up a document's meaning or message, headings will guide them. Even when readers are committed enough to read every word, headings can help them preview a document before they begin reading.

TIP: While headings can be useful, they cannot substitute for transitions between paragraphs (see 3d). Keep this in mind as you write college essays.

Phrasing headings

Headings should be as brief and as informative as possible. Certain styles of headings—the most common being *-ing* phrases, noun phrases, questions, and imperative sentences—work better for some purposes, audiences, and subjects than others.

Whatever style you choose, use it consistently. Headings on the same level of organization should be written in parallel structure (see 9), as in the following examples from a report, a history textbook, a financial brochure, and a nursing manual, respectively.

-ING PHRASES AS HEADINGS
Safeguarding the earth's atmosphere
Charting the path to sustainable energy
Conserving global forests

NOUN PHRASES AS HEADINGS

The antiwar movement

The civil rights movement

The feminist movement

QUESTIONS AS HEADINGS

How do I buy shares?

How do I redeem shares?

How has the fund performed in the past three years?

IMPERATIVE SENTENCES AS HEADINGS

Ask the patient to describe current symptoms.

Take a detailed medical history.

Record the patient's vital signs.

Placing and formatting headings

Headings on the same level of organization should be placed and formatted in a consistent way. If you have more than one level of heading, you might center your first-level headings and make them boldface; then you might make the second-level headings left-aligned and italicized, like this:

First-level heading

Second-level heading

A college paper with headings typically has only one level, and the headings are often centered, as in the sample paper on pages 674–83. Business memos often include headings. Important headings can be highlighted by using white space around them. Less important headings can be downplayed by using less white space or by running them into the text.

58c Use lists to guide readers.

Lists are easy to read or scan when they are displayed, item by item, rather than run into your text. You might choose to display the following kinds of lists:

- steps in a process
- advice or recommendations
- items to be discussed
- criteria for evaluation (as in checklists)
- parts of an object

Lists are usually introduced with an independent clause followed by a colon (*All mammals share the following five characteristics:*). Periods are not used after items in a list unless the items are complete sentences. Lists are most readable when they are presented in parallel grammatical form (see 9).

If you are describing a sequence or a set of steps, number your list with arabic numerals (1, 2, 3) followed by periods. If the order of items is not important, you can use bullets (circles or squares) or dashes to draw readers' eyes to a list.

Although lists can be useful visual cues, don't overdo them. Too many will clutter a document.

58d Add visuals to support your purpose.

Visuals can convey information concisely and powerfully. Charts, graphs, and tables, for example, can simplify complex numerical information. Images—including photographs and diagrams—often express an idea more vividly than words can. With access to the Internet, digital photography, and word processing or desktop publishing software, you can download or create your own visuals to enhance your document. Keep in mind that if you download a visual—or use published information to create your own visual—you must credit your source (see 48).

Choosing appropriate visuals

Use visuals to supplement your writing, not to substitute for it. Always consider how a visual supports your purpose and how your audience might respond to it. A student writing about electronic surveillance in the workplace, for example, used a cartoon to illustrate her point about employees' personal use of the Internet at work (see 54c). Another student, writing about treatments for childhood obesity, created a table to display data she had found in two different sources and discussed in her paper (see 56f).

As you draft and revise a document, choose carefully the visuals that support your main point, and avoid overloading your text with too many images. The chart on pages 736–37 describes eight types of visuals and their purposes.

Placing and labeling visuals

A visual may be placed in the text of a document, near a discussion to which it relates, or it can be put in an appendix, labeled, and referred to in the text.

Placing visuals in the text of a document can be tricky. Usually you will want the visual to appear close to the sentences that relate to it, but page breaks won't always allow this placement. At times you may need to insert the visual at a later point and tell readers where it can be found; sometimes you can make the text flow, or wrap, around the visual. No matter where you place a visual, refer to it in your text. Don't expect visuals to speak for themselves.

Making the most of your handbook

Guidelines for using visuals vary by academic discipline.

▶ English and other humanities: 54a
▶ Social sciences: 56e
▶ History: 57e

Most of the visuals you include in a document will require some sort of label. A label, which is typically placed above or below the visual, should be brief but descriptive. Most commonly, a visual is labeled with the word "Figure" or the abbreviation "Fig.," followed by a number: *Fig. 4.* Sometimes a title might be included to explain how the visual relates to the text: *Fig. 4. Voter turnout by age.*

Using visuals responsibly

Most word processing and spreadsheet software will allow you to produce your own visuals. If you create a chart, a table, or a graph using information from your research, you must cite the source of the information even though the visual is your own. The visual on page 735 credits the source of its data.

VISUAL WITH A SOURCE CREDITED

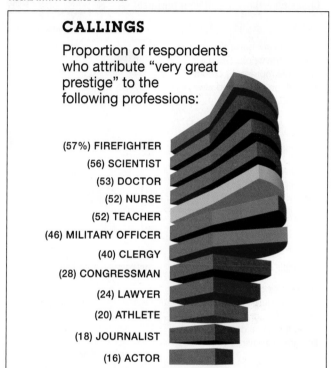

CALLINGS

Proportion of respondents who attribute "very great prestige" to the following professions:

(57%) FIREFIGHTER
(56) SCIENTIST
(53) DOCTOR
(52) NURSE
(52) TEACHER
(46) MILITARY OFFICER
(40) CLERGY
(28) CONGRESSMAN
(24) LAWYER
(20) ATHLETE
(18) JOURNALIST
(16) ACTOR

Source: The New York Times Company, September 21, 2008, from data by the Harris Poll,
July 2008.

If you download a photograph from the Web or scan an image from a magazine or book, you must credit the person or organization that created it, just as you would cite any other source you use in a college paper (see 48). Make sure any cropping or other changes you make to the visual do not distort the meaning of the original. If your document is written for publication outside the classroom, you will need to request permission to use any visual you borrow.

Choosing visuals to suit your purpose

Pie chart

Pie charts compare a part or parts to the whole. Segments of the pie represent percentages of the whole (and always total 100 percent).

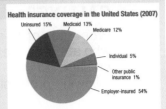

Health insurance coverage in the United States (2007)

Uninsured 15% Medicaid 13% Medicare 12%
Individual 5%
Other public insurance 1%
Employer-insured 54%

Line graph

Line graphs highlight trends over a period of time or compare numerical data.

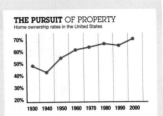

THE PURSUIT OF PROPERTY
Home ownership rates in the United States

70%
60%
50%
40%
30%
20%
1930 1940 1950 1960 1970 1980 1990 2000

Bar graph

Bar graphs can be used for the same purpose as line graphs. This bar graph displays the same data as in the line graph above.

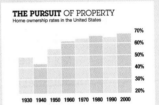

THE PURSUIT OF PROPERTY
Home ownership rates in the United States

70%
60%
50%
40%
30%
20%
1930 1940 1950 1960 1970 1980 1990 2000

Table

Tables organize complicated numerical information into a digestible format.

Prices of daily doses of AIDS drugs
($US)

Drug	Brazil	Uganda	Côte d'Ivoire	US
3TC (Lamivudine)	1.66	3.28	2.95	8.70
ddC (Zalcitabine)	0.24	4.17	3.75	8.80
Didanosine	2.04	5.26	3.48	7.25
Efavirenz	6.96	n/a	6.41	13.13
Indinavir	10.32	12.79	9.07	14.93
Nelfinavir	4.14	4.45	4.39	6.47
Nevirapine	5.04	n/a	n/a	8.48
Saquinavir	6.24	7.37	5.52	6.50
Stavudine	0.56	6.19	4.10	9.07
ZDV/3TC	1.44	7.34	n/a	18.78
Zidovudine	1.08	4.34	2.43	10.12

Source: UNAIDS, 2000

Sources [top to bottom]: Kaiser Foundation; US Census Bureau; US Census Bureau; UNAIDS.

Photograph

Photographs vividly depict
people, scenes, or objects
discussed in a text.

Diagram

Diagrams, useful in scientific
and technical writing, concisely illustrate processes,
structures, or interactions.

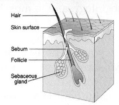

Flowchart

Flowcharts show structures or
steps in a process. (See also
p. 227 for another example of
a flowchart.)

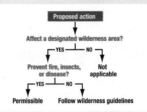

Map

Maps indicate distances,
historical information, or
demographics.

Sources [top to bottom]: Fred
Zwicky; NIAMS; Arizona Board of
Regents; Lynn Hunt et al.

59 Use standard academic formatting.

Instructors have certain expectations about how a college paper should look. If your instructor provides guidelines for formatting an essay, a report, a research paper, or another document, you should follow them. Otherwise, use the manuscript format that is recommended for your academic discipline.

In most English and other humanities classes, you will be asked to use the MLA (Modern Language Association) format (see 54a). In most social science classes, such as psychology and sociology, and in most business and health-related classes, you will be asked to use APA (American Psychological Association) format (see 56e). In history and some other humanities classes, you will be asked to use *Chicago* format (see 57e).

Most composition instructors require MLA format, which is illustrated in the sample on pages 739–40. For more detailed MLA manuscript guidelines and a sample MLA-style research paper, see 54.

60 Use standard business formatting.

This section provides guidelines for preparing business letters, résumés, and memos.

60a Use established conventions for business letters.

In writing a business letter, be direct, clear, and courteous, but do not hesitate to be firm if necessary. State your purpose or request at the beginning of the letter and include only relevant information in the body. By being as direct and concise as possible, you show that you value your reader's time.

For the format of the letter, use established business conventions. The sample business letter on page 741 is typed in what is known as *full block* style. Paragraphs are not indented and are typed single-spaced, with double-spacing between them.

MLA ESSAY FORMAT

½"
Orlov 1

Anna Orlov

Professor Willis

English 101

17 March 2009

Online Monitoring:

A Threat to Employee Privacy in the Wired Workplace

Title is centered.

½"
As the Internet has become an integral tool of businesses, company policies on Internet usage have become as common as policies regarding vacation days or sexual harassment. A 2005 study by the American Management Association and ePolicy Institute found that 76% of companies monitor employees' use of the Web, and the number of companies that block employees' access to certain Web sites has increased 27% since 2001 (1). Unlike other company rules, however, Internet usage policies often include language authorizing companies to secretly monitor their employees, a practice that raises questions about rights in the workplace. Although companies often have legitimate concerns that lead them to monitor employees' Internet usage—from expensive security breaches to reduced productivity—the benefits of electronic surveillance are outweighed by its costs to employees' privacy and autonomy.

1"

Double-spacing is used throughout.

While surveillance of employees is not a new phenomenon, electronic surveillance allows employers to monitor workers with unprecedented efficiency. In his book *The Naked Employee*, Frederick Lane describes offline ways in which employers have been permitted to intrude on employees' privacy for decades, such as drug testing, background checks, psychological exams, lie detector tests, and in-store video surveillance. The difference, Lane argues, between these old methods of data gathering and electronic surveillance involves quantity:

1"

MLA ESSAY FORMAT (*continued*)

½″
1″   Orlov 6

Heading is centered.

Works Cited

Adams, Scott. *Dilbert and the Way of the Weasel*. New York: Harper, 2002. Print.

American Management Association and ePolicy Institute. "2005
½″ Electronic Monitoring and Surveillance Survey." *American Management Association*. Amer. Management Assn., 2005. Web. 15 Feb. 2009.

1″

"Automatically Record Everything They Do Online! Spector Pro 5.0 FAQ's." *Netbus.org*. Netbus.Org, n.d. Web. 17 Feb. 2009.

Flynn, Nancy. "Internet Policies." *ePolicy Institute*. ePolicy Inst., n.d. Web. 15 Feb. 2009.

1″

Frauenheim, Ed. "Stop Reading This Headline and Get Back to Work." *CNET News.com*. CNET Networks, 11 July 2005. Web. 17 Feb. 2009.

Gonsalves, Chris. "Wasting Away on the Web." *eWeek.com*. Ziff Davis Enterprise Holdings, 8 Aug. 2005. Web. 16 Feb. 2009.

Kesan, Jay P. "Cyber-Working or Cyber-Shirking? A First Principles Examination of Electronic Privacy in the Workplace." *Florida Law Review* 54.2 (2002): 289-332. Print.

Double-spacing is used throughout; no extra space between entries.

Lane, Frederick S., III. *The Naked Employee: How Technology Is Compromising Workplace Privacy*. New York: Amer. Management Assn., 2003. Print.

Tam, Pui-Wing, et al. "Snooping E-mail by Software Is Now a Workplace Norm." *Wall Street Journal* 9 Mar. 2005: B1+. Print.

Tynan, Daniel. "Your Boss Is Watching." *PC World*. PC World Communications, 6 Oct. 2004. Web. 17 Feb. 2009.

Verespej, Michael A. "Inappropriate Internet Surfing." *Industry Week*. Penton Media, 7 Feb. 2000. Web. 16 Feb. 2009.

This style is usually preferred when the letter is typed on letterhead stationery, as in the example.

Below the signature, aligned at the left, you may include the abbreviation *Enc.* to indicate that something is enclosed with the letter or the abbreviation *cc* followed by a colon and the name of someone who is receiving a copy of the letter.

BUSINESS LETTER IN FULL BLOCK STYLE

LatinoVoice

March 16, 2009 ──────── Date

Jonathan Ross
Managing Editor
Latino World Today   Inside
2971 East Oak Avenue   address
Baltimore, MD 21201

Dear Mr. Ross: ──────── Salutation

Thank you very much for taking the time yesterday to speak to the University of Maryland's Latino Club. A number of students have told me that they enjoyed your presentation and found your job search suggestions to be extremely helpful.

As I mentioned to you when we first scheduled your appearance, the club publishes a monthly newsletter, *Latino Voice.* Our purpose is to share up-to-date information and expert advice with members of the university's Latino population. Considering how much students benefited from your talk, I would like to publish excerpts from it in our newsletter.

Body —

I have taken the liberty of transcribing parts of your presentation and organizing them into a question-and-answer format for our readers. When you have a moment, would you mind looking through the enclosed article and letting me know if I may have your permission to print it? I would be happy, of course, to make any changes or corrections that you request. I'm hoping to include this article in our next newsletter, so I would need your response by April 4.

Once again, Mr. Ross, thank you for sharing your experiences with us. You gave an informative and entertaining speech, and I would love to be able to share it with the students who couldn't hear it in person.

Sincerely, ──────── Close

Jeffrey Richardson

──────── Signature

Jeffrey Richardson
Associate Editor

Enc.

210 Student Center University of Maryland **College Park MD 20742**

60b Write effective résumés and cover letters.

An effective résumé gives relevant information in a clear and concise form. You may be asked to produce a traditional résumé, a scannable résumé, or a Web résumé. The cover letter gives a prospective employer a reason to look at your résumé. The trick is to present yourself in a favorable light without including unnecessary details.

Cover letters Always include a cover letter to introduce yourself, state the position you seek, and tell where you learned about it. The letter should also highlight past experiences that qualify you for the position and emphasize what you can do for the employer (not what the job will do for you). End the letter with a suggestion for a meeting, and tell your prospective employer when you will be available.

Traditional résumés Traditional résumés are produced on paper, and they are screened by people, not by computers. Because screeners often face stacks of applications, they may spend very little time looking at each résumé. Therefore, you will need to make your résumé as reader-friendly as possible. Here are a few guidelines:

- Limit your résumé to one page if possible, two pages at the most. (If your résumé is longer than a page, repeat your name at the top of the second page.)
- Organize your information into clear categories—Education, Experience, and so on.
- Present the information in each category in reverse chronological order to highlight your most recent accomplishments.
- Use bulleted lists or some other simple, clear visual device to organize information.
- Use strong, active verbs to state your accomplishments. Use present-tense verbs (*manage*) for current activities and past-tense verbs (*managed*) for past activities.

TRADITIONAL RÉSUMÉ

Jeffrey Richardson

121 Knox Road, #6
College Park, MD 20740
301–555–2651
jrichardson@jrichardson.localhost

OBJECTIVE	To obtain an editorial internship with a magazine
EDUCATION Fall 2006– present	University of Maryland • BA expected in June 2010 • Double major: English and Latin American studies • GPA: 3.7 (on a 4-point scale)
EXPERIENCE Fall 2008– present	Associate editor, *Latino Voice*, newsletter of Latino Club • Assign and edit feature articles • Coordinate community outreach
Fall 2007– present	Photo editor, *The Diamondback*, college paper • Shoot and organize photos for print and online publication • Oversee photo staff assignments; evaluate photos
Summer 2008	Intern, *The Globe,* Fairfax, Virginia • Wrote stories about local issues and personalities • Interviewed political candidates • Edited and proofread copy • Coedited "The Landscapes of Northern Virginia: A Photoessay"
Summers 2007, 2008	Tutor, Fairfax County ESL Program • Tutored Latino students in English as a Second Language • Trained new tutors
ACTIVITIES	Photographers' Workshop, Latino Club
PORTFOLIO	Available at http://jrichardson.localhost/jrportfolio.htm
REFERENCES	Available on request

Scannable résumés Scannable résumés might be submitted on paper, by e-mail, or through an online employment service. The résumés are scanned and searched electronically, and a database matches keywords in the job description with keywords in the résumés. A human screener reads the résumés selected by the database.

In general, follow these guidelines when preparing a scannable résumé:

- Include a Keywords section that lists words likely to be searched by a scanner. Use nouns (*manager*), not verbs (*manage* or *managed*).
- Use standard résumé headings (for example, Education, Experience, References).
- Avoid special characters, graphics, or font styles.
- Avoid formatting such as tabs, indents, columns, or tables.

Web résumés Posting your résumé on a Web site is an easy way to provide recent information about your goals and accomplishments. Most guidelines for traditional résumés apply to Web résumés; keep the following guidelines in mind as well.

- Make the opening screen of your Web site simple and concise. Provide links to your résumé and to any other relevant pages, such as an electronic portfolio.
- Consider providing your résumé in HTML format and as a PDF file.
- Include your name, address, phone number, and e-mail address at the top of your résumé page.
- Always list the date that you last updated the résumé.

60c Write clear and concise memos.

Usually brief and to the point, a memo reports information, makes a request, or recommends an action. The format of a memo, which varies from company to company, is designed for easy distribution, quick reading, and efficient filing.

BUSINESS MEMO

COMMONWEALTH PRESS

MEMORANDUM

February 26, 2009

To:	Editorial assistants, Advertising Department
cc:	Stephen Chapman
From:	Helen Brown
Subject:	New database software

The new database software will be installed on your computers next week. I have scheduled a training program to help you become familiar with the software and with our new procedures for data entry and retrieval.

Training program
A member of our IT staff will teach in-house workshops on how to use the new software. If you try the software before the workshop, please be prepared to discuss any problems you encounter.

We will keep the training groups small to encourage hands-on participation and to provide individual attention. The workshops will take place in the training room on the third floor from 10:00 a.m. to 2:00 p.m.

Lunch will be provided in the cafeteria.

Sign-up
Please sign up by March 1 for one of the following dates by adding your name in the department's online calendar:

- Wednesday, March 4
- Friday, March 6
- Monday, March 9

If you will not be in the office on any of those dates, please let me know by March 1.

Most memos display the date, the name of the recipient, the name of the sender, and the subject on separate lines at the top. Many companies have preprinted forms for memos, and most word processing programs have memo templates. Memos are often distributed via e-mail.

The subject line of a memo, on paper or in e-mail, should describe the topic as clearly and concisely as possible, and the introductory paragraph should get right to the point. In addition, the body of the memo should be well organized and easy to skim. To promote skimming, use headings where possible and set off any items that deserve special attention (in a list, for example, or in boldface). A sample memo appears on page 745.

60d Write effective e-mail messages.

In business and academic contexts, you will want to show readers that you value their time. Your e-mail message may be just one of many that your readers have to wade through. Here are some strategies for writing effective e-mails:

- Use a meaningful, concise subject line to help readers sort through messages and set priorities.
- Put the most important part of your message at the beginning so it will be seen without scrolling.
- For long, detailed messages, provide a summary at the beginning.
- Write concisely, and keep paragraphs fairly short.
- Avoid writing in all capital letters or all lowercase letters.
- Use an appropriate tone.
- Before forwarding an e-mail message, check that the original sender has no objections.
- Be sparing with boldface, italics, and special characters; not all e-mail systems handle such elements consistently.
- Proofread for typos and obvious errors that are likely to slow down readers.

Part XI
Grammar Basics

61 Parts of speech

Traditional grammar recognizes eight parts of speech: noun, pronoun, verb, adjective, adverb, preposition, conjunction, and interjection. Many words can function as more than one part of speech. For example, depending on its use in a sentence, the word *paint* can be a noun (*The paint is wet*) or a verb (*Please paint the ceiling next*).

A quick-reference chart of the parts of speech appears on pages 760–62.

61a Nouns

A noun is the name of a person, place, thing, or concept.

> N   N   N
> The *lion* in the *cage* growled at the *zookeeper*.

Nouns sometimes function as adjectives modifying other nouns. Because of their dual roles, nouns used in this manner may be called *noun/adjectives*.

> N/ADJ   N/ADJ
> The *leather* notebook was tucked in the *student's* backpack.

Nouns are classified in a variety of ways. *Proper* nouns are capitalized, but *common* nouns are not (see 45a). For clarity, writers choose between *concrete* and *abstract* nouns (see 18b). The distinction between *count* nouns and *noncount* nouns can be especially helpful to multilingual writers (see 29a). Most nouns have singular and plural forms; *collective* nouns may be either singular or plural, depending on how they are used (see 21f and 22b). *Possessive* nouns require an apostrophe (see 36a).

EXERCISE 61–1 Underline the nouns (and noun/adjectives) in the following sentences. Answers to lettered sentences appear in the back of the book. Example:

The best <u>part</u> of <u>dinner</u> was the <u>chef's</u> newest <u>dessert</u>.

a. The stage was set for a confrontation of biblical proportions.
b. The courage of the mountain climber was an inspiration to the rescuers.
c. The need to arrive before the guest of honor motivated us to navigate the thick fog.
d. The defense attorney made a final appeal to the jury.
e. A national museum dedicated to women artists opened in 1987.

1. Truthfulness is a virtue lacking in many public officials.
2. The Wright Brothers used a wind tunnel to test their airplane designs.
3. The miners' work clothes were clogged with fine black dust.
4. Virginia Woolf wrote that women needed their own income and their own space.
5. The child's language was a charming combination of her father's English and her mother's French.

hackerhandbooks.com/bedhandbook > Grammar exercises > Grammar basics
> E-ex 61–5 and 61–6

61b Pronouns

A pronoun is a word used in place of a noun. Usually the pronoun substitutes for a specific noun, known as its *antecedent*.

When the *battery* wears down, we recharge *it.*

Although most pronouns function as substitutes for nouns, some can function as adjectives modifying nouns. Because they have the form of a pronoun and the function of an adjective, such pronouns may be called *pronoun/adjectives.*

PN / ADJ
This bird was at the same window yesterday morning.

Pronouns are classified as personal, possessive, intensive and reflexive, relative, interrogative, demonstrative, indefinite, and reciprocal.

Personal pronouns   Personal pronouns refer to specific persons or things. They always function as noun equivalents.

Singular: I, me, you, she, her, he, him, it

Plural: we, us, you, they, them

Possessive pronouns   Possessive pronouns indicate ownership.

Singular: my, mine, your, yours, her, hers, his, its

Plural: our, ours, your, yours, their, theirs

Some of these possessive pronouns function as adjectives modifying nouns: *my, your, his, her, its, our, their.*

Intensive and reflexive pronouns   Intensive pronouns emphasize a noun or another pronoun (The senator *herself* met us at the door). Reflexive pronouns, which have the same form as intensive pronouns, name a receiver of an action identical with the doer of the action (Paula cut *herself*).

Singular: myself, yourself, himself, herself, itself

Plural: ourselves, yourselves, themselves

Relative pronouns   Relative pronouns introduce subordinate clauses functioning as adjectives (The writer *who won the award* refused to accept it). In addition to introducing the clause, the relative pronoun, in this case *who*, points back to a noun or pronoun that the clause modifies (*writer*). (See 63e.)

who, whom, whose, which, that

Some textbooks also treat *whichever, whoever, whomever, what,* and *whatever* as relative pronouns. These words introduce noun clauses; they do not point back to a noun or pronoun. (See "Noun clauses" in 63e.)

Interrogative pronouns   Interrogative pronouns introduce questions (*Who* is expected to win the election?).

who, whom, whose, which, what

Demonstrative pronouns Demonstrative pronouns identify or point to nouns. Frequently they function as adjectives (*This* chair is my favorite), but they may also function as noun equivalents (*This* is my favorite chair).

> this, that, these, those

Indefinite pronouns Indefinite pronouns refer to nonspecific persons or things. Most are always singular (*everyone, each*); some are always plural (*both, many*); a few may be singular or plural (see 21e). Most indefinite pronouns function as noun equivalents (*Something* is burning), but some can also function as adjectives (*All* campers must check in at the lodge).

all	anything	everyone	nobody	several
another	both	everything	none	some
any	each	few	no one	somebody
anybody	either	many	nothing	someone
anyone	everybody	neither	one	something

Reciprocal pronouns Reciprocal pronouns refer to individual parts of a plural antecedent (By turns, the penguins fed *one another*).

> each other, one another

NOTE: Pronouns can cause a variety of problems for writers. See pronoun-antecedent agreement (22), pronoun reference (23), distinguishing between pronouns such as *I* and *me* (24), and distinguishing between *who* and *whom* (25).

EXERCISE 61–2 Underline the pronouns (and pronoun/adjectives) in the following sentences. Answers to lettered sentences appear in the back of the book. Example:

> <u>We</u> were intrigued by the video <u>that</u> the fifth graders
>
> produced as <u>their</u> final technology project.

a. The governor's loyalty was his most appealing trait.
b. In the fall, the geese that fly south for the winter pass through our town in huge numbers.
c. Carl Sandburg once said that even he himself did not understand some of his poetry.
d. I appealed my parking ticket, but you did not get one.
e. Angela did not mind gossip as long as no one gossiped about her.

1. The Tigers stood unhappily in front of their dugout while the victorious Jaguars tossed their hats in the air.
2. Nothing fascinated the toddler like something that was not his.
3. We understood that we were expected to submit our dissertations in triplicate.
4. The trick-or-treaters helped themselves to their neighbors' candy.
5. She found herself peering into the mouth of a creepy cave.

hackerhandbooks.com/bedhandbook > Grammar exercises > Grammar basics
> E-ex 61–7 and 61–8

61c Verbs

The verb of a sentence usually expresses action (*jump, think*) or being (*is, become*). It is composed of a main verb possibly preceded by one or more helping verbs.

> MV
> The horses *exercise* every day.

> HV   MV
> The task force report *was* not *completed* on schedule.

> HV HV   MV
> No one *has been defended* with more passion than our pastor.

Notice that words, usually adverbs, can intervene between the helping verb and the main verb (was *not* completed). (See 61e.)

Helping verbs

There are twenty-three helping verbs in English: forms of *have*, *do*, and *be*, which may also function as main verbs; and nine modals, which function only as helping verbs. *Have, do,* and *be* change form to indicate tense; the nine modals do not.

FORMS OF *HAVE*, *DO*, AND *BE*

have, has, had

do, does, did

be, am, is, are, was, were, being, been

MODALS

can, could, may, might, must, shall, should, will, would

The verb phrase *ought to* is often classified as a modal as well.

Main verbs

The main verb of a sentence is always the kind of word that would change form if put into these test sentences:

BASE FORM	Usually I (*walk*, *ride*).
PAST TENSE	Yesterday I (*walked*, *rode*).
PAST PARTICIPLE	I have (*walked*, *ridden*) many times before.
PRESENT PARTICIPLE	I am (*walking*, *riding*) right now.
-S FORM	Usually he / she / it (*walks*, *rides*).

If a word doesn't change form when slipped into the test sentences, you can be certain that it is not a main verb. For example, the noun *revolution*, though it may seem to suggest an action, can never function as a main verb. Just try to make it behave like one (*Today I revolution . . . Yesterday I revolutioned . . .*) and you'll see why.

When both the past-tense and the past-participle forms of a verb end in *-ed*, the verb is regular (*walked*, *walked*). Otherwise, the verb is irregular (*rode*, *ridden*). (See 27a.)

The verb *be* is highly irregular, having eight forms instead of the usual five: the base form *be*; the present-tense forms *am*, *is*, and *are*; the past-tense forms *was* and *were*; the present participle *being*; and the past participle *been*.

Helping verbs combine with the various forms of main verbs to create tenses. For a survey of tenses, see 28a.

NOTE: Some verbs are followed by words that look like prepositions but are so closely associated with the verb that they are a part of its meaning. These words are known as *particles*. Common verb-particle combinations include *bring up, call off, drop off, give in, look up, run into,* and *take off.*

> Sharon *packed up* her broken laptop and *sent* it *off* to the repair shop.

TIP: You can find more information about using verbs in other sections of the handbook: active verbs (8), subject-verb agreement (21), standard English verb forms (27), verb tense and mood (27f and 27g), and ESL challenges with verbs (28).

EXERCISE 61–3 Underline the verbs in the following sentences, including helping verbs and particles. If a verb is part of a contraction (such as *is* in *isn't* or *would* in *I'd*), underline only the letters that represent the verb. Answers to lettered sentences appear in the back of the book. Example:

> The ground under the pine trees <u>was</u>n't wet from the rain.

a. My grandmother always told me a soothing story before bed.
b. There were fifty apples on the tree before the frost killed them.
c. Morton brought down the box of letters from the attic.
d. Stay on the main road and you'll arrive at the base camp before us.
e. The fish struggled vigorously but was trapped in the net.

1. Do not bring that issue up again.
2. Galileo lived the last years of his life under house arrest because of his revolutionary theories about the universe.
3. Cynthia asked for a raise, but she didn't expect one immediately.
4. We should plant the roses early this year.
5. The documentary was engrossing. It humanized World War II.

hackerhandbooks.com/bedhandbook > Grammar exercises > Grammar basics
> E-ex 61–9 and 61–10

61d Adjectives

An adjective is a word used to modify, or describe, a noun or pronoun. An adjective usually answers one of these questions: Which one? What kind of? How many?

ADJ
the *frisky* horse [Which horse?]

ADJ   ADJ
cracked old plates [What kind of plates?]

ADJ
nine months [How many months?]

Adjectives usually precede the words they modify. They may also follow linking verbs, in which case they describe the subject. (See 62b.)

ADJ
The decision was *unpopular.*

The definite article *the* and the indefinite articles *a* and *an* are also classified as adjectives.

ART   ART   ART
A defendant should be judged on *the* evidence provided to *the* jury, not on hearsay.

Some possessive, demonstrative, and indefinite pronouns can function as adjectives: *their, its, this, all* (see 61b). And nouns can function as adjectives when they modify other nouns: *apple pie* (the noun *apple* modifies the noun *pie;* see 61a).

TIP: You can find more details about using adjectives in 26. If you are a multilingual writer, you may also find help with articles and specific uses of adjectives in 29, 30g, and 30h.

61e Adverbs

An adverb is a word used to modify, or qualify, a verb (or verbal), an adjective, or another adverb. It usually answers one of these questions: When? Where? How? Why? Under what conditions? To what degree?

Pull *firmly* on the emergency handle. [Pull how?]

Read the text *first* and *then* work the exercises. [Read when? Work when?]

Adverbs modifying adjectives or other adverbs usually in-tensify or limit the intensity of the word they modify.

ADV   ADV
Be *extremely* kind, and you will *probably* have many friends.

Adverbs modifying adjectives and other adverbs are not movable. It is not correct to write "Be kind *extremely*" or "*Extremely* be kind."

Adverbs can modify prepositional phrases, subordinate clauses, or whole sentences (independent clauses).

The budget is *barely* on target.

We will try to attend, *especially* if you will be there.

Certainly Joe did not intend to insult you.

The negators *not* and *never* are classified as adverbs. A word such as *cannot* contains the helping verb *can* and the adverb *not*. A contraction such as *can't* contains the helping verb *can* and a contracted form of the adverb *not*.

TIP: You can find more details about using adverbs in 26b–26d. Multilingual writers can find more about the placement of adverbs in 30f.

EXERCISE 61–4 Underline the adjectives and circle the adverbs in the following sentences. If a word is a noun or pronoun function-ing as an adjective, underline it and mark it as a noun/adjective or pronoun/adjective. Also treat the articles *a*, *an*, and *the* as adjec-tives. Answers to lettered sentences appear in the back of the book. Example:

Searching for an available room during the convention

was not an easy task.

a. Generalizations lead to weak, unfocused essays.
b. The Spanish language is wonderfully flexible.
c. The wildflowers smelled especially fragrant after the steady rain.
d. I'd rather be slightly hot than bitterly cold.
e. The cat slept soundly in its wicker basket.

1. Success can be elusive to those who object to working hard.
2. After three hours, the discussion had dwindled from a lively sprint to a tedious crawl.
3. She made a fairly earnest attempt at solving the most difficult calculus problems.
4. The black bear sniffed eagerly at the broken honeycomb.
5. The bacteria in the dish grew steadily over twenty-four hours.

hackerhandbooks.com/bedhandbook > Grammar exercises > Grammar basics
> E-ex 61–11 to 61–14

61f Prepositions

A preposition is a word placed before a noun or pronoun to form a phrase modifying another word in the sentence. The prepositional phrase nearly always functions as an adjective or as an adverb.

>   ᴾ   ᴾ   ᴾ
> The road *to* the summit travels *past* craters *from* an extinct volcano.

To the summit functions as an adjective modifying the noun *road*; *past craters* functions as an adverb modifying the verb *travels*; *from an extinct volcano* functions as an adjective modifying the noun *craters*. (For more on prepositional phrases, see 63a.)

English has a limited number of prepositions. The most common are included in the following list.

about	beside	from	outside	toward
above	besides	in	over	under
across	between	inside	past	underneath
after	beyond	into	plus	unlike
against	but	like	regarding	until
along	by	near	respecting	unto
among	concerning	next	round	up
around	considering	of	since	upon
as	despite	off	than	with
at	down	on	through	within
before	during	onto	throughout	without
behind	except	opposite	till	
below	for	out	to	

Some prepositions are more than one word long. *Along with, as well as, in addition to, next to*, and *rather than* are common examples.

TIP: Prepositions are used in idioms such as *capable of* and *try to* (see 18d). For a discussion of specific issues for multilingual writers, see 31.

61g Conjunctions

Conjunctions join words, phrases, or clauses, and they indicate the relation between the elements joined.

Coordinating conjunctions　A coordinating conjunction is used to connect grammatically equal elements. The coordinating conjunctions are *and, but, or, nor, for, so*, and *yet*.

> The sociologist interviewed children *but* not their parents.
>
> Write clearly, *and* your readers will appreciate your efforts.

In the first sentence, *but* connects two noun phrases; in the second, *and* connects two independent clauses.

Correlative conjunctions　Correlative conjunctions come in pairs. Like coordinating conjunctions, they connect grammatically equal elements.

> either . . . or　　　　　　whether . . . or
> neither . . . nor　　　　　both . . . and
> not only . . . but also

> *Either* the painting was brilliant *or* it was a forgery.

Subordinating conjunctions　A subordinating conjunction introduces a subordinate clause and indicates the relation of the clause to the rest of the sentence. (See 63e.) The most common subordinating conjunctions are *after, although, as, as if,* *because, before, if, in order that, once, since, so that, than, that, though, unless, until, when, where, whether,* and *while.*

> *When* the fundraiser ends, we expect to have raised more than half a million dollars.

Conjunctive adverbs   Conjunctive adverbs connect independent clauses and indicate the relation between the clauses. They can be used with a semicolon to join two independent clauses in one sentence, or they can be used alone with an independent clause. The most common conjunctive adverbs are *finally, furthermore, however, moreover, nevertheless, similarly, then, therefore,* and *thus.* (See p. 762 for a longer list.)

> The photographer failed to take a light reading; *therefore,* all the pictures were underexposed.

> During the day, the kitten sleeps peacefully. *However,* when night falls, the kitten is wide awake and ready to play.

Conjunctive adverbs can appear at the beginning or in the middle of a clause.

> When night falls, *however,* the kitten is wide awake and ready to play.

TIP: The ability to distinguish between conjunctive adverbs and coordinating conjunctions will help you avoid run-on sentences and make punctuation decisions (see 20, 32a, and 32b). The ability to recognize subordinating conjunctions will help you avoid sentence fragments (see 19).

61h Interjections

An interjection is a word used to express surprise or emotion (*Oh! Hey! Wow!*).

hackerhandbooks.com/bedhandbook > Grammar exercises > Grammar basics
> E-ex 61–15 and 61–16

Parts of speech

- A **noun** names a person, place, thing, or concept.

  Repetition does not transform a *lie* into *truth*.

- A **pronoun** substitutes for a noun.

  Before the attendant let *us* board the small plane, *he* weighed *us*
  and *our* baggage.

  Personal pronouns: I, me, you, he, him, she, her, it, we, us,
  they, them

  Possessive pronouns: my, mine, your, yours, her, hers, his, its,
  our, ours, their, theirs

  Intensive and reflexive pronouns: myself, yourself, himself,
  herself, itself, ourselves, yourselves, themselves

  Relative pronouns: that, which, who, whom, whose

  Interrogative pronouns: who, whom, whose, which, what

  Demonstrative pronouns: this, that, these, those

  Indefinite pronouns

all	each	many	one
another	either	neither	several
any	everybody	nobody	some
anybody	everyone	none	somebody
anyone	everything	no one	someone
anything	few	nothing	something
both			

  Reciprocal pronouns: each other, one another

- A **helping verb** comes before a main verb.

  Modals: can, could, may, might, must, shall, should, will, would
  (*also* ought to)

→

Forms of *be*: be, am, is, are, was, were, being, been

Forms of *have*: have, has, had

Forms of *do*: do, does, did

(The forms of *be*, *have*, and *do* may also function as main verbs.)

- A **main verb** shows action or a state of being.

  MV
  The novel *opens* with a tense description of a grim murder, but

  HV   MV
  the author *does* not *maintain* the initial level of suspense.

  A main verb will always change form when put into these positions in sentences:

Usually I _____ .	(*walk, ride*)
Yesterday I _____ .	(*walked, rode*)
I have _____ many times before.	(*walked, ridden*)
I am _____ right now.	(*walking, riding*)
Usually he _____ .	(*walks, rides*)

  The highly irregular verb *be* has eight forms: *be, am, is, are, was, were, being, been*.

- An **adjective** modifies a noun or pronoun, usually answering one of these questions: Which one? What kind of? How many? The articles *a*, *an*, and *the* are also adjectives.

  PN/ADJ N/ADJ ADJ   ADJ   PN/ADJ
  Our family's strong ties gave us *welcome* comfort in *our* grief.

- An **adverb** modifies a verb, an adjective, or an adverb, usually answering one of these questions: When? Where? Why? How? Under what conditions? To what degree?

  ADV   ADV
  Young people *often* approach history *skeptically*.

- A **preposition** indicates the relationship between the noun or pronoun that follows it and another word in the sentence.

  P   P
  A journey *of* a thousand miles begins *with* a single step.

→

Parts of speech, *continued*

Common prepositions

about	besides	like	since
above	between	near	than
across	beyond	next	through
after	but	next to	throughout
against	by	of	till
along	concerning	off	to
along with	considering	on	toward
among	despite	onto	under
around	down	opposite	underneath
as	during	out	unlike
as well as	except	outside	until
at	for	over	unto
because of	from	past	up
before	in	plus	upon
behind	in addition to	rather than	with
below	inside	regarding	within
beside	into	respecting	without

- A **conjunction** connects words or word groups.

  Coordinating conjunctions: and, but, or, nor, for, so, yet

  Subordinating conjunctions: after, although, as, as if, because, before, even though, if, in order that, once, since, so that, than, that, though, unless, until, when, where, whether, while

  Correlative conjunctions: either . . . or; neither . . . nor; not only . . . but also; both . . . and; whether . . . or

  Conjunctive adverbs: accordingly, also, anyway, besides, certainly, consequently, conversely, finally, furthermore, hence, however, incidentally, indeed, instead, likewise, meanwhile, moreover, nevertheless, next, nonetheless, otherwise, similarly, specifically, still, subsequently, then, therefore, thus

- An **interjection** expresses surprise or emotion (*Oh! Wow! Hooray!*).

62   Sentence patterns

Most English sentences flow from subject to verb to any
objects or complements. The vast majority of sentences conform to one of these five patterns:

> subject / verb / subject complement
>
> subject / verb / direct object
>
> subject / verb / indirect object / direct object
>
> subject / verb / direct object / object complement
>
> subject / verb

Adverbial modifiers (single words, phrases, or clauses) may be
added to any of these patterns, and they may appear nearly
anywhere—at the beginning, the middle, or the end.

Predicate is the grammatical term given to the verb plus its
objects, complements, and adverbial modifiers.

For a quick-reference chart of sentence patterns, see page
769.

62a Subjects

The subject of a sentence names who or what the sentence
is about. The *complete subject* is usually composed of a *simple
subject*, always a noun or pronoun, plus any words or word
groups modifying the simple subject.

The complete subject

To find the complete subject, ask Who? or What?, insert the verb,
and finish the question. The answer is the complete subject.

┌─────── COMPLETE SUBJECT ───────┐
The devastating effects of famine can last for many years.

Who or what lasts for many years? *The devastating effects of
famine.*

```
┌────────── COMPLETE SUBJECT ──────────┐
```
Adventure novels that contain multiple subplots are often
made into successful movies.

Who or what are made into movies? *Adventure novels that con-*
tain multiple subplots.

```
                          ┌ COMPLETE SUBJECT ┐
```
Within one city neighborhood, income levels can vary greatly.

Who or what can vary greatly? *Income levels.* Notice that
Within one city neighborhood, income levels is not a sensible answer to the question. *Within one city neighborhood* is a prepositional phrase modifying the verb *can vary.* Since sentences
frequently open with such modifiers, it is not safe to assume
that the subject must always appear first in a sentence.

The simple subject

To find the simple subject, strip away all modifiers in the complete subject. This includes single-word modifiers such as *the*
and *devastating*, phrases such as *of famine*, and subordinate
clauses such as *that contain multiple subplots.*

```
         ┌─SS─┐
```
The devastating effects of famine can last for many years.

```
         ┌─SS─┐
```
Adventure novels that contain multiple subplots are often made
into successful movies.

```
                                 ┌─SS─┐
```
Within one city neighborhood, *income levels* can vary greatly.

A sentence may have a compound subject containing two
or more simple subjects joined with a coordinating conjunction such as *and, but,* or *or.*

```
       ┌──── SS ────┐          ┌─SS─┐
```
Great commitment and a little luck make a successful actor.

Understood subjects

In imperative sentences, which give advice or issue commands, the subject is understood but not actually present in

the sentence. The subject of an imperative sentence is understood to be *you*.

> [*You*] Put your clothes in the hamper.

Subject after the verb

Although the subject ordinarily comes before the verb (*the planes took off*) occasionally it does not. When a sentence begins with *There is* or *There are* (or *There was* or *There were*), the subject follows the verb. The word *There* is an expletive in such inverted constructions, an empty word serving merely to get the sentence started.

> ┌─SS─┐
> There are *eight planes waiting to take off.*

Occasionally a writer will invert a sentence for effect.

> ┌─SS─┐
> Joyful is *the child whose school closes for snow.*

Joyful is an adjective, so it cannot be the subject. Turn this sentence around and its structure becomes obvious.

> The *child* whose school closes for snow is joyful.

In questions, the subject frequently appears in an unusual position, sandwiched between parts of the verb.

> ┌────SS────┐
> Do *Kenyan marathoners* train year-round?

Turn the question into a statement, and the words will appear in their usual order: *Kenyan marathoners do train year-round.* (*Do train* is the verb.)

For more about unusual sentence patterns, see 62c.

TIP: The ability to recognize the subject of a sentence will help you edit for a variety of problems: sentence fragments (19), subject-verb agreement (21), choice of pronouns such as *I* and *me* (24), missing subjects (30b), and repeated subjects (30c).

EXERCISE 62–1 In the following sentences, underline the complete subject and write *SS* above the simple subject(s). If the subject is an understood *you*, insert *you* in parentheses. Answers to lettered sentences appear in the back of the book. Example:

> ┌─SS─┐ ┌─SS─┐
> <u>Parents and their children</u> often look alike.

a. The hills and mountains seemed endless, and the snow atop them glistened.
b. In foil fencing, points are scored by hitting an electronic target.
c. Do not stand in the aisles or sit on the stairs.
d. There were hundreds of fireflies in the open field.
e. The evidence against the defendant was staggering.

1. The size of the new building caused an uproar in the town.
2. Eat heartily. You need your strength.
3. In the opinion of the court, siblings must be kept together.
4. All of the books in the old library smelled like mothballs.
5. There were no tour buses at the customs booth.

hackerhandbooks.com/bedhandbook > Grammar exercises > Grammar basics
> E-ex 62–4 and 62–5

62b Verbs, objects, and complements

Section 61c explains how to find the verb of a sentence. A sentence's verb is classified as linking, transitive, or intransitive, depending on the kinds of objects or complements the verb can (or cannot) take.

Linking verbs and subject complements

Linking verbs connect the subject to a subject complement, a word or word group that completes the meaning of the subject by renaming or describing it. They fit into the sentence pattern subject/verb/subject complement.

If the subject complement renames the subject, it is a noun or noun equivalent (sometimes called a *predicate noun*).

> ┌──────────── S ────────────┐ ┌─ V ─┐ ┌─ SC ─┐
> An e-mail requesting personal information may be a scam.

If the subject complement describes the subject, it is an adjective or adjective equivalent (sometimes called a *predicate adjective*).

$$\overline{\text{Last month's temperatures}}^{\;S}\;\overline{\text{were}}^{\;V}\;\overset{SC}{\text{mild.}}$$

Whenever they appear as main verbs (rather than helping verbs), the forms of *be*—*be, am, is, are, was, were, being, been*—usually function as linking verbs. In the preceding examples, for instance, the main verbs are *be* and *were*.

Verbs such as *appear, become, feel, grow, look, make, seem, smell, sound,* and *taste* are sometimes linking, depending on the sense of the sentence.

Before we knew it, $\overline{\text{our toddler's disjointed words}}^{\;S}$ $\overline{\text{had become}}^{\;V}$

$\overset{SC}{\text{sentences.}}$

As it thickens, $\overline{\text{the sauce}}^{\;S}$ $\overline{\text{will look}}^{\;V}$ $\overset{SC}{\text{unappealing.}}$

When you suspect that a verb such as *becomes* or *looks* is linking, check to see if the word or words following it rename or describe the subject. In the preceding examples, *sentences* renames *words*, and *unappealing* describes *sauce*.

Transitive verbs and direct objects

A transitive verb takes a direct object, a word or word group that names a receiver of the action. It fits into the sentence pattern subject/verb/direct object.

$$\overline{\text{The hungry cat}}^{\;S}\;\overset{V}{\text{clawed}}\;\overline{\text{the bag of dry food.}}^{\;DO}$$

The simple direct object is always a noun or pronoun, in this case *bag*. To find it, simply strip away all modifiers.

Transitive verbs usually appear in the active voice, with the subject doing the action and a direct object receiving the action.

Active-voice sentences can be transformed into the passive voice, with the subject receiving the action instead. (See 62c.)

Transitive verbs, indirect objects, and direct objects

The direct object of a transitive verb is sometimes preceded by an indirect object, a noun or pronoun telling to whom or for whom the action of the sentence is done. It fits into the sentence pattern subject/verb/indirect object/direct object.

> S V IO ┌── DO ──┐   S ┌─ V ─┐ IO ┌─ DO ─┐
> You give her some yarn, and she will knit you a scarf.

The simple indirect object is always a noun or pronoun. To test for an indirect object, insert the word *to* or *for* before the word or word group in question. If the sentence makes sense, the word or word group is an indirect object.

> You give [to] *her* some yarn, and she will knit [for] *you* a scarf.

An indirect object may be turned into a prepositional phrase using *to* or *for*: *You give some yarn to her, and she will knit a scarf for you.*

Only certain transitive verbs take indirect objects. Some examples are *ask, bring, find, get, give, hand, lend, make, offer, pay, promise, read, send, show, teach, tell, throw,* and *write.*

Transitive verbs, direct objects, and object complements

The direct object of a transitive verb is sometimes followed by an object complement, a word or word group that renames or describes the object. It fits into the sentence pattern subject/verb/direct object/object complement.

> S   V   DO   ┌────── OC ──────┐
> People often consider chivalry a thing of the past.

> ┌─ S ─┐ V   DO ┌────── OC ──────┐
> The kiln makes clay firm and strong.

When the object complement renames the direct object, it is a noun or pronoun (such as *thing*). When it describes the direct object, it is an adjective (such as *firm* and *strong*).

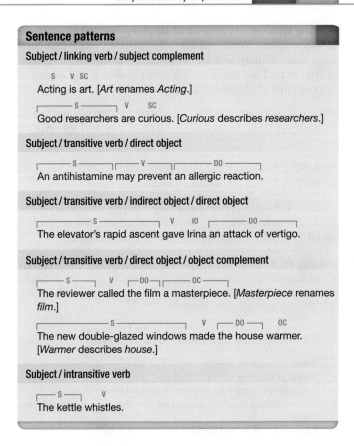

Sentence patterns

Subject / linking verb / subject complement

S   V SC
Acting is art. [*Art* renames *Acting*.]

————— S —————   V   SC
Good researchers are curious. [*Curious* describes *researchers*.]

Subject / transitive verb / direct object

————— S ————— ———— V ———— ———— DO ————
An antihistamine may prevent an allergic reaction.

Subject / transitive verb / indirect object / direct object

————————— S —————————   V   IO   ———— DO ————
The elevator's rapid ascent gave Irina an attack of vertigo.

Subject / transitive verb / direct object / object complement

———— S ————   V   —DO— ———— OC ————
The reviewer called the film a masterpiece. [*Masterpiece* renames *film*.]

————————— S —————————   V   —— DO ——   OC
The new double-glazed windows made the house warmer.
[*Warmer* describes *house*.]

Subject / intransitive verb

—— S ——   V
The kettle whistles.

Intransitive verbs

Intransitive verbs take no objects or complements. Their sentence pattern is subject/verb.

———— S ————   V
The audience laughed.

———— S ————   V
The driver accelerated in the straightaway.

Nothing receives the actions of laughing and accelerating in these sentences, so the verbs are intransitive. Notice that such verbs may or may not be followed by adverbial modifiers. In the second sentence, *in the straightaway* is an adverbial prepositional phrase modifying *accelerated*.

NOTE: The dictionary will tell you whether a verb is transitive or intransitive. Some verbs have both transitive and intransitive functions.

TRANSITIVE Sandra *flew* her small plane over the canyon.

INTRANSITIVE A flock of migrating geese *flew* overhead.

In the first example, *flew* has a direct object that receives the action: *her small plane*. In the second example, the verb is followed by an adverb (*overhead*), not by a direct object.

EXERCISE 62–2 Label the subject complements and direct objects in the following sentences, using the labels *SC* and *DO*. If a subject complement or direct object consists of more than one word, bracket and label all of it. Example:

┌───DO───┐
The sharp right turn confused most drivers.

a. Textbooks are expensive.
b. Samurai warriors never fear death.
c. Successful coaches always praise their players' efforts.
d. St. Petersburg was the capital of the Russian Empire for two centuries.
e. The medicine tasted bitter.

1. Solar flares emit UV radiation.
2. The friends' quarrel was damaging their relationship.
3. Feng shui is the practice of achieving harmony between the physical and the spiritual in one's environment.
4. A well-made advertisement captures viewers' attention.
5. The island's climate was neither too hot nor too rainy.

EXERCISE 62–3 Each of the following sentences has either an indirect object followed by a direct object or a direct object followed by an object complement. Label the objects and complements, using the labels *IO*, *DO*, and *OC*. If an object or a complement consists of more than one word, bracket and label all of it. Example:

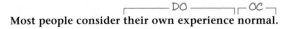

Most people consider their own experience normal.

a. Stress can make adults and children weary.
b. Zita has made community service her priority this year.
c. Consider the work finished.
d. We showed the agent our tickets, and she gave us boarding passes.
e. The dining hall offered students healthy meal choices.

1. Send the registrar your scholarship form today.
2. The independent research institute gives its scholars the freedom to work without government or military interference.
3. Computer viruses make networks vulnerable.
4. Give me a book's title, and I can tell you the author.
5. The dire forecast made us extremely cautious about riding out the storm at home.

hackerhandbooks.com/bedhandbook > Grammar exercises > Grammar basics
> E-ex 62–6 to 62–9

62c Pattern variations

Although most sentences follow one of the five patterns in the chart on page 769, variations of these patterns commonly occur in questions, commands, sentences with delayed subjects, and passive transformations.

Questions and commands

Questions are sometimes patterned in normal word order, with the subject preceding the verb.

S ⎡— V —⎤
Who will have the most hits this season?

Just as frequently, however, the pattern of a question is inverted, with the subject appearing between the helping and main verb or after the verb.

HV S   MV
Will he have the most hits this season?

V ┌──── S ────┐
Why is the number of hits an important statistic?

In commands, the subject of the sentence is an understood *you*.

S   V
[You] Pay attention to the road.

Sentences with delayed subjects

Writers sometimes choose to delay the subject of a sentence to achieve a special effect such as suspense or humor.

V ┌──── S ────┐
Behind the phony tinsel of Hollywood lies the real tinsel.

The subject of the sentence is also delayed in sentences opening with the expletive *There* or *It*. When used as expletives, the words *There* and *It* have no strict grammatical function; they serve merely to get the sentence started.

V ┌──── S ────┐
There are thirty thousand spectators in the stadium.

V ┌──── S ────┐
It is best to avoid trans fats.

The subject in the second example is an infinitive phrase. (See 63b.)

Passive transformations

Transitive verbs, those that can take direct objects, usually appear in the active voice. In the active voice, the subject does the action and a direct object receives the action.

┌──── S ────┐ V ┌──── DO ────┐
ACTIVE   The fireworks display dazzled the viewers on the

┌────┐
Esplanade.

Sentences in the active voice may be transformed into the passive voice, with the subject receiving the action instead.

```
                 ┌──────── S ────────┐   HV      MV
PASSIVE          The viewers on the Esplanade were dazzled by the fire-
                 works display.
```

What was once the direct object (*the viewers on the Esplanade*) has become the subject in the passive-voice transformation, and the original subject appears in a prepositional phrase beginning with *by*. The *by* phrase is frequently omitted in passive-voice constructions.

PASSIVE   The viewers on the Esplanade were dazzled.

Verbs in the passive voice can be identified by their form alone. The main verb is always a past participle, such as *dazzled* (see 61c), preceded by a form of *be* (*be, am, is, are, was, were, being, been*): *were dazzled.* Sometimes adverbs intervene (*were usually dazzled*).

TIP: Avoid using the passive voice when the active voice would be more appropriate (see 8a).

63   Subordinate word groups

Subordinate word groups include phrases and clauses. Phrases are subordinate because they lack a subject and a verb; they are classified as prepositional, verbal, appositive, and absolute (see 63a–63d). Subordinate clauses have a subject and a verb, but they begin with a word (such as *although*, *that*, or *when*) that marks them as subordinate (see 63e).

63a Prepositional phrases

A prepositional phrase begins with a preposition such as *at*, *by*, *for*, *from*, *in*, *of*, *on*, *to*, or *with* (see 61f) and usually ends with a noun or noun equivalent: *on the table*, *for him*, *by sleeping late*. The noun or noun equivalent is known as the *object of the preposition*.

Prepositional phrases function either as adjectives modifying nouns or pronouns or as adverbs modifying verbs, adjectives, or other adverbs.

When functioning as an adjective, a prepositional phrase nearly always appears immediately following the noun or pronoun it modifies.

The hut had *walls of mud.*

Adjective phrases usually answer one or both of the questions Which one? and What kind of? If we ask Which walls? or What kind of walls? we get a sensible answer: *walls of mud.*

Adverbial prepositional phrases that modify the verb can appear nearly anywhere in a sentence.

James *walked* his dog *on a leash.*

Sabrina *will in time adjust* to life in Ecuador.

During a mudslide, the terrain *can change* drastically.

If a prepositional phrase is movable, you can be certain that it is adverbial.

In the cave, the explorers found well-preserved prehistoric drawings.

The explorers found well-preserved prehistoric drawings *in the cave.*

Adverbial word groups usually answer one of these questions: When? Where? How? Why? Under what conditions? To what degree?

James walked his dog *how? On a leash.*

Sabrina would adjust to life in Ecuador *when? In time.*

The terrain can change drastically *under what conditions*?
During a mudslide.

In questions and subordinate clauses, a preposition may
appear after its object.

What are you afraid *of*?

We avoided the bike trail *that* John had warned us *about*.

The object of a preposition might itself be modified by a
prepositional phrase.

There are many *paths to the top of the mountain*.

The complete object of *to* is *the top of the mountain*. The prepositional phrase *of the mountain* modifies the noun *top*. And
the prepositional phrase *to the top of the mountain* modifies the
noun *paths*.

EXERCISE 63–1 Underline the prepositional phrases in the following sentences. Tell whether each phrase is an adjective or an
adverb phrase and what it modifies in the sentence. Answers to
lettered sentences appear in the back of the book. Example:

> **Flecks of mica glittered in the new granite floor.** *(Adjective
> phrase modifying "Flecks"; adverb phrase modifying "glittered")*

a. In northern Italy, some people speak German as their first
language.
b. William completed the hike through the thick forest with ease.
c. To my boss's dismay, I was late for work again.
d. The traveling exhibit of Mayan artifacts gave viewers new insight into pre-Columbian culture.
e. In 2002, the euro became the official currency in twelve European countries.

1. The Silk Road was an old trade route between China and other
parts of the world.
2. Dough with too much flour yields heavy baked goods.

3. On one side of the barricades were revolutionary students; on the other was a government militia.
4. You can tell with just one whiff whether the milk is fresh.
5. At first, we couldn't decide whether to take the car or the train, but in the end we decided to take the train.

hackerhandbooks.com/bedhandbook > Grammar exercises > Grammar basics
> E-ex 63–4 to 63–6

63b Verbal phrases

A verbal is a verb form that does not function as the verb of a clause. Verbals include infinitives (the word *to* plus the base form of the verb), present participles (the *-ing* form of the verb), and past participles (the verb form usually ending in *-d*, *-ed*, *-n*, *-en*, or *-t*). (See 27a and 61c.)

INFINITIVE	PRESENT PARTICIPLE	PAST PARTICIPLE
to dream	dreaming	dreamed
to choose	choosing	chosen
to build	building	built
to grow	growing	grown

Instead of functioning as the verb of a clause, a verbal functions as an adjective, a noun, or an adverb.

ADJECTIVE	*Broken* promises cannot be fixed.
NOUN	Constant *complaining* becomes wearisome.
ADVERB	Can you wait *to celebrate*?

Verbals with objects, complements, or modifiers form verbal phrases.

In my family, *singing loudly* is more appreciated than *singing well.*

Governments exist *to protect the rights of minorities.*

The verbal *singing* is modified by the adverbs *loudly* and *well*; the verbal *to protect* is followed by a direct object, *the rights of minorities.*

Like single-word verbals, verbal phrases function as adjectives, nouns, or adverbs. Verbal phrases are ordinarily classified as participial, gerund, and infinitive.

Participial phrases

Participial phrases always function as adjectives. Their verbals are either present participles (such as *dreaming*, *asking*) or past participles (such as *stolen*, *reached*).

Participial phrases frequently appear immediately following the noun or pronoun they modify.

Congress shall make no *law abridging the freedom of speech or of the press*.

Truth kept in the dark will never save the world.

Unlike other adjectival word groups (prepositional phrases, infinitive phrases, adjective clauses), which must always follow the noun or pronoun they modify, participial phrases are often movable. They can precede the word they modify.

Being a weight-bearing joint, the *knee* is among the most frequently injured.

They may also appear at some distance from the word they modify.

Last night we saw a *play* that affected us deeply, *written with profound insight into the lives of immigrants*.

Gerund phrases

Gerund phrases are built around present participles (verb forms that end in *-ing*), and they always function as nouns:

usually as subjects, subject complements, direct objects, or objects of a preposition.

┌────── S ──────┐
Rationalizing a fear can eliminate it.

┌────────── SC ──────────┐
The key to good sauce is browning the mushrooms.

┌────── DO ──────┐
Lizards usually enjoy sunning themselves.

The American Heart Association has documented the benefits

┌────────── OBJ OF PREP ──────────┐
of diet and exercise in reducing the risk of heart attack.

Infinitive phrases

Infinitive phrases, usually constructed around *to* plus the base form of the verb (*to call*, *to drink*), can function as nouns, as adjectives, or as adverbs.

When functioning as a noun, an infinitive phrase may appear in almost any noun slot in a sentence, usually as a subject, subject complement, or direct object.

┌────────── S ──────────┐
To live without health insurance is risky.

┌────────────── DO ──────────────┐
The orchestra wanted to make its premier season memorable.

Infinitive phrases functioning as adjectives usually appear immediately following the noun or pronoun they modify.

The Twentieth Amendment gave women the *right to vote.*

The infinitive phrase modifies the noun *right.* Which right? *The right to vote.*

Adverbial infinitive phrases usually qualify the meaning of the verb, telling when, where, how, why, under what conditions, or to what degree an action occurred.

Volunteers *rolled up* their pants *to wade through the flood waters.*

Why did they roll up their pants? *To wade through the flood waters.*

NOTE: In some constructions, the infinitive is unmarked; in other words, the *to* does not appear. (See 28f.)

Graphs and charts can help researchers [*to*] *present complex data.*

EXERCISE 63–2 Underline the verbal phrases in the following sentences. Tell whether each phrase is participial, gerund, or infinitive and how each is used in the sentence. Answers to lettered sentences appear in the back of the book. Example:

Do you want <u>to watch that documentary</u>? (Infinitive phrase used as direct object of "Do want")

a. Updating your software will fix the computer glitch.
b. The challenge in decreasing the town budget is identifying non-essential services.
c. Cathleen tried to help her mother by raking the lawn.
d. Understanding little, I had no hope of passing my biology final.
e. Working with animals gave Steve a sense of satisfaction.

1. Driving through South Carolina, we saw kudzu growing out of control along the roadside.
2. Some people now use a patch to repel mosquitoes.
3. We helped the schoolchildren find their way to the station.
4. Painting requires the ability to keep a steady hand.
5. My father could not see a weed without pulling it out of the ground.

hackerhandbooks.com/bedhandbook > Grammar exercises > Grammar basics
> E-ex 63–7 and 63–8

63c Appositive phrases

Though strictly speaking they are not subordinate word groups, appositive phrases function somewhat as adjectives do, to describe nouns or pronouns. Instead of modifying nouns or pronouns, however, appositive phrases rename them. In form they are nouns or noun equivalents.

Appositives are said to be "in apposition" to the nouns or pronouns they rename.

> Bloggers, *conversationalists at heart*, are the online equivalent of radio talk show hosts.

Conversationalists at heart is in apposition to the noun *Bloggers*.

63d Absolute phrases

An absolute phrase modifies a whole clause or sentence, not just one word, and it may appear nearly anywhere in the sentence. It consists of a noun or noun equivalent usually followed by a participial phrase.

> *Her words reverberating in the hushed arena*, the senator urged the crowd to support her former opponent.

> The senator urged the crowd to support her former opponent, *her words reverberating in the hushed arena*.

63e Subordinate clauses

Subordinate clauses are patterned like sentences, having subjects and verbs and sometimes objects or complements. But they function within sentences as adjectives, adverbs, or nouns. They cannot stand alone as complete sentences.

A subordinate clause usually begins with a subordinating conjunction or a relative pronoun. The chart on page 783 classifies these words according to the kinds of clauses (adjective, adverb, or noun) they introduce.

Adjective clauses

Like other word groups functioning as adjectives, adjective clauses modify nouns or pronouns. An adjective clause nearly always appears immediately following the noun or pronoun it modifies.

A *flower that is planted in summer* will grow quickly.

The coach chose *players who would benefit from intense drills*.

To test whether a subordinate clause functions as an adjective, ask the adjective questions: Which one? What kind of? The answer should make sense. Which flower? *The flower that is planted in summer.* What kind of players? *Players who would benefit from intense drills.*

Most adjective clauses begin with a relative pronoun (*who, whom, whose, which,* or *that*), which marks them as grammatically subordinate. In addition to introducing the clause, the relative pronoun points back to the noun that the clause modifies.

A *book that goes unread* is a writer's worst nightmare.

Relative pronouns are sometimes "understood."

The things [*that*] *we cherish most* are the things [*that*] *we might lose.*

Occasionally an adjective clause is introduced by a relative adverb, usually *when, where,* or *why.*

The aging actor returned to the *stage where he had made his debut as Hamlet half a century earlier.*

The parts of an adjective clause are often arranged as in sentences (subject/verb/object or complement).

                                      S   V   DO
Sometimes it is our closest friends who disappoint us.

Frequently, however, the object or complement appears first, violating the normal order of subject/verb/object.

                             DO   S   V
They can be the very friends whom we disappoint.

TIP: For punctuation of adjective clauses, see 32e and 33e. For advice about avoiding repeated words in adjective clauses, see 30d.

Adverb clauses

Adverb clauses usually modify verbs. In such cases, they may appear nearly anywhere in a sentence—at the beginning, at the end, or in the middle. Like other adverbial word groups, they tell when, where, why, how, under what conditions, or to what degree an action occurred or a situation existed.

When the sun went down, the hikers *prepared* their camp.

Laurabeth *would have made* the basketball team *if she hadn't broken her ankle*.

When did the hikers prepare their camp? *When the sun went down.* Under what conditions would Laurabeth have made the team? *If she hadn't broken her ankle.*

Adverb clauses are usually movable when they modify a verb. In the preceding examples, for instance, the adverb clauses can be moved without affecting the meaning of the sentences.

The hikers prepared their camp *when the sun went down.*

If she hadn't broken her ankle, Laurabeth would have made the basketball team.

When an adverb clause modifies an adjective or an adverb, it is not movable; it must appear next to the word it modifies. In the following examples, the *when* clause modifies the adjective *Uncertain*, and the *than* clause modifies the adverb *better*.

Uncertain *when the baby would be born*, Ray and Leah stayed close to home.

Jackie can dance better *than I can walk.*

Adverb clauses always begin with a subordinating conjunction (see the chart on p. 783 for a list). Subordinating conjunctions introduce clauses and express their relation to the rest of the sentence.

> **Words that introduce subordinate clauses**
>
> **Words introducing adverb clauses**
>
> **Subordinating conjunctions:** after, although, as, as if, because, before, even though, if, in order that, since, so that, than, that, though, unless, until, when, where, whether, while
>
> **Words introducing adjective clauses**
>
> **Relative pronouns:** that, which, who, whom, whose
> **Relative adverbs:** when, where, why
>
> **Words introducing noun clauses**
>
> **Relative pronouns:** that, which, who, whom, whose
> **Other pronouns:** whoever, whomever, what, whatever, whichever
> **Other subordinating words:** how, if, when, whenever, where, wherever, whether, why

Adverb clauses are sometimes elliptical, with some of their words being understood but not appearing in the sentence.

> *When* [*it is*] *renovated*, the dorm will hold six hundred students.

Noun clauses

Because they do not function as modifiers, noun clauses are not subordinate in the same sense as adjective and adverb clauses are. They are called subordinate only because they cannot stand alone: They must function within a sentence, always as nouns.

A noun clause functions just like a single-word noun, usually as a subject, subject complement, direct object, or object of a preposition.

┌─────── S ───────┐
Whoever leaves the house last must double-lock the door.

┌─────────── DO ───────────┐
Copernicus argued that the sun is the center of the universe.

A noun clause begins with a word that marks it as subordinate (see the list on p. 783). The subordinating word may or may not play a significant role in the clause. In the preceding example sentences, *Whoever* is the subject of its clause, but *that* does not perform a function in its clause.

As with adjective clauses, the parts of a noun clause may appear out of their normal order (subject/verb/object).

DO   S   V

New Mexico is where we live.

The parts of a noun clause may also appear in normal order.

S   V   ┌──DO──┐

Loyalty is what keeps a friendship strong.

EXERCISE 63–3 Underline the subordinate clauses in the following sentences. Tell whether each clause is an adjective, adverb, or noun clause and how it is used in the sentence. Answers to lettered sentences appear in the back of the book. Example:

> Show the committee the latest draft <u>before you print the</u>
>
> <u>final report.</u> (*Adverb clause modifying "Show"*)

a. The city's electoral commission adjusted the voting process so that every vote would count.
b. A marketing campaign that targets baby boomers may not appeal to young professionals.
c. After the Tambora volcano erupted in the southern Pacific in 1815, no one realized that it would contribute to the "year without a summer" in Europe and North America.
d. The concept of peak oil implies that at a certain point there will be no more oil to extract from the earth.
e. Details are easily overlooked when you are rushing.

1. What her internship taught her was that she worked well with children with special needs.
2. Whether you like it or not, you cannot choose your family.

3. The meteorologist who underestimated the total snowfall of
   the first winter storm was right on target about the second
   storm.
4. If Ramon didn't have to work every afternoon, he would be
   willing to sign up for the yoga class with Andrea.
5. The book that we saw in the shop in Dublin was not available
   when we returned home.

hackerhandbooks.com/bedhandbook > Grammar exercises > Grammar basics
> E-ex 63–9 to 63–12

64 Sentence types

Sentences are classified in two ways: according to their structure (simple, compound, complex, and compound-complex)
and according to their purpose (declarative, imperative, interrogative, and exclamatory).

64a Sentence structures

Depending on the number and types of clauses they contain,
sentences are classified as simple, compound, complex, or
compound-complex.

Clauses come in two varieties: independent and subordinate. An independent clause contains a subject and a predicate,
and it either stands alone or could stand alone. A subordinate
clause also contains a subject and a predicate, but it functions
within a sentence as an adjective, an adverb, or a noun; it cannot stand alone. (See 63e.)

Simple sentences

A simple sentence is one independent clause with no subordinate clauses.

———————————— INDEPENDENT CLAUSE ————————————
Without a passport, Eva could not visit her grandparents in
‾‾‾‾‾‾‾‾|
Hungary.

This sentence contains a subject (*Eva*), a verb with an adverb modifier (*could not visit*), a direct object (*her grandparents in Hungary*), and two prepositional phrases (*Without a passport* and *in Hungary*).

A simple sentence may contain compound elements—a compound subject, verb, or object, for example—but it does not contain more than one full sentence pattern. The following sentence is simple because its two verbs (*comes in* and *goes out*) share a subject (*Spring*).

————————— INDEPENDENT CLAUSE —————————
Spring comes in like a lion and goes out like a lamb.

Compound sentences

A compound sentence is composed of two or more independent clauses with no subordinate clauses. The independent clauses are usually joined with a comma and a coordinating conjunction (*and*, *but*, *or*, *nor*, *for*, *so*, *yet*) or with a semicolon. (See 14a.)

INDEPENDENT — CLAUSE —   INDEPENDENT — CLAUSE —
The car broke down, but a rescue van arrived within minutes.

————— INDEPENDENT CLAUSE —————   — INDEPENDENT CLAUSE—
A shark was spotted near shore; people left immediately.

Complex sentences

A complex sentence is composed of one independent clause with one or more subordinate clauses. (See 63e.)

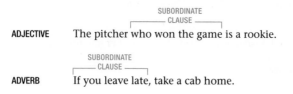

SUBORDINATE — CLAUSE —
ADJECTIVE   The pitcher who won the game is a rookie.

SUBORDINATE — CLAUSE —
ADVERB   If you leave late, take a cab home.

SUBORDINATE
┌────── CLAUSE ──────┐
NOUN   What matters most to us is a quick commute.

Compound-complex sentences

A compound-complex sentence contains at least two independent clauses and at least one subordinate clause. The following sentence contains two full sentence patterns that can stand alone.

┌────── INDEPENDENT CLAUSE ──────┐   ┌────── INDEPENDENT CLAUSE ──────
Tell the doctor how you feel, and she will decide whether

┌──────────
you can go home.

And each independent clause contains a subordinate clause, making the sentence both compound and complex.

┌────── INDEPENDENT CLAUSE ──────┐   ┌────── INDEPENDENT CLAUSE ──────
      ┌───── SUB CL ─────┐   ┌──────
Tell the doctor how you feel, and she will decide whether

┌───── SUB CL ─────┐
you can go home.

64b Sentence purposes

Writers use declarative sentences to make statements, imperative sentences to issue requests or commands, interrogative sentences to ask questions, and exclamatory sentences to make exclamations.

DECLARATIVE   The echo sounded in our ears.

IMPERATIVE   Love your neighbor.

INTERROGATIVE   Did the better team win tonight?

EXCLAMATORY   We're here to save you!

EXERCISE 64–1   Identify the following sentences as simple, compound, complex, or compound-complex. Identify the subordinate clauses and classify them according to their function: adjective, adverb, or noun. (See 63e.) Answers to lettered sentences appear in the back of the book. Example:

The deli in Courthouse Square was crowded with lawyers

at lunchtime. (Simple)

a. Fires that are ignited in dry areas spread especially quickly.
b. The early Incas were advanced; they used a calendar and developed a decimal system.
c. Elaine's jacket was too thin to block the wintry air.
d. Before we leave for the station, we always check the Amtrak Web site.
e. Decide when you want to leave, and I will be there to pick you up.

1. The fact is that the network outage could have been avoided.
2. Those who lose a loved one in a tragic accident may find group therapy comforting.
3. The outlets in the garment district are the best places to find Halloween costumes.
4. There were six lunar Apollo missions, but people usually remember Apollo 13 best.
5. Our generator kicks in whenever we lose power.

hackerhandbooks.com/bedhandbook > Grammar exercises > Grammar basics
> E-ex 64–2

Glossary of Usage

This glossary includes words commonly confused (such as *accept* and *except*), words commonly misused (such as *aggravate*), and words that are nonstandard (such as *hisself*). It also lists colloquialisms and jargon. Colloquialisms are casual expressions that may be appropriate in informal speech but are inappropriate in formal writing. Jargon is needlessly technical or pretentious language that is inappropriate in most contexts. If an item is not listed here, consult the index. For irregular verbs (such as *sing, sang, sung*), see 27a. For idiomatic use of prepositions, see 18d.

> **Grammar checkers** can point out commonly confused words and suggest that you check your usage. It is up to you, however, to determine the correct word for your intended meaning.

hackerhandbooks.com/bedhandbook > Language Debates
 > Absolute concepts such as *unique*
 bad versus *badly*
 however at the beginning of a sentence
 lie versus *lay*
 myself
 that versus *which*
 who versus *which* or *that*
 who versus *whom*
 you

a, an Use *an* before a vowel sound, *a* before a consonant sound: *an apple, a peach*. Problems sometimes arise with words beginning with *h* or *u*. If the *h* is silent, the word begins with a vowel sound, so use *an*: *an hour, an honorable deed*. If the *h* is pronounced, the word begins with a consonant sound, so use *a*: *a hospital, a historian, a hotel*. Words such as *university* and *union* begin with a consonant sound (a *y* sound), so use *a*: *a union*. Words such as *uncle* and *umbrella* begin with a vowel sound, so use *an*: *an underground well*. When an abbreviation or an acronym begins with a vowel sound, use *an*: *an EKG, an MRI, an AIDS prevention program*.

accept, except *Accept* is a verb meaning "to receive." *Except* is usually a preposition meaning "excluding." *I will accept all the packages except that one*. *Except* is also a verb meaning "to exclude." *Please except that item from the list*.

789

adapt, adopt *Adapt* means "to adjust or become accustomed"; it is usually followed by *to*. *Adopt* means "to take as one's own." *Our family adopted a Vietnamese child, who quickly adapted to his new life.*

adverse, averse *Adverse* means "unfavorable." *Averse* means "opposed" or "reluctant"; it is usually followed by *to*. *I am averse to your proposal because it could have an adverse impact on the economy.*

advice, advise *Advice* is a noun, *advise* a verb. *We advise you to follow John's advice.*

affect, effect *Affect* is usually a verb meaning "to influence." *Effect* is usually a noun meaning "result." *The drug did not affect the disease, and it had adverse side effects. Effect* can also be a verb meaning "to bring about." *Only the president can effect such a dramatic change.*

aggravate *Aggravate* means "to make worse or more troublesome." *Overgrazing aggravated the soil erosion.* In formal writing, avoid the use of *aggravate* meaning "to annoy or irritate." *Her babbling annoyed* (not *aggravated*) *me.*

agree to, agree with *Agree to* means "to give consent to." *Agree with* means "to be in accord with" or "to come to an understanding with." *He agrees with me about the need for change, but he won't agree to my plan.*

ain't *Ain't* is nonstandard. Use *am not, are not* (*aren't*), or *is not* (*isn't*). *I am not* (not *ain't*) *going home for spring break.*

all ready, already *All ready* means "completely prepared." *Already* means "previously." *Susan was all ready for the concert, but her friends had already left.*

all right *All right* is written as two words. *Alright* is nonstandard.

all together, altogether *All together* means "everyone or everything in one place." *Altogether* means "entirely." *We were not altogether certain that we could bring the family all together for the reunion.*

allude To *allude* to something is to make an indirect reference to it. Do not use *allude* to mean "to refer directly." *In his lecture, the professor referred* (not *alluded*) *to several pre-Socratic philosophers.*

allusion, illusion An *allusion* is an indirect reference. An *illusion* is a misconception or false impression. *Did you catch my allusion to Shakespeare? Mirrors give the room an illusion of depth.*

a lot *A lot* is two words. Do not write *alot. Sam lost a lot of weight.* See also *lots, lots of.*

among, between See *between, among.*

amongst In American English, *among* is preferred.

amoral, immoral *Amoral* means "neither moral nor immoral"; it also means "not caring about moral judgments." *Immoral* means "morally wrong." *Until recently, most business courses were taught from an amoral perspective. Murder is immoral.*

amount, number Use *amount* with quantities that cannot be counted; use *number* with those that can. *This recipe calls for a large amount of sugar. We have a large number of toads in our garden.*

an See *a, an.*

and etc. *Et cetera* (*etc.*) means "and so forth"; *and etc.* is redundant. See also *etc.*

and/or Avoid the awkward construction *and/or* except in technical or legal documents.

angry at, angry with Use *angry with*, not *angry at*, when referring to a person. *The coach was angry with the referee.*

ante-, anti- The prefix *ante-* means "earlier" or "in front of"; the prefix *anti-* means "against" or "opposed to." *William Lloyd Garrison was a leader of the antislavery movement during the antebellum period. Anti-* should be used with a hyphen when it is followed by a capital letter or a word beginning with *i.*

anxious *Anxious* means "worried" or "apprehensive." In formal writing, avoid using *anxious* to mean "eager." *We are eager* (not *anxious*) *to see your new house.*

anybody, anyone *Anybody* and *anyone* are singular. (See 21e and 22a.)

anymore Reserve the adverb *anymore* for negative contexts, where it means "any longer." *Moviegoers are rarely shocked anymore by profanity.* Do not use *anymore* in positive contexts. Use *now* or *nowadays* instead. *Summer jobs for high school students are so scarce nowadays* (not *anymore*) *that more students are turning to volunteer opportunities.*

anyone See *anybody, anyone.*

anyone, any one *Anyone,* an indefinite pronoun, means "any person at all." *Any one,* the pronoun *one* preceded by the adjective *any,* refers to a particular person or thing in a group. *Anyone from the winning team may choose any one of the games on display.*

anyplace In formal writing, use *anywhere.*

anyways, anywheres *Anyways* and *anywheres* are nonstandard. Use *anyway* and *anywhere.*

as Do not use *as* to mean "because" if there is any chance of ambiguity. *We canceled the picnic because* (not *as*) *it began raining. As* here could mean "because" or "when."

as, like See *like, as.*

as to *As to* is jargon for *about. He inquired about* (not *as to*) *the job.*

averse See *adverse, averse.*

awful The adjective *awful* and the adverb *awfully* are not appropriate in formal writing.

awhile, a while *Awhile* is an adverb; it can modify a verb, but it cannot be the object of a preposition such as *for.* The two-word form *a while* is a noun preceded by an article and therefore can be the object of a preposition. *Stay awhile. Stay for a while.*

back up, backup *Back up* is a verb phrase. *Back up the car carefully. Be sure to back up your hard drive. Backup* is a noun meaning "a copy of electronically stored data." *Keep your backup in a safe place. Backup* can also be used as an adjective. *I regularly create backup disks.*

bad, badly *Bad* is an adjective, *badly* an adverb. *They felt bad about ruining the surprise. Her arm hurt badly after she slid into second base.* (See 26c.)

being as, being that *Being as* and *being that* are nonstandard expressions. Write *because* instead. *Because* (not *Being as*) *I slept late, I had to skip breakfast.*

beside, besides *Beside* is a preposition meaning "at the side of" or "next to." *Annie Oakley slept with her gun beside her bed. Besides* is a preposition meaning "except" or "in addition to." *No one besides Terrie can have that ice cream. Besides* is also an adverb meaning "in addition." *I'm not hungry; besides, I don't like ice cream.*

between, among Ordinarily, use *among* with three or more entities, *between* with two. *The prize was divided among several contestants. You have a choice between carrots and beans.*

bring, take Use *bring* when an object is being transported toward you, *take* when it is being moved away. *Please bring me a glass of water. Please take these forms to Mr. Scott.*

burst, bursted; bust, busted *Burst* is an irregular verb meaning "to come open or fly apart suddenly or violently." Its past tense is *burst.* The past-tense form *bursted* is nonstandard. *Bust* and *busted* are slang for *burst* and, along with *bursted,* should not be used in formal writing.

can, may The distinction between *can* and *may* is fading, but some writers still observe it in formal writing. *Can* is traditionally reserved for ability, *may* for permission. *Can you speak French? May I help you?*

capital, capitol *Capital* refers to a city, *capitol* to a building where lawmakers meet. *Capital* also refers to wealth or resources. *The capitol has undergone extensive renovations. The residents of the state capital protested the development plans.*

censor, censure *Censor* means "to remove or suppress material considered objectionable." *Censure* means "to criticize severely." *The administrations's policy of censoring books has been censured by the media.*

cite, site *Cite* means "to quote as an authority or example." *Site* is usually a noun meaning "a particular place." *He cited the zoning law in his argument against the proposed site of the gas station.* Locations on the Internet are usually referred to as *sites. The library's Web site improves every week.*

climactic, climatic *Climactic* is derived from *climax,* the point of greatest intensity in a series or progression of events. *Climatic* is derived from *climate* and refers to meteorological conditions. *The climactic period in the dinosaurs' reign was reached just before severe climatic conditions brought on an ice age.*

coarse, course *Coarse* means "crude" or "rough in texture." *The coarse weave of the wall hanging gave it a three-dimensional quality. Course* usually refers to a path, a playing field, or a unit of study; the expression *of course* means "certainly." *I plan to take a course in car repair this summer. Of course, you are welcome to join me.*

compare to, compare with *Compare to* means "to represent as similar." *She compared him to a wild stallion. Compare with* means "to examine similarities and differences." *The study compared the language ability of apes with that of dolphins.*

complement, compliment *Complement* is a verb meaning "to go with or complete" or a noun meaning "something that completes." *Compliment* as a verb means "to flatter"; as a noun, it means "flattering remark." *Her skill at rushing the net complements his skill at volleying. Martha's flower arrangements receive many compliments.*

conscience, conscious *Conscience* is a noun meaning "moral principles." *Conscious* is an adjective meaning "aware or alert." *Let your conscience be your guide. Were you conscious of his love for you?*

continual, continuous *Continual* means "repeated regularly and frequently." *She grew weary of the continual telephone calls. Continuous* means "extended or prolonged without interruption." *The broken siren made a continuous wail.*

could care less *Could care less* is nonstandard. Write *couldn't care less* instead. *He couldn't* (not *could*) *care less about his psychology final.*

could of *Could of* is nonstandard for *could have*. *We could have* (not *could of*) *taken the train.*

council, counsel A *council* is a deliberative body, and a *councilor* is a member of such a body. *Counsel* usually means "advice" and can also mean "lawyer"; a *counselor* is one who gives advice or guidance. *The councilors met to draft the council's position paper. The pastor offered wise counsel to the troubled teenager.*

criteria *Criteria* is the plural of *criterion,* which means "a standard or rule or test on which a judgment or decision can be based." *The only criterion for the scholarship is ability.*

data *Data* is a plural noun technically meaning "facts or propositions." But *data* is increasingly being accepted as a singular noun. *The new data suggest* (or *suggests*) *that our theory is correct.* (The singular *datum* is rarely used.)

different from, different than Ordinarily, write *different from. Your sense of style is different from Jim's.* However, *different than* is acceptable to avoid an awkward construction. *Please let me know if your plans are different than* (to avoid *from what*) *they were six weeks ago.*

differ from, differ with *Differ from* means "to be unlike"; *differ with* means "to disagree with." *She differed with me about the wording of the agreement. My approach to the problem differed from hers.*

disinterested, uninterested *Disinterested* means "impartial, objective"; *uninterested* means "not interested." *We sought the advice of a disinterested counselor to help us solve our problem. Mark was uninterested in anyone's opinion but his own.*

don't *Don't* is the contraction for *do not. I don't want any. Don't* should not be used as the contraction for *does not,* which is *doesn't. He doesn't* (not *don't*) *want any.*

due to *Due to* is an adjective phrase and should not be used as a preposition meaning "because of." *The trip was canceled because of* (not *due to*) *lack of interest. Due to* is acceptable as a subject complement and usually follows a form of the verb *be. His success was due to hard work.*

each *Each* is singular. (See 21e and 22a.)

effect See *affect, effect.*

e.g. In formal writing, replace the Latin abbreviation *e.g.* with its English equivalent: *for example* or *for instance.*

either *Either* is singular. (See 21e and 22a.) For *either . . . or* constructions, see 21d and 22d.

elicit, illicit *Elicit* is a verb meaning "to bring out" or "to evoke." *Illicit* is an adjective meaning "unlawful." *The reporter was unable to elicit any information from the police about illicit drug traffic.*

emigrate from, immigrate to *Emigrate* means "to leave one country or region to settle in another." *In 1903, my great-grandfather emigrated from Russia to escape the religious pogroms.* *Immigrate* means "to enter another country and reside there." *More than fifty thousand Bosnians immigrated to the United States in the 1990s.*

eminent, imminent *Eminent* means "outstanding" or "distinguished." *We met an eminent professor of Greek history.* *Imminent* means "about to happen." *The snowstorm is imminent.*

enthused Many people object to the use of *enthused* as an adjective. Use *enthusiastic* instead. *The children were enthusiastic* (not *enthused*) *about going to the circus.*

etc. Avoid ending a list with *etc.* It is more emphatic to end with an example, and in most contexts readers will understand that the list is not exhaustive. When you don't wish to end with an example, *and so on* is more graceful than *etc.* (See also *and etc.*)

eventually, ultimately Often used interchangeably, *eventually* is the better choice to mean "at an unspecified time in the future," and *ultimately* is better to mean "the furthest possible extent or greatest extreme." *He knew that eventually he would complete his degree. The existentialists considered suicide the ultimately rational act.*

everybody, everyone *Everybody* and *everyone* are singular. (See 21e and 22a.)

everyone, every one *Everyone* is an indefinite pronoun. *Every one,* the pronoun *one* preceded by the adjective *every,* means "each individual or thing in a particular group." *Every one* is usually followed by *of. Everyone wanted to go. Every one of the missing books was found.*

except See *accept, except.*

expect Avoid the informal use of *expect* meaning "to believe, think, or suppose." *I think* (not *expect*) *it will rain tonight.*

explicit, implicit *Explicit* means "expressed directly" or "clearly defined"; *implicit* means "implied, unstated." *I gave him explicit instructions not to go swimming. My mother's silence indicated her implicit approval.*

farther, further *Farther* usually describes distances. *Further* usually suggests quantity or degree. *Chicago is farther from Miami than I thought. I would be grateful for further suggestions.*

fewer, less Use *fewer* for items that can be counted; use *less* for items that cannot be counted. *Fewer people are living in the city. Please put less sugar in my tea.*

finalize *Finalize* is jargon meaning "to make final or complete." Use ordinary English instead. *The architect prepared final drawings* (not *finalized the drawings*).

firstly *Firstly* sounds pretentious, and it leads to the ungainly series *firstly, secondly, thirdly,* and so on. Write *first, second, third* instead.

further See *farther, further.*

get *Get* has many colloquial uses. In writing, avoid using *get* to mean the following: "to evoke an emotional response" (*That music always gets to me*); "to annoy" (*After a while his sulking got to me*); "to take revenge on" (*I got back at her by leaving the room*); "to become" (*He got sick*); "to start or begin" (*Let's get going*). Avoid using *have got to* in place of *must. I must* (not *have got to*) *finish this paper tonight.*

good, well *Good* is an adjective, *well* an adverb. (See 26c.) *He hasn't felt good about his game since he sprained his wrist last season. She performed well on the uneven parallel bars.*

graduate Both of the following uses of *graduate* are standard: *My sister was graduated from UCLA last year. My sister graduated from UCLA last year.* It is nonstandard, however, to drop the word *from*: *My sister graduated UCLA last year.* Though this usage is common in informal English, many readers object to it.

grow Phrases such as *to grow the economy* and *to grow a business* are jargon. Usually the verb *grow* is intransitive (it does not take a direct object). *Our business has grown very quickly.* Use *grow* in a transitive sense, with a direct object, to mean "to cultivate" or "to allow to grow." *We plan to grow tomatoes this year. John is growing a beard.*

hanged, hung *Hanged* is the past-tense and past-participle form of the verb *hang* meaning "to execute." *The prisoner was hanged at dawn. Hung* is the past-tense and past-participle form of the verb *hang* meaning "to fasten or suspend." *The stockings were hung by the chimney with care.*

hardly Avoid expressions such as *can't hardly* and *not hardly,* which are considered double negatives. *I can* (not *can't*) *hardly describe my surprise at getting the job.* (See 26e.)

has got, have got *Got* is unnecessary and awkward in such constructions. It should be dropped. *We have* (not *have got*) *three days to prepare for the opening.*

he At one time *he* was commonly used to mean "he or she." Today such usage is inappropriate. (See 17f and 22a.)

he/she, his/her In formal writing, use *he or she* or *his or her*. For alternatives to these wordy constructions, see 17f and 22a.

hisself *Hisself* is nonstandard. Use *himself*.

hopefully *Hopefully* means "in a hopeful manner." *We looked hopefully to the future.* Some usage experts object to the use of *hopefully* as a sentence adverb, apparently on grounds of clarity. To be safe, avoid using *hopefully* in sentences such as the following: *Hopefully, your son will recover soon.* Instead, indicate who is doing the hoping: *I hope that your son will recover soon.*

however In the past, some writers objected to the conjunctive adverb *however* at the beginning of a sentence, but current experts allow placing the word according to the intended meaning and emphasis. All of the following sentences are correct. *Pam decided, however, to attend Harvard. However, Pam decided to attend Harvard.* (She had been considering other schools.) *Pam, however, decided to attend Harvard.* (Unlike someone else, Pam opted for Harvard.) (See 32f.)

hung See *hanged, hung*.

i.e. In formal writing, replace the Latin abbreviation *i.e.* with its English equivalent: *that is*.

if, whether Use *if* to express a condition and *whether* to express alternatives. *If you go on a trip, whether to Nebraska or Italy, remember to bring traveler's checks.*

illusion See *allusion, illusion*.

immigrate See *emigrate from, immigrate to*.

imminent See *eminent, imminent*.

immoral See *amoral, immoral*.

implement *Implement* is a pretentious way of saying "do," "carry out," or "accomplish." Use ordinary language instead. *We carried out* (not *implemented*) *the director's orders.*

imply, infer *Imply* means "to suggest or state indirectly"; *infer* means "to draw a conclusion." *John implied that he knew all about computers, but the interviewer inferred that John was inexperienced.*

in, into *In* indicates location or condition; *into* indicates movement or a change in condition. *They found the lost letters in a box after moving into the house.*

in regards to *In regards to* confuses two different phrases: *in regard to* and *as regards*. Use one or the other. *In regard to* (or *As regards*) *the contract, ignore the first clause.*

irregardless *Irregardless* is nonstandard. Use *regardless*.

is when, is where These mixed constructions are often incorrectly used in definitions. *A run-off election is a second election held to break a tie* (not *is when a second election is held to break a tie*). (See 11c.)

its, it's *Its* is a possessive pronoun; *it's* is a contraction for *it is*. (See 36c and 36e.) *It's always fun to watch a dog chase its tail.*

kind(s) *Kind* is singular and should be treated as such. Don't write *These kind of chairs are rare.* Write instead *This kind of chair is rare. Kinds* is plural and should be used only when you mean more than one kind. *These kinds of chairs are rare.*

kind of, sort of Avoid using *kind of* or *sort of* to mean "somewhat." *The movie was somewhat* (not *sort of*) *boring.* Do not put *a* after either phrase. *That kind of* (not *kind of a*) *salesclerk annoys me.*

lay, lie See *lie, lay.*

lead, led *Lead* is a metallic element; it is a noun. *Led* is the past tense of the verb *lead. He led me to the treasure.*

learn, teach *Learn* means "to gain knowledge"; *teach* means "to impart knowledge." *I must teach* (not *learn*) *my sister to read.*

leave, let *Leave* means "to exit." Avoid using it with the nonstandard meaning "to permit." *Let* (not *Leave*) *me help you with the dishes.*

less See *fewer, less.*

let, leave See *leave, let.*

liable *Liable* means "obligated" or "responsible." Do not use it to mean "likely." *You're likely* (not *liable*) *to trip if you don't tie your shoelaces.*

lie, lay *Lie* is an intransitive verb meaning "to recline or rest on a surface." Its principal parts are *lie, lay, lain. Lay* is a transitive verb meaning "to put or place." Its principal parts are *lay, laid, laid.* (See 27b.)

like, as *Like* is a preposition, not a subordinating conjunction. It can be followed only by a noun or a noun phrase. *As* is a subordinating conjunction that introduces a subordinate clause. In casual speech, you may say *She looks like she hasn't slept* or *You don't know her like I do.* But in formal writing, use *as. She looks as if she hasn't slept. You don't know her as I do.* (See also 61f and 61g.)

loose, lose *Loose* is an adjective meaning "not securely fastened." *Lose* is a verb meaning "to misplace" or "to not win." *Did you lose your only loose pair of work pants*?

lots, lots of *Lots* and *lots of* are informal substitutes for *many, much,* or *a lot.* Avoid using them in formal writing.

mankind Avoid *mankind* whenever possible. It offends many readers because it excludes women. Use *humanity, humans, the human race,* or *humankind* instead. (See 17f.)

may See *can, may.*

maybe, may be *Maybe* is an adverb meaning "possibly." *May be* is a verb phrase. *Maybe the sun will shine tomorrow. Tomorrow may be brighter.*

may of, might of *May of* and *might of* are nonstandard for *may have* and *might have. We might have* (not *might of*) *had too many cookies.*

media, medium *Media* is the plural of *medium. Of all the media that cover the Olympics, television is the medium that best captures the spectacle of the events.*

most *Most* is informal when used to mean "almost" and should be avoided. *Almost* (not *Most*) *everyone went to the parade.*

must of See *may of.*

myself *Myself* is a reflexive or intensive pronoun. Reflexive: *I cut myself.* Intensive: *I will drive you myself.* Do not use *myself* in place of *I* or *me. He gave the flowers to Melinda and me* (not *myself*). (See also 24b.)

neither *Neither* is singular. (See 21e and 22a.) For *neither . . . nor* constructions, see 21d and 22d.

none *None* may be singular or plural. (See 21e.)

nowheres *Nowheres* is nonstandard. Use *nowhere* instead.

number See *amount, number.*

of Use the verb *have,* not the preposition *of,* after the verbs *could, should, would, may, might,* and *must. They must have* (not *must of*) *left early.*

off of *Off* is sufficient. Omit *of. The ball rolled off* (not *off of*) *the table.*

OK, O.K., okay All three spellings are acceptable, but avoid these expressions in formal speech and writing.

parameters *Parameter* is a mathematical term that has become jargon for "fixed limit," "boundary," or "guideline." Use ordinary English instead. *The task force worked within certain guidelines* (not *parameters*).

passed, past *Passed* is the past tense of the verb *pass. Ann passed me another slice of cake. Past* usually means "belonging to a former time" or "beyond a time or place." *Our past president spoke until past midnight. The hotel is just past the next intersection.*

percent, per cent, percentage *Percent* (also spelled *per cent*) is always used with a specific number. *Percentage* is used with a descriptive term such as *large* or *small*, not with a specific number. *The candidate won 80 percent of the primary vote. A large percentage of registered voters turned out for the election.*

phenomena *Phenomena* is the plural of *phenomenon*, which means "an observable occurrence or fact." *Strange phenomena occur at all hours of the night in that house, but last night's phenomenon was the strangest of all.*

plus *Plus* should not be used to join independent clauses. *This raincoat is dirty; moreover* (not *plus*), *it has a hole in it.*

precede, proceed *Precede* means "to come before." *Proceed* means "to go forward." *As we proceeded up the mountain path, we noticed fresh tracks in the mud, evidence that a group of hikers had preceded us.*

principal, principle *Principal* is a noun meaning "the head of a school or an organization" or "a sum of money." It is also an adjective meaning "most important." *Principle* is a noun meaning "a basic truth or law." *The principal expelled her for three principal reasons. We believe in the principle of equal justice for all.*

proceed, precede See *precede, proceed.*

quote, quotation *Quote* is a verb; *quotation* is a noun. Avoid using *quote* as a shortened form of *quotation*. *Her quotations* (not *quotes*) *from current movies intrigued us.*

raise, rise *Raise* is a transitive verb meaning "to move or cause to move upward." It takes a direct object. *I raised the shades. Rise* is an intransitive verb meaning "to go up." *Heat rises.*

real, really *Real* is an adjective; *really* is an adverb. *Real* is sometimes used informally as an adverb, but avoid this use in formal writing. *She was really* (not *real*) *angry.* (See 26b.)

reason . . . is because Use *that* instead of *because. The reason she's cranky is that* (not *because*) *she didn't sleep last night.* (See 11c.)

reason why The expression *reason why* is redundant. *The reason* (not *The reason why*) *Jones lost the election is clear.*

relation, relationship *Relation* describes a connection between things. *Relationship* describes a connection between people. *There is a relation between poverty and infant mortality. Our business relationship has cooled over the years.*

respectfully, respectively *Respectfully* means "showing or marked by respect." *Respectively* means "each in the order given." *He respectfully submitted his opinion to the judge. John, Tom, and Larry were a butcher, a baker, and a lawyer, respectively.*

sensual, sensuous *Sensual* means "gratifying the physical senses," especially those associated with sexual pleasure. *Sensuous* means "pleasing to the senses," especially those involved in the experience of art, music, and nature. *The sensuous music and balmy air led the dancers to more sensual movements.*

set, sit *Set* is a transitive verb meaning "to put" or "to place." Its past tense is *set*. *Sit* is an intransitive verb meaning "to be seated." Its past tense is *sat*. *She set the dough in a warm corner of the kitchen. The cat sat in the doorway.*

shall, will *Shall* was once used in place of the helping verb *will* with *I* or *we*: *I shall, we shall*. Today, however, *will* is generally accepted even when the subject is *I* or *we*. The word *shall* occurs primarily in polite questions (*Shall I find you a pillow?*) and in legalistic sentences suggesting duty or obligation (*The applicant shall file form A by December 31*).

should of *Should of* is nonstandard for *should have*. *They should have* (not *should of*) *been home an hour ago.*

since Do not use *since* to mean "because" if there is any chance of ambiguity. *Because* (not *Since*) *we won the game, we have been celebrating with a pitcher of root beer. Since* here could mean "because" or "from the time that."

sit See *set, sit*.

site See *cite, site*.

somebody, someone *Somebody* and *someone* are singular. (See 21e and 22a.)

something *Something* is singular. (See 21e.)

sometime, some time, sometimes *Sometime* is an adverb meaning "at an indefinite or unstated time." *Some time* is the adjective *some* modifying the noun *time* and means "a period of time." *Sometimes* is an adverb meaning "at times, now and then." *I'll see you sometime soon. I haven't lived there for some time. Sometimes I see him at the library.*

suppose to Write *supposed to*.

sure and Write *sure to*. *We were all taught to be sure to* (not *sure and*) *look both ways before crossing a street.*

take See *bring, take*.

than, then *Than* is a conjunction used in comparisons; *then* is an adverb denoting time. *That pizza is more than I can eat. Tom laughed, and then we recognized him.*

that See *who, which, that.*

that, which Many writers reserve *that* for restrictive clauses, *which* for nonrestrictive clauses. (See 32e.)

theirselves *Theirselves* is nonstandard for *themselves. The crash victims pushed the car out of the way themselves* (not *theirselves*).

them The use of *them* in place of *those* is nonstandard. *Please take those* (not *them*) *flowers to the patient in room 220.*

then, than See *than, then.*

there, their, they're *There* is an adverb specifying place; it is also an expletive (placeholder). Adverb: *Sylvia is lying there unconscious.* Expletive: *There are two plums left. Their* is a possessive pronoun. *Fred and Jane finally washed their car. They're* is a contraction of *they are. They're later than usual today.*

they The use of *they* to indicate possession is nonstandard. Use *their* instead. *Cindy and Sam decided to sell their* (not *they*) *1975 Corvette.*

this kind See *kind(s).*

to, too, two *To* is a preposition; *too* is an adverb; *two* is a number. *Too many of your shots slice to the left, but the last two were just right.*

toward, towards *Toward* and *towards* are generally interchangeable, although *toward* is preferred in American English.

try and *Try and* is nonstandard for *try to. The teacher asked us all to try to* (not *try and*) *write an original haiku.*

ultimately, eventually See *eventually, ultimately.*

unique Avoid expressions such as *most unique, more straight, less perfect, very round.* Either something is unique or it isn't. It is illogical to suggest degrees of uniqueness. (See 26d.)

usage The noun *usage* should not be substituted for *use* when the meaning is "employment of." *The use* (not *usage*) *of insulated shades has cut fuel costs dramatically.*

use to Write *used to.*

utilize *Utilize* means "to make use of." It often sounds pretentious; in most cases, *use* is sufficient. *I used* (not *utilized*) *the laser printer.*

wait for, wait on *Wait for* means "to be in readiness for" or "to await." *Wait on* means "to serve." *We're only waiting for* (not *waiting on*) *Ruth to take us to the museum.*

ways *Ways* is colloquial when used to mean "distance." *The city is a long way* (not *ways*) *from here.*

weather, whether The noun *weather* refers to the state of the atmosphere. *Whether* is a conjunction referring to a choice between alternatives. *We wondered whether the weather would clear.*

well, good See *good, well.*

where Do not use *where* in place of *that. I heard that* (not *where*) *the crime rate is increasing.*

which See *that, which* and *who, which, that.*

while Avoid using *while* to mean "although" or "whereas" if there is any chance of ambiguity. *Although* (not *While*) *Gloria lost money in the slot machine, Tom won it at roulette.* Here *While* could mean either "although" or "at the same time that."

who, which, that Do not use *which* to refer to persons. Use *who* instead. *That,* though generally used to refer to things, may be used to refer to a group or class of people. *The player who* (not *that* or *which*) *made the basket at the buzzer was named MVP. The team that scores the most points in this game will win the tournament.*

who, whom *Who* is used for subjects and subject complements; *whom* is used for objects. (See 25.)

who's, whose *Who's* is a contraction of *who is; whose* is a possessive pronoun. *Who's ready for more popcorn? Whose coat is this?* (See 36c and 36e.)

will See *shall, will.*

would of *Would of* is nonstandard for *would have. She would have* (not *would of*) *had a chance to play if she had arrived on time.*

you In formal writing, avoid *you* in an indefinite sense meaning "anyone." (See 23d.) *Any spectator* (not *You*) *could tell by the way John caught the ball that his throw would be too late.*

your, you're *Your* is a possessive pronoun; *you're* is a contraction of *you are. Is that your new bike? You're in the finals.* (See 36c and 36e.)

Answers to Tutorials and Lettered Exercises

1. A verb has to agree with its subject. (21)
2. Avoid sentence fragments. (19)
3. It's important to use apostrophes correctly. (36)
4. If your sentence begins with a long introductory word group, use a comma to separate the word group from the rest of the sentence. (32b)
5. Watch out for dangling modifiers. (12e)

Tutorial 2, page xxviii

1. The index entry "*each*" mentions that the word is singular, so you might not need to look further to realize that the verb should be *has*, not *have*. The first page reference takes you to section 21, which explains in more detail why *has* is correct. The index entry "*has* vs. *have*" also leads you to section 21.
2. The index entry "*lying* vs. *laying*" takes you to section 27b, where you will learn that *lying* (meaning "reclining or resting on a surface") is correct.
3. Look up "*only*" and you will be directed to section 12a, which explains that limiting modifiers such as *only* should be placed before the words they modify. The sentence should read *We looked at only two houses before buying the house of our dreams.*
4. Looking up "*you*, inappropriate use of" leads you to section 23d and the Glossary of Usage, which explain that *you* should not be used to mean "anyone in general." You can revise the sentence by using *a person* or *one* instead of *you*, or you can restructure the sentence completely: *In Saudi Arabia, accepting a gift is considered ill mannered.*
5. The index entries "*I* vs. *me*" and "*me* vs. *I*" take you to section 24, which explains why *her sister and me* is correct.

Tutorial 3, page xxix

1. Section 32c states that, although usage varies, most experts advise using a comma between all items in a series — to prevent possible misreadings or ambiguities. To find this section, you would probably use the menu system.
2. You and the student would consult section 29, on articles. This section is easy to locate in the menu system.
3. In the menu system, you will find "Writing MLA papers" and then section 52, "Integrating sources."
4. You can send your interns to sections 21 and 27c, which you can find in the menu system if you know to look under "Subject-verb agreement" or "Standard English verb forms." If you aren't sure about the grammatical terminology, you can look in the index under "-*s*, as verb ending" or "Verbs, -*s* form of."
5. The index entry "Tenses, verb" contains a subentry "present, in writing about literature." This leads you to discussions about present tense and

about how to avoid shifting tenses. The entry "Literature, writing about" contains an entry "shifts in tense, avoiding," which directs you to how and why to avoid shifting tenses.

Tutorial 4, page xxx

1. Changing attitudes toward alcohol have *affected* the beer industry.
2. It is *human* nature to think wisely and act foolishly.
3. Correct
4. Our goal this year is to *increase* our profits by 9 percent.
5. Most sleds are pulled by no *fewer* than two dogs and no more than ten.

Tutorial 5, page xxxi

Alim, H. Samy. "360 Degreez of Black Art Comin at You: Sista Sonia Sanchez and the Dimensions of a Black Arts Continuum." *BMa: The Sonia Sanchez Literary Review* 6.1 (2000): 15-33. Print.

Chang, Jeff. *Can't Stop, Won't Stop: A History of the Hip-Hop Generation.* New York: St. Martin's, 2005. Print.

Davis, Kimberly. "The Roots Redefine Hip-Hop's Past." *Ebony* June 2003: 162-64. *Expanded Academic ASAP.* Web. 13 Apr. 2008.

Randall, Kay. "Studying a Hip Hop Nation." *University of Texas at Austin.* U of Texas at Austin, 9 Oct. 2008. Web. 13 Aug. 2009.

Sugarhill Gang. "Rapper's Delight." *Sugarhill Gang.* DBK Works, 2008. CD.

Exercise 6–1, page 128

a. hasty generalization; b. false analogy; c. biased language; d. faulty cause-and-effect reasoning; e. *either . . . or* fallacy

Exercise 8–1, page 146

Possible revisions:

a. The Prussians defeated the Saxons in 1745.
b. Ahmed, the producer, manages the entire operation.
c. The travel guides expertly paddled the sea kayaks.
d. Emphatic and active; no change
e. Protesters were shouting on the courthouse steps.

Exercise 9–1, page 150

Possible revisions:

a. Police dogs are used for finding lost children, tracking criminals, and detecting bombs and illegal drugs.
b. Hannah told her rock climbing partner that she bought a new harness and that she wanted to climb Otter Cliffs.
c. It is more difficult to sustain an exercise program than to start one.
d. During basic training, I was told not only what to do but also what to think.
e. Jan wanted to drive to the wine country or at least to Sausalito.

Exercise 10–1, page 155

Possible revisions:

a. A grapefruit or an orange is a good source of vitamin C.
b. The women entering VMI can expect haircuts as short as those of the male cadets.
c. Looking out the family room window, Sarah saw that her favorite tree, which she had climbed as a child, was gone.
d. The graphic designers are interested in and knowledgeable about producing posters for the balloon race.
e. Reefs are home to more species than any other ecosystem in the sea.

Exercise 11–1, page 159

Possible revisions:

a. Using surgical gloves is a precaution now taken by dentists to prevent contact with patients' blood and saliva.
b. A career in medicine, which my brother is pursuing, requires at least ten years of challenging work.
c. The pharaohs had bad teeth because tiny particles of sand found their way into Egyptian bread.
d. Recurring bouts of flu caused the team to forfeit a record number of games.
e. This box contains the key to your future.

Exercise 12–1, page 164

Possible revisions:

a. More research is needed to evaluate effectively the risks posed by volcanoes in the Pacific Northwest.
b. Many students graduate from college with debt totaling more than fifty thousand dollars.
c. It is a myth that humans use only 10 percent of their brains.
d. A coolhunter is a person who can find the next wave of fashion in the unnoticed corners of modern society.
e. Not all geese fly beyond Narragansett for the winter.

Exercise 12–2, page 168

Possible revisions:

a. Though Martha was only sixteen, UCLA accepted her application.
b. To replace the gear mechanism, you can use the attached form to order the part by mail.
c. As I settled in the cockpit, the pounding of the engine was muffled only slightly by my helmet.
d. After studying polymer chemistry, Phuong found computer games less complex.
e. When I was a young man, my mother enrolled me in tap dance classes.

Exercise 13–3, page 175

Possible revisions:

a. An incredibly talented musician, Ray Charles mastered R&B, soul, and gospel styles. He even performed country music well.

b. Environmentalists point out that shrimp farming in Southeast Asia is polluting water and making farmlands useless. They warn that governments must act before it is too late.

c. We observed the samples for five days before we detected any growth. *Or* The samples were observed for five days before any growth was detected.

d. In his famous soliloquy, Hamlet contemplates whether death would be preferable to his difficult life and, if so, whether he is capable of committing suicide.

e. The lawyer told the judge that Miranda Hale was innocent and asked that she be allowed to prove the allegations false. *Or* The lawyer told the judge, "Miranda Hale is innocent. Please allow her to prove the allegations false."

Exercise 13–4, page 175

Possible revisions:

a. Courtroom lawyers have more than a touch of theater in their blood.

b. The interviewer asked if we had brought our proof of citizenship and our passports.

c. Reconnaissance scouts often have to make fast decisions and use sophisticated equipment to keep their teams from being detected.

d. After the animators finish their scenes, the production designer arranges the clips according to the storyboard and makes synchronization notes for the sound editor and the composer.

e. Madame Defarge is a sinister figure in Dickens's *A Tale of Two Cities*. On a symbolic level, she represents fate; like the Greek Fates, she knits the fabric of individual destiny.

Exercise 14–1, page 181

Possible revisions:

a. Williams played for the Boston Red Sox from 1936 to 1960, and he managed the Washington Senators and Texas Rangers for several years after retiring as a player.

b. In 1941, Williams finished the season with a batting average of .406; no player has hit over .400 for a season since then.

c. Although he acknowledged that Joe DiMaggio was a better all-around player, Williams felt that he was a better hitter than DiMaggio.

d. Williams was a stubborn man; for example, he always refused to tip his cap to the crowd after a home run because he claimed that fans were fickle.

e. Williams's relationship with the media was unfriendly at best; he sarcastically called baseball writers the "knights of the keyboard" in his memoir.

Exercise 14–2, page 183

Possible revisions:

a. The X-Men comic books and Japanese woodcuts of kabuki dancers, all part of Marlena's research project on popular culture, covered the tabletop and the chairs.

b. Our waitress, costumed in a kimono, had painted her face white and arranged her hair in a lacquered beehive.

c. Students can apply for a spot in the leadership program, which teaches thinking and communication skills.
d. Shore houses were flooded up to the first floor, beaches were washed away, and Brant's Lighthouse was swallowed by the sea.
e. Laura Thackray, an engineer at Volvo Car Corporation, addressed women's needs by designing a pregnant crash-test dummy.

Exercise 14–3, page 185

Possible revisions:

a. These particles, known as "stealth liposomes," can hide in the body for a long time without detection.
b. Irena, a competitive gymnast majoring in biochemistry, intends to apply her athletic experience and her science degree to a career in sports medicine.
c. Because students, textile workers, and labor unions have loudly protested sweatshop abuses, apparel makers have been forced to examine their labor practices.
d. Developed in a European university, IRC (Internet relay chat) was created as a way for a group of graduate students to talk about projects from their dorm rooms.
e. The cafeteria's new menu, which has an international flavor, includes everything from enchiladas and pizza to pad thai and sauerbraten.

Exercise 14–4, page 188

Possible revisions:

a. Working as an aide for the relief agency, Gina distributed food and medical supplies.
b. Janbir, who spent every Saturday learning tabla drumming, noticed with each hour of practice that his memory for complex patterns was growing stronger.
c. When the rotor hit, it gouged a hole about an eighth of an inch deep in my helmet.
d. My grandfather, who was born eighty years ago in Puerto Rico, raised his daughters the old-fashioned way.
e. By reversing the depressive effect of the drug, the Narcan saved the patient's life.

Exercise 15–1, page 195

Possible revisions:

a. Across the hall from the fossils exhibit are the exhibits for insects and spiders.
b. After growing up desperately poor in Japan, Sayuri becomes a successful geisha.
c. What caused Mount St. Helens to erupt? Researchers believe that a series of earthquakes in the area was a contributing factor.
d. Ice cream typically contains 10 percent milk fat, but premium ice cream may contain up to 16 percent milk fat and has considerably less air in the product.
e. If home values climb, the economy may recover more quickly than expected.

Exercise 16–1, page 202

Possible revisions:

a.   Martin Luther King Jr. set a high standard for future leaders.
b.   Alice has loved cooking since she could first peek over a kitchen tabletop.
c.   Bloom's race for the governorship is futile.
d.   A successful graphic designer must have technical knowledge and an eye for color and balance.
e.   You will deliver mail to all employees.

Exercise 17–1, page 206

Possible revisions:

a.   When I was young, my family was poor.
b.   This conference will help me serve my clients better.
c.   The meteorologist warned the public about the possible dangers of the coming storm.
d.   Government studies show a need for after-school programs.
e.   Passengers should try to complete the customs declaration form before leaving the plane.

Exercise 17–4, page 214

Possible revisions:

a.   Dr. Geralyn Farmer is the chief surgeon at University Hospital. Dr. Paul Green is her assistant.
b.   All applicants want to know how much they will earn.
c.   Elementary school teachers should understand the concept of nurturing if they intend to be effective.
d.   Obstetricians need to be available to their patients at all hours.
e.   If we do not stop polluting our environment, we will perish.

Exercise 18–2, page 219

Possible revisions:

a.   We regret this delay; thank you for your patience.
b.   Ada's plan is to acquire education and experience to prepare herself for a position as property manager.
c.   Tiger Woods, the ultimate competitor, has earned millions of dollars just in endorsements.
d.   Many people take for granted that public libraries have up-to-date computer systems.
e.   The effect of Gao Xinjian's novels on Chinese exiles is hard to gauge.

Exercise 18–3, page 220

Possible revisions:

a.   Queen Anne was so angry with Sarah Churchill that she refused to see her again.
b.   Correct
c.   The parade moved off the street and onto the beach.
d.   The frightened refugees intend to make the dangerous trek across the mountains.
e.   What type of wedding are you planning?

Exercise 18–4, page 223

Possible revisions:

a. John stormed into the room like a hurricane.
b. Some people insist that they'll always be available to help, even when they haven't been before.
c. The Cubs easily beat the Mets, who were in trouble early in the game today at Wrigley Field.
d. We worked out the problems in our relationship.
e. My mother accused me of evading her questions when in fact I was just saying the first thing that came to mind.

Exercise 19–1, page 233

Possible revisions:

a. Listening to the CD her sister had sent, Mia was overcome with a mix of emotions: happiness, homesickness, nostalgia.
b. Cortés and his soldiers were astonished when they looked down from the mountains and saw Tenochtitlán, the magnificent capital of the Aztecs.
c. Although my spoken Spanish is not very good, I can read the language with ease.
d. There are several reasons for not eating meat. One reason is that dangerous chemicals are used throughout the various stages of meat production.
e. To learn how to sculpt beauty from everyday life is my intention in studying art and archaeology.

Exercise 20–1, page 241

Possible revisions:

a. The city had one public swimming pool that stayed packed with children all summer long.
b. The building is being renovated, so at times we have no heat, water, or electricity.
c. The view was not what the travel agent had described. Where were the rolling hills and the shimmering rivers?
d. All those gnarled equations looked like toxic insects; maybe I was going to have to rethink my major.
e. City officials had good reason to fear a major earthquake: Most [*or* most] of the business district was built on landfill.

Exercise 20–2, page 242

Possible revisions:

a. Wind power for the home is a supplementary source of energy that can be combined with electricity, gas, or solar energy.
b. Correct
c. In the Middle Ages, when the streets of London were dangerous places, it was safer to travel by boat along the Thames.
d. "He's not drunk," I said. "He's in a state of diabetic shock."
e. Are you able to endure extreme angle turns, high speeds, frequent jumps, and occasional crashes? Then supermoto racing may be a sport for you.

Exercise 21–2, page 255

a. One of the main reasons for elephant poaching is the profits received from selling the ivory tusks.
b. Correct
c. A number of students in the seminar were aware of the importance of joining the discussion.
d. Batik cloth from Bali, blue and white ceramics from Delft, and a bocce ball from Turin have made Angelie's room the talk of the dorm.
e. Correct

Exercise 22–1, page 261

Possible revisions:

a. Every presidential candidate must appeal to a wide variety of ethnic and social groups to win the election.
b. David lent his motorcycle to someone who allowed a friend to use it.
c. The aerobics teacher motioned for all the students to move their arms in wide, slow circles.
d. Correct
e. Applicants should be bilingual if they want to qualify for this position.

Exercise 23–1, page 266

Possible revisions:

a. Some professors say that engineering students should have hands-on experience with dismantling and reassembling machines.
b. Because she had decorated her living room with posters from chamber music festivals, her date thought that she was interested in classical music. Actually she preferred rock.
c. In my high school, students didn't need to get all A's to be considered a success; they just needed to work to their ability.
d. Marianne told Jenny, "I am worried about your mother's illness." [or ". . . about my mother's illness."]
e. Though Lewis cried for several minutes after scraping his knee, eventually his crying subsided.

Exercise 24–1, page 273

a. Correct [But the writer could change the end of the sentence: . . . *than he is.*]
b. Correct [But the writer could change the end of the sentence: . . . *that she was the coach.*]
c. She appreciated his telling the truth in such a difficult situation.
d. The director has asked you and me to draft a proposal for a new recycling plan.
e. Five close friends and I rented a station wagon, packed it with food, and drove two hundred miles to Mardi Gras.

Exercise 25–1, page 279

a. The roundtable featured scholars whom I had never heard of. [or . . . scholars I had never heard of.]
b. Correct
c. Correct

d. Daniel always gives a holiday donation to whoever needs it.
e. So many singers came to the audition that Natalia had trouble deciding whom to select for the choir.

Exercise 26–1, page 286

Possible revisions:

a. Did you do well on last week's chemistry exam?
b. With the budget deadline approaching, our office has hardly had time to handle routine correspondence.
c. Correct
d. The customer complained that he hadn't been treated nicely.
e. Of all my relatives, Uncle Roberto is the cleverest.

Exercise 27–1, page 293

a. When I get the urge to exercise, I lie down until it passes.
b. Grandmother had driven our new hybrid to the sunrise church service on Savage Mountain, so we were left with the station wagon.
c. A pile of dirty rags was lying at the bottom of the stairs.
d. How did the computer know that the gamer had gone from the room with the blue ogre to the hall where the gold was heaped?
e. Abraham Lincoln took good care of his legal clients; the contracts he drew for the Illinois Central Railroad could never be broken.

Exercise 27–2, page 299

a. The glass sculptures of the Swan Boats were prominent in the brightly lit lobby.
b. Visitors to the glass museum were not supposed to touch the exhibits.
c. Our church has all the latest technology, even a closed-circuit television.
d. Christos didn't know about Marlo's promotion because he never listens. He is [or He's] always talking.
e. Correct

Exercise 27–3, page 307

Possible revisions:

a. Correct
b. Watson and Crick discovered the mechanism that controls inheritance in all life: the workings of the DNA molecule.
c. When city planners proposed rezoning the waterfront, did they know that the mayor had promised to curb development in that neighborhood?
d. Correct
e. Correct

Exercise 28–1, page 314

a. In the past, tobacco companies denied any connection between smoking and health problems.
b. There is nothing in the world that TV has not touched on.
c. I want to register for a summer tutoring session.
d. By the end of the year, the state will have tested 139 birds for avian flu.
e. The benefits of eating fruits and vegetables have been promoted by health care providers.

Exercise 28–2, page 315

a.   A major league pitcher can throw a baseball more than ninety-five miles per hour.
b.   The writing center tutor will help you revise your essay.
c.   A reptile must adjust its body temperature to its environment.
d.   Correct
e.   My uncle, a cartoonist, could sketch a face in less than two minutes.

Exercise 28–3, page 323

Possible revisions:

a.   The electrician might have discovered the broken circuit if she had gone through the modules one at a time.
b.   If Verena wins a scholarship, she will go to graduate school.
c.   Whenever there is a fire in our neighborhood, everybody comes out to watch.
d.   Sarah will take the paralegal job unless she gets a better offer.
e.   If I lived in Budapest with my cousin Szusza, she would teach me Hungarian cooking.

Exercise 28–4, page 326

a.   I enjoy riding my motorcycle.
b.   The tutor told Samantha to come to the writing center.
c.   The team hopes to work hard and win the championship.
d.   Ricardo and his brothers miss surfing during the winter.
e.   The babysitter let Roger stay up until midnight.

Exercise 29–1, page 335

a.   Doing volunteer work often brings satisfaction.
b.   As I looked out the window of the plane, I could see Cape Cod.
c.   Melina likes to drink her coffee with lots of cream.
d.   Correct
e.   I completed my homework assignment quickly. *Or* I completed the homework assignment quickly.

Exercise 30–1, page 341

a.   There are some cartons of ice cream in the freezer.
b.   I don't use the subway because I am afraid.
c.   The prime minister is the most popular leader in my country.
d.   We tried to get in touch with the same manager whom we spoke to earlier.
e.   Recently there have been a number of earthquakes in Turkey.

Exercise 30–2, page 343

Possible revisions:

a.   Although freshwater freezes at 32 degrees Fahrenheit, ocean water freezes at 28 degrees Fahrenheit.
b.   Because we switched cable packages, our channel lineup has changed.
c.   The competitor confidently mounted his skateboard.
d.   My sister performs the *legong*, a Balinese dance, well.
e.   Correct

Exercise 30–3, page 345

a. Listening to everyone's complaints all day was irritating.
b. The long flight to Singapore was exhausting.
c. Correct
d. After a great deal of research, the scientist made a fascinating discovery.
e. That blackout was one of the most frightening experiences I've ever had.

Exercise 30–4, page 346

a. an attractive young Vietnamese woman
b. a dedicated Catholic priest
c. her old blue wool sweater
d. Joe's delicious Scandinavian bread
e. many beautiful antique jewelry boxes

Exercise 31–1, page 348

a. Whenever we eat at the Centerville Café, we sit at a small table in the corner of the room.
b. Correct
c. On Thursday, Nancy will attend her first home repair class at the community center.
d. Correct
e. We decided to go to a restaurant because there was no fresh food in the refrigerator.

Exercise 32–1, page 356

a. Alisa brought the injured bird home and fashioned a splint out of Popsicle sticks for its wing.
b. Considered a classic of early animation, *The Adventures of Prince Achmed* used hand-cut silhouettes against colored backgrounds.
c. If you complete the enclosed evaluation form and return it within two weeks, you will receive a free breakfast during your next stay.
d. Correct
e. Roger had always wanted a handmade violin, but he couldn't afford one.

Exercise 32–2, page 357

a. J. R. R. Tolkien finished writing his draft of *The Lord of the Rings* trilogy in 1949, but the first book in the series wasn't published until 1954.
b. In the first two minutes of its ascent, the space shuttle had broken the sound barrier and reached a height of over twenty-five miles.
c. German shepherds can be gentle guide dogs, or they can be fierce attack dogs.
d. Some former professional cyclists claim that the use of performance-enhancing drugs is widespread in cycling, and they argue that no rider can be competitive without doping.
e. As an intern, I learned most aspects of the broadcasting industry, but I never learned about fundraising.

Exercise 32–3, page 360

a. The cold, impersonal atmosphere of the university was unbearable.

b. An ambulance threaded its way through police cars, fire trucks, and irate citizens.
c. Correct
d. After two broken arms, three cracked ribs, and one concussion, Ken quit the varsity football team.
e. Correct

Exercise 32–4, page 361

a. NASA's rovers on Mars are equipped with special cameras that can take close-up, high-resolution pictures of the terrain.
b. Correct
c. Correct
d. Love, vengeance, greed, and betrayal are common themes in Western literature.
e. Many experts believe that shark attacks on surfers are a result of the sharks' mistaking surfboards for small injured seals.

Exercise 32–5, page 365

a. Choreographer Alvin Ailey's best-known work, *Revelations*, is more than just a crowd-pleaser.
b. Correct
c. Correct
d. A member of an organization that provides job training for teens was also appointed to the education commission.
e. Brian Eno, who began his career as a rock musician, turned to meditative compositions in the late seventies.

Exercise 32–6, page 371

a. Cricket, which originated in England, is also popular in Australia, South Africa, and India.
b. At the sound of the starting pistol, the horses surged forward toward the first obstacle, a sharp incline three feet high.
c. After seeing an exhibition of Western art, Gerhard Richter escaped from East Berlin and smuggled out many of his notebooks.
d. Corrie's new wet suit has an intricate blue pattern.
e. The cookies will keep for two weeks in sturdy, airtight containers.

Exercise 32–7, page 371

a. On January 15, 2008, our office moved to 29 Commonwealth Avenue, Mechanicsville, VA 23111.
b. Correct
c. Ms. Carlson, you are a valued customer whose satisfaction is very important to us.
d. Mr. Mundy was born on July 22, 1939, in Arkansas, where his family had lived for four generations.
e. Correct

Exercise 33–1, page 377

a. Correct
b. Tricia's first artwork was a bright blue clay dolphin.

c. Some modern musicians (trumpeter John Hassell is an example) blend several cultural traditions into a unique sound.
d. Myra liked hot, spicy foods such as chili, kung pao chicken, and buffalo wings.
e. On the display screen was a soothing pattern of light and shadow.

Exercise 34–1, page 382

a. Do not ask me to be kind; just ask me to act as though I were.
b. When men talk about defense, they always claim to be protecting women and children, but they never ask the women and children what they think.
c. When I get a little money, I buy books; if any is left, I buy food and clothes.
d. Correct
e. Wit has truth in it; wisecracking is simply calisthenics with words.

Exercise 34–2, page 383

a. Strong black coffee will not sober you up; the truth is that time is the only way to get alcohol out of your system.
b. Margaret was not surprised to see hail and vivid lightning; conditions had been right for violent weather all day.
c. There is often a fine line between right and wrong, good and bad, truth and deception.
d. Correct
e. Severe, unremitting pain is a ravaging force, especially when the patient tries to hide it from others.

Exercise 35–1, page 386

a. Correct [Either *It* or *it* is correct.]
b. If we have come to fight, we are far too few; if we have come to die, we are far too many.
c. The travel package includes a round-trip ticket to Athens, a cruise through the Cyclades, and all hotel accommodations.
d. The news article portrays the land use proposal as reckless, although 62 percent of the town's residents support it.
e. Psychologists Kindlon and Thompson (2000) offer parents a simple starting point for raising male children: "Teach boys that there are many ways to be a man" (p. 256).

Exercise 36–1, page 391

a. Correct
b. The innovative shoe fastener was inspired by the designer's young son.
c. Each day's menu features a different European country's dish.
d. Sue worked overtime to increase her family's earnings.
e. Ms. Jacobs is unwilling to listen to students' complaints about computer failures.

Exercise 37–1, page 398

a. As for the advertisement "Sailors have more fun," if you consider chipping paint and swabbing decks fun, then you will have plenty of it.

b.   Correct
c.   After winning the lottery, Juanita said that she would give half the money to charity.
d.   After the movie, Vicki said, "The reviewer called this flick 'trash of the first order.' I guess you can't believe everything you read."
e.   Correct

Exercise 39–1, page 407

a.   A client has left his or her [*or* a] cell phone in our conference room.
b.   The films we made of Kilauea on our trip to Hawaii Volcanoes National Park illustrate a typical spatter cone eruption.
c.   Correct
d.   Correct
e.   Of three engineering fields—chemical, mechanical, and materials—Keegan chose materials engineering for its application to toy manufacturing.

Exercise 40–1, page 412

a.   Correct
b.   Some combat soldiers are trained by government diplomats to be sensitive to issues of culture, history, and religion.
c.   Correct
d.   How many pounds have you lost since you began running four miles a day?
e.   Denzil spent all night studying for his psychology exam.

Exercise 41–1, page 415

a.   The carpenters located three maple timbers, twenty-one sheets of cherry, and ten oblongs of polished ebony for the theater set.
b.   Correct
c.   Correct
d.   Eight students in the class had been labeled "learning disabled."
e.   The Vietnam Veterans Memorial in Washington, DC, had 58,132 names inscribed on it when it was dedicated in 1982.

Exercise 42–1, page 418

a.   Howard Hughes commissioned the *Spruce Goose*, a beautifully built but thoroughly impractical wooden aircraft.
b.   The old man screamed his anger, shouting to all of us, "I will not leave my money to you worthless layabouts!"
c.   I learned the Latin term *ad infinitum* from an old nursery rhyme about fleas: "Great fleas have little fleas upon their back to bite 'em, / Little fleas have lesser fleas and so on *ad infinitum*."
d.   Correct
e.   Neve Campbell's lifelong interest in ballet inspired her involvement in the film *The Company*, which portrays a season with the Joffrey Ballet.

Exercise 44–1, page 431

a.   Correct
b.   The swiftly moving tugboat pulled alongside the barge and directed it away from the oil spill in the harbor.
c.   Correct

d.   Your dog is well known in our neighborhood.
e.   Roadblocks were set up along all the major highways leading out of the city.

Exercise 45–1, page 436

a.   Assistant Dean Shirin Ahmadi recommended offering more world language courses.
b.   Correct
c.   Kalindi has an ambitious semester, studying differential calculus, classical Hebrew, brochure design, and Greek literature.
d.   Lydia's aunt and uncle make modular houses as beautiful as modernist works of art.
e.   We amused ourselves on the long flight by discussing how spring in Kyoto stacks up against summer in London.

Exercise 61–1, page 748

a. stage, confrontation, proportions; b. courage, mountain (noun/adjective), climber, inspiration, rescuers; c. need, guest, honor, fog; d. defense (noun/adjective), attorney, appeal, jury; e. museum, women (noun/adjective), artists, 1987

Exercise 61–2, page 751

a. his; b. that, our (pronoun/adjective); c. that, he, himself, some, his (pronoun/adjective); d. I, my (pronoun/adjective), you, one; e. no one, her

Exercise 61–3, page 754

a. told; b. were, killed; c. brought down; d. Stay, 'll [will] arrive; e. struggled, was trapped

Exercise 61–4, page 756

a. Adjectives: weak, unfocused; b. Adjectives: The (article), Spanish, flexible; adverb: wonderfully; c. Adjectives: The (article), fragrant, the (article) steady; adverb: especially; d. Adjectives: hot, cold; adverbs: rather, slightly, bitterly; e. Adjectives: The (article), its (pronoun/adjective), wicker (noun/adjective); adverb: soundly

Exercise 62–1, page 766

a. Complete subjects: The hills and mountains, the snow atop them, simple subjects: hills, mountains, snow; b. Complete subject: points; simple subject: points; c. Complete subject: (You); d. Complete subject: hundreds of fireflies; simple subject: hundreds; e. Complete subject: The evidence against the defendant; simple subject: evidence

Exercise 62–2, page 770

a. Subject complement: expensive; b. Direct object: death; c. Direct object: their players' efforts; d. Subject complement: the capital of the Russian Empire; e. Subject complement: bitter

Exercise 62–3, page 770

a. Direct objects: adults and children; object complement: weary; b. Direct object: community service; object complement: her priority; c. Direct object: the work; object complement: finished; d. Indirect objects: agent, us; direct objects: our tickets, boarding passes; e. Indirect object: students; direct object: healthy meal choices

Exercise 63–1, page 775

a. In northern Italy, as their first language (adverb phrases modifying *speak*); b. through the thick forest (adjective phrase modifying *hike*); with ease (adverb phrase modifying *completed*); c. To my boss's dismay (adverb phrase modifying *was*); for work (adverb phrase modifying *late*); d. of Mayan artifacts (adjective phrase modifying *exhibit*); into pre-Columbian culture (adjective phrase modifying *insight*); e. In 2002, in twelve European countries (adverb phrases modifying *became*)

Exercise 63–2, page 779

a. Updating your software (gerund phrase used as subject); b. decreasing the town budget (gerund phrase used as object of the preposition *in*); identifying nonessential services (gerund phrase used as subject complement); c. to help her mother by raking the lawn (infinitive phrase used as direct object); raking the lawn (gerund phrase used as object of the preposition *by*); d. Understanding little (participial phrase modifying *I*); passing my biology final (gerund phrase used as object of the preposition *of*); e. Working with animals (gerund phrase used as subject)

Exercise 63–3, page 784

a. so that every vote would count (adverb clause modifying *adjusted*); b. that targets baby boomers (adjective clause modifying *campaign*); c. After the Tambora volcano erupted in the southern Pacific in 1815 (adverb clause modifying *realized*); that it would contribute to the "year without a summer" in Europe and North America (noun clause used as direct object of *realized*); d. that at a certain point there will be no more oil to extract from the earth (noun clause used as direct object of *implies*); e. when you are rushing (adverb clause modifying *are overlooked*)

Exercise 64–1, page 787

a. Complex; that are ignited in dry areas (adjective clause); b. Compound; c. Simple; d. Complex; Before we leave for the station (adverb clause); e. Compound-complex; when you want to leave (noun clause)

Index

ESL Menu

A complete section on major ESL challenges:

ESL and Academic English notes in other sections:

A List of Charts

IX Researched Writing

X Document Design

XI Grammar Basics

Revision Symbols
Boldface numbers refer to sections of the handbook.

A List of Grammatical Terms

Boldface numbers refer to sections of the handbook.

Detailed Menu